MILITARY RULES OF EVIDENCE MANUAL

By

Stephen A. Saltzburg
Professor of Law, University of Virginia

Lee D. Schinasi
Major, Judge Advocate General's Corps

David A. Schlueter
Major, Judge Advocate General's Corps

THE MICHIE COMPANY

Law Publishers

CHARLOTTESVILLE, VIRGINIA

1981

The views of the authors do not purport to reflect the positions of the Department of the Army or Department of Defense.

TABLE OF CONTENTS

VI. Witnesses

VIII. Hearsay

IX. Authentication and Identification

X. Contents of Writings, Recordings, and Photographs

XI. Miscellaneous Rules

FOREWORD

For several decades the admission of evidence in courts-martial has been governed by detailed rules contained in a chapter of the Manual for Courts-Martial. Meanwhile trial judges in federal courts and in most state courts were seeking guidance on evidentiary questions from a mass of sometimes conflicting precedents and from treatises like that of Dean Wigmore — who, incidentally, had been closely associated with drafting the chapter on Rules of Evidence in the Manual for Courts-Martial.

Various organizations, like the American Law Institute and the National Conference of Commissioners on Uniform State Laws, proposed codes of evidence; but the adoption of such codes was sparse. Finally, however, after a lengthy process in which many lawyers, judges, and law professors, as well as the Congress, played a part, the Federal Rules of Evidence were adopted. Once that was done — and in light of the mandate in Article 36 of the Uniform Code of Military Justice, 10 U.S.C. § 836, that the President, "so far as he considers practicable," shall apply "the rules of evidence generally recognized in the trial of criminal cases in the United States district courts" — it was only a matter of time until the President prescribed that the Federal Rules of Evidence should be used in courts-martial. As the result of two years of efforts by a working group comprised of representatives of each Armed Service, the Court of Military Appeals, and the General Counsel of the Defense Department and with substantial encouragement from the American Bar Association and other bar groups, that time finally arrived on September 1, 1980.

However, the Military Rules of Evidence go much further than their civilian counterpart. Like the chapter on Rules of Evidence contained in several editions of the Manual for Courts-Martial, the Military Rules deal with subjects such as the exclusionary rules and privileges, which are not within the compass of the Federal Rules. Thus, there are Military Rules concerning self-incrimination, Rule 301; warnings about rights, Rule 305; unlawful searches and seizures, Rule 311; bodily intrusions for blood specimens and the like, Rule 312; and eye-witness identifications, Rule 321. Similarly, there is specific provision for lawyer-client, husband-wife, penitent-clergy, and informer privileges and for privileges concerning classified and other government information. *See* Rules 501-512. Perhaps, after thorough testing at trial and appellate levels, the Military Rules on such topics will provide a model for expanding the scope of the Federal Rules into areas that to this point have been left uncharted.

The Court of Military Appeals has not yet had occasion to review fully a case tried under the Military Rules of Evidence. However, last summer the members of the Court received a "cram course" from two officers who had participated actively in drafting the Rules. One obvious conclusion to be drawn from this course was that the new Rules have made substantial changes in the prior military law of evidence. I can foresee that many of these changes will generate petitions for review and that my Brothers on the Court and I will be searching for guidance as to the intent of various Rules. Furthermore, I perceive that a lawyer who does not recognize the changes made by the new Rules will jeopardize his client's cause, since failure to make a specific objection or offer of proof or to request a limiting instruction will generally constitute a waiver. *See*

Rules 103(a), 105. Likewise, military judges who fail to grasp the significance of changes wrought by the Military Rules of Evidence will encounter difficulty in making the detailed findings which the Rules sometimes require. *See, e.g.,* Rule 304(d)(4).

In performing their respective tasks, those concerned with administering military justice will benefit greatly from having at hand the MILITARY RULES OF EVIDENCE MANUAL. There the reader can readily locate the analysis of each Rule by its drafters and the authors' incisive editorial comment, which highlights not only the main features of each rule but also latent problems of interpreting it.

A rule which is not understood cannot be followed. Fortunately, the authors have dedicated themselves to meeting the need for a well-grounded, comprehensive understanding of the Military Rules of Evidence. Their well-prepared, instructive Manual will contribute immeasurably to a comprehension of the intricacies of the Rules. I feel sure that I shall use this Manual often and to advantage; and I believe it will be a valuable addition to the growing library of volumes on military law.

ROBINSON O. EVERETT
Chief Judge
U.S. Court of Military Appeals

Washington, D.C.
1981

INTRODUCTION

I. Our Purposes

One purpose of this book is to offer assistance to military lawyers and judges who are now bound to use the Military Rules of Evidence in courts-martial. Although many of the Military Rules follow the Federal Rules of Evidence, there are changes. More importantly, the Military Rules contain lengthy material not found in the Federal Rules of Evidence. These Rules will be a challenge to lawyers and judges who must master them almost immediately in order to protect the rights of the parties they represent and to provide fair trials. We attempt to explain what the Rules do, how they work, what problems may be encountered in using them, and sometimes how the problems may be solved. Since the military courts have not yet had occasion to use the Rules in many cases, it is too early to give definitive answers to many questions. It is our goal to identify the principal areas of concern under these Rules and to provide what help we can.

Ours is the collaborative effort of two military lawyers and one civilian lawyer. We have attempted to combine the practical insights that come from working within a special system like the military with the observations, and sometimes the criticisms, of one who is outside that system and who may approach it with a different perspective than many military lawyers share. By combining practical insights with a fresh look, we hope to be able to provide a balanced view of the Military Rules of Evidence and to identify strengths and weaknesses of many of the Rules that we talk about. But our effort is primarily to explain and to help, not to suggest reforms or to offer academic discussions about various aspects of evidence law. We take the system as it is and want to help those who work in it do the best job possible in order to promote justice and fair play for the military and its members.

Another purpose of our writing is to make available not only to military lawyers, but also to civilian lawyers interested in criminal justice, litigation and evidence, information about military processes. Each of us has developed great respect for the fundamental fairness of the military system and admiration for many of the rules that have been created to protect the interests of those accused of offenses. Contrary to the image that many civilian lawyers have of the military system, often the military system is far more protective of accused persons than its civilian counterpart. Military justice is not perfect any more than civilian justice is, but some military procedures, once they are understood properly, may prove to be attractive to civilian courts. We very much hope that this book will provide a basis for comparing civilian and military evidence and procedural systems in an effort to improve both.

As military cases are decided, we plan to annotate them and to supplement the book yearly so that military lawyers and judges and civilian lawyers interested in military justice can have a convenient and up-to-date reference. Also, we hope to keep the book to a manageable size so that military personnel can carry it wherever they travel in the world to handle courts-martial.

II. Background of the Military Rules of Evidence

Historically, evidentiary rules applicable in court-martial practice have been derived from several sources:

(i) *The Uniform Code of Military Justice,* 10 U.S.C. § 801-940;

(ii) *The Manual for Courts-Martial,* United States, 1969 (Rev.);

(iii) Rules of Evidence recognized in the practice of criminal cases in Federal District Courts; and

(iv) Case law from the Courts of Military Review (Army, Air Force, Coast Guard, and Navy) and the United States Court of Military Appeals.

The foundation for all of this is the Constitution itself which directs in Article 1, § 8 that the Congress will regulate the armed forces. The Uniform Code of Military Justice (U.C.M.J.) represents Congressional rulemaking and itself provides some evidentiary rules. *See, e.g.,* Article 31 (right against self-incrimination) and Article 49 (depositions). But the most important provision lies in Article 36, which states:

(a) Pretrial, trial, and post-trial procedures, including modes of proof, for cases arising under this chapter triable in courts-martial, military commissions and other military tribunals, and procedures for courts of inquiry, may be prescribed by the President by regulations which shall, so far as he considers practicable, apply the principles of law and the rules of evidence generally recognized in the trial of criminal cases in the United States district courts, but which may not be contrary to or inconsistent with this chapter.

(b) All rules and regulations made under this article shall be uniform insofar as practicable and shall be reported to Congress.

This provision serves as the underlying authority for specifically promulgating the rules of evidence which have since 1951 appeared in Chapter XXVII of the Manual for Courts-Martial. Although the evidentiary rules have generally been considered to have the force and effect of statutory law, *see, e.g., United States v. Lucas,* 1 C.M.A. 19, 1 C.M.R. 19 (1951), they must always be tested against the Constitution and the Uniform Code of Military Justice. Conflict with either or both of those higher sources will fall the *Manual* provision. *See, e.g., United States v. Jacoby,* 11 C.M.A. 428, 29 C.M.R. 244 (1960); *United States v. Douglas,* 1 M.J. 354 (C.M.A. 1976); *United States v. Ware,* 1 M.J. 282 (C.M.A. 1976). But if the *Manual* affords greater rights to the accused, then the *Manual* provision, rather than the Constitution or the U.C.M.J. will control. And under the former *Manual* ¶ 137, federal practice served as a model when an issue was not otherwise covered in the *Manual.* The common law could be applied if federal practice was not inconsistent with it.

This basic scheme of military evidentiary law still is intact. What has changed dramatically is the content of Chapter XXVII of the *Manual.* All of the former "cook-book" type discussions of the applicable rules of evidence are gone. In its place the President has placed eighty some tersley-worded rules that comprise the new Military Rules of Evidence.

The formal road to this major change in military practice was relatively short when compared to the lengthy process used to formulate the Federal Rules. This abbreviated process was due in large part to the fact that many of the Military Rules are simply an adoption of the rules adopted by Congress for the federal courts. Although Congress actively participated in drafting of the Federal Rules, it had no part in promulgating the Military Rules. They were initially drafted by a special committee of the Joint Service Committee on Military Justice Working Group. This committee submitted its work to the parent body — the Joint Service Committee on Military Justice. This body has the task of periodically reviewing and submitting proposals for revision of both the U.C.M.J. and the *Manual.* The final product was then reviewed by the Department of Defense and the Office of Management and Budget. The latter in turn circulated it to the Department of Justice. The Rules were finally signed by President Carter on March 12, 1980. Minor amendments were made on September 1, 1980, the effective date of the Rules. Unlike the process used for adopting the Federal Rules, the procedure here did not generally involve public input.

Generally speaking, the Military Rules are substantially similar to the Federal Rules of Evidence in Sections I, II, IV, and VI through XI. (The word "section" rather than "article" was used by the drafters to avoid potential confusion with articles of the U.C.M.J.).

Section III contains rules concerning self-incrimination, search and seizure, and eyewitness identification. Of particular interest are rules governing the procedures to be used for litigating constitutional issues. *See, e.g.,* Rule 304 (confessions and admissions); Rule 312 (an innovative rule governing bodily views and intrusions); and Rule 302 (a rule creating a limited privilege for communications by an accused to a sanity board).

The Section III Rules provide a combination of both procedural and evidentiary prescriptions. At first blush there appears to be a question as to whether these Rules are properly within the confines of the President's Article 36 powers. The drafters' *Analysis* is silent on this point. It seems safe to conclude that even though these Rules plainly are designed in part to affect out-of-court behavior, they are written so as to focus on evidence, trials and the creation of evidence. Thus, they can be viewed as being sufficiently procedural or evidentiary to withstand challenge. *Cf. United States v. Frederick,* 3 M.J. 230 (C.M.A. 1977) (outside President's authority to promulgate matters affecting substantive law).

The Rules in Section III do not establish defenses nor do they establish the elements of offenses. It also seems safe to conclude that because these Rules carry forward many of the long-standing pre-Rules provisions on the same subject matter, Congress has implicitly approved the President's authority in this area by failing to limit that authority; Article 36 was amended as recently as 1979 and the legislative history on that change reflects no misgivings or reservations on this issue. Rather, the 1979 changes were designed to make more clear the President's broad powers in prescribing rules of procedure and evidence. The same view would govern any challenge to privilege rules, discussed next. We note that there is no limitation on the President's power to promulgate procedural rules that is comparable to the Rules Enabling Act, 28 U.S.C. § 2072, which requires some deference to state substantive law in certain contexts.

Section V adopts many of the Supreme Court's proposed Federal Rules of Evidence on privileges which were not adopted by the Congress. The drafters chose the route of laying out specific privileges rather than following the development of privileges under common law. There is no treatment of presumptions (found in Article III of the Federal Rules of Evidence) in the Military Rules.

On the whole, the Rules place a greater burden on the defense than previously existed to either articulate in timely fashion specific objections or risk waiver. They provide that all relevant evidence should be admitted unless some evidence rule, statute or constitutional principle requires exclusion. Ultimately, they should speed up and simplify the litigation process and probably permit more evidence to be considered at trial. The trial judge is given broad powers to promote fair trial and fair treatment of parties and witnesses. Some of these powers go well beyond existing military authorities.

There can be no doubt that the adoption of the Military Rules of Evidence is a bold, exciting, and innovative step. The title itself, according to the drafters, is intended to make it clear that "military evidentiary law should echo the civilian federal law to the extent practicable," but should also reflect the "unique and critical reasons" behind a separate military justice system. *See* the drafters' *Analysis* for Rule 1103.

III. *Using the Book*

Throughout the Rules the reader will see that various terms, unique to military law, have been substituted in place of those terms found in federal practice. Before discussing the format of this book it might be helpful for the sake of those not familiar with the military criminal legal system to briefly lay out the procedural process, highlighting terms which the reader will see again in the Rules, our comments, and the drafters' *Analysis*.

Although anyone subject to the U.C.M.J. may *prefer* court-martial *charges,* it is usually the *accused's* immediate commanding officer who informally investigates the alleged offense (a violation of the punitive articles of the U.C.M.J.) and prepares the sworn charges. The charge sheet (DD Form 458) is forwarded up the chain of command with recommendations as to the type of court-martial which may try the case: summary, special, or general. The *summary court-martial,* to which the accused must consent, is composed of one officer who generally acts as both prosecutor and judge. This officer need not be, but generally is, an armed forces lawyer. The next higher court is the *special court-martial,* which may be composed of either a *military judge* alone or a *court* consisting of not less than three officers sitting as *court-members.* The U.C.M.J. does provide that a special court-martial can be conducted with members but without a military judge, but this is rare. A *general court-martial* is generally reserved for the more serious offenses and consists of a military judge and at least five officers serving as court-members. The procedural steps leading to the general court-martial are more complex than the other two types of courts. The process includes a thorough, independent *Article 32 Investigation* by an officer, often a lawyer, who questions witnesses and considers the available evidence in deciding whether probable cause exists to send the case to trial. At this investigation, the accused is represented by counsel and has the opportunity to cross-examine witnesses.

Sending a case to trial consists of a *convening authority referring* the case to a designated court for trial. This convening authority is a commander authorized by the U.C.M.J. to convene courts. For example, commanding generals of installations are usually general court-martial convening authorities. These individuals also may become involved in acting on pretrial requests for defense witnesses or other discovery. *See, e.g.,* Rules 505, 506.

Preliminary matters, such as arraignment, entering of pleas, and hearing motions to suppress are handled at a pretrial session referred to as the *Article 39(a)* session. At trial (both merits and sentencing), the *accused* is represented by a defense counsel (appointed military counsel, individual military counsel, or civilian counsel). The government is represented by the *trial counsel.* After trial, the results are reviewed by the convening authority and his legal advisor, the *staff judge advocate,* who reviews it for legal sufficiency. Depending on the type of court and the punishment, the case may be automatically reviewed by the various service appellate courts and the United States Court of Military Appeals.

That foundation having been laid, we turn our attention to the actual mechanics and format of this book. The format consists of three parts: (A) The official text of each Rule; (B) our editorial comment; and (C) the drafters' *Analysis.*

A. OFFICIAL TEXT OF THE RULE

This part contains the exact text of each Rule as prescribed by President Carter in Executive Order 12198, March 12, 1980, and any amendments to date. *See, e.g.,* Executive Order 12233 of 1 September 1980.

B. EDITORIAL COMMENT

Each Rule is followed by an explanation of the Rule, how it compares with the comparable Federal Rule, and how it affects pre-Rules military practice. The comments are intended to be brief, making suggestions for the practitioner where appropriate. This section is not so much a how-to discussion as it is a starting point for an understanding of what each Rule says and how the Rule might be applied by military courts. Citations are held to a minimum to maintain readability. Where potential problems exist with a Rule we set those out, not for the purpose of setting forth definitive answers, but rather to better enable counsel and judges to focus on troublesome aspects of the Rules and to enable them to benefit from the experience of the federal courts.

C. DRAFTERS' ANALYSIS

Serving as a legislative history of sorts, the non-binding drafters' *Analysis* explains the drafters' intent and should be helpful in discerning what the drafters had in mind in formulating the Rules as they did. The drafters' *Analysis* should be especially helpful in understanding rules or provisions not included in the Federal Rules of Evidence.

Executive Order 12198 of March 12, 1980

By virtue of the authority vested in me by the Uniform Code of Military Justice (title 10, United States Code, ch. 47), and as President of the United States, I hereby prescribe the following amendments to the Manual for Courts-Martial, United States, 1969 (revised edition), prescribed by Executive Order No. 11476 as amended by Executive Order No. 11835 and Executive Order No. 12018.

EDITORIAL COMMENT

On 12 March 1980, the President of the United States prescribed a new evidentiary code for military practice. His action was only the final step in a two year process aimed at totally rewriting Chapter XXVII of the *Manual for Courts-Martial*. This revision was a joint effort in every sense of the term. Members from all services, departments, courts and agencies served by the Rules contributed to their development.

As the Rules themselves clearly demonstrate, the drafters attempted to adopt federal practice to the greatest extent possible, while still allowing for the necessities of a world wide criminal practice.

In order to assist military and civilian attorneys, and the bench in using these Rules, the drafters have provided a detailed *Analysis* describing their intentions. This drafters' *Analysis* is not binding, however, and it is not part of the Executive Order itself. It also does not constitute or represent any official position with respect to the Rules. The drafters' *Analysis* should be of great assistance as it highlights what the drafters intended and often traces each Rule back to its federal and *Manual* foundations.

The drafters' *Analysis* has limitations, however. Sometimes there is little detailed information addressing known uncertainties in the Rule. There are also apparent conflicts between some Rules and the drafters' *Analysis* itself. We attempt to point out the problems with the drafters' *Analysis* as we proceed.

The President's action in promulgating the new Rules and the 1 September 1980 amendments, *see* Executive Order 12233, should improve military practice. The Rules will be more easily understood and uniformly applied than those they replaced. And they represent a convenient reference source for virtually all military evidence law.

DRAFTERS' ANALYSIS OF THE 1980 AMENDMENTS TO THE MANUAL FOR COURTS-MARTIAL

The Military Rules of Evidence, Chapter XXVII of the Manual for Courts-Martial, were the product of a two year effort participated in by the General Counsel of the Department of Defense, the United States Court of Military Appeals, the Military Departments, and the Department of Transportation. The Rules were drafted by the Evidence Working Group of the Joint Service Committee on Military Justice, which consisted of Commander James Pinnell, JAGC, U.S. Navy, then Major John Bozeman,

JAGC, U.S. Army (from April 1978 until July 1978), Major Fredric Lederer, JAGC, U.S. Army (from August, 1978), Major James Potuk, U.S. Air Force, Lieutenant Commander Tom Snook, U.S. Coast Guard, and Mr. Robert Mueller and Ms. Carol Wild Scott of the United States Court of Military Appeals. Mr. Andrew Effron represented the Office of the General Counsel of the Department of Defense on the Committee. The draft rules were reviewed and, as modified, approved by the Joint Service Committee on Military Justice. Aspects of the Rules were reviewed by the Code Committee as well. *See* Article 67(g). The Rules were approved by the General Counsel of the Department of Defense and forwarded to the White House via the Office of Management and Budget which circulated the Rules to the Departments of Justice and Transportation.

The following Analysis was prepared primarily by Major Fredric Lederer, U.S. Army, of the Evidence Working Group of the Joint Service Committee on Military Justice and was approved by the Joint Service Committee on Military Justice and reviewed in the Office of the General Counsel of the Department of Defense. The Analysis presents the intent of the drafting committee, seeks to indicate the source of the various changes to the Manual, and generally notes when substantial changes to military law result from the amendments. This Analysis is not, however, part of the Executive Order modifying the present Manual nor does it constitute the official views of the Department of Defense, the Department of Transportation, the Military Departments, or of the United States Court of Military Appeals.

The Analysis does not identify technical changes made to adapt the Federal Rules of Evidence to military use. Accordingly, the Analysis does not identify changes made to make the Rules gender neutral or to adapt the Federal Rules to military terminology by substituting, for example, "court members" for "jury" and "military judge" for "court." References within the Analysis to "the present Manual" refer to the Manual for Courts-Martial, 1969 (rev. ed) (Executive Order 11,476, as amended by Executive Order 11,835 and Executive Order 12,018) as it existed prior to the effective date of the 1980 amendments. References to the "Federal Rules of Evidence Advisory Committee" refer to the Advisory Committee on the Rules of Evidence appointed by the Supreme Court, which prepared the original draft of the Federal Rules of Evidence.

2

SECTION I. GENERAL PROVISIONS

Rule 101. Scope.

(a) Applicability. These rules are applicable in courts-martial, including summary courts-martial, to the extent and with the exceptions stated in rule 1101.

(b) Secondary sources. If not otherwise prescribed in this Manual or these rules, and insofar as practicable and not inconsistent with or contrary to the Uniform Code of Military Justice or this Manual, courts-martial shall apply:

(1) First, the rules of evidence generally recognized in the trial of criminal cases in the United States district courts; and

(2) Second, when not inconsistent with subdivision (b)(1), the rules of evidence at common law.

(c) Rule of construction. Except as otherwise provided in these rules, the term "military judge" includes the president of a special court-martial without a military judge and a summary court-martial officer.

EDITORIAL COMMENT

This introductory rule describes the circumstances under which the new Military Rules of Evidence will be applied. Although Rule 101 must be read together with Rule 1101 and Rule 104(a), essentially it states that the Military Rules of Evidence will be applicable in all courts-martial, specifically including summary courts-martial. Rule 1101 defines courts-martial to include all proceedings conducted under the provisions of Article 39(a) U.C.M.J., proceedings in revision, fact-finding proceedings ordered by appellate authorities, and those related to non-summary contempt actions.

Rule 104(a) generally qualifies Rule 101(a)'s broad application by indicating that most preliminary questions heard at pretrial Article 39(a) sessions will not be governed by the Rules of Evidence, nor will most evidentiary rulings and related fact-finding that occurs during trial (*see* our discussion of Rule 104(a)). A similar result obtains during sentencing proceedings, where ¶ 75*c* of the *Manual for Courts-Martial* requires that virtually all evidentiary constraints be relaxed (*see* our discussion of Rule 1101(c)).

Rule 101(a) leaves military practice largely unchanged, as the prior evidentiary format found in the *Manual* was similarly applicable to all courts-martial. In fact, ¶ 137 of the *Manual* vested the summary court officer with discretionary powers similar to those of a trial judge, particularly with respect to questions concerning the admissibility of evidence.   •

To the extent that summary courts still will be conducted by non-attorneys, the new rules may produce substantial problems. Previously, the summary court officer could rely on the lay approach taken by the *Manual* with respect to evidence practice. The text of the *Manual* not only specified what evidentiary rule was to be used, and specified it in lay terms in many instances, but also it detailed how the rule should be applied. The *Manual* provided examples and required the examples to be adhered to strictly by both lay summary court officers and attorneys practicing before special and general courts-martial. The resultant "cookbook approach" to criminal practice worked very well for lay persons. But with the adoption of the Military Rules of Evidence, the explanatory "how to do it" material is excised from the *Manual*. Thus, the non-attorney summary court officer may find the judicial mission much more difficult to accomplish.

In *Middendorf v. Henry,* 425 U.S. 25 (1976), the Supreme Court held that military personnel did not have a right to counsel in a summary court-martial proceeding. It is arguable that the adoption of rules of evidence, which make the proceedings more uniform and more legalistic, could change this result. We view this as doubtful, however, because of the Court's emphasis on the uniqueness of the military mission and the overall procedures that are employed in a summary proceeding.

Rule 101(b) seems to settle the difficult question of what authority controls court-martial practice when the *Manual*, the Uniform Code of Military Justice, and the new Rules of Evidence fail to provide a governing standard. Subdivision (b) of the Rule specifies two additional sources of evidence authority. Once it is demonstrated that none of the three standard reference sources referred to above is sufficient, resort can be made to the rules of evidence generally recognized in United States District Courts, although the similarity between the Military Rules and the Federal Rules of Evidence makes it unlikely that the District Courts will have much to add to the Military Rules. Resort can also be made to common law authority. The only limitation on the use of these additional sources is that neither source can be used if it is inconsistent with or contrary to the U.C.M.J. or the *Manual*.

This Military Rule is as vague as Federal Rule of Evidence 501 as to what "common law" means. We assume that the drafters of the Rule intended the term to be read broadly to include common law decisions that are found throughout the United States. The drafters' *Analysis* to the Rule suggests that prior military determinations would be considered to be common law authority within the meaning of the Rule. This is a sensible approach, and our view is that existing military precedent probably will prove to be the most persuasive authority available on open questions, since this authority indicates the view that military courts have reached on the basis of their examination of common law evidence traditions throughout the United States.

Military courts called upon to interpret the Military Rules of Evidence will find much useful guidance in the opinions of civilian courts that have interpreted the Federal Rules of Evidence. Since the drafters of the Military Rules made an effort to conform the Military Rules to the Federal Rules of Evidence whenever possible, it appears that military courts should endeavor to keep the interpretation of the Military Rules in harmony with the interpretation given the Federal Rules of Evidence, especially when the civilian courts are unanimous or nearly so in their interpretation of a Federal Rule. An advantage to both military judges and military lawyers of conformity is that the civilian authorities will be readily accessible and often will find their way into law school curricula, meaning that they will be better known to new military lawyers than are the decisions of the military courts.

We would emphasize, however, that where the Military Rules make a conscious effort to depart from the Federal Rules, it would be counterproductive for military courts to emulate the decisions of civilian courts. If the drafters have made an effort to provide a different rule, one that recognizes the special needs of the military, this Rule should be interpreted with the choice to be different in mind. Thus, when military courts look to the rules of evidence that are used by District Courts as an auxiliary source of authority under Rule 101(b), military courts should be careful to distinguish the Rules used by District Courts that are explicitly or implicitly rejected by the Military Rules, which probably ought not to be followed, and those rules which supplement evidence Rules that are accepted by military courts, which can readily be borrowed.

The basic mandate of subdivision (b) substantially reiterates the existing approach of military courts and is consistent with the designs of Congress. Article 36(a) of the Code requires that modes of proof in criminal cases — including pretrial, trial and post-trial proceedings — follow those that are generally recognized in the United States District Courts. Paragraph 137 of the *Manual* adopts the language of Article 36. In *United States v. Nivens,* 21 C.M.A. 420, 423, 45 C.M.R. 194, 197 (1972), the Court of Military Appeals stated as follows: "This court has repeatedly held that federal practice applies to courts-martial if not incompatible with military law or with the special requirements of the military establishment." *See also United States v. Moore,* 14 C.M.A. 635, 34 C.M.R. 415 (1964).

Subdivision (c) makes clear that when the Rules use the term "military judge," the term is intended to include the president of the special court-martial that has no military judge and also a summary court-martial officer. Other Rules distinguish between courts-martial with a military judge and those without. Our Editorial Comments will point out the distinctions at appropriate points.

DRAFTERS' ANALYSIS

(a) Applicability. Rule 101(a) is taken generally from Federal Rule of Evidence 101. It emphasizes that these Rules are applicable to summary as well as to special and general courts-martial. *See* "Rule of Construction," Rule 101(c). Rule 1101 expressly indicates that the rules of evidence are inapplicable to investigative hearings under Article 32, proceedings for pretrial advice, search authorization proceedings, vacation proceedings, and certain other proceedings. Although the Rules apply to sentencing, they may be "relaxed" under Rule 1101(c) and ¶ 75c of the *Manual*.

The limitation in subdivision (a) applying the Rules to courts-martial is intended expressly to recognize that these Rules are not applicable to military commissions, provost courts, and courts of inquiry unless otherwise required by competent authority. *See* ¶ 2 of the *Manual*. The Rules, however, serve as a "guide" for such tribunals. *Id.*

The Military Rules of Evidence are inapplicable to proceedings conducted pursuant to Article 15 of the Uniform Code of Military Justice.

The decisions of the United States Court of Military Appeals and of the Courts of Military Review must be utilized in interpreting these Rules. While specific decisions of the Article III courts involving rules which are common both to the Military Rules and the Federal Rules should be considered very persuasive, they are not binding; *see* Article 36 of the Uniform Code of Military Justice. It should be noted, however, that a significant policy consideration in adopting the Federal Rules of Evidence was to ensure, where possible, common evidentiary law.

(b) Secondary Sources. Rule 101 (b) is taken from ¶ 137 of the present *Manual* which has its origins in Article 36 of the Uniform Code of Military Justice. Rule 101(a) makes it clear that the Military Rules of Evidence are the primary source of evidentiary law for military practice. Notwithstanding their wide scope, however, Rule 101(b) recognizes that recourse to secondary sources may occasionally be necessary. Rule 101(b) prescribes the sequence in which such sources shall be utilized.

Rule 101(b) (1) requires that the first such source be the "rules of evidence generally recognized in the trial of criminal cases in the United States district courts." To the extent that a Military Rule of Evidence reflects an express modification of a Federal Rule of Evidence or a federal evidentiary procedure, the President has determined that the unmodified Federal Rule or procedure is, within the meaning of Article 36(a), either not "practicable" or is "contrary to or inconsistent with" the Uniform Code of Military Justice. Consequently, to the extent to which the Military Rules do not dispose of an issue, the Article III federal practice when practicable and not inconsistent or contrary to the Military Rules shall be applied. In determining whether there is a rule of evidence "generally recognized," it is anticipated that ordinary legal research shall be involved with primary emphasis being placed upon the published decisions of the three levels of the Article III courts.

Under Rule 1102, which concerns amendments to the Federal Rules of Evidence, no amendment to the Federal Rules shall be applicable to courts-martial until 180 days after the amendment's effective date unless the President shall direct its earlier adoption. Thus, such an amendment cannot be utilized as a secondary source until 180 days has passed since its effective date or until the President has directed its adoption, whichever occurs first. An amendment will not be applicable at any time if the President so directs.

It is the intent of the committee that the expression, "common law" found within Rule 101(b) (2) be construed in its broadest possible sense. It should include the federal common law and what may be denominated military common law. Prior military cases may be cited as authority under Rule 101(b) (2) to the extent that they are based upon a present *Manual* provision which has been retained in the Military Rules of Evidence or to the extent that they are not inconsistent with the "rules of evidence generally recognized in the trial of criminal cases in the United States district courts," deal with matters "not otherwise prescribed in this *Manual* or these rules," and are "practicable and not inconsistent with or contrary to the Uniform Code of Military Justice or this *Manual.*"

*(c) **Rule of Construction.*** Rule 101(c) is intended to avoid unnecessary repetition of the expressions, "president of a special court-martial without a military judge" and "summary court-martial officer." "Summary court-martial officer" is used instead of "summary court-martial" for purposes of clarity. A summary court-martial officer is considered to function in the same role as a military judge notwithstanding possible lack of legal training. As previously noted in ¶ 137 of the *Manual,* "a summary court-martial has the same discretionary power as a military judge concerning the reception of evidence." Where the application of these Rules in a summary court-martial or a special court-martial without a military judge is different from the application of the Rules in a court-martial with a military judge, specific reference has been made.

Disposition of Present Manual. That part of ¶ 137 of the present *Manual* not reflected in Rule 101 is found in other rules, *see, e.g.,* Rules 104, 401, 403. The reference in ¶ 137 to privileges arising out of treaty or executive agreement has been deleted as being unnecessary. *See generally* Rule 501.

Rule 102. Purpose and Construction

These rules shall be construed to secure fairness in administration, elimination of unjustifiable expense and delay, and promotion of growth and development of the law of evidence to the end that the truth may be ascertained and proceedings justly determined.

EDITORIAL COMMENT

Rule 102 is a statement of philosophy and goals, not a specific rule on how trials are to be conducted. It is an aspirational and hortatory rule, different from anything in previous *Manual* renditions. Six objectives worthy of attainment are included in the Rule's few lines: (1) Securing fairness in the administration of justice; (2) eliminating unjustifiable delay; (3) eliminating unjustifiable expense; (4) promoting the growth and development of the law; (5) enhancing the truth-finding process; and (6) justly determining the guilt or innocence of an accused.

There is no mention in the Rule of military exigencies, and no recognition that the requirement for discipline or mission may have a bearing on court-martial practice. It could be argued that the drafters' failure to address these concerns means that the traditional conceptual battle between defense and government counsel as to whether the proceeding is actually one of justice or military discipline has been laid to rest. It is unfortunate that neither the Rule nor the drafters' *Analysis* speaks to these matters, although each fuels the defense position by default.

The very clear language of the Rule mandates that it is to be used to "construe" the remaining Rules. Thus, the Rule provides ammunition for both defense and government counsel to use in their application of other evidentiary provisions. Government counsel can always oppose a defense offer of evidence by arguing that to permit the evidence to be admitted would cause unjustifiable expense to the government and needlessly delay the proceedings, while ultimately adding nothing to the truth-finding process. Defense counsel's rejoinder will be to suggest that the court cannot adequately determine the issue before it without the evidence in question, and thus the interests of justice and the Rules themselves will be frustrated if the evidence is not admitted. Defense counsel's requests to suppress government evidence will emphasize the need for proceedings to be "justly determined," whereas the government will stress the importance of truth-finding. The fact is that there is authority in Rule 102 for almost any argument anyone would care to make. Admitting evidence takes time and may be expensive; yet it may aid the search for truth. On the other hand, it may distract the court and impair the search. Exclusion of evidence denies the court evidence, but may speed up and improve fact-finding. Because everyone can argue from this Rule, it is likely to help no one very much.

When Rule 102 is used, its language indicates that it is intended to aid in the construction — *i.e.,* the legitimate application — of other specific Rules.

The Rule, in our view, should not be used as an independent source of authority to override specific dictates of other Rules. The question whether Rule 102 may be an independent evidence source has caused some uncertainty in the federal courts. In *United States v. Batts,* 558 F.2d 513 (9th Cir. 1977), the court initially decided a Rule 608(b) issue in the government's favor, ruling it had been proper to establish, with extrinsic evidence on rebuttal, that the accused had previously sold cocaine, which he had denied on cross-examination. Unable to uphold the use of extrinsic evidence under Rule 608(b)'s provisions, the court decided that Rule 102 could be used to create an exception to 608(b). Ultimately, the court withdrew its original decision, 573 F.2d 599 (9th Cir. 1977), and affirmed the conviction, this time in reliance on Rule 404(b). Had the earlier decision stood, Rule 102 would have been a threat to the very idea of an evidence code with specific rules defined in advance, since Rule 102 would always be available to provide an escape from specific rules. Drawing a line between the interpretation of other rules, which is required, and the disregard for other rules, which is improper, will not always be easy. But it must be done.

A proper use of Rule 102 is evident in *United States v. Jackson,* 405 F. Supp. 938 (E.D.N.Y. 1975). There the Rule was employed to balance government and defense contentions with respect to impeachment of witnesses. No specific Rule governed, and both sides made claims worthy of consideration. So, the judge ruled in a way that accommodated the concerns of both parties. Sound reliance on Rule 102 is also found in *United States v. Bibbs,* 564 F.2d 1165 (5th Cir. 1977). There the issue at bar concerned how Rule 613(b)'s provisions for using *prior* inconsistent statements might control counsel's use of *subsequent* inconsistent statements. The Fifth Circuit resolved this problem by determining that because the Rules were silent on the question, the trial judge was free to fashion an evidentiary approach which would comport with Rule 102's guidance and Congress' intent.

Because Rule 102 is so broadly written, it places great responsibility upon counsel and judges. Rule 103's requirements for making and protecting the record must be adequately employed in order to assure a reasoned basis for its invocation in a particular case.

Military due process will always be the final standard against which an interpretation of any Rule must be measured. Adequate recognition of this concept has consistently been a theme in the Court of Military Appeals' decisions, since it was first announced in *United States v. Clay,* 1 C.M.A. 74, 1 C.M.R. 74 (1951). Shortly thereafter, the United States Supreme Court recognized the new standard in *Burns v. Wilson,* 346 U.S. 137 (1953), and with it a new independence and respect for court-martial practice. *Burns* represents the High Court's view that military justice can be trusted to adjudicate criminal cases and criminal punishments as long as the Court of Military Appeals adheres "to those basic guarantees which have long been recognized and honored by the military courts." 346 U.S. at 143. However, the court warned that if it or the various federal circuit courts determine that military practice has become "bent on fixing guilt by dispensing with rudimentary fairness," (*id.*) then it would be forced to become more involved in overseeing the operation of military tribunals.

In the years which have elapsed since *Burns* was decided, the Supreme Court and the federal district courts have continued to recognize court-martial practice as being both fair and just; they consistently have refused to interfere in its administration. *See, e.g., Parker v. Levy,* 417 U.S. 733 (1974), and *Schlesinger v. Councilman,* 420 U.S. 738 (1975) (where Articles 133 and 134's general punitive prohibitions were affirmed); *Middendorf v. Henry,* 425 U.S. 25 (1976) (approving summary court-martial proceedings without defense counsel); *Curry v. Secretary of the Army,* 595 F.2d 873 (D.C. Cir. 1979) (rejecting contentions that the convening authority's actions in the court-martial process were unconstitutional). *But see O'Callahan v. Parker,* 395 U.S. 258 (1969) (where court-martial jurisdiction was substantially limited).

In applying the new Rules, military courts must endeavor to retain the trust and confidence earned over so long a period of time. The Rules provide possibilities for judicial discretion which, if abused, could vitiate fundamental concepts of fairness and thereby threaten the credibility of military justice.

A final question is whether a military judge trying a case alone must follow the Rules as he would were the decision in the case to be made by members of the court. Rule 101 makes clear that the Rules apply in all courts-martial, which means those tried to members of the court *and* those tried to a judge alone. Of course, the judge who sits both as evidence umpire and fact finder may hear evidence that is inadmissible. But the law demands that the judge endeavor to set this evidence aside in reaching a decision in the case.

It is arguable that judges are more capable than jurors in dealing with hearsay. But free admission of hearsay evidence in trials before military judges would raise serious confrontation and fundamental fairness problems. The fact that judges understand that hearsay evidence has its problems does not mean that a judge who is unable to examine a declarant is much better able than members of the court would be to determine how much weight to allocate to the hearsay. The trouble with hearsay is that it might be erroneous for several different reasons — the declarant may have lied, the declarant's memory may have failed, or the declarant may have erred in perceiving events, for example — but without the declarant present, even a trained judge cannot evaluate very well the chance of error in particular instances. Rules 801, 803, and 804 permit some out-of-court statements to be admitted for their truth; when these Rules are not satisfied hearsay should be excluded. The Supreme Court has recognized this and has held that it is just as erroneous for a judge to admit hearsay in a bench trial as in a jury trial. *Moore v. United States,* 429 U.S. 20 (1976).

This is not to suggest that, when hearsay is improperly admitted, an appellate court will reverse a case tried to a trial judge alone as quickly as it will a case tried to members of the court. Indeed, appellate courts often assume that the trial judge disregarded any inadmissible evidence in reaching a decision, unless the trial judge plainly indicated otherwise. It does suggest, however, that trial judges should follow the Rules when they try cases if they want to act properly.

10

It would be proper for a judge to take into account the fact that members of the court might be more likely to be prejudiced by certain evidence than a judge. Thus, holdings under Rules like 403, 608(c), and 609(a) might differ in cases tried to a judge alone from rulings in cases tried to members of the court.

It is possible that Rule 102 will be somewhat less important in the overall scheme of Military Rules than in the Federal Rules. The drafters of the Military Rules attempted to fill gaps in the Federal Rules in order to reduce the necessity of having judges answer questions left open by the Rules through ad hoc decisions. Thus, resort to Rule 102 may be infrequent in military courts.

DRAFTERS' ANALYSIS

Rule 102 is taken without change from Federal Rule of Evidence 102 and is without counterpart in the present *Manual for Courts-Martial.* It provides a set of general guidelines to be used in construing the Military Rules of Evidence. It is, however, only a rule of construction and not a license to disregard the Rules in order to reach a desired result.

Rule 103. Rulings on Evidence

(a) Effect of erroneous ruling. Error may not be predicated upon a ruling which admits or excludes evidence unless the ruling materially prejudices a substantial right of a party, and

   (1) Objection. In case the ruling is one admitting evidence, a timely objection or motion to strike appears of record, stating the specific ground of objection, if the specific ground was not apparent from the context; or

   (2) Offer of proof. In case the ruling is one excluding evidence, the substance of the evidence was made known to the military judge by offer or was apparent from the context within which questions were asked.

The standard provided in this subdivision does not apply to errors involving requirements imposed by the Constitution of the United States as applied to members of the armed forces except insofar as the error arises under these rules and this subdivision provides a standard that is more advantageous to the accused than the constitutional standard.

(b) Record of offer and ruling. The military judge may add any other or further statement which shows the character of the evidence, the form in which it was offered, the objection made, and the ruling thereon. The military judge may direct the making of an offer in question and answer form.

(c) Hearing of members. In a court-martial composed of a military judge and members, proceedings shall be conducted, to the extent practicable, so as to prevent inadmissible evidence from being suggested to the members by any means, such as making statements or offers of proof or asking questions in the hearing of the members.

(d) Plain error. Nothing in this rule precludes taking notice of plain errors that materially prejudice substantial rights although they were not brought to the attention of the military judge.

EDITORIAL COMMENT

From a military practitioner's point of view, Rule 103 will probably alter court-martial practice more than any other provision contained in the new Military Rules. This is because the Rule places the responsibility of raising and preserving evidentiary issues squarely and almost entirely upon counsel, not upon the trial or appellate courts. As a result, if a proper record is not made at trial, no relief will be available on appeal.

It cannot be said that counsel have borne similar responsibilities in the past. Particularly in practicing before the Court of Military Appeals, appellate defense counsel often have been permitted, if not encouraged by the court, to raise allegations of error having no foundation in the trial record. *Cf.* Fidell, *The Specification of Appellate Issues by the United States Court of Military Appeals,* 31 JAG J. 99 (1980). Rule 103 rejects this approach for several reasons: First, it permits careless litigation below. In some instances, it even encourages the sloppy handling of issues, as when defense counsel is concerned that the trial judge may be less sympathetic to facts than the appellate court. Second, the government may be denied a fair chance to be heard on appeal. If an appellate court will permit defense counsel to save claims not raised at trial and then to raise and litigate them on a cold appellate record or upon post-trial affidavits, the defense, knowing in advance that claims have been withheld, will have a substantial advantage. Thus, the interests of justice may suffer. When this happens before the Court of Military Appeals, a body with no fact-finding power (*see* Article 67(d), U.C.M.J.), the situation becomes particularly egregious.

Third, the absence of a proper record may lead to inappropriate decisions, and inconsistent reasoning by an appellate court. Such a body cannot work well in a vacuum, resolving questions based on what it, detached from the trial proceedings, *thinks* the proper issues should have been, as opposed to what the record discloses the actual issues *were*. Decisions, which are not narrowed and sharpened in the trial court, may be unfortunate.

An example is *United States v. Reagan,* 7 M.J. 490 (C.M.A. 1980). There, defense counsel framed their case at trial around the government's lack of probable cause in making a search. Naturally, the prosecution directed its efforts and evidence against that allegation. When the case was ultimately reviewed by the Court of Military Appeals, that body permitted the defense to change its theory of attack, and litigate whether the search violated the Supplementary Agreements to the North Atlantic Treaty Organization Status of Forces Agreement, not whether probable cause existed. Based on the record presented to it, the Court of Military Appeals had little difficulty in finding a Treaty violation and reversed the conviction. In dissenting, Judge Cook questioned the wisdom of the majority's ruling, and highlighted the difficulties involved in adequately resolving unlitigated, complex issues on appeal. This, of course, was a probable cause issue only; it did not affect the underlying facts of the case. But it serves as a reminder of the need to present questions in the first instance to the trial court.

Fourth, the failure to make proper objections and offers of proof at trial means that appeals, which might be unnecessary if the trial court were properly informed of the contentions of the parties, will occur. When issues are withheld at trial, the trial court is denied an opportunity to provide a correct result the first time around.

Rule 103 should change all this, although it remains to be seen whether the Court of Military Appeals' paternalistic tendencies will be abandoned in favor of a more traditional appellate practice. This is not to suggest that plain error will not be taken into account on appeal. As we indicate below, it will. It is to suggest, however, that the concept should be used sparingly.

An examination of the Rule itself will demonstrate just how much responsibility counsel must shoulder now.

Rule 103(a) first states that no error may be found to exist on appeal unless that error materially prejudices a substantial right of a party. Because the new Rules are applicable to only military *criminal* cases, the term "party" must be taken to mean the accused. The language "materially prejudices a substantial right of a party" is somewhat different from that found in the Federal Rule, although it is substantively similar (the federal language is "a substantial right of a party is affected"). This difference is necessitated by Article 59(a) of the Code which states "A finding or sentence of a court-martial may not be held incorrect on the ground of an error of law unless the error materially prejudices the substantial rights of the accused."

Application of this language has not proved easy for the military courts. They have struggled with the same sorts of questions about the effects of errors on trials that have plagued civilian courts.

In some instances the military courts, particularly the Court of Military Appeals, have adopted prophylactic rules that must be followed if a conviction is to be sustained. Violation of these rules can result in reversal, even if no claim of prejudice in an individual case can or could be made. This may be observed in *United States v. Green,* 1 M.J. 453 (C.M.A. 1976) and *United States v. King,* 3 M.J. 458 (C.M.A. 1977), where the court enforced inflexible guilty plea procedural requirements, even though the accused in both cases failed to establish prejudice. In *United States v. Groce,* 3 M.J. 369 (C.M.A. 1977) the court reversed a conviction, believing that a court-member had been asleep during the judge's instructions, even though the accused failed to establish the issue at trial, and was unable to demonstrate prejudice on appeal. *United States v. Castrillon-Moreno,* 7 M.J. 414 (C.M.A. 1979) restates the holding in *Green,* again reversing a conviction without concern for prejudice or harm to the accused. *Cf. United States v. Passini,* 10 M.J. 108 (C.M.A. 1980) where the court demonstrated an intention to withdraw from *King's* strict requirements.

This approach is not unique to the military courts; the United States Supreme Court has indicated that it will not apply the harmless error rule to certain kinds of errors. *See, e.g., Holloway v. Arkansas,* 435 U.S. 475 (1978). But prophylactic rules are the exception. The rule is that the effect of error must be tested by looking to the impact of the error on the proceeding.

When a federal constitutional error is committed, the Court of Military Appeals has stated that the decision of the Supreme Court in *Chapman v. California,* 386 U.S. 18 (1967), must be followed. *See, e.g., United States v. Bonavita,* 21 C.M.A. 407, 409, 45 C.M.R. 181, 183 (1972); *United States v. Ward,* 1 M.J. 176 (C.M.A. 1975). *Chapman* requires reversal unless a constitutional error is harmless beyond a reasonable doubt, which, the court has indicated, means there is no reasonable possibility that error affected the decision in the trial court. *See Harrington v. California,* 395 U.S. 250 (1969); *Schneble v. Florida,* 405 U.S. 427 (1972); *Milton v. Wainwright,* 407 U.S. 371 (1972). *Cf. Hicks v. Oklahoma,* 100 S. Ct. 2227 (1980) (finding a violation of due process where the trial jury that was to sentence a defendant was erroneously informed that it had to give a mandatory sentence if it convicted, and a properly instructed jury might have returned a different verdict.) The Rule makes clear that the standard for testing a constitutional error must be at least as protective of defendants as the standard for testing other errors. A per se rule, such as those described above, sometimes may apply to all errors.

Where the violation is other than constitutional, the Court of Military Appeals, in *United States v. Barnes,* 8 M.J. 115 (C.M.A. 1979) specifically adopted the Supreme Court's approach in *Kotteakos v. United States,* 328 U.S. 750, 764-765 (1946) as its standard. In *Kotteakos,* the High Court held that non-constitutional error produces harm when it has a substantial influence on the findings. In reaching this result, the court rejected contentions that if sufficient evidence of guilt existed without considering the tainted testimony, a conviction could still be affirmed; it required an analysis of the effect of error in the trial court.

The majority in *Barnes* specified that non-constitutional errors would be harmless under two circumstances: first, if the government could establish "that the finder of fact had not been influenced by it," or second, that the error had but a slight effect on the resolution of the issues in the instant case (8 M.J. at 116).

While application of these tests, particularly in the non-constitutional area, must be on an *ad hoc* basis, affirmative answers to the following questions may suggest that an error was harmful: Did the error go to the heart of the defense's case? Did the error discredit the accused, prohibit the accused from discrediting a key government witness, or prohibit the accused from proving an affirmative defense? Did the error result in admission of important evidence used to convict the accused? Was erroneously admitted evidence continually referred to in the government's case? If evidence favorable to the defense was erroneously suppressed by the trial judge, was the accused deprived of important and unique evidence? Did the exclusion of the defense's evidence make the government's evidence appear stronger than it otherwise might have appeared?

If the important thing under both the *Chapman* and *Kotteakos* lines of cases is the affect of error on the trial proceedings, it is not immediately apparent why a constitutional error is more worrisome than a non-constitutional mistake. Indeed, some commentators and courts have suggested that the *Chapman* test should be used for all errors, since it is consistent with the notion that reasonable doubts as to guilt, including legal guilt, should be resolved in favor of the defendant. *See* Saltzburg, *The Harm of Harmless Error,* 59 Va. L. Rev. 988 (1973). Some courts that purport to distinguish between kinds of errors slip into the *Chapman* test in reviewing non-constitutional claims, without apparently realizing it. *See, e.g., United States v. Rice,* 550 F.2d 1364 (5th Cir. 1977); *United States v. Martinez,* 588 F. 2d 495 (5th Cir. 1979). But other courts purport to make a distinction between the claims. *See, e.g., United States v. Valle-Valdez,* 554 F.2d 911 (9th Cir. 1977). Our view is that the *Chapman* test should be utilized for all errors. One advantage of this approach is that it signals the prosecution and trial judges that all errors are to be considered serious. Another advantage is that it makes clear to lower courts the importance of ruling correctly on all issues. A third advantage is that it complements the requirement that defense counsel preserve all claims at trial by assuring counsel that claims properly raised will not lightly be dismissed on appeal. A final advantage is that it avoids the need in some cases for courts to decide whether an error is simply an evidence mistake or an error of constitutional proportions. Avoidance of unnecessary constitutional decisions would seem to be desirable in light of the numerous and difficult constitutional claims that cannot be avoided. Although our approach is not currently the law, it could be suggested to military courts, since no particular standard is specified by the Rule.

Rules 103(a)(1) and (2) are the drafters' tools for enforcing the general prohibitions against appellate relief without an adequate trial record. Pursuant to Rule 103(a)(1), a timely and specific objection must be lodged with respect to the introduction of any allegedly improper evidence. If the evidence for some reason is already before the finder of fact, then a motion to strike the evidence must be made. It is important to note that both the motion to strike and any objection to the evidence must be specific, identifying the evidence objected to, and the grounds upon which it is contended the objection or motion should be sustained. The only exception to these requirements arises when the basis for an objection is obvious. However, it should be pointed out that what may appear to be obvious at trial may be unclear on appeal, and a careful lawyer always will state grounds for objecting. Rule 103(a) does not define what a timely objection is. Traditionally, timeliness has meant objecting before the witness has had an opportunity to answer the question, thereby prohibiting counsel from gambling that the answer might be helpful to his case. We believe the traditional approach should be followed, but that trial judges should recognize that sometimes counsel will not be aware of grounds for objection until a question is answered.

Neither the Rules nor the drafters' *Analysis* indicates exactly how appellate courts will define "specific ground of objection." Viewed from defense counsel's position, it is whatever will be enough to adequately make a record of what counsel believes is wrong with the proffered evidence or the form of the question. Recent federal decisions in this area point out that in order for a Rule 103(a)(1) objection to be properly made, it must be tied to the particular rule of evidence at bar. *See, e.g., United States v. Sims,* 617 F.2d 1371 (9th Cir. 1980) (court would not consider Rule 803(8) when only Rule 803(6) was raised at trial); *United States v. O'Brien,* 601 F.2d 1067 (9th Cir. 1979) (counsel did not rely on Rule 1006 at trial and could not rely on it on appeal); *United States v. Long,* 574 F.2d 761 (3d Cir. 1978) (objection failed to rely on Rule 703 and would not be considered on appeal); *United States v. Fendley,* 522 F.2d 181 (5th Cir. 1975) (no specific objection to foundation for business record, hence no appellate consideration).

Rule 103(a)(2) applies when an objection has been successful and the trial judge has decided to exclude evidence. If the proponent of the evidence is to retain for appeal the question of whether the trial judge's ruling was proper, an offer of proof must be made. As with Rule 103(a)(1), such an offer will not be required where it is clear from the record exactly what was involved. If, for example, defense counsel attempts to examine a witness whose testimony is hearsay, but the defense claims that it falls within an exception to the hearsay rule, yet government counsel successfully objects, defense counsel must then make an offer of proof—*i.e.,* indicate in a clear way what the excluded testimony would have been. Similarly, if an expert witness is excluded, defense counsel must indicate what testimony would have been offered.

Pre-existing *Manual* provisions, though uniformly ignored on appeal, were similar to Rule 103(a)(2). Under ¶ 154c (now redesignated as ¶ 154(*f*), an offer of proof was strictly a defense counsel's tool, and was to be used any time the trial judge prevented the accused from introducing evidence. Paragraph 154c provided for defense counsel to make a concise statement setting forth the substance of the excluded evidence. In *United States v. Young,* 49 C.M.R. 133 (A.F.C.M.R. 1974), one of the few appellate decisions in point, the court held that a defense counsel's offer of proof must be more than his mere hope of what the expected testimony would be. The offer of proof must portray, in fact, what the witness in question would ultimately have added to the proceedings. Because trial defense counsel in *Young* failed to accomplish this, the offer of proof was rejected, both at trial and on appeal, as incomplete.

It should be clear that there is a difference between an offer of proof following a judge's decision to exclude evidence and representations of fact that are actually used in lieu of evidence by the court to resolve a disputed question. In *United States v. Barbeau,* 9 M.J. 569 (A.F.C.M.R. 1980), the Air Force Court of Review had occasion to reject the propriety of offers of proof by both sides, which the trial judge used as a basis for deciding whether there was in personam jurisdiction. It is clear that counsel may stipulate to certain facts, including facts about personal as opposed to subject matter jurisdiction — *see, e.g., United States v. Bertleson,* 3 M.J. 314 (C.M.A. 1977) (discussing "confessional" stipulations); *United States v. Long,* 3 M.J. 400 (C.M.A. 1977) (allowing "non-confessional" stipulations) — but it also is clear that offers to prove critical facts are not to be used as substitutes for proof, absent stipulations. Of course, counsel may represent to the court that a witness is available to testify — *see United States v. Burrow,* 16 C.M.A. 94, 36 C.M.R. 250 (1966) — or that certain counsel may or may not be available to a defendant — *see United States v. Vanderpool,* 10 C.M.R. 664 (A.F.B.R. 1953) — but these representations are not evidence in the case.

Neither ¶ 154c, nor Rule 103(a) (2) and the drafters' *Analysis* accompanying it discusses what form an offer of proof should take. Offers of proof can be made in several ways.

First, counsel may obtain permission from the trial court to question a witness as if the objection had been overruled. Rule 103(b) explicitly recognizes this form of an offer. This technique permits the trial and appellate courts to view the actual testimony in the form it would have taken. The difficulty here is that this procedure may take a great deal of time, and naturally it must be conducted out of the court-members' presence. Second, counsel can simply state for the record what his investigation and preparation indicates the witness will testify to, establishing the basis for such knowledge. Depending on the complexity of this offer, it may be possible to have it at side bar, thus saving time while protecting the record. Third, counsel, fearing exclusion of evidence, could summarize in writing the testimony of the witness and offer the summary to the court.

United States v. Winkle, 587 F.2d 705 (5th Cir. 1979), indicates what happens when a proper offer is not made. There the accused contended on appeal that the trial court had erred in excluding certain testimony. Although it seems the court of appeals agreed with appellant's legal contentions, it failed to grant relief, because the record did not contain an adequate offer of proof disclosing precisely what the excluded testimony would have been. The court did note that the various circuits (much like the military) have not uniformly applied Rule 103(a)(2). Some, as in *Charter v. Chleborad,* 551 F.2d 246 (8th Cir. 1977) have been very lenient with respect to counsel's offer of proof. But the *Winkle* court warned that it "will not even consider the propriety of the decision to exclude the evidence at issue if no offer of proof was made at trial." 587 F.2d at 710. The court suggested that a proper offer contains: (A) a statement concerning the nature of the testimony in question; (B) an indication of the issue that the testimony would affect; and (C) a showing of how the issue would be affected. The court warned that mere conclusions with respect to these criteria will not be sufficient. We suggest that the format provided in *Winkle* is an excellent model for the military to follow. *See also United States v. Vitale,* 596 F.2d 688 (5th Cir. 1979) and *United States v. Muncy,* 526 F.2d 1261 (5th Cir. 1976) (refusing to consider the propriety of evidence rulings); *United States v. Clark,* 617 F.2d 180 (9th Cir. 1980) (no error found in refusal by trial judge to allow the defense to recall a witness, since no offer of proof was made).

Rule 103(b) is designed to insure that counsel's offers of proof will be accurately preserved for appellate review by giving the trial judge discretion to enhance any offering. The trial court may add a comment which can be used to explain the character or form of the offer, the objection, or the trial court's own ruling. As such, Rule 103(b) provides the bench with an opportunity to make special findings concerning the reasons for its ruling, taking into consideration everything that occurs at trial.

Rule 103(c) is largely self-explanatory and is consistent with previous military practice. It provides that, to the extent practicable, the court-members should be protected from hearing inadmissible statements, offers of proof, or questions which might adversely affect the trial's outcome. As a result, all such matter should be handled at side bar, or with the members excused. Judge Weinstein suggests that continuously conducting proceedings outside the court-members' presence, or at side bar, may be disruptive and confusing to the finders of fact. He also suggests that the bench employ the following technique against counsel who continuously insist upon interrupting the proceedings with frivolous objections: "[I]t may be helpful to explain to him before the jury why the evidence is relevant, what the theory of the proponent's case is, and how the inquiry tends to support that theory," J. WEINSTEIN & M. BERGER, WEINSTEIN'S EVIDENCE, § 103[05].

Rule 103 (d) allows appellate courts to recognize plain errors that materially prejudice an accused's substantial rights, even though defense counsel may have failed to make a timely objection, an offer of proof, or motion to strike. It is in effect an escape clause from Rule 103's general mandatory provisions. Unfortunately subdivisions (a) and (d) of the Rule are confusing when read together. Since Rule 103(a) does not permit a claim of error unless a ruling at trial materially prejudices a substantial right of party, at first blush it would seem to overlap almost completely with Rule 103(d). If Rule 103(d) permits reversal any time that an error materially prejudices substantial rights, whether or not an error was preserved below, it would take the teeth out of the procedural requirements of subdivision (a). How is the apparent overlap in the Rules to be handled?

Our suggestion is that Rule 103(d) should be limited to errors that are indeed "plain," which means that there is no excuse for their occurrence. Such a reading of the Rule would assure that the accused is not unfairly tried because of inadequate or ill-prepared defense counsel. It would also hold the prosecution and the trial court responsible to see that obvious errors are corrected. But it would not permit defense counsel to intentionally conceal non-obvious claims for use on appeal. This reading places the burden on counsel to raise and preserve most claims, but indicates that the responsibility for correcting obvious, or *plain,* mistakes is shared by all trial participants. Consistent with our view is the suggestion in some cases that if defense counsel makes an effort to state a proper objection and alerts the court and opposing counsel to a claim, even if the objection is not quite right an appellate court might be more likely to find plain error than if defense counsel stands mute. *See, e.g., United States v. Check,* 582 F.2d 668, 677 n. 28 (2d Cir. 1978).

Because a trial judge shares responsibility for plain errors, when it appears that an error is about to occur, or has already occurred, the judge may want to inquire of defense counsel, outside the earshot of the court-members, to see whether counsel has inadvertently or erroneously acted, or whether counsel is pursuing a particular course intentionally, for strategic reasons. Not only would this make a good record for appeal, but more importantly it would protect those accused against some of the human errors that are going to occur in litigation. We see no reason not to protect against obvious mistakes, as long as the court is careful not to interfere with the defense tactics of competent counsel.

DRAFTER'S ANALYSIS

(a) Effect of erroneous ruling. Rule 103(a) is taken from the Federal Rule with a number of changes. The first, the use of the language, "the ruling materially prejudices a substantial right of a party" in place of the Federal Rule's "a substantial right of a party is affected" is required by Article 59(a) of the Uniform Code of Military Justice. Rule 103(a) comports with present military practice.

The second significant change is the addition of material relating to constitutional requirements and explicity states that errors of constitutional magnitude may require a higher standard than the general one required by Rule 103(a). For example the harmless error rule, when applicable to an error of constitutional dimensions, prevails over the general rule of Rule 103(a). Because Section III of these Rules embodies Constitutional rights, two standards of error may be at issue; one involving the Military Rules of Evidence, and one involving the underlying constitutional rule. In such a case, the standard of error more advantageous to the accused will apply.

Rule 103(a)(1) requires that a timely motion or objection generally be made in order to preserve a claim or error. This is similar to but more specific than present practice. In making such a motion or objection, the party has a right to state the specific grounds of the objection to the evidence. Failure to make a timely and sufficiently specific objection may waive the objection for purposes of both trial and appeal. In applying Federal Rule 103(a), the Article III courts have interpreted the Rule strictly and held the defense to an extremely high level of specificity. *See, e.g., United States v. Rubin,* 609 F.2d 51, 61-63 (2d Cir. 1979) (objection to form of witness's testimony did not raise or preserve an appropriate hearsay objection); *United States v. O'Brien,* 601 F.2d 1067 (9th Cir. 1979) (objection that prosecution witness was testifying from material not in evidence held inadequate to raise or preserve an objection under Rule 1006). As indicated in the *Analysis* of Rule 802, Rule 103 significantly changes military law insofar as hearsay is concerned. Unlike present law under which hearsay is absolutely incompetent, the Military Rules of Evidence simply treat hearsay as being inadmissible upon adequate objection; *see* Rules 803, 103(a). Note in the context of Rule 103(a) that ¶ 53g of the *Manual* states: "Both sides in a case are entitled to an opportunity to present and support their respective contentions, upon any matter presented to the court for decision."

An "offer of proof" is a concise statement by counsel setting forth the substance of the expected testimony or other evidence. *See* present *Manual* ¶ 145c.

Rule 103(a) prescribes a standard by which errors will be tested on appeal. Although counsel at trial need not indicate how an alleged error will "materially prejudice a substantial right" in order to preserve error, such a showing, during or after the objection or offer, may be advisable as a matter of trial practice to further illuminate the issue for both the trial and appellate bench.

(b);(c) Record of offer and ruling: Hearing of members. — Rules 103(b) and (c) are taken from the Federal Rules with minor changes in terminology to adapt them to military procedure.

(d) Plain error. Rule 103(d) is taken from the Federal Rule with a minor change of terminology to adapt it to military practice and the substitution of "materially prejudices" substantial rights for "affecting" substantial rights to conform it to Article 59(a) of the Uniform Code of Military Justice.

Rule 104. Preliminary Questions

(a) Questions of admissibility generally. Preliminary questions concerning the qualification of a person to be a witness, the existence of a privilege, the admissibility of evidence, an application for continuance, or the availability of a witness shall be determined by the military judge. In making these determinations the military judge is not bound by the rules of evidence except those with respect to privileges.

(b) Relevancy conditioned on fact. When the relevancy of evidence depends upon the fulfillment of a condition of fact, the military judge shall admit it upon, or subject to, the introduction of evidence sufficient to support a finding of the fulfillment of the condition. A ruling on the sufficiency of evidence to support a finding of fulfillment of a condition of fact is the sole responsibility of the military judge, except where these rules or this Manual provide expressly to the contrary.

(c) Hearing of members. Except in cases tried before a special court-martial without a military judge, hearings on the admissibility of statements of an accused under rules 301-306 shall in all cases be conducted out of the hearing of the members. Hearings on other preliminary matters shall be so conducted when the interests of justice require or, when an accused is a witness, if the accused so requests.

(d) Testimony by accused. The accused does not, by testifying upon a preliminary matter, become subject to cross-examination as to other issues in the case.

(e) Weight and credibility. This rule does not limit the right of a party to introduce before the members evidence relevant to weight or credibility.

EDITORIAL COMMENT

This Rule follows the structure of the Federal Rule, but makes some language changes. Essentially, it codifies a traditional approach to the division of function between judge and court members. It should be kept in mind that this is a procedural, not a substantive, Rule. Section III of the Military Rules defines the content of many criminal procedure rules, and Sections V, VI, VII, VIII, and X set forth some basic evidence rules that judges will look to in making 104 rulings.

Rule 104(a) is generally based on its federal counterpart, although the drafters have altered it slightly to accommodate existing military authority. The Rule provides that the trial judge will resolve most preliminary questions that require application of procedural or evidentiary rules and that the judge will do so without the court-members present. *See* Rule 104(c). Five particular issues are reserved for the trial judge: (1) Whether an individual is fit to be a witness (*see* our discussion of Rule 601 which treats witness competency); (2) whether there is a privilege protecting a witness from disclosing information he might have (*see* Section V generally); (3) whether an evidence or procedure rule or a constitutional doctrine prevents the admission of evidence (*see* Section III generally); (4) whether a continuance should be granted; and (5) whether a request for witnesses should be honored. The Rule goes on to mandate that in resolving such issues the trial judge is not bound by the rules of evidence, except with respect to privileges. Although the drafters' *Analysis* suggests that it is unclear whether inadmissible evidence may be utilized by a judge making a 104(a) ruling, especially on a constitutional question, the prevailing practice is for judges to use such evidence. It is doubtful that the Rule will be held unconstitutional. *See generally United States v. Matlock,* 415 U.S. 164, 175 (1974).

The Military Rule differs from the Federal Rule in two minor respects. Applications for continuance and requests for witnesses are specifically mentioned in the Military Rule; they are not specifically covered by the Federal Rule. The military drafters felt these additional requirements were necessary due to the world-wide nature of court-martial practice. Witness production could not efficiently be litigated if, for example, the hearsay prohibitions in Section VIII were controlling. With trial forums and witnesses thousands of miles apart, litigation concerning witness production would be impossible. As a result *Manual* ¶ 137's provisions were drafted into the new rules. Even though Federal Rule 104(a) is not as explicit, federal judges exercise the same authority conferred upon military judges. Federal Rule 1101 makes the evidence rules inapplicable when the judge considers such matters.

Because of Rule 104, many questions about how judges make evidence rulings now have been answered. However, questions of who has the burden of proof, and what standard of proof applies to Rule 104(a) questions are not addressed. We anticipate this void will be filled by traditional military practice. *See* ¶ 57*a* of the *Manual;* Saltzburg, *Standards of Proof and Preliminary Questions of Fact,* 27 STAN. L. REV. 271 (1975).

Privileges receive more favorable treatment under Rule 104(a) than do other evidence rules. This is not surprising. When it comes to the other evidence rules, courts trained in how to treat evidence issues can handle inadmissible evidence well enough to permit its use on a preliminary issue — one that is not a fact going to the merits of the case. But a privilege need only be violated once before its benefits largely are lost. So the Rule opts to allow privileges to retain their utility throughout proceedings.

When the trial judge is called upon to make a Rule 104(a) determination, a hearing may be necessary. At the hearing the trial judge may have to resolve credibility issues in order to decide whether evidence should be admitted or must be excluded. The most troublesome situation for trial judges arises when an evidence issue coincides with an ultimate fact in the case, the typical example being the evidence question of whether a conspiracy existed that justifies admission of a statement under Rule 801(d)(2)(E) in a case where the ultimate question on the merits is whether a conspiracy existed. Our treatment of Rule 801(d)(2)(E) covers this situation.

Generally, the important thing to keep in mind is that the trial judge decides questions of how evidence rules, procedural rules and constitutional concepts affect offers and objections to evidence. The judge must administer the legal concepts, and in doing so, may have to do fact-finding. But the fact-finding that relates to the questions of guilt and innocence and criminal responsibility is left to members of the court. Although there sometimes is an identity of issues, the trial judge's ruling on a preliminary question only determines whether or not evidence is to be admitted; the court-members have the final say on the weight to be given evidence.

Subdivision (b) of Rule 104 should be consulted whenever counsel objects that evidence is irrelevant. The trial judge alone determines whether the evidence is relevant and whether there is a sufficient factual predicate to permit the evidence to come before the court-members. If one piece of evidence is relevant only if another piece also is offered, the trial judge might admit the evidence and strike it if the link is not made, or he might ask counsel to demonstrate that the link can be made before admitting the evidence.

Rule 104(b) has language not found in the Federal Rule. The additional language makes applicable what is implicit in the Federal Rule. The last sentence of subdivision (b) specifies that the trial judge will determine the sufficiency of evidence to support a finding by members of the court, unless some other evidence rule or *Manual* provision dictates otherwise. It is difficult to imagine when the trial judge will be required to admit evidence that could not support a finding by members of the court. The drafters' *Analysis* does not explain what they had in mind. Perhaps, however, the drafters were concerned with Rules like Rule 201, which allows the judge to judicially notice a fact (which means that the judge has already found it to be beyond reasonable dispute). The trial judge probably ought to admit counter-evidence that satisfies the evidence rules in order to avoid making the noticed fact appear to be uncontradictory.

In the usual case, Rule 104(b) requires the trial judge to ask himself at least one, and possibly two, questions when evidence is offered and an objection on relevance grounds is made. Always, the judge must ask the following questions: Will the court-members believe this evidence might be helpful in deciding the case accurately? If the answer is "no," the judge excludes the evidence as irrelevant under Rule 402. If the answer is "yes," the judge asks another question: Is there sufficient evidence to warrant a reasonable court-member in concluding that it is to be believed? If the answer is "no," the evidence is excluded. If the answer is "yes," the evidence is admitted. It is very important that the judge not decide whether *he* believes the evidence under Rule 104(b); the judge only decides whether a reasonable court-member could believe it. If one piece of evidence must be connected with another to be useful, the judge asks the questions stated here with respect to the two pieces of evidence together.

When Rules 104(a) and 104(b) are put together, it seems that the judge protects the court-members under (b) by assuring that evidence is relevant if believed, and that there is enough evidence for the jury to believe it. Under Rule 104(a) the judge himself must be satisfied that the principle of evidence, procedure or constitutional law has been satisfied. For instance, the judge decides whether a communication was made in confidence to a lawyer, or whether it was part of plea bargaining. Once he decides, he knows whether to admit or to exclude the evidence.

Subdivision (c) discusses under what circumstances the court-members should be excluded from hearing these issues discussed. In substance the Rule is much like its federal counterpart, although it has been tailored to meet military requirements. It is possible, for example, to have a trial before a special court-martial that sits without a military judge, although this does not happen frequently. Under these circumstances all issues, legal and factual, must be decided by the laymen members; they would be expected to act as trial judges act in bench trials (or as three judge federal courts act when they try cases), only without the legal training of the judges. Rule 104 is largely useless in a lay trial without a judge. We will not pursue this matter any further, as military trials without judges are now mainly of historical importance only. However, when trial is conducted before a military judge and court-members, Rule 104(c) *requires* that the members be excused during litigation arising under Rules 301-306. With respect to hearings on other preliminary issues, the Rule is permissive, indicating such litigation should be conducted out of the court-members' presence under two circumstances: (1) When the interests of justice require, and (2) when the accused is a witness on a preliminary question and so requests.

In large part, Rule 104(c) is a re-codification of existing *Manual* and UCMJ provisions. Article 39(a) of the UCMJ allows the bench to convene sessions outside the court-members' presence when resolving motions, objections, and matters which may be prejudicial to the defense. The Code also states, in very general terms, that the judge shall exclude the members when regulations or other competent authority requires. Specifically included within this category are evidentiary concerns falling within Article 36. Paragraph 67e of the *Manual* also is relevant; it permits the judge to rule on objections when made, or after taking them under advisement. Paragraph 57a(2) requires the trial court to protect the members from inadvertent examination of inadmissible evidence. *See also Manual* ¶ 57g, which generally discusses this area.

Recent military cases have struggled with the question of when the trial judge should rule on suppression and related motions. In *United States v. Allen*, 6 M.J. 633 (C.G.C.M.R. 1978) the court indicated that the choice as to whether such issues should be litigated at trial or during pretrial Article 39(a) sessions was a matter falling within the trial judge's sound discretion, and no substitution of judgment would occur on appeal absent abuse. *See United States v. Gainer*, 7 M.J. 1009 (N.C.M.R. 1979); *United States v. Freeman*, 15 C.M.A. 126, 35 C.M.R. 98 (1964) for similar holdings. However, Section III of the Military Rules of Evidence has altered this precedent, now requiring the bench to rule on all suppression and related motions prior to plea. This should prove to be of substantial benefit to the defense, offering in effect two bites at the apple (assuming the defense will renew a motion at trial), and providing valuable insight into the possible benefits of obtaining a pretrial agreement following a loss at the suppression hearing.

Subdivision (c) provides that hearings on the admissibility of an accused's statements, covered by Rules 301-306, must be held outside the hearing of court-members. If other hearings are to be conducted outside their presence, a party may have to request that this be done. *United States v. Fowler,* 605 F.2d 181, 185 (5th Cir. 1979) reinforces the importance of defense requests in this area. A failure to make a request may be considered a waiver of the issue, and no appellate relief will be available.

Rule 104(d) discusses another protection given the accused during preliminary question litigation: If the accused decides it is in his best interest to testify, he is not subject to cross-examination concerning any other issue in the case. In this respect the Rule is meant to encourage the accused to take the stand, and in so doing, to improve the fact-finding process by providing additional evidence. The accused's testimony almost certainly cannot constitutionally be used against him on the merits. *See Simmons v. United States,* 390 U.S. 377 (1968). It probably cannot be used for impeachment purposes either despite *Harris v. New York,* 401 U.S. 222 (1971) and *Jenkins v. Anderson,* 100 S. Ct. 2124 (1980) because of Rule 304(f). This subdivision reaffirms existing military authority, while reducing the latitude given government counsel in cross-examining the accused. *See* ¶ 149*b* of the *Manual.*

Rule 104(e) again highlights the importance of thorough trial preparation, and the alternatives available to opposing counsel after losing a preliminary question issue. The new provision states that nothing in Rule 104 prohibits opposing counsel from challenging the weight to be given evidence and the credibility of witnesses. Additional evidence can be offered to make the challenge. Thus, this subdivision is a reminder that the trial judge's decision to admit evidence does not mean the evidence must be believed by the court-members. Thorough trial preparation may provide opposing counsel with the means to establish that even though evidence is admitted, it is entitled to no weight.

DRAFTERS' ANALYSIS

(a) *Questions of admissibility generally.* Rule 104(a) is taken generally from the Federal Rule. Language in the Federal Rule requiring that admissibility shall be determined by the "court, subject to the provisions of subdivision (b)" has been struck to ensure that, subject to Rule 1008, questions of admissibility are solely for the military judge and not for the court-members. The deletion of the language is not intended, however, to negate the general interrelationship between subdivisions (a) and (b). When relevancy is conditioned on the fulfillment of a condition of fact, the military judge shall "admit it upon, or subject to, the introduction of evidence sufficient to support a finding of the fulfillment of the condition."

Pursuant to language taken from Federal Rule of Evidence 104(a), the rules of evidence, other than those with respect to privileges, are inapplicable to "preliminary questions concerning the qualification of a person to be a witness, the existence of a privilege, the admissibility of evidence. . . ." These exceptions are new to military law and may substantially change military practice. The Federal Rule has been modified, however, by inserting language relating to applications for continuances and determinations of witness availability. The change, taken from present *Manual* ¶ 137, is required by the worldwide disposition of the armed forces which makes matters relating to continuances and witness availability particularly difficult, if not impossible, to resolve under the normal rules of evidence — particularly the hearsay rule.

A significant and unresolved issue stemming from the language of Rule 104(a) is whether the rules of evidence shall be applicable to evidentiary questions involving constitutional or statutory issues such as those arising under Article 31. Thus it is unclear, for example, whether the rules of evidence are applicable to a determination of the voluntariness of an accused's statement. While the Rule strongly suggests that rules of evidence are not applicable to admissibility determinations involving constitutional issues, the issue is unresolved at present.

(b) Relevancy conditioned on fact. Rule 104(b) is taken from the Federal Rule except that the following language has been added: "A ruling on the sufficiency of evidence to support a finding of fulfillment of a condition of fact is the sole responsibility of the military judge." This material was added in order to clarify the rule and to explicitly preserve contemporary military procedure. *Manual* ¶ 57. Under the Federal Rule, it is unclear whether and to what extent evidentiary questions are to be submitted to the jury as questions of admissibility. Rule 104(b) has thus been clarified to eliminate any possibility, except as required by Rule 1008, that the court-members will make an admissibility determination. Failure to clarify the rule would produce unnecessary confusion in the minds of the court-members and unnecessarily prolong trials. Accordingly, adoption of the language of the Federal Rules without modification is impracticable in the armed forces.

(c) Hearing of members. Rule 104(c) is taken generally from the Federal Rule. Introductory material has been added because of the impossibility of conducting a hearing out of the presence of the members in a special court-martial without a military judge. "Statements of an accused" has been used in lieu of "confessions" because of the phrasing of Article 31 of the Uniform Code of Military Justice, which has been followed in Rules 301-306.

(d) Testimony by accused. Rule 104(d) is taken without change from the Federal Rule. Application of this Rule in specific circumstances is set forth in Rules 304(f), 311(f), and 321(e).

(e) Weight and credibility. Rule 104(e) is taken without change from the Federal Rule.

Rule 105. Limited Admissibility

When evidence which is admissible as to one party or for one purpose but not admissible as to another party or for another purpose is admitted, the military judge, upon request, shall restrict the evidence to its proper scope and instruct the members accordingly.

EDITORIAL COMMENT

Evidence can be admitted during the course of a criminal trial for many purposes. Some evidence is what courts call "substantive," which means that it relates to the ultimate question of guilt or innocence. Some substantive evidence is admissible on all questions in a case. But other substantive evidence may be admissible on one issue but not another; if this is the case, the evidence comes in for a limited purpose. Sometimes evidence is not substantive because it is offered to prove something that is not an element of a case. For example, it may be offered to shed light on the value a trier of fact should give to witnesses or evidence; this often is called credibility or rehabilitation evidence. It also is offered for a limited purpose. A lay court-member often will find it difficult to cabin evidence offered for a limited purpose and, as a result, may tend to misapply the evidence. *See, e.g., Gross v. United States*, 394 F.2d 216, 222 (8th Cir. 1968). Rule 105 addresses this problem.

Rule 105 follows traditional common law and military authority and permits evidence to be admitted for a limited purpose. Thus, even though a witness' testimony may be objectionable for some purposes, the fact that it is admissible for even one purpose may be sufficient to bring it before the fact finder. In theory, this is acceptable since the evidence is helpful on the point for which it is offered. In practice, it causes problems, however, that are attributable to the difficulty of confining evidence to some, but not all, issues.

Rule 105 categorizes the usual limitations that may be placed upon the use of evidence. First, in joint trials, evidence may be used against one accused even though it is inadmissible against a co-accused. One familiar situation arises when admissions of a nontestifying accused that implicate another accused are offered against the declarant, although they are not admissible against the other accused. *See Bruton v. United States*, 391 U.S. 123 (1968); *Parker v. Randolph*, 442 U.S. 62 (1979); *United States v. Pringle*, 3 M.J. 308 (C.M.A. 1977). *See also* Rule 306. Second, evidence may be admissible on one issue, but not on others. Whenever evidence is used for a limited purpose, such as impeaching a witness, the evidence falls into this second category. Of course, some evidence may be admissible against some, but not all, defendants on some, but not all, issues.

The Rule provides that the trial judge should appropriately instruct court-members about any limitations that are to be placed on the use of evidence. However, an instruction need not be given unless counsel specifically request it. Once a proper request is made, the instruction must be given. *See, e.g., United States v. Washington*, 592 F.2d 680 (2d Cir. 1979).

Rule 105 does not detail what satisfies the phrase "upon request." Is it enough for counsel to request that the bench do "whatever the law requires?" We suggest that Rule 103(a) (relevant here, of course, because all Rule 105 problems involve objections to the use of evidence for some purposes) would require more; it would, in fact, require that counsel specify what restricting instruction is desired. For example, if the testimony in question is extrinsic offense evidence, offered for the sole purpose of establishing a modus operandi, defense counsel would be well advised to request a limiting instruction in terms specifically tied to Rule 404(b). Counsel should request that the testimony be identified as evidence generally excluded by the law because of its tendency to distract and prejudice court-members; that the court admitted the evidence for a limited purpose only, in an effort to establish the identity of the guilty person; that the evidence can be used for that purpose and that purpose alone; and that the fact finder must not draw any other inferences from the evidence. Careful counsel would even offer the court specific language for the instruction based upon samples contained in the judge's guide or handbook, or some similar competent authority. Only after this specific request is satisfactorily made on the record can counsel be certain he has satisfied this Rule and Rule 103(a).

Careful trial judges will settle for no less and will require that requests for limiting instructions be specific and complete. If the bench does less, it is gambling on being able to adequately instruct without a well-defined factual or legal predicate. Rule 105 is designed to avoid this by placing the responsibility for instructions upon *counsel*, not the judge. Another advantage of asking for an appropriate instruction is that the judge may learn that no good instruction can be formulated and may decide, therefore, to exclude the evidence under Rule 403.

Despite the responsibility lodged with counsel, it is possible that reviewing military courts may perceive a particular issue as so potentially prejudicial, notwithstanding the defense's failure to ask for an instruction, that the bench's failure to give one sua sponte may be error. In this event, Rule 103(d)'s provision for plain error may be invoked. Sage trial judges can avoid problems by following our suggestion under Rule 103(d) and asking defense counsel on the record whether the failure to ask for an obvious limiting instruction is tactical or inadvertent. If defense counsel indicates the decision is tactical, the record will be well protected. If the failure to request the instruction is inadvertent, the counsel will ask for the instruction and protect the defendant. *See, e.g., United States v. Caldwell*, 9 M.J. 534 (A.C.M.R. 1980) (pointing out that the propriety of defense counsel's tactical decisions should not be measured based on successful accomplishment). Of course, the trial judge should also protect the prosecution from inadvertent errors.

Nothing in Rule 105 states when the restricting instruction should be given. The Rule only requires that, if requested, the trial judge should instruct the members. Obviously two separate opportunities are available: One at the time the evidence is admitted, and the other when the trial judge gives his final instructions to the court-members. It seems appropriate for the bench to inquire of counsel as to when he desires the instruction be given. This added step will place counsel's position firmly on the record and limit appellate second-guessing. In most cases counsel will want, and should get, two instructions. If both are given, the chances improve that the court-members will be able to confine the evidence to its proper purpose. Of course, two instructions could unduly emphasize the evidence. This is why counsel should be consulted.

The drafters' *Analysis* to Rule 105 indicates that the new provision overturns a landmark Court of Military Appeals decision, *United States v. Grunden*, 2 M.J. 116 (C.M.A. 1977). *Grunden* has produced substantial debate. A brief analysis of it, interpreted through the new Rules and federal experience, may help determine how the Court of Military Appeals will see Rule 105 in the future.

Airman First Class Grunden was tried for several specifications of espionage-related offenses. During the government's proof, numerous incidents of uncharged misconduct were introduced. Out of the court-members' presence the trial judge asked defense counsel whether he wanted limiting instructions with respect to the extrinsic offense evidence. The trial judge was relying upon ¶ 57a's provisions that court-members should be advised "of any limitations applicable to evidence which has been admitted for a limited purpose." *See also* ¶ 138g. After consultation with his client, defense counsel indicated he did not want a limiting instruction. Although they were unspecified at trial, defense counsel's tactics seem obvious. Grunden was being tried for a serious offense, and the government's evidence was very complicated. It was all the court-members could do to follow the proof and understand what the government was attempting to establish. The uncharged misconduct was camouflaged in this maze of evidence, and defense counsel may well have thought that any instruction about the evidence would only emphasize it. Sensitive to these tactical constraints, the trial judge acceded to the defense's wishes. On review the Court of Military Appeals rejected the trial judge's decision with the following statement:

> No evidence can so fester in the minds of court members as to the guilt or innocence of the accused as to the crime charged as evidence of uncharged misconduct. Its use must be given the weight of judicial comment, i.e., an instruction as to its limited use. [2 M.J. at 119.]

A strong dissent by Judge Cook indicated that the majority's resolution might lead to future incidents of self-induced error by defense counsel, and was inconsistent with the court's previous decision in *United States v. Morales*, 1 M.J. 87 (1975), recognizing the validity of deferring to defense counsel's tactical decisions, particularly when they are affirmatively stated.

Grunden is important here because it is not simply a case where defense counsel failed to request an instruction the reviewing court thought should have been given; it is a case where all parties at trial agreed that the interests of justice would be better served without the instruction. Nonetheless, the court's prophylactic rule seemed to require limiting instructions for all extrinsic offense evidence.

Although we know of no similar federal mandate in the area, there is some authority to support *Grunden*. In *United States v. Diaz*, 585 F.2d 116 (5th Cir.

1978), a case litigated before the effective date of the Federal Rules of Evidence, appellant was tried for several drug related offenses. After he testified, government counsel established that Diaz had previous convictions for similar misconduct. All evidence was allowed to reach the jury, without counsel or the bench indicating any desire for a restricting instruction. On review, the Court of Appeals determined that the sole issue was whether the trial judge should have given a limiting instruction sua sponte. Recognizing that the circuits were divided on this issue, the court took great pains to explain why reversal was required. The majority held that the burden for requesting limiting instructions rests in the first instance with the defense counsel. If he fails to request them, then *government* counsel should do so. Both having failed here, the responsibility passed to the bench:

> We recognize the salutary rule that empowers the trial judge to exercise discretion in determining what curative instruction is required and hold only that when, during a jury trial, evidence is introduced that the defendant has a prior conviction for the same offense for which he is being tried, both counsel and the court have a duty to minimize the risk that the jury would infer guilt on the cocaine charges from the fact of previous convictions on cocaine charges. Thus, in this situation where no cautionary instruction is given to the jury, prejudicial error has intervened. [585 F.2d at 118.]

After the effective date of the Federal Rules, most federal courts have reached different results. In *United States v. Barnes,* 586 F.2d 1052 (5th Cir. 1978), the same court that decided *Diaz* reached the opposite result on similar facts. In *Barnes,* the questioned evidence concerned an extrinsic offense admitted under Rule 404(b) that was potentially more devastating than the prior conviction admitted under Rule 609 in *Diaz*'s case. Yet the court affirmed the conviction by focusing on counsel's tactical considerations, specifically failing to find sufficient prejudicial error to justify relief under 103(d)'s plain error provisions. The court recognized that defense counsel waived the instruction because he did not desire to "emphasize potentially damaging evidence." 586 F.2d at 1059. The court indicated, however, that it did not intend to rule out the possibility of plain error under other facts. *See also United States v. Vitale,* 596 F.2d 688 (5th Cir. 1979), where the court applied the same logic and reached the same result with respect to properly admitted hearsay as to which there was no cautionary instruction.

Since *Grunden* was decided, military appellate courts have become much more sensitive to the federal treatment of instructional issues. It appears that the Court of Military Appeals is attempting to find a way to live with *Grunden* in light of contrary civilian authority. An example is *United States v. James,* 5 M.J. 382, 383 (C.M.A. 1978) where the court limited the sua sponte requirements for instructions to evidence amounting to "acts sufficient to support independent criminal charges of equal gravity as those charge[d]." The court failed to grant relief where the charges were "part of the chain of events that leads to the consummation of the crime charged." *Id.* In *United States v. Kick,* 7 M.J. 82, 86 (C.M.A. 1979) a negligent homicide prosecution, the court clearly withdrew from its earlier position in holding that the uncharged misconduct "did not rise to the level of prejudicial error, since the incident demonstrates no general predisposition to commit the offense of negligent homicide." This was so despite testimony indicating that the accused was drinking before the crime, and that he had previously been arrested for disorderly conduct and a five day unauthorized absence. The court's affirmance in light of this "tenuous" evidence was a clear withdrawal from *Grunden*, and a movement toward embracing Rule 105's provisions. This interpretation must also have motivated the Army Court of Military Review to affirm a conviction in *United States v. Seivers*, 9 M.J. 612 (A.C.M.R. 1980). There the appellant was charged with possessing marijuana, and the government introduced extrinsic offense evidence which was objected to by the defense. However, defense counsel failed to request a limiting instruction, and as a result, none was provided. Recognizing the friction between *Grunden* and *James*, the court found no fault with the trial judge's actions and affirmed the conviction.

More recently, in *United States v. Wray*, 9 M.J. 361 (C.M.A. 1980) the court took another step away from *Grunden's* strict mandates. There, after three instances of uncharged misconduct were testified to, the prosecutor inquired as to whether a limiting instruction should be given. The bench then asked the defense if one was desired, and defense counsel responded by stating: "We don't want it. The defense feels that it would merely draw attention to what has been said." 9 M.J. at 362. Defense counsel went on to decline the bench's invitation for even a "general statement as to uncharged misconduct." *Id.* In affirming conviction the Court of Military Appeals alluded to Rules 105 and 103(d) finding that "there is no reason for adhering to the anomoly of finding error when the military judge follows the request of defense counsel in omitting an instruction on a collateral matter." *Id.*

Nothing in Rule 105 or in the federal courts' interpretation of it appears to change the basic common law and military justice philosophy that the trial judge "is more than a mere referee, and as such he is required to assure that the accused receives a fair trial," *United States v. Graves*, 1 M.J. 50 (C.M.A. 1975). The trial judge is "not relieved of his independent duty to take [appropriate] action," *United States v. Morales*, 1 M.J. 87 (C.M.A. 1975). By working with counsel, the judge can assure the defendant a fair trial without impairing the presentation of a defense. *See generally,* Saltzburg, *The Unnecessarily Expanding Role of the American Trial Judge*, 64 VA. L. REV. 1 (1978).

One final point should be made concerning Rule 105's generally applicability. The provision requires trial judges to do two things with respect to limited admissibility evidence—one is to restrict its use; the other is to instruct the members accordingly. It appears to us that, although the Rule is most clearly applicable to member trials, it should also be of assistance during bench trials. Although the judge is presumed to know the law and to properly apply it—*United States v. McConnico*, 7 M.J. 302 (C.M.A. 1979); *United States v. Montgomery*, 20 C.M.A. 35, 39, 42 C.M.R. 227, 231 (1970)—the principle actually operates more effectively in theory than practice. We believe that it is appropriate for counsel to ask the trial judge in a bench trial how he intends to use certain evidence. If this occurs, the judge should inform counsel of his intentions. We believe a terse response, such as "I'll use it appropriately," ought not to be sufficient. A more detailed explanation not only will help counsel to effectively present the case, but it also will be beneficial to the trial judge who wants to do justice by giving the parties an opportunity to correct the errors that even the most careful jurist may make during the heat of litigation.

DRAFTERS' ANALYSIS

Rule 105 is taken without change from the Federal Rule. In view of its requirement that the military judge restrict evidence to its proper scope "upon request," it overrules *United States v. Grunden,* 2 M.J. 116 (C.M.A. 1977) (holding that the military judge must sua sponte instruct the members as to use of evidence of uncharged misconduct) and related cases insofar as they *require* the military judge to sua sponte instruct the members. *See e.g.,* S. SALTZBURG & K. REDDEN, FEDERAL RULES OF EVIDENCE MANUAL 50 (2d ed. 1977); *United States v. Sangrey,* 586 F.2d 1312 (9th Cir. 1978); *United States v. Barnes,* 586 F.2d 1052 (5th Cir. 1978); *United States v. Bridwell,* 583 F.2d 1135 (10th Cir. 1978); *but see United States v. Ragghianti,* 560 F.2d 1376 (9th Cir. 1977). This is compatible with the general intent of both the Federal and Military Rules in that they place primary if not full responsibility upon counsel for objecting to or limiting evidence. Note that Rule 306, dealing with statements of co-accused, is more restrictive and protective than Rule 105. The military judge may, of course, choose to instruct sua sponte but need not do so. Failure to instruct sua sponte could potentially require a reversal only if such failure could be considered "plain error" within the meaning of Rule 103(d). Most failures to instruct sua sponte, or to instruct, cannot be so considered in light of current case law.

Rule 106. Remainder of or Related Writings or Recorded Statements

When a writing or recorded statement or part thereof is introduced by a party, an adverse party may require that party at that time to introduce any other part or any other writing or recorded statement which ought in fairness to be considered contemporaneously with it.

EDITORIAL COMMENT

Rule 106 specifies that when a writing or recorded statement is offered, an opposing party may require the proponent, "at that time," to introduce any other portion of the document in question, or an entirely different document when "fairness" demands. The object here is to allow the finder of fact to consider documentary evidence or a recorded statement in its proper context, as soon as it is offered, not at some later time. The Rule applies to all writings and to statements recorded in writing or on tape.

The legislative history indicates that the federal version of Rule 106 was specifically intended to exclude oral testimony from its coverage. Although the drafters' *Analysis* to Military Rule 106 is silent on this point, we envision that the same limitation will be applicable. We do see one situation, however, in which oral testimony should be deemed to be covered by Rule 106; it is where secondary evidence is allowed as an exception to the best evidence rule. *See* our discussion of Rule 1004. If oral testimony used in lieu of a writing or recording were outside the Rule, its proponent would be relieved from having to admit other evidence "which ought in fairness" be considered as part of a single package. In effect, this would make oral secondary evidence different from written secondary evidence, which still is a writing under the Rule. We believe the better approach is to treat all secondary evidence similarly, and to require the proponent to place it in context upon proper motion, even though we appreciate the counter-argument which is that unless a writing or recording is actually presented, there is no danger that a jury will give it undue weight and therefore no need for a special rule. In any event, a trial judge can use Rule 611(a) to prevent unfairness.

Past *Manual* provisions failed to provide a mechanism for dealing with the unadmitted portions of documentary evidence. While ¶ 140a(6) did specifically permit defense counsel to "fill in" the exculpatory nature of an accused's pretrial statement, its scope was obviously limited. *See United States v. McConnico*, 7 M.J. 302 (C.M.A. 1979) (applying ¶ 140a(6) to statements made by accessories). *See also* our discussion of Rule 304(h)(2) which adopts the previous *Manual* philosophy. When Rule 304(h)(2) applies, oral as well as written and recorded statements are covered. Both Rules may be used in the same case.

The purpose of Rule 106 is to avoid having one side obtain an unfair advantage by offering into evidence a portion of a document or recorded statement and conveying a misleading impression of it, which the other side will then have to try to erase at a later time, either on cross-examination or during its own case. If first impressions are lasting, then misleading first impressions may be hard to eradicate. Rule 106 seeks to avoid the need to erase them. If one document should be read as a whole, or if a tape recorded statement can only be fairly understood if played in connection with several other statements, admission of evidence as a unit may promote initial clarity, save time by presenting evidence as an understandable whole, and avoid the recalling of witnesses and the duplication of foundations for evidence. Moreover, it may avoid confusing the court-members about the nature and contents of the documents or recordings that are offered into evidence.

The new provision is not without its difficulties. The Rule does suggest that "fairness" will control the process, but fairness is the watchword of all court-martial discretionary decisions. We recommend that "fairness" be read to require the admission of additional evidence when the same subject matter, issue, defense, or element of proof is explained thereby. This result is particularly appropriate when the proponent's document or recording mentions or indicates that other written or recorded evidence is involved. In a close case, we would urge favoring admission of evidence under the Rule, since little damage can come from giving court-members a complete initial picture of a writing or recording.

But care must be taken that the Rule is not read so broadly that it vitiates other limitations on evidence. This is particularly important in criminal litigation where admissible evidence may be contained in a sanitized or redacted statement, and it is imperative that the entire statement not be used.

In fact, one of the most important concepts for lawyers and judges to keep in mind in using Rule 106 is that it does not provide a rule of admissibility. All that Rule 106 does is to provide for an order of proof. Thus, if a written confession is offered by the government, but a portion has been deleted, the offered portions are surely going to be admissible as admissions under Rule 801(d). But the other portions might not be admissions. They might, however, be part of the admissions and thus admissible, going to the weight to be given the admissions. The government surely will not be able to offer portions of a confession taken out of context, because the probative value of the statements could be exaggerated. If a court traditionally would have allowed the remaining statements to be admitted, Rule 106 indicates that they can be admitted sooner rather than later.

If, however, a defendant confesses on one day, gets a lawyer the next day, and repudiates his confession on the third day, the repudiation of the confession probably is classic, self-serving hearsay and inadmissible under Rule 802. If it is not admissible, it will never come in, and a request to have it admitted in connection with the initial confession should be rejected by a trial court.

Of course, there are going to be cases in which the relationship between statements will present hard questions. All that Rule 106 says is that if statements are so related that they should be considered together and the Rules of Evidence would allow all the statements to be admitted, they may be considered as a unit when the first statement is offered.

It is easy to exaggerate the importance of the part of Rule 106 that allows one party to force the other party to introduce a complete writing or recording or set of writings and recordings. Of course, at common law, one side might have to wait until it presented its evidence to complete proof initially presented by the other side. This Rule states that a wait is no longer required. Although the party offering the writing or recorded statement is required to offer evidence that he might not want to offer, the evidence would come into the case anyway, so all that really happens is that the timing of the evidence is changed. Since all parties can impeach all witnesses, including hearsay declarants, there is little danger of unfairness in having one side offer a complete writing or recorded statement at the first opportunity.

It may seem that parties will try to avoid Rule 106 by using oral testimony in lieu of writings, since oral testimony generally is outside the scope of the Rule. This prospect is an unlikely one. First, it should be noted that people who have writings that work to their advantage are not likely to give up the opportunity of using them, since writings and recorded statements may be much more likely to be believed than ordinary testimony. This is especially the case if an opponent will offer the writing in any event, and it may look as if the oral testimony was an attempt to avoid presenting the document. Second, in a number of instances, there may be no alternative to offering a document, since no witness with personal knowledge may be available to testify. Third, the burden of Rule 106 is not so onerous that it is likely to dissuade litigants from offering writings and recorded statements. Finally, in military trials, the fact that the judge and the court-members can call for evidence means that documents and recorded statements may be requested even if the parties do not offer them, which may make a failure to present them embarrassing to a party who is asked to produce them.

Any provision as broad as Rule 106 will always provide an opportunity for abuse, allowing opposing counsel to constantly interrupt a proponent's case, and requiring him to place unimportant contextual evidence before the fact finder. We trust that the military judge's effective use of Rule 611(a) will minimize this liability. Moreover, we believe the new provision will greatly assist court-members, insuring that inaccuracies and misinterpretations will be minimized. Also, because a witness will now only need to testify on one occasion, and not be required to return for the opponent's case, trials should be speedier, and witness inconvenience, so devastating in a military context, will be greatly reduced.

A number of federal courts have analogized to Rule 106 in holding that if a cross-examiner uses a writing to examine a witness, the other side may be able to see the writing and perhaps have it introduced into evidence to show that the witness' testimony is not really impeached by the writing, although the Rule is not strictly applicable. *See, e.g., United States v. Baron,* 602 F.2d 1248 (7th Cir. 1979); *United States v. Salsedo,* 607 F.2d 318 (9th Cir 1979); *United States v. Juarez,* 549 F.2d 1113 (7th Cir. 1977). *See also United States v. Lyon,* 567 F.2d 777, 784 (8th Cir. 1977), cert. denied, 435 U.S. 918 (1978) (similar reasoning used to justify admission of hearsay under the residual exception). As long as it is recognized that the cases draw analogies that are imperfect, we have no problem with them. We repeat, however, that Rule 106 is a timing rule, not a rule of additional admissibility. Thus, the analogies are helpful to the extent that they stand for the proposition that one side should not take unfair advantage by suggesting that a document says something that it really does not say. But to the extent that these cases expand the rules of admissibility for purposes of impeachment, which in our view may well be permissible under Rules 401 and 607, the analogy breaks down.

DRAFTERS' ANALYSIS

Rule 106 is taken from the Federal Rule without change. In view of the tendency of fact finders to give considerable evidentiary weight to written matters, the Rule is intended to preclude the misleading situation that can occur if a party presents only part of a writing or recorded statement. In contrast to ¶ 140a of the present *Manual,* which applies only to statements by an accused, the new Rule is far more expansive and permits a party to require the opposing party to introduce evidence. That aspect of ¶ 140a(b) survives as Rule 304(h) (2) and allows the defense to complete an alleged confession or admission offered by the prosecution. When a confession or admission is involved, the defense may employ both Rules 106 and 304(h) (2), as appropriate.

SECTION II. JUDICIAL NOTICE

Rule 201. Judicial Notice of Adjudicative Facts

(a) Scope of rule. This rule governs only judicial notice of adjudicative facts.

(b) Kinds of facts. A judicially noticed fact must be one not subject to reasonable dispute in that it is either (1) generally known universally, locally, or in the area pertinent to the event or (2) capable of accurate and ready determination by resort to sources whose accuracy cannot reasonably be questioned.

(c) When discretionary. The military judge may take judicial notice, whether requested or not. The parties shall be informed in open court when, without being requested, the military judge takes judicial notice of an adjudicative fact essential to establishing an element of the case.

(d) When mandatory. The military judge shall take judicial notice if requested by a party and supplied with the necessary information.

(e) Opportunity to be heard. A party is entitled upon timely request to an opportunity to be heard as to the propriety of taking judicial notice and the tenor of the matter noticed. In the absence of prior notification, the request may be made after judicial notice has been taken.

(f) Time of taking notice. Judicial notice may be taken at any stage of the proceeding.

(g) Instructing members. The military judge shall instruct the members that they may, but are not required to, accept as conclusive any matter judicially noticed.

EDITORIAL COMMENT

Judicial notice of facts serves as a substitute for testimonial, documentary, or real evidence. In the interest of judicial economy, this doctrine relieves a proponent from formally proving certain facts that reasonable persons would not dispute. Rule 201 is substantially similar to its federal counterpart and permits judicial notice of "adjudicative" facts. It defines how judicial notice should be used, the kinds of facts which may be judicially noticed, and the specific procedures for taking judicial notice. Rule 201 replaces *Manual* ¶ 147 *a* and changes both the substance and procedure of military practice.

Subdivision (a) defines the Rule's scope. It covers only adjudicative facts — *i.e.*, those facts of the case which are normally resolved by the fact finder. Professor Kenneth Culp Davis in his Administrative Law Treatise (1958) notes that:

> When a court or an agency finds facts concerning the immediate parties — who did what, where, when, how, and with what motive or intent — the court or agency is performing an adjudicative function, and the facts are conveniently called adjudicative facts. . . .
>
> Stated in other terms, the adjudicative facts are those to which the law is applied in the process of adjudication. . . . [2 Administrative Law Treatise 353.]

Legislative facts, those facts which relate to questions of law, policy, or legal reasoning, are not addressed in the Military Rules. Judicial notice of law, however, is specifically recognized in Rule 201A (see our discussion). For a good discussion on the distinction between adjudicative and legislative facts *see* Note, *Judicial Notice: Rule 201 of the Federal Rules of Evidence*, 28 U. Fla. L. Rev. 723 (1976).

The absence of any direction on the taking of judicial notice of legislative facts is a weakness the Military Rule shares with its federal counterpart. *See* S. Saltzburg & K. Redden, Federal Rules of Evidence Manual 60-62 (2d ed. 1977). Because legislative facts are not within the scope of Rule 201, it appears that military judges can notice what they want, when they want, as long as facts are deemed to be legislative. Parties wishing to be heard can, of course, submit briefs or memoranda to the judge, but they may never know exactly what legislative facts the judge is noticing. It should be noted that military judges may give the parties notice about legislative facts, the Rule does not require notice, but would not bar it. Often, the parties' input might be helpful to the judge. The drafters' *Analysis* is not particularly helpful in distinguishing between adjudicative and legislative facts. Federal decisions suggest that the two categories are often confused, or at least are difficult to differentiate. *See, e.g., Atkins v. United States*, 556 F.2d 1028 (Ct. Cl. 1977), cert. denied, 434 U.S. 1009 (1978); *Goodman v. Stalford, Inc.*, 411 F. Supp. 889 (D.N.J. 1976). A conservative approach would dictate that where the military judge contemplates taking judicial notice of facts which fall into gray areas, he should so indicate on the record and afford counsel an opportunity to question whether Rule 201 governs.

Rule 201 limits the adjudicative facts that may be noticed. Subdivision (b) permits notice of facts which are not subject to reasonable dispute. They must either be generally known under (b)(1), or capable of ready and accurate confirmation under (b)(2). They must also be otherwise admissible under the Rules — *i.e.,* if, under the Military Rules of Evidence, the parties would not have been able to have the facts admitted, the facts cannot be judicially noticed either. The Rule is a substitute for proof, not an exemption from the usual Rules of Evidence. Subdivision (b)(1) modified the Federal Rule to reflect the unique needs of a widely-dispersed military community by allowing judicial notice of facts which are "generally known universally, locally, or in the area pertinent to the event." Examples of the kind of facts that may be noticed are found in drafters' *Analysis,* which incorporates verbatim a portion of the pre-empted *Manual* ¶ 147a.

Noticeably absent in Rule 201 is the authority to judicially notice a wide range of signatures and seals, which had been specifically recognized in ¶ 147 *a* and, in effect, amounted to a method of self-authentication. *See, e.g., United States v. Stein,* 14 C.M.R. 376 (A.B.R. 1954) (court could take judicial notice of signature of person authenticating record of trial). Rule 902, paragraphs (4) and (10) which are discussed *infra,* should fill the gap, however.

Subdivisions (c) and (d) address the question of when judicial notice may, and must, be taken. These provisions slightly modify pre-Rules practice, which simply required the proponent to request judicial notice and furnish authority for the fact to be noticed, unless it was a matter of common knowledge. *Manual* ¶ 147a.

Subdivision (c) permits the military judge to take judicial notice on his own motion. The first sentence is identical to the Federal Rule, but the second sentence is new and requires the military judge to announce when he has taken judicial notice on his own motion if the fact noticed is essential to establishing an element of the case. This notice requirement was included by the drafters to meet the "clear implication" of subdivision (e), which offers counsel an opportunity to be heard, and to satisfy the requirement of *Garner v. Louisiana,* 368 U.S. 157 (1961). In *Garner,* pursuant to a Louisiana statute, black defendants were convicted for disturbing the peace when they sat in a restaurant section reserved for whites. The Supreme Court resisted state arguments that the trial court must have sub silentio taken judicial notice of the racial unrest in Louisiana. Finding no evidence in the record to support the State's position, the Court noted that it would not turn the doctrine of judicial notice into a pretext for dispensing with a trial. The Court stated:

> Furthermore, unless an accused is informed at the trial of the facts of which the court is taking judicial notice, not only does he not know upon what evidence he is being convicted, but, in addition, he is deprived of any opportunity to challenge the deductions drawn from such notice or to dispute the notoriety or truth of the facts allegedly relied upon. Moreover, there is no way by which an appellate court may review the facts and law of a case and intelligently decide whether the findings of the lower court are supported by the evidence where the evidence is unknown. Such an assumption would be a denial of due process. [368 U.S. at 173].

This requirement has not been uniformly applied in the federal courts, when the facts noticed have not been controversial. *Compare United States v. Harris,* 530 F.2d 576 (4th Cir. 1976) (Court of Appeals in bank robbery case could take judicial notice that a bank chartered with the name including "National Bank" was in fact a national bank) *with United States v. Jones,* 580 F.2d 219 (6th Cir. 1978) (appellate court could not notice on appeal a fact not noticed at trial, *i.e.,* whether a telephone company was in interstate commerce). The requirement was applied by the Court of Military Appeals in *United States v. Williams,* 3 M.J. 155 (C.M.A. 1977). A conviction for violating a regulation was reversed, because the regulation in question was neither received in evidence nor judicially noticed. The court looked to Federal Rule 201 and concluded that it did not compel an appellate court to assume that a trial court had sub silentio considered the missing regulation; thus, the decision rejected the approach of the courts in *United States v. Atherton,* 1 M.J. 581 (A.C.M.R. 1975) and *United States v. Levesque,* 47 C.M.R. 285 (A.F.C.M.R. 1973). 3 M.J. at 157. n.2. *See also* our comments at Rule 201A on taking judicial notice of law.

Under subdivision (d) a military judge must take judicial notice if the proponent presents the necessary supporting information, which need not itself be admissible. If the supporting evidence is admissible, the military judge, instead of judicially noticing the fact, may admit the evidence. The military judge may, of course, decide that judicial notice is not appropriate. But if notice is appropriate, it shall be taken. This is important, even though the proponent of the noticed fact may have some evidence to support it; the taking of notice effectively tells the members of the court that the proponent need not offer additional evidence of the fact, and places the imprimatur of the judge on the fact.

Subdivision (e) is identical to the Federal Rule and provides that counsel must be provided an opportunity to address the propriety of taking judicial notice. This provision generally comports with at least the spirit of *Manual* ¶ 147a, which had required the proponent to give sufficient notice to opposing counsel when reliance was placed on a specific source.

Subdivision (f) provides that judicial notice may be taken either at the trial or appellate level. It is identical to the Federal Rule and is apparently subject to the second sentence of Rule 201(c), which, as noted above, would prevent an appellate court from filling evidentiary gaps by noticing an essential adjudicative fact for the first time on appeal. This subdivision should not restrict appellate courts from continuing to judicially notice, for example, a counsel's qualifications, *United States v. Craft,* 44 C.M.R. 664 (A.C.M.R. 1971), a military judge's certification, *United States v. Gray,* 47 C.M.R. 693 (A.C.M.R. 1973), or matters in other cases pending before the court, *United States v. Surry,* 6 M.J. 800 (A.C.M.R. 1978). Nor should it restrict an appellate court from drawing inferences from the evidence actually admitted or judicially noticed. *See generally,* Adamkewicz, *Appellate Consideration of Matters Outside the Record of Trial,* 32 Mil. L. Rev. 1, 27-31 (1966); Feld, *What is the Appellate Record? Appellate Inferences and Judicial Notice,* 20 JAG J. 51 (1965).

Subdivision (g) is derived from the second sentence of the Federal Rule and requires the military judge to instruct the court-members that they may, but are not required to, consider as conclusive those adjudicative facts which have been judicially noticed. Since the court-members may reject the noticed fact, it would seem that the opponent of the fact should be able to offer evidence to rebut it. Such evidence must satisfy the other evidence rules, however. Often, admissible evidence of a fact beyond reasonable dispute will be difficult to find. Even if no rebuttal evidence is offered, the instruction to the court-members is permissive so that they can reject the noticed fact, as they can reject any fact in a case.

DRAFTERS' ANALYSIS

(a) Scope of Rule. Rule 201 (a) provides that Rule 201 governs judicial notice of adjudicative facts. In so doing, the Rule replaces present *Manual* § 147a. The Federal Rules of Evidence Advisory Committee defined adjudicative facts as "simply the facts of the particular case" and distinguished them from legislative facts which it defined as "those which have relevance to legal reasoning and the lawmaking process, whether in the formulation of a legal principle or ruling by a judge or court or in the enactment of a legislative body," reprinted in S. SALTZBURG & K. REDDEN, FEDERAL RULES OF EVIDENCE MANUAL 63 (2d ed. 1977). The distinction between the two types of facts, originated by Professor Kenneth Davis, can on occasion be highly confusing in practice and resort to any of the usual treatises may be helpful.

(b) Kinds of facts. Rule 201 (b) was taken generally from the Federal Rule. The limitation within FED. R. EVID. 201 (b) (1) to facts known "within the territorial jurisdiction of the trial court" was replaced, however, by the expression, "generally known universally, locally, or in the area pertinent to the event." The worldwide disposition of the armed forces rendered the original language inapplicable and impracticable within the military environment. Notice of signatures, appropriate under present *Manual* ¶ 147a, will normally be inappropriate under this Rule. Rules 902 (4) and (10) will, however, usually yield the same result as under ¶ 147a of the present *Manual*.

When they qualify as adjudicative facts under Rule 201, the following are examples of matters of which judicial notice may be taken:

> The ordinary division of time into years, months, weeks and other periods; general facts and laws of nature, including their ordinary operations and effects; general facts of history; generally known geographical facts; such specific facts and propositions of generalized knowledge as are so universally known that they cannot reasonably be the subject of dispute; such facts as are so generally known or are of such common notoriety in the area in which the trial is held that they cannot reasonably be the subject of dispute; and specific facts and propositions of generalized knowledge which are capable of immediate and accurate determination by resort to easily accessible sources of reasonably indisputable accuracy.

(c) When discretionary. While the first sentence of the subdivision is taken from the Federal Rule, the second sentence is new and is included as a result of the clear implication of subdivision (e) and of the holding in *Garner v. Louisiana*, 368 U.S. 157, 173-74 (1961). In *Garner,* the Supreme Court rejected the contention of the State of Louisiana that the trial judge had taken judicial notice of certain evidence stating that:

> There is nothing in the records to indicate that the trial judge did in fact take judicial notice of anything. To extend the doctrine of judicial notice ... would require us to allow the prosecution to do through argument to this Court what it is required by due process to do at the trial, and would be to turn the doctrine into a pretext for dispensing with a trial of the facts of which the court is taking judicial notice, not only does he not know upon what evidence he is being convicted, but, in addition, he is reprived of any opportunity to challenge the deductions drawn from such notice or to dispute the notoriety or truth of the facts allegedly relied upon.

368 U.S. at 173.

(d) When mandatory. Rule 201 (d) provides that the military judge shall take notice when requested to do so by a party who supplies the military judge with the necessary information. The military judge must take judicial notice only when the evidence is properly within this Rule, is relevant under Rule 401, and is not inadmissible under these Rules.

(e) Opportunity to be heard; Time of taking notice; Instructing members. Subdivisions (e), (f) and (g) of Rule 201 are taken from the Federal Rule without change.

Rule 201A. Judicial Notice of Law

(a) Domestic law. The military judge may take judicial notice of domestic law. Insofar as a domestic law is a fact that is of consequence to the determination of the action, the procedural requirements of rule 201 apply.

(b) Foreign law. A party who intends to raise an issue concerning the law of a foreign country shall give reasonable written notice. The military judge, in determining foreign law, may consider any relevant material or source including testimony whether or not submitted by a party or admissible under these rules. Such a determination shall be treated as a ruling on a question of law.

EDITORIAL COMMENT

Complementing Rule 201, which permits judicial notice of adjudicative facts, Rule 201A allows a military judge to judicially notice domestic or foreign law. Although it has no counterpart in the Federal Rules of Evidence, it joins several comparable State provisions. *See, e.g.,* Rule 202, Alaska Rules of Evidence.

Subdivision (a) addresses judicial notice of domestic law. The first sentence of this subdivision is patterned after *Manual* ¶ 147a which allowed judicial notice of a wide range of domestic law. Some of the examples listed in ¶ 147a have been included in the drafters' *Analysis;* others, however, have been omitted and are now apparently treated as adjudicative or legislative facts. For example, ¶ 147a permitted judicial notice of "contents of official informational bulletins, manuals, and pamphlets and similar official publications of any agency of the federal government of the United States. . . ." *See, e.g., United States v. Houston,* 4 M.J. 729 (A.F.C.M.R. 1978) (citing Federal Rule of Evidence 201(b), the court ruled that the military judge could judicially notice a Department of Defense information bulletin on the drug PCP). Interestingly, the drafters include within the definition of "domestic law," international law which, the drafters indicate, in turn includes the laws of war, general maritime law and the law of air and space. *See* drafters' *Analysis infra.* This is consistent with Supreme Court cases. *See, e.g., The Soctia,* 81 U.S. (14 Wall.) 170, 188 (1871); *The Paguete Habana,* 175 U.S. 677, 700 (1900). Although international law is assumed to be part of our domestic law, it may be more difficult to ascertain than most laws. For an excellent group of articles on the discovery and application of international law (and also foreign law), *see* the *Second Annual Sokol Colloquium on Private International Law,* 18 Va. J. Int'l L., 609 (1978).

The second sentence of subdivision (a) directs that where the law in question is a "fact that is of consequence to the determination of the action," Rule 201's procedural requirements must be met. This would almost always be the case where violation of a regulation is the gravamen of the offense charged or a matter in defense; the regulation must be brought before the court and judicial notice is a way to do it. Apparently this requirement was included to provide notice to the opponent, and an opportunity to be heard. *See generally* our discussion of Rule 201, and in particular our discussion of Rule 201(c). It is difficult to determine whether the second sentence of subdivision (a) is intended to state that if domestic law is relevant, it should be noticed according to Rule 201, or whether the Rule intends that Rule 201 will be utilized only in a narrower class of cases, in which questions of law are somehow especially factual. We suspect that the former reading is intended, and find support for this in the drafters' *Analysis* which states that the procedural requirements of Rule 201 must be applied where the "law" constitutes the adjudicative fact.

It should be noted that only the procedural sections of Rule 201 should be utilized; these do not include subdivision (g) since it would be improper to tell the court-members they need not follow the law. *See, e.g., United States v. Gould,* 536 F.2d 216 (8th Cir. 1976), in which the court stated that judicial notice that "cocaine hydrochloride is a Schedule II controlled substance under the laws of the United States" was a legislative fact that does not traditionally go to the jury.

Note that neither Rule 201A nor Rule 201, which may be applicable under subdivision (a), require attachment to the record of a copy of the law in question although the drafters' *Analysis* suggests that practice — a carryover from *Manual* ¶ 147a.

Subdivision (b) permits judicial notice of foreign law. It is derived from Federal Rule of Criminal Procedure 26.1 and provides no major changes to pre-Rules practice grounded in *Manual* ¶ 147b. One noticeable change is the new requirement of reasonable *written* notice to the opponent; *Manual* ¶ 147b required only "sufficient notice."

The notice requirement seems to reflect the drafters' reasonable judgment that to resolve questions of foreign law, the parties and the court may need extra time to gather sources of information, to understand them, and to apply them to the facts of a case.

The procedural requirements of Rule 201 do not apply to subdivision (b). Here again, because a determination of foreign law is treated as a question of law, the court-members may be instructed to accept as conclusive the existence and content of the foreign law that is noticed. Treatment of the issue as a matter of law should meet any claims of violation of Sixth Amendment right to confrontation problems raised by consideration of sources not subject to cross-examination. *See generally,* Reznaeck, *The New Federal Rules of Criminal Procedure,* 54 GEO. L. J. 1276, 1307 (1966) (discussion of Federal Rule of Criminal Procedure 26.1). *See also* Cohn, *The New Federal Rules of Civil Procedure,* 54 GEO. L. J. 1204, 1241 (1966) (discussion of Rule 44.1 which is substantially similar to Fed. R. Crim. P. 26.1).

Although the military judge is free to employ his own resources to determine the law, the parties should be called upon to address the matter. Again, the Rule does not mandate attachment of supporting evidence to the record of trial but the drafters' *Analysis* suggests its inclusion, a practice formerly required by *Manual* ¶ 147b.

In some jurisdictions courts do not require judges to take notice of foreign law, because such law is sometimes difficult to find and apply accurately. The same jurisdictions usually mandate that some domestic law be noticed. Rule 201A appears to make judicial notice of all law optional, although the intent of the drafters with respect to domestic law is not crystal clear, since Rule 201A (a) refers back to the procedural sections of Rule 201, and one procedural section arguably is subdivision (d) which would make notice mandatory.

Although it is plain to us that the wording of Rule 201A is confusing and its intent is difficult to discern, we believe that the best approach to the Rule is as follows: Questions of law in any case are going to be questions for the judge, not for the court-members. Whether law is domestic or foreign, if it bears on litigation, the judge must decide what the law for the case shall be. When domestic law is involved, generally the judge will have little problem. Usually, the parties and the court will refer to the same statutes and published regulations in resolving domestic legal questions. Even though private acts and local ordinances may be less familiar than the United States Code and the Code of Federal Regulations, it is reasonable to assume that most domestic law will be neither unique nor unusually difficult to find. Foreign law will be more difficult to ascertain. Experts may have to assist the parties and the court in understanding foreign languages and foreign legal systems. But, the trial judge will still want to proceed by having the parties produce their sources so that the judge can examine them and the parties can address each other's sources.

A basic pragmatic difference between using foreign and domestic law is that ascertaining the former is likely to take more time and involve more presentation of material to the court than ascertaining the latter. Yet, the basic procedures should be the same. Although the judge is authorized by Rule 201A (b) to consider material not submitted by a party, we believe that it is necessary for the judge to indicate to the parties what sources he is considering. This is especially important when the judge is referring to sources written in another language, but it always is important when unusual material is used to inform the judge. It is one thing to assume that all parties can find the United States Code or the Supreme Court Reports. In foreign law cases, however, it is quite another thing to assume that all will have access to foreign-law materials. If the judge has peculiar access, he should assure that the parties are able to see his materials so that there is a check on the predictable mistakes that can be made when an American judge looks to another country's law.

DRAFTERS' ANALYSIS

In general. Rule 201A is new. Not addressed by the Federal Rules of Evidence, the subject matter of the Rule is treated as a procedural matter in the Article III courts; *see, e.g.,* FED. R. CRIM. P. 26.1. Adoption of a new evidentiary rule was thus required. Rule 201A is generally consistent in principle with present *Manual* ¶ 147a.

Domestic law. Rule 201A(a) recognizes that law may constitute the adjudicative fact within the meaning of Rule 201(a) and requires that when that is the case, *i.e.,* insofar as a domestic law is a fact that is of consequence to the determination of the action, the procedural requirements of Rule 201 must be applied. When domestic law constitutes only a legislative fact, *see* the *Analysis* to Rule 201(a), the procedural requirements of Rule 201 may be utilized as a matter of discretion. For purposes of this Rule, it is intended that "domestic law" include: treaties of the United States; executive agreements between the United States and any State thereof, foreign country or international organization or agency; the laws and regulations pursuant thereto of the United States, of the District of Columbia, and of a State, Commonwealth, or possession; international law, including the laws of war; general maritime law and the law of air and space; and the common law. This definition is taken without change from present *Manual* ¶ 147*a* except that reference to the law of space has been added. "Regulations" of the United States include regulations of the armed forces.

When a party requests that domestic law be noticed, or when the military judge sua sponte takes such notice, a copy of the applicable law should be attached to the record of trial unless the law in question can reasonably be anticipated to be easily available to any possible reviewing authority.

Foreign law. Rule 201A(b) is taken without significant change from FED. R. CRIM. P. 26.1 and recognizes that notice of foreign law may require recourse to additional evidence including testimony of witnesses. For purposes of this Rule, it is intended that "foreign law" include the laws and regulations of foreign countries and their political subdivisions and of international organizations and agencies. Any material or source received by the military judge for use in determining foreign law, or pertinent extracts therefrom, should be included in the record of trial as an exhibit.

SECTION III. EXCLUSIONARY RULES AND RELATED MATTERS CONCERNING SELF-INCRIMINATION, SEARCH AND SEIZURE, AND EYEWITNESS IDENTIFICATION

Rule 301. Privilege Concerning Compulsory Self-Incrimination.
    (a) General rule.
    (b) Standing.
        (1) In general.
        (2) Judicial advice.
    (c) Exercise of the privilege.
        (1) Immunity generally.
        (2) Notification of immunity or leniency.
    (d) Waiver by a witness.
    (e) Waiver by the accused.
    (f) Effect of claiming the privilege.
        (1) Generally.
        (2) On cross-examination.
        (3) Pretrial.
    (g) Instructions.

Rule 302. Privilege Concerning Mental Examination of an Accused.
    (a) General rule.
    (b) Exceptions.
    (c) Release of evidence.
    (d) Noncompliance by the accused.
    (e) Procedure.

Rule 303. Degrading Questions.

Rule 304. Confessions and Admissions.
    (a) General rule.
    (b) Exception.
    (c) Definitions.
        (1) Confession.
        (2) Admission.
        (3) Involuntary.
    (d) Procedure.
        (1) Disclosure.
        (2) Motions and objections.
        (3) Specificity.
        (4) Rulings.
        (5) Effect of guilty plea.
    (e) Burden of proof.
        (1) In general.
        (2) Weight of the evidence.
        (3) Derivative evidence.
    (f) Defense evidence.
    (g) Corroboration.
        (1) Quantum of evidence needed.
        (2) Procedure.
    (h) Miscellaneous.
        (1) Oral statements.
        (2) Completeness.
        (3) Certain admissions by silence.

Rule 305. Warnings About Rights.
    (a) General rule.
    (b) Definitions.
        (1) Persons subject to the Uniform Code of Military Justice.
        (2) Interrogation.

(c) Warnings concerning the accusation, right to remain silent, and use of statements.
(d) Counsel rights and warnings.
    (1) General rule.
    (2) Counsel.
(e) Notice to counsel.
(f) Exercise of rights.
(g) Waiver.
    (1) General rule.
    (2) Counsel.
(h) Nonmilitary interrogations.
    (1) General rule.
    (2) Foreign interrogations.

Rule 306. Statements by One of Several Accused.

Rule 311. Evidence Obtained from Unlawful Searches and Seizures.
(a) General rule.
    (1) Objection.
    (2) Adequate interest.
(b) Exception.
(c) Nature of search or seizure.
    (1) Military personnel.
    (2) Other officials.
    (3) Officials of a foreign government.
(d) Motions to suppress and objections.
    (1) Disclosure.
    (2) Motion or objection.
    (3) Specificity.
    (4) Rulings.
(e) Burden of proof.
    (1) In general.
    (2) Derivative evidence.
    (3) Specific motion or objections.
(f) Defense evidence.
(g) Scope of motions and objections challenging probable cause.
    (1) Generally.
    (2) False statements.
(h) Objections to evidence seized unlawfully.
(i) Effect of guilty plea.

Rule 312. Bodily Views and Intrusions.
(a) General rule.
(b) Visual examination of the body.
    (1) Consensual.
    (2) Involuntary.
(c) Intrusion into body cavities.
    (1) For purposes of seizure.
    (2) For purposes of search.
(d) Seizure of bodily fluids.
(e) Other intrusive searches.
(f) Intrusions for valid medical purposes.
(g) Medical qualifications.

Rule 313. Administrative Inspections and Inventories in the Armed Forces.
(a) General rule.
(b) Inspections.
(c) Inventories.

Rule 314. Searches Not Requiring Probable Cause.
(a) General rule.
(b) Border searches.
(c) Searches upon entry to United States installations, aircraft, and vessels abroad.
(d) Searches of government property.

   (e) Consent searches.
      (1) General rule.
      (2) Who may consent.
      (3) Scope of consent.
      (4) Voluntariness.
      (5) Burden of proof.
   (f) Frisks incident to a lawful stop.
      (1) Stops.
      (2) Frisks.
   (g) Searches incident to a lawful apprehension.
      (1) General rule.
      (2) Search for weapons and destructible evidence.
      (3) Examination for other persons.
   (h) Searches within jails, confinement facilities, or similar facilities.
   (i) Emergency searches to save life or for related purposes.
   (j) Searches of open fields and woodlands.
   (k) Other searches.

Rule 315. Probable Cause Searches.
   (a) General rule.
   (b) Definitions.
      (1) Authorization to search.
      (2) Search warrant.
   (c) Scope of authorization.
      (1) Persons.
      (2) Military property.
      (3) Persons and property within military control.
      (4) Nonmilitary property within a foreign country.
   (d) Power to authorize.
      (1) Commander.
      (2) Delegee.
      (3) Military judge.
   (e) Power to search.
   (f) Basis for search authorizations.
      (1) Probable cause requirement.
      (2) Probable cause determination.
   (g) Exigencies.
      (1) Insufficient time.
      (2) Lack of communications.
      (3) Search of operable vehicle.
      (4) Not required by Constitution.
   (h) Execution.
      (1) Notice.
      (2) Inventory.
      (3) Foreign searches.
      (4) Search warrants.

Rule 316. Seizures.
   (a) General rule.
   (b) Seizure of property.
   (c) Apprehension.
   (d) Seizure of property or evidence.
      (1) Abandoned property.
      (2) Consent.
      (3) Government property.
      (4) Other property.
         (A) Authorization.
         (B) Exigent circumstances.
         (C) Plain view.
   (e) Power to seize.

Rule 317. Interception of Wire and Oral Communications.
   (a) General rule.

(b) Authorization for judicial applications in the United States.
(c) Regulations.

Rule 321. Eyewitness Identification.
    (a) General rule.
        (1) Admissibility.
        (2) Exclusionary rule.
    (b) Definition of "unlawful."
        (1) Lineups and other identification processes.
        (2) Lineups: right to counsel.
            (A) Military lineups.
            (B) Nonmilitary lineups.
    (c) Motions to suppress and objections.
        (1) Disclosure.
        (2) Motion or objection.
        (3) Specificity.
    (d) Burden of proof.
        (1) Right to counsel.
        (2) Unnecessarily suggestive identification.
    (e) Defense evidence.
    (f) Rulings.
    (g) Effect of guilty pleas.

DRAFTERS' ANALYSIS

Military Rules of Evidence 301-306, 311-317, and 321 are new and have no equivalent in the Federal Rules of Evidence. They represent a partial codification of the law relating to self-incrimination, confessions and admissions, search and seizure, and eye-witness identification. They are often rules of criminal procedure as well as evidence and have been located in this section due to their evidentiary significance. They replace Federal Rules of Evidence 301 and 302 which deal with civil matters exclusively.

The Committee believed it imperative to codify the material treated in Section III because of the large numbers of lay personnel who hold important roles within the military criminal legal system. Non-lawyer legal officers aboard ship, for example, do not have access to attorneys and law libraries. In all cases, the Rules represent a judgment that it would be impracticable to operate without them. *See* Article 36. The Rules represent a compromise between specificity, intended to ensure stability and uniformity within the armed forces, and generality, intended usually to allow change via case law. In some instances they significantly change present procedure. *See, e.g.,* Rule 304(d) (procedure for suppression motions relating to confessions and admissions).

Rule 301. Privilege Concerning Compulsory Self-Incrimination.

(a) General rule. The privileges against self-incrimination provided by the Fifth Amendment to the Constitution of the United States and Article 31 of the Uniform Code of Military Justice are applicable only to evidence of a testimonial or communicative nature. The privilege most beneficial to the individual asserting the privilege shall be applied.

(b) Standing.

(1) **In general.** The privilege of a witness to refuse to respond to a question the answer to which may tend to incriminate the witness is a personal one that the witness may exercise or waive at the discretion of the witness.

(2) **Judicial advice.** If a witness who is apparently uninformed of the privileges under this rule appears likely to incriminate himself or herself, the military judge should advise the witness of the right to decline to make any answer that might tend to incriminate the witness and that any self-incriminating answer the witness might make can later be used as evidence against the witness. Counsel for any party or for the witness may request the military judge to so advise a witness provided that such a request be made out of the hearing of the witness and, except in a special court-martial without a military judge, the members. Failure to so advise a witness does not make the testimony of the witness inadmissible.

(c) Exercise of the privilege.
If a witness states that the answer to a question may tend to incriminate him or her, the witness may not be required to answer unless facts and circumstances are such that no answer the witness might make to the question could have the effect of tending to incriminate the witness or that the witness has, with respect to the question, waived the privilege against self-incrimination. A witness may not assert the privilege if the witness is not subject to criminal penalty as a result of an answer by reason of immunity, running of the statute of limitations, or similar reason.

(1) **Immunity generally.** The minimum grant of immunity adequate to overcome the privilege is that which under either paragraph 68*h* of this Manual or other proper authority provides that neither the testimony of the witness nor any evidence obtained from that testimony may be used against the witness at any subsequent trial other than in a prosecution for perjury, false swearing, the making of a false official statement, or failure to comply with an order to testify after the military judge has ruled that the privilege may not be asserted by reason of immunity.

(2) **Notification of immunity or leniency.** When a prosecution witness before a court-martial has been

granted immunity or leniency in exchange for testimony, the grant shall be reduced to writing and shall be served on the accused prior to arraignment or within a reasonable time before the witness testifies. If notification is not made as required by this rule, the military judge may grant a continuance until notification is made, prohibit or strike the testimony of the witness, or enter such other order as may be required.

(d) Waiver by a witness. A witness who answers a question without having asserted the privilege against self-incrimination and thereby admits a self-incriminating fact may be required to disclose all information relevant to that fact except when there is a real danger of further self-incrimination. This limited waiver of the privilege applies only at the trial in which the answer is given, does not extend to a rehearing or new or other trial, and is subject to rule 608(b).

(e) Waiver by the accused. When an accused testifies voluntarily as a witness, the accused thereby waives the privilege against self-incrimination with respect to the matters concerning which he or she so testifies. If the accused is on trial for two or more offenses and on direct examination testifies concerning the issue of guilt or innocence as to only one or some of the offenses, the accused may not be cross-examined as to guilt or innocence with respect to the other offenses unless the cross-examination is relevant to an offense concerning which the accused has testified. This waiver is subject to rule 608(b).

(f) Effect of claiming the privilege.

(1) Generally. The fact that a witness has asserted the privilege against self-incrimination in refusing to answer a question cannot be considered as raising any inference unfavorable to either the accused or the government.

(2) On cross-examination. If a witness asserts the privilege against self-incrimination on cross-examination, the military judge, upon motion, may strike the direct testimony of the witness in whole or in part, unless the matters to which the witness refuses to testify are purely collateral.

(3) Pretrial. The fact that the accused during official questioning and in exercise of rights under the Fifth Amendment to the Constitution of the United States or Article 31, remained silent, refused to answer a certain question, requested counsel, or requested that the questioning be terminated is inadmissible against the accused.

(g) Instructions. When the accused does not testify at trial, defense counsel may request that the members of the court be instructed to disregard that fact and not draw any adverse inference from it. Defense counsel may request that the members not be so instructed. Defense counsel's election shall be binding upon the military judge except that the military judge may give the instruction when the instruction is necessary in the interests of justice.

EDITORIAL COMMENT

Rule 301 codifies the privilege against self-incrimination and sets forth a procedural framework that is designed to protect the right of witnesses, including the accused, not to incriminate themselves and to provide guidance as to the reach of the privilege in military proceedings.

Pre-Rules case law, which dealt primarily with the military's statutory right against self-incrimination, found in Article 31 of the Uniform Code of Military Justice, had interpreted the statutory privilege as providing protections not afforded persons in civilian courts where the sole source of authority was the Fifth Amendment. Subdivision (a) of Rule 301 recognizes that both the constitutional and statutory protections are available to a service-member, and directs that the privilege most beneficial to the individual asserting it shall be applied, a suggestion that would seem to indicate that the drafters intended that the protection of pre-Rules decisions would still be available under the Military Rules of Evidence.

Although subdivision (a) adopts language found in the former *Manual* provision, which limited the privilege against self-incrimination to evidence of a testimonial or communicative nature, in pre-Rules decisions that language did not inhibit the military courts from extending the Article 31 privilege to protect against compulsory production of voiceprints, handwriting exemplars and even bodily fluids (such as blood and urine). Thus, decisions of the United States Supreme Court limiting the scope of the constitutional privilege against self-incrimination to "testimonial incrimination" were not necessarily controlling in military courts. *See, e.g., Schmerber v. California,* 384 U.S. 757 (1966); *United States v. Wade,* 388 U.S. 218 (1967); *Gilbert v. California,* 388 U.S. 263 (1967); *United States v. Dionisio,* 410 U.S. 1 (1973).

However, after the effective date of the Rules, but without relying on Rule 301, the Court of Military Appeals effected several major changes in the breadth of the Article 31 privilege. In *United States v. Armstrong,* 9 M. J. 374 (C.M.A. 1980) the court conducted an in-depth re-examination of Article 31 and concluded that Congress had intended the statutory protection to be co-extensive with the Fifth Amendment privilege — no more and no less. Applying the currently dominant "testimonial compulsion" approach to the Fifth Amendment, the court concluded that body fluids (blood, urine, etc.) are not protected under Article 31. 9 M.J. at 383. Citing civilian precedents, the court in *United States v. Lloyd,* 10 M.J. 172 (C.M.A. 1981) continued its sweep and stated that Article 31 did not extend to handwriting and voice exemplars. Together these cases reverse a number of military decisions (some are noted in the drafters' *Analysis*) which had clearly interpreted Article 31 in a broad fashion.

It also seems clear that an accused is to be protected against impliedly admitting something by the production of evidence. *See generally* Lederer, *Rights Warnings in the Armed Services,* 72 Mil. L. Rev. 1 (1976) (discussion of "verbal acts"). If the act of producing evidence is tantamount to some sort of admission, then the privilege against self-incrimination, even the constitutional version, may well provide protection. *See Fisher v. United States,* 425 U.S. 391 (1976).

If the government is able to gather its evidence in compliance with the Fourth Amendment and the evidence incriminates the accused, it is unlikely today that any self-incrimination problem will be recognized. Whereas *Boyd v. United States,* 116 U.S. 616 (1886), once suggested that use of papers seized from a suspect would violate the Fifth Amendment if used against the suspect, there no longer seems to be much force in this position. *See Fisher v. United States, supra; Andresen v. Maryland,* 427 U.S. 463 (1976). Rule 312 should be consulted when "bodily evidence" has been seized from the accused and is offered as evidence. That Rule treats the obtaining of bodily evidence, including fluids, as primarily a Fourth Amendment problem, and thus is consistent with the developing case law.

The drafters' *Analysis* notes that the privilege against self-incrimination is not violated when a person is compelled to produce a record or writing that is held in a representative, rather than a personal, capacity. This is consistent with the decisions of the United States Supreme Court that interpret the constitutional privilege. *See Wilson v. United States,* 221 U.S. 361 (1911). *See also United States v. Lloyd* (production of military ID card not protected.

Subdivision (b) makes clear that the privilege against self-incrimination is a personal one. It belongs to the witness and only the witness may choose to exercise or waive it. The second part of subdivision (b) indicates that the military judge should advise a witness, who appears to be uninformed about the constitutional and statutory privileges, about the right to decline to make any answer that might be incriminating. Any counsel in the case, including counsel for the witness, may request that the judge so advise the witness. Like Rule 103(c), this Rule is designed to protect against the members of the court hearing the suggestion that the witness should invoke the privilege. If proceedings are conducted outside the hearing of court-members, they are unlikely to draw improper adverse inferences from the fact that a witness was warned about the possible wisdom of refusing to answer questions. The responsibility of warning witnesses is consistent with existing military law. *See, e.g., United States v. Milburn,* 8 M.J. 110 (C.M.A. 1979). If the procedure is followed, witnesses should have a full opportunity to avail themselves of the privileges against self-incrimination provided by the Constitution and the statute, and no counsel should be able to seek an unfair advantage by suggesting to the members of the court that a witness has a need to invoke the protections of the privilege against self-incrimination. *See also* Rule 512.

Subdivision (c) indicates that if a witness refuses to testify on the ground that answers to questions may tend to be incriminating, the witness may not be required to answer, unless it is clear that no answer the witness might make could possibly result in self-incrimination. Often, it is clear from the nature of the question and the information sought that answers could be incriminating. When it is not clear, however, it is a responsibility of the military judge to make a determination, using an objective standard, of whether an answer might possibly be incriminating. If so, the witness is entitled to the privilege. *See Hoffman v. United States,* 341 U.S. 479 (1951).

The last sentence of the first paragraph of subdivision (c) states that a witness may not assert the privilege if the witness would not be subject to "criminal penalty" as a result of an answer. It is important to note that the drafters of the Rule state in their *Analysis* that they do not intend to define "criminal penalty." Military cases have held that the threat of an administrative discharge less than honorable gives rise to the protection of the privilege against self-incrimination, because the discharge is sufficiently penal in nature to be considered "criminal." *See United States v. Ruiz,* 23 C.M.A. 181, 48 C.M.R. 797 (1974). Thus, it is important to keep in mind the possibility that the privilege against self-incrimination may be invoked when a witness could receive an administrative discharge, less than honorable (as a result of answering questions), even though the questions would not relate to an offense punishable under the Uniform Code of Military Justice or under civilian law.

Subdivision (c)(1) indicates that use immunity, approved by the United States Supreme Court in *Kastigar v. United States,* 406 U.S. 441 (1972), is sufficient to displace both the constitutional and statutory privileges against self-incrimination. Such immunity protects a witness against the use of statements made and the fruits thereof in subsequent proceedings, except proceedings for perjury type offenses committed pursuant to the grant of immunity. Military courts have followed the prevailing rule that there is no absolute right on the part of a defendant to have immunity conferred upon defense witnesses, although in some cases immunity has been granted. *See, e.g., United States v. Griffin,* 8 M.J. 66 (C.M.A. 1979). *See also United States v. Villines,* 9 M.J. 807 (N.C.M.R. 1980); *United States v. Martin,* 9 M.J. 731 (N.C.M.R. 1979). There is some authority that the Sixth Amendment may require immunity for defense witnesses in some circumstances. *See Government of the Virgin Islands v. Smith,* 615 F.2d 964 (3d Cir. 1980). *See also United States v. Lenz,* 616 F.2d 960 (6th Cir. 1980).

If immunity, or some other form of clemency or leniency, is extended to a prosecution witness, subdivision (c)(2) requires the government to have the promise or grant reduced to writing and served upon the defense. *See also* Federal Rule of Criminal Procedure 16(g). It is important to note that this section is written broadly. It is not confined to transactional or use immunity. It extends to any form of leniency that is granted to a witness. The notice to the defense, which may be waived, *United States v. Carroll,* 4 M.J. 674 (N.C.M.R. 1977), should state the terms of the promise, but need not state the reasons why the promise was made, *United States v. Webster,* 1 M.J. 216 (C.M.A. 1975). Existing case law places the burden on the military judge to determine what relief is appropriate if the prosecutor fails to provide timely notice. *See, e.g., United States v. Saylor,* 6 M.J. 647 (N.C.M.R. 1978). For a discussion of grants of immunity, *see* Green, *Grants of Immunity and Military Law, 1971-1976,* 73 MIL. L. REV. 1 (1976).

The privilege against self-incrimination may be waived under subdivision (d) when a witness answers a question without asserting the privilege against self-incrimination and thereby admits an incriminating fact. Under these circumstances the witness can be compelled to disclose all information relevant to the fact "except when there is a real danger of further self-incrimination." The Rule indicates that a witness who is willing to talk about incriminating matters cannot close the door on the inquiry once the real damage associated with revelation of information already has been done. But when additional statements might prove to be more harmful to the witness, the privilege against self-incrimination remains effective as to the additional answers. *See generally,* Note, *Testimonial Waiver of the Privilege Against Self-Incrimination,* 92 HARVARD L. REV 1752 (1979).

Subdivision (e) covers the accused who takes the stand to testify. It provides that an accused waives the privilege against self-incrimination "with respect to the matters concerning which he or she so testifies." This is consistent with Rule 611(b), which limits the scope of cross-examination to the scope of direct. Subdivision (e) makes clear that an accused who is being tried for more than one offense may testify as to some, but not all, of the offenses without waiving the privilege as to offenses not covered by the accused's testimony. The approach is to allow the accused to waive the privilege against self-incrimination in a limited way, and to provide the government a fair opportunity to examine the accused on the testimony actually given.

One of the difficult problems that military judges will face is how to reconcile Rule 301(e) with Rule 404(b). In many cases the government will charge several offenses simultaneously, and will take the position that evidence about each offense is relevant to all crimes charged. The evidence may show intent, common plan or scheme, guilty knowledge, etc. If an accused takes the stand to testify about one of several charges and the government claims that evidence about other charges is relevant to the one charge testified to by the accused, must the accused answer questions about the other charges? If the accused is forced to answer, it is doubtful that members of the court will be able to confine the testimony to the one charge on which the accused has chosen to testify. And if the accused invokes the privilege against self-incrimination and refuses to answer questions, invocation of the privilege before members of the court may prove to be damaging to the defense. In this situation, a severance may be desirable so that the prosecution is entitled to ask the defendant all relevant questions about the crime about which the defendant testifies, but the defendant is not put to the Hobson's choice of having to answer questions relating to charges to which he or she did not testify, or invoking the privilege before the members of the court. *Cf. Manual ¶33h.* If a severance is granted, testimony by the accused on cross-examination should not be used in subsequent prosecutions, since Rule 301(e) indicates that the accused should be able to testify as to one charge and only one charge. If testimony given on one charge were used on other charges, the spirit of the Rule would be violated. Severance is not common in military courts. If successfully opposed by the government, arguably the government should have to forego Rule 404(b) cross-examination. *See generally United States v. Kelly,* 7 C.M.A. 218, 22 C.M.R. 8 (1956).

It should be noted that Rule 608(b) provides that a witness who takes the stand does not waive the privilege against self-incrimination when examined with respect to matters that relate only to credibility. An accused is treated like any other witness under that Rule. A matter relates only to credibility when it does not tend to prove anything about the events that are disputed, but it is offered to suggest only that a witness is not worthy of belief.

Should a witness invoke the privilege, the court-members may be instructed that no unfavorable inference may be drawn against either the prosecution or the defense. This is consistent with subdivision (f)(1). The assumption of section (f)(1) is that the privilege against self-incrimination is properly invoked. Section (2) indicates that if a witness asserts the privilege against self-incrimination on cross-examination and refuses to answer questions relating to matters testified on direct examination, the testimony of the witness may be stricken in whole or in part. The only exception is where the matters to which the witness refuses to testify are collateral to the main issues at trial. *See, e.g., United States v. Terrell,* 4 M.J. 720 (A.C.M.R. 1977) aff'd on other grounds, 6 M.J. 13 (C.M.A. 1978). It is not clear what happens when an accused takes the stand to testify and refuses to answer questions on cross-examination. May the government choose to use the refusal of the accused to answer as evidence against the accused and comment upon it? Or is striking of the direct examination the sole remedy? The drafters' *Analysis* provides little guidance as to the appropriate answer under the Rule. *See* Rule 512. One possible approach is to ask the accused which remedy for refusal to answer he or she elects. This would provide a useful remedy, and also would make it virtually impossible for the accused to register any complaint about the fairness of the remedy. *See* Callahan, *Criminal Procedure — Striking Testimony of Witnesses Who Refuse to Answer on Cross-Examination,* 43 Mo. L. Rev. 334 (1978).

Section (3) of subdivision (f) provides that if an accused exercised either his constitutional right to remain silent or his statutory right not to incriminate himself during official questioning prior to trial, that fact may not be used as evidence against the accused. *See also* Rules 304(h)(3) and 512. Existing military case law offers even more protection than the evidence rule. In *United*

States v. Noel, 3 M.J. 328 (C.M.A. 1977), the court stated that an accused's pretrial silence was protected, even though he had not been informed of his right to remain silent under Article 31(b) U.C.M.J. Because he was a suspect and entitled to be warned about the right to remain silent, the court said silence could not be used against him. *Compare Jenkins v. Anderson,* 100 S. Ct. 2124 (1980) (pre-arrest silence could be used against defendant). It is important to note that this provision includes protections against the use not only of the accused's silence but also of any requests to terminate questioning, *see* Rule 305(f), and any request to see counsel. *See United States v. Ross,* 7 M.J. 174 (C.M.A. 1979).

The final subdivision of the Rule states that when an accused does not testify at trial, defense counsel may request that the members of the court be instructed not to draw an adverse inference from the defendant's failure to take the stand. The Rule also states that defense counsel may request that the members not be instructed on the point. *See also* Rule 512. The choice by defense counsel is binding on the military judge, except when the military judge believes that an instruction is necessary in the interest of justice. This subdivision seems to limit some of the discretion that had been given the military judge in pre-Rules case law. *See, e.g., United States v. Grunden,* 2 M.J. 116 (C.M.A. 1977). Generally, the instruction is viewed as protection for the accused, and if the accused believes that the instruction would do more harm than good, it should not be given. The United States Supreme Court has held that it is not constitutional error to give an instruction over the objection of the defendant. *Lakeside v. Oregon,* 435 U.S. 333 (1978). But the Court recognized that in general the wishes of the accused should be respected, since little point is served in giving an instruction that is designed to protect the accused under circumstances where the accused believes that the instruction is going to deny him a fair trial. *But see United States v. Jackson,* 6 M.J. 116 (C.M.A. 1979).

Nothing in the last subdivision bars a judge from instructing the court-members that they may consider the absence of evidence on a point in the course of its fact finding, so long as such an instruction is not tantamount to a reminder that the accused has not testified. Similarly, it is common for counsel to argue that evidence is uncontradicted. Most courts do not condemn such argument and distinguish it from a suggestion concerning the accused's failure to testify. An instruction or agrument that the members should consider that there is uncontradicted evidence may be improper if the accused is "the only person who could have challenged or contradicted such evidence." *United States v. Bartemio,* 547 F.2d 341 (7th Cir. 1974). *Compare United States v. Saint John,* 23 C.M.A. 20, 48 C.M.R. 312 (1974). *See also* 14 A.L.R.3d 723, 728, 763 (1967).

DRAFTERS' ANALYSIS

(a) General rule. Rule 301 (a) is consistent with the rule currently expressed in the first paragraph of ¶ 150*b* of the *Manual* but omits the phrasing of the privileges and explicitly states that as both variations apply the accused or witness receives the protection of whichever privilege may be the more beneficial. The fact that the privilege extends to a witness as well as an accused is inherent within the new phrasing which does not distinguish between the two.

The Rule states that the privileges are applicable only to "evidence of a testimonial or communicative nature," *Schmerber v. California,* 384 U.S. 757, 761 (1966). The meaning of "testimonial or communicative" for the purpose of Article 31 of the Uniform Code of Military Justice is not fully settled. Past decisions of the Court of Military Appeals have extended the Article 31 privilege against self-incrimination to voice and handwriting exemplars and perhaps under certain conditions to bodily fluids. *United States v. Ruiz,* 23 C.M.A. 181, 48 C.M.R. 797 (1974). Because of the unsettled law in the area of bodily fluids, it is not the intent of the Committee to adopt any particular definition of "testimonial or communicative." It is believed, however, that the decisions of the United States Supreme Court construing the Fifth Amendment, *e.g., Schmerber v. California,* 384 U.S. 757 (1966), should be persuasive in this area. Although the right against self-incrimination has a number of varied justifications, its primary purposes are to shield the individual's thought processes from government inquiry and to permit an individual to refuse to *create* evidence to be used against him. Taking a bodily fluid sample from the person of an individual fails to involve either concern. The fluid in question already exists; the individual's actions are irrelevant to its seizure except insofar as the health and privacy of the individual can be further protected through his or her cooperation. No persuasive reason exists for Article 31 to be extended to bodily fluids. To the extent that due process issues are involved in bodily fluid extractions, Rule 312 provides adequate protections.

The privilege against self-incrimination does not protect a person from being compelled by an order or force to exhibit his or her body or other physical characteristics as evidence. Similarly, the privilege is not violated by taking the fingerprints of an individual, in exhibiting or requiring that a scar on the body be exhibited, in placing an individual's feet in tracks, or by trying shoes or clothing on a person or in requiring the person to do so, or by compelling a person to place a hand, arm, or other part of the body under ultra-violet light for identification or other purposes.

The privilege is not violated by the use of compulsion in requiring a person to produce a record or writing under his or her control containing or disclosing incriminating matter when the record or writing is under control in a representative rather than a personal capacity as, for example, when it is in his or her control as the custodian for a non appropriated fund. Soo, *o.g.,* ¶ 150*b* of tho prooont *Manual; United Statoo v. Sellers,* 12 C.M.A. 262, 30 C.M.R. 262 (1961); *United States v. Haskins,* 11 C.M.A. 365, 29 C.M.R. 181 (1960).

(b) Standing.

(1) In general. Rule 301(b) (1) recites the first part of the third paragraph of ¶ 150*b* of the present *Manual* without change except that the present language indicating that neither counsel nor the court may object to a self-incriminating question put to the witness has been deleted as being unnecessary.

(2) Judicial advice. A clarified version of the military judge's responsibility under ¶ 150*b* of the present *Manual* to warn an uninformed witness of the right against self-incrimination has been placed in Rule 301 (b) (2). The revised procedure precludes counsel asking in open court that a witness be advised of his or her rights, a practice which the Committee deemed of doubtful propriety.

(c) Exercise of the privilege. The first sentence of Rule 301 (c) restates generally the first sentence of the second paragraph of ¶ 150*b* of the present *Manual.* The language "unless it clearly appears to the military judge" was deleted. The test involved is purely objective.

The second sentence of Rule 301 (c) is similar to the second and third sentence of the second paragraph of ¶ 150*b* of the present *Manual* but the language has been rephrased. The present *Manual's* language states that the witness can be required to answer if for "any other reason, he can successfully object to being tried for any offense as to which the answer may supply information tending to incriminate him . . . ." Rule 301 (c) provides: "A witness may not assert the privilege if the witness is not subject to criminal penalty as a result of an answer by reason of immunity, running of the statute of limitations, or similar reason." It is believed that the new language is simpler and more accurate as the privilege is properly defined in terms of consequence rather than in terms of "being tried." In the absence of a possible criminal penalty, to include the mere fact of conviction, there is no risk of self-incrimination. It is not the intent of the Committee to adopt any particular definition of "criminal penalty." It should be noted, however, that the courts have occasionally found that certain consequences that are technically non-criminal are so similar in effect that the privilege should be construed to apply. *See, e.g., Spevack v. Klein,* 385 U.S. 511 (1967); *United States v. Ruiz,* 23 C.M.A. 181, 48 C.M.R. 797 (1974). Thus, the definition of "criminal penalty" may depend upon the facts of a given case as well as the applicable case law.

It should be emphasized that an accused, unlike a witness, need not take the stand to claim the privilege.

(1) Immunity generally. Rule 301 (c) (1) recognizes that "testimonial" or "use plus fruits" immunity is sufficient to overcome the privilege against self-incrimination, *cf. United States v. Rivera,* 1 M.J. 107 (C.M.A. 1975), reversing on other grounds, 49 C.M.R. 259 (A.C.M.R. 1974), and declares that such immunity is adequate for purposes of the *Manual.* The Rule recognizes that immunity may be granted under federal statutes as well as under ¶ 68*h* of the *Manual.*

(2) Notification of immunity or leniency. The basic disclosure provision of Rule 301 (c) (2) is taken from *United States v. Webster,* 1 M.J. 216 (C.M.A. 1975). Disclosure should take place prior to arraignment in order to conform with the timing requirements of Rule 304 and to ensure efficient trial procedure.

(d) Waiver by a witness. The first sentence of Rule 301 (d) repeats without change the third sentence of the third subparagraph of ¶ 150*b* of the present *Manual.*

The second sentence of the Rule restates the second section of the present subparagraph but with a minor change of wording. The present text reads: "The witness may be considered to have waived the privilege to this extent by having made the answer, but such a waiver will not extend to a rehearing or new or other trial," while the new language is: "This limited waiver of the privilege applies only at the trial in which the answer is given, does not extend to a rehearing or new or other trial, and is subject to Rule 608(b)."

(e) Waiver by the accused. Except for the reference to Rule 608(b), Rule 301(e) generally restates the fourth sentence of the third subparagraph of present ¶ 149*b* (1) of the *Manual.* "Matters" was substituted for "issues" for purposes of clarity.

The mere act of taking the stand does not waive the privilege. If an accused testifies on direct examination only as to matters not bearing upon the issue of guilt or innocence of any offense for which the accused is being tried, as in Rule 304 (f), the accused may not be cross-examined on the issue of guilt or innocence at all. *See* ¶ 149*b* (1) of the present *Manual* and Rule 608 (b).

The last sentence of the third subparagraph of ¶ 149*b* (1) of the present *Manual* has been deleted as unnecessary. The Analysis statement above, "The mere act of taking the stand does not waive the privilege," reinforces the fact that waiver depends upon the actual content of the accused's testimony.

The last sentence of Rule 301 (e) restates without significant change the sixth sentence of the third subparagraph of present ¶ 149*b* (1).

(f) Effect of claiming the privilege.

(1) Generally. Rule 301(f)(1) is taken without change from the fourth subparagraph of ¶ 150*b* of the present *Manual.* It should be noted that it is ethically improper to call a witness with the intent of having the witness claim a valid

privilege against self-incrimination in open court, *see, e.g.,* ABA STANDARDS RELATING TO THE ADMINISTRATION OF CRIMINAL JUSTICE, STANDARDS RELATING TO THE PROSECUTION FUNCTION AND THE DEFENSE FUNCTION, Prosecution Standard 3-5.7(c); Defense Standard 4-7.6(c) (Approved draft 1979).

Whether and to what extent a military judge may permit comment on the refusal of a witness to testify after his or her claimed reliance on the privilege against self-incrimination has been determined by the judge to be invalid is a question not dealt with by the Rule and one which is left to future decisions for resolution.

(2) On cross-examination. This provision is new and is intended to clarify the situation in which a witness who has testified fully on direct examination asserts the privilege against self-incrimination on cross-examination. It incorporates the prevailing civilian rule, which has also been discussed in military cases. *See, e.g., United States v. Colon-Atienza,* 22 C.M.A. 399, 47 C.M.R. 336 (1973); *United States v. Rivas,* 3 M.J. 282 (C.M.A. 1977). Where the assertion shields only "collateral" matters — *i.e.,* evidence of minimal importance (usually dealing with a rather distant fact solicited for impeachment purposes) — it is not appropriate to strike direct testimony. A matter is collateral when sheltering it would create little danger of prejudice to the accused. Where the exercise of the privilege reaches the core of the direct testimony or prevents a full inquiry into the credibility of the witness, however, striking of the direct testimony would appear mandated. Cross-examination includes for the purpose of Rule 301 the testimony of a hostile witness called as if on cross-examination. *See* Rule 607. Depending upon the circumstances of the case, a refusal to strike the testimony of a government witness who refuses to answer defense questions calculated to impeach the credibility of the witness may constitute prejudicial limitation of the accused's right to cross-examine the witness.

(3) Pretrial. Rule 301(f)(3) is taken generally from ¶ 140*a* (4) of the present *Manual* and follows the decisions of the United States Supreme Court in *United States v. Hale,* 422 U.S. 171 (1975) and *Doyle v. Ohio,* 426 U.S. 610 (1976). *See also United States v. Brooks,* 12 C.M.A. 423, 31 C.M.R. 9 (1961); *United States v. McBride,* 50 C.M.R. 126 (A.F.C.M.R. 1975). The present *Manual* provision has been expanded to include a request to terminate questioning.

(g) Instructions. Rule 301(g) has no counterpart in the present *Manual.* It is designed to address the potential for prejudice that may occur when an accused exercises his or her right to remain silent. Traditionally, the court members have been instructed to disregard the accused's silence and not to draw any adverse inference from it. However, counsel for the accused may determine that this very instruction may emphasize the accused's silence, creating a prejudicial effect. Although the Supreme Court has held that it is not unconstitutional for a judge to instruct a jury over the objection of the accused to disregard the accused's silence, it has also stated: "It may be wise for a trial judge not to give such a cautionary instruction over a defendant's objection." *Lakeside v. Oregon,* 435 U.S., 333.340-41 (1978). Rule 301 (g) recognizes that the decision to ask for a cautionary instruction is one of great tactical importance for the defense and generally leaves that decision solely within the hands of the defense. Although the military judge may give the instruction when it is necessary in the interests of justice, the intent of the Committee is to leave the decision in the hands of the defense in all but the most unusual cases. *See also* Rule 105. The military judge may determine the content of any instruction that is requested to be given.

(h) Miscellaneous. The last portion of paragraph 150*b* dealing with exclusion of evidence obtained in violation of due process has been deleted and its content placed in the new Rules on search and seizure. *See e.g.,* Rule 312, Bodily Views and Intrusions. The exclusionary rule now found in the last subparagraph of present ¶ 150*b* has been deleted as being unnecessary in view of the general exclusionary rule in Rule 304.

Rule 302. Privilege Concerning Mental Examination of an Accused

(a) General rule. The accused has a privilege to prevent any statement made by the accused at a mental examination ordered under paragraph 121 of this Manual and any derivative evidence obtained through use of such a statement from being received into evidence against the accused on the issue of guilt or innocence or during sentencing proceedings. This privilege may be claimed by the accused notwithstanding the fact that the accused may have been warned of the rights provided by rule 305 at the examination.

(b) Exceptions.

　　(1) There is no privilege under this rule when the accused first introduces into evidence such statements or derivative evidence.

　　(2) An expert witness for the prosecution may testify as to the reasons for the expert's conclusions and the reasons therefor as to the mental state of the accused if expert testimony offered by the defense as to the mental condition of the accused has been received in evidence, but such testimony may not extend to statements of the accused except as provided in (1).

(c) Release of evidence. If the defense offers expert testimony concerning the mental condition of the accused, the military judge, upon motion, shall order the release to the prosecution of the full contents, other than any statements made by the accused, of any report prepared pursuant to paragraph 121 of this Manual. If the defense offers statements made by the accused at such examination, the military judge may upon motion order the disclosure of such statements made by the accused and contained in the report as may be necessary in the interests of justice.

(d) Noncompliance by the accused. The military judge may prohibit an accused who refuses to cooperate in a mental examination authorized under paragraph 121 of this Manual from presenting any expert medical testimony as to any issue that would have been the subject of the mental examination.

(e) Procedure. The privilege in this rule may be claimed by the accused only under the procedure set forth in rule 304 for an objection or a motion to suppress.

EDITORIAL COMMENT

Insanity, the lack of mental responsibility, is a complete defense. Once raised, the prosecution must show beyond a reasonable doubt that the accused was mentally responsible at the time of the offense. Rule 302 fully recognizes that burden but in tandem with a new *Manual* ¶ 121 substantially changes the treatment of the defense at both trial and pre-trial stages.

Previous *Manual* provisions, grounded in cases such as *United States v. Babbidge,* 18 C.M.A. 327, 40 C.M.R. 39 (1969), provided that in return for raising the insanity defense through expert testimony, the accused could be compelled to submit to a psychiatric examination. Any statements made by the accused during the sanity board's inquiry were not admissible against him at trial unless they were preceded with rights warnings or the defense first offered them at trial. *United States v. Frederick,* 3 M.J. 230 (C.M.A. 1977). Submission to the sanity board was considered a qualified waiver of the privilege against self-incrimination.

Rule 302, comparable in intent to Rule 12.2 of the Federal Rule of Criminal Procedure, revives the availability of the privilege against self-incrimination in compelled sanity board proceedings and limits disclosure of any statements to the prosecution. *See also* 18 U.S.C. § 4244 (statements made by defendant at sanity hearing are inadmissible on issue of guilt). The Rule must be read in conjunction with the new *Manual* ¶ 121. We have included the text of ¶ 121 at the end of our comment for the reader's convenience. *See also* Yustas, *Mental Evaluation of an Accused Under the Military Rules of Evidence: An Excellent Balance,* THE ARMY LAWYER, May 1980 at 24.

In brief summary, *Manual* ¶ 121 now requires that an inquiry into the mental condition of the accused must be ordered if during pretrial or trial proceedings there is a resonable basis to believe that the accused is insane or was insane at the time of the offense. The matter must be referred to a board of one or more physicians. At least one member of the board should be a psychiatrist. In addition to its general findings, the board will be directed to include specific and distinct findings as to specified issues, including the ALI standard of mental responsibility adopted by the Court of Military Appeals in *United States v. Frederick, supra. See* Taylor, *Building the Cuckoo's Nest,* THE ARMY LAWYER, June 1978 at 32. When the board has completed its investigation, disclosure of its findings is closely controlled. Its "ultimate conclusions" are, in effect, given to all parties involved in the case. The "full report" may be given to other medical personnel for medical purposes. It may also be released to others, except to the prosecution, if authorized by the convening authority or military judge. It must be given to the defense counsel and, upon request, must be given to the accused's "commanding officer." The contents and supporting data for the board's findings may not be disclosed to individuals not entitled to the full report unless the military judge orders it. In addition to these limitations on the board's disclosure, ¶ 121 prohibits anyone, other than the military judge, defense counsel or accused, from disclosing to the prosecution any statement by the accused or its derivative evidence. Note that these disclosure limitations speak primarily to limiting what the sanity board may reveal to specified parties. However, once the material is out of the board's hands, all persons subject to the Uniform Code of Military Justice are prohibited from making further disclosures to the prosecutor.

The drafters recognized that a sanity board's report often is used in determining what disposition should be made of charges against an accused. Their concern apparently centered on the potential use of an accused's compelled statements at a later trial. Rule 302 is therefore an attempt to insure that if the disclosure provisions of *Manual* ¶ 121 somehow do not prevent the prosecution from seeing the accused's statements, ample protection will still exist with respect to the use of the statements.

Subdivision (a) states the general rule. If the accused has submitted to a compelled sanity board inquiry under *Manual* ¶ 121, he has a privilege to block use of his statements made at that inquiry and any evidence derived from those statements. The Rule does not require rights warnings and indeed the drafters' *Analysis* points out that for purposes of invoking the Rule they are meaningless, since subdivision (d) compels the accused to cooperate upon pain of effectively losing his insanity defense. The privilege takes the form of testimonial immunity. That is, the accused's statements have been compelled and to admit them could violate the Fifth Amendment. *See generally New Jersey v. Portash,* 440 U.S. 450 (1979).

Neither the Rule nor the drafters' *Analysis* defines the term "statement," but read in conjunction with the broad protections offered by Article 31(a), U.C.M.J., "statement" for purposes of Rule 302 should include inculpatory, exculpatory and neutral statements. Arguably, verbal acts which present physical evidence to the board could also be protected. *See generally* our discussion of Rule 301.

Because the privilege in Rule 302 is equated with testimonial immunity, counsel and judges should find the military case law on that topic to be helpful in deciding whether derivative use has been made of the accused's statements. The military courts have given a very broad reading to derivative evidence to the point where even the remotest connection between the offered evidence and the prior immunized testimony will make the evidence "derivative." *See, e.g., United States v. Daley,* 3 M.J. 541 (A.C.M.R. 1977) (prosecution could not use immunized testimony given four years earlier to impeach accused); *United States v. Eastman,* 2 M.J. 417 (A.C.M.R. 1975) (Article 32 investigating officer, drafter of pretrial advice, and Staff Judge Advocate should not have read immunized testimony of accused in acting on charges).

The Rule 302 privilege, however, is limited. It extends only to the case on the merits and to sentencing. The accused therefore cannot complain if his statements are considered by the chain of command, the Article 32 investigating officer, or are used during a pretrial hearing to determine, for example, whether he is competent to stand trial. However, once the statements or the board's report are disclosed, the prosecution is potentially tainted. Where the prosecution has directly or indirectly learned of the accused's statements, the government is placed in the delicate position of either: (1) proceeding with trial in hopes of showing that neither the statements nor derivative evidence will be used; (2) assigning a new trial counsel who has not been privy to the information; or (3) transferring prosecution of the case to another jurisdiction in hopes of completely extinguishing any taint.

The privilege of Rule 302 is limited by the fact that it does not protect statements by the accused at mental examinations other than a compelled *Manual* ¶ 121 examination.

The defense may waive the privilege through a failure to object, *see* Rule 302(e), or by first offering, under subdivision (b), the accused's statements or their derivative evidence. The Rule does not specify what manner of introducing the statements will vitiate the privilege, but the drafters' *Analysis* urges that only explicit use will open the door for the prosecution. Limiting application of (b)(1) to only explicit introduction of either the statements or derivative evidence seems an easy-to-apply standard. In practice, however, the door sometimes is opened inadvertently or negligently, but clearly enough for the prosecution to respond. Only the most wary defense counsel should make any reference or allusion to covered evidence here unless he clearly intends to make use of the statements and is willing to see the government respond. The government should not be permitted to "push" the door open through its examination of defense witnesses.

The Rule is particularly cloudy with respect to the basis of offered lay testimony. According to the *Analysis,* a lay witness' testimony is not derivative unless the witness has read the sanity board's report. This seems too narrow and does not take into account the case where a "lay" sanity defense might be derivatively and very effectively built on statements made by the accused to the board. In that case, the lay testimony should be considered to be derivative for purposes of (b)(1). That broad treatment of the term "derivative" would be more in line with the policies of subdivision (a).

The Rule as originally written would have permitted the prosecution to respond to lay defense witnesses with expert testimony as long as no reference was made to specific statements by the accused. However, subdivision (b)(2) was changed on 1 September 1980 to permit prosecution use of experts only after the defense used its experts. Now, following an adverse finding of sanity under ¶ 121, the defense can nonetheless theoretically rely on lay testimony and block expert rebuttal by the prosecution.

Subdivision (c) is a disclosure provision governing release of the sanity board's report and the accused's statements to the prosecution. Note that it is the defense which determines to a great extent what information may be disclosed to the prosecution. If the defense presents no expert testimony on the issue of the accused's mental condition, the prosecution will not see the board's report, even if a *Manual* ¶ 121 board was held. If the defense chooses not to use any of the accused's statements to the board, the prosecution will not see them. Rule 302(c) contains both *must* and *may* provisions. The military judge, upon motion, *must* release the full contents of the report if expert testimony is offered by the defense. The military judge *may,* upon motion, release all or some of the accused's statements if the defense opens the door by offering statements. While the defense counsel must be ever aware of the possibility of triggering disclosure, the prosecution must be prepared to utilize the disclosure provisions of subdivision (c). When disclosure is ordered the prosecution should be granted a reasonable time to review the released information and to consider its potential use.

Subdivision (d) follows pre-Rules law and provides that if the accused fails to cooperate in the ordered sanity board examination, the defense is precluded from using expert testimony "as to any issue that would have been the subject of the mental examination." Implied in this limitation is the slim possibility that the defense might be able to present expert testimony on the mental state of the accused if it can satisfactorily establish that the subject matter of the expert's testimony covers matters which would not have been covered at the sanity board. A refusal to submit to the board will not bar lay testimony. If expert testimony has already been given it should be struck, but the prosecution should be wary of making comments on the accused's refusal to cooperate with the board, because to do so might under the circumstances of the refusal constitute a comment on the accused's right to remain silent. *See generally* Rules 301(f)(3) and 512.

Subdivision (e) directs that Rule 304 is the only mechanism for claiming the privilege. If the strict disclosure limitations of *Manual* ¶ 121 have been followed, it is not likely that the prosecution will be providing notice prior to arraignment as required by Rule 304 (d)(1). However, that should not prevent the defense from raising the issue prior to plea in anticipation that the prosecution may learn of statements or derivative evidence during trial. If the prosecutor has no access to statements, this pre-plea motion could do no more than make a record and put the prosecutor on notice that the defense will object if and when 302 evidence is obtained and offered by the government. Defense counsel should not be required to make this effort. A timely motion during trial should suffice. Where the defense places into evidence sanity board statements of the accused, *see* 302(c), and the prosecution intends to use other pretrial statements made at the sanity board, theoretically it should still give notice to the defense of its intent. Defense counsel should at that point object or risk waiver. Where the defense properly raises the possibility, either prior to or after plea, that improper disclosure has been made in violation of *Manual* ¶ 121, the prosecution must be prepared to show either (1) that it has no knowledge of the sanity report or its contents or (2) that it does have knowledge of the report and its contents but that no statement made by the accused or any derivative evidence will be used. Throughout, the standard to be employed by the military judge is a preponderance of the evidence with the burden resting on the prosecution to establish the admissibility of the evidence. *See* Rule 304 (e).

As we noted earlier, Rule 302 is closely linked with *Manual* ¶ 121. For the sake of convenience, we include here the text of that provision:

121. INQUIRY. If it appears to any commanding officer who considers the disposition of charges as indicated in 32, 33, and 35 or to any investigating officer (34), trial counsel, defense counsel or, as provided by 122, military judge or member of the court, that there is reason to believe that the accused is insane (120*d*) or was insane at the time of the alleged offense (120*b*), that fact and the basis of the belief or observation should be submitted through appropriate channels to the officer authorized to

order an inquiry into the mental condition of the accused. The submission may be accompanied by a formal application for a mental examination under this paragraph. Prior to referral of charges, such inquiry may be ordered by the convening authority with immediate responsibility for the disposition of the charges. After referral of charges, the inquiry may be ordered by the military judge; provided, however, that the convening authority may order such an inquiry after referral of charges but prior to commencement of the first session of the court-martial conducted pursuant to Article 39(a) when a military judge is not reasonably available. The military judge may order a mental examination of the accused whenever he deems it appropriate notwithstanding any prior determination by the convening authority.

When the report or the observations of the officer authorized to order an inquiry under this paragraph indicates a reasonable basis for such inquiry, the matter shall be referred to a board of one or more physicians for their observation and report as to the sanity of the accused. At least one member of the board should be a psychiatrist.

When a mental examination is ordered under this paragraph, the order shall contain the reasons for doubting the sanity of the accused or requesting the examination. In addition to other requirements, the order shall require the board to make separate and distinct findings as to each of the following questions:

At the time of the alleged criminal conduct did the accused have a mental disease or defect? The terms "mental disease or defect" do not include an abnormality manifested only by repeated criminal or otherwise antisocial conduct.

What is the clinical psychiatric diagnosis?

Did the accused, at the time of the alleged criminal conduct and as a result of such mental disease or defect, lack substantial capacity to appreciate the criminality of his conduct?

Did the accused, at the time of the alleged criminal conduct and as a result of such mental disease or defect, lack substantial capacity to conform his conduct to the requirements of law?

Does the accused possess sufficient mental capacity to understand the nature of the proceedings against him and to conduct or cooperate intelligently in his defense (120d)?

Such other questions as may be appropriate may also be included.

In addition to the above requirements, the order shall specify:

That upon completion of the board's investigation, only a statement of the board's ultimate conclusions as to all questions specified in the order shall be submitted to the officer ordering the examination, the individual's commanding officer, the investigating officer, if any, appointed pursuant to Article 32, and to all counsel in the case, the convening authority, and, after referral, to the military judge;

That the full report of the board may be released by the board or other medical personnel only to other medical personnel for medical purposes, unless otherwise authorized by the convening authority or, after referral of charges by the military judge, except that a copy of the full report shall be furnished to the defense and, upon request, to the commanding officer of the accused; and

That neither the contents of the report nor any matter considered by the board during its investigation shall be released by the board or other medical personnel to any individual not authorized to receive the full report, except pursuant to an order by the military judge.

No individual, other than the defense counsel, accused, or, after referral of charges, the military judge, shall disclose to the trial counsel any statement made by the accused to the board or any evidence derived from that statement. See Military Rule of Evidence 302.

The board should place the accused under observation, examine him, and conduct any further investigation that it deems necessary to comply with the order.

Based upon the report, further action in the case may be suspended, the charges may be dismissed by an officer competent to convene a court-martial appropriate to try the offense charged, administrative action may be taken to discharge the accused from the service on the grounds of his mental disability, or, subject to Military Rule of Evidence 302, the charges may be referred to trial. Additional mental examinations may be directed at any stage of the proceedings as circumstances may require.

DRAFTERS' ANALYSIS

Introduction. The difficulty giving rise to Rule 302 and its conforming changes is a natural consequence of the tension between the right against self-incrimination and the favored position occupied by the insanity defense. If an accused could place a defense expert on the stand to testify to his lack of mental responsibility and yet refuse to cooperate with a government expert, it would place the prosecution in a disadvantageous position. The courts have attempted to balance the competing needs and have arrived at what is usually, although not always, an adequate compromise: when an accused has raised a defense of insanity through expert testimony, the prosecution may compel the accused to submit to government psychiatric examination on pain of being prevented from presenting any defense expert testimony (or of striking what expert testimony has already been presented). However, at trial the expert may testify *only* as to his or her conclusions and their basis and not as to the contents of any statements made by the accused during the examination. *See, e.g., United States v. Albright,* 388 F.2d 719 (4th Cir. 1968); *United States v. Babbidge,* 18 C.M.A. 327, 40 C.M.R. 39 (1969). *See generally,* Lederer, *Rights Warnings in the Armed Services,* 72 MIL. L. REV. 1 (1976); Holladay, *Pretrial Mental Examinations Under Military Law: A Re-Examination,* 16 A.F.L. REV. 14 (1974). This compromise, which originally was a product of case law, is based on the premise that raising an insanity defense is an implied partial waiver of the privilege against self-incrimination and has since been codified in the Federal Rules of Criminal Procedure, FED. R. CRIM. P. 12-2, and present *Manual* ¶¶ 140a, 122b, 150b. The compromise, however, does not fully deal with the problem in the military.

In contrast to the civilian accused who is more likely to have access to a civilian doctor as an expert witness for the defense — a witness with no governmental status — the military accused normally must rely upon the military doctors assigned to the local installation. In the absence of a doctor-patient privilege, anything said can be expected to enter usual government medical channels. Once in those channels there is nothing in the present *Manual* that prevents the actual psychiatric report from reaching the prosecution and release of such information appears to be common in contemporary practice. As a result, even when the actual communications made by the accused are not revealed by the expert witness in open court, under the present *Manual* they may be studied by the prosecution and may be used to discover other evidence later admitted against the accused. This raises significant derivative evidence problems, *cf. United States v. Rivera,* 23 C.M.A. 430, 50 C.M.R. 389 (1975). One military judge's attempt to deal with this problem by issuing a protective order was commended by the Court of Military Appeals in an opinion that contained a caveat from Judge Duncan that the trial judge may have exceeded his authority in issuing the order, *United States v. Johnson,* 22 C.M.A. 424, 47 C.M.R. 402 (1973).

Further complicating this picture is the literal language of Article 31(b) which states, in part, that "No person subject to this chapter may . . . request a statement from, an accused or a person suspected of an offense without first informing him . . ." [of his rights]. Accordingly, a psychiatrist who complies with the literal meaning of Article 31(b) may effectively and inappropriately destroy the very protections created by *Babbidge* and related cases, while hindering the examination itself. At the same time, the validity of warnings and any consequent "waiver" under such circumstances is most questionable because *Babbidge* never considered the case of an accused forced to choose between a waiver and a prohibited or limited insanity defense. Also left open by the present compromise is the question of what circumstances, if any, will permit a prosecutor to solicit the actual statements made by the suspect during the mental examination. In *United States v. Frederick,* 3 M.J. 230 (C.M.A. 1977), the Court of Military Appeals held that the defense counsel had opened the door via his questioning of the witness and thus allowed the prosecution a broader examination of the expert witness than would otherwise have been allowed. At present, what constitutes "opening the door" is unclear. An informed defense counsel must proceed with the greatest of caution being always concerned that what may be an innocent question may be considered to be an "open sesame."

Under the present *Manual* interpretation of *Babbidge, supra,* the accused may refuse to submit to a government examination until after the actual presentation of defense expert testimony on the insanity issue. Thus, trial may have to be adjourned for a substantial period in the midst of the defense case. This is conducive to neither justice nor efficiency.

A twofold solution to these problems has been developed. Rule 302 provides a form of testimonial immunity intended to protect an accused from use of anything he may say during a mental examination ordered pursuant to ¶ 121 of the *Manual.* Paragraph 121 has been modified to sharply limit actual disclosure of information obtained from the accused during the examination. Together, these provisions should adequately protect the accused from disclosure of any statements made during the examination. This will encourage the accused to cooperate fully in the examination while protecting the Fifth Amendment and Article 31 rights of the accused.

Paragraph 121 has been retitled to eliminate "Before Trial" and is thus made applicable before and during trial. Pursuant to paragraph 121, an individual's belief or observations reflecting possible need for a mental examination of the accused should be submitted to the convening authority with immediate responsibility for the disposition of the charges or, after referral, to the military judge or president of a special court-martial without a military judge. This submission may, but need not, be accompanied by a formal application for a mental examination. While the convening authority may act on a submission under paragraph 121 after referral, he or she may do so only when a military judge is not reasonably available.

Paragraph 121 has been revised to reflect the new test for insanity set forth in *United States v. Frederick,* 3 M.J. 230 (C.M.A. 1977), and to require sufficient information for the fact finder to be able to make an intelligent decision rather than necessarily relying solely upon the expert's conclusion. Further questions, tailored to the individual case, may also be propounded. Thus, in an appropriate case, the following might be asked:

> Did the accused, at the time of the alleged offense and as a result of such mental disease or defect, lack substantial capacity to (possess actual knowledge), (entertain a specific intent), (premeditate a design to kill)?
> What is the accused's intelligence level?
> Was the accused under the influence of alcohol or other drugs at the time of the offense? If so, what was the degree of intoxication and was it voluntary? Does the diagnosis of alcoholism, alcohol or drug induced organic brain syndrome or pathologic intoxication apply?

As the purpose of the revision of paragraph 121 and the creation of Rule 302 is purely to protect the privilege against self-incrimination of an accused undergoing a mental examination related to a criminal case, both paragraph 121 and Rule 302 are inapplicable to proceedings not involving criminal consequences.

The order to the sanity board required by paragraph 121 affects only members of the board and other medical personnel. Upon request by a commanding officer of the accused, that officer shall be furnished a copy of the board's full report. The commander may then make such use of the report as may be appropriate (including consultation with a judge advocate) subject only to the restriction on release to the trial counsel and to Rule 302. The restriction is fully applicable to all persons subject to the Uniform Code of Military Justice. Thus, it is intended that the trial counsel receive only the board's conclusions unless the defense should choose to disclose specific matter. The report itself shall be released to the trial counsel, minus any statements made by the accused, when the defense raises a sanity issue at trial and utilizes an expert witness in its presentation. Rule 302(c).

Although Rule 302(a) does not apply to determinations of the competency of the accused to stand trial, paragraph 121 does prohibit access to the sanity board report by the trial counsel except as specifically authorized. In the event that the competency of an accused to stand trial is at issue, the trial counsel may request, pursuant to paragraph 121, that the military judge disclose the sanity board report to the prosecution. In such a case, a trial counsel who has read the report will be disqualified from prosecuting the case in chief if Rule 302(a) is applicable.

As indicated above, paragraph 121 requires that the sanity board report be kept within medical channels except insofar as it will be released to the defense and, upon request, to the commanding officer of the accused. The paragraph expressly prohibits any person from supplying the trial counsel with information relating to the contents of the report. Care should be taken not to misconstrue the intent of the provision. The trial counsel is dealt with specifically because in the normal case it is only the trial counsel who is involved in the preparation of the case at the stage at which a sanity inquiry is likely to take place. Exclusion of evidence will result, however, even if the information is provided to persons other than the trial counsel if such information is the source of derivative evidence. Rule 302 explicitly allows suppression of any evidence resulting from the accused's statement to the sanity board, and evidence derivative thereof, with limited exceptions as found in Rule 302. This is consistent with the theory behind the revision which treats the accused's communication to the sanity board as a form of coerced statement required under a form of testimonial immunity. For example, a commander who has obtained the sanity board's report may obtain legal advice from a judge advocate, including the staff judge advocate, concerning the content of the sanity board's report. If the judge advocate uses the information in order to obtain evidence against the accused or provides it to another person who used it to obtain evidence to be used in the case, Rule 302 authorizes exclusion. Commanders must take great care when discussing the sanity board report with others, and judge advocates exposed to the report must also take great care to operate within the Rule.

(a) General rule. Rule 302(a) provides that, absent defense offer, neither a statement made by the accused at a mental examination ordered under paragraph 121 nor derivative evidence thereof shall be received into evidence against the accused at trial on the merits or during sentencing when the Rule is applicable. This should be treated as a question of testimonial immunity for the purpose of determining the applicability of the exclusionary rule in the area. The Committee does not express an opinion as to whether statements made at such a mental examination or derivative evidence thereof may be used in making an adverse determination as to the disposition of the charges against the accused.

Subject to Rule 302(b), Rule 302(a) makes statements made by an accused at a paragraph 121 examination inadmissible even if Article 31(b) and counsel warnings have been given. This is intended to resolve problems arising from the literal interpretation of Article 31 discussed above. It protects the accused and enhances the validity of the examination.

(b) Exceptions. Rule 302(b) is taken from present law; *see Manual* paragraph 122 *b.* The waiver provision of Rule 302(b)(1) applies only when the defense makes explicit use of statements made by the accused to a sanity board or derivative evidence thereof. The use of lay testimony to present an insanity defense is not derivative evidence when the witness has not read the report.

(c) Release of evidence. Rule 302(c) is new and is intended to provide the trial counsel with sufficient information to reply to an insanity defense raised via expert testimony. The Rule is so structured as to permit the defense to choose how much information will be available to the prosecution by determining the nature of the defense to be made. If the accused fails to present an insanity defense or does so only through lay testimony, for example, the trial counsel will not receive access to the report. If the accused presents a defense, however, which includes specific incriminating statements made by the accused to the sanity board, the military judge may order disclosure to the trial counsel of "such statements . . . as may be necessary in the interest of justice."

Inasmuch as the revision of paragraph 121 and the creation of Rule 302 is intended primarily to deal with the situation in which the accused denies committing an offense and only raises an insanity defense as an alternative defense, the defense may consider that it is appropriate to disclose the entire sanity report to the trial counsel in a case in which the defense concedes the commission of the offense but is raising as its sole defense the mental state of the accused.

(d) Non-compliance by the accused. Rule 302(d) restates present law and is in addition to any other lawful sanctions. As Rule 302 and the revised paragraph 121 adequately protect the accused's right against self-incrimination at a sanity board, sanctions other than that found in Rule 302(d) should be statutorily and constitutionally possible. In an unusual case these sanctions might include prosecution of an accused for disobedience of a lawful order to cooperate with the sanity board.

(e) Procedure. Rule 302(e) recognizes that a violation of paragraph 121 or Rule 302 is in effect a misuse of immunized testimony — the coerced testimony of the accused at the sanity board — and thus results in an involuntary statement which may be challenged under Rule 304.

Rule 303. Degrading Questions

No person may be compelled to make a statement or produce evidence before any military tribunal if the statement or evidence is not material to the issue and may tend to degrade that person.

EDITORIAL COMMENT

The common law recognized a privilege against disclosing facts involving one's disgrace or infamy. 8 WIGMORE § 2215(7). A person could not be forced to give personally degrading evidence if it did not relate to an issue in question. At one point, the privilege almost became part of the Fifth Amendment. *See* L. LEVY, ORIGINS OF THE FIFTH AMENDMENT 317 (1968). Article 31(c), U.C.M.J. adopted the common law proscription and, although most jurisdictions have abandoned the privilege, Rule 303 is apparently an attempt to revive what commonly has been recognized as a dead letter in military practice.

The Rule has no equivalent in the Federal Rules and would seem to be of doubtful utility in courts-martial practice because of other general rules of exclusion, requirements of relevancy or protections against harassment. *See, e.g.,* Rules 403, 611(a). The drafters, however, find the Rule useful in carrying forward the spirit of Rule 412 in Article 32 U.C.M.J. investigations. The drafters plainly state in their *Analysis* that Article 32 investigations are "military tribunals" under the Rule. They also state that evidence barred by Rule 412 is degrading and immaterial, thus falling within the ambit of Rule 303. However, the public policy arguments suggested by the drafters for limiting examination of the Rule 412 witness at a pretrial investigation would not prevent consideration of other witnesses' testimony or evidence from being considered in determining whether charges should be referred to trial. Under Rule 412, no covered evidence may be received from anyone. This is not the case with a pretrial investigation in which the victim is generally not present when the investigation takes place. Neither Rule 303 nor the drafters' *Analysis* suggest just how the privilege might be asserted nor whether the judge or the Article 32 investigating officer should advise the victim or any other witness of the privilege. *See generally,* Rule 301(b)(2) (advice concerning privilege against self-incrimination). Nonetheless the privilege here is personal and although one of the parties may bring it to the attention of a witness, the decision to invoke it rests solely with the witness who would be degraded by answering. Government counsel can respect the Rule by not asking any witnesses for evidence that would be barred under Rule 412. Defense counsel probably cannot be stopped from asking, however, when the questions are put to witnesses who know about someone else's sexual activity.

DRAFTERS' ANALYSIS

Rule 303 restates Article 31(c). The content of present paragraph 150a has been omitted.

A specific application of Rule 303 is in the area of sexual offenses. Under present law the victims of such offenses are often subjected to a probing and degrading cross-examination related to past sexual history — an examination usually of limited relevance at best. Rule 412 of the Military Rules of Evidence now prohibits such questioning, but Rule 412 is, however, not applicable to Article 32 hearings as it is only a rule of evidence; Rule 1101. Rule 303 and Article 31(c), on the other hand, are rules of privilege applicable to all persons, military or civilian, and are thus fully applicable to Article 32 proceedings. Although Rule 303 (Article 31(c)), applies only to "military tribunals," it is apparent that Article 31(c) was intended to apply to courts-of-inquiry, and implicitly to Article 32 hearings. *The Uniform Code of Military Justice, Hearings on H.R. 2498 Before a Subcomm. of the House Comm. on Armed Services,* 81st Cong., 1st Sess. 975 (1949). The Committee intends that the expression "military tribunals" in Rule 303 includes Article 32 hearings.

Congress found the information now safeguarded by Rule 412 to be degrading. *See e.g.,* Cong. Rec. H119944-45 (Daily ed. Oct. 10, 1978) (Remarks of Rep. Mann). As the material within the constitutional scope of Rule 412 is inadmissible at trial, it is thus not relevant let alone "material." Consequently that data within the lawful coverage of Rule 412 is both immaterial and degrading and thus is within the ambit of Rule 303 (Article 31(c)).

Rule 303 is therefore the means by which the substance of Rule 412 applies to Article 32 proceedings, and no person may be compelled to answer a question that would be prohibited by Rule 412. As Rule 412 permits a victim to refuse to supply irrelevant and misleading sexual information at trial, so too does the substance of Rule 412 through Rule 303 permit the victim to refuse to supply such degrading information at an Article 32 for use by the defense or the convening authority. *See generally* Rule 412 and the *Analysis* thereto. It should also be noted that it would clearly be unreasonable to suggest that Congress in protecting the victims of sexual offenses from the degrading and irrelevant cross-examination formerly typical of sexual cases would have intended to permit the identical examination at a military preliminary hearing that is not even presided over by a legally trained individual. Thus public policy fully supports the application of Article 31(c) in this case.

Rule 304. Confessions and Admissions

(a) General rule. An involuntary statement or any derivative evidence therefrom may not be received in evidence against an accused who made the statement if the accused makes a timely motion to suppress or an objection to the evidence under this rule.

(b) Exception. Where the statement is involuntary only in terms of noncompliance with the requirements concerning counsel under rules 305(d), 305(e), and 305(g), this rule does not prohibit use of the statement to impeach by contradiction the in-court testimony of the accused or the use of such statement in a later prosecution against the accused for perjury, false swearing, or the making of a false official statement.

(c) Definitions. As used in these rules:

> *(1) Confession.* A "confession" is an acknowledgment of guilt.
>
> *(2) Admission.* An "admission" is a self-incriminating statement falling short of an acknowledgment of guilt, even if it was intended by its maker to be exculpatory.
>
> *(3) Involuntary.* A statement is "involuntary" if it is obtained in violation of the self-incrimination privilege or due process clause of the Fifth Amendment to the Constitution of the United States, Article 31, or through the use of coercion, unlawful influence, or unlawful inducement.

(d) Procedure.

> *(1) Disclosure.* Prior to arraignment, the prosecution shall disclose to the defense the contents of all statements, oral or written, made by the accused that are relevant to the case, known to the trial counsel, and within the control of the armed forces.
>
> *(2) Motions and objections.*
>
>> (A) Motions to suppress or objections under this rule or rules 302 or 305 to statements that have been disclosed shall be made by the defense prior to submission of a plea. In the absence of such motion or objection, the defense may not raise the issue at a later time except as permitted by the military judge for good cause shown. Failure to so move or object constitutes a waiver of the objection.
>>
>> (B) If the prosecution intends to offer against the accused a statement made by the accused that was not disclosed prior to arraignment, the prosecution shall

provide timely notice to the military judge and to counsel for the accused. The defense may enter an objection at that time and the military judge may make such orders as are required in the interests of justice.

(C) If evidence is disclosed as derivative evidence under this subdivision prior to arraignment, any motion to suppress or objection under this rule or rules 302 or 305 shall be made in accordance with the procedure for challenging a statement under (A). If such evidence has not been so disclosed prior to arraignment, the requirements of (B) apply.

(3) Specificity. The military judge may require the defense to specify the grounds upon which the defense moves to suppress or object to evidence. If defense counsel, despite the exercise of due diligence, has been unable to interview adequately those persons involved in the taking of a statement, the military judge may make any order required in the interests of justice, including authorization for the defense to make a general motion to suppress or general objection.

(4) Rulings. A motion to suppress or an objection to evidence made prior to plea shall be ruled upon prior to plea unless the military judge, for good cause, orders that it be deferred for determination at trial, but no such determination shall be deferred if a party's right to appeal the ruling is affected adversely.
Where factual issues are involved in ruling upon such motion or objection, the military judge shall state essential findings of fact on the record.

(5) Effect of guilty plea. A plea of guilty to an offense that results in a finding of guilty waives all privileges against self-incrimination and all motions and objections under this rule with respect to that offense regardless of whether raised prior to plea.

(e) Burden of proof. When an appropriate motion or objection has been made by the defense under this rule, the prosecution has the burden of establishing the admissibility of the evidence. When a specific motion or objection has been required under subdivision (d)(3), the burden on the prosecution extends only to the grounds upon which the defense moved to suppress or object to the evidence.

(1) In general. The military judge must find by a preponderance of the evidence that a statement by the

accused was made voluntarily before it may be received into evidence. When trial is by a special court-martial without a military judge, a determination by the president of the court that a statement was made voluntarily is subject to objection by any member of the court. When such objection is made, it shall be resolved pursuant to paragraph 57f of this Manual.

(2) Weight of the evidence. If a statement is admitted into evidence, the military judge shall permit the defense to present relevant evidence with respect to the voluntariness of the statement and shall instruct the members to give such weight to the statement as it deserves under all the circumstances. When trial is by military judge without members, the military judge shall determine the appropriate weight to give the statement.

(3) Derivative evidence. Evidence that is challenged under this rule as derivative evidence may be admitted against the accused if the military judge finds by a preponderance of the evidence either that the statement was made voluntarily or that the evidence was not obtained by use of the statement.

(f) Defense evidence. The defense may present evidence relevant to the admissibility of evidence as to which there has been an objection or motion to suppress under this rule. An accused may testify for the limited purpose of denying that the accused made the statement or that the statement was made voluntarily. Prior to the introduction of such testimony by the accused, the defense shall inform the military judge that the testimony is offered under this subdivision. When the accused testifies under this subdivision, the accused may be cross-examined only as to the matter on which he or she testifies. Nothing said by the accused on either direct or cross-examination may be used against the accused for any purpose other than in a prosecution for perjury, false swearing, or the making of a false official statement.

(g) Corroboration. An admission or a confession of the accused may be considered as evidence against the accused on the question of guilt or innocence only if independent evidence, either direct or circumstantial, has been introduced that corroborates the essential facts admitted to justify sufficiently an inference of their truth. Other uncorroborated confessions or admissions of the accused that would themselves require corroboration may not be

used to supply this independent evidence. If the independent evidence raises an inference of the truth of some but not all of the essential facts admitted, than the confession or admission may be considered as evidence against the accused only with respect to those essential facts stated in the confession or admission that are corroborated by the independent evidence. Corroboration is not required for a statement made by the accused before the court by which the accused is being tried, for statements made prior to or contemporaneously with the act, or for statements offered under a rule of evidence other than that pertaining to the admissibility of admissions or confessions.

> *(1) Quantum of evidence needed.* The independent evidence necessary to establish corroboration need not be sufficient of itself to establish beyond a reasonable doubt the truth of facts stated in the admission or confession. The independent evidence need raise only an inference of the truth of the essential facts admitted. The amount and type of evidence introduced as corroboration is a factor to be considered by the trier of fact in determining the weight, if any, to be given to the admission or confession.
>
> *(2) Procedure.* The military judge alone shall determine when adequate evidence of corroboration has been received. Corroborating evidence usually is to be introduced before the admission or confession is introduced but the military judge may admit evidence subject to later corroboration.

(h) Miscellaneous.

> *(1) Oral statements.* A voluntary oral confession or admission of the accused may be proved by the testimony of anyone who heard the accused make it, even if it was reduced to writing and the writing is not accounted for.
>
> *(2) Completeness.* If only part of an alleged admission or confession is introduced against the accused, the defense, by cross-examination or otherwise, may introduce the remaining portions of the statement.
>
> *(3) Certain admissions by silence.* A person's failure to deny an accusation of wrongdoing concerning an offense for which at the time of the alleged failure the person was under official investigation or was in confinement, arrest, or custody does not support an inference of an admission of the truth of the accusation.

EDITORIAL COMMENT

An accused's involuntary statements and any derivative evidence obtained through those statements may be excluded upon timely objection or motion. Rule 304 sets out this general rule of exclusion, which is applicable also to Rules 301 and 305; it also includes an exception to the general rule, a definition of the term "involuntary," and procedural rules for determining the admissibility of an accused's statements.

Key to any application of Rule 304 is the definition given to the term "involuntary" in subdivision (c)(3). The broad connotations of that term under pre-Rules practice have been adopted in this Rule. Involuntary statements (inculpatory or exculpatory), including silent admissions and verbal acts which were obtained through words or actions, may be inadmissible. The Rule implicitly recognizes that a wide variety of tactics may produce involuntary statements and the drafters' *Analysis* cites a number of common examples. Under the Rule, all derivative evidence obtained through the use of an involuntary statement is as inadmissible as the statement itself. No distinction is made between involuntary statements obtained through official action and those resulting from private action. *Cf. Manual* ¶ 150*b*.

The exception to the general rule of exclusion is found in subdivision (b) which changes pre-Rules practice. An accused's pretrial statements that are defective only in that they were not preceded with proper right to counsel warnings or notice to counsel under Rule 305 may be used for impeaching an accused or in a subsequent perjury type prosecution if the statements are otherwise voluntary. Other involuntary statements may not be used for any purpose by the prosecution. The drafters' *Analysis* indicates that this exception only applies to the use of a statement that is valid except insofar as it was not preceded by a proper waiver under Rule 305(g). To this extent, subdivision (b) is grounded in *Harris v. New York,* 401 U.S. 222 (1971), and overrules pre-Rules case law. *See, e.g., United States v. Jordan,* 20 C.M.A. 614, 44 C.M.R. 44 (1971). Statements obtained after defective Article 31(b) warnings are still considered involuntary and within the general rule of exclusion in subdivision (a).

The core of Rule 304 lies in subdivisions (d) and (e) which make major changes to motions practice in courts-martial. Subdivision (d) governs the procedures for litigating admissibility and subdivision (e) addresses the prosecution's burden of proof. These two provisions generally mirror similar procedural requirements in Rule 311 (unlawful searches and seizures) and Rule 321 (eyewitness identification). Each of these three Rules contains common elements which include:

(i) Disclosure by the prosecution of its evidence;

(ii) Procedures for objecting or making timely motions to suppress;

(iii) A possible requirement of specificity in the suppression motion or objection;

(iv) A specified burden of proof on the prosecution; and

(v) A requirement for the judge sua sponte to state essential findings of fact.

Because of this commonality, much of what we say here will also be applicable to understanding the operation of Rules 311 and 321. *See generally,* Basham, *Suppression Motions Under the Military Rules of Evidence,* THE ARMY LAWYER, May 1980 at 17.

Subdivision (d)(1) requires the prosecution to disclose to the defense, prior to arraignment, all of the accused's statements which are (i) relevant to the case, (ii) known to the prosecution, and (iii) within the control of the armed forces. This requirement is not hinged on the prosecutor's intended use and contains no sanction for failing to comply. In addressing a similar disclosure provision in Rule 12 of the Federal Rules of Criminal Procedure, the Advisory Committee in its Notes on the 1974 Amendments to the Rules stated that excluding evidence for failure to notify would be too burdensome considering other broad discovery rights. That rational is equally applicable in military practice. Untimely disclosure should support a continuance, however. This would be consistent with (d)(2)(B) which recognizes that disclosure may occur after arraignment and further provides that the military judge may take whatever action is appropriate.

Subdivision (d)(2) requires the judge to decide the admissibility of the statements and derivative evidence *prior* to the plea. *See* (d)(2)(A) and (d)(2)(B). This changes pre-Rules practice which had permitted the judge to defer hearing the issue until after the plea. *See, e.g., United States v. Kelly,* 4 M.J. 845 (A.C.M.R. 1978), pet. denied, 5 M.J. 267 (C.M.A. 1978). Failure to raise the issue prior to the plea will bar a post-plea objection unless the defense can show good cause. And according to (d)(2)(A) and (d)(5), the issue of admissibility may be waived either by a failure to raise the issue or by entering a plea of guilty.

Under pre-Rules practice, the prosecution carried the burden of proving the voluntariness of a statement unless the defense explicitly waived the issue. Now, the prosecution need only proceed with its proof when the defense explicitly raises the issue in a motion or objection. To raise the issue, the defense need only make an offer of proof and be timely and specific in raising its point. *See* Rule 103(a). No evidence need be presented by the defense.

Litigation of voluntariness will normally be narrowed and more quickly disposed of through (d)(3) which permits a military judge to require the defense to specify the basis for its motion or objection. Hypertechnical objections or motions are not necessary, but the grounds should be specific enough to permit the parties to focus sharply on the real issues. If the defense has not been able to adequately question witnesses to the taking of the statement, the judge may grant appropriate relief, including permission to enter only a general objection to the statement. Thus, a delay in disclosure by the prosecution may eliminate any need for a specific objection.

Because the prosecution must only meet the *stated* defense objection, *see* subdivision (e), it is usually to the advantage of the defense to stand on more general grounds. If, however, the judge has required a specific objection and the prosecution meets it, other defects not objected to may be waived. It is the prosecution's right to insist upon, and the judge's right to require, specificity unless there is good reason why an objection cannot be particularized.

Therefore, the Rule clearly places a greater burden on the defense to carefully review the circumstances of the accused's statements and to identify with specificity all of those defects upon which it is relying. Banking on a general objection or motion will no longer do. The drafters' *Analysis* illustrates the form that various specific objections might take.

Subdivision (d)(4) is patterned after Rule 12(e) of the Federal Rules of Criminal Procedure and requires the military judge to rule on the admissibility of the accused's statements prior to the plea unless some good reason exists for deferring the ruling until trial. Where the prosecution responds to the defense motion to suppress by noting that it does not intend to offer the accused's statement but cannot promise that it would never offer it, the military judge could defer ruling, but also could appropriately deny the motion and permit the defense to later object at trial if the statement is offered. The language concerning a party's right to appeal the ruling is taken verbatim from Rule 12(e) of the Federal Rules of Criminal Procedure, which covers more than just motions to suppress evidence. It takes into consideration the federal practice of interlocutory appeals of motions rulings that protects the government's right to take an appeal without violating the defendant's right not to be placed twice in jeopardy. *See* 18 U.S.C. 3731 (1976) (appeals of rulings). *See also United States v. Winnie Mae Manufacturing Co.,* 451 F. Supp. 642 (C.D. Cal. 1978) (ruling under Rule 12(e) should be made before court picks jury and before jeopardy attaches so as not to deprive government of right to appeal).

Although the ability of either side to appeal a suppression motion ruling is doubtful under current military practice, *see Dettinger v. United States,* 7 M.J. 216 (C.M.A. 1979) (extraordinary relief may be granted to either side under limited circumstances), the timing of the ruling obviously impacts on the defense decision regarding a plea and potentially may affect the prosecution's decision to proceed with trial where, for example, the judge rules the accused's confession inadmissible after jeopardy has attached.

Simply admitting or excluding the evidence generally will not suffice under the Rule if the facts are in dispute. The military judge is now required under (d)(4) to state "essential findings of fact" on the record. These sua sponte findings should not be confused with the more formalized special findings of fact which may be requested under Article 51(d), U.C.M.J. *See generally* Schinasi, *Special Findings: Their Use at Trial and On Appeal,* 87 Mil. L. Rev. 73 (1980). The (d)(4) findings should be detailed and thorough enough to permit the appellate authorities to determine whether the judge's reasoning was sound. Conclusory statements should be avoided. The Rule does not specify when these findings should be made, but implicit in the Rule is the intent to resolve the question of admissibility prior to the plea. Delaying the statement of findings, as does deferral of the ruling itself, causes uncertainty for parties who must decide finally on what plea to enter and finalize preparation of an orderly and timely presentation of evidence. In framing the findings, a military judge may want to ask counsel to contribute suggested language, but he should not rely on a counsel's refusal to do so as grounds for not making the findings.

Subdivision (e) does away with the two-step "Massachusetts Rule" used in litigating the admissibility of an accused's statement. Now the issue is litigated only before the military judge — *see* Rule 104(a), (c) — who applies a preponderance of the evidence standard to both the statement, (e)(1), and any derivative evidence, (e)(3).

In litigating admissibility, the defense may present evidence including testimony of the accused who may take the stand for the limited purpose of showing either that he did not make the statement or that it was made involuntarily. *See* subdivision (f), which follows *Manual* ¶ 140*a*(3) and (6). If the accused does take the stand, the defense must first announce that the testimony will be offered for the limited purpose of determining admissibility of evidence. Later use of the testimony for any purpose other than in a perjury type prosecution is prohibited by subdivision (f). The accused can be cross-examined during the hearing but only on matters about which he testifies. The cross-examination, like the direct examination, cannot be used for any purpose by the government at trial. *See also* Rule 104(d). If the accused's statement is admitted as voluntary, the defense is limited to presenting relevant evidence which relates to the "voluntariness" of the statement in order to support an argument that little or no weight should be attached to the statement. If such defense evidence is offered, the court-members should be instructed to decide what weight the accused's statement deserves under the circumstances. *See* subdivision (e)(2). Neither the Rule nor the drafters' *Analysis* address the matter, but it would seem that the prosecution should be permitted to rebut the defense evidence.

Subdivision (g), which substantially adopts pre-Rules practice, requires "corroboration" of both confessions and admissions before they may be considered as evidence on the question of guilt or innocence. The corroboration must come from independent evidence which is sufficient to justify an inference that the facts admitted by the accused are true. Only those essential facts which are corroborated may be considered by the fact-finder. The Rule recognizes that the quantum of evidence is generally slight and can be either direct or circumstantial. *See* subdivision (g)(1). The big change in this area is one of procedure. Under (g)(2) the military judge now decides finally the question of whether sufficient corroborative evidence has been produced to permit consideration of the admitted statement. *Cf. United States v. Seigle,* 22 C.M.A. 403, 47 C.M.R. 340 (1973) (members to be instructed on requirement of corroboration before considering confession). However, the amount and type of corroborating evidence are factors which may be considered by the members in deciding what weight the accused's confession or admission should receive.

Subdivision (h) contains three miscellaneous provisions which carry forward pre-Rules practice. Paragraph (1) permits proof of an oral statement through testimony without accounting for any written rendition of the statement which may have been made. *See Manual* ¶ 140*a*(6). This is entirely consistent with the Best Evidence Rule stated in Rule 1002. Paragraph (2) adopts *Manual* ¶ 140 *a*(6) and permits the defense counsel to complete both oral and written statements of the accused offered by the prosecution. *See also* Rule 106 which would permit the defense to require the prosecution to complete an offered written statement. Finally, Paragraph (3) recognizes that silence in the face of official accusations or even official suspicion does not support an inference that the accusations are true. *See also* Rule 301(f)(3). However, silence when confronted with accusations by private parties may constitute an admission by silence. *See, e.g., United States v. Cain,* 5 M.J. 844 (A.C.M.R. 1978) (accused remained silent when confronted by robbery victim).

DRAFTERS' ANALYSIS

(a) General rule. The exclusionary rule found in Rule 304(a) is applicable to Rules 301-305, and basically restates present law which appears in present *Manual* paragraphs 140*a*(6), and 150*b*. Rule 304(b) does permit, however, limited impeachment use of evidence that is excludable on the merits. A statement that is not involuntary within the meaning of Rule 304(c)(3), Rule 305(a), or Rule 302(a) is voluntary and will not be excluded under this Rule.

The seventh paragraph of ¶ 150*b* of the present *Manual* attempts to limit the derivative evidence rule to *statements* obtained through *compulsion* that is "applied by, or at the instigation or with the participation of, an *official or agent of the United States, or any State thereof or political subdivision of either, who was acting in a governmental capacity . . .*," (emphasis added). Rule 304, however, makes all derivative evidence inadmissible. Although some support for the present *Manual* limitation can be found in the literal phrasing of Article 31(d), the intent of the Article as indicated in the commentary presented during the House hearings, *The Uniform Code of Military Justice, Hearing on H.R. 2498 Before a Subcomm. of the House Comm. on Armed Services,* 81st Cong., 1st Sess. 984 (1949), was to exclude "evidence" rather than just "statements." Attempting to allow admission of evidence obtained from statements which were the product of coercion, unlawful influence or unlawful inducement would appear to be both against public policy and unnecessarily complicated. Similarly, the present *Manual's* attempt to limit the exclusion of derivative evidence to that obtained through compulsion caused by "government agents" has been deleted in favor of the simpler exclusion of all derivatives evidence. This change, however, does not effect the limitation, as expressed in current case law, that the warning requirements apply only when the interrogating individual is either a civilian law enforcement officer or an individual subject to the Uniform Code of Military Justice acting in an official disciplinary capacity or in a position of authority over a suspect or accused. The House hearings indicate that all evidence obtained in violation of Article 31 was to be excluded and all persons subject to the Uniform Code of Military Justice may violate Article 31(a). Consequently, the attempted present *Manual* restriction could affect at most only derivative evidence obtained from involuntary statements compelled by private citizens. Public policy demands that private citizens not be encouraged to take the law into their own hands and that law enforcement agents not be encouraged to attempt to circumvent an accused's rights via proxy interrogation.

It is clear that truly spontaneous statements are admissible as they are not "obtained" from an accused or suspect. An apparently volunteered statement which is actually the result of coercive circumstances intentionally created or used by interrogators will be involuntary, *Cf. Brewer v. Williams,* 430 U.S. 387 (1977), Rule 305(b)(2). *Manual* language dealing with this area has been deleted as being unnecessary.

(b) Exception. Rule 304(b) adopts *Harris v. New York,* 401 U.S. 222 (1971) insofar as it would allow use for impeachment or at a later trial for perjury, false swearing or the making of a false official statement, of statements taken in violation of the counsel warnings required under Rule 305(d)-(e). Under ¶¶ 140*a*(2) and 153*b* of the present *Manual,* use of such statements is not permissible. *United States v. Girard,* 23 C.M.A.

263, 49 C.M.R. 438 (1975); *United States v. Jordan*, 20 C.M.A. 614, 44 C.M.R. 44 (1971). The Court of Military Appeals has recognized expressly the authority of the President to adopt the holding in *Harris* on impeachment. *Jordan, supra,* 20 C.M.A. 614, 617, 44 C.M.R. 44, 47, and Rule 304(b) adopts *Harris* to military law. A statement obtained in violation of Article 31(b), however, remains inadmissible for all purposes, as is a statement that is otherwise involuntary under Rules 302, 304(b)(3) or 305(a). It was the intent of the Committee to permit use of a statement which is involuntary because the *waiver* of *counsel* rights under Rule 305(g) was absent or improper which is implicit in Rule 304(b)'s reference to Rule 305(d).

(c) Definitions.

(1) Confession and Admission. Rules 304(c)(1) & (2) express without change the present *Manual* definitions found in ¶ 140a(1).

Silence may constitute an admission when it does not involve a reliance on the privilege against self-incrimination or related rights. Rule 301(f)(3). For example, if an imputation against a person comes to his or her attention under circumstances that would reasonably call for a denial of its accuracy if the imputation were not true, a failure to utter such a denial could possibly constitute an admission by silence. Note, however, in this regard, Rule 304(h)(3), and Rule 801(a)(2).

(2) Involuntary. The definition of "involuntary" in Rule 304(c)(3) summarizes the present definition of "not voluntary" as found in present *Manual* ¶ 140a(2). The examples in ¶ 140a(2) of the present *Manual* are set forth in this paragraph. A statement obtained in violation of the warning and waiver requirements of Rule 305 is "involuntary." Rule 305(a).

The language governing statements obtained through the use of "coercion, unlawful influence, and unlawful inducement," found in Article 31(d), makes it clear that a statement obtained by any person, regardless of status, that is the product of such conduct is involuntary. Although it is unlikely that a private citizen may run afoul of the prohibition of unlawful influence or inducement, such a person clearly may coerce a statement and such coercion will yield an involuntary statement.

A statement made by the accused during a mental examination ordered under ¶ 121 is treated as an involuntary statement under Rule 304. *See* Rule 302(a). The basis for this rule is that ¶ 121 and Rule 302 compel the accused to participate in the government examination or face a judicial order prohibiting the accused from presenting any expert testimony on the issue of mental responsibility.

Insofar as Rule 304(c)(3) is concerned, some examples which may by themselves or in conjunction with others constitute coercion, unlawful influence, or unlawful inducement in obtaining a confession or admission or:

Infliction of bodily harm including questioning accompanied by deprivation of the necessities of life such as food, sleep or adequate clothing;

Threats of bodily harm;

Imposition of confinement or deprivation of privileges or necessities because a statement was not made by the accused, or threats thereof if a statement is not made;

Promises of immunity or clemency as to any offense allegedly committed by the accused;

Promises of reward or benefit, or threats of disadvantage likely to induce the accused to make the confession or admission.

There is no change in the principle, set forth in the fifth paragraph of ¶ 140 a(2) of the present *Manual*, that a statement obtained "in an interrogation conducted in accordance with all applicable rules is not involuntary because the interrogation was preceded by one that was not so conducted if it clearly appears that all improper influences of the preceding interrogation had ceased to operate on the mind of the accused or suspect at the time that he or she made the statement." In such a case, the effect of the involuntary statement is sufficiently attenuated to permit a determination that the later statement was not *"obtained in violation of"* the rights and privileges found in Rules 304(c)(3) and 305(a) (emphasis added).

(d) Procedure. Rule 304(d) makes a significant change in present procedure. Under ¶ 140a(2) of the present *Manual* the prosecution must prove a statement to be voluntary before it can be admitted in evidence absent explicit defense waiver. Rule 304(d) is intended to reduce the number of unnecessary objections to evidence on voluntariness grounds and to narrow what litigation remains by requiring the defense to move to suppress or to object to evidence covered by this rule. Failure to so move or object constitutes a waiver of the motion or objection. This follows civilian procedure in which the accused is provided an opportunity to assert the privilege against self-incrimination and related rights but may waive any objection to evidence obtained in violation of the privilege through failure to object.

(1) Disclosure. Present procedure is changed in order to assist the defense in formulating its challenges. The prosecution is required to disclose prior to arraignment all statements by the accused known to the prosecution which are relevant to the case (including matters likely to be relevant in rebuttal and sentencing) and within military control. Disclosure should be made in writing in order to prove compliance with the Rule and to prevent misunderstandings. As a general matter, the trial counsel is not authorized to obtain statements made by the accused at a sanity board convened under ¶ 121 with limited exceptions set forth therein. If the trial counsel has knowledge of such statements, they must be disclosed. Regardless of trial counsel's knowledge, the defense is entitled to receive the full report of the sanity board under ¶ 121.

(2) Motions and objections. The defense is required under Rule 304(d)(2) to challenge evidence disclosed prior to arraignment under Rule 304(d)(1) prior to submission of plea. In the absence of a motion or objection prior to plea, the defense may not raise the issue at a later time except as permitted by the military judge for good cause shown. Failure to challenge disclosed evidence waives the objection. This is a change from present law under which objection traditionally has been made after plea but may be made, at the discretion of the military judge, prior to plea. This change brings military law into line with civilian federal procedure and resolves what is presently a variable and uncertain procedure.

Litigation of a defense motion to suppress or an objection to a statement made by the accused or to any derivative evidence should take place at a hearing held outside the presence of the court members. *See, e.g.,* Rule 104(c).

(3) Specificity. Rule 304(d)(3) permits the military judge to require the defense to specify the grounds for an objection under Rule 304, but if the defense has not had adequate opportunity to interview those persons present at the taking of a statement, the military judge may issue an appropriate order including granting a continuance for purposes of interview or permitting a general objection. In view of the waiver that results in the event of failure to object, defense counsel must have sufficient information in order to decide whether to object to the admissibility of a statement by the accused. Although telephone or other long distance communication may be sufficient to allow a counsel to make an informed decision, counsel may consider a personal interview to be essential in this area and in such a case counsel is entitled to personally interview the witnesses to the taking of a statement before specificity can be required. When such an interview is desired but despite due diligence counsel has been unable to interview adequately those persons included in the taking of a statement, the military judge has authority to resolve the situation. Normally this would include the granting of a continuance for interviews or other appropriate relief. If an adequate opportunity to interview is absent, even if this results solely from the witness' unwillingness to speak to the defense, then the specificity requirement does not apply. Lacking adequate opportunity to interview, the defense may be authorized to enter a general objection to the evidence. If a general objection has been authorized, the prosecution must present evidence to show affirmatively that the statement was voluntary in the same manner as it would be required to do under present law. Defense counsel is not required to meet the requirements of ¶ 115 of the *Manual* in order to demonstrate "due diligence" under the Rule. Nor shall the defense be required to present evidence to raise a matter under the Rule. The defense shall present its motion by offer of proof, but it may be required to present evidence in support of the motion should the prosecution first present evidence in opposition to the motion.

If a general objection to the prosecution evidence is not authorized, the defense may be required by Rule 304(d)(3) to make specific objection to prosecution evidence. It is not the intent of the Committee to require extremely technical pleading, but enough specificity to reasonably narrow the issue is desirable. Examples of defense objections include but are not limited to one or more of the following non-exclusive examples:

That the accused was a suspect but not given Article 31(b) or Rule 305(c) warnings prior to interrogation.

That although 31(b) or Rule 305(c) warnings were given, counsel warnings under Rule 305(d) were necessary and not given (or given improperly).[1]

That despite the accused's express refusal to make a statement, she was questioned and made an admission.[2]

That the accused requested counsel but was interrogated by the military police without having seen counsel.[3]

That the accused was induced to make a statement by a promise of leniency by his squadron commander.[4]

That an accused was threatened with prosecution of her husband if she failed to make a statement.[5]

---

1. Rule 305(d); United States v. Tempia, 16 C.M.A. 629, 37 C.M.R. 249 (1967).

2. *See, e.g.* Rule 305(f), Michigan v. Mosley, 423 U.S. 96; United States v. Westmore, 17 C.M.A. 406, 38 C.M.R. 204 (1968).

3. *See, e.g.* Rule 305(a) and (d), United States v. Gaines, 21 C.M.A. 236, 45 C.M.R. 10 (1972).

4. *See, e.g.* Rule 304(b)(3), Manual for Courts-Martial, United States, 1969 (Rev. ed.). ¶ 140a(2); People v. Pineda, 182 Colo. 388, 513 P.2d 452 (1973).

5. *See, e.g.* Rule 304(b)(3), Jarriel v. State, 317 So. 2d 141 (Fla. App. 1975).

That the accused was held incommunicado and beaten until she confessed.[6]

That the accused made the statement in question only because he had previously given a statement to his division officer which was involuntary because it was improperly warned.[7]

Although the prosecution retains at all times the burden of proof in this area, a specific defense objection under this Rule must include enough facts to enable the military judge to determine whether the objection is appropriate. These facts will be brought before the court via recital by counsel; the defense will not be required to offer evidence in order to raise the issue. If the prosecution concurs with the defense recital, the facts involved will be taken as true for purposes of the motion and evidence need not be presented. If the prosecution does not concur and the defense facts would justify relief if taken as true, the prosecution will present its evidence and the defense will then present its evidence. The general intent of this provision is to narrow the litigation as much as may be possible without affecting the prosecution's burden.

In view of the Committee's intent to narrow litigation in this area, it has adopted a basic structure in which the defense, when required by the military judge to object with specificity, has total responsibility in terms of what objection, if any, to raise under this Rule. Note, however, ¶ 54c.

(4) Rulings. Rule 304(d)(4) is taken without significant change from Federal Rule of Criminal Procedure 12(e). As a plea of guilty waives all self-incrimination or voluntariness objections, Rule 304(d)(5), it is contemplated that litigation of confession issues raised before the plea will be fully concluded prior to plea. Cases involving trials by military judge alone in which the accused will enter a plea of not guilty are likely to be the only ones in which deferral of ruling is even theoretically possible. If the prosecution does not intend to use against the accused a statement challenged by the accused under this Rule but is unwilling to abandon any potential use of such statement, two options exist. First, the matter can be litigated before plea, or second, if the accused clearly intends to plead not guilty regardless of the military judge's ruling as to the admissibility of the statements in question, the matter may be deferred until such time as the prosecution indicates a desire to use the statements.

(5) Effect of guilty plea. Rule 304(d)(5) restates present law; *see, e.g., United States v. Dusenberry,* 23 C.M.A. 287, 49 C.M.R. 536 (1975).

(e) Burden of proof. Rule 304(e) substantially changes military law. Under the present system, the armed forces do not follow the rule applied in the civilian federal courts. Instead the present *Manual* utilizes the minority "Massachusetts Rule," sometimes known as the "Two Bite Rule." Under this procedure the defense first raises a confession or admission issue before the military judge who determines it on a preponderance basis; if the judge determines the issue adversely to the accused, the defense may raise the issue again before the members. In such a case, the members must be instructed not to consider the evidence in question unless they find it to have been voluntary beyond a reasonable doubt. The Committee determined that this bifurcated system unnecessarily complicated the final instructions to the members to such an extent as to substantially confuse the important matters before them. In view of the preference expressed in Article 36 for the procedure used in the trial of criminal cases

---

6. *See, e.g.* Rule 304(b)(3), Payne v. Arkansas, 356 U.S. 560 (1958).

7. *See, e.g.* Rule 304(b)(3), United States v. Seay, 1 M.J. 201 (C.M.A. 1975).

in the United States district courts, the Committee adopted the majority "Orthodox Rule" as used in Article III courts. Pursuant to this procedure, the military judge determines the admissibility of confessions or admissions using a preponderance basis. No recourse exists to the court members on the question of admissibility. In the event of a ruling on admissibility adverse to the accused, the accused may present evidence to the members as to voluntariness for their consideration in determining what weight to give to the statements in question.

It should be noted that under the Rules the prosecution's burden extends *only* to the specific issue raised by the defense under Rule 304(d), should specificity have been required pursuant to Rule 304(d)(3).

(1) In general. Rule 304(e)(1) requires that the military judge find by a preponderance that a statement challenged under this rule was made voluntarily. When trial is before a special court-martial without a military judge, the ruling of the President of the court is subject to objection by any member. The President's decision may be overruled pursuant to the procedure found in ¶ 57 *f.* The Committee authorized use of this procedure in view of the importance of the issue and the absence of a legally trained presiding officer.

(2) Weight of the evidence. Rule 304(e)(2) allows the defense to present evidence with respect to voluntariness to the members for the purpose of determining what weight to give to the statement. When trial is by judge alone, the evidence received by the military judge on the question of admissibility also shall be considered by the military judge on the question of weight without the necessity of a formal request to do so by counsel. Additional evidence may, however, be presented to the military judge on the matter of weight if counsel chooses to do so.

(3) Derivative evidence. Rule 304(e)(3) recognizes that derivative evidence is distinct from the primary evidence dealt with by Rule 304, *i.e.,* statements. The prosecution may prove that notwithstanding an involuntary statement, the evidence in question was not "obtained by use of" it and is not derivative.

(f) Defense evidence. Rule 304(f) generally restates the present law as found in present *Manual* ¶ 140a(3) and (6). Under the Rule, the defense must specify that the accused plans to take the stand under this subdivision. This is already normal practice and is intended to prevent confusion. Testimony given under this subdivision may not be used at the same trial at which it is given for any other purpose to include impeachment. The language, "the accused may be cross-examined only as to matter on which he or she so testifies" permits otherwise proper and relevant impeachment of the accused. *See, e.g.,* Rules 607-609; 613.

(g) Corroboration. Rule 304(g) restates the present law of corroboration with one major procedural change. At present, no instruction on the requirement of corroboration is required *unless* the evidence is substantially conflicting, self-contradictory, uncertain or improbable and there is a defense request for such an instruction. *United States v. Seigle,* 22 C.M.A. 403, 47 C.M.R. 340 (1973). The holding in *Seigle* is consistent with the present *Manual's* view that the issue of admissibility may be decided by the members, but it is inconsistent with the position taken in Rule 304(d) that admissibility is the sole responsibility of the military judge. Inasmuch as the Rule requires corroborating evidence as a condition precedent to admission of the statement, submission of the issue to the members would seem to be both unnecessary and confusing. Consequently, the Rule does not follow *Seigle* insofar as the case allows the issue to be submitted to the members. The members must still weigh the evidence when

determining the guilt or innocence of the accused, and the nature of any corroborating evidence is an appropriate matter for the members to consider when weighing the statement before them.

The corroboration rule requires only that evidence be admitted which would support an inference that the essential facts admitted in the statement are true. For example, presume that an accused charged with premeditated murder has voluntarily confessed that, intending to kill the alleged victim, she concealed herself so that she might surprise the victim at a certain place and that when the victim passed by, she plunged a knife in his back. At trial, the prosecution introduces independent evidence that the victim was found dead as a result of a knife wound in his back at the place where, according to the confession, the incident occurred. This fact would corroborate the confession because it would support an inference of the truth of the essential facts admitted in the confession.

(h) Miscellaneous.

(1) Oral statements. Rule 304(h)(1) is taken verbatim from present *Manual* paragraph 140*a*(6). It recognizes that although an oral statement may be transcribed, the oral statement is separate and distinct from the transcription and that accordingly the oral statement may be received into evidence without violation of the best evidence rule unless the specific writing is in question, *see* Rule 1002. So long as the oral statement is complete, no specific rule would require the prosecution to offer the transcription. The defense could of course offer the writing when it would constitute proper impeachment.

(2) Completeness. Rule 304(h)(2) is taken without significant change from present *Manual* paragraph 140*a*(6). Although Rule 106 allows a party to require an adverse party to complete an otherwise incomplete written statement in an appropriate case, Rule 304(h)(2) allows the defense to complete an incomplete statement regardless of whether the statement is oral or in writing. As Rule 304(h)(2) does not by its terms deal only with oral statements, it provides the defense in this area with the option of using either Rule 106 or 304(h)(2) to complete a written statement.

(3) Certain admissions by silence. Rule 304(h)(3) is taken from ¶ 140*a*(4) of the present *Manual*. That part of the remainder of ¶ 140*a*(4) dealing with the existence of the privilege against self-incrimination is now set forth in Rule 301(f)(3). The remainder of ¶ 140*a*(4) has been set forth in the *Analysis* to subdivision (d)(2), dealing with an admission by silence, or has been omitted as being unnecessary.

Rule 305. Warnings About Rights

(a) General rule. A statement obtained in violation of this rule is involuntary and shall be treated under rule 304.

(b) Definitions. As used in this rule:

(1) Person subject to the Uniform Code of Military Justice. A "person subject to the Uniform Code of Military Justice" includes a person acting as a knowing agent of a military unit or of a person subject to the Uniform Code of Military Justice.

(2) Interrogation. "Interrogation" includes any formal or informal questioning in which an incriminating response either is sought or is a reasonable consequence of such questioning.

(c) Warnings concerning the accusation, right to remain silent, and use of statements. A person subject to the Uniform Code of Military Justice who is required to give warnings under Article 31 may not interrogate or request any statement from an accused or a person suspected of an offense without first: (1) informing the accused or suspect of the nature of the accusation; (2) advising the accused or suspect that the accused or suspect has the right to remain silent; and (3) advising the accused or suspect that any statement made may be used as evidence against the accused or suspect in a trial by court-marital.

(d) Counsel rights and warnings.

(1) General rule. When evidence of a testimonial or communicative nature within the meaning of the Fifth Amendment to the Constitution of the United States either is sought or is a reasonable consequence of an interrogation, an accused or a person suspected of an offense is entitled to consult with counsel as provided by paragraph (2) of this subdivision, to have such counsel present at the interrogation, and to be warned of these rights prior to the interrogation if —

(A) The interrogation is conducted by a person subject to the Uniform Code of Military Justice who is required to give warnings under Article 31 and the accused or suspect is in custody, could reasonably believe himself or herself to be in custody, or is otherwise deprived of his or her freedom of action in any significant way; or

(B) The interrogation is conducted by a person subject to the Uniform Code of Military Justice acting in a law enforcement capacity, or an agent of such a person, the interrogation is conducted subsequent to preferral of charges or the imposition of pretrial restraint under paragraph 20 of this Manual, and the interrogation concerns the offenses or matters that were the subject of the preferral of charges or were the cause of the imposition of pretrial restraint.

(2) Counsel. When a person entitled to counsel under this rule requests counsel, a judge advocate or law specialist within the meaning of Article 1 or an individual certified in accordance with Article 27(b) shall be provided by the United States at no expense to the person and without regard to the person's indigency or lack thereof before the interrogation may proceed. In addition to counsel supplied by the United States, the person may retain civilian counsel at no expense to the United States. Unless otherwise provided by regulations of the Secretary concerned, an accused or suspect does not have a right under this rule to have military counsel of his or her own selection.

(e) Notice to counsel. When a person subject to the Uniform Code of Military Justice who is required to give warnings under subdivision (c) intends to question an accused or person suspected of an offense and knows or reasonably should know that counsel either has been appointed for or retained by the accused or suspect with respect to that offense, the counsel must be notified of the intended interrogation and given a reasonable time in which to attend before the interrogation may proceed.

(f) Exercise of rights. If a person chooses to exercise the privilege against self-incrimination or the right to counsel under this rule, questioning must cease immediately.

(g) Waiver.

(1) General rule. After receiving applicable warnings under this rule, a person may waive the rights described therein and in rule 301 and make a statement. The waiver must be made freely, knowingly, and intelligently. A

written waiver is not required. The accused or suspect must acknowledge affirmatively that he or she understands the rights involved, affirmatively decline the right to counsel and affirmatively consent to making a statement.

(2) Counsel. If the right to counsel in subdivision (d) is applicable and the accused or suspect does not decline affirmatively the right to counsel, the prosecution must demonstrate by a preponderance of the evidence that the individual waived the right to counsel. In addition, if the notice to counsel in subdivision (e) is applicable, a waiver of the right to counsel is not effective unless the prosecution demonstrates by a preponderance of the evidence that reasonable efforts to notify the counsel were unavailing or that the counsel did not attend an interrogation scheduled within a reasonable period of time after the required notice was given.

(h) Nonmilitary interrogations.

(1) General rule. When a person subject to the Uniform Code of Military Justice is interrogated by an official or agent of the United States, of the District of Columbia, or of a State, Commonwealth, or possession of the United States, or any political subdivision of such a State, Commonwealth, or possession, and such official or agent is not required to give warnings under subdivision (c), the person's entitlement to rights warnings and the validity of any waiver of applicable rights shall be determined by the principles of law generally recognized in the trial of criminal cases in the United States district courts involving similar interrogations.

(2) Foreign interrogations. Neither warnings under subdivisions (c) or (d), nor notice to counsel under subdivision (e) are required during an interrogation conducted abroad by officials of a foreign government or their agents unless such interrogation is conducted, instigated, or participated in by military personnel or their agents or by those officials or agents listed in subdivision (h)(1). A statement obtained during such an interrogation is involuntary within the meaning of rule 304(b)(3) if it is obtained through the use of coercion, unlawful influence, or unlawful inducement. An interrogation is not "participated

in" by military personnel or their agents or by the officials or agents listed in subdivision (h)(1) merely because such a person was present at an interrogation conducted in a foreign nation by officials of a foreign government or their agents, or because such a person acted as an interpreter or took steps to mitigate damage to property or physical harm during the foreign interrogation.

EDITORIAL COMMENT

Before interrogating a suspect or accused, investigators may be required to give rights warnings and to obtain a voluntary waiver of those rights. Rule 305 incorporates much of *Manual* ¶ 140 and codifies a large amount of case law in addressing the military's two distinct "rights warnings." Also included are provisions which define the term "interrogation" and require notice to counsel before questioning. As a general rule, statements obtained in violation of Rule 305 will be considered involuntary under Rule 304. The exception, stated in Rule 304(b), permits limited use of statements obtained in violation of 304(d), (e), and implicitly (g), if the statements are otherwise voluntary. *See* our discussion of Rule 304.

It is clear that not every encounter between an investigator and another individual must be preceded by rights warnings; they are only required before interrogation of a suspect or accused by individuals required to give the warnings. The terms "suspect" and "accused" are not defined in the Rule but military cases have applied a two-pronged subjective-objective test in determining whether an individual was a suspect when questioned. *See, e.g., United States v. Tibbetts,* 1 M.J. 1024 (N.C.M.R. 1976). "Interrogation" is defined in subdivision (b)(2) which provides intentionally broad coverage — broad enough to include the definitions noted in *Brewer v. Williams,* 430 U.S. 387 (1977) and *Rhode Island v. Innis,* 440 U.S. 934 (1980). In those cases the Court recognized that conversations or actions which could reasonably be expected to elicit a response should be considered the equivalent of formal questioning. To date, the military courts have generally frowned upon attempts to circumvent warnings requirements through subtle conversations. *See, e.g., United States v. Borodzik,* 21 C.M.A. 95, 44 C.M.R. 149 (1971) (Investigators indirectly questioned accused through his wife). "Innocent" questioning is apparently untouched by the Rule which turns on intentional elicitation of incriminating responses. *Cf. United States v. Dowell,* 10 M.J. 36 (C.M.A. 1980) (court declined to question good faith of commander whose actions in advising accused of additional charges was equivalent of interrogation).

Subdivisions (c) and (d) are the central provisions of the Rule. They lay out the two rights warnings recognized in military practice: the Article 31(b), U.C.M.J. warnings and the right to counsel warnings. As a general rule, the Article 31(b) warnings are to be given prior to any interrogation of a suspect or accused. Right to counsel warnings need be given only in those situations detailed in 305(d)(1).

The required Article 31(b) warnings are incorporated in subdivision (c). Before questioning an accused or suspect, persons subject to the U.C.M.J. required to give warnings must first advise the accused or suspect that:

(1) He is suspected or accused of a particular offense; and

(2) He has a right to remain silent; and

(3) Any statement made may be used against him at the court-martial.

These three elements generally follow the statutory wording of Article 31(b); but (c)(2) is different. Article 31(b) only requires that the individuals be told of the right "not to have to make any statement regarding the offense of which he is accused or suspected . . . ." The broader language of (c)(2) was included to emphasize that absolute silence is an option. The more protective language of the Rule should control.

Although the Rule addresses the questions of when rights warnings are required and who must receive the warnings, it does not specifically confront the crucial question of who must give the warnings. The drafters intentionally left that issue for resolution by the military courts which in the past have applied both an "official questioning" test and "position of authority" test. *See, e.g., United States v. Seay*, 1 M.J. 201 (C.M.A. 1975) (commander conducting official interrogation of suspect should have given Article 31(b) warnings); *United States v. Dohle*, 1 M.J. 223 (C.M.A. 1975) (noncommissioned officer in position of authority over suspect should have given Article 31(b) warnings).

The military courts have not generally required undercover agents or informants to give rights warnings. *See, e.g., United States v. Kirby*, 8 M.J. 8 (C.M.A. 1979) (no warnings necessary where informant was mere volunteer in getting information); *United States v. Duga*, 10 M.J. 206 (C.M.A. 1981) (court adopted useful two-pronged test for determining who must warn). *Cf. United States v. Johnstone*, 5 M.J. 744 (A.F.C.M.R. 1978), pet. granted, 6 M.J. 145 (C.M.A. 1978) (on other grounds) (informant was *de facto* government agent who should have given warnings). Medical personnel also are usually exempt. *See, e.g., United States v. Fischer*, 21 C.M.A. 223, 44 C.M.R. 277 (1972).

Civilian investigators may be required to give Article 31(b) warnings if they are acting as agents for the military. *See* subdivisions (b)(1) and (h). *See also United States v. Kellam*, 2 M.J. 338 (A.F.C.M.R. 1976) (local deputy sheriff working with military). And under Rule 301(b)(2) military judges may be required to give warnings.

Subdivision (d) generally addresses the requirement of right to counsel warnings. Specifically, subdivision (d)(1) recognizes that Article 31(b) warnings may not be enough. Under certain conditions a suspect or accused has a right to consult with counsel, that is defined in (d)(2) and discussed later, a right to have counsel present, and finally the right to be warned of the first two rights. The exact content of the warnings is not set out in the Rule but the drafters' *Analysis* suggests appropriate language. The conditions stated in the Rule which trigger the rights to counsel might be summarized as follows:

(i) A suspect or accused is being interrogated, *see* (d)(1); and

(ii) Testimonial or communicative evidence is sought, *see* (d)(1); and

(iii) The accused or suspect is in custody, could reasonably believe himself to be in custody or is otherwise significantly deprived of his freedom of action, *see* (d)(1)(A); or

(iv) The interrogation is conducted after initiation of charges or imposition of restraint, *see* (d)(1)(B).

These items are considered in the following discussion.

By limiting the counsel warnings requirement only to those interrogations designed to elicit "testimonial or communicative" evidence, the drafters have attempted to distinguish between evidence protected by Article 31, U.C.M.J. but not necessarily the Fifth Amendment, *e.g.,* voiceprints or handwriting exemplars. Only Fifth Amendment rights trigger counsel warnings. In light of the broad interpretations given to the protections of Article 31 by the military courts, *see* Rule 301, the distinction, although technically sound, may be too fine for practical day-to-day use by military investigators.

The crux of the requirement to give counsel warnings rests in (d)(1)(A) and (d)(1)(B). Subdivision (d)(1)(A) restates the traditional custodial interrogation criteria. *See Miranda v. Arizona,* 384 U.S. 436 (1966), *United States v. Tempia,* 16 C.M.A. 629, 37 C.M.R. 249 (1967), and *Manual* ¶ 140. *See generally,* Lederer, *Miranda v. Arizona — The Law Today,* 78 Mil. L. Rev. 107 (1977), Schlueter, Tempia, Turner, McOmber *and the Military Rules of Evidence: A Right to Counsel Trio with the New Look,* The Army Lawyer, April 1980, at 1. "Custody" here is measured through an objective standard. But the cases should remind counsel that the term "custody" is deceptively simple. Police station interrogations are not automatically custodial, *see Oregon v. Mathiason,* 429 U.S. 492 (1977) (questioning in police station was not custodial). Interrogations in the suspect's home are not necessarily non-custodial. *See Orozco v. Texas,* 394 U.S. 324 (1969) (suspect not free to leave own room at 4 a.m.). The issue of custody also potentially raises Fourth Amendment considerations. If the custody amounts to seizure of the person, the prosecution may be required to establish either that probable cause supported seizure of the suspect or that the suspect voluntarily consented to the custodial interrogation. *See Dunaway v. New York,* 442 U.S. 200 (1979). *See also* Rules 311 and 316.

The counsel warnings under (d)(1)(A) are to be given when the interrogation is conducted by a person required to give Article 31 (b) warnings. Thus our earlier discussion of who must give Article 31(b) warnings is equally applicable here.

Subdivision (d)(1)(B) is new to military practice and is grounded on Sixth Amendment right to counsel considerations. *See Brewer v. Williams,* 430 U.S. 387 (1977); *Massiah v. United States,* 377 U.S. 201 (1964); and *United States v. Henry,* 444 U.S. 824 (1980). Right to counsel warnings must precede interrogations of suspects or accuseds taking place after either (i) preferral of charges or (ii) imposition of pretrial confinement, arrest, or restriction and (iii) the questioning relates to offenses charged or offenses serving as the basis for the restraint. This provision is apparently not linked with Article 31(b) warnings as is (d)(1)(A) and is triggered by interrogation conducted by persons acting in a law enforcement capacity or their agents. Thus, a commander questioning an accused on purely administrative matters after charges have been preferred would apparently not have to give the counsel warnings. *Cf. United States v. Dowell,* 10 M.J. 36 (C.M.A. 1980) (commander advising accused of additional charges was functional equivalent of interrogation). However, undercover agents or informants questioning or conversing with the same accused in hopes of getting more information would be required to give counsel warnings. In *United States v. Henry,* 444 U.S. 824 (1980), some members of the Court said that use of a purely passive listening post would not necessarily violate the Sixth Amendment rights of an indicted accused. It would not seem to be an interrogation under this Rule.

Subdivision (d)(2) defines "counsel" as that term is to be used in conjunction with the counsel warnings spelled out in (d)(1). The provision makes two changes in pre-Rules practice. First, the right to consult with an individual military lawyer of the suspect's selection is gone unless the Secretaries of the services reinstate it. Military case law had recognized that investigators could limit the pool of available lawyers for interrogations; *see, e.g., United States v. Harris,* 7 M.J. 154 (C.M.A. 1979), but had not directly confronted the question of whether the right could be completely abrogated. This change could cause Sixth Amendment problems where the suspect or accused has previously entered into an attorney-client relationship with a particular counsel. *See, e.g., United States v. Turner,* 5 M.J. 148 (C.M.A. 1978) and Rule 305(e). Secondly, the provision also overrules decisions such as *United States v. Hofbauer,* 5 M.J. 409 (C.M.A. 1978), which had indicated that the right to appointed counsel turned on a requirement of indigency.

Subdivision (e) effects a major extension of military case law. It requires investigators to give pre-interrogation notice to the suspect's or the accused's counsel, *United States v. McOmber,* 1 M.J. 380 (C.M.A. 1976). The military courts have generally limited this unique notice requirement to those cases where the investigator had *actual* knowledge that counsel was representing the suspect or accused. *See, e.g., United States v. Harris,* 7 M.J. 154 (C.M.A. 1979); *United States v. Littlejohn,* 7 M.J. 200 (C.M.A. 1979). Rule 305(e) now requires notice where the investigator knows or *reasonably should know* that a counsel is involved. To avoid the problem of later discovering that the suspect had a counsel, the prudent investigator should simply ask the subject if he has counsel; that should remove all doubt. Rule 305(e) however does apply pre-Rules case law, which excepts the notice requirement from those interrogations regarding an offense different from the one for which a suspect is receiving the assistance of counsel. *United States v. McDonald,* 9 M.J. 81 (C.M.A. 1980) (federal agent not required to give notice to counsel representing accused on military offense). *Cf. United States v. Dowell,* 10 M.J. 36 (C.M.A. 1980) (commander should have given to counsel where additional charges related to original charges).

After receiving the appropriate rights warnings, the suspect or accused may either invoke the rights or waive them in whole or in part. If the individual indicates a desire to remain silent or wishes to see a counsel, the interrogation must cease. Rule 305(f). *See also* Rule 301 (f)(2). Both civilian and military case law, however, recognize that investigators may at some later point attempt to continue the interrogation. We believe that existing case law presents a flexible workable rule. That is, questioning may be later continued but a heavy burden rests on the prosecution to show that the individual's rights to counsel were scrupulously honored. *United States v. Hill,* 5 M.J. 114 (C.M.A. 1978). *See also Michigan v. Mosley,* 423 U.S. 96 (1975). Judge Fletcher's dissenting opinion in *United States v. Hill, supra,* presents a good discussion of the options normally available to investigators when the right to counsel is involved. Factors which should be considered in assessing the protection of the suspect's rights include: temporal proximity of the invocation of the right and any later statements; whether the investigators encouraged or discouraged invocation of the right; whether attempts were made by either the investigators or the suspect to contact or to obtain counsel; the surrounding facts and circumstances of the interrogation; and the suspect's mental and physical condition. *See, e.g., United States v. Quintana,* 5 M.J. 484 (C.M.A. 1978).

The right to remain silent and the various counsel rights may be waived but the prosecution must be prepared under subdivision (g) to show that the rights were freely, knowingly and intelligently waived in an affirmative manner — either orally or in writing. Subdivision (g)(1) sets out a three-pronged affirmative waiver requirement: the suspect or accused must state that he understands his rights, that he declines his right to counsel and that he consents to making a statement. Subdivision (g)(2) sets out further guidance with regard to waiver of counsel rights. Should an affirmative waiver be lacking insofar as subdivision (d) counsel rights are concerned, the prosecution may show by a preponderance of the evidence that the rights were waived. This follows *North Carolina v. Butler,* 441 U.S. 369 (1979). The right to remain silent must still be affirmatively waived.

Subdivision (g)(2) also states that a waiver of rights to counsel where notice to counsel would be required, *see* 305 (e), is not effective until after reasonable efforts have been made to contact the counsel or counsel did not attend the interrogation after being given a reasonable opportunity to do so. These prerequisites also must be established by a preponderance of the evidence.

Finally, subdivision (h) addresses the issue of nonmilitary interrogations and provides that with regard to domestic civilian interrogations of military personnel, the principles of federal law will control unless the civilian interrogators are acting as agents of the military, in which case Rule 305 will control. Foreign interrogations will also be governed by Rule 305 if military authorities or their agents conducted, instigated or participated in such interrogations. Otherwise they will be tested only for voluntariness under Rule 304(b)(3), insofar as the offered statements may have resulted from coercion, unlawful influence, or unlawful inducement.

DRAFTERS' ANALYSIS

(a) ***General Rule.*** Rule 305(a) makes statements obtained in violation of Rule 305, *e.g.,* statements obtained in violation of Article 31(b) and the right to counsel, involuntary within the meaning of Rule 304. This approach eliminates any distinction between statements obtained in violation of the common law voluntariness doctrine (which is, in any event, included within Article 31(d)) and those statements obtained

in violation, for example, of *Miranda* (*Miranda v. Arizona*, 384 U.S. 436 (1966)) warning requirements. This is consistent with the approach taken in the present *Manual. E.g.,* present *Manual* ¶ 140a(2).

(b) Definitions.

(1) Person subject to the Uniform Code of Military Justice. Rule 305(b) (1) makes it clear that under certain conditions a civilian may be a "person subject to the Uniform Code of Military Justice" for purposes of warning requirements, and would be required to give Article 31(b) (Rule 305(c)) warnings. *See, generally, United States v. Penn,* 18 C.M.A. 194, 39 C.M.R. 194 (1969). Consequently civilian members of the law enforcement agencies of the Armed Forces, *e.g.,* the Naval Investigative Service and the Air Force Office of Special Investigations, will have to give Article 31 (Rule 305(c)) warnings. This provision is taken in substance from ¶ 140a(2) of the present *Manual.*

(2) Interrogation. Rule 305(b)(2) defines interrogation to include the situation in which an incriminating response is either sought or is a reasonable consequence of such questioning. The definition is expressly not a limited one and interrogation thus includes more than the putting of questions to an individual. *See, e.g. Brewer v. Williams,* 430 U.S. 387 (1977).

The Rule does not specifically deal with the situation in which an "innocent" question is addressed to a suspect and results unexpectedly in an incriminatory response which could not have been foreseen. This legislative history and the cases are unclear as to whether Article 31 allows nonincriminatory questioning, *see* Lederer, *Rights Warnings in the Armed Services,* 72 MIL. R. REV. 1, 32-33 (1976), and the issue is left open for further development.

(c) Warnings concerning the accusation, right to remain silent, and use of statements. Rule 305(c) basically requires that those persons who are required by statute to give Article 31(b) warnings give such warnings. The Rule refrains from specifying who must give such warnings in view of the unsettled nature of the case law in the area.

It was not the intent of the Committee to adopt any particular interpretation of Article 31(b) insofar as who must give warnings except as provided in Rule 305(b) (1) and the Rule explicitly defers to Article 31 for the purpose of determining who must give warnings. The Committee recognized that numerous decisions of the Court of Military Appeals and its subordinate courts have dealt with this issue. These courts have rejected literal application of Article 31(b), but have not arrived at a conclusive rule. *See, e.g., United States v. Dohle,* 1 M.J. 223 (C.M.A. 1975). The Committee was of the opinion, however, that both Rule 305(c) and Article 31(b) should be construed at a minimum, and in compliance with numerous cases, as requiring warnings by those personnel acting in an official disciplinary or law enforcement capacity. Decisions such as *United States v. French,* 25 C.M.R. 851 (A.F.B.R. 1958), *aff'd in relevant part,* 10 C.M.A. 171, 27 C.M.R. 245 (1959) (undercover agent) are not affected by the Rule.

Spontaneous or volunteered statements do not require warnings under Rule 305. The fact that a person may have known of his or her rights under the Rule is of no importance if warnings were required but not given.

Normally, neither a witness nor an accused need be warned under any part of this Rule when taking the stand to testify at a trial by court-martial. *See,* however, Rule 301(b) (2).

The Rule requires in Rule 305(c)(2) that the accused or suspect be advised that he or she has the "right to remain silent" rather than the statutory Article 31(b) warning which is limited to silence on matters relevant to the underlying offense. The new language was inserted upon the suggestion of the Department of Justice in order to provide clear advice to the accused as to the absolute right to remain silent. *See, Miranda v. Arizona,* 384 U.S. 436 (1966).

(d) Counsel rights and warnings. Rule 305(d) provides the basic right to counsel at interrogations and requires that an accused or suspect entitled to counsel at an interrogation be warned of that fact. The Rule restates the basic counsel entitlement for custodial interrogations found in both present ¶ 140*a*(2) of the *Manual* for Courts-Martial and *United States v. Tempia,* 16 C.M.A. 629, 37 C.M.R. 249 (1967), and recognizes that the right to counsel attaches after certain procedural steps have taken place.

(1) General rule. Rule 305(d) (1) makes it clear that the right to counsel only attaches to an interrogation in which an individual's Fifth Amendment privilege against self-incrimination is involved. This is a direct result of the different coverages of the statutory and constitutional privileges. The Fifth Amendment to the Constitution of the United States is the underpinning of the Supreme Court's decision in *Miranda v. Arizona,* 384 U.S. 436 (1966) which is in turn the origin of the military right to counsel at an interrogation. *United States v. Tempia,* 16 C.M.A. 629, 37 C.M.R. 249 (1967). Article 31, on the other hand, does not provide any right to counsel at an interrogation; *but see United States v. McOmber,* 1 M. J. 380 (C.M.A. 1976). Consequently, interrogations which involve only the Article 31 privilege against self-incrimination do not include a right to counsel. Under present law such interrogations include requests for voice and handwriting samples and perhaps requests for bodily fluids. *Compare United States v. Dionisio,* 410 U.S. 1 (1973); *United States v. Mara,* 410 U.S. 19 (1973); and *Schmerber v. California,* 384 U.S. 757 (1966) *with United States v. White,* 17 C.M.A. 211, 38 C.M.R. 9 (1967); *United States v. Greer,* 3 C.M.A. 576, 13 C.M.R. 132 (1953); and *United States v. Ruiz,* 23 C.M.A. 181, 48 C.M.R. 797 (1974). Rule 305(d)(1) requires that an individual who is entitled to counsel under the Rule be advised of the nature of that right before an interrogation involving evidence of a testimonial or communicative nature within the meaning of the Fifth Amendment (an interrogation as defined in Rule 305(b)(2) and modified in this case by Rule 305(d) (1)) may lawfully proceed. Although the Rule does not specifically require any particular wording or format for the right to counsel warning, reasonable specificity is required. At a minimum, the right to counsel warning must include the following substantive matter:

(1) That the accused or suspect has the right to be represented by a lawyer at the interrogation if he or she so desires;

(2) That the right to have counsel at the interrogation includes the right to consult with counsel and to have counsel at the interrogation;

(3) That if the accused or suspect so desires, he or she will have a military lawyer appointed to represent the accused or suspect at the interrogation at no expense to the individual, and the accused or suspect may obtain civilian counsel at no expense to the government in addition to or instead of free military counsel.

It is important to note that these warnings are in addition to such other warnings and waiver questions as may be required by Rule 305.

Rule 305(d) (1) (A) follows the plurality of civilian jurisdictions by utilizing an objective test in defining "custodial" interrogation. *See also United States v. Temperly,* 22 C.M.A. 383, 47 C.M.R. 235 (1973). Unfortunately, there is no national consensus as to the exact nature of the test that should be used. The language used in the Rule results from an analysis of *Miranda v. Arizona,* 384 U.S. 436 (1966) which leads to the conclusion that *Miranda* is predominately a voluntariness decision concerned with the effects of that psychological coercion inherent in official questioning. *See, e.g.,* Lederer, *Miranda v. Arizona — The Law Today,* 78 MIL. L. REV. 107, 130 (1977).

The variant chosen adopts an objective test that complies with *Miranda's* intent by using the viewpoint of the suspect. The objective nature of the test, however, makes it improbable that a suspect would be able to claim a custodial status not recognized by the interrogator. The test makes the actual belief of the suspect irrelevant because of the belief that it adds nothing in practice and would unnecessarily lengthen trial.

Rule 305(d)(1)(B) codifies the Supreme Court's decisions in *Brewer v. Williams,* 430 U.S. 387 (1977) and *Massiah v. United States,* 377 U.S. 201 (1964). As modified by *Brewer, Massiah* requires that an accused or suspect be advised of his or her right to counsel prior to interrogation, whether open or surreptitious, if that interrogation takes place after either arraignment or indictment. As the Armed Forces lack any equivalent to those civilian procedural points, the initiation of the formal military criminal process has been utilized as the functional equivalent. Accordingly, the right to counsel attaches if an individual is interrogated after preferral of charges or imposition of pretrial arrest, restriction or confinement. The right is not triggered by apprehension or temporary detention. Undercover investigation prior to the formal beginning of the criminal process will not be affected by this, but jailhouse interrogations will generally be prohibited. *Compare* Rule 305(d)(1)(B) *with United States v. Hinkson,* 17 C.M.A. 126, 37 C.M.R. 390 (1967) and *United States v. Gibson,* 3 C.M.A. 746, 14 C.M.R. 164 (1954).

(2) Counsel. Rule 305(d)(2) sets forth the basic right to counsel at interrogations required under present *Manual* ¶ 140a(2). The Rule rejects the interpretation of ¶ 140a(2) set forth in *United States v. Hofbauer,* 5 M.J. 409 (C.M.A. 1978) and *United States v. Clark,* 22 C.M.A. 570, 48 C.M.R. 77 (1974) which held that the *Manual* only provided a right to military counsel at an interrogation in the event of financial indigency — minimum *Miranda* rule.

Rule 305(d)(2) clarifies present practice insofar as it explicitly indicates that no right to individual military counsel of the suspect's or accused's choice exists. *See, e.g., United States v. Wilcox,* 3 M.J. 863 (C.M.A. 1977).

(e) Notice to Counsel. Rule 305(e) is taken from *United States v. McOmber,* 1 M.J. 380 (C.M.A. 1976). The holding of that case has been expanded slightly to clarify the situation in which an interrogator does not have actual knowledge that an attorney has been appointed for or retained by the accused or suspect with respect to the offenses, but reasonably should be so aware. In the absence of the expansion, present law places a premium on law enforcement ignorance and has the potential for encouraging perjury. The change rejects the view expressed in *United States v. Roy,* 4 M.J. 840 (A.C.M.R. 1978) which held that in the absence of bad faith a criminal investigator who interviewed the accused one day before the scheduled Article 32 investigation was not in violation of *McOmber* because he was unaware of the appointment of counsel.

Factors which may be considered in determining whether an interrogator should have reasonably known that an individual had counsel for purposes of this Rule include:

Whether the interrogator knew that the person to be questioned had requested counsel;

Whether the interrogator knew that the person to be questioned had already been involved in a pretrial proceeding at which he would ordinarily be represented by counsel;

Any regulations governing the appointment of counsel;

Local standard operating procedures;

The interrogator's military assignment and training; and

The interrogator's experience in the area of military criminal procedure.

The standard involved is purely an objective one.

(f) Exercise of rights. Rule 305(f) restates present law in that it requires all questioning to cease immediately upon the exercise of either the privilege against self-incrimination or the right to counsel. *See Michigan v. Mosley,* 423 U.S. 96 (1975). The Rule expressly does not deal with the question of whether or when questioning may be resumed following an exercise of a suspect's rights and does not necessarily prohibit it. The Committee notes that both the Supreme Court, *see, e.g., Brewer v. Williams,* 430 U.S. 387 (1977); *Michigan v. Mosley,* 423 U.S. 96 (1975), and the Court of Military Appeals, *see, e.g., United States v. Hill,* 5 M.J. 114 (C.M.A. 1978); *United States v. Collier,* 1 M.J. 358 (C.M.A. 1976), have yet to fully resolve this matter.

(g) Waiver. The waiver provision of Rule 305(g) restates current military practice and is taken in part from ¶ 140a(2) of the present *Manual.*

Rule 305(g) (1) sets forth the general rule for waiver and follows *Miranda v. Arizona,* 384 U.S. 436, 475 (1966). The Rule requires that an affirmative acknowledgment of the right be made before an adequate waiver may be found. *See Manual* ¶ 30b. Thus, three waiver questions are required under Rule 305(g):

(1) Do you understand your rights?

(2) Do you want a lawyer?

(3) Are you willing to make a statement?

The specific wording of the questions is not detailed by the Rule and any format may be used so long as the substantive content is present.

Notwithstanding the above, Rule 305(g) (2), following *North Carolina v. Butler,* 441 U.S. 369 (1979), recognizes that the right to counsel, and only the right to counsel, may be waived even absent an affirmative declination. The burden of proof is on the prosecution in such a case to prove by a preponderance that the accused waived the right to counsel.

The second portion of Rule 305(g)(2) dealing with notice to counsel is new. The intent behind the basic notice provision, Rule 305(e), is to give meaning to the right to counsel by preventing interrogators who know or reasonably should know that an individual has counsel from circumventing the right to counsel by obtaining a waiver from that person without counsel present. Permitting a *Miranda* type waiver in such a situation clearly would defeat the purpose of the Rule. Rule 305(g) (2) thus permits a waiver of the right to counsel when notice to counsel is required only if it can be demonstrated either that the counsel, after reasonable efforts, could not be notified, or that the counsel did not attend the interrogation which was scheduled within a reasonable period of time after notice was given.

A statement given by an accused or suspect who can be shown to have his rights as set forth in this Rule and who intentionally frustrated the diligent attempt of the interrogator to comply with this Rule shall not be involuntary solely for failure to comply with the rights warning requirements of this Rule or of the waiver requirements. *United States v. Sikorski,* 21 C.M.A. 345, 45 C.M.R. 119 (1972).

(h) Non-military interrogations. Paragraph 140a(2) of the present *Manual,* which governs civilian interrogations of military personnel basically restates the holding of *Miranda v. Arizona,* 384 U.S. 436 (1966). Recognizing that the Supreme Court may modify the *Miranda* rule, the Committee has used the language in Rule 305(h) (1) to make practice in this area dependent upon the way the federal district courts would handle such interrogations. *See* Article 36.

Rule 305(h)(2) clarifies the law of interrogations as it relates to interrogations conducted abroad by officials of a foreign government or their agents when the interrogation is not conducted, instigated, or participated in by military personnel or their agents. Such an interrogation does not require rights warnings under subdivisions (c) or (d) or notice to counsel under subdivision (e). The only test to be applied in such a case is that of common law voluntariness: whether a statement obtained during such an interrogation was obtained through the use of "coercion, unlawful influence, or unlawful inducement." Article 31(d).

Whether an interrogation has been "conducted, instigated, or participated in by military personnel or their agents" is a question of fact depending on the circumstances of the case. The Rule makes it clear that United States personnel do not participate in an interrogation merely by being present at the scene of the interrogation, *see United States v. Jones,* 6 M.J. 226 (C.M.A. 1979) and the *Analysis* to Rule 311(c), or by taking steps which are in the best interests of the accused. Also, an interrogation is not "participated in" by military personnel or their agents who act as interpreters during the interrogation if there is no other participation. *See* Rule 311(c). The omission of express reference to interpreters in Rule 305(h)(2) was inadvertent.

Rule 306. Statements by One of Several Accused

When two or more accused are tried at the same trial, evidence of a statement made by one of them which is admissible only against him or her or only against some but not all of the accused may not be received in evidence unless all references inculpating an accused against whom the statement is inadmissible are deleted effectively or the maker of the statement is subject to cross-examination.

EDITORIAL COMMENT

In a joint trial, the prosecution may wish to introduce extrajudicial statements of one or more accused persons. In order to insure protection of the confrontation rights of an accused, the extrajudicial statements of a co-accused must not be admitted unless they are purged of any reference to the accused or the maker of the offered statement is subject to cross-examination. This Rule of law, grounded in *Bruton v. United States,* 391 U.S. 123 (1968), forms the basis for Rule 306. The Rule follows pre-Rules practice noted in *Manual* ¶ 140 *b* and adopted in military decisions. *See, e.g., United States v. Pringle,* 3 M.J. 308 (C.M.A. 1977) and *United States v. Green,* 3 M.J. 320 (C.M.A. 1977). In both of these cases the Court of Military Appeals addressed the issue of whether the admitted statements of a co-accused had been sufficiently purged of references to the accused.

Litigation under this Rule will more often than not center on the question of effective deletion of references to the accused. The *Pringle* and *Green* decisions serve to remind counsel that simply whiting out the accused's name will normally not suffice. All direct, contextual and implied references should be removed. To further insure effective redaction the court may have to delete all references, make contextual changes when necessary, and then read the statement to the court-members. *See, e.g., United States v. Gay,* 522 F.2d 429 (6th Cir. 1975) (effective redaction consisted of deletion of accused's name, rephrasing, instructions to jury, and not permitting jury to see document). *See also United States v. Dority,* 487 F.2d 846 (6th Cir. 1973).

If the statement cannot be effectively purged, then a severance should be liberally granted — *see Manual* ¶ 69*d* — unless the maker of the statement takes the stand and thus is subject to cross-examination, in which case his extrajudicial statements need not be purged of references to the accused. It is unclear whether the military courts will find a possibility of cross-examination to be present when in reality cross-examination is difficult, if not impossible. See *California v. Green,* 399 U.S. 149 (1970); *Nelson v. O'Neil,* 402 U.S. 622 (1971).

Another possible exception may arise in a case involving interlocking confessions: i.e., both a co-accused's extrajudicial statement and an accused's confession are offered. The Supreme Court in *Parker v. Randolph,* 442 U.S. 62 (1979), ruled that *Bruton* was not applicable to interlocking confessions. But because of the absence of a majority opinion in *Parker,* the drafters opted for continued application of the *Bruton* rule to interlocking confessions. Thus, even where interlocking confessions are offered, the parties must still be sensitive to the redaction requirements of Rule 306.

For a thorough discussion of the *Bruton* problem, *see* Haddad, *Post-Bruton Developments: A Reconsideration of the Confrontation Rationale, and a Proposal for a Due Process Evaluation of Limiting Instructions,* 18 Am. Crim. L. Rev. 1 (1980).

DRAFTERS' ANALYSIS

Rule 306 is taken from the fifth subparagraph of present ¶ 140*b* of the *Manual* for Courts-Martial and states the holding of *Bruton v. United States,* 391 U.S. 123 (1968). The remainder of the associated material in the *Manual* is primarily concerned with the co-conspirator's exception to the hearsay rule and has been superseded by adoption of the Federal Rules of Evidence. *See* Rule 801.

When it is impossible to effectively delete all references to a co-accused, alternative steps must be taken to protect the co-accused. This may include the granting of a severance.

The Committee was aware of the Supreme Court's decision in *Parker v. Randolph,* 442 U.S. 62 (1979) dealing with interlocking confessions. In view of the lack of a consensus in *Parker,* however, the Committee determined that the case did not provide sufficient precise basis for drafting a rule, and decided instead to apply *Bruton* to interlocking confessions.

Rule 311. Evidence Obtained From Unlawful Searches and Seizures

(a) General rule. Evidence obtained as a result of an unlawful search or seizure made by a person acting in a governmental capacity is inadmissible against the accused if:

(1) Objection. The accused makes a timely motion to suppress or an objection to the evidence under this rule; and

(2) Adequate interest. The accused had a reasonable expectation of privacy in the person, place or property searched; the accused had a legitimate interest in the property or evidence seized when challenging a seizure; or the accused would otherwise have grounds to object to the search or seizure under the Constitution of the United States as applied to members of the armed forces.

(b) Exception. Evidence that was obtained as a result of an unlawful search or seizure may be used to impeach by contradiction the in-court testimony of the accused.

(c) Nature of search or seizure. A search or seizure is "unlawful" if it was conducted, instigated, or participated in by:

(1) Military personnel. Military personnel or their agents and was in violation of the Constitution of the United States as applied to members of the armed forces, an Act of Congress applicable to trials by court-martial that requires exclusion of evidence obtained in violation thereof, or rules 312-317;

(2) Other officials. Other officials or agents of the United States, of the District of Columbia, or of a State, Commonwealth, or possession of the United States or any political subdivision of such a State, Commonwealth, or possession and was in violation of the Constitution of the United States, or is unlawful under the principles of law generally applied in the trial of criminal cases in the United States district courts involving a similar search or seizure; or

(3) Officials of a foreign government. Officials of a foreign government or their agents and was obtained as a result of a foreign search or seizure which subjected the accused to gross and brutal maltreatment.

A search or seizure is not "participated in" merely because a person is present at a search or seizure conducted in a foreign nation by officials of a foreign government or their agents, or because a person acted as an interpreter or took steps to mitigate damage to property or physical harm during the foreign search or seizure.

(d) Motions to suppress and objections.

(1) Disclosure. Prior to arraignment, the prosecution shall disclose to the defense all evidence seized from the person or property of the accused, or believed to be owned by the accused, that it intends to offer into evidence against the accused at trial.

(2) Motion or objection.

(A) When evidence has been disclosed under subdivision (d)(1), any motion to suppress or objection under this rule shall be made by the defense prior to submission of a plea. In the absence of such motion or objection, the defense may not raise the issue at a later time except as permitted by the military judge for good cause shown. Failure to so move or object constitutes a waiver of the motion or objection.

(B) If the prosecution intends to offer evidence seized from the person or property of the accused that was not disclosed prior to arraignment, the prosecution shall provide timely notice to the military judge and to counsel for the accused. The defense may enter an objection at that time and the military judge may make such orders as are required in the interest of justice.

(C) If evidence is disclosed as derivative evidence under this subdivision prior to arraignment, any motion to suppress or objection under this rule shall be made in accordance with the procedure for challenging evidence under (A). If such evidence has not been so disclosed prior to arraignment, the requirements of (B) apply.

(3) Specificity. The military judge may require the defense to specify the grounds upon which the defense moves to suppress or object to evidence. If defense counsel, despite the exercise of due diligence, has been unable to interview adequately those persons involved in the search or seizure, the military judge may enter any order required by the interests of justice, including authorization for the defense to make a general motion to suppress or a general objection.

(4) Rulings. A motion to suppress or an objection to evidence made prior to plea shall be ruled upon prior to plea unless the military judge, for good cause, orders that it be deferred for determination at the trial of the general issue or until after findings, but no such determination shall be deferred if a party's right to appeal the ruling is affected adversely. Where factual issues are involved in ruling upon such motion or objection, the military judge shall state essential findings of fact on the record.

(e) Burden of proof.

(1) In general. When an appropriate motion or objection has been made by the defense under subdivision (d), the prosecution has the burden of proving by a preponderance of the evidence that evidence was not obtained as a result of an unlawful search or seizure.

(2) Derivative evidence. Evidence that is challenged under this rule as derivative evidence may be admitted against the accused if the military judge finds by a preponderance of the evidence that the evidence was not obtained as a result of an unlawful search or seizure.

(3) Specific motions or objections. When a specific motion or objection has been required under subdivision (d)(3), the burden on the prosecution extends only to the grounds upon which the defense moved to suppress or object to the evidence.

(f) Defense evidence. The defense may present evidence relevant to the admissibility of evidence as to which there has been an appropriate motion or objection under this rule. An accused may testify for the limited purpose of contesting the legality of the search or seizure giving rise to the challenged evidence. Prior to the introduction of such testimony by the accused, the defense shall inform the military judge that the testimony is offered under this subdivision. When the accused

testifies under this subdivision, the accused may be cross-examined only as to the matter on which he or she testifies. Nothing said by the accused on either direct or cross-examination may be used against the accused for any purpose other than in a prosecution for perjury, false swearing, or the making of a false official statement.

(g) *Scope of motions and objections challenging probable cause.*

(1) *Generally.* If the defense challenges evidence seized pursuant to a search warrant or search authorization on the grounds that the warrant or authorization was not based upon probable cause, the evidence relevant to the motion is limited to evidence concerning the information actually presented to or otherwise known by the authorizing officer, except as provided in paragraph (2).

(2) *False statements.* If the defense makes a substantial preliminary showing that a government agent included a false statement knowingly and intentionally or with reckless disregard for the truth in the information presented to the authorizing officer, and if the allegedly false statement is necessary to the finding of probable cause, the defense, upon request, shall be entitled to a hearing. At the hearing, the defense has the burden of establishing by a preponderance of the evidence the allegation of falsity or reckless disregard for the truth. If the defense meets its burden, the prosecution has the burden of proving by a preponderance of the evidence, with the false information set aside, that the remaining information presented to the authorizing officer is sufficient to establish probable cause. If the prosecution does not meet its burden, the objection or motion shall be granted unless the search is otherwise lawful under these rules.

(h) *Objections to evidence seized unlawfully.* If a defense motion or objection under this rule is sustained in whole or in part, the members may not be informed of that fact except insofar as the military judge must instruct the members to disregard evidence.

(i) *Effect of guilty plea.* A plea of guilty to an offense that results in a finding of guilty waives all issues under the Fourth

Amendment to the Constitution of the United States and rules 311-317 with respect to that offense whether or not raised prior to plea.

EDITORIAL COMMENT

Evidence obtained in a manner violative of the Fourth Amendment as it is applied to military practice will be excluded. Rule 311 specifies under what circumstances the evidence is not admissible and details the procedures for litigating admissibility.

The general rule of exclusion is stated in subdivision (a) which provides that unlawfully obtained evidence will be excluded if the defense contests admissibility in a timely fashion and can show that the accused had an "adequate interest", or standing, in the property searched or seized. Specifically, the accused must have had either (1) a reasonable expectation of privacy in the person or place searched; or (2) a legitimate (i.e., a lawful) interest in the seized evidence; or (3) can show that his interest rests on other grounds cognizable under the Constitution. The two distinct interests, personal privacy and legitimate interests, were included in the Rule to emphasize that the interests involved in a search are not necessarily the same as those involved in a seizure. The third, an open-ended category of "other grounds," should provide flexibility for future case law. These interests are in line with recent Supreme Court cases. *See, e.g., Rakas v. Illinois,* 439 U.S. 128 (1978); *United States v. Salvucci,* 444 U.S. 989 (1980); *Rawlings v. Kentucky,* 444 U.S. 989 (1980).

The exception to the general rule of exclusion is found in subdivision (b). Evidence obtained by an unlawful search or seizure may be admissible for the limited purpose of impeaching the accused's testimony. This is in accord with *Manual* ¶ 152 and with the Supreme Court's position on the subject in *United States v. Havens,* 444 U.S. 962 (1980). *See also Walder v. United States,* 347 U.S. 62 (1954).

The Rule implicitly recognizes that not all intrusions into areas in which the accused has an adequate interest are necessarily unlawful. Subdivision (c), for example, continues pre-Rules case law and proscribes only governmental or official actions. Purely private searches or seizures are not included. *See, e.g., United States v. Rosado,* 2 M.J. 763 (A.C.M.R. 1976). Specifically, searches or seizures by military personnel or their agents, (c)(1), are to be measured for legality against the Constitution, applicable Acts of Congress, and by Rules 312 to 317, which set out in more detail a variety of lawful intrusions. Intrusions by civilian authorities are governed by the laws recognized in the federal courts, (c)(2), and foreign searches and seizures under (c)(3) are unlawful only if they involve gross and brutal maltreatment. In the case of intrusions by foreign officials, subdivision (c)(3) rests in part on *United States v. Jordan,* 1 M.J. 334 (C.M.A. 1976), and follows *United States v. Jones,* 6 M.J. 226 (C.M.A. 1979), to the extent that mere presence of American officials at the scene will not in itself trigger application of American law. There must be some causal connection between the American officials and the foreign intrusion.

The key procedures for challenging and litigating the admissibility of evidence obtained by searches and seizures are outlined in subdivisions (d) through (f). With only minor exceptions these subdivisions mirror provisions in Rules 304 and 321 and are part and parcel of major changes to the military's motion practice. Because much of what we note in Rule 304, is equally applicable here, we will only briefly address Rule 311 procedures.

Unlike Rule 304(d)(1) which requires broad disclosure of an accused's statements, Rule 311(d)(1) only requires the prosecution to disclose evidence which it intends to introduce. Once disclosed the burden rests on the defense to raise the issue and to do so, if possible, prior to entering a plea. If disclosure is made for the first time during trial, a timely objection must be made at that point. The issue of admissibility may be waived by failing to move to suppress or to object, (d)(2), or by entering a plea of guilty. See subdivision (i). The motion to suppress generally must be ruled on prior to the entry of a plea.

The prosecution must prove under subdivision (e) by a preponderance of the evidence that the offered evidence was not obtained through an unlawful search or seizure; however, Rule 314(e)(5) notes that where the prosecution is relying upon a consent search, it bears the burden of showing consent by "clear and convincing" evidence. See United States v. Middleton, 10 M.J. 123, 132, n. 17 (court applied standard set out in Rule 314(e)(5)). Subdivision (e)(2) recognizes that, as under pre-Rules practice, the prosecution may introduce derivative evidence if it can show that notwithstanding an illegal search, the evidence resulted from an independent source, United States v. Waller, 3 M.J. 32 (C.M.A. 1977), or that the initial illegality was attenuated, Wong Sun v. United States, 371 U.S. 471 (1963).

Subdivision (f) provides that an accused can testify for the limited purpose of contesting the legality of the search or seizure. The defense must however announce beforehand that the testimony is being offered under (f), thereby limiting the scope of cross-examination and the prosecution's later use of the testimony at trial.

Where the defense is challenging a search based upon probable cause, see Rule 315, subdivision (g)(1) generally limits the scope of the challenge to that information actually considered by the authorizing officer. The question whether the defense may ever go behind that information is addressed in (g)(2), which is based upon the Supreme Court's decision in Franks v. Delaware, 442 U.S. 928 (1978), and is consistent with pre-Rules case law. See, e.g., United States v. Turck, 49 C.M.R. 49 (A.F.C.M.R. 1974). The provision sets out a two-step procedure. First, the defense must make a substantial preliminary showing that the information presented to the authorizing officer included a false statement made by a governmental agent which was either made (a) knowingly and intentionally or (b) with reckless disregard for the truth, and that the alleged false statement was necessary to support probable cause. Once that burden is met, the defense is entitled to a hearing on the matter. The Rule is silent as to the manner of making this preliminary showing, but an offer of proof should suffice. During the hearing, the defense must prove willful or reckless falsity by a preponderance of the evidence. If the defense is successful, the burden shifts to the prosecution to establish by a preponderance of the evidence that, without considering the false statement, the judicial officer was presented with probable cause. Failing that, the defense challenge will be sustained. Of course, if a search is lawful without regard to the warrant, suppression will not be required.

Subdivision (h), not based upon any prior *Manual* provision, was intended to clarify practice concerning what information may be given to the court-members. If the judge has determined under Rule 311 that evidence is inadmissible, the members should not be told of the ruling. Under the Rule, and also under Rule 104(c), the court-members ought not even to know about the suppression dispute. But if evidence has been admitted and is to be stricken, they must be informed that they are to disregard the evidence. If an instruction is not likely to be effective, a mistrial may have to be declared. If the ruling is to admit evidence, the judge should say nothing about the search and seizure question to court-members. That the search was lawful does not affect the probative value of the evidence.

DRAFTERS' ANALYSIS

Rules 311-317 express the manner in which the Fourth Amendment to the Constitution of the United States applies to trials by court-martial. *Cf. Parker v. Levy,* 417 U.S. 733 (1974).

(a) General rule. Rule 311(a) restates the basic exclusionary rule for evidence obtained from an unlawful search or seizure and is taken generally from ¶ 152 of the present *Manual* although much of the language of ¶ 152 has been deleted for purposes of both clarity and brevity. The Rule requires suppression of derivative as well as primary evidence and follows the present *Manual* rule by expressly limiting exclusion of evidence to that resulting from unlawful searches and seizures involving governmental activity. Those persons whose actions may thus give rise to exclusion are listed in Rule 311(c) and are taken generally from ¶ 152 with some expansion for purposes of clarity. Rule 311 recognizes that discovery of evidence may be so unrelated to an unlawful search or seizure as to escape exclusion because it was not "obtained as a result" of that search or seizure.

The Rule recognizes that searches and seizures are distinct acts the legality of which must be determined independently. Although a seizure will usually be unlawful if it follows an unlawful search, a seizure may be unlawful even if preceded by a lawful search. Thus, adequate cause to seize may be distinct from the legality of the search or observation which preceded it. Note in this respect Rule 316(d)(4)(c), Plain View.

(1) Objection. Rule 311(a)(1) requires that a motion to suppress or as appropriate, an objection be made before evidence can be suppressed. Absent such motion or objection, the issue is waived. Rule 311(i).

(2) Adequate interest. Rule 311(a)(2) represents a complete redrafting of the standing requirements now found in ¶ 152 of the present *Manual.* The Committee viewed the Supreme Court decision in *Rakas v. Illinois,* 439 U.S. 128 (1978) as substantially modifying the *Manual* language. Indeed, the very use of the term, "standing" was considered obsolete by a majority of the committee. The Rule distinguishes between searches and seizures. To have sufficient interest to challenge a search, a person must have "a reasonable expectation of privacy in the person, place, or property searched." "Reasonable expectation of privacy" was used in lieu of "legitimate expectation of privacy," often used in *Rakas, supra,* as

the committee believed the two expressions to be identical. The committee also considered that the expression "reasonable expectation" has a more settled meaning. Unlike the case of a search, an individual must have an interest distinct from an expectation of privacy to challenge a seizure. When a seizure is involved rather than a search, the only invasion of one's rights is the removal of the property in question. Thus, there must be some recognizable right to the property seized. Consequently, the Rule requires a "legitimate interest in the property or evidence seized." This will normally mean some form of possessory interest. Adequate interest to challenge a seizure does not per se give adequate interest to challenge a prior search that may have resulted in the seizure.

The Rule also recognizes an accused's right to challenge a search or seizure when the right to do so would exist under the Constitution. Among other reasons, this provision was included because of the Supreme Court's decision in *Jones v. United States,* 362 U.S. 257 (1960) which created what has been termed the "automatic standing rule." The viability of *Jones* after *Rakas* and other cases is unclear, and the Rule will apply *Jones* only to the extent that *Jones* is constitutionally mandated.

(b) Exception. Rule 311(b) states the holding of *Walder v. United States,* 347 U.S. 62 (1954), and restates with minor change the rule as found in ¶ 152 of the present *Manual.*

(c) Nature of search or seizure. Rule 311(c) defines "unlawful" searches and seizures and makes it clear that the treatment of a search or seizure varies depending on the status of the individual or group conducting the search or seizure.

(1) Military personnel. Rule 311(c)(1) generally restates present law. A violation of a military regulation alone will not require exclusion of any resulting evidence. However, a violation of such a regulation that gives rise to a reasonable expectation of privacy may require exclusion. *Compare United States v. Dillard,* 8 M.J. 213 (C.M.A. 1980) *with United States v. Caceres,* 440 U.S. 741 (1979).

(2) Other officials. Rule 311(c)(2) requires that the legality of a search or seizure performed by officials of the United States, of the District of Columbia, or of a state, commonwealth, or possession or political subdivision, thereof, be determined by the principles of law applied by the United States district courts when resolving the legality of such a search or seizure.

(3) Officials of a foreign government. This provision is taken in part from *United States v. Jordan,* 1 M.J. 334 (C.M.A. 1976). After careful analysis, a majority of the committee concluded that that portion of the *Jordan* opinion which purported to require that such foreign searches be shown to have compiled with foreign law is dicta and lacks any specific legal authority to support it. Further the committee noted the fact that most foreign nations lack any law of search and seizure and that in some cases, *e.g. Germany,* such law as may exist is purely theoretical and not subject to determination. The *Jordan* requirement thus unduly complicates trial without supplying any protection to the accused. Consequently, the Rule omits this requirement in favor of a basic due process test. In determining which version of the various due process phrasings to utilize, a majority of the committee chose to use the language now found in ¶ 150b of the present *Manual* rather than the language found in *Jordan* (which requires that the evidence not shock the conscience of the court) believing the *Manual* language is more appropriate to the circumstances involved.

Rule 311(c) also indicates that persons who are present at a foreign search or seizure conducted in a foreign nation have "not participated in" that search or seizure due either to their mere presence or because of any actions taken to mitigate possible damage to property or person. The Rule thus clarifies *United States v. Jordan*, 1 M.J. 334 (C.M.A. 1976) which stated that the Fourth Amendment would be applicable to searches and seizures conducted abroad by foreign police when United States personnel participate in them. The Court's intent in *Jordan* was to prevent American authorities from sidestepping Constitutional protections by using foreign personnel to conduct a search or seizure that would have been unlawful if conducted by Americans. That intention is safeguarded by the Rule, which applies the Rules and the Fourth Amendment when military personnel or their agents conduct, instigate, or participate in a search or seizure. The Rule only clarifies the circumstances in which a United States official will be deemed to have participated in a foreign search or seizure. This follows dicta in *United States v. Jones*, 6 M.J. 226, 230 (C.M.A. 1979) which would require an "element of causation," rather than mere presence. It seems apparent that an American servicemember is far more likely to be well served by United States presence — which might mitigate foreign conduct — than by its absence. Further, international treaties frequently require United States cooperation with foreign law enforcement. Thus, the Rule serves all purposes by prohibiting conduct by United States officials which might improperly support a search or seizure which would be unlawful if conducted in the United States while protecting both the accused and international relations.

The Rule also permits use of United States personnel as interpreters viewing such action as a neutral activity normally of potential advantage to the accused. Similarly the Rule permits personnel to take steps to protect the person or property of the accused because such actions are clearly in the best interests of the accused.

(d) Motion to suppress and objections. Rule 311(d) provides for challenging evidence obtained as a result of an allegedly unlawful search or seizure. The procedure, normally that of a motion to suppress, is intended with a small difference in the disclosure requirements to duplicate that required by Rule 304(d) for confessions and admissions, the *Analysis* of which is equally applicable here.

Rule 311(d)(1) differs from Rule 304(c)(1) in that it is applicable only to evidence that the prosecution intends to offer against the accused. The broader disclosure provision for statements by the accused was considered unnecessary. Like Rule 304(d)(2)(C), Rule 311(d)(2)(C) provides expressly for derivative evidence disclosure of which is not mandatory as it may be unclear to the prosecution exactly what is derivative of a search or seizure. The Rule thus clarifies the situation.

(e) Burden of proof. Rule 311(e) requires that a preponderance of the evidence standard be used in determining search and seizure questions, *Lego v. Twomey*, 404 U.S. 477 (1972). Where the validity of a consent to search or seize is involved, a higher standard of "clear and convincing," is applied by Rule 314(e). This restates present law.

(f) Defense evidence. Rule 311(f) restates present law and makes it clear that although an accused is sheltered from any use at trial of a statement made while challenging a search or seizure, such statement may be used in a subsequent "prosecution for perjury, false swearing or the making of a false official statement."

(g) Scope of motions and objections challenging probable cause. Rule 311(g)(2) follows the Supreme Court decision in *Franks v. Delaware*, 442 U.S. 928 (1978), *see also United States v. Turck*, 49 C.M.R. 49, 53 (A.F.C.M.R. 1974), with minor modifications made to adopt the decision to military procedures. Although *Franks* involved perjured affidavits by police, Rule 311(a) is made applicable to information given by government agents because of the governmental status of members of the armed services. The Rule is not intended to reach misrepresentations made by informants without any official connection.

(h) Objections to evidence seized unlawfully. Rule 311(h) is new and is included for reasons of clarity.

(i) Effect of guilty plea. Rule 311(i) restates present law. *See, e.g., United States v. Hamil,* 15 C.M.A. 110, 35 C.M.R. 82 (1964).

Rule 312. Bodily Views and Intrusions

(a) General rule. Evidence obtained from bodily views and intrusions conducted in accordance with this rule is admissible at trial when relevant and not otherwise inadmissible under these rules.

(b) Visual examination of the body.

> *(1) Consensual.* Visual examination of the unclothed body may be made with the consent of the individual subject to the inspection in accordance with rule 314(e).

> *(2) Involuntary.* An involuntary display of the unclothed body including a visual examination of body cavities, may be required only if conducted in reasonable fashion and authorized under the following provisions of these rules: inspections and inventories under rule 313; searches under rules 314(b) and 314(c) if there is a real suspicion that weapons, contraband or evidence of crime is concealed on the body of the person to be searched; searches within jails and similar facilities under rule 314(h) if reasonably necessary to maintain the security of the institution or its personnel; searches incident to lawful apprehension under rule 314(g); emergency searches under rule 314(i); and probable cause searches under rule 315. An examination of the unclothed body under this paragraph should be conducted whenever practicable by a person of the same sex as that of the person being examined; provided, however, that failure to comply with this requirement does not make an examination an unlawful search within the meaning of rule 311.

(c) Intrusion into body cavities. A reasonable nonconsensual physical intrusion into the mouth, nose, and ears may be made when a visual examination of the body under subdivision (b) is permissible. Nonconsensual intrusions into other body cavities may be made:

> *(1) For purposes of seizure.* To remove weapons, contraband, or evidence of crime discovered under subdivisions (b) and (c)(2) of this rule or under rule 316(d)(4)(C) if such intrusion is made in a reasonable fashion by a person with appropriate medical qualifications; or

(2) **For purposes of search.** To search for weapons, contraband, or evidence of crime; if authorized by a search warrant or search authorization under rule 315 and conducted by a person with appropriate medical qualifications.

Notwithstanding this paragraph, a search under rule 314(h) may be made without a search warrant or authorization if such search is based upon a real suspicion that the individual is concealing weapons, contraband, or evidence of crime.

(d) **Seizure of bodily fluids.** Nonconsensual extraction of bodily fluids, including blood and urine, may be made from the body of an individual pursuant to a search warrant or a search authorization under rule 315. Nonconsensual extraction of bodily fluids may be made without such warrant or authorization, notwithstanding rule 315(g), only when there is a clear indication that evidence of crime will be found and that there is reason to believe that the delay that would result if a warrant or authorization were sought could result in the destruction of the evidence. Involuntary extraction of bodily fluids under this rule must be done in a reasonable fashion by a person with appropriate medical qualifications.

(e) **Other intrusive searches.** Nonconsensual intrusive searches of the body made to locate or obtain weapons, contraband, or evidence of crime and not within the scope of subdivisions (b) or (c) may be made only upon search warrant or search authorization under rule 315 and only if such search is conducted in a reasonable fashion by a person with appropriate medical qualifications and does not endanger the health of the person to be searched. Compelling a person to ingest substances for the purposes of locating the property described above or to compel the bodily elimination of such property is a search within the meaning of this section. Notwithstanding this rule, a person who is neither a suspect nor an accused may not be compelled to submit to an intrusive search of the body for the sole purpose of obtaining evidence of crime.

(f) **Intrusions for valid medical purposes.** Nothing in this rule shall be deemed to interfere with the lawful authority of the armed forces to take whatever action may be necessary to preserve the health of a service member. Evidence or contraband

115

obtained from an examination or intrusion conducted for a valid medical purpose may be seized and is not evidence obtained from an unlawful search or seizure within the meaning of rule 311.

(g) Medical qualifications. The Secretary concerned may prescribe appropriate medical qualifications for persons who conduct searches and seizures under this rule.

EDITORIAL COMMENT

Whenever evidence is obtained from an examination or search of an accused's body, there are potential self-incrimination, Fourth Amendment, and due process problems. Rule 312 is an innovative effort to address two of these. It centers on Fourth Amendment issues, but also, implicitly covers due process issues, as it controls consensual and nonconsensual intrusions of the body. Bodily evidence obtained in violation of this Rule is treated as the product of an unlawful search under Rule 311.

The Rule does not address self-incrimination problems. These normally are not present in the civilian system which has rejected application of the Fifth Amendment privilege to most bodily evidence issues. *See, e.g., Schmerber v. California,* 384 U.S. 757 (1966) (blood sample taken from accused). *See generally,* Eckhart, *Intrusions Into the Body,* 52 MIL. L. REV. 141 (1971). *See also,* 25 A.L.R.2d 1407. A different rule may apply to military practice where Article 31(a), U.C.M.J., potentially provides broader self-incrimination protections. *See* our discussion of Rule 301. The military courts have not applied Article 31 protections to external body evidence such as teeth, *United States v. Martin,* 9 M.J. 731 (N.C.M.R. 1979) or hair, *United States v. Pyburn,* 47 C.M.R. 896 (A.F.C.M.R. 1973). *See also United States v. Rosato,* 3 C.M.A. 143, 11 C.M.R. 143 (1953) (accused or suspect may be required to trim or grow a beard, submit to fingerprinting, try on clothes, place foot in track or exhibit scars). Recently, the Court of Military Appeals indicated that Article 31 would not protect body fluids, *United States v. Armstrong,* 9 M.J. 374 (1980) or handwriting or voice exemplars, *United States v. Lloyd,* 10 M.J. 172 (1981). This marks a clear departure from prior military case law and brings the military's treatment of this area more in line with civilian precedents. Article 31 protections are potentially available where a servicemember is told or asked to produce evidence. *See, e.g., United States v. Whipple,* 4 M.J. 773 (C.G.C.M.R. 1978) (handing over drugs was a "statement," a verbal act, to be tested for voluntariness). The implicit statement that may accompany an act also may cause civilian courts to provide Fifth Amendment protections, something discussed in *Fisher v. United States,* 425 U.S. 391 (1976).

Where Article 31 or self-incrimination protections exist, the authorities may request voluntary relinquishment in the same way they do when they are interrogating a suspect — *i.e.,* after giving appropriate rights warnings. *See* Rule 305. Or they may compel the individual to relinquish the evidence after granting immunity from criminal consequences, a solution implicitly recognized in *United States v. Ruiz,* 23 C.M.A. 181, 48 C.M.R. 797 (1974). *See*

generally, Schlueter, *Bodily Evidence and Rule 312, M.R.E.,* THE ARMY LAW-
YER, May 1980, at 35. It is not necessary to seek a waiver, however; an
alternative for the government is to proceed under valid search and seizure
procedures. If evidence is properly seized without compelling the accused to
incriminate himself, then it may be used.

Rule 312 applies a sliding scale approach to bodily evidence problems: the
greater the Fourth Amendment intrusion, the broader the protection. At the
least intrusive end of the scale are those slight intrusions such as visual
examinations of the body. At the other end are gross intrusions, like surgical
procedures to recover evidence.

Subdivision (b) permits visual examination of an unclothed body. This
superficial examination may be conducted either with the consent of the
servicemember, *see* Rule 314(e) (outlining valid consent searches) or without
consent. But if consent is lacking, (b)(1) requires that the examination be
conducted reasonably and in conjunction with one or more of the following
authorized intrusions:

(a) Inspection or inventory, Rule 313;

(b) Border search or its military equivalent if there is a real suspicion
that weapons, contraband, or evidence of a crime are concealed on the
individual, Rule 314(b) and (c);

(c) Confinement facility search, Rule 314(h);

(d) Search incident to apprehension, Rule 314(g);

(e) Emergency search, Rule 314(i); or

(f) Probable cause search, Rule 315.

The Rule states a preference that a member of the same sex as the suspect
conduct the examination, which may include a visual examination of body
cavities. However, failure to follow the "same sex" preference is not grounds for
invalidating a search. Subdivision (b) is consistent with federal practice. *See
e.g., United States v. Mendenhall,* — U.S. — (1980) (accused consented to strip
search); *Bell v. Wolfish,* 441 U.S. 520 (1979) (prison searches); *United States
v. Himmelwright,* 551 F.2d 991 (5th Cir. 1977) (drugs discovered during visual
examination of suspect's vagina); *Committee for G.I. Rights v. Callaway,* 518
F.2d 466 (D.C. Cir. 1975) (visual rectal inspections of servicemembers).

Intrusions into body cavities are controlled by subdivision (c) which
separates the cavities into two categories; the first includes the mouth, nose
and ears while the second is comprised of all "other body cavities." Consensual
physical intrusions are implicitly allowed for both categories. But each receives
separate treatment for purposes of nonconsensual intrusions. Reasonable
nonconsensual intrusions into the mouth, ears or nose are permitted whenever
a visual inspection of the body is allowed under subdivision (b)(2).

Nonconsensual intrusions into other body cavities are further categorized
into those involving "seizures" and those involving "searches." Contraband
evidence or weapons may be seized from these other cavities without the
individual's consent if they are discovered during a proper visual examination
under (b), a properly authorized search under (c)(2), or pursuant to "plain
view," Rule 316(d)(4)(C). Searches of this second category of body cavities must

comply with probable cause search requirements detailed in Rule 315, except that a confinement facility search, Rule 314(h), may be conducted without prior authorization if the search is based on a real suspicion that the individual is concealing weapons, contraband or evidence on his person. *See Bell v. Wolfish, supra.* In situations involving either searches or seizures of these "other" cavities, personnel with appropriate medical qualifications, *see* (g), *infra,* must be called upon to execute the intrusion, and they must make any intrusion "in a reasonable fashion."

Seizure of body fluids is governed by subdivision (d). They may be involuntarily extracted pursuant to a warrant or authorization, *see* Rule 315. In order to proceed under Rule 315(g) without a warrant or search authorization to seize body fluids, probable cause alone is not enough, nor are exigent circumstances; Rule 312(d) also requires that there be clear indication that evidence of crime will be found and that delay could result in the destruction of the evidence. This exception is generally consistent with *Manual* ¶ 152. Seizures of body fluids must be reasonably executed by personnel with appropriate medical qualifications.

Subdivision (e) covers those intrusions which do not fit into either visual examinations of the body under (b) or intrusions into body cavities under (c). Nonconsensual intrusions for weapons, contraband or evidence must be supported by warrant or authorization, *see* Rule 315, must be reasonably performed by persons with appropriate medical qualifications and must not endanger the health of the individual. Intrusive searches conducted solely to recover evidence may be conducted only upon an accused or suspect. This provision demonstrates a flexible balancing test used in a number of civilian jurisdictions where surgical intrusions are in issue. Implicit here is consideration of the government's need for the evidence, the proposed procedures, and the privacy interests and health of the individual. *See generally,* Note, *Search and Seizure: Compelled Surgical Intrusions?* 27 BAYLOR L. REV. 305 (1975). A helpful template here is contained in *United States v. Crowder,* 543 F.2d 312 (D.C. Cir. 1976), cert. denied, 429 U.S. 1062 (1977) discussed in Minton, *Criminal Procedure, Surgical Removal of Evidence,* 43 Mo. L. REV. 133 (1978). In permitting two bullets recovered from the defendant's thigh and wrist to be admitted, the court noted that (1) surgical removal was the only way to obtain the evidence, (2) the defendant was offered an opportunity to argue against the application for surgery, (3) he was offered an opportunity to appeal the order authorizing the surgery, and (4) skilled doctors took all necessary precautions in performing the minor surgery.

Subdivision (e) is not limited, however, to surgical intrusions. Also covered are forced ingestions of substances designed to locate evidence or force its elimination. Simply allowing nature to take its course would not be a search within subdivision (e) nor would it raise Article 31 U.C.M.J. issues. *See United States v. Woods,* 3 M.J. 264 (C.M.A. 1977) where officials recovered from accused's stool a packet of heroin which he had swallowed eight days earlier. The court treated the evidence as "abandoned" property. *See also* Rule 316(d)(1).

Serving as a sort of catch-all for any bodily intrusion is subdivision (f) which recognizes the broad authority of the armed forces to maintain the health of its members. Key here is the requirement of "valid medical purpose." Simply labelling an examination or intrusion as such will normally not suffice, especially where the action involves a law enforcement official and the patient is a suspect. The Rule recognizes, however, that evidence recovered during valid medical treatment is admissible. *See, e.g., United States v. Miller,* 15 C.M.A. 320, 35 C.M.R. 292 (1965) (evidence of alcohol content in blood taken for purely diagnostic purposes). *See also* Rule 314(i).

Throughout the Rule, there are requirements that intrusions into the body be conducted by persons with appropriate medical qualifications. Subdivision (g) notes only that the Secretary concerned may prescribe the appropriate qualifications. The drafters' *Analysis* suggests that in the absence of Secretarial direction, the normal procedures of the local medical facility should control. The term is obviously broad and should be read to recognize that what may be appropriate qualifications to take a blood sample will not necessarily be sufficient where surgical intrusions are required.

The requirement for medical qualifications points out the necessity of providing due process protections in an area where the "shock the conscience" test is ever-present. *Rochin v. California,* 342 U.S. 165 (1952). Meeting the requirements of Rule 312 will normally suffice because the drafters have incorporated reasonableness requirements. Yet, even a reasonably executed intrusion may be so extreme so as to shock the conscience. *See, e.g., People v. Scott,* 21 Cal. App. 3d 284, 578 P.2d 123 (1978) (court-ordered bodily intrusion, which consisted of massaging prostate gland to obtain semen sample, was regarded as extreme as regurgitation in *Rochin*).

DRAFTERS' ANALYSIS

(a) *General rule.* Rule 312(a) limits all nonconsensual inspections, searches or seizures by providing standards for examinations of the naked body and bodily intrusions. An inspection, search or seizure that would be lawful but for noncompliance with this Rule is unlawful within the meaning of Rule 311.

(b) *Visual examination of the body.* Rule 312(b) governs searches and examinations of the naked body and thus controls what has often been loosely termed, "strip searches." Rule 312(b) permits visual examinations of the naked body in a wide but finite range of circumstances. In doing so, the Rule strictly distinguishes between visual examination of body cavities and actual intrusion into them. Intrusion is governed by Rule 312(c) and (e). Visual examination of the male genitals is permitted when a visual examination is permissible under this subdivision. Examination of cavities may include, when otherwise proper under the Rule, requiring the individual being viewed to assist in the examination.

Examination of body cavities within the prison setting has been vexatious. *See, e.g., Hanley v. Ward,* 584 F.2d 609 (2d Cir. 1978); *Wolfish v. Levi,* 573 F.2d 118, 131 (2d Cir.), *reversed sub nom. Bell v. Wolfish,* 441 U.S. 520 (1979); *Daughtery v. Harris,* 476 F.2d 292 (10th Cir.), *cert. denied,* 414 U.S. 872 (1973); *Frazier v. Ward,* 426 F. Supp. 1354, 1362-67 (N.D.N.Y. 1977); *Hodges v. Klein,* 412 F. Supp. 896 (D.N.J. 1976). Institutional security must be protected while at the same time only those privacy intrusions necessary should be imposed on the individual. The problem is particularly acute in this area of inspection of body cavities as such strong social taboos are involved. Rule 312(b)(2) allows examination of body cavities when reasonably necessary to maintain the security of the institution or its personnel. *See, e.g., Bell v. Wolfish,* 441 U.S. 520 (1979). Examinations likely to be reasonably necessary include examination upon entry or exit from the institution, examination subsequent to a personal visit, or examination pursuant to a reasonably clear indication that the individual is concealing property within a body cavity. *Frazier v. Ward,* 426 F. Supp. 1354 (N.D.N.Y. 1977); *Hodges v. Klein,* 412 F. Supp. 896 (D.N.J. 1976). Great deference should be given to the decisions of the commanders and staff of military confinement facilities. The concerns voiced by the Court of Appeals for the Tenth Circuit in *Daughtery v. Harris,* 476 F.2d 292 (10th Cir. 1973) about escape and related risks are likely to be particularly applicable to military prisoners because of their training in weapons and escape and evasion tactics.

As required throughout Rule 312, examination of body cavities must be accomplished in a reasonable fashion. This incorporates *Rochin v. California,* 342 U.S. 165 (1952), and recognizes society's particularly sensitive attitude in this area. Where possible, examination should be made in private and by members of the same sex as the person being examined.

(c) Intrusion into body cavities. Actual intrusion into body cavities, *e.g.,* the anus and vagina, may represent both a significant invasion of the individual's privacy and a possible risk to the health of the individual. Rule 312(c) allows seizure of property discovered in accordance with Rules 312(b), 312(c)(2), or 316(d)(4)(c) but requires that intrusion into such cavities be accomplished by personnel with appropriate medical qualifications. The Rule thus does not specifically require that the intrusion be made by a doctor, nurse, or other similar medical personnel although Rule 312(g) allows the Secretary concerned to prescribe who may perform such procedures. It is presumed that an object easily located by sight can normally be easily extracted. The requirement for appropriate medical qualifications, however, recognizes that circumstances may require more qualified personnel. This may be particularly true, for example, for extraction of foreign matter from a pregnant woman's vagina. Intrusion should normally be made either by medical personnel or by persons with appropriate medical qualifications who are members of the same sex as the person involved.

The Rule distinguishes between seizure of property previously located and intrusive searches of body cavities by requiring the Rule 312(c)(2) that such searches be made only pursuant to a search warrant or authorization, based upon probable cause, and conducted by persons with appropriate medical qualifications. Exigencies do not permit such searches without warrant or authorization unless Rule 312(f) is applicable. In the absence of express regulations issued by the Secretary concerned pursuant to Rule 312(g), the determination as to which personnel are qualified to conduct an intrusion should be made in accordance with the normal procedures of the applicable medical facility.

Recognizing the peculiar needs of confinement facilities and related institutions, *see, e.g., Bell v. Wolfish,* 441 U.S. 520 (1979), Rule 312(c) authorizes body cavity searches without prior search warrant or authorization when there is a "real suspicion that the individual is concealing weapons, contraband, or evidence of crime."

(d) Seizure of bodily fluids. Seizure of fluids from the body may involve self-incrimination questions pursuant to Article 31 of the Uniform Code of Military Justice, and appropriate case law should be consulted prior to involuntary seizure. *See generally* Rule 301(a) and its *Analysis.* The committee does not intend an individual's expelled breath to be within the definition of "bodily fluids."

The present *Manual* ¶ 152 authorization for seizure of bodily fluids when there has been inadequate time to obtain a warrant or authorization has been slightly modified. The present language that there be "clear indication that evidence of crime will be found and that there is reason to believe that delay will threaten the destruction of evidence" has been modified to authorize such a seizure if there is reason to believe that the delay "could result in the destruction of the evidence." Personnel involuntarily extracting bodily fluids must have appropriate medical qualifications.

Rule 312 does not prohibit compulsory urinalysis, whether random or not, made for appropriate medical purposes, *see* Rule 312(f), and the product of such a procedure if otherwise admissible may be used in evidence at a court-martial.

(e) Other intrusive searches. The intrusive searches governed by Rule 312(e) will normally involve significant medical procedures including surgery and include any intrusion into the body including x-rays. Applicable civilian cases lack a unified approach to surgical intrusions, *see, e.g., United States v. Crowder,* 543 F.2d 312 (D.C. Cir. 1976); *Adams v. State,* 299 N.E. 2d 834 (Ind. 1973); *Creamer v. State,* 299 Ga. 511, 192 S.E. 2d 350 (1972), Note, *Search and Seizure: Compelled Surgical Intrusion?* 27 Baylor L. Rev. 305 (1975) and cases cited therein, other than to rule out those intrusions which are clearly health threatening. Rule 312(e) balances the government's need for evidence with the individual's privacy interest by allowing intrusion into the body of an accused or suspect upon search authorization or warrant when conducted by persons with "appropriate medical qualifications," and by prohibiting intrusion when it will endanger the health of the individual. This allows, however, considerable flexibility and leaves the ultimate issue to be determined under a due process standard of reasonableness. As the public's interest in obtaining evidence from an individual other than an accused or suspect is substantially less than that person's right to privacy in his or her body, the Rule prohibits the involuntary intrusion altogether if its purpose is to obtain evidence of crime.

(f) Intrusions for valid medical purposes. Rule 312(f) makes it clear that the Armed Forces retain their power to ensure the health of their members. A procedure conducted for valid medical purposes may yield admissible evidence. Similarly, Rule 312 does not affect in any way any procedure necessary for diagnostic or treatment purposes.

(g) Medical qualifications. Rule 312(g) permits but does not require the Secretaries concerned to prescribe the medical qualifications necessary for persons to conduct the procedures and examinations specified in the Rule.

Rule 313. Inspections and Inventories in the Armed Forces

(a) General rule. Evidence obtained from inspections and inventories in the armed forces conducted in accordance with this rule is admissible at trial when relevant and not otherwise inadmissible under these rules.

(b) Inspections. An "inspection" is an examination of the whole or part of a unit, organization, installation, vessel, aircraft, or vehicle, including an examination conducted at entrance and exit points, conducted as an incident of command the primary purpose of which is to determine and to ensure the security, military fitness, or good order and discipline of the unit, organization, installation, vessel, aircraft, or vehicle. An inspection may include but is not limited to an examination to determine and to ensure that any or all of the following requirements are met: that the command is properly equipped, functioning properly, maintaining proper standards of readiness, sea or airworthiness, sanitation and cleanliness, and that personnel are present, fit, and ready for duty. An inspection also includes an examination to locate and confiscate unlawful weapons and other contraband when such property would affect adversely the security, military fitness, or good order and discipline of the command and when (1) there is a reasonable suspicion that such property is present in the command or (2) the examination is a previously scheduled examination of the command. An examination made for the primary purpose of obtaining evidence for use in a trial by court-martial or in other disciplinary proceedings is not an inspection within the meaning of this rule. Inspections shall be conducted in a reasonable fashion and shall comply with rule 312, if applicable. Inspections may utilize any reasonable natural or technological aid and may be conducted with or without notice to those inspected. Unlawful weapons, contraband, or other evidence of crime located during an inspection may be seized.

(c) Inventories. Unlawful weapons, contraband, or other evidence of crime discovered in the process of an inventory, the primary purpose of which is administrative in nature, may be seized. Inventories shall be conducted in a reasonable fashion and shall comply with rule 312, if applicable. An examination made for the primary purpose of obtaining evidence for use in a trial by

court-martial or in other disciplinary proceedings is not an inventory within the meaning of this rule.

EDITORIAL COMMENT

Inspections and inventories are governed by Rule 313, which now codifies large portions of pre-Rules military and civilian case law.

Rule 313 in an attempt to reinstate pre-Rules case law which had generally supported the commander's broad authority to inspect persons and places under his control. *See* Hunt, *Inspections,* 54 MIL. L. REV. 225 (1971). In doing so, it limits the effect of more recent cases such as *United States v. Thomas,* 1 M.J. 397 (C.M.A. 1976) and *United States v. Roberts,* 2 M.J. 31 (C.M.A. 1976). These cases had placed limitations on a commander's authority to administratively measure and maintain the unit's discipline and readiness. Regardless of whether inspections are considered as a brand of reasonable searches or simply as administrative intrusions, and regardless of which rationale is relied upon to support the constitutionality of Rule 313 (*see* drafters' *Analysis* for three alternative rationales), inspections now seem to be firmly planted in military law. *See United States v. Middleton,* 10 M.J. 123 (C.M.A. 1981).

Subdivision (b) addresses inspections and defines them as command examinations of persons and places for the primary purpose of insuring fitness, security and discipline. Contained in the Rule are a number of nonexclusive, general reasons for conducting inspections:

(i) To insure that command is properly equipped and functioning properly;

(ii) To maintain readiness, sea or airworthiness, sanitation and cleanliness; or

(iii) To insure that personnel are present, fit and ready for duty.

These inspections clearly are consistent with pre-Rules practice, although the more commonly recognized terms which were readily associated with these purposes — e.g., "shakedown" or "health and welfare" inspections — are missing from the Rule. Apparently, the only prerequisite for conducting this more general type of inspection is that the examination be reasonable and not for the primary purpose of obtaining evidence. The command should be prepared to demonstrate, if challenged, the purposes and manner of the intrusion. *See* Rule 311.

Inspections conducted for the specific purposes of locating and confiscating weapons and contraband are more restricted. First, the command must be prepared to demonstrate that such items would adversely affect the command's security, fitness or discipline. Second, this type of inspection must be justified either on the basis that there is reasonable suspicion that such items are in the command or on the basis that the inspection was prearranged. Inspections for weapons and contraband were apparently singled out because of the unique threat these items pose to the armed forces. This is especially true for inspections designed for the sole purpose of locating and confiscating drugs.

But because these inspections are most often closely linked with criminal prosecution and are therefore suspect, the drafters included the "reasonable suspicion" and "previously scheduled" criteria. Although minimal, they are intended to meet the danger of subterfuge searches. In *United States v. Middleton,* 10 M.J. 123 (C.M.A. 1981) the Court of Military Appeals applied pre-Rules criteria in assessing the validity of an inspection but noted that under Rule 313 contraband discovered during an inspection could be admissible if sufficient safeguards were present to insure that the inspection was not a subterfuge.

Subdivision (b) does not provide specifics as to who may conduct inspections but the drafters suggest that unless otherwise limited "any individual placed in a command or appropriate supervisory position may inspect the personnel and property within his or her control." This broad language, in conjunction with the permissible "discretion" in actually conducting the inspection also envisioned by the drafters, could prove troublesome. This could be particularly true in the case of a gate inspection, where pre-Rules cases clearly disallowed any discretion to be exercised. *United States v. Harris,* 5 M.J. 44 (C.M.A. 1978). Where possible, inspections, especially for contraband and weapons, should be closely monitored and preferably conducted as "command" examinations.

Although the Rule is silent as to actual methods or techniques for conducting inspections, the test is reasonableness. The timing, underlying reasons and manner of the intrusion are obviously key factors to be considered. However, reasonableness will not save the inspection if the primary purpose of the examination is to gather evidence for disciplinary action. In that case, Rule 313 is not applicable. As long as a valid inspection is conducted, any evidence or contraband discovered may be lawfully seized. *See* Rule 316.

Included in subdivision (b) is the provision authorizing the use of "natural or technological aids" as long as their use is reasonable. The most common aid no doubt will be drug detection dogs which have been used for some time in both military and civilian practice. Because Rule 316's prescriptions for lawful seizures govern in any inspection, drug detection dogs may be viewed as providing requisite probable cause for either seizure or a further search, Rule 315. *See, e.g., United States v. Grosskreutz,* 5 M.J. 344 (C.M.A. 1978) (alert by dog in parking lot provided adequate probable cause to search car). *See also, United States v. Middleton,* 10 M.J. 123 (C.M.A. 1981) (dog alerted during inspection).

Subdivision (c) simply codifies well-established pre-Rules law permitting admissibility of evidence discovered during administrative inventories. As in subdivision (b), these intrusions must be reasonably conducted and must not be accomplished for the primary purpose of obtaining evidence. The drafters intentionally left open the question of the lawful scope of inventories.

One of the problems we foresee with this Rule is the potential for abuse which may arise from relying upon the Rule as an alternate basis for making an intrusion. For example, suppose a commander authorizes a probable cause search of a government desk for drugs. At trial the prosecution argues first that the requirements for a probable cause search, Rule 315, were met. In the alternative, no probable cause was needed under Rule 314(d) because the property searched was the government's. May the prosecution continue to argue that under Rule 313 this was an "inspection" for contraband and thus rely on the "reasonable suspicion" requirement? The *Analysis* draws attention to the lurking misuse of inspections to cover subterfuge searches. This would be especially true it seems where the "inspection" is narrowed to one person or one desk, etc., and where the intrusion commences as a probable cause search. As under pre-Rules practice, the matter will most often turn on the motive, intent, and good faith of the commander who initiates the intrusions.

DRAFTERS' ANALYSIS

Although inspections have long been recognized as being necessary and legitimate exercises of a commander's powers and responsibilities, *see, e.g., United States v. Gebhart,* 10 C.M.A. 606, 610 n.2, 28 C.M.R. 172, 176 n.2 (1959), the present *Manual* for courts-martial omits discussion of inspections except to note that the ¶ 152 restriction on seizures is not applicable to "administrative inspections." The reason for the omission is likely that military inspections per se have traditionally been considered administrative in nature and free of probable cause requirements; *Cf. Frank v. Maryland,* 359 U.S. 360 (1959). Inspections that have been utilized as subterfuge searches have been condemned. *See, e.g., United States v. Lange,* 15 C.M.A. 486, 35 C.M.R. 458 (1965). Recent decisions of the United States Court of Military Appeals have attempted, generally without success, to define "inspection" for Fourth Amendment evidentiary purposes, *see, e.g., United States v. Thomas,* 1 M.J. 397 (C.M.A. 1976) [three separate opinions], and have been concerned with the intent, scope and method of conducting inspections. *See, e.g., United States v. Harris,* 5 M.J. 44 (C.M.A. 1978).

(a) General rule. Rule 313 codifies the law of military inspections and inventories. Traditional terms used to describe various inspections, *e.g.,* "shakedown inspection" or "gate search," have been abandoned as being conducive to confusion.

Rule 313 does not govern inspections or inventories not conducted within the armed forces. These civilian procedures must be evaluated under Rule 311(c)(2). In general, this means that such inspections and inventories need only be permissible under the Fourth Amendment in order to yield evidence admissible at a court-martial.

Seizure of property located pursuant to a proper inspection or inventory must meet the requirements of Rule 316.

(b) Inspections. Rule 313(b) defines "inspection" as an "examination . . . conducted as an incident of command the primary purpose of which is to determine and to ensure the security, military fitness, or good order and discipline of the unit, organization, installation, vessel, aircraft, or vehicle." Thus, an inspection is conducted for the primary function of ensuring mission readiness, and is a function of the inherent duties and responsibilities of those in the military chain of command. Because inspections are intended to discover, correct and deter conditions detrimental to military efficiency and safety, they must be considered as a condition precedent to the existence of any effective armed force and inherent in the very concept of a military unit. Inspections as a general legal concept have their constitutional origins in the very provisions of the Constitution which authorize the armed forces of the United States. Explicit authorization for inspections has thus been viewed in the past as unnecessary, but in light of the present ambiguous state of the law; *see, e.g., United States v. Thomas, supra; United States v. Roberts,* 2 M.J. 31 (C.M.A. 1976), such authorization appears desirable. Rule 313 is

thus, in addition to its status as a rule of evidence authorized by Congress under Article 36, an express Presidential authorization for insepctions with such authorization being grounded in the President's powers as Commander-in-Chief.

The interrelationship of inspections and the Fourth Amendment is complex. The constitutionality of inspections is apparent and has been well recognized; *see, e.g., United States v. Gebhart,* 10 C.M.A. 606, 610 n.2, 28 C.M.R. 172, 176 n.2 (1959). There are three distinct rationales which support the constitutionality of inspections.

The first such rationale is that inspections are not technically "searches" within the meaning of the Fourth Amendment. *Cf. Air Pollution Variance Board v. Western Alfalfa Corp.,* 416 U.S. 861 (1974); *Hester v. United States,* 265 U.S. 57 (1924). The intent of the framers, the language of the amendment itself, and the nature of military life render the application of the Fourth Amendment to a normal inspection questionable. As the Supreme Court has often recognized, the "military is, 'by necessity, a specialized society separate from civilian society.' " *Brown v. Glines,* — U.S. —, —, 62 L. Ed. 2d 540, 547 (1980) *citing Parker v. Levy,* 417 U.S. 733, 743 (1974). As the Supreme Court noted in *Glines, supra,* "Military personnel must be ready to perform their duty whenever the occasion arises. To ensure that they always are capable of performing their mission promptly and reliably, the military services 'must insist upon a respect for duty and a discipline without counterpart in civilian life.' " — U.S. at —, 62 L. Ed. 2d 540, 547 (1980) [citations omitted]. An effective armed force without inspections is impossible — a fact amply illustrated by the unfettered right to inspect vested in commanders throughout the armed forces of the world. As recognized in *Glines, supra,* and *Greer v. Spock,* 424 U.S. 828 (1976), the way that the Bill of Rights applies to military personnel may be different from the way it applies to civilians. Consequently, although the Fourth Amendment is applicable to members of the armed forces, inspections may well not be "searches" within the meaning of the Fourth Amendment by reason of history, necessity and constitutional interpretation. If they are "searches", they are surely reasonable ones, and are constitutional on either or both of two rationales.

As recognized by the Supreme Court, highly regulated industries are subject to inspections without warrant, *United States v. Biswell,* 406 U.S. 311 (1972); *Colonnade Catering Corp. v. United States,* 397 U.S. 72 (1970), both because of the necessity for such inspections and because of the "limited threats to . . . justifiable expectations of privacy." *United States v. Biswell, supra,* at 316. The court in *Biswell, supra,* found that regulations of firearms traffic involved "large interests"; that "inspection is a crucial part of the regulatory scheme"; and that when a firearms dealer enters the business "he does so with the knowledge that his business records, firearms, and ammunition will be subject to effective inspection," 406 U.S. 315, 316. It is clear that inspections within the armed forces are at least as important as regulation of firearms; that without such inspections effective regulation of the armed forces is impossible; and that all personnel entering the armed forces can be presumed to know that the reasonable expectation of privacy within the armed forces is exceedingly limited by comparison with civilian expectations. *See, e.g., Committee for G.I. Rights v. Callaway,* 518 F.2d 466 (D.C. Cir. 1975). Under *Collonnade Catering, supra,* and *Biswell, supra,* inspections are thus reasonable searches and may be made without warrant.

An additional rationale for military inspections is found within the Supreme Court's other administrative inspection cases. *See Marshall v. Barlow's, Inc.,* 436 U.S. 307 (1978); *Camara v. Municipal Court,* 387 U.S. 523 (1967); *See v. City of Seattle,* 387 U.S. 541 (1967). Under these precedents an administrative inspection is constitutionally acceptable for health and safety purposes so long as such an inspection is first authorized by warrant. The warrant involved, however, need not be upon probable cause in the traditional sense, rather the warrant may be issued "if reasonable legislative or administrative standards for conducting an area inspection are satisfied. . . ." *Camara, supra,* 387 U.S. at 538. Military inspections are intended for health and safety reasons in a twofold sense: they protect the health and safety of the personnel in peacetime in a fashion somewhat analogous to that which protects the health of those in a civilian environment, and, by ensuring the presence and proper condition of armed forces personnel, equipment and environment, they protect those personnel from becoming unnecessary casualties in the event of combat. Although *Marshall v. Barlow's Inc., Camara,* and *See, supra,* require warrants, the intent behind the warrant requirement is to ensure that the person whose property is inspected is adequately notified that local law requires inspection, that the person is notified of the limits of the inspection, and that the person is adequately notified that the inspector is acting with proper authority. *Camara v. Municipal Court,* 387 U.S. 523, 532 (1967). Within the armed forces, the warrant requirement is met automatically if an inspection is ordered by a commander as commanders are empowered to grant warrants. *United States v. Ezell,* 6 M.J. 307 (C.M.A. 1979). More importantly, the concerns voiced by the court are met automatically within the military environment in any event as the rank and assignment of those inspecting and their right to do so are known to all. To the extent that the search warrant requirement is intended to prohibit inspectors from utilizing inspections as subterfuge searches, a normal inspection fully meets the concern, and Rule 313(b) expressly prevents such subterfuges. The fact that an inspection that is primarily administrative in nature may result in a criminal prosecution is unimportant. *Camara v. Municipal Court,* 387 U.S. 523, 530-31 (1967). Indeed, administrative inspections may inherently result in prosecutions because such inspections are often intended to discover health and safety defects the presence of which are criminal offenses. *Id.* at 531. What is important, to the extent that the Fourth Amendment is applicable, is protection from unreasonable violations of privacy. Consequently, Rule 313(b) makes it clear that an otherwise valid inspection is not rendered invalid solely because the inspector has as his or her purpose a *secondary* "purpose of obtaining evidence for use in a trial by court-martial or in other disciplinary proceedings. . . ." An examination made, however, with a *primary* purpose of prosecution is no longer an administrative inspection. Inspections are, as has been previously discussed, lawful acceptable measures to ensure the survival of the American armed forces and the accomplishment of their mission. They do not infringe upon the limited reasonable expectation of privacy held by service personnel. It should be noted, however, that it is possible for military personnel to be granted a reasonable expectation of privacy greater than that minimum inherently recognized by the Constitution. An installation commander might, for example, declare a BOQ sacrosanct and off limits to inspections. In such a rare case the reasonable expectation of privacy held by the relevant personnel could prevent or substantially limit the power to inspect under the Rule. *See* Rule 311(c). Such extended expectations of privacy may, however, be negated with adequate notice.

An inspection may be made "of the whole or part" of a unit, organization installation, vessel, aircraft, or vehicle . . . [and is] conducted as an incident of command." Inspections are usually quantitative examinations insofar as they do not normally single out specific individuals or small groups of individuals. There is, however, no requirement that the entirety of a unit or organization be inspected. Unless authority to do so has been withheld by competent superior authority, any individual placed in a command or appropriate supervisory position may inspect the personnel and property within his or her control.

Inspections for contraband such as drugs have posed a major problem. Initially, such inspections were viewed simply as a form of health and welfare inspection, *see, e.g. United States v. Unrue,* 22 C.M.A. 466, 47 C.M.R. 556 (1973). More recently, however, the Court of Military Appeals has tended to view them solely as searches for evidence of crime. *See, e.g., United States v. Roberts,* 2 M.J. 31 (C.M.A. 1976); *but see United States v. Harris,* 5 M.J. 44, 58 (1978). Illicit drugs, like unlawful weapons, represent, however, a potential threat to military efficiency of disastrous proportions. Consequently, it is entirely appropriate to treat inspections intended to rid units of contraband that would adversely affect military fitness as being health and welfare inspections, *see, e.g., Committee for G.I. Rights v. Callaway,* 518 F.2d 466 (D.C. Cir. 1975), and the Rule does so.

A careful analysis of the applicable case law, military and civilians, easily supports this conclusion. Military cases have long recognized the legitimacy of "health and welfare" inspections and have defined those inspections as examinations intended to ascertain and ensure the readiness of personnel and equipment. *See, e.g., United States v. Gebhart,* 10 C.M.A. 606, 610 n.2, 28 C.M.R. 172, 176 n.2 (1959): "[these] types of searches are not to be confused with inspections of military personnel . . . conducted by a commander in furtherance of the security of his command"; *United States v. Brashears,* 45 C.M.R. 438 (A.C.M.R.), *rev'd on other grounds,* 21 C.M.A. 522, 45 C.M.R. 326 (1972). Among the legitimate intents of a proper inspection is the location and confiscation of unauthorized weapons. *See, e.g., United States v. Grace,* 19 C.M.A. 409, 410, 42 C.M.R. 11, 12 (1970). The justification for this conclusion is clear; unauthorized weapons are a serious danger to the health of military personnel and therefore to mission readiness. Contraband that "would affect adversely the security, military fitness, or good order and discipline" is thus identical with unauthorized weapons insofar as their effects can be predicted. Rule 313(b) authorizes inspections for contraband, and is expressly intended to authorize inspections for unlawful drugs. As recognized by the Court of Military Appeals in *United States v. Unrue,* 22 C.M.A. 466, 469-70, 47 C.M.R. 556, 559-60 (1973), unlawful drugs pose unique problems. If uncontrolled, may create an "epidemic," 47 C.M.R. at 559. Their use is not only contagious as peer pressure in barracks, aboard ship and in units, tends to impel the spread of improper drug use, but the effects are known to render units unfit to accomplish their missions. Viewed in this light, it is apparent that inspection for those drugs which would "affect adversely the security, military fitness, or good order and discipline of the command" is a proper administrative intent well within the decisions of the United States Supreme Court. *See, e.g., Camara v. Municipal Court,* 387 U.S. 523 (1967; *United States v. Unrue,* 22 C.M.A. 446, 471, 47 C.M.A. 556, 561 (1973) [Judge Duncan dissenting]. This conclusion is buttressed by the fact that members of the military have a diminished expectation of privacy, and that inspections for such contraband are "reasonable" within the meaning of the Fourth Amendment. *See, e.g., Committee for G.I. Rights v. Callaway,* 518 F.2d 466 (D.C. Cir. 1975). Although there are a number of decisions of the Court of Military Appeals that have called the legality of inspections for unlawful drugs into question, *see United States v. Thomas, supra; United States v. Roberts,* 2 M.J. 31 (C.M.A. 1977), those decisions with their multiple opinions are not dispositive. Particularly important to this conclusion is the opinion of Judge Perry in *United States v. Roberts, supra.* Three significant themes are present in the opinion: lack of express authority for such inspections, the perception that unlawful drugs are merely evidence of crime, and the high risk that inspections may be used for subterfuge searches. The new Rule is intended to resolve these matters fully. The Rule, as part of an express Executive Order, supplies the explicit authorization for inspections then lacking. Secondly, the Rule is intended to make plain the fact that an inspection that has as its object the prevention and correction of conditions harmful to readiness is far more than a hunt for evidence. Indeed, it is the express judgment of the Committee that the uncontrolled use of unlawful drugs within the armed forces creates a readiness crisis and that continued use of such drugs is totally incompatible with the possibility of effectively fielding military forces capable of accomplishing their assigned mission. Thirdly, Rule 313(b) specifically deals with the subterfuge question in order to prevent improper use of inspections.

Rule 313(b) requires that before an inspection intended "to locate and confiscate unlawful weapons or other contraband, that would affect adversely the . . . command" may take place, there must be either "a reasonable suspicion that such property is present in the command" or the inspection must be "a previously scheduled examination of the command." The former requirement requires that an inspection not previously scheduled be justified by "reasonable suspicion that such property is present in the command." This standard is intentionally minimal and requires only that the person ordering the inspection have a suspicion that is, under the circumstances, reasonable in nature. Probable cause is not required. Under the latter requirement, an inspection shall be scheduled sufficiently far enough in advance as to eliminate any reasonable probability that the inspection is being used as a subterfuge, *i.e.,* that it is being used to search a given individual for evidence of crime when probable cause is lacking. Such scheduling may be made as a matter of date or event. In other words, inspections may be scheduled to take place on any specific date, *e.g.,* a commander may decide on the first of a month to inspect on the 7th, 9th and 21st, or on the occurrence of a specific event beyond the usual control of the commander, *e.g.,* whenever an alert is ordered, forces are deployed, a ship sails, the stock market reaches a certain level of activity, etc. It should be noted that "previously scheduled" inspections that vast discretion in the inspector are permissible when otherwise lawful. So long as the examination, *e.g.,* an entrance gate inspection, has been previously scheduled, the fact that reasonable exercise of discretion is involved in singling out individuals to be inspected is not improper; such inspection must not be in violation of the Equal Protection Clause of the Fifth Amendment or be used as a subterfuge intended to allow search of certain specific individuals.

The Rule applies special restrictions to contraband inspections because of the inherent possibility that such inspections may be used as subterfuge searches. Although a lawful inspection may be conducted with a secondary motive to prosecute those found in possession of contraband, the primary motive must be administrative in nature. The Rule recognizes the fact that commanders are ordinarily more concerned with removal of contraband from units — thereby eliminating its negative effects on unit readiness — than with prosecution of those found in possession of it. The fact that possession of contraband is itself unlawful renders the probability that an inspection may be a subterfuge somewhat higher than that for an inspection not intended to locate such material.

An inspection which has as its intent, or one of its intents, in whole or in part, the discovery of contraband, however slight, must comply with the specific requirements set out in the Rule for inspections for contraband. An inspection which does not have such an intent need not so comply and will yield admissible evidence if contraband is found incidentally by the inspection. Contraband is defined as material the possession of which is by its very nature unlawful. Material may be declared to be unlawful by appropriate statute, regulation or order. For example, if liquor is prohibited aboard ship, a shipboard inspection for liquor must comply with the rules for inspections for contraband.

Before unlawful weapons or other contraband may be the subject of an inspection under Rule 313(b), there must be a determination that "such property would affect adversely the security, military fitness, or good order and discipline of the command." In the event of an adequate defense challenge under Rule 311 to an inspection for contraband, the prosecution must establish by a preponderance that such property would in fact so adversely affect the command. Although the question is an objective one, its resolution depends heavily on factors unique to the personnel or location inspected. If such contraband would adversely affect the ability of the command to complete its assigned mission in any significant way, the burden is met. The nature of the assigned mission is unimportant for that is a matter within the prerogative of the chain of command only. The expert testimony of those within the chain of command of a given unit is worthy of great weight as the only purpose for permitting such an inspection is to ensure military readiness. The physiological or psychological effects of a given drug on an individual are normally irrelevant except insofar as such evidence is relevant to the question of the user's ability to perform duties without impaired efficiency. As inspections are generally quantitative examinations, the nature and amount of contraband sought is relevant to the question of the government's burden. The existence of five unlawful drug users in an Army division, for example, is unlikely to meet the Rule's test involving adverse effect, but five users in an Army platoon may well do so.

The Rule does not require that personnel to be inspected be given preliminary notice of the inspection although such advance notice may well be desirable as a matter of policy or in the interests, as perhaps in gate inspections, of establishing an alternative basis, such as consent, for the examination.

Rule 313(b) requires that inspections be conducted in a "reasonable fashion." The timing of an inspection and its nature may be of importance. Inspections conducted at a highly unusual time are not inherently unreasonable — especially when a legitimate reason for such timing is present. However, a 0200 inspection, for example, may be unreasonable depending upon the surrounding circumstances.

The Rule expressly permits the use of "any reasonable or natural technological aid." Thus, dogs may be used to detect contraband in an otherwise valid inspection for contraband. This conclusion follows directly from the fact that inspections for contraband conducted in compliance with Rule 313 are lawful. Consequently, the technique of inspection is generally unimportant under the new rules. The committee did, however, as a matter of policy require that the natural or technological aid be "reasonable."

Rule 313(b) recognizes and affirms the commander's power to conduct administrative examinations which are primarily non-prosecutorial in purpose. Personnel directing inspections for contraband must take special care to ensure that such inspections comply with Rule 313(b) and thus do not constitute improper general searches or subterfuges.

(c) **Inventories.** Rule 313(c) codifies current law by recognizing the admissibility of evidence seized via bona fide inventory. The rationale behind this exception to the usual probable cause requirement is that such an inventory is not prosecutorial in nature and is a reasonable intrusion. *See, e.g., South Dakota v. Opperman,* 428 U.S. 364 (1976).

An inventory may not be used as a subterfuge search, *United States v. Mossbauer,* 20 C.M.A. 584, 44 C.M.R. (1971), and the basis for an inventory and the procedure utilized may be subject to challenge in any specific case. Inventories of the property of detained individuals have usually been sustained. *See, e.g., United States v. Brashears,* 21 C.M.A 552, 45 C.M.R. 326 (1972).

The committee does not, however, express an opinion as to the lawful scope of an inventory. *See, e.g., South Dakota v. Opperman,* 428 U.S. 364 (1976), in which the court did not determine the propriety of opening the locked trunk or glovebox during the inventory of a properly impounded automobile.

Inventories will often be governed by regulation.

Rule 314. Searches Not Requiring Probable Cause

(a) General rule. Evidence obtained from reasonable searches not requiring probable cause conducted pursuant to this rule is admissible at trial when relevant and not otherwise inadmissible under these rules.

(b) Border searches. Border searches for customs or immigration purposes may be conducted when authorized by Act of Congress.

(c) Searches upon entry to United States installations, aircraft, and vessels abroad. In addition to the authority to conduct inspections under rule 313(b), a commander of a United States military installation, enclave, or aircraft on foreign soil, or in foreign or international airspace, or a United States vessel in foreign or international waters, may authorize appropriate personnel to search persons or the property of such persons upon entry to the installation, enclave, aircraft, or vessel to ensure the security, military fitness or good order and discipline of the command. Such searches may not be conducted at a time or in a manner contrary to an express provision of a treaty or agreement to which the United States is a party. Failure to comply with a treaty or agreement, however, does not render a search unlawful within the meaning of rule 311. A search made for the primary purpose of obtaining evidence for use in a trial by court-martial or other disciplinary proceeding is not authorized by this subdivision.

(d) Searches of government property. Government property may be searched under this rule unless the person to whom the property is issued or assigned has a reasonable expectation of privacy therein at the time of the search. Under normal circumstances, a person does not have a reasonable expectation of privacy in government property that is not issued for personal use. Wall or floor lockers in living quarters issued for the purpose of storing personal possessions normally are issued for personal use; but the determination as to whether a person has a reasonable expectation of privacy in government property issued for personal use depends on the facts and circumstances at the time of the search.

(e) Consent searches.

   (1) General rule. Searches may be conducted of any person or property with lawful consent.

(2) **Who may consent.** A person may consent to a search of his or her person or property, or both, unless control over such property has been given to another. A person may grant consent to search property when the person exercises control over that property.

(3) **Scope of consent.** Consent may be limited in any way by the person granting consent, including limitations in terms of time, place, or property and may be withdrawn at any time.

(4) **Voluntariness.** To be valid, consent must be given voluntarily. Voluntariness is a question to be determined from all the circumstances. Although a person's knowledge of the right to refuse to give consent is a factor to be considered in determining voluntariness, the prosecution is not required to demonstrate such knowledge as a prerequisite to establishing a voluntary consent. Mere submission to the color of authority of personnel performing law enforcement duties or acquiescence in an announced or indicated purpose to search is not a voluntary consent.

(5) **Burden of proof.** Consent must be shown by clear and convincing evidence. The fact that a person was in custody while granting consent is a factor to be considered in determining the voluntariness of the consent, but it does not affect the burden of proof.

(f) Frisks incident to a lawful stop.

(1) **Stops.** A person authorized to apprehend by paragraph 19a of this Manual and others performing law enforcement duties may stop another person temporarily when the person making the stop has information or observes unusual conduct that leads him or her reasonably to conclude in light of his or her experience that criminal activity may be afoot. The purpose of the stop must be investigatory in nature.

(2) **Frisks.** When a lawful stop is performed, the person stopped may be frisked for weapons when that person is reasonably believed to be armed and presently dangerous. Contraband or evidence located in the process of a lawful frisk may be seized.

(g) Searches incident to a lawful apprehension.

(1) General rule. A person who has been lawfully apprehended may be searched.

(2) Search for weapons and destructible evidence. A search may be conducted for weapons or destructible evidence in the area within the immediate control of a person who has been apprehended. The area within the person's "immediate control" is the area which the individual searching could reasonably believe that the person apprehended could reach with a sudden movement to obtain such property.

(3) Examination for other persons. When an apprehension takes place at a location in which other persons reasonably might be present who might interfere with the apprehension or endanger those apprehending, a reasonable examination may be made of the general area in which such other persons might be located.

(h) Searches within jails, confinement facilities, or similar facilities. Searches within jails, confinement facilities, or similar facilities may be authorized by persons with authority over the institution.

(i) Emergency searches to save life or for related purposes. In emergency circumstances to save life or for a related purpose, a search may be conducted of persons or property in a good faith effort to render immediate medical aid, to obtain information that will assist in the rendering of such aid, or to prevent immediate or ongoing personal injury.

(j) Searches of open fields or woodlands. A search of open fields or woodlands is not an unlawful search within the meaning of rule 311.

(k) Other searches. A search of a type not otherwise included in this rule and not requiring probable cause under rule 315 may be conducted when permissible under the Constitution of the United States as applied to members of the armed forces.

EDITORIAL COMMENT

A variety of reasonable searches, sometimes referred to as administrative searches, have been upheld by both military and civilian courts even though no probable cause justifies the searches. Rule 314, which makes no substantial change in pre-Rules practice, gathers and codifies nine specific types of searches not requiring probable cause. The listing covers a variety of familiar intrusions.

Subdivisions (b) and (c) recognize the lawfulness and necessity of protecting the places and property under the control of the Armed Forces of the United States. Subdivision (b) addresses reasonable border searches but requires congressional authorization before servicemembers may act. Subdivision (c) follows the underlying rationale of border-type searches expressed in *United States v. Rivera,* 4 M.J. 215 (C.M.A. 1978), and authorizes commanders to conduct searches of persons or property entering overseas installations, enclaves, aircraft or vessels as long as they are conducted to insure security, fitness or good order. This provision adds to the commander's power under Rule 313 to conduct inspections at entrances and exits to military places and property, and like Rule 313, it provides that searches conducted for the primary purpose of gathering evidence for trial or disciplinary proceedings are not permitted. But this Rule, unlike 313, does not require the command to show that weapons or contraband searches are required because of the adverse effect of the illicit material. *See* Rule 313(b). The reason for the difference is that Rule 314(c) is limited to "entry searches" whereas Rule 313 is much broader and could be abused absent limitations.

Subdivision (c) also speaks to the problem whether these overseas searches must in any respect comply with existing treaties or agreements. The Rule notes that these overseas searches should not be conducted in disregard of the manner and time requirements of any applicable treaty or agreement. On the other hand, the failure to follow the treaty or agreement does not render the search invalid. This Rule apparently varies from pre-Rules case law which had required strict compliance with applicable treaties. *See United States v. Paige,* 7 M.J. 480 (C.M.A. 1979). Apparently, the change recognizes that it is more reasonable to expect personnel to comply with these Rules, which are readily available to them, than it is to expect them to know all the specifics of every treaty to which the United States may be a party.

Subdivision (d) could, as the drafters' *Analysis* notes, be considered more as a question of "adequate interest" or standing under Rule 311(a)(2). Servicemembers generally have no standing to assert that any privacy interests have been violated if the property searched is subject to government control. *See, e.g., United States v. Weshenfelder,* 20 C.M.A. 416, 43 C.M.R. 256 (1971) (search of government desk used by accused). A suppression motion usually falls for lack of an expectation of privacy. Subdivision (d) makes it clear that an accused with a legitimate possessory interest that is shared with others does not necessarily have an expectation of privacy that bars a search and seizure. Note also that in *United States v. Middleton,* 10 M.J. 123 (C.M.A. 1981) the Court of Military Appeals stated that during a legitimate health and welfare inspection the area of inspection becomes "public" as to the commander.

Subdivision (e) is grounded in *Schneckloth v. Bustamonte,* 412 U.S. 218 (1973), and generally continues pre-Rules law governing consent searches, except that the drafters have attempted to clarify who may grant the consent. *See Manual* ¶ 152. The key term in (e)(2) is "control." Thus, where the property to be searched is jointly controlled by a third party, that party may grant the requisite consent. *See Stoner v. California,* 376 U.S. 483 (1964); *United States v. Boyce,* 3 M.J. 711 (A.F.C.M.R. 1977). *See generally* Eisenberg, *Hell Hath No Fury Like ... A Hostile Third Party Granting Consent to Search,* THE ARMY LAWYER, May 1979 at 1. As before, persons granting consent may specifically define the limits of the search. *See United States v. Castro,* 23 C.M.A. 166, 48 C.M.R. 782 (1974). The Rule does not provide any hard and fast guidelines for determining voluntariness but rather recognizes that voluntariness turns on the facts of each case. The Rule does, however, clarify the importance of four factors: (i) knowledge on the part of the consenting person of the right not to consent need not be proved, but is one factor to be considered in assessing voluntariness; (ii) mere submission to color of authority is not consent; (iii) whether the consenting person was in custody at the time of granting consent also is just another factor to be considered in assessing the totality of the circumstances. *See United States v. Watson,* 423 U.S. 411 (1976); *United States v. Justice,* 13 C.M.A. 31, 32 C.M.R. 31 (1962); and (iv) prefatory rights warnings are not required, *see United States v. Morris,* 1 M.J. 352 (C.M.R. 1976), but are often helpful to the prosecution in showing voluntariness.

The prosecution's burden under 314(e)(5) is now "clear and convincing", *cf. Manual* ¶ 152 ("clear and positive"), and falls somewhere between the preponderance and reasonable doubt standards. *United States v. Middleton,* 10 M.J. 123, 132, n. 17 (C.M.A. 1981). *See also* Rule 316(d)(2) (consent to seizures of property).

Stop and frisk searches, which are limited investigatory intrusions, are covered in subdivision (f), which is consistent with pre-Rules case law. *Terry v. Ohio,* 392 U.S. 1 (1968); *United States v. Edwards,* 3 M.J. 921 (A.C.M.R. 1977). The Rule recognizes that facts supporting a temporary "stop" do not necessarily support a subsequent "frisk," which is limited to checking for weapons if the person stopped is reasonably believed to be armed and presently dangerous. Note that "stops" may only be made by persons authorized by *Manual* ¶ 19a to apprehend; by commissioned, warrant and noncommissioned officers; by Air Force security police, shore patrol and military police executing their duties; and by other persons designated to perform guard or police duties. Although the Rule does not address the issues of duration or type of questioning which may take place after the stop, those making such stops should be sensitive to the possibility that the person detained may be a suspect entitled to rights warnings before being questioned. *See* Rule 305. Questions designed simply to establish identity or reasons for particular actions should normally not require threshold rights warnings. *See United States v. Davenport,* 9 M.J. 364 (C.M.A. (1980); *United States v. Ballard,* 17 C.M.A. 96, 37 C.M.R. 360 (1967); *United States v. Kincheloe,* 7 M.J. 873 (C.G.C.M.R. 1979). *See generally United States v. Mendenhall,* — U.S. — (1980) (not a "seizure" to simply stop individual and ask for identification) (Stewart and Rehnquist, JJ.). *But see Brown v. Texas,* 440 U.S. 903 (1979) (defendant forcibly detained and questioned without justification).

Subdivision (g) follows *Manual* ¶ 152 and states the applicable standards for traditional searches incident to apprehension. Once a lawful apprehension is effected — conducted by proper authorities acting on probable cause — the person may be searched without further justification, (g)(2), and the presence of others determined (g)(3). The Rule specifically limits the scope of this type of search to weapons and evidence which can be destroyed and are within the person's immediate control. *See, e.g., United States v. Chadwick,* 433 U.S. 1 (1977). What constitutes "immediate control" will obviously turn on the facts, although an apprehending official's actions will later be measured against a reasonableness test — *i.e.,* was it reasonable for him to think that the items could have been destroyed or used to injure him? Any decision to search the premises, *i.e.,* conduct a "fan-out", for other persons will also be tested for good faith. If the apprehension is unlawful, any resulting derivative evidence, such as incriminating statements, may be tainted. *See, e.g., Dunaway v. New York,* 442 U.S. 200 (1979).

The broad authority to conduct non-probable cause searches in jails or similar facilities is recognized in subdivision (h). In the balance, any Fourth Amendment rights prisoners or detainees might have are usually subordinated to overriding interests in the security of the facility. But that does not remove the ever-present requirement of reasonableness. *Bell v. Wolfish,* 441 U.S. 520 (1979). Under Rule 312, these searches may include visual examinations of the body and searches of body cavities. Rule 312(b), (c).

Subdivision (i) is new to the *Manual* and covers those situations where good faith efforts to render immediate medical attention include a search for identification or information. *See United States v. Yarborough,* 50 C.M.R. 149 (A.F.C.M.R. 1975) (NCO properly detained and searched accused in order to obtain necessary medical aid). But a search merely to obtain information from an accident victim for purposes of completing an accident report is not within this provision. *See United States v. Ferguson,* 2 M.J. 651 (A.F.C.M.R. 1976), pet. denied, 2 M.J. 154 (C.M.A. 1976). Emergency actions might also properly include bodily instrusions under Rule 312.

The "open fields" doctrine is codified in subdivision (j) which follows *Manual* ¶ 152. Whether such intrusions are even searches within the Fourth Amendment is subject to debate. The drafters' *Analysis* points out that under certain circumstances the searched fields or woodlands may involve privacy rights which trigger the amendment's application. *Hester v. United States,* 265 U.S. 57 (1924); *Air Pollution Variance Board v. Western Alfafa Corp.,* 416 U.S. 861 (1974).

Subdivision (k) leaves the door open for recognition of other unlisted types of searches which would fit into the mold of Rule 314. Although it is difficult to foresee the searches and seizures this last provision ultimately will cover, the provision surely will be significant. Rule 314 provides protections that in some instances may go beyond those provided by the decisions of the United States Supreme Court. The drafters' *Analysis* states that it is intended that the additional protections should remain in effect even if the Supreme Court should reduce those available to a civilian accused. But when nothing specific in this Rule or other Rules provides protections, the decisions of the Supreme Court will govern under subdivision (k).

DRAFTERS' ANALYSIS

The list of non-probable cause searches contained within Rule 314 is intended to encompass most of the non-probable cause searches common in the military environment. The term "search" is used in Rule 314 in its broadest non-technical sense. Consequently, a "search" for purposes of Rule 314 may include examinations that are not "searches" within the narrow technical sense of the Fourth Amendment. *See, e.g.,* Rule 314(j).

Insofar as Rule 314 expressly deals with a given type of search, the Rule pre-empts the area in that the Rule must be followed even should the Supreme Court issue a decision more favorable to the government. If such a decision involves a non-probable cause search of a *type* not addressed in Rule 314, it will be fully applicable to the Armed Forces under Rule 314(k) unless other authority prohibits such application.

(a) General rule. Rule 314(a) provides that evidence obtained from a search conducted pursuant to Rule 314 and not in violation of another Rule, *e.g.,* Rule 312, Bodily Views and Intrusions, is admissible when relevant and not otherwise inadmissible.

(b) Border searches. Rule 314(b) recognizes that military personnel may perform border searches when authorized to do so by Congress.

(c) Searches upon entry to United States installations, aircraft, and vessels abroad. Rule 314(c) follows the opinion of Chief Judge Fletcher in *United States v. Rivera,* 4 M.J. 215 (C.M.A. 1978), in which he applied, 4 M.J. 215, 216 n.2, the border search doctrine to entry searches of United States installations or enclaves on foreign soil. The search must be reasonable and its intent, in line with all border searches, must be primarily prophylactic. This authority is additional to any other powers to search or inspect that a commander may hold.

Although Rule 314(c) is similar to Rule 313(b), it is distinct in terms of its legal basis. Consequently, a search performed pursuant to Rule 314(c) need not comply with the burden of proof requirement found in Rule 313(b) for contraband inspections even though the purpose of the 314(c) examination is to prevent introduction of contraband into the installation, aircraft or vessel.

A Rule 314(c) examination must, however, be for a purpose denominated in the rule and must be rationally related to such purpose. A search pursuant to Rule 314(c) is possible only upon entry to the installation, aircraft or vessel, and an individual who chooses not to enter removes any basis for search pursuant to Rule 314(c). The Rule does not indicate whether discretion may be vested in the person conducting a properly authorized Rule 314(c) search. It was the opinion of members of the Committee, however, that such discretion is proper considering the Rule's underlying basis.

(d) Searches of government property. Rule 314(d) restates present law, *see, e.g., United States v. Weshenfelder,* 20 C.M.A. 416, 43 C.M.R. 256 (1971), and recognizes that personnel normally do not have sufficient interest in government property to have a reasonable expectation of privacy in it. Although the Rule could be equally well denominated as a lack of adequate interest, *see, e.g.,* Rule 311(a)(2), it is more usually expressed as a nonprobable cause search. The Rule recognizes that certain government property may take on aspects of private property allowing an individual to develop a reasonable expectation of privacy surrounding it. Wall or floor lockers in living quarters issued for the purpose of storing personal property will normally, although not necessarily, involve a reasonable expectation of privacy. It was the intent of the Committee that such lockers give rise to a rebuttable presumption that they do have an expectation of privacy, and that insofar as other government property is concerned such property gives rise to a rebuttable presumption that such an expectation is absent.

Public property, such as streets, parade grounds, parks, and office buildings, rarely if ever involves any limitations upon the ability to search.

(e) Consent searches.

(1) General rule. The present *Manual* Rule is found in paragraph 152, the relevant sections of which state:

> A search of one's person with his freely given consent, or of property with the freely given consent of a person entitled in the situation involved to waive the right to immunity from an unreasonable search, such as an owner, bailee, tenant, or occupant as the case may be under the circumstances [is lawful].

> If the justification for using evidence obtained as a result of a search is that there was a freely given consent to the search, that consent must be shown by clear and positive evidence.

Although Rule 314(e) generally restates the present law without substantive change, the language has been recast. The basic rule for consent searches is taken from *Schneckloth v. Bustamonte*, 412 U.S. 218 (1973).

(2) Who may consent. The *Manual* language illustrating when third parties may consent to searches has been omitted as being insufficient and potentially misleading and has been replaced by Rule 314(e)(2). The Rule emphasizes the degree of control that an individual has over property and is intended to deal with circumstances in which third parties may be asked to grant consent. *See, e.g., Frazier v. Cupp*, 394 U.S. 731 (1969); *Stoner v. California*, 376 U.S. 483 (1964); *United States v. Mathis*, 16 C.M.A. 511, 37 C.M.R. 142 (1967). It was the Committee's intent to restate current law in this provision and not to modify it in any degree. Consequently, whether an individual may grant consent to a search of property not his own is a matter to be determined on a case by case basis.

(3) Scope of consent. Rule 314(e)(3) restates present law. *See, e.g., United States v. Castro*, 23 C.M.A. 166, 48 C.M.R. 782 (1974); *United States v. Cady*, 22 C.M.A. 408, 47 C.M.R. 345 (1973).

(4) Voluntariness. Rule 314(e)(3) requires that a consent be voluntary to be valid. The second sentence is taken in substance from *Schneckloth v. Bustamonte*, 412 U.S. 218, 248-49 (1973).

The specific inapplicability of Article 31(b) warnings follows *Schneckloth* and complies with the *United States v. Morris*, 1 M.J. 352 (C.M.A. 1976) (opinion by Chief Judge Fletcher with Judge Cook concurring in the result). Although not required, such warnings are, however, a valuable indication of a voluntary consent. The Committee does not express an opinion as to whether rights warnings are required prior to obtaining an admissible statement as to ownership or possession of property from a suspect when that admission is obtained via a request for consent to search.

(5) Burden of proof. Although not constitutionally required, the burden of proof in ¶ 152 of the present *Manual* for consent searches has been retained in a slightly different form — "clear and convincing" in place of "clear and positive" — on the presumption that the basic nature of the military structure renders consent more suspect than in the civilian community. "Clear and convincing evidence" is intended to create a burden of proof between the preponderance and beyond a reasonable doubt standards. The Rule expressly rejects a different

burden for custodial consents. The law in this area evidences substantial confusion stemming initially from language used in *United States v. Justice*, 13 C.M.A. 31, 34, 32 C.M.R. 31, 34 (1962): "It [the burden of proof] is an especially heavy obligation if the accused was in custody . . .", which was taken in turn from a number of civilian federal court decisions. While custody should be a factor resulting in an especially careful scrutiny of the circumstances surrounding a possible consent, there appears to be no legal or policy reason to require a higher burden of proof.

(f) **Frisks incident to a lawful stop.** Rule 314(f) recognizes a frisk as a lawful search when performed pursuant to a lawful stop. The primary authority for the stop and frisk doctrine is *Terry v. Ohio*, 392 U.S. 1 (1968), and the present *Manual* lacks any reference to either stops or frisks. Hearsay may be used in deciding to stop and frisk. *See, e.g., Adams v. Williams*, 407 U.S. 143 (1972).

The Rule recognizes the necessity for assisting police or law enforcement personnel in their investigations but specifically does not address the issue of the lawful duration of a stop nor of the nature of the questioning, if any, that may be involuntarily addressed to the individual stopped. *See Brown v. Texas*, 440 U.S. 903 (1979) generally prohibiting such questioning in civilian life. Generally, it would appear that any individual who can be lawfully stopped is likely to be a suspect for the purposes of Article 31(b). Whether identification can be demanded of a military suspect without Article 31(b) warnings is an open question and may be dependent upon whether the identification of the suspect is relevant to the offense possibly involved. *See* Lederer, *Rights Warnings in the Armed Services*, 72 MIL. L. REV. 1, 40-41 (1976).

(g) Searches incident to a lawful apprehension. The present *Manual* Rule is found in paragraph 152 and states:

> A search conducted as an incident of lawfully apprehending a person, which may include a search of his person, of the clothing he is wearing, and of property which, at the time of apprehension, is in his immediate possession or control, or of an area from within which he might gain possession of weapons or destructible evidence; and a search of the place where the apprehension is made [is lawful];

Rule 314(g) restates the principle found within the *Manual* text but utilizes new and clarifying language. The Rule expressly requires that an apprehension be lawful.

(1) **General rule.** The Rule 314(g)(1) expressly authorizes the search of the person of a lawfully apprehended individual without further justification.

(2) **Search for weapons and destructible evidence.** Rule 314(g)(2) delimits the area that can be searched pursuant to an apprehension and specifies that the purpose of the search is only to locate weapons and destructible evidence. This is a variation of the authority presently in the Manual and is based upon the Supreme Court's decision in *Chimel v. California*, 395 U.S. 752 (1969). It is clear from the Court's decision in *United States v. Chadwick*, 433 U.S. 1 (1977) that the scope of a search pursuant to a lawful apprehension must be limited to those areas which an individual could reasonably reach and utilize. The search of the area within the immediate control of the person apprehended is thus properly viewed as a search based upon necessity — whether one based upon the safety of those persons apprehending or upon the necessity to safeguard evidence. *Chadwick*, holding that police could not search a sealed footlocker pursuant to an arrest, stands for the proposition that the *Chimel* search must be limited by its rationale.

That portion of the present *Manual* subparagraph dealing with intrusive body searches has been incorporated into Rule 312. Similarly that portion of the *Manual* dealing with search incident to hot pursuit of a person has been incorporated into that portion of Rule 315 dealing with exceptions to the need for search warrants or authorizations.

(3) Examination for other persons. Rule 314(g)(3) is intended to protect personnel performing apprehensions. Consequently, it is extremely limited in scope and requires a good faith and reasonable belief that persons may be present who might interfere with the apprehension or apprehending individuals. Any search must be directed towards the finding of such persons and not evidence.

An unlawful apprehension of the accused may make any subsequent statement by the accused inadmissible, *Dunaway v. New York,* 442 U.S. 200 (1979).

(h) Searches within jails, confinement facilities, or similar facilities. Personnel confined in a military confinement facility or housed in a facility serving a generally similar purpose will normally yield any normal Fourth Amendment protections to the reasonable needs of the facility. *See, e.g., United States v. Maglito,* 20 C.M.A. 456, 43 C.M.R. 296 (1971). *See also* Rule 312.

(i) Emergency searches to save life or for related purposes. This type of search is not found within the present *Manual* provision but is in accord with prevailing civilian and military case law. *See, e.g., United States v. Yarborough,* 50 C.M.R. 149, 155 (A.F.C.M.R. 1975). Such a search must be conducted in good faith and may not be a subterfuge in order to circumvent an individual's Fourth Amendment protections.

(j) Searches of open fields or woodlands. This type of search is taken from present *Manual* paragraph 152. Originally recognized in *Hester v. United States,* 265 U.S. 57 (1924), this doctrine was revived by the Supreme Court in *Air Pollution Variance Board v. Western Alfalfa Corp.,* 416 U.S. 861 (1974). Arguably, such a search is not a search within the meaning of the Fourth Amendment. In *Hester,* Mr. Justice Holmes simply concluded that "the special protection accorded by the 4th Amendment to the people in their 'persons, houses, papers, and effects' is not extended to the open fields." 265 U.S. at 59. In relying on *Hester,* the Court in *Air Pollution Variance Board* noted that it was "not advised that he [the air pollution investigator] was on premises from which the public was excluded." 416 U.S. 865. This suggests that the doctrine of open fields is subject to the caveat that a reasonable expectation of privacy may result in application of the Fourth Amendment to open fields.

(k) Other searches. Rule 314(k) recognizes that searches of a *type* not specified within the Rule but proper under the Constitution are also lawful.

Rule 315. Probable Cause Searches

(a) General rule. Evidence obtained from searches requiring probable cause conducted in accordance with this rule is admissible at trial when relevant and not otherwise inadmissible under these rules.

(b) Definitions. As used in these rules:

(1) Authorization to search. An "authorization to search" is an express permission, written or oral, issued by competent military authority to search a person or an area for specified property or evidence or for a specific person and to seize such property, evidence, or person. It may contain an order directing subordinate personnel to conduct a search in a specified manner.

(2) Search warrant. A "search warrant" is an express permission to search and seize issued by competent civilian authority.

(c) Scope of authorization. A search authorization may be issued under this rule for a search of:

(1) Persons. The person of anyone subject to military law or the law of war wherever found;

(2) Military property. Military property of the United States or of nonappropriated fund activities of an armed force of the United States wherever located;

(3) Persons and property within military control. Persons or property situated on or in a military installation, encampment, vessel, aircraft, vehicle, or any other location under military control, wherever located; or

(4) Nonmilitary property within a foreign country.

(A) Property owned, used, occupied by, or in the possession of an agency of the United States other than the Department of Defense when situated in a foreign country. A search of such property may not be conducted without the concurrence of an appropriate representative of the agency concerned. Failure to obtain such concurrence, however, does not render a search unlawful within the meaning of rule 311.

(B) Other property situated in a foreign country. If the United States is a party to a treaty or agreement that governs a search in a foreign country, the search shall be conducted in accordance with the treaty or agreement. If there is no treaty or agreement, concurrence should be obtained from an appropriate representative of the foreign country with respect to a search under paragraph (4)(B) of this subdivision. Failure to obtain such concurrence or noncompliance with a treaty or agreement, however, does not render a search unlawful within the meaning of rule 311.

(d) *Power to authorize.* Authorization to search pursuant to this rule may be granted by an impartial individual in the following categories:

(1) *Commander.* A commanding officer, officer in charge, or other person serving in a position designated by the Secretary concerned as either a position analogous to an officer in charge or a position of command, who has control over the place where the property or person to be searched is situated or found, or, if that place is not under military control, having control over persons subject to military law or the law of war;

(2) *Delegee.* An impartial person to whom the authority has been delegated by a person empowered to authorize a search under (1) except insofar as the power to delegate is restricted by the Secretary concerned; or

(3) *Military judge.* A military judge or magistrate if authorized under regulations prescribed by the Secretary of Defense or the Secretary concerned.

An otherwise impartial authorizing official does not lose that character merely because he or she is present at the scene of a search or is otherwise readily available to persons who may seek the issuance of a search authorization; nor does such an official lose impartial character merely because the official previously and impartially authorized investigative activities when such previous authorization is similar in intent or function to a pretrial authorization made by the United States district courts.

(e) *Power to search.* Any commissioned officer, warrant officer, petty officer, noncommissioned officer, and, when in the execution of guard or police duties, any criminal investigator, member of the Air Force security police, military police, or shore

patrol, or person designated by proper authority to perform guard or police duties, or any agent of any such person, may conduct or authorize a search when a search authorization has been granted under this rule or a search would otherwise be proper under subdivision (g).

(f) Basis for search authorizations.

(1) Probable cause requirement. A search authorization issued under this rule must be based upon probable cause.

(2) Probable cause determination. Probable cause to search exists when there is a reasonable belief that the person, property, or evidence sought is located in the place or on the person to be searched. Before a person may conclude that probable cause to search exists, he or she must first have a reasonable belief that the information giving rise to the intent to search is believable and has a factual basis. A search authorization may be based upon hearsay evidence in whole or in part. A determination of probable cause under this rule shall be based upon any or all of the following:

(1) Written statements communicated to the authorizing officer;

(2) Oral statements communicated to the authorizing official in person, via telephone, or by other appropriate means of communication; or

(3) Such information as may be known by the authorizing official that would not preclude the officer from acting in an impartial fashion.

The Secretary of Defense or the Secretary concerned may prescribe additional requirements.

(g) Exigencies. A search warrant or search authorization is not required under this rule for search based upon probable cause when:

(1) Insufficient time. There is a reasonable belief that the delay necessary to obtain a search warrant or search authorization would result in the removal, destruction, or concealment of the property or evidence sought;

(2) Lack of communications. There is a reasonable military operational necessity that is reasonably believed to prohibit or prevent communication with a person empowered to grant a search warrant or authorization and there is a reasonable belief that the delay necessary to obtain a search warrant or search authorization would result in the removal, destruction, or concealment of the property or evidence sought;

(3) Search of operable vehicle. An operable vehicle is to be searched, except in circumstances where a search warrant or authorization is required by the Constitution of the United States, this Manual or these rules; or

(4) Not required by Constitution. A search warrant or authorization is not otherwise required by the Constitution of the United States as applied to members of the armed forces.

For purposes of this rule, a vehicle is presumed to be "operable" unless a reasonable person would have known at the time of search that the vehicle was not functional for purposes of transportation.

(h) Execution.

(1) Notice. If the person whose property is to be searched is present during a search conducted pursuant to a search authorization granted under this rule, the person conducting the search should when possible notify him or her of the act of authorization and the general substance of the authorization. Such notice may be made prior to or contemporaneously with the search. Failure to provide such notice does not make a search unlawful within the meaning of rule 311.

(2) Inventory. Under regulations prescribed by the Secretary concerned, and with such exceptions as may be authorized by the Secretary, an inventory of the property seized shall be made at the time of a seizure under this rule or as soon as practicable thereafter. At an appropriate time, a copy of the inventory shall be given to a person from whose possession or premises the property was taken. Failure to make an inventory, furnish a copy thereof, or otherwise comply with this paragraph does not render a search or seizure unlawful within the meaning of rule 311.

(3) Foreign searches. Execution of a search authorization outside the United States and within the jurisdiction of a foreign nation should be in conformity with existing agreements between the United States and the foreign nation. Noncompliance with such an agreement does not make an otherwise lawful search unlawful.

(4) Search warrants. The execution of a search warrant affects admissibility only insofar as exclusion of evidence is required by the Constitution of the United States or an applicable Act of Congress.

EDITORIAL COMMENT

Searches requiring probable cause are addressed in Rule 315. An absence of probable cause or authorization that is unexcused under the Rule may result in any evidence seized being inadmissible under Rule 311. Rule 315 generally follows pre-Rules law, sets forth applicable definitions, and indicates who may authorize these searches, the requirements of probable cause, and permissible exceptions to the requirements for proper authorization to search.

A minor change in practice occurs in subdivision (b), which now makes a distinction in terminology between civilian and military authorization to conduct probable cause searches. The military's "authorization to search" is either an oral or written direction to conduct searches for and to seize specific items. Civilian authorizations are referred to by the traditional term, "search warrant." Subdivision (b) limits authorizations to "specified" property and "specific" persons in order to comply with the particularity requirement of the Fourth Amendment.

Subdivision (c) defines the scope of the authorization and covers persons, military property, persons and property within military control (civilians) and nonmilitary property in a foreign country. *See Manual* ¶ 152. This last category, noted in (c)(4), is simply designed to promote coordination and good will between the military and other United States agencies and between the United States and foreign governments. Note that when a treaty exists, it should be followed and that, absent a treaty, concurrence of the foreign government should be sought. However failure to follow the Rules guidelines under (c)(4) does not trigger the exclusionary provisions of Rule 311. Searches potentially involving foreign governments are also addressed in Rules 311(c)(3), 314(c), and 315(h)(3).

The long standing authority of impartial commanders to authorize probable cause searches of persons or property under their control has been codified in subdivision (d) which recognizes similar authority in delegees and military judges. The term "commander" in this Rule is a question of position rather than rank and is broad enough to include warrant and noncommissioned officers and enlisted personnel who may actually be serving either as commanders of units designated as commands or in a position equivalent to "officers-in-charge." *See* Article 1 (4), U.C.M.J. (term applies to Navy, Marine Corps and Coast Guard).

Cf. United States v. Carter, 1 M.J. 318 (C.M.A. 1976) (constitutionally impermissible to saddle noncommissioned officers who determine the necessity for searches with the responsibility of implementing appropriate procedures). Likewise, the term "delegees" in (c)(2) is not limited to officers, although most commanding officers have traditionally delegated their search powers to other officers. The drafters' *Analysis* indicates this is likely to continue to be the case. The drafters' *Analysis* also suggests that "[d]elegees should be mature experienced impartial individuals possessing judicial temperament." We doubt that the choice of a delegee will be subject to a post-search challenge, however.

The preferable practice here is to execute any delegation in writing to a specific individual. The drafters note that a military judge could be a delegee under (c)(2), and subdivision (c)(3) specifically recognizes that the services generally may authorize military judges and magistrates to authorize searches without particularized authorization by a commander. *See, e.g.,* Army Regulation 27-10, Chapter 14 (authorizing military judges to authorize searches of designated persons and places).

The key requirement under (d) is that the authorizing official be "impartial." Subdivision (d), according to the drafters, is an attempt to clarify the Court of Military Appeals' decision in *United States v. Ezell,* 6 M.J. 307 (C.M.A. 1979). There the court recognized that commanders are not per se disqualified to authorize probable cause searches, but that commanders may be disqualified where they have been active participants in gathering evidence which will be relied upon to support probable cause. Cited as examples by the court were commanders who had approved use of informants, controlled buys, surveillance operations and drug detection dogs. *See generally, United States v. Rivera,* 10 M.J. 55 (C.M.A. 1980) (commander disqualified where he investigated source of probable cause). However, in *United States v. Powell,* 8 M.J. 260 (C.M.A. 1980) the court interpreted *Lo-Ji Sales, Inc. v. New York,* 442 U.S. 319 (1979), and declined to extend *Ezell* to a situation where the commander was merely present at the scene. It noted, however, that presence at the scene is a strong factor indicating involvement in the enforcement process. Subdivision (d) is therefore apparently in harmony with pre-Rules case law insofar as it addresses the mere presence question. However, the Rule may not be entirely consistent with *Ezell* insofar as (d) attempts to permit commanders to retain the mantle of impartiality even where they have authorized investigative activities. The military courts have, as does the Rule, drawn comparisons between the search authorization powers of commanders and civilian magistrates. But, the court in *Ezell* also recognized that the military commander is often involved in wide-ranging and necessary law enforcement functions and expressed concern for the ability of commanders to authorize the gathering of evidence, a police function, and then later to impartially weigh that evidence in determining whether to authorize a search, a judicial function. *See generally,* Cooke, *United States v. Ezell: Is the Commander a Magistrate? Maybe,* THE ARMY LAWYER, August 1979 at 9. To be consistent with *Ezell,* the commander's neutral authorization of investigative activities under Rule 315 must be viewed by the courts as primarily a judicial function, equivalent to the pretrial function of civilian judges.

Subdivision (e) states who is authorized to actually conduct properly authorized probable cause searches:

(i) commissioned officers;

(ii) warrant and petty officers;

(iii) noncommissioned officers;

(iv) criminal investigators (see drafters' *Analysis*), members of the Air Force security police, military police, or shore patrol when acting in execution of guard or police duties;

(v) persons designed to perform guard or police duties; and

(vi) agents of these persons.

These same individuals may also authorize or conduct exigency searches under subdivision (g), which does not require prior search authorizations. *See, e.g., United States v. Hessler,* 4 M.J. 303 (C.M.A. 1978) (valid warrantless search by staff duty officer).

The heart of Rule 315 lies in subdivision (f) which specifies the basis for search authorizations — probable cause. The traditional two-pronged test of *Aguilar v. Texas,* 378 U.S. 108 (1964) spelled out in more detail in *Spinelli v. United States,* 393 U.S. 410 (1969) and *United States v. Harris,* 403 U.S. 573 (1971), and formerly found in *Manual* ¶ 152, is restated in (f)(2): an authorizing official must reasonably believe that the information he is receiving is believable and supported by facts. This information, which may include hearsay, must be based on written or oral statements or facts otherwise known to the authorizing official so long as those facts do not render him partial.

The new provision varies slightly from the *Manual's* language in ¶ 152, which noted that where informants were providing the necessary information, the authorizing official must have first concluded that the informant was reliable or his information credible. Subdivision (f)(2) states a similar standard but requires that the information not only be "believable," but also that it have a factual basis. Thus, both prongs of the two-pronged *Aguilar* test must be satisfied. Note that Rule 311(g), *supra,* discusses the litigation of probable cause searches which may have been based on false statements. The drafters' *Analysis* provides several common examples of applications of the *Aguilar* test. *See also United States v. Land,* 10 M.J. 103 (C.M.A. 1980) (discussion of "citizen informant").

The Rule makes no mention of any requirement that the information be presented under oath or affirmation. However, the drafters were aware of *United States v. Fimmano,* 8 M.J. 197 (C.M.A. 1980) (requiring oath or affirmation) and contemplated compliance with that case.

Subdivision (g) contains exceptions to the general Rule that probable cause searches must be supported by search authorizations. Under (g)(1), time may be an exigency if there is a reasonable belief (which probably means "probable cause") that removal, destruction or concealment of items would result from any delay needed to get authorization. This exception could include the "hot pursuit" rule in *Warden v. Hayden,* 387 U.S. 294 (1967). Apparently, lack of communication with the authorizing official will be an exigency under (g)(2) only where there is an accompanying reasonable belief that as in (g)(1), delay

will result in loss of the item sought. The automobile exception is included in
(g)(3). The vehicle, excluding a government vehicle which would be covered by
Rule 314(d), must be operable — "functional for purposes of transportation."
The Rule presumes that vehicles are operable. But if a reasonable person would
have known that a vehicle could not be used for transportation at the time of
the search, no exigency is recognized.

Some miscellaneous rules for executing the searches are noted in subdivision
(h) which addresses: (1) notification to the person whose property is being
searched of the authorization; (2) the requirement of conducting an inventory
of the items seized; (3) conformance with applicable treaties or agreements
with foreign nations; and (4) applicable law where the authorization is by
search warrant. *See* (b)(2). However, failure to comply with the first three
provisions does not result in an illegal search under Rule 311.

DRAFTERS' ANALYSIS

(a) *General rule.* Rule 315 states that evidence obtained pursuant to the Rule is
admissible when relevant and not otherwise inadmissible under the Rules.

(b) *Definitions.*

(1) *Authorization to search.* Rule 315(b)(1) defines an "authorization to
search" as an express permission to search issued by proper military authority,
whether commander or judge. As such, it replaces the term "search warrant"
which is used in the Rules only when referring to a permission to search given
by proper civilian authority. The change in terminology reflects the unique
nature of the armed forces and of the role played by commanders.

(2) *Search warrant.* The expression "search warrant" refers only to authority
to search issued by proper civilian authority.

(c) *Scope of authorization.* Rule 315(c) is taken generally from ¶ 152(1)-(3) of the
present *Manual* except that military jurisdiction to search upon military installations
or in military aircraft, vessels or vehicle has been clarified. Although civilians and
civilian institutions on military installations are subject to a search pursuant to a
proper search authorization, the effect of any applicable federal statute or regulation
must be considered. *E.g.,* the Right to Financial Privacy Act of 1978, 12 U.S.C.
§§ 340-3422, and DOD Directive 5400.12 (Obtaining Information From Financial
Institutions).

Rule 315(c)(4) is a modification of present law. Subdivision (c)(4)(A) is intended to
ensure cooperation between Department of Defense agencies and other government
agencies by requiring prior consent to DOD searches involving such other agencies.
Although Rule 315(c)(4)(B) follows the present *Manual* in permitting searches of "other
property in a foreign country" to be authorized pursuant to subdivision (d), subdivision
(c) requires that all applicable treaties be complied with or that prior concurrence with
an appropriate representative of the foreign nation be obtained if no treaty or
agreement exists. The Rule is intended to foster cooperation with host nations and
compliance with all existing international agreements. The Rule does not require
specific approval by foreign authority of each search (unless, of course, applicable treaty
requires such approval); rather the Rule permits prior blanket or categorical approvals.
Because Rule 315(c)(4) is designed to govern intra-governmental and international
relationships rather than relationships between the United States and its citizens, a
violation of these provisions does not render a search unlawful.

(d) Power to authorize. Rule 315(d) grants power to authorize searches to impartial individuals of the included classifications. The closing portion of the subdivision clarifies the decision of the Court of Military Appeals in *United States v. Ezell*, 6 M.J. 307 (C.M.A. 1979) by stating that the mere presence of an authorizing officer at a search does not deprive the individual of an otherwise neutral character. This is in conformity with the decision of the United States Supreme Court in *Lo-Ji Sales, Inc. v. New York*, 442 U.S. 319 (1979) from which the first portion of the language has been taken. The subdivision also recognizes the propriety of a commander granting a search authorization after taking a pretrial action equivalent to that which may be taken by a federal district judge. For example, a commander might authorize use of a drug detector dog, an action arguably similar to the granting of wiretap order by a federal judge, without necessarily depriving himself or herself of the ability to later issue a search authorization. The question would be whether the commander has acted in the first instance in an impartial judicial capacity.

(1) Commander. Rule 315(d)(1) restates the present Rule by recognizing the power of commanders to issue search authorizations upon probable cause. The Rule explicitly allows non-officers serving in a position designated by the secretary concerned as a position of command to issue search authorizations. If a non-officer assumes command of a unit, vessel or aircraft, and the command position is one recognized by regulations issued by the secretary concerned, *e.g.,* command of a company, squadron, vessel or aircraft, the non-officer commander is empowered to grant search authorizations under this subdivision whether the assumption of command is pursuant to express appointment or devolution of command. The power to do so is thus a function of position rather than rank.

The Rule also allows persons serving as officers-in-charge or in a position designated by the secretary as a position analogous to an officer-in-charge to grant search authorizations. The term "officer-in-charge" is statutorily defined, Article 1(4), as pertaining only to the Navy, Coast Guard and Marine Corps, and the change will allow the Army and Air Force to establish an analogous position should they desire to do so, in which case the power to authorize searches would exist although such individuals would not be "officers-in-charge" as that term is used in the U.C.M.J.

(2) Delegee. Rule 315(d)(2) restates present law and explicitly permits the power to issue search authorizations to be delegated to non-officers. Delegees should be mature experienced impartial individuals possessing judicial temperament. Delegation normally should be made to an officer, but delegation to senior non-commissioned or petty officers may be made in appropriate case.

Rule 315(d)(2) permits a commander to delegate the power to authorize searches to a military judge. This power is distinct from the power of the secretary concerned under subdivision (d)(3) to authorize military judges, normally as a group, to authorize searches. Although a lawful delegation may be made across service lines, a commander may not require an individual receiving such a delegation to function as an authorizing officer unless that individual is under the command of the commander delegating the power.

(3) Military judge. Rule 315(d)(3) permits military judges to issue search authorizations when authorized to do so by the secretary concerned. Military magistrates may also be empowered to grant search authorizations. This recognizes the practice now in use in the Army but makes such practice discretionary with the specific service involved.

(e) Power to search. Rule 315(e) specifically denominates those persons who may conduct or authorize a search upon probable cause either pursuant to a search authorization or when such an authorization is not required for reasons of exigencies. The Rule recognizes, for example, that all officers and non-commissioned officers have inherent power to perform a probable cause search without obtaining of a search authorization under the circumstances set forth in Rule 315(g). The expression "criminal investigator" within Rule 315(e) includes members of the Army Criminal Investigation Command, the Marine Corps Criminal Investigation Division, the Naval Investigative Service, the Air Force Office of Special Investigations, and Coast Guard special agents.

(f) Basis for search authorizations. Rule 315(f) requires that probable cause be present before a search can be conducted under the Rule and utilizes the basic definition of probable cause found in present *Manual* ¶ 152.

For reasons of clarity the Rule sets forth a simple and general test to be used in all probable cause determinations: probable cause can exist only if the authorizing individual has a "reasonable belief that the information giving rise to the intent to search is believable and has a factual basis." This test is taken from the "two prong test" of *Aguilar v. Texas,* 378 U.S. 108 (1964), which was incorporated in ¶ 152 of the present *Manual.* The Rule expands the test beyond the hearsay and informant area. The "factual basis" requirement is satisfied when an individual reasonably concludes that the information, if reliable, adequately apprises the individual that the property in question is what it is alleged to be and is where it is alleged to be. Information is "believable" when an individual reasonably concludes that it is sufficiently reliable to be believed.

The twin test of "believability" and "basis in fact" must be met in all probable cause situations. The method of application of the tests will differ, however, depending upon circumstances. The following examples are illustrative:

(1) An individual making a probable cause determination who observes an incident first hand is only required to determine if the observation is reliable and that the property is likely to be what it appears to be.

For example, an officer who believes that she sees an individual in possession of heroin must first conclude that the observation was reliable *(i.e.,* if her eyesight was adequate — should glasses have been worn — and if there was sufficient time for adequate observation) and that she has sufficient knowledge and experience to be able to reasonably believe that the substance in question was in fact heroin.

(2) An individual making a probable cause determination who relies upon the in-person report of an informant must determine both that the informant is believable and that the property observed is likely to be what the observer believes it to be. The determining individual may rely upon the demeanor of the informant in order to determine whether the observer is believable. An individual known to have a "clean record" and no bias against the individual to be affected by the search is likely to be credible.

(3) An individual making a probable cause determination who relies upon the report of an informant not present before the authorizing individual must determine both that the informant is credible and that the property observed is likely to be what the informant believed it to be. The determining individual may utilize one or more of the following factors, among others, in order to determine whether the informant is believable:

(A) *Prior record as a reliable informant* — Has the informant given information in the past which proved to be accurate?

(B) *Corroborating detail* — Has enough detail of the informant's information been verified to imply that the remainder can reasonably be presumed to be accurate?

(C) *Statement against interest* — Is the information given by the informant sufficiently adverse to the fiscal or penal interest of the informant to imply that the information may reasonably be presumed to be accurate?

(D) *Good citizen* — Is the character of the informant, as known by the individual making the probable cause determination, such as to make it reasonable to presume that the information is accurate?

Mere allegations may not be relied upon. For example, an individual may not reasonably conclude that an informant is reliable simply because the informant is so named by a law enforcement agent. The individual making the probable cause determination must be supplied with specific details of the informant's past actions to allow that individual to personally and reasonably conclude that the informant is reliable.

Information transmitted through law enforcement or command channels is presumed to have been reliably transmitted. This presumption may be rebutted by an affirmative showing that the information was transmitted with intentional error.

The Rule permits a search authorization to be issued based upon information transmitted by telephone or other means of communication.

The Rule also permits the secretaries concerned to impose additional procedural requirements for the issuance of search authorizations.

In *United States v. Fimmano*, 8 M.J. 197 (C.M.A. 1980) the Court of Military Appeals held that individuals presenting information to an authorizing officer in the course of requesting a search authorization must present that information under oath or affirmation. The decision was not codified in Rule 315 because of its late date and the fact that a petition for reconsideration had been filed in the case. Notwithstanding its absence from Rule 315, compliance is required. Subsequent to *Fimmano* a number of the armed forces further implemented *Fimmano* by regulation. Such regulations are authorized under subdivision (f).

(g) Exigencies. Rule 315(g) restates present law and delimits those circumstances in which a search warrant or authorization is unnecessary despite the ordinary requirement for one. In all such cases probable cause is required.

Rule 315(g)(1) deals with the case in which the time necessary to obtain a proper authorization would threaten the destruction or concealment of the property or evidence sought.

Rule 315(g)(2) recognizes that military necessity may make it tactically impossible to attempt to communicate with a person who could grant a search authorization. Should a nuclear submarine on radio silence, for example, lack a proper authorizing individual, (perhaps for reasons of disqualification), no search could be conducted if the Rule were otherwise unless the ship broke radio silence and imperiled the vessel or its mission. Under the Rule this would constitute an "exigency". "Military operational necessity" includes similar necessity incident to the Coast Guard's performance of its maritime police mission.

The Rule also recognizes in subdivision (g)(3) the "automobile exception" created by the Supreme Court. *See, e.g., United States v. Chadwick*, 433 U.S. 1 (1977); *South Dakota v. Opperman*, 428 U.S. 364 (1976); *Texas v. White*, 423 U.S. 67 (1975), and, subject to the constraints of the Constitution, the *Manual* or the Rules, applies it to all vehicles. While the exception will thus apply to vessels and aircraft as well as to automobiles, trucks, et al, it must be applied with great care. In view of the Supreme Court's reasoning that vehicles are both mobile and involve a diminished expectation of privacy, the larger a vehicle is, the more unlikely it is that the exception will apply. The exception has no application to government vehicles as they may be searched without formal warrant or authorization under Rule 314(d).

   (h) Execution. Rule 314(h)(1) provides for service of a search warrant or search authorization upon a person whose property is to be searched when possible. Noncompliance with the Rule does not, however, result in exclusion of the evidence. Similarly, Rule 314(h)(2) provides for the inventory of seized property and provision of a copy of the inventory to the person from whom the property was seized. Noncompliance with the subdivision does not, however, make the search or seizure unlawful. Under Rule 315(h)(3) compliance with foreign law is required when executing a search authorization outside the United States but noncompliance does not trigger the exclusionary rule.

Rule 316. Seizures

(a) General rule. Evidence obtained from seizures conducted in accordance with this rule is admissible at trial if the evidence was not obtained as a result of an unlawful search and if the evidence is relevant and not otherwise inadmissible under these rules.

(b) Seizure of property. Probable cause to seize property or evidence exists when there is a reasonable belief that the property or evidence is an unlawful weapon, contraband, evidence of crime, or might be used to resist apprehension or to escape. Before a person may conclude that probable cause to seize property is present, the person must first have a reasonable belief that the information giving rise to the intent to seize is believable and has a factual basis.

(c) Apprehension. Apprehension is governed by paragraph 19 of this Manual.

(d) Seizure of property or evidence.

(1) Abandoned property. Abandoned property may be seized without probable cause and without a search warrant or search authorization. Such seizure may be made by any person.

(2) Consent. Property or evidence may be seized with consent consistent with the requirements applicable to consensual searches under rule 314.

(3) Government property. Government property may be seized without probable cause and without a search warrant or search authorization by any person listed in subdivision (e), unless the person to whom the property is issued or assigned has a reasonable expectation of privacy therein, as provided in rule 314(d), at the time of the seizure.

(4) Other property. Property or evidence not included in paragraph (1) — (3) may be seized for use in evidence by any person listed in subdivision (e) if:

(A) Authorization. The person is authorized to seize the property or evidence by a search warrant or a search authorization under rule 315;

(B) Exigent circumstances. The person has probable cause to seize the property or evidence and under rule 315(g) a search warrant or search authorization is not required; or

153

   (C) Plain view. The person while in the course of otherwise lawful activity observes in a reasonable fashion property or evidence that the person has probable cause to seize.

 (e) Power to seize. Any commissioned officer, warrant officer, petty officer, noncommissioned officer, and, when in the execution of guard or police duties, any criminal investigator, member of the Air Force security police, military police, or shore patrol, or individual designated by proper authority to perform guard or police duties, or any agent of any such person, may seize property pursuant to this rule.

EDITORIAL COMMENT

 Seizure of property and persons is the subject of Rule 316 which recognizes the separate requirement of probable cause for seizure, some exceptions to that requirement, and denotes who has the power to seize. The Rule generally follows *Manual* ¶ 152 and makes no substantial change in pre-Rules law.

 Subdivision (b) lays out the two-pronged probable cause requirement. It is comparable to 315(f)(2), and requires that the property in question be reasonably believed to be an unlawful weapon, contraband, evidence of crime or something that might be used to escape or to resist apprehension. Thus, a pistol found in a barracks room might be properly seized if it fits into one or more of the foregoing categories — *e.g.,* regulations prohibit its possession, it could be used to resist apprehension, or it is a suspected murder weapon.

 Seizures of persons are, according to subdivision (c), governed by *Manual* ¶ 19, which in turn specifies who may apprehend. *See also* Rule 314(g) (searches incident to lawful apprehension) and 314(f) (stop and frisks). The apprehension also must be based on probable cause. See, e.g., United States v. Texidor Perez, 7 M.J. 356 (C.M.A. 1979); United States v. Wilson, 6 M.J. 214 (C.M.A. 1979). Illegal apprehensions are treated as illegal seizures under this Rule and evidence derived from them may be challenged under Rule 311.

 Exceptions to the general requirement of probable cause are found in subdivision (d). Abandoned property may be seized without probable cause by anyone. *See, e.g., Abel v. United States,* 362 U.S. 217 (1960); *United States v. Weckner,* 3 M.J. 546 (A.C.M.R. 1977) (accused threw heroin out a window). The concept of abandonment was not specifically included in the *Manual* and often is treated as a standing question since the abandonment of property is tantamount to giving up any reasonable expectation of privacy with respect to it. *See* Rule 311 (a) (2). Consensual seizures, under (d)(2) are governed in the same manner as consent searches under Rule 314(e). Government property may be seized by anyone listed in subdivision (e) without probable cause unless an expectation of privacy exists in the property. *See* Rule 314 (d).

 Subdivision (d)(4) permits seizures of property or evidence not covered in (d) (1) to (d)(3). The seizures must be accomplished by the persons listed in subdivision (e) and must rest on probable cause that the property is of the kind noted in subdivision (b). If probable cause exists, then the seizure may be executed either (1) pursuant to a valid search authorization, Rule 315, or (2) under exigent circumstances, Rules 315(g), 316 or (3) after observing items in plain view. The plain view provision is derived from the ALI Model Code of Pre-arraignment Procedure § SS 260.6 (1975) and does not include a requirement that the "view" be inadvertent. *Compare Coolidge v. New Hampshire*, 403 U.S. 443 (1971). It does mandate that the view be accomplished in a "reasonable fashion," although the drafters have deferred to the courts the task of defining what is reasonable. *See generally* Rintamaki, *Plain View Searching*, 60 MIL. L. REV. 28 (1973). *See also United States v. Kim*, 415 F. Supp. 1252 (D. Hawaii 1976) (use of binoculars was not plain view); *United States v. Hessler*, 4 M.J. 303 (C.M.A. 1978) (plain smell theory applied).

Subdivision (e) lists the individuals who may seize property under Rule 316 and is comparable to Rule 315(e), which designates those with the power to search.

DRAFTERS' ANALYSIS

(a) General rule. Rule 316 (a) provides that evidence obtained pursuant to the Rule is admissible when relevant and not otherwise inadmissible under the Rules. Rule 316 recognizes that searches are distinct from seizures. Although rare, a seizure need not be preceded by a search. Property may, for example, be seized after being located pursuant to plain view, *see* subdivision (d) (4) (C). Consequently, the propriety of a seizure must be considered independently of any preceding search.

(b) Seizure of property. Rule 316 (b) defines probable cause in the same fashion as defined by Rule 315 for probable cause searches. *See* the *Analysis* to Rule 315 (f) (2). The justifications for seizing property are taken from present *Manual* ¶ 152. Their number has, however, been reduced for reason of brevity. No distinction is made between "evidence of crime" and "instrumentalities or fruits of crime." Similarly, the proceeds of crime are also "evidence of crime."

(c) Apprehension. Apprehensions are, of course, seizures of the person and unlawful apprehensions may be challenged as an unlawful seizure. *See, e.g., Dunaway v. New York*, 442 U.S. 200 (1979); *United States v. Texidor-Perez*, 7 M.J. 356 (C.M.A. 1979). *See generally*, paragraph 19 of the *Manual*.

(d) Seizure of property or evidence.

(1) Abandoned property. Rule 316 (d) restates present law, not addressed specifically by the present *Manual* chapter, by providing that abandoned property may be seized by anyone at anytime.

(2) Consent. Rule 316(d)(2) permits seizure of property with appropriate consent pursuant to Rule 314 (e). The prosecution must demonstrate a voluntary consent by clear and convincing evidence.

(3) Government property. Rule 316(d)(3) permits seizure of government property without probable cause unless the person to whom the property is issued or assigned has a reasonable expectation of privacy therein at the time of seizure. In this regard note Rule 314 (d), and its analysis.

(4) Other property. Rule 316(d)(4) provides for seizure of property or evidence not otherwise addressed by the Rule. There must be justification to exercise control over the property. Although property may have been lawfully located, it may not be seized for use at trial unless there is a reasonable belief that the

property is of a type discussed in Rule 316(b). Because the Rule is inapplicable to seizures unconnected with law enforcement, it does not limit the seizure of property for a valid administrative purpose such as safety.

Property or evidence may be seized upon probable cause when seizure is authorized or directed by a search warrant or authorization, Rule 316 (d)(4)(A); when exigent circumstances pursuant to Rule 315 (g) permit proceeding without such a warrant or authorization; or when the property or evidence is in plain view or smell, Rule 316 (d) (4) (C).

Although most plain view seizures are inadvertent, there is no necessity that a plain view discovery be inadvertent — notwithstanding dicta in some court cases; *see, e.g., Coolidge v. New Hampshire,* 403 U.S. 443 (1971). The Rule allows a seizure pursuant to probable cause when made as a result of plain view. The language used in Rule 316 (d)(4)(C) is taken from the ALI MODEL CODE OF PREARRAIGNMENT PROCEDURE § SS 260.6 (1975). The Rule requires that the observation making up the alleged plain view be "reasonable". Whether intentional observation from outside a window, via flashlight or binoculars, for example, is observation in a "reasonable fashion" is a question to be considered on a case by case basis. Whether a person may properly enter upon private property in order to affect a seizure of matter located via plain view is not resolved by the Rule and is left to future case development.

(e) Power to seize. Rule 316(e) conforms with Rule 315(e) and has its origins in *Manual* ¶ 19.

Rule 317. Interception of Wire and Oral Communications

(a) *General rule.* Wire or oral communications constitute evidence obtained as a result of an unlawful search or seizure within the meaning of rule 311 when such evidence must be excluded under the Fourth Amendment to the Constitution of the United States as applied to members of the armed forces or if such evidence must be excluded under a statute applicable to members of the armed forces.

(b) *Authorization for judicial applications in the United States.* Under section 2516(1) of title 18, United States Code, the Attorney General, or any Assistant Attorney General specially designated by the Attorney General may authorize an application to a federal judge of competent jurisdiction for, and such judge may grant in conformity with section 2518 of title 18, United States Code, an order authorizing or approving the interception of wire or oral communications by the Department of Defense, the Department of Transportation, or any Military Department for purposes of obtaining evidence concerning the offenses enumerated in section 2516(1) of title 18, United States Code, to the extent such offenses are punishable under the Uniform Code of Military Justice.

(c) *Regulations.* Notwithstanding any other provision of these rules, members of the armed forces or their agents may not intercept wire or oral communications for law enforcement purposes unless such interception:

    (1) takes place in the United States and is authorized under subdivision (b);

    (2) takes place outside the United States and is authorized under regulations issued by the Secretary of Defense or the Secretary concerned; or

    (3) is authorized under regulations issued by the Secretary of Defense or the Secretary concerned and is not unlawful under section 2511 of title 18, United States Code.

EDITORIAL COMMENT

In recent years growing attention has focused on the admissibility of evidence obtained through eavesdropping. *See generally* 11 A.L.R.3d 1296. Rule 317 recognizes that such evidence may have been illegally "seized" and therefore inadmissible under Rule 311. This area of the law already is so complicated and fraught with pitfalls in view of the statutory, regulatory and decisional law that exists that the drafters opted for a short, simple Rule which directs the practitioner to applicable Constitutional decisions, federal statutes and military regulations. *See generally,* Eisenberg, *Hercules Unchained: A Simplified Approach to Wiretap, Investigative Monitoring, and Eavesdrop Activity,* THE ARMY LAWYER, Oct. 1980 at 1.

Subdivision (a) notes that evidence of oral or wire (e.g., telephonic) communications is inadmissible if it is obtained in violation of the Fourth Amendment (*see, e.g., Katz v. United States,* 389 U.S. 347 (1967)) or a statute. The basic statutory scheme is set forth in Chapter 119, of the United States Code (§§ 2510-2520). *See United States v. Sturdivant,* 9 M.J. 923 (A.C.M.R. 1980) (not violation of statute to eavesdrop on telephone conversation regarding drug transaction). Violation of military directives or regulations will apparently not trigger exclusion under subdivision (a), a result inconsistent with *United States v. Dillard,* 8 M.J. 213 (C.M.A. 1980) (evidence excluded where no compliance with military regulation governing searches). It is generally consistent with *United States v. Caceres,* 440 U.S. 741 (1979) (violation of departmental regulation did not trigger exclusion of evidence).

Subdivision (b) prescribes that requests for interception of wire or oral communications within the United States will be processed under the provisions of 18 U.S.C. §§ 2516 and 2518. Interception under (b) is limited to those offenses listed in § 2516 and punishable under the Uniform Code of Military Justice. This subdivision indicates that the Attorney General or his special designate may authorize the military to seek approval of eavesdropping orders. This is consistent with 18 U.S.C. § 2516(1). Subdivision (c)(1) indicates that the statutory constraints of Chapter 119, 18 U.S.C., are applicable *only* to interceptions occurring within the United States. *See Berlin Democratic Club v. Rumsfeld,* 410 F. Supp. 144 (D.C. Cir. 1976); *United States v. Cotroni,* 527 F.2d 708 (2d Cir. 1975), cert. denied, 426 U.S. 906 (1976). Interceptions taking place overseas are controlled only by regulations. *See, e.g.,* Army Regulation 390-53, Interception of Wire and Oral Communications for Law Enforcement Purposes. Wiretapping outside the United States has been the subject of some litigation and there seems to be a trend toward requiring some form of judicial scrutiny before tapping is undertaken. Whether this is required by the Fourth Amendment is not yet clearly established.

The drafters' *Analysis* indicates an intention to limit (c) to nonconsensual interceptions, although the language of subdivision (c) does not make this clear.

In *United States v. United States District Court,* 407 U.S. 297 (1972), the Supreme Court indicated that some national security surveillance may be outside the warrant requirement. *See also Zweibon v. Mitchell,* 516 F.2d 594 (D.C. Cir. 1975), *cert. denied,* 425 U.S. 944 (1976). The statute, 18 U.S.C. § 2511(3), recognizes this possibility too.

DRAFTERS' ANALYSIS

(a) General rule. The area of interception of wire and oral communications is unusually complex and fluid. At present, the area is governed by the Fourth Amendment, applicable federal statute, DOD directive, and regulations prescribed by the Service Secretaries. In view of this situation, it is preferable to refrain from codification and to vest authority for the area primarily in the Department of Defense or secretary concerned. Rule 317(c) thus prohibits interception of wire and oral communications for law enforcement purposes by members of the armed forces except as authorized by 18 U.S.C. § 2516, Rule 317(b), and, when applicable, by regulations issued by the Secretary of Defense or the secretary concerned. Rule 317(a), however, specifically requires exclusion of evidence resulting from noncompliance with Rule 317(c) only when exclusion is required by the Constitution or by an applicable statute. Insofar as a violation of a regulation is concerned, *compare United States v. Dillard,* 8 M.J. 213 (C.M.A. 1980) *with United States v. Caceres,* 440 U.S. 741 (1979).

(b) Authorization for judicial applications in the United States. Rule 317(b) is intended to clarify the scope of 18 U.S.C. § 2516 by expressly recognizing the Attorney General's authority to authorize applications to a federal court by the Department of Defense, Department of Transportation, or the military departments for authority to intercept wire or oral communications.

(c) Regulations. Rule 317(c) requires that interception of wire or oral communications in the United States be first authorized by statute, see Rule 317(b), and interceptions abroad by appropriate regulation. *See* the *Analysis* to Rule 317(a). The Committee intends Rule 317(c) to limit only interceptions that are nonconsensual under chapter 119 of title 18 of the United States Code.

Rule 321. Eyewitness Identification

(a) General rule.

(1) Admissibility. Testimony concerning a relevant out of court identification by any person is admissible, subject to an appropriate objection under this rule, if such testimony is otherwise admissible under these rules. The witness making the identification and any person who has observed the previous identification may testify concerning it. When in testimony a witness identifies the accused as being, or not being, a participant in an offense or makes any other relevant identification concerning a person in the courtroom, evidence that on a previous occasion the witness made a similar identification is admissible to corroborate the witness' testimony as to identity even if the credibility of the witness has not been attacked directly, subject to appropriate objection under this rule.

(2) Exclusionary rule. An identification of the accused as being a participant in an offense, whether such identification is made at the trial or otherwise, is inadmissible against the accused if (A) the accused makes a timely motion to suppress or an objection to the evidence under this rule and if the identification is the result of an unlawful lineup or other unlawful identification process conducted by the United States or other domestic authorities; or (B) exclusion of the evidence is required by the due process clause of the Fifth Amendment to the Constitution of the United States as applied to members of the armed forces. Evidence other than an identification of the accused that is obtained as a result of an unlawful lineup or unlawful identification process is inadmissible against the accused if the accused makes a timely motion to suppress or an objection to the evidence under this rule and if exclusion of the evidence is required under the Constitution of the United States as applied to members of the armed forces.

(b) Definition of "unlawful".

(1) Lineups and other identification processes. A lineup or other identification process is "unlawful" if it is (A) conducted by persons subject to the Uniform Code of

Military Justice or their agents and is unnecessarily suggestive or otherwise in violation of the due process clause of the Fifth Amendment to the Constitution of the United States as applied to members of the armed forces; or (B) conducted by other authorities of the United States, of the District of Columbia, or of a State, Commonwealth, or possession of the United States, or any political subdivision of such a State, Commonwealth, or possession and is unnecessarily suggestive or otherwise in violation of the due process clause of the Fifth Amendment to the Constitution of the United States.

(2) Lineups: right to counsel. A lineup is "unlawful" if it is conducted in violation of the following rights to counsel:

(A) Military lineups. An accused or suspect is entitled to counsel if, after preferral of charges or imposition of pretrial restraint under paragraph 20 of this Manual for the offense under investigation, the accused is subjected by persons subject to the Uniform Code of Military Justice or their agents to a lineup for the purpose of identification. When a person entitled to counsel under this rule requests counsel, a judge advocate or law specialist within the meaning of Article 1 or a person certified in accordance with Article 27(b) shall be provided by the United States at no expense to the accused or suspect and without regard to indigency or lack thereof before the lineup may proceed. The accused or suspect may waive the rights provided in this rule if the waiver is freely, knowingly, and intelligently made.

(B) Nonmilitary lineups. When a person subject to the Uniform Code of Military Justice is subjected to a lineup for purposes of identification by an official or agent of the United States, of the District of Columbia, or of a State, Commonwealth, or possession of the United States, or any political subdivision of such a State, Commonwealth, or possession, and the provisions of paragraph (A) do not apply, the person's entitlement to counsel and the validity of any waiver of applicable rights shall be determined by the

principles of law generally recognized in the trial of criminal cases in the United States district courts involving similar lineups.

(c) Motions to suppress and objections.

(1) Disclosure. Prior to arraignment, the prosecution shall disclose to the defense all evidence of a prior identification of the accused at a lineup or other identification process that it intends to offer into evidence against the accused at trial.

(2) Motion or objection.

(A) When such evidence has been disclosed, any motion to suppress or objection under this rule shall be made by the defense prior to submission of a plea. In the absence of such motion or objection, the defense may not raise the issue at a later time except as permitted by the military judge for good cause shown. Failure to so move constitutes a waiver of the motion or objection.

(B) If the prosecution intends to offer such evidence and the evidence was not disclosed prior to arraignment, the prosecution shall provide timely notice to the military judge and counsel for the accused. The defense may enter an objection at that time and the military judge may make such orders as are required in the interests of justice.

(C) If evidence is disclosed as derivative evidence under this subdivision prior to arraignment, any motion to suppress or objection under this rule shall be made in accordance with the procedure for challenging evidence under (A). If such evidence has not been so disclosed prior to arraignment, the requirements of (B) apply.

(3) Specificity. The military judge may require the defense to specify the grounds upon which the defense moves to suppress or object to evidence. If defense counsel, despite the exercise of due diligence, has been unable to interview adequately those persons involved in the lineup or other identification process, the military judge may enter any order required by the interests of justice, including authorization for the defense to make a general motion to suppress or a general objection.

*(d) **Burden of proof.*** When a specific motion or objection has been required under subdivision (c)(3), the burden on the prosecution extends only to the grounds upon which the defense moved to suppress or object to the evidence. When an appropriate objection under this rule has been made by the defense, the issue shall be determined by the military judge as follows:

*(1) **Right to counsel.*** When an objection raises the right to presence of counsel under this rule, the prosecution must prove by a preponderance of the evidence that counsel was present at the lineup or that the accused, having been advised of the right to the presence of counsel, voluntarily and intelligently waived that right prior to the lineup. When the military judge determines that an identification is the result of a lineup conducted without the presence of counsel or an appropriate waiver, any later identification by one present at such unlawful lineup is also a result thereof unless the military judge determines that the contrary has been shown by clear and convincing evidence.

*(2) **Unnecessarily suggestive identification.*** When an objection raises the issues of an unnecessarily suggestive identification process or other violation of due process under this rule, the prosecution must prove by a preponderance of the evidence that the lineup or other identification process was not so unnecessarily suggestive, in light of the totality of the circumstances, as to create a very substantial likelihood of irreparable mistaken identity; provided, however, that if the military judge determines that the identification process, although unnecessarily suggestive, did not create a very substantial likelihood of irreparable mistaken identity, a later identification may be admitted into evidence if the government proves by clear and convincing evidence that the subsequent identification is not the result of the improper identification.

*(e) **Defense evidence.*** The defense may present evidence relevant to the issue of the admissibility of evidence as to which there has been an appropriate motion or objection under this rule. An accused may testify for the limited purpose of contesting the legality of the lineup or identification process giving rise to the

challenged evidence. Prior to the introduction of such testimony by the accused, the defense shall inform the military judge that the testimony is offered under this subdivision. When the accused testifies under this subdivision, the accused may be cross-examined only as to the matter on which he or she testifies. Nothing said by the accused on either direct or cross-examination may be used against the accused for any purpose other than in a prosecution for perjury, false swearing, or the making of a false official statement.

(f) Rulings. A motion to suppress or an objection to evidence made prior to plea under this rule shall be ruled upon prior to plea unless the military judge, for good cause, orders that it be deferred for determination at the trial of the general issue or until after findings, but no such determination shall be deferred if a party's right to appeal the ruling is affected adversely. Where factual issues are involved in ruling upon such motion or objection, the military judge shall state his or her essential findings of fact on the record.

(g) Effect of guilty pleas. A plea of guilty to an offense that results in a finding of guilty waives all issues under this rule with respect to that offense whether or not raised prior to the plea.

EDITORIAL COMMENT

The various military rules governing the admissibility of eyewitness identification are now located in Rule 321 which makes several substantial changes in military practice.

Subdivision (a) (1) states the general rule of admissibility. Under pre-Rules practice out-of-court statements of identification were considered hearsay and could be admitted only if they fit into the "bolstering" requirements of *Manual* ¶153*a* or under an exception to the hearsay rule. *See United States v. Burge,* 1 M.J. 408 (C.M.A. 1976) (identifying statement qualified as spontaneous exclamation). This is now changed by Rule 321. Subdivision (a)(1) provides that relevant out-of-court identifications are admissible if they satisfy the other Rules of Evidence. It is not clear on the face of the Rule, but the drafters apparently intended to permit this identification evidence even absent an in-court identification. Of course, the out-of-court identification must be independently admissible if it is to be used for its truth. An out-of-court identification may also be used to bolster an in-court identification — not for the truth of the identification — even if the witness' credibility has not been attacked. So used, the evidence presents no hearsay problems.

The fact that Rule 321 (a) interrelates with Rule 801(d)(1)(C) means that it is easy to confuse the Rules governing testimony about identifications. We think that running through four examples should help in understanding both Rules.

1. If an eyewitness to a crime testifies and makes an in-court identification while testifying, then Rule 801(d)(1)(C) allows prior identifications by this person to be used as substantive evidence — *i.e.,* for the truth of the identification, not merely for corroboration. The eyewitness himself is allowed to disclose the prior out-of-court identifications. Rule 321(a) would not be at all important once Rule 801 permits a broader use of the prior identification evidence.

2. If another witness is called to testify that he saw the eyewitness make the out-of-court identification that is admitted under 1, *supra,* this is admissible as corroborative evidence under Rule 321(a).

3. If the eyewitness who made the out-of-court identification is not present to testify, then the witness in number 2 *supra,* who saw the identification cannot testify about it, unless the identification fits within a hearsay exception — *e.g.,* it is an excited utterance by the eyewitness.

4. Even if the out-of-court identification by an unavailable witness under 3, *supra,* is admitted pursuant to a hearsay exception, other out-of-court identifications that this eyewitness may have made, which are not within the hearsay exception, are not admissible for corroboration under Rule 321(a), since the only corroboration that is permitted relates to testimony of a witness who makes an in-court identification.

Subdivision (a)(2) addresses the exclusion of certain evidence. Evidence of an out-of-court or in-court identification is inadmissible if it resulted either directly or indirectly from an "unlawful" lineup or identification process (as defined in subdivision (b)). Derivative evidence may also be inadmissible.

Under subdivision (b), both lineups and *all* other identification procedures (i.e. showups, photo arrays) may be unlawful because they are unnecessarily suggestive or otherwise deny an accused due process. Although it is not clear in the Rule, the drafters seem to have treated the term "unnecessarily suggestive" as a "technical" term which incorporates the unreliability standard of *Manson v. Brathwaite,* 432 U.S. 98 (1977). Unnecessarily suggestive identification procedures are therefore unlawful if they lead to a substantial likelihood of irreparable mistaken identification. *See also* (d)(2).

Also, lineups, but not other procedures may be unlawful if the accused's right to counsel is not honored. Here the Rule makes another significant change in pre-Rules practice. Under *Manual* ¶153a the accused's right to counsel was triggered if he was a suspect at the time of the lineup. *See, e.g., United States v. Longoria,* 43 C.M.R. 676 (A.C.M.R. 1971), pet. denied 43 C.M.R. 413 (1971). Now, under (b)(2)(A), the right to counsel at a military lineup is generally triggered much later — after preferral of charges, pretrial arrest, restriction or confinement — and generally follows *Kirby v. Illinois,* 406 U.S. 682 (1972) (although in *Kirby* a warrantless arrest or confinement was not enough to trigger the right). The Rule requires the appointment of one military lawyer. No provision is made for either a civilian or individually requested military counsel. "Line-up" for the purpose of the right to counsel could include a one-man showup but would normally not include a photographic identification — *United States v. Ash,* 413 U.S. 300 (1973); *United States v. Gillespie,* 3 M.J. 721 (A.C.M.R. 1977) — identification at the scene of the crime — *United States v. Smith,* 2 M.J. 562 (A.C.M.R. 1976) — or an accidental confrontation, *United States v. Young,* 44 C.M.R. 670 (A.F.C.M.R. 1971). The right to counsel at domestic, nonmilitary lineups is to be governed by federal practice. The drafters assumed that foreign lineups not participated in by United States authorities would not include a right to counsel. However, unreliable evidence resulting from foreign identifications may be excluded under (a)(2)(B).

Subdivisions (c) through (g) generally reflect the procedural handling of admission or exclusion of identification evidence and with only minor exceptions mirror similar procedural requirements of Rules 304 (confessions and admissions) and 311 (evidence obtained from searches and seizures). Our discussion of Rule 304 should be helpful here.

One special procedural section is subdivision (d), which addresses the prosecution's burden of proof when an appropriate motion or objection is lodged. Subdivision (d)(1) follows *Manual* ¶153a and provides that where the right to counsel issue is raised, the prosecution must prove by a preponderance of the evidence that counsel was either present or his presence was properly waived. That failing, any resulting identification evidence is inadmissible. A subsequent identification may be admissible, however, if the military judge is satisfied by clear and convincing evidence that it was not tainted by the first unlawful lineup.

Where the defense attacks the pretrial identification process as being unnecessarily suggestive, the prosecution's burden under (d)(2) extends to showing that under the circumstances the evidence is not unreliable, that is, there is not a substantial likelihood of irreparable mistaken identification. *See Manson v. Brathwaite,* 432 U.S. 98 (1977); *Neil v. Biggers,* 409 U.S. 188 (1972); *Stovall v. Denno,* 388 U.S. 293 (1967). In *Biggers* the Court cited a number of factors which should be considered in assessing the reliability of the evidence:

(a) Opportunity to view the accused at the time of the offense;

(b) Degree of attention;

(c) Accuracy of prior descriptions of the accused;

(d) Level of certainty shown by the witness at the identification process;

(e) Interval of time between offense and the identification.

See generally, Gasperini, *Eyewitness Identification Under the Military Rules of Evidence,* THE ARMY LAWYER, May 1980 at 42.

It should be noted that the wording of Rule 321(b), and also of 321(d)(2), is much less clear than is the apparent intent of the drafters as expressed in their *Analysis.* Rule 321(b) refers to "unnecessarily suggestive" procedures. It would seem to focus on the need for suggestion, rather than simply on whether a suggestive procedure nonetheless is reliable. Yet, the drafters' *Analysis* states that the language does not mean what it appears to mean and that the focus really is on reliability. Rule 321(d)(2) compounds the problem. It provides that once a proper challenge to an identification is made, the prosecutor must prove by a preponderance of the evidence that the procedure was not so unnecessarily suggestive as to create a very substantial likelihood of irreparable mistaken identity. This might appear to more clearly focus on reliability, but the fact is that the subdivision goes on to say that if the military judge "determines that the identification process, although unnecessarily suggestive, did not create a very substantial likelihood of irreparable mistaken identity, a later identification may be admitted ... if the government proves by clear and convincing evidence that the subsequent identification is not the result of the improper identification." What is unexplained is why the prior identification is "improper" if reliability, not unnecessary suggestiveness, is the test. Once again, the drafters' *Analysis* simply indicates that reliability is the key. Yet, there plainly must have been some hesitancy on the part of the drafters to ignore the problems presented by unnecessarily suggestive procedures and to embrace reliability as the sole test of fairness.

DRAFTERS' ANALYSIS

(a) General rule.

(1) Admissibility. The first sentence of Rule 321(a)(1) is the basic rule of admissibility of eyewitness identification and provides that evidence of a relevant out-of-court identification is admissible when otherwise admissible under the Rules. The intent of the provision is to allow any relevant out-of-court identification without any need to comply with a condition precedent such as an in-court identification, a significant change from the present Rule as found in paragraph 153*a*.

The language "if such testimony is otherwise admissible under these rules" is primarily intended to ensure compliance with the hearsay rule, Rule 802. It should be noted that Rule 801 (d) (1) (C) states that a statement of "identification of a person made after perceiving the person" is not hearsay when "the declarant testifies at the trial or hearing and is subject to cross-examination concerning the statement." An eyewitness identification normally will be admissible if the declarant testifies. The Rule's statement, "the witness making the identification and any person who has observed the previous identification may testify concerning it", is not an express exception authorizing the witness to testify to an out-of-court identification notwithstanding the hearsay rule, rather it is simply an indication that in appropriate circumstances, *see* Rules 803 and 804, a witness to an out-of-court identification may testify concerning it.

The last sentence of subdivision (a) (1) is intended to clarify procedure by emphasizing that an in-court identification may be bolstered by an out-of-court identification notwithstanding the fact that the in-court identification has not been attacked.

(2) Exclusionary rule. Rule 321 (a) (2) provides the basic exclusionary rule for eyewitness identification testimony. The substance of the Rule is taken from present *Manual* paragraph 153*a* as modified by the new procedure for suppression motions. *See* Rules 304 and 311. Subdivision (a) (2) (A) provides that evidence of an identification will be excluded if it was obtained as a result of an "unlawful identification process conducted by the United States or other domestic authorities" while subdivision (a) (2) (B) excludes evidence of an identification if exclusion would be required by the due process clause of the Fifth Amendment to the Constitution. Under the burden of proof, subdivision (d)(2), an identification is not inadmissible if the prosecution proves by a preponderance of the evidence that the identification process was not so unnecessarily suggestive, in light of the totality of the circumstances, as to create a very substantial likelihood of irreparable mistaken identity. It is the unreliability of the evidence which is determinative. *Manson v. Brathwaite,* 432 U.S. 98 (1977). "United States or other domestic authorities" includes military personnel.

Although it is clear that an unlawful identification may taint a later identification, it is unclear at present whether an unlawful identification requires suppression of evidence other than identification of the accused. Consequently, the Rule requires exclusion of nonidentification derivative evidence only when the Constitution would so require.

(b) Definition of "unlawful".

(1) Lineups and other identification processes. Rule 321(b) defines "unlawful line-ups or other identification processes." When such a procedure is conducted by persons subject to the Uniform Code of Military Justice or their agents, it will be unlawful if it is "unnecessarily suggestive or otherwise in violation of the due process clause of the Fifth Amendment to the Constitution of the United States as applied to members of the armed forces." The expression, "unnecessarily suggestive" itself is a technical one and refers to an identification that is in violation of the due process clause because it is unreliable. *See Manson v. Brathwaite, supra; Stovall v. Denno,* 388 U.S. 293 (1967); *Neil v. Biggers,* 409 U.S. 188 (1972). *See also Foster v. California,* 394 U.S. 440 (1969). An identification is not unnecessarily suggestive in violation of the due process clause if the identification process was not so unnecessarily suggestive, in light of the totality of the circumstances, as to create a very substantial likelihood of irreparable mistaken identity. *See Manson v. Brathwaite, supra,* and subdivision (d) (2).

Subdivision (1)(A) differs from subdivision (1)(B) only in that it recognizes that the Constitution may apply differently to members of the armed forces than it does to civilians.

Rule 321 (b) (1) is applicable to all forms of identification processes including showups and lineups.

(2) Lineups: right to counsel. Rule 321(b)(2) deals only with lineups. The Rule does declare that a lineup is "unlawful" if it is conducted in violation of the right to counsel. Like Rules 305 and 311, Rule 321 (b) (2) distinguishes between lineups conducted by persons subject to the Uniform Code of Military Justice or their agents and those conducted by others.

Subdivision (b)(2)(A) is the basic right to counsel for personnel participating in military lineups. A lineup participant is entitled to counsel only if that participant is in pretrial restraint (pretrial arrest, restriction or confinement) under paragraph 20 of the *Manual* or has had charges preferred against him or her. Mere apprehension or temporary detention does not trigger the right to counsel under the Rule. This portion of the Rule substantially changes military law and adapts the Supreme Court's decision in *Kirby v. Illinois,* 406 U.S. 682, 689 (1972) (holding that the right to counsel attached only when "adversary judicial criminal proceedings" have been initiated or "the government has committed itself to prosecute") to unique military criminal procedure. *See also* Rule 305(d)(1)(B).

Note that *interrogation* of a suspect will require rights warnings, perhaps including a warning of a right to counsel, even if counsel is unnecessary under Rule 321. *See* Rule 305.

As previously noted, the Rule does not define "lineup" and recourse to case law as necessary. International exposure of the suspect to one or more individuals for purposes of identification is likely to be a lineup. *Stovall v. Denno,* 388 U.S. 293, 297 (1967), although in rare cases of emergency (*e.g.,* a dying victim) such an identification may be considered a permissible "showup" rather than a "lineup".

Truly accidental confrontations between victims and suspects leading to an identification by the victim are not generally considered "lineups"; *cf. United States ex rel. Ragazzini v. Brierley,* 321 F. Supp. 440 (W.D. Pa. 1970). Photographic identifications are not "lineups" for purposes of the right to counsel. *United States v. Ash,* 413 U.S. 300, n.;2 (1973). If a photographic identification is used, however, the photographs employed should be preserved for use at trial in the event that the defense should claim that the identification was "unnecessarily suggestive." *See* subdivision (b) (1) *supra.*

A lineup participant who is entitled to counsel is entitled to only one lawyer under the Rule and is specifically entitled to free military counsel without regard to the indigency or lack thereof of the participant. No right to civilian counsel or military counsel of the participant's own selection exists under the Rule, *United States v. Wade,* 388 U.S. 218 n.27 (1967). A lineup participant may waive any applicable right to counsel so long as the participant is aware of the right to counsel and the waiver is made "freely, knowingly, and intelligently." Normally a warning of the right to counsel will be necessary for the prosecution to prove an adequate waiver should the defense adequately challenge the waiver. *See, e.g., United States v. Ayers,* 426 F.2d 524 (2d Cir. 1970). *See also* Model Rules for Law Enforcement, Eye Witness Identification, Rule 404 (1974) cited in E. IMWINKELRIED, P. GIANNELLI, F. GILLIGAN & F. LEDERER, CRIMINAL EVIDENCE 366 (1979).

Subdivision (b) (2) (B) grants a right to counsel at non-military lineups within the United States only when such a right to counsel is recognized by "the principles of law generally recognized in the trial of criminal cases in the United States district courts involving similar lineups." The Rule presumes that an individual participating in a foreign lineup conducted by officials of a foreign nation without American participation has no right to counsel at such a lineup.

(c) *Motions to suppress and objections.* Rule 321(c) is identical in application to Rule 311(d). *See* the *Analysis* to Rules 304 and 311.

(d) *Burden of proof.* Rule 321(d) makes it clear that when an eyewitness identification is challenged by the defense, the prosecution need reply only to the specific cognizable defense complaint. *See also* Rules 304 and 311. The subdivision distinguishes between defense challenges involving alleged violations of the right to counsel and those involving alleged unnecessarily suggestive identifications.

(1) *Right to counsel.* Subdivision (d) (1) requires that when an alleged violation of the right to counsel has been raised, the prosecution must either demonstrate by a preponderance of the evidence that counsel was present or that the right to counsel was waived voluntarily and intelligently. The Rule also declares that if the right to counsel is violated at a lineup that results in an identification of the accused, any later identification is considered a result of the prior lineup as a matter of law unless the military judge determines by clear and convincing evidence that the later identification is not the result of the first lineup. Subdivision (d) (1) is taken in substance from present *Manual* paragraph 153a.

(2) *Unnecessarily suggestive identification.* Rule 321 (d) (2) deals with an alleged unnecessarily suggestive identification or with any other alleged violation of due process. The subdivision makes it clear that the prosecution must show, when the defense has raised the issue, that the identification in question was not, based upon a preponderance of the evidence, "so unnecessarily suggestive, in light of the totality of the circumstances, as to create a very substantial likelihood of irreparable mistaken identity." This rule is taken from the Supreme Court's decisions of Neil v. Biggers, 409 U.S. 188 (1972) and Stovall v. Denno, 388 U.S. 293 (1967), and unlike subdivision (d)(1), applies to all identification processes whether lineups or not. The Rule recognizes that the nature of the identification process itself may well be critical to the reliability of the identification and provides for exclusion of unreliable evidence regardless of its source. If the prosecution meets its burden, the mere fact that the identification process was unnecessary or suggestive does not require exclusion of the evidence. *Manson v. Brathwaite, supra.*

If the identification in question is subsequent to an earlier, unnecessarily suggestive identification, the later identification is admissible if the prosecution can show by clear and convincing evidence that the later identification is not the result of the earlier improper examination. This portion of the Rule is consistent both with present *Manual* paragraph 153*a* and *Kirby v. Illinois,* 406 U.S. 682 (1972).

(e) Defense evidence. Rule 321 (e) is identical with the analagous provisions in Rules 304 and 311 and generally restates present law.

(f) Rulings. Rule 321 (f) is identical with the analagous provisions in Rules 304 and 321 and substantially changes present law. *See* the *Analysis* to Rule 304(d)(4).

(g) Effect of guilty pleas. Rule 321 (g) is identical with the analagous provisions in Rules 304 and 311 and restates present law.

SECTION IV. RELEVANCY AND ITS LIMITS

Rule 401. Definition of "Relevant Evidence"

"Relevant evidence" means evidence having any tendency to make the existence of any fact that is of consequence to the determination of the action more probable or less probable than it would be without the evidence.

EDITORIAL COMMENT

A basic tenet of American jurisprudence is that finders of fact may consider only relevant evidence. Rule 401 codifies traditional federal practice and adopts a logical approach to relevance, although the language of the Rule is somewhat different than that used in past military authority. *See* ¶ 74 *a* (3) of the *Manual* which has been amended to indicate that both circumstantial and direct evidence can satisfy the relevancy criteria.

Under Rule 401, evidence is relevant if it has "any tendency" to make an issue in the case "more or less probable" than it would have been without the evidence. By using the phrase "any tendency," the drafters have not attempted to make evidence meet a higher "legal relevance" standard, which has sometimes been used in military courts. Anything that can help rationally decide disputed issues is relevant. *See, e.g., United States v. Ives,* 609 F.2d 930, 933 (9th Cir. 1979) where the court held that weak, even remote, defense evidence of mental responsibility was erroneously rejected by the trial judge. *See also United States v. McCullers,* 7 M.J. 824 (A.C.M.R. 1979).

It is important to note that the Rule does not use the word "materiality." Instead, it uses the term "fact that is of consequence to the determination of the action" to refer to the type of issue on which evidence can be offered. The drafters of the Federal Rule, from which the Military Rule is taken, felt that the word "materiality" was overused and had so many different meanings that

171

it was unhelpful. (In the *Manual* ¶ 137 "materiality" was said to mean the same thing as "relevance.") But the difference is one of form and not substance. Anything that would have been "material" prior to the adoption of the Rules should be of consequence to the determination of the action. An objection on relevant grounds covers everything traditionally covered by a "materiality" objection.

The words chosen by the drafters of the Federal Rule are almost as ambiguous as the word "materiality." Does "of consequence" mean an important issue or any issue? The answer in our view is that it means any issue that is fairly raised in the case. The previous *Manual* ¶ 137 had indicated that evidence could be rejected if it did not tend to prove a disrupted issue or if it was remote. A proper analysis under Rule 401 leads to the conclusion that remoteness is not a question to be resolved under this Rule, unless evidence is so remote that it is of no help in a case. *See, e.g., United States v. Bassett,* 4 M.J. 736, 739 (1978). If it is of any value at all, then it qualifies under the Rule. However, it might still be excluded under Rule 403.

Relevancy must be established with respect to every item of evidence. No evidence possesses inherent relevance. The trial judge has four basic choices with respect to how he should rule on relevancy issues: (1) exclude the evidence; (2) admit all the evidence; (3) admit all the evidence subject to a limiting instruction; (4) admit part of the evidence and exclude part. In deciding which ruling to make, trial judges should require counsel to do three things: (1) describe the evidence; (2) explain its nexus to the consequential issue at bar; and (3) indicate how the offered evidence will establish the fact in question. Although the primary responsibility for meeting these requirements rests with counsel (Rule 103), it may be in the trial judge's best interest to assist in this demonstration, particularly when difficult instructional issues are likely to result (Rule 105).

In many instances it will be obvious why evidence is relevant, and no purpose would be served by spending valuable judicial resources rehearsing what is clear to everyone participating at trial. But in some cases the relation of evidence to an issue in the case is obscure. The trial judge should not hesitate in such cases to ask for the explanation suggested above, and opposing counsel should insist upon it.

Once the explanation is made, the trial judge should be careful to analyze whether an issue really is of consequence to the action. For example, if the government offers evidence to show modus operandi when identity is not in dispute, the evidence could not be of consequence to the action since the parties are not fighting about the issue to which the evidence is directed.

The trial judge also should take care to assure that the evidence is relevant to an issue that the law allows parties to prove. For example, evidence that a defendant charged with murder or rape is an aggressive person is excluded under Rule 404(a), when offered by the government in the first instance. An argument that such character evidence is relevant and should be admitted cannot overcome the specific rule that excludes evidence whether relevant or not. If, however, the defendant opens the door, relevant character evidence might be admitted.

It is important, we think, for the trial judge to make a decision on whether evidence is relevant before moving on to consider Rule 403. There are two reasons for this. First, irrelevant evidence never is admitted at trial. Rule 402 keeps it out. Thus, if evidence is irrelevant there is no need to try to identify specific prejudice and to strike a balance. Irrelevant evidence cannot help and cannot be used; there is no balancing to be done. Second, Rule 403 requires that a balance be struck between the probative value and the prejudicial effect of evidence. The best way to ascertain probative value is to decide why evidence is relevant. This can be done by considering the three things we described above. Then the trial judge is in a position to recognize the costs associated with exclusion of evidence and to use Rule 403 properly. *See generally United States v. McRary,* 616 F.2d 181, 184 (5th Cir. 1980) discussing the interrelation of Rules 401, 402 and 403; Saltzburg, *A Special Aspect of Relevance: Countering Negative Inferences Associated with the Absence of Evidence,* 66 Cal. L. Rev. 1011, 1014-15 (1978).

DRAFTERS' ANALYSIS

The definition of "relevant evidence" found within Rule 401 is taken without change from the Federal Rule and is substantially similar in effect to that used by present *Manual* ¶ 137. The Rule's definition may be somewhat broader than the *Manual's,* as the Rule defines as relevant any evidence that has "any tendency to make the existence of any fact . . . more probable or less probable than it would be without the evidence," while the *Manual* defines as "not relevant" evidence "too remote to have any appreciable probative value. . . ." To the extent that the *Manual's* definition includes considerations of "legal relevance," those considerations are adequately addressed by such other Rules as Rules 403 and 609. *See, e.g.,* E. Imwinkelried, P. Giannelli, F. Gilligan & F. Lederer, Criminal Evidence 62-65 (1979) [which, after defining "logical relevance" as involving only probative value, states at 63 that "under the rubric of 'legal relevance,' the courts have imposed an additional requirement that the item's probative value outweighs any attendant probative dangers."]. The Rule is similar to the present *Manual* in that it abandons any reference to "materiality" in favor of a single standard of "relevance." Notwithstanding the specific terminology used, however, the concept of materiality survives in the Rule's condition that to be relevant evidence must involve a fact "which is of consequence to the determination of the action."

Rule 402. Relevant Evidence Generally Admissible; Irrelevant Evidence Inadmissible

All relevant evidence is admissible, except as otherwise provided by the Constitution of the United States as applied to members of the armed forces, the Uniform Code of Military Justice, these rules, this Manual, or any Act of Congress applicable to members of the armed forces. Evidence which is not relevant is not admissible.

EDITORIAL COMMENT

Rule 401 defines relevance, and this Rule states that all relevant evidence is admissible, except evidence falling into any one of five categories. These include evidence which violates: (1) the Constitution, as it is applied to the military; (2) the Uniform Code of Military Justice; (3) the Manual for Courts-Martial; (4) the Military Rules of Evidence; and (5) any Congressional limitation which might specifically concern court-martials. Evidence falling in these categories cannot be admitted even though it is relevant. For example, if an accused's pretrial statement is not properly preceded by Article 31 U.C.M.J. warnings, it would nonetheless be relevant to determining his guilt or innocence, but for policy reasons it has traditionally been suppressed. *See* our discussion of Rule 305. Other relevant evidence may be admitted, but it need not always be, since a provision like Military Rule of Evidence 403 may result in exclusion. Irrelevant evidence is never admissible. It cannot help in the effort to reach an accurate and fair result.

Application of Rule 402 should be less difficult than it might appear from its reference to various sources of law. Essentially, the Rule requires that three questions may have to be addressed before evidence is admitted. First, does the evidence qualify under Rule 401's definition? Second, will the evidence violate any of the five prohibitions listed in Rule 402? Third, will the evidence satisfy any rule that requires a judicial assessment of the probative value of the evidence and the possible reliability or prejudice problems presented by the evidence. *See, e.g.,* Rules 403, 611, 803(6), 803(24), 804(b)(5) and 1003.

Rule 402's requirements are not that different from those formerly contained in ¶137 of the *Manual*. Although the Military and Federal versions of Rule 402 are slightly different in content, they should produce very similar results.

Questions may arise concerning what the bench should do when counsel fail to object to irrelevant evidence. Is there a *sua sponte* obligation to protect the court-members from irrelevant evidence? We believe that a judge who fears that evidence cannot be relevant is well advised to ask why the evidence is offered. If no valid answer is provided, an objection should be expected and should be sustained. If however, the judge mistakenly thinks the evidence is relevant, says nothing and hears no objection, there should be no reversal, unless the introduction of the irrelevant evidence amounts to plain error under Rule 103(d). There is no reason to encourage counsel to sit on relevancy objections in the hope of introducing his own irrelevant matters in rebuttal, thus making it necessary for the court to decide whether one party can "fight fire with fire."

DRAFTERS' ANALYSIS

Rule 402 is taken without significant change from the Federal Rule. The Federal Rule's language relating to limitations imposed by "the Constitution of the United States, by Act of Congress, by these rules, or by other rules prescribed by the Supreme Court pursuant to statutory authority" has been replaced by material tailored to the unique nature of the Military Rules of Evidence. Rule 402 recognizes that the Constitution may apply somewhat differently to members of the armed forces than to civilians, and the Rule deletes the Federal Rule's reference to "other rules prescribed by the Supreme Court" because such Rules do not apply directly in courts-martial. *See* Rule 101(b)(2).

Rule 402 provides a general standard by which irrelevant evidence is always inadmissible and by which relevant evidence is generally admissible. Qualified admissibility of relevant evidence is required by the limitations in Sections III and V and by such other Rules as 403 and 609 which intentionally utilize matters such as degree of probative value and judicial efficiency in determining whether relevant evidence should be admitted.

Rule 402 is not significantly different in its effect from ¶ 137 of the present *Manual* which it replaces, and procedures used under the present *Manual* in determining relevance generally remain valid. Offers of proof are encouraged when items of doubtful relevance are proffered, and it remains possible, subject to the discretion of the military judge, to offer evidence "subject to later connection." Use of the latter technique, however, must be made with. great care to avoid the possibility of bringing inadmissible evidence before the members of the court.

It should be noted that Rule 402 is potentially the most important of the new rules. Neither the Federal Rules of Evidence nor the Military Rules of Evidence resolve all evidentiary matters; *see, e.g.,* Rule 101(b). When specific authority to resolve an evidentiary issue is absent, Rule 402's clear result is to make relevant evidence admissible.

Rule 403. Exclusion of Relevant Evidence on Grounds of Prejudice, Confusion, or Waste of Time

Although relevant, evidence may be excluded if its probative value is substantially outweighed by the danger of unfair prejudice, confusion of the issues, or misleading the members, or by considerations of undue delay, waste of time, or needless presentation of cumulative evidence.

EDITORIAL COMMENT

Rule 403 for the first time codifies the power of the trial judge to exclude probative evidence on the ground that its admission would do more harm than good. Previous *Manual* renditions, particularly ¶ 137, failed to adequately address the judge's power to exclude such evidence. Judicial decisions filled the void and recognized the need for balancing. *See United States v. Bartholomew*, 1 C.M.A. 314, 307, 3 C.M.R. 41, 48 (1952) (recognizing that any danger of unfair prejudice from using gruesome photographs was "overborne" by the evidence's probative value).

Rule 403 may be the most important new Rule. It provides that any evidence, no matter how probative, may be rejected if its probative value is substantially outweighed by the danger that it will result in any of six evils: (1) Unfair prejudice, (2) confusion on an important issue, (3) misleading court-members, (4) undue delay, (5) waste of time, or (6) presentation of needlessly cumulative evidence. (The last three are somewhat redundant.)

There is little doubt that the trial judge is given enormous leeway under this Rule to judge the merits and demerits of admitting any evidence that satisfies the other Rules of Evidence. To rule properly the trial judge will have to pay close attention to the other evidence in the case, to the theory of admissibility relied upon by the proponent of the evidence, and to the possible misuse or detrimental influence of the evidence which the opponent fears. Here, as elsewhere under the Rules, the better counsel do their job in educating the judge about their concerns, the more enlightened the judge's ruling is likely to be.

Striking an appropriate balance under the Rule requires an analysis of several concepts that are quite different. Probative value involves a logical process of reasoning favored by the law. Prejudicial effect means some unwelcome influence on the logical process and is disfavored. The time concerns of the Rule speak to questions of scarce judicial resources and not to probative value or prejudice. Weighing such different concepts against each other to reach an accommodation under the Rule is indeed a demanding task.

The use of the word "substantially" in the Rule suggests that in close cases the drafters intended that evidence should be admitted rather than excluded. If evidence is admitted, the trial judge can give explanatory or cautionary instructions to the court-members, and it is possible that the court-members will properly use the evidence. But if evidence is excluded, the court-members will not see it and will have no opportunity to derive any benefit from it. The Rule wants the trial judge to be confident that the evidence will do more harm than good before excluding it and removing it entirely from the case. In making a ruling, the judge should consider the utility of limiting instructions, the deletion of part, but not all, of prejudicial evidence, and any other technique short of overall exclusion before depriving a party of probative material.

There is some dispute among the commentators as to how the judge should strike the balance. Most would assume that the judge should consider that the cost of excluding evidence is the deprivation of the proponent's opportunity to ask the court-members to give the evidence its maximum probative force, which the members could do if the evidence were admitted. The difference of opinion comes in the approach to the prejudicial effect of evidence. One commentator would assume that the evidence has the lowest possible prejudicial effect. Another would assume that evidence is likely to be as prejudicial as it might possibly be. A third view is that the judge should carefully analyze the nature of the case, the court-members, the other evidence in the case and the way the case has been presented in order to estimate the real likelihood in the particular case that the evidence would prejudice the court-members hearing the case. This is the approach that makes the most sense to us, since it accepts the Rule's implicit assumption that the members can be improperly influenced by evidence, but it assumes that a careful case-by-case balancing of probative value and prejudicial effect is needed to make the Rule work correctly. The various approaches are spelled out in S. SALTZBURG & K. REDDEN, FEDERAL RULES OF EVIDENCE MANUAL (1980 Supp.) at 42. We adopt the approach suggested there.

In our view, the words "unfairly prejudicial" signify that the danger to be avoided is the use of the evidence for something other than its logical, probative force. An emotional reaction to evidence would distort the fact-finding function and could be prejudicial. The possibility that court-members would dramatically overestimate the value of evidence or be confused as to its meaning should be treated as "prejudicial" effects. The balance is between the prejudice that the law wishes to avoid and the probative value that the law wants to have.

As difficult as the balancing is, it can be aided by special findings in which the trial judge gives reasons for his decision. *See* Schinasi, *Special Findings: Their Use at Trial and on Appeal,* 87 MIL. L. REV. 73 (1980). Substantial authority supports the use of special findings in virtually all Rule 403 determinations. This is so particularly because the Rule operates on an *ad hoc* basis and requires the evaluation of diverse factual and legal concepts.

Special findings will provide trial and appellate courts with two obvious benefits. First, appellate courts will be able to appreciate the formula used to resolve complex issues below. As a result, reversals for abuse of discretion will be greatly reduced. The second benefit of special findings is that they provide counsel with an opportunity to correct erroneous resolutions in the trial court, rather than months or years later on appeal.

Recent federal decisions indicate that there is some controversy over special findings. In *United States v. Potter,* 616 F.2d 384 (9th Cir. 1980), a physician was convicted for illegally prescribing medication. In discussing the judge's use of Rule 403 and extrinsic offense evidence, (see Rule 404(b)) the court held that sua sponte special findings were not necessary. In *United States v. Slade,* — F.2d — (D.C. Cir. 1980) the court reversed a conviction because the trial judge excluded key evidence without explanation. Had special findings been offered, the court might have come out differently. *United States v. Milhollan,* 599 F.2d 518 (3d Cir. 1979) makes the useful suggestion that the problems attendant to sua sponte special findings can be alleviated by counsel merely requesting them when a Rule 403 resolution is made. Counsel must make very sure that an actual 403 objection is made, not just a relevance objection, or no findings will be required, and no review under Rule 403 will be possible. *See United States v. Long,* 574 F.2d 761 (3d Cir. 1978).

We believe special findings should accompany Rule 403 rulings following proper objections. They can, and often should be, oral, thus relieving trial judges from the unnecessary work of making written findings. Article 51(d) UCMJ; and ¶ 4*i,* Manual for Courts Martial.

Although Rule 403 has broad applicability, we anticipate its greatest use in two areas. The first deals with evidence about other acts of the accused. In the federal system, Rule 403 is generally applied with Rule 404, and together they are the most often cited provisions in the Federal Rules of Evidence. The military has had a similar experience. Even before the Military Rules of Evidence were adopted, several appellate courts had already used Rule 403 in connection with an accused's acts. In *United States v. Dawkins,* 2 M.J. 898, 900 (A.C.M.R. 1976), for example, the court used Rule 403 with Rule 404 in the same manner as in the federal circuit courts. The government introduced extensive extrinsic offense evidence as part of its attack on the accused's alibi defense. Finding that the trial judge had "achieved a reasonable balance between the need for using available evidence and the risk of undue harm to an accused," the court affirmed the trial judge and approved his use of limiting instructions and his careful preparation of the evidence to insure that Rule 403 would not be violated.

The second area in which Rule 403 often will be used involves physical, documentary, and scientific evidence. Physical evidence tends to be viewed by laymen as being particularly important, even when it actually has little value in a case. A classic example occurs in drug prosecutions where the accused is charged with possessing large amounts of marijuana. The prosecution often will parade the voluminous quantities of contraband before the court-members in an attempt to highlight the offense's seriousness. Such conduct rarely assists in determining whether or not the accused actually committed the charged offense, but for some reason having the drugs present, and paraded in large quantities, seems to make the accused's conviction more likely. This should not be encouraged. Judicious use of Rule 403 would permit the government to prove the substance was marijuana, but not to display it to the court-members. Judges should be wary of approaches like that of the government in *United States v. Lowe,* 569 F.2d 1113 (10th Cir. 1978) where the prosecution was able to prove a kidnapped baby's identity by displaying the child to its mother, notwithstanding defense counsel's offer to stipulate to identity. The parent-child reunion in court added nothing to what the stipulation would have established and threatened to add an emotional element to the case.

Probably the most common documentary evidence problem concerns photographic evidence. Prosecutors traditionally attempt to aggravate criminal misconduct by showing slides, movies and still photographs of the victim. Although military courts have not yet reached uniformity in this area, they generally apply a Rule 403 type balance. In *United States v. Bellamy*, 47 C.M.R. 319, 322 (A.C.M.R. 1973) the prosecution admitted a photograph of a homicide victim for identification purposes. On appeal, the court defined the allegation of error in Rule 403 terms: "The problem presented is whether the probative value of the photograph outweighs the nature of the inflammatory exhibit." The Army Court of Review affirmed admission even though trial defense counsel had attempted to stipulate to the victim's identity. *See also United States v. Noreen*, 48 C.M.R. 228, 233 (A.C.M.R. 1973), where the reviewing court affirmed a conviction even though photographs of the homicide victim had been admitted *after* the crucial facts were established and defense counsel had indicated he would not contest the issue. Applying a 403-type approach the court held, "[in] our opinion the probative value . . . outweighed the inflammatory nature of this evidence." In *United States v. Tua*, 4 M.J. 761 (A.C.M.R. 1977) the Army Court of Review was faced with photographs and a movie film depicting a particularly savage beating. Affirming conviction, the court opined, without mentioning Rule 403, that because the evidence was admissible for legitimate purposes, its "shock value" was overridden by its probative value. It recognized that in such cases any evidence will excite the court members, but said that factor alone did not render it inadmissible. In our view, none of these cases adequately handled the Rule 403 issue. When an issue is undisputed it is difficult to see how evidence tending to prove it is relevant under Rule 401. Even if it is slightly relevant, the prejudicial effect of showing gruesome photos to the court-members should be obvious. It should also not be permitted. *Cf. United States v. Mohel*, 604 F.2d 748 (2d Cir. 1979) (conviction reversed because proper stipulation was refused). *See Manual* ¶ 54f's amended treatment of stipulations. *See also United States v. Grassi*, 602 F.2d 1192 (5th Cir. 1979).

The Army Court of Review has specifically used Rule 403 in determining the value of expert testimony. In *United States v. Hicks*, 7 M.J. 561, 566 (A.C.M.R. 1979) defense counsel requested that the government obtain an expert in the area of eyewitness identification. Defense counsel wanted to use this witness to discredit key government testimony. The trial judge denied the defense's request. Relying on Rule 403, the court affirmed conviction, indicating that the proffered testimony "would create a substantial danger of undue prejudice and confusion because of its aura of special reliability and trustworthiness, and that it would have limited probative value directed, as it is, to the expert's thesis rather than the actual eyewitness accounts."

Finally it should be noted that Rule 403 is a check on evidence admissibility; it is not a license to ignore Rule 402's prohibitions concerning irrelevancy, nor any other provision's specific limitations. Rule 403 is a one-way street; it can make relevant evidence inadmissible, but it cannot make irrelevant or otherwise inadmissible evidence admissible. For example, hearsay evidence that satisfies Rule 801, 803, or 804 is admissible, but can be excluded under Rule 403. *See, e.g., United States v. Salisbury,* 50 C.M.R. 175, 181 (A.C.M.R. 1975) (using Rule 403 to test hearsay statements offered against the accused). Hearsay evidence not qualifying for admission under Section VIII is never admissible under Rule 403.

DRAFTERS' ANALYSIS

Rule 403 is taken without change from the Federal Rule of Evidence. The Rule incorporates the concept often known as "legal relevance", see the *Analysis* to Rule 401, and provides that evidence may be excluded for the reasons stated notwithstanding its character as relevant evidence. The Rule vests the military judge with wide discretion in determining the admissibility of evidence that comes within the Rule.

If a party views specific evidence as being highly prejudical, it may be possible to stipulate to the evidence and thus avoid its presentation to the court-members. *United States v. Grassi,* 602 F.2d 1192 (5th Cir. 1979), a prosecution for interstate transportation of obscene materials, illustrates this point. The defense offered to stipulate that certain films were obscene in order to prevent the jury from viewing the films, but the prosecution declined to join in the stipulation. The trial judge sustained the prosecution's rejection of the stipulation and the Fifth Circuit upheld the judge's decision. In its opinion, however, the Court of Appeals adopted a case-by-case balancing approach recognizing both the inportance of allowing probative evidence to be presented and the use of stipulations as a tool to implement the policies inherent in Rule 403. Insofar as the latter is concerned, the court expressly recognized the power of a federal district judge to compel the prosecution to accept a defense tendered stipulation.

Rule 404. Character Evidence Not Admissible to Prove Conduct; Exceptions; Other Crimes

(a) Character evidence generally. Evidence of a person's character or a trait of a person's character is not admissible for the purpose of proving that the person acted in conformity therewith on a particular occasion, except:

> *(1) Character of the accused.* Evidence of a pertinent trait of the character of the accused offered by an accused, or by the prosecution to rebut the same;

> *(2) Character of victim.* Evidence of a pertinent trait of character of the victim of the crime offered by an accused, or by the prosecution to rebut the same, or evidence of a character trait of peacefulness of the victim offered by the prosecution in a homicide or assault case to rebut evidence that the victim was an aggressor;

> *(3) Character of witness.* Evidence of the character of a witness, as provided in rules 607, 608, and 609.

(b) Other crimes, wrongs, or acts. Evidence of other crimes, wrongs or acts is not admissible to prove the character of a person in order to show that the person acted in conformity therewith. It may, however, be admissible for other purposes, such as proof of motive, opportunity, intent, preparation, plan, knowledge, identity, or absence of mistake or accident.

EDITORIAL COMMENT

Rule 404 addresses the use which can be made of character evidence in general, and extrinsic offense evidence in particular. Although the military Rule is broader than its federal counterpart, it is likely that the two Rules will produce similar results.

The Rule basically is a codification of the common law; it serves as a replacement for paragraphs 138*f* and *g* of the *Manual.* Two major sections make up the Rule: subdivision (a) concerning general character evidence; and subdivision (b) dealing with proof of other crimes, wrongs or similar acts (called extrinsic offense evidence in the federal courts, and previously known as uncharged misconduct in the military).

Subdivision (a) indicates that a person's character traits generally cannot be used to establish that he acted on a particular occasion in conformity with them; *e.g.,* that he committed the charged offense because he is a certain type of person. However, the Rule does list several exceptions to this general prohibition.

Subdivision (a)(1) addresses the character of the accused. It permits evidence of an accused's *pertinent* character traits to be admitted by the *defense.* This

181

IK to show Chambers is peaceful man on the assault charge

means that if the accused is charged with larceny, he can establish that he is an honest person. However, once the accused uses such evidence, the government can then rebut it with similar testimony.

This aspect of the Rule constitutes a significant departure from, and a limitation upon, previous court-martial practice which allowed evidence of general good military character to be admitted. Although the military version of 404(a)(1) is identical with its federal counterpart in prohibiting such evidence, the drafters' *Analysis* suggests that the defense will still be able to introduce general good military character if the accused is charged with a uniquely military offense. It might have been preferable for the drafters to amend the Rule itself to reflect this result, rather than attempting to accomplish it through the non-binding drafters' *Analysis*. Apparently, the word "pertinent," which presumably means the relevant trait or traits that the judge believes relate to the charged conduct, is the key. If military character is pertinent, it can be used.

Subdivision (a)(2) of the Rule addresses the admissibility of character evidence aimed at the victim of an assault or homicide. The Military Rule expands its federal counterpart, which allows such evidence to be used only in homicide cases. Both provisions contain two distinct applications, one for the defense, and one for the government. The defense can always use (a)(2) to establish that the victim of an assault or homicide has character traits which tend to demonstrate that he (the victim) may have been responsible for the charged offense. When the defense uses such evidence the government can rebut it with similar testimony. The Rule also provides that the government can offer evidence to show that the victim has character traits of peacefulness in an attempt to rebut any allegation that the victim was the aggressor in an assault or homicide prosecution.

The drafters' *Analysis* justifies this expansion of the Federal Rule on military necessity grounds. Servicemembers are required to live in close quarters. As a result, an excessive number of assault offenses occur. The expanded Rule covers a large amount of court-martial litigation and increases the defense and government's ability to properly educate the triers of fact about a character trait that is helpful in evaluating who acted improperly in assaulting another.

Rule 404(a)(3) does not provide substantive guidance with respect to character evidence. It directs attention to Rules 607, 608, and 609. These Rules cover impeachment of witnesses, which is permissible in accordance with Section VI, Rule 404 notwithstanding.

Although Rules 607, 608, and 609 are highlighted in the Rule, other provisions also are important in applying Rule 404. Primary among them is Rule 403. It is likely to be invoked whenever Rule 404(b) is relied upon. *See, e.g., United States v. Ricardo,* 619 F.2d 1124, 1231 (5th Cir. 1980) and our discussion of Rule 403. Also important is Rule 405, which specifies the methods for proving witness character, and Rule 406, which addresses habit and routine practice evidence.

Perhaps the easiest way to understand subsection (b) of Rule 404 is to separate its two sentences. The first sentence establishes that extrinsic offense evidence cannot be used to demonstrate that a person, usually the accused, has acted in conformity with his past crimes, wrongs, or similar acts. The principle at work is that specific acts may not be used to prove the kind of person someone is in order to show how he probably acted on a particular occasion. This is consistent with the limitation on proof of character in Rule 405. The sentence applies whether or not the extrinsic offense ever resulted in apprehension, referral, preferral, or conviction.

However, this broad prohibition is virtually subsumed by the Rule's second sentence which allows extrinsic offense evidence to be admitted for specific purposes listed in the Rule and other relevant purposes not barred by subdivision (a). Among the specific purposes mentioned in 404(b) are those already common in military practice; *i.e.,* motive, intent, knowledge, plan, scheme, and absence of mistake.

The most important aspect of subsection (b) is that it may be used to introduce evidence of the acts of an accused, even though he does not testify in his own behalf. This means Rule 404(b) can be used as part of the government's case in chief as substantive evidence to be considered by the finder of fact in determining guilt or innocence, not just as a matter affecting credibility.

It is no wonder that subdivision (b) is so heavily litigated in federal courts, and it will be no surprise to see it hotly contested in military courts. Any time that the prosecution attempts to offer other acts of the accused as part of its substantive proof there is a very real problem of prejudice. *See United States v. Beechum,* 582 F.2d 898 (5th Cir. 1978) (en banc), cert. denied, 440 U.S. 920 (1979). These other acts ordinarily involve some kind of wrongdoing or misbehavior. No matter how carefully the court-members are instructed that the evidence is not to be used for a determination of whether the accused is a good or bad person, there is a possibility of misuse. The worse the act, the greater the chance that court-members may lose sympathy for the accused and decide against him because he is a bad person — something that the law does not allow.

This is why Rule 403's balance is so important in connection with Rule 404(b) rulings. In deciding whether to admit or to exclude evidence, trial judges should be aware of the constant danger of prejudice and should pay close attention to the kind of act that is to be proved. The first determination to be made is whether the act tends to prove the specific thing for which it is offered. Closely related to this is the question of whether the matter is actually disputed. If, for example, a person admits an act but claims insanity, modus operandi evidence offered to show identity should not be admitted. It would not aid in the resolution of a disputed matter.

In many cases intent will be an element of the government's case, but the kind of act that the accused committed is almost always an intentional act. In such a case, it is wise for the court to decline to admit evidence of other acts to prove intent until the defendant has an opportunity to put on evidence. *See, e.g., United States v. Brunson,* 549 F.2d 348 (5th Cir.), cert. denied, 434 U.S. 842 (1977); *United States v. Danzey,* 594 F.2d 905 (2d Cir. 1979). If the defendant challenges intent, then on rebuttal the prosecution can offer the evidence of the other acts. Where intent is more clearly an issue in a case, evidence of other crimes need not be held in reserve. *See, e.g., United States v. Juarez,* 561 F.2d 65 (7th Cir. 1977).

It is common for the prosecution to use short-hand expressions like modus operandi, common plan or scheme, etc., to account for an offer of evidence of other acts. A trial judge must be certain to make the prosecution state exactly what issue it is trying to prove in order to see whether the evidence is probative, how probative it is, and whether it should be admitted in light of the other evidence in the case and the ever present danger of prejudice.

American jurisdictions differ in phrasing rules like 404(b) in exclusionary or inclusionary terms. Some jurisdictions bar evidence of other criminal acts except when offered for specific purposes. Others admit the evidence for any purpose except to show that the accused is a bad person. Actually, the Military Rule and its federal counterpart have elements of both approaches. The Rule admits evidence for all purposes except to show bad character. But it also lists common examples of purposes for which evidence can be offered. Some courts have referred to the Rule as inclusionary. *See, e.g., United States v. Benedetto,* 571 F.2d 1246 (2d Cir. 1978). We find nothing to be gained from such labels. The Rule plainly allows evidence of other acts to be admitted in many circumstances, but Rule 403 just as plainly requires exclusion in many instances. A careful balance is required. *See United States v. Beechum, supra; United States v. Nolan,* 551 F.2d 266 (10th Cir. 1977).

The Rule does not specify the kind of proof that is needed. No court requires that other acts be proved beyond a reasonable doubt. Some purport to require clear and convincing evidence of the other acts, however. *See, e.g., United States v. Calvert,* 523 F.2d 895 (8th Cir. 1975), cert. denied, 424 U.S. 911 (1976). We find no warrant for the clear and convincing evidence standard in the language of the Rule. The proper questions to be asked are whether the evidence is offered for a proper purpose, whether it is relevant, and whether it should be excluded because of problems covered by Rule 403. Now, this is not to say that the strength of the government's proof is unimportant. It appears that the strength of the evidence of other acts relates to the probative value of such evidence and is appropriately weighed in Rule 403 balancing. But if there is good proof, perhaps not clear and convincing, of an act that is not very prejudicial and not time-consuming to prove, it can be admitted under our reading of Rule 404(b) and Rules 401 and 402.

In *United States v. Janis,* 1 M.J. 395, 397 (C.M.A. 1976) the court established that three criteria must be satisfied before extrinsic offense evidence could be admitted. First, there must be a "nexus in time, place and circumstances between the offense charged and the uncharged misconduct." The court was very liberal in applying the test, finding that a three-year interval was not too remote. Second, the extrinsic offense would have to be established by "plain, clear and conclusive" evidence to be admissible. Finally, the court adopted a Rule 403 balance indicating that the extrinsic offense evidence would be excluded if it threatened the "fairness of the trial process," and its prejudicial impact outweighed its probative value. Again the court was liberal, striking the balance in favor of excluding the evidence only if it was inflammatory. *See also United States v. Anderson,* 9 M.J. 530 (A.C.M.R. 1980); and *United States v. Whiting,* 9 M.J. 501 (A.F.C.M.R. 1980) where *Janis* was effectively implemented. These cases are close to the approach that we suggest. We would only urge more sensitivity to Rule 403 concerns.

Whether an extrinsic offense can be used if the accused was previously acquitted of it divides the federal circuits. In *United States v. Mespoulede,* 597 F.2d 329 (2d Cir. 1979) and *United States v. Day,* 591 F.2d 861 (D.C. Cir. 1979) the courts determined that the government was estopped from using such evidence. *See also United States v. Keller,* 624 F.2d 1154 (3d Cir. 1980). But in *United States v. Rocha,* 553 F.2d 615 (9th Cir. 1977), and *United States v. Brown,* 562 F.2d 1144 (9th Cir. 1977), the court held that such evidence was admissible and valuable to juries as it helped them interpret an accused's defense.

Most judicial attention has focused on the typical case in which the prosecution is offering evidence against an accused. It should be remembered, however, that an accused might be able to offer evidence of the bad acts of a witness to show a motive to lie. *See, e.g., United States v. Alvarez-Lopez,* 559 F.2d 1155 (9th Cir. 1977). And the accused might offer evidence of his own other acts to explain why certain conduct charged by the government actually was part of a legal pattern of events. *See, e.g., United States v. Garvin,* 565 F.2d 519 (8th Cir. 1977).

DRAFTERS' ANALYSIS

(a) Character evidence generally. Rule 404(a) replaces present *Manual* ¶ 138f and is taken without substantial change from the Federal Rule. Rule 404(a) provides, subject to three exceptions, that character evidence is not admissible to show that a person acted in conformity therewith.

Rule 404(a)(1) allows only evidence of a pertinent trait of character of the accused to be offered in evidence by the defense. This is a significant change from ¶ 138f of the present *Manual* which also allows evidence of "general good character" of the accused to be received in order to demonstrate that the accused is less likely to have committed a criminal act. Under the new Rule, evidence of general good character is inadmissible because only evidence of a specific trait is acceptable. It is the intention of the Committee, however, to allow the defense to introduce evidence of good military character when that specific trait is pertinent. Evidence of good military character would be admissible, for example, in a prosecution for disobedience of orders. The prosecution may present evidence of a character trait only in rebuttal to receipt in evidence of defense character evidence. This is consistent with present military law.

Rule 404(a) (2) is taken from the Federal Rule with minor charges. The Federal Rule allows the prosecution to present evidence of the character trait of peacefulness of the victim "in a homicide case to rebut evidence that the victim was the first aggressor". Thus, the Federal Rule allows prosecutorial use of character evidence in a homicide case in which self-defense has been raised. The limitation to homicide cases appeared to be inappropriate and impracticable in the military environment. All too often, assaults involving claims of self-defense take place in the densely populated living quarters common to military life. Whether aboard ship or within barracks, it is considered essential to allow evidence of the character trait of peacefulness of the victim. Otherwise, a substantial risk would exist of allowing unlawful assaults to go undeterred. The Federal Rule's use of the expression "first aggressor" was modified to read, "an aggressor" as substantive military law recognizes that even an individual who is properly exercising the right of self-defense may overstep and become an aggressor. The remainder of Rule 404(a)(2) allows the defense to offer evidence of a pertinent trait of character of the victim of a crime and restricts the prosecution to rebuttal of that trait.

Rule 404(a)(3) allows character evidence to be used to impeach or support the credibility of a witness pursuant to Rules 607-609.

(b) *Other crimes, wrongs, or acts.* Rule 404(b) is taken without change from the Federal Rule, and is substantially similar to the present *Manual* Rule found in ¶ 138 g. While providing that evidence of other crimes, wrongs, or acts is not admissible to prove a predisposition to commit a crime, the Rule expressly permits use of such evidence on the merits when relevant to another specific purpose. Rule 404(b) provides examples rather than a list of justifications for admission of evidence of other misconduct. Other justifications, such as the tendency of such evidence to show the accused's consciousness of guilt of the offense charged, expressly permitted in *Manual* ¶ 138g(4), remain effective. Such a purpose would, for example, be an acceptable one. Rule 404(b), like *Manual* ¶ 138g, expressly allows use of evidence of misconduct not amounting to conviction. Like the *Manual*, the Rule does not, however, deal with use of evidence of other misconduct for purposes of impeachment. *See* Rules 608 and 609. Evidence offered under Rule 404(b) is subject to Rule 403.

Rule 405. Methods of Proving Character

(a) Reputation or opinion. In all cases in which evidence of character or a trait of character of a person is admissible, proof may be made by testimony as to reputation or by testimony in the form of an opinion. On cross-examination, inquiry is allowable into relevant specific instances of conduct.

(b) Specific instances of conduct. In cases in which character or a trait of character of a person is an essential element of an offense or defense, proof may also be made of specific instances of the person's conduct.

(c) Affidavits. The defense may introduce affidavits or other written statements of persons other than the accused concerning the character of the accused. If the defense introduces affidavits or other written statements under this subdivision, the prosecution may, in rebuttal, also introduce affidavits or other written statements regarding the character of the accused. Evidence of this type may be introduced by the defense or prosecution only if, aside from being contained in an affidavit or other written statement, it would otherwise be admissible under these rules.

(d) Definitions. "Reputation" means the estimation in which a person generally is held in the community in which the person lives or pursues a business or profession. "Community" in the armed forces includes a post, camp, ship, station, or other military organization regardless of size.

EDITORIAL COMMENT

Rule 405 delineates the types of character evidence that can be used at trial if any character evidence is allowed under Rule 404. Subdivision (a) recognizes that other Rules will have to be consulted for determining whether character evidence will be admissible. It enlarges traditional court-martial practice under *Manual* ¶ 138f(1) and (2), and adds substantially to the treatment of character evidence found in Federal Rule 405.

The new Rule provides three methods for proving a witness' character: (1) by reputation testimony, (2) by opinion testimony, and (3) by evidence of specific conduct.

Subdivision (a) mandates that the proponent of character evidence will generally be limited to reputation or opinion testimony. Reputation evidence can be defined as that information which the witness knows about an individual from having heard community discussion about him. It is not the witness' personal belief as to an individual's reputation that matters; it is his knowledge of what others say about him that counts.

The Rule's drafters were particularly concerned about defining "reputation." Satisfied with previous court-martial practice, they engrafted ¶ 138f(1)'s definition into the new Rule in subdivision (d). As a result, some of the uncertainty generated by the federal version of Rule 405 has been eliminated. Sensitive to the military's needs, Rule 405(d) encompasses virtually any duty station to which a service member could be assigned, regardless of its size or population.

When offering reputation evidence, counsel must insure that an adequate foundation has been laid for its admission. The following questions may be valuable in determining admissibility. (1) Is the character witness familiar with the individual's reputation in some relevant community? (2) Is the witness competent to speak for the community with respect to the individual's reputation? In other words, is the witness sufficiently linked to the community to really know of the individual's reputation? (3) Is the witness' reputation knowledge timely with respect to the issue it addresses? And (4), does the reputation relate to the character trait that can be proven under Rule 404? Affirmative answers to all four questions are necessary for admissibility.

Rule 405(a) also provides that opinion evidence may be used. This is new to federal practice, but it has long been a part of military law. *See Manual* ¶ 138 f(1). It is thought that much evidence admitted as reputation evidence actually is camouflaged opinion testimony. By allowing both opinion and reputation evidence to be admitted, the Rule enables character witnesses to testify accurately and honestly. Thus, Rule 405(a) permits counsel to ask a witness what his personal opinion of an individual's character is. Opinion evidence presents a danger that the impact of this testimony will often depend not so much on the nature of the testimony itself as on the stature of the witness offering it. This is particularly so in the military where the finder of fact is more likely to be influenced by a senior officer than by a junior enlisted man. While cautionary instructions and vigorous *voir dire* should be aimed at eliminating this possibility, counsel and trial judges must be aware of the problem. Unfortunately, opinion evidence also provides an effective means for venting personal hostilities and similar irrelevant considerations, which also must be guarded against.

The most effective way of testing a witness' opinion or reputation knowledge is by cross-examining that witness with respect to specific instances of conduct, a practice not provided for under ¶ 138f(2) of the previous *Manual.* Rule 405(a) authorizes this approach, which usually involves asking a witness "Have you heard" type questions. "Have you heard" questions may not be appropriate when examining opinion witnesses. Here counsel may ask "Do you know" questions, since it is the witness' own belief, not the community's, which is important.

Such questions received Supreme Court approbation in *Michelson v. United States,* 335 U.S. 469 (1948), although the court noted that the questions are suggestive and therefore troublesome. It is a strange cross-examination, because the cross-examiner is not allowed to prove the existence of the acts about which he asks. The purpose of the questions is to test the witness who provides character evidence. Any questions about what the witness knows or has heard, like all suggestive questions, must be based on a good faith belief that the act occurred. If the witness admits hearing or knowing of the act, he can explain how reputation or his opinion has been affected by what he has heard or knows. If the witness denies having heard or knowing of the act, the court-members may not believe the witness is being truthful, but the trial judge may be well advised to admonish court-members that information contained in questions is not evidence. There is no time limit on acts; any may be asked about. *See United States v. Edwards,* 549 F.2d 362 (5th Cir.), cert. denied sub nom. *United States v. Matassini,* 434 U.S. 828 (1977). But Rules 403 and 611(a) can be used to prevent unfairly prejudicial or wasteful questioning.

Often overlooked under the Rule is the fact that the character with which the Rule is concerned is character at the time of the crime charged. This is in contrast with character evidence offered on the credibility of a testifying witness, which makes the time that the witness testifies controlling. Under Rules 404 and 405, cross-examination should be limited to acts that would have occurred prior to the crime charged, because the court wants to test character at that time. Also, it usually should be improper to ask a character witness whether the charges brought in the very case before the court have affected reputation or opinion. The government is not permitted by charge to blemish character and then to take advantage of the blemish. *See United States v. Senak,* 527 F.2d 129 (7th Cir. 1975), cert. denied, 425 U.S. 907 (1976). When reputation evidence is offered it is really hearsay testimony. However, Rule 803(19) provides for its admissibility.

Under subdivision (b) specific conduct evidence is not admissible to demonstrate that an individual had a certain character trait and acted in conformity with it. Rather, specific instances of conduct can only be used to establish an *wallet* essential element of an offense or defense. Thus, even an accused who is permitted to prove a pertinent trait under Rule 404(a) may not do so with specific act evidence. Character might be an element of a defense if entrapment is claimed and the government wants to prove predisposition. Specific acts might be used in this context.

Subdivision (c) of the Military Rule has no counterpart in Federal Rule 405. It was incorporated without change from ¶ 146*b* of the *Manual,* and is designed to permit *defense* counsel to use affidavits or other documentary evidence to establish the *accused's* character. Subdivision (c) is a necessary device in an international judicial system. Because the Rule can only be initiated by the accused, there should be no Sixth Amendment problems with it. While the provision does permit the government to make use of similar evidence in rebuttal, the accused can avoid any unfavorable results here by merely foregoing its use himself.

DRAFTERS' ANALYSIS

(a) Reputation or opinion. Rule 405(a) is taken without change from the Federal Rule. The first portion of the Rule is identical in effect with the military rule found in ¶ 138*f*(1) of the present *Manual.* An individual testifying under the Rule must have an

adequate relationship with the community, (see Rule 405(c)) in the case of reputation, or with the given individual in the case of opinion, in order to testify. The remainder of Rule 405(a) expressly permits inquiry on cross-examination "into relevant specific instances of conduct." This is at variance with present military practice under which such an inquiry is prohibited. *See, e.g.,* ¶ 138f(2) (Character of the accused). Reputation evidence is exempted from the hearsay rule, Rule 803(21).

(b) *Specific instances of conduct.* Rule 405(b) is taken without significant change from the Federal Rule. Reference to "charge, claim, or defense" has been replaced with "offense or defense" in order to adapt the Rule to military procedure and terminology.

(c) *Affidavits.* Rule 405(c) is not found within the Federal Rules and is taken verbatim from material now found in ¶ 146b of the present *Manual.* Use of affidavits or other written statements is required due to the worldwide disposition of the armed forces which makes it difficult if not impossible to obtain witnesses — particularly when the sole testimony of a witness is to be a brief statement relating to the character of the accused. This is particularly important for offenses committed abroad or in a combat zone, in which case the only witnesses likely to be necessary from the United States are those likely to be character witnesses. The Rule exempts statements used under it from the hearsay rule insofar as the mere use of an affidavit or other written statement is subject to that Rule.

(d) *Definitions.* Rule 405(d) is not found within the Federal Rules of Evidence and has been included because of the unique nature of the armed forces. The definition of "reputation" is taken generally from present *Manual* ¶ 138f(1) and the definition of "community" is an expansion of that now found in the same paragraph. The definition of "community" has been broadened to add "regardless of size" to indicate that a party may proffer evidence of reputation within any specific military organization, whether a squad, company, division, ship, fleet, group, or wing, branch, or staff corps, for example. Rule 405(d) makes it clear that evidence may be offered of an individual's reputation in either the civilian or military community or both.

Rule 406. Habit; Routine Practice

Evidence of the habit of a person or of the routine practice of an organization, whether corroborated or not and regardless of the presence of eyewitnesses, is relevant to prove that the conduct of the person or organization on a particular occasion was in conformity with the habit or routine practice.

EDITORIAL COMMENT

Rules 404 and 405 generally bar evidence of previous conduct when offered to establish that an individual or organization has acted in conformity with its past. However, Rule 406 specifically permits its use under two circumstances. First, with respect to individuals, evidence of a person's habit is admissible to show that the individual's conduct on a specific occasion was consistent with his conduct on past occasions. Second, evidence of an organization's past routine practices is admissible to demonstrate that the organization acted consistently with those practices. Both evidence of habit and routine practice may be admitted even though no corroborating testimony exists. As a result, a single witness may be sufficient to establish the events. Similarly, the specific act being testified to need not have occurred in the witness' presence. It is sufficient if the witness merely knows of the events based on his familiarity with the organization or individual involved. These results are consistent with *Manual* ¶ 138*h*.

The drafters have left the terms "habit" and "routine practice" undefined in the Rule and its *Analysis.* Rule 406 acts must be regular, consistent and specific. Five questions must be asked under the Rule. (1) How often has the individual been observed performing the same conduct? (2) How similar is the past conduct with the conduct sought to be proved? (3) How unique is the conduct? (4) How uniformly or consistently has the conduct been performed? And (5), does the conduct appear to be virtually automatic rather than discretionary in nature?

Evidence is most likely to be admitted when its proponent is able to demonstrate that the individual performed the past acts without planning, with what Wigmore refers to as "invariable regularity," a form of semi-automatic action. The more counsel can offer detail to demonstrate this, the more likely a trial court will be to view it as habitual. *See United States v. Krejce,* 5 M.J. 701 (N.C.M.R. 1978) (government able to rely on a recruiting sergeant's past habits to establish a proper enlistment; conviction reversed on other grounds). Similarly, when applying this logic to routine business or organization practices, counsel should be concerned with the frequency of the conduct more than uniqueness. An event which continually occurs is more likely to be viewed as a routine practice, than one which rarely and unpredictably happens.

In order to prove either habit or routine practice, counsel should produce witnesses with personal knowledge of the conduct involved. The greater the number of perceived incidents, the more powerful the case for admission. Here it is clearly better to call one witness who has observed habitual performance many times, than many witnesses who have each observed the practice a single time.

Rule 406 is often used in the military and federal courts without being labeled as habit or routine-practice evidence. For instance, military forums are accustomed to applying a presumption of regularity with respect to certain governmental actions. *See generally United States v. Weaver,* 1 M.J. 111, 115 (C.M.A. 1975); *Kitchens v. Smith,* 401 U.S. 847 (1971). Similarly, evidence which is offered as an exception to the hearsay rule under the business entry or official document exception, also draws from Rule 406 (*see* Rules 803(6) and (8) respectively).

DRAFTERS' ANALYSIS

Rule 406 is taken without change from the Federal Rule. It is similar in effect to ¶ 138*h* of the present *Manual.* It is the intent of the Committee to include within Rule 406's use of the word, "organization", military organizations regardless of size. *See, e.g.,* Rule 405 and the *Analysis* to that Rule.

Rule 407. Subsequent Remedial Measures

When, after an event, measures are taken which, if taken previously, would have made the event less likely to occur, evidence of the subsequent measures is not admissible to prove negligence or culpable conduct in connection with the event. This rule does not require the exclusion of evidence of subsequent measures when offered for another purpose, such as proving ownership, control, or feasibility of precautionary measures, if controverted, or impeachment.

EDITORIAL COMMENT

Rule 407 addresses incidents of negligent or culpable conduct and is directed primarily at non-criminal litigation. The Military Rule simply copies the Federal Rule, as there is no comparable provision in previous editions of the *Manual.*

The new Rule specifies that proof of measures that an individual may have taken after an event, which would have made the event less likely to have occurred had they happened before the event, are not admissible to show that the individual's original action was negligent or culpable. Although the drafters' *Analysis* does not indicate how Rule 407 will affect court-martial practice, we envision an impact on at least two offenses: Article 134, negligent homicide; and Article 119(b)(1), involuntary manslaughter resulting from a culpably negligent act.

Although negligent conduct is generally not sufficient to invoke criminal sanctions, military necessity has caused Congress to control and punish areas of conduct beyond those in the civilian community. In *United States v. Kick,* 7 M.J. 82 (C.M.A. 1979), the court affirmed a conviction despite appellant's contention that his negligent act should not have resulted in criminal liabilities. For an example of how Rule 407 might affect negligent homicide cases, *see* S. SALTZBURG & K. REDDEN, FEDERAL RULES OF EVIDENCE MANUAL 162-163 (2d ed. 1977).

Under some circumstances — whenever the evidence is offered for a purpose other than to show negligence or culpable conduct — proof of an individual's subsequent actions may be admissible just as in civil cases. The Rule lists some examples — *e.g.,* to establish control of or ownership of an automobile which might have been used to commit an offense. Subsequent conduct might also be used to establish that the instrument of criminality was in the accused's possession when an offense occurred.

DRAFTERS' ANALYSIS

Rule 407 is taken from the Federal Rules without change, and has no express equivalent in the present *Manual.*

Rule 408. Compromise and Offer to Compromise

Evidence of (1) furnishing or offering or promising to furnish, or (2) accepting or offering or promising to accept, a valuable consideration in compromising or attempting to compromise a claim which was disputed as to either validity or amount, is not admissible to prove liability for or invalidity of the claim or its amount. Evidence of conduct or statements made in compromise negotiations is likewise not admissible. This rule does not require the exclusion of any evidence otherwise discoverable merely because it is presented in the course of compromise negotiations. This rule also does not require exclusion when the evidence is offered for another purpose, such as proving bias or prejudice of a witness, negativing a contention of undue delay, or proving an effort to obstruct a criminal investigation or prosecution.

EDITORIAL COMMENT

Rule 408 discusses the admissibility of evidence originating in offers to compromise or to settle civil suits. It protects these discussions much the way Rule 410 does plea negotiations. This provision was taken from the Federal Rule without alteration. Because it concerns non-criminal proceedings, it has no foundation in previous *Manual* editions.

The drafters' *Analysis* does not indicate how Rule 408 will affect court-martial practice. This is probably due to the Rule's narrow civil applicability. However, circumstances may arise where the accused might be civilly liable for damages inflicted as a result of his criminal misconduct. Here, Rule 408 would generally prohibit the admission of evidence concerning any offer to settle or statement made in connection therewith from being admitted during the court-martial itself. Or, if the United States brings a civil suit against a person, settlement negotiations in that suit should not generally be admissible in a related criminal proceeding.

It may be that the most important function of this Rule will be to assure someone facing both civil and criminal liability that simultaneous bargaining with the government about both forms of liability will result in protection under both this Rule and Rule 410. There is one problem with simultaneous bargaining, however. The legislative history of Federal Rule 410, which will be important in interpreting Military Rule 410, indicates that statements made in the course of legitimate plea bargaining may not be used to impeach an accused at trial if bargaining breaks down. Rule 408 is less clear on the impeachment question. Some commentators have suggested that the last sentence of the Rule would permit impeachment use of statements made in settlement negotiations. Others have argued that this approach would inhibit free and open bargaining in which the parties do not have to fear a mistake or a slip of the tongue. Our own position is that impeachment use should not be permitted, since simultaneous bargaining would be impaired were Rules 408 and 410 read differently on the impeachment issue. We do not believe that our reading encourages parties to misstate facts during settlement negotiations, since misstatements of fact are generally rejected by opponents and tend to reveal a weakness in the case of the misrepresenting party. Our approach would avoid having one party "set up" another by seeking during compromise negotiations to elicit some, but not all, facts in a form that might appear to create a contradiction with any full story that is told at trial. One way counsel can assure that statements will not be used for impeachment purposes is to put everything in hypothetical form. Safe lawyers will proceed this way whenever simultaneous bargaining is attempted, since the answer to the question whether impeachment is allowed under Rule 408 is so controversial.

In applying Rule 408, courts must remember that the Rule only protects against the use of compromise offers relating to claims that are disputed as to either validity or amount. Someone who admits liability cannot say to someone else "I will never pay you the $100 that I admittedly owe you unless you sue me, but I'll give you $50 to forget the whole thing" and claim the protection of the Rule. The claim would be admitted under these circumstances, and the Rule does not encourage persons to refuse to pay admitted claims.

Similarly, the Rule only protects offers involving a valuable consideration. What this means is that something of legitimate value must be offered. A threat to kill someone unless a settlement is reached would not be an offer of anything of value that the law regards as legitimate. Thus, it would be outside the coverage of the Rule.

Unlike the common law, the Rule does protect against statements made in compromise negotiations, even though these statements are not inextricably bound up in a settlement offer. As noted above, the philosophy of the Rule is to promote bargaining in a free and open atmosphere, although the impeachment question poses some difficulty here.

The fact that something is revealed in settlement does not bar its being discovered and used should the case go to trial. There is no immunity against the use of evidence that one party is entitled to obtain from the other just because the evidence was revealed for the first time during settlement. Under the Rule, the settlement negotiations themselves are not to be used as evidence, but no part of the Rule is intended to permit one party to immunize against trial use evidence that might otherwise be available.

Finally, it should be noted that the last sentence of the Rule, read in conjunction with the opening sentence, makes it clear that the limitation on the use of evidence in this Rule applies only when the evidence is offered to prove liability for or invalidity of a claim or the amount of a claim. It does not apply when the evidence is offered for another purpose, such as one of those suggested in the final sentence of the Rule. But, if there is sufficient danger that the jury would misuse evidence on the liability of amount questions, Rule 403 could be used to bar evidence otherwise admissible under the last sentence.

DRAFTERS' ANALYSIS

Rule 408 is taken from the Federal Rules without change, and has no express equivalent in the present *Manual*.

Rule 409. Payment of Medical and Similar Expenses

Evidence of furnishing or offering or promising to pay medical, hospital, or similar expenses occasioned by an injury is not admissible to prove liability for the injury.

EDITORIAL COMMENT

Rule 409 simply states that testimony indicating that a party has paid or promised to pay hospital or medical expenses is not admissible to establish his liability for the injury. The Military Rule has been taken directly from the Federal Rule, and cannot be traced to a specific *Manual* provision.

The drafters' *Analysis* indicates that 409 may not apply to criminal cases at all because by its terms "it deals only with questions of liability — normally only a civil matter." We would agree with the drafters if the term "liability" is used as a word of art meaning civil, tort-like liability for injury or damage. However, if "liability" is defined as meaning responsibility, then the Rule would apply to court-martial practice to the same degree as Rule 407. *See* our discussion, *supra.* If this is the case, then prosecutions for criminal assaults and similar offenses also could be affected.

If this Rule applies in criminal cases, it is especially important to remember that it only bars admission of payments or promises to pay, not factual statements or admissions made in connection therewith. Hence, in not protecting against admission of statements this Rule is less protective than Rule 408.

Assuming that the Rule is applicable in courts-martial, there may arise a question whether a payment or promise to pay can be used to prove the identity of an assailant. Is identity different from liability? Arguments can be made both ways. One argument would be that identity is being used to establish criminal liability and should not be allowed. The countervailing argument is that liability is otherwise proved, and that the Rule only protects against using the evidence to show negligence or failure to meet a standard of care on the theory that the evidence is of only slight value; if used to prove identity, arguably the evidence has greater probative force. At the moment, there is little law supporting either argument.

DRAFTERS' ANALYSIS

Rule 409 is taken from the Federal Rules without change. It has no present military equivalent and is intended to be applicable to courts-martial to the same extent that it is applicable to civilian criminal cases. Unlike Rules 407 and 408 which although primarily applicable to civil cases are clearly applicable to criminal cases, it is arguable that Rule 409 may not apply to criminal cases as it deals only with questions of "liability" — normally only a civil matter. The Rule has been included in the Military Rules to ensure its availability should it, in fact, apply to criminal cases.

Rule 410. Inadmissibility of Pleas, Plea Discussions, and Related Statements

Except as otherwise provided in this rule, evidence of a plea of guilty, later withdrawn, or a plea of nolo contendere, or of an offer to plead guilty or nolo contendere to the crime charged or any other crime, or of statements made in connection with, and relevant to any of the foregoing pleas or offers, is not admissible in any court-martial proceeding against the person who made the plea or offer. However, evidence of a statement made in connection with, and relevant to, a plea of guilty, later withdrawn, a plea of nolo contendere, or an offer to plead guilty or nolo contendere to the crime charged or any other crime, is admissible in a court-martial proceeding for perjury or false statement if the statement was made by the defendant under oath, on the record, and in the presence of counsel. An "offer to plead guilty" includes a statement made by the accused solely for the purpose of requesting disposition under an authorized procedure for administrative action in lieu of trial by court-martial; "on the record" includes the written statement submitted by the accused in furtherance of such request.

EDITORIAL COMMENT

Although the Rule set out above is official on the date this book was published, Congress amended the Federal version of it on 1 December 1980. Because Military Rule 1102 provides that federal amendments "shall apply to the Military Rules of Evidence 180 days after the effective date of such amendments unless" the President takes a contrary action, we have set out the new Rule in anticipation of its adoption. While our comments apply to both Rules, they should be considered in light of the amendments.

The new Federal Rule is designed to address three problems caused by its predecessor. First, the scope of out of court statements protected by the Rule is now limited to those made to a "prosecuting attorney." Statements made to other law enforcements personnel are outside the Rule's protection. Second, the new provision adopts a "rule of completeness" approach to those statements actually obtained from the accused. See our discussion of Rule 106 for an interpretation of this change. Third, the amended Rule expressly addresses statements made during in-court providence or judicial inquiries. The 1 December 1980 version of Federal Rule 410 is set out below.

Except as otherwise provided in this rule, evidence of the following is not, in any civil or criminal proceeding, admissible against the defendant who made the plea or was a participant in the plea discussions:

(1) a plea of guilty which was later withdrawn;

(2) a plea of nolo contendere;

(3) any statement made in the course of any proceedings under Rule 11 of the Federal Rules of Criminal Procedure or comparable state procedure regarding either of the foregoing pleas; or

(4) any statement made in the course of plea discussions with an attorney for the prosecuting authority which do not result in a plea of guilty or which result in a plea of guilty later withdrawn.

However, such a statement is admissible (i) in any proceeding wherein another statement made in the course of the same plea or plea discussions has been introduced and the statement ought in fairness be considered contemporaneously with it, or (ii) in a criminal proceeding for perjury or false statement if the statement was made by the defendant under oath, on the record and in the presence of counsel.

Military Rule 410 is modeled after its federal counterpart, although some changes have been made to conform the Rule to standard court-martial procedures. Although not evident on its face, Rule 410 controls two separate aspects of criminal practice: (1) the use which can be made of statements rendered by the accused during a judicial (or providence) inquiry (*see United States v. Care,* 18 C.M.A. 535, 40 C.M.R. 247 (1969)); and (2) new protections accorded any statement the accused might make during plea bargaining.

The Rule's first sentence codifies current court-martial practice. It states that any evidence obtained from the accused in connection with a plea generally cannot be used against him. An interesting application of this Rule is contained in *United States v. Schackelford,* 2 M.J. 17 (C.M.A. 1977). There the accused impeached his guilty plea during the providence inquiry. Subsequently, the case was tried to a court with members. After the accused testified on direct examination, the trial judge asked him more than 50 questions aimed at displaying the untruthful nature of his testimony. In reversing the conviction, the court found that the trial judge had unfairly disparaged the defense by improperly using information obtained during the providence inquiry. The court further held that such conduct has long been prohibited by the Uniform Code of Military Justice (*see* Article 45), military precedent (*see United States v. Barben,* 14 C.M.A. 198, 33 C.M.R. 410 (1963)), and Supreme Court guidance (*see Kercheval v. United States,* 274 U.S. 220 (1927)). Judge Cook's concurring opinion particularly highlighted the impropriety of using the accused's guilty plea statements against him in such fashion.

Although Rule 410 generally is consistent with *Schackelford,* and prior military practice, it also provides an exception. The Rule's second sentence indicates that if the accused makes a false statement during a colloquy with the trial judge, the false statement can be used as the basis for a perjury prosecution. For the exception to apply, three conditions must be satisfied: (1) The false statement must be given by the accused under *oath;* (2) it must be made on the record (which might include a written statement by the accused asking for disposition by administrative action); and (3) it must be rendered in counsel's presence. Current military practice does not require that the accused be sworn prior to discussing his guilt with the trial judge. As a result, the military's ability to use the "false statement" exception to the new Rule is conditioned upon a change in existing practice. The bench will now have to insure that the accused is sworn before the providence inquiry begins. Such a procedure may have a tendency to chill the accused's desire to openly admit his guilt in court. This cost may be offset by the healthy aspect of having the accused think carefully about what he is saying to the judge.

The second and more controversial aspect of Rule 410 is that it implicitly provides that any statement which the accused may make as part of a plea negotiation is not admissible against him. In effect, this application of the Rule is an extention of Article 31 and *United States v. Tempia,* 16 C.M.A. 629, 37 C.M.R. 249 (1967), in that now even properly warned and otherwise voluntary statements may be suppressed because when the accused made the statement, it was part of an effort to reach a possible pretrial agreement.

There are some people who would like to see plea bargaining abolished altogether, believing that it coerces defendants into waiving their trial rights upon pain of higher sentences following trials. Advocates of plea bargaining point out the advantages of allowing parties to obtain a certainty in bargaining that is not available at trial. It may be that the coercive aspects of plea bargaining are less worrisome in military than in civilian courts, because sentencing practices in military courts appear to be somewhat more uniform than in their civilian counterparts.

In any event, as long as plea bargaining is recognized as important and desirable, there is little dispute that procedures should not impair the bargaining process. Thus, in the federal courts, it has been recognized that it is desirable to allow the defendant to bargain with the prosecutor and to protect statements made in bargaining from admissibility at trial so that the bargaining can be as free and open as possible. Rule 410 implicitly covers plea bargaining. The problem that the federal courts have faced and that will have to be faced under the Military Rule is whether a situation in which an accused talks with a government agent (or attorney for the prosecution under the new Federal Rule), amounts to bargaining or is simply a form of interrogation of conversation. Only bargaining is covered by the Rule.

The original version of the Federal Rule, like its December 1980 amendment, only covers bargaining between an attorney for the government and a defendant. Some federal courts supported this approach before the amendment. *See, e.g., United States v. Stirling,* 571 F.2d 708 (2d Cir. 1978), cert. denied, 439 U.S. 824 (1978). Others adopted a more expansive approach. *See, e.g., United States v. Robertson,* 582 F.2d 1356 (5th Cir. 1978) (en banc). Still others adopted a middle position, restricting the definition of bargaining to communications between the accused and the attorney for the government or his authorized agent. *See, e.g., United States v. Grant,* 622 F.2d 308 (8th Cir. 1980).

To determine the admissibility of an accused's pretrial statement under the current Rule a court will focus on such questions as: (1) Was there an actual negotiation? (2) If so, was it between the accused and a representative of the government with power to bind the government? (3) Was the negotiation for the accused's benefit? (4) Was the negotiation relevant to and concerned specifically with the accused's offer to plead guilty in exchange for a limitation on punishment?

In asking these questions, most courts have adopted something close to the two-step approach announced in *United States v. Robertson, supra.* The court will first look to the accused's *subjective* intent to bargain for a plea, then balance it against the *objective* circumstances that surround and define the intent, ultimately seeking to determine whether it was reasonable for the accused to believe an agreement was possible. *See, e.g., United States v. Castillo,* 615 F.2d 878 (9th Cir. 1980), where the court found both the objective and subjective criteria to be missing because the accused was constantly aware that the agent did not have authority to bind the government.

Perhaps the most difficult cases to deal with are those where the accused's initial statement to authorities clearly indicates his willingness to confess if some form of pretrial agreement is possible. When the accused utters such a "preamble," the burden should shift to the government agent to carefully and clearly inform the accused that no deal can result from their conversation. However, if the accused is left uninformed of this reality, or if the accused is encouraged to make further statements because of his mistaken belief, then such statements will probably be suppressed. *See, e.g., United States v. Herman,* 544 F.2d 791, 799 (5th Cir. 1977). To be safe, commanders and military policemen should refrain from the customary practice of informing the accused that anything he says to them or any assistance he offers them will be made known to the convening authority or some other individual in power. Appellate courts may well find that such a conversation renders any statements made thereafter inadmissible. However, *see United States v. White,* 617 F.2d 1131 (5th Cir. 1980), where the court found that no violation of Rule 410 occurred where the government agent told the accused that the United States attorney would be informed of his cooperation.

Our view is that bargaining between an official authorized to make charging or sentencing concessions and the accused is the clearest kind of bargaining covered by the Rule. Statements made in a context in which a reasonable person in the shoes of an accused would believe that he was speaking with someone authorized to plea bargain for the government and to offer concessions in return for the accused's cooperation also should be covered. Without this expansion, it would be possible for agents of the government to lead an accused to think they were lawyers and to appear to be engaged in plea bargaining. Objective appearances should govern. We suspect that over time this is the way the cases will come out, even if they have to use a combination of Rule 410 and coerced confession principles.

Finally, the last sentence of the Military Rule adds a provision not needed in the federal model. It provides that if the accused requests a discharge from the service through administrative channels, in lieu of trial, then any statement rendered in this request will be inadmissible. This aspect of the Rule codifies existing practice.

DRAFTERS' ANALYSIS

Rule 410 is taken generally from the Federal Rule. It extends to plea bargaining as well as to statements made during a providency inquiry, civilian or military. *E.g., United States v. Care,* 18 C.M.A. 535, 40 C.M.R. 247 (1969). The last sentence was added to the Rule in recognition of the unique possibility of administrative disposition, usually separation, in lieu of court-martial. Denominated differently within the various armed forces, this administrative procedure often requires a confession as a prerequisite. As modified, Rule 410 protects an individual against later use of a statement submitted in furtherance of such a request for administrative disposition. The definition of "on the record" was required because no "record" in the judicial sense exists insofar as request for administrative disposition is concerned. It is the belief of the Committee that a copy of the written statement of the accused in such a case is, however, the functional equivalent of such a record.

Although the expression, "false statement" was retained in the Rule, it is the Committee's intent that it be construed to include all related or similar military offenses.

A modification of Rule 410 was proposed by the Supreme Court, but the effective date has been delayed by Congress. Consequently, the Rules adopt the present Rule 410; those modifications sanctioned by Congress will become applicable insofar as authorized under Rule 1102.

Rule 411. Liability Insurance

Evidence that a person was or was not insured against liability is not admissible upon the issue whether the person acted negligently or otherwise wrongfully. This rule does not require the exclusion of evidence of insurance against liability when offered for another purpose, such as proof of agency, ownership, or control, or bias or prejudice of a witness.

EDITORIAL COMMENT

Rule 411 prohibits the admission of evidence tending to establish that a person was or was not insured against liability if offered to show possible negligent or wrongful conduct. It allows such testimony to prove agency, ownership, control, prejudice or bias of a witness. These provisions are taken without alteration from the Federal Rule and have no foundation in the *Manual*.

Although Rule 409 is primarily a rule of civil, not criminal, applicability, it may affect a military accused who is charged with negligent homicide or involuntary manslaughter. *See* our discussion of Rule 407. The drafters have stated that the Rule should be applied so that it is consistent with federal practice.

DRAFTERS' ANALYSIS

Rule 411 is taken from the Federal Rule without change. Although it would appear to have potential impact upon some criminal cases, *e.g.*, some negligent homicide cases, its actual application to criminal cases is uncertain. It is the Committee's intent that Rule 411 be applicable to courts-martial only to the extent that it is applicable to crimimal cases.

Rule 412. Nonconsensual Sexual Offenses; Relevance of Victim's Past Behavior

(a) Notwithstanding any other provision of these rules or this Manual, in a case in which a person is accused of a nonconsensual sexual offense, reputation or opinion evidence of the past sexual behavior of an alleged victim of such nonconsensual sexual offense is not admissible.

(b) Notwithstanding any other provision of these rules or this Manual, in a case in which a person is accused of a nonconsensual sexual offense, evidence of a victim's past sexual behavior other than reputation or opinion evidence is also not admissible, unless such evidence other than reputation or opinion evidence is —

(1) admitted in accordance with subdivisions (c)(1) and (c)(2) and is constitutionally required to be admitted; or

(2) admitted in accordance with subdivision (c) and is evidence of —

(A) past sexual behavior with persons other than the accused, offered by the accused upon the issue of whether the accused was or was not, with respect to the alleged victim, the source of semen or injury; or

(B) past sexual behavior with the accused and is offered by the accused upon the issue of whether the alleged victim consented to the sexual behavior with respect to which the nonconsensual sexual offense is alleged.

(c)(1) If the person accused of committing a nonconsensual sexual offense intends to offer under subdivision (b) evidence of specific instances of the alleged victim's past sexual behavior, the accused shall serve notice thereof on the military judge and the trial counsel.

(2) The notice described in paragraph (1) shall be accompanied by an offer of proof. If the military judge determines that the offer of proof contains evidence described in subdivision (b), the military judge shall conduct a hearing, which may be closed, to determine if such evidence is admissible. At such hearings the parties may call witnesses, including the alleged victim, and offer relevant evidence. In a case before a court-martial composed of a military judge and members, the military judge shall conduct such hearings outside the presence of the members pursuant to Article 39(a).

(3) If the military judge determines on the basis of the hearing described in paragraph (2) that the evidence which the accused seeks to offer is relevant and that the probative value of such evidence outweighs the danger of unfair prejudice, such evidence shall be admissible in the trial to the extent an order made by the military judge specifies evidence which may be offered and areas with respect to which the alleged victim may be examined or cross-examined.

(d) For purposes of this rule, the term "past sexual behavior" means sexual behavior other than the sexual behavior with respect to which a nonconsensual sexual offense is alleged.

(e) A "nonconsensual sexual offense" is a sexual offense in which consent by the victim is an affirmative defense or in which the lack of consent is an element of the offense. This term includes rape, forcible sodomy, assault with intent to commit rape or forcible sodomy, indecent assault, and attempts to commit such offenses.

EDITORIAL COMMENT

Traditional prosecution of sexual offenses too often tended to place both the accused and the victim on trial. While the government alleged the accused's culpability, the defense attacked the victim's sexual history. This approach not only demeaned victims, but also often confused the finders of fact, and wasted the court's time.

"Trying the victim" was permitted, if not encouraged, by ¶ 153b(2)(b) of the *Manual.* It allowed defense counsel to present opinion and reputation evidence dealing with every facet of the victim's past sexual behavior, from associations to specific instances of illicit sexual intercourse. The only codified limitation here was the *Manual's* prohibition against remote evidence. *See, e.g., United States v. Lewis,* 6 M.J. 581 (A.C.M.R. 1978), where the court permitted defense counsel to cross-examine the prosecutrix about her previous sexual relationships; the fact that in the past six months she had sexual relations 15 times; and that she used birth control pills during the time in question.

Critics of such questioning properly claimed that ¶ 153b(2)(b) and similar common-law practices produced irrelevant evidence that tended to mislead and distract the triers of fact, while needlessly embarrassing the victim. The Privacy for Rape Victims Act of 1978, signed into law on 28 October 1978 as Federal Rule of Evidence 412, was designed to curtail such abuses. The military's adoption and modification of that Rule promises to alter litigation in this area. *See generally* Tanford and Bocchino, *Rape Shield Laws and the Sixth Amendment,* 128 U. of PENN. L. REV. 544 (Jan. 1980).

Rule 412 is relatively long, but it is logically constructed. The military drafters have attempted to cure many of the defects contained in the federal version. To a significant extent, they have succeeded. Initially military practitioners should recognize that 412 covers a wider range of criminal conduct than the Federal Rule. Subdivisions (a) and (b) broadly address nonconsensual sexual offenses while the federal version is limited to only rape or assault with intent to commit rape. In order to clarify these differences, the military drafters added subdivision (e) to the Rule. It specifies that nonconsensual sexual offenses include rape, forcible sodomy, all forms of assaults, attempts, plus any other sexual offense where consent is an element of the charge or defense. As the *Analysis* suggests, such an extension of the Federal Rule is quite important. The drafters concluded that no justification exists to limit the Rule's application to only designated offenses.

Before discussing Rule 412's provisions, it is important to recognize that the drafters intended it to exclusively control the use of character and conduct evidence of the victim in sexual offense prosecutions. Both subdivisions (a) and (b) mandate that no other provision of the Rules shall override Rule 412. This is particularly important as Rules 404 and 405 generally conflict with Rule 412's design. Rules 404 and 405 cover the use of character evidence of the accused, however.

Subdivision (a) of Rule 412 prohibits the defense from ever offering reputation or opinion evidence concerning a victim's past sexual behavior. Simply stated, this means that defense counsel can no longer ask questions about the victim's general morality, sexual life style, or sexual habits. Subdivision (b) adds that other evidence of a victim's past sexual behavior — *i.e.,* specific conduct — is also prohibited except in specified, limited circumstances.

The three exceptions to subdivision (b) are critical to its constitutionality and its application. Each one can only be invoked after subdivision (c)'s procedural requirements are satisfied.

Subdivision (b)(2)(A) allows the defense to present evidence concerning the victim's past sexual activity with someone other than the accused if such evidence will establish that another individual was the source of any semen or injury inflicted upon the prosecutrix. If the government contends that semen or injury is attributable to the accused, the accused must be given a full opportunity to ask questions and to discover whether someone else might have been the actual source. Were this opportunity denied, the accused would be denied a defense. Thus, the accused is not required to provide the court with the individual's name, address and social security number in order to make use of this exception. Any questions tending to prove the source of injury or semen should be acceptable. Of course, questions about events removed in time would be irrelevant to prove the source of semen and might even be irrelevant on the source of an injury, depending on its nature and duration.

Subdivision (b)(2)(B) allows the defense to present evidence of past sexual conduct between the accused and the prosecutrix to establish that the charged sexual behavior was consensual. The Rule places no time constraints upon such evidence, and we see no need for any additional protections to be added to Rules 401 and 403. The defense's position actually becomes stronger if the accused is able to establish that a course of sexual conduct covers ten or twenty years. A twenty-year gap between events might make the stale evidence irrelevant or more confusing than helpful, however.

The third exception of Rule 412's limitations is the Rule's most elusive provision. Subparagraph (b)(1) permits the defense to introduce any evidence which is "constitutionally required to be admitted." The only qualification is that such testimony cannot be in the form of opinion or reputation evidence. This exception is an attempt to save the Rule from being held unconstitutional as applied. The first two exceptions discussed are narrow enough that injustice might result in special circumstances were they the exclusive exceptions.

However, subdivision (b)(1) may create more problems than it solves. An accused may want to show that based on the victim's reputation, he believed his conduct was consensual, thus providing a foundation for a defense based on reasonable mistake of fact. But the Rule bars all reputation evidence. The drafters' *Analysis* recognizes the problem and implies that the Constitution may require admission of some reputation evidence; yet the Rule as drafted places the exception in subdivision (b), which only allows proof other than reputation or opinion. The drafters have failed to even suggest a definition of what "constitutionally required" means. Their *Analysis* indicates that proof establishing the victim to be a prostitute may fall within the exception, but they do not identify under what circumstances this should be permitted. A prostitute does not lose her ability to reject sexual advances merely because of her vocation. The Supreme Court has expressed its concern that the accused must be afforded a fair opportunity to establish a defense. In *Chambers v. Mississippi,* 410 U.S. 284 (1973), the High Court found a violation of the accused's Sixth and Fourteenth Amendment rights because he was prohibited from offering reliable and needed evidence. Similarly, in *Davis v. Alaska,* 415 U.S. 308 (1974), the Court reversed conviction because the accused was prohibited from thoroughly cross-examining a key government witness whose background and criminal record were protected by state juvenile statutes. But the Court has not yet clearly indicated when an evidence rule must give way to the accused's right to offer proof in support of a defense. Thus, this final exception is unclear. It also is unnecessary. Any limitation on a constitutional right would be disregarded whether or not such a Rule existed. Perhaps its real function is to explicitly recognize that serious constitutional questions are likely to be raised with frequency and to put judges and lawyers on the alert.

Subdivision (c) imposes procedural and notice requirements which must be implemented when one of the exceptions to the Rule is used. Initially, (c)(1) requires that before the defense can make use of its specific act evidence, notice must be given to the government and to the military judge. Unlike the Federal Rule, (c)(1) fails to specify a time requirement for such notice. The drafters' *Analysis* indicates that the 15-day federal limitation was rejected because of the military's stringent speedy trial requirements. Defense counsel should provide the government with sufficient notice to facilitate litigation. If notice is late, a continuance is preferred to exclusion of evidence. *Cf.* Rule 311(d). If defense counsel, due to inadvertence, simple mistake, or outright negligence, is prohibited from presenting admissible evidence, appellate courts will certainly evaluate the record of trial under competency of counsel standards, as well as Rule 412 requirements. Often, they will be forced to view defense counsel as inadequate and thus grant new trials if evidence was excluded because of counsel's conduct. Such a result benefits neither side and can be avoided if a continuance is the preferred remedy for tardiness.

Subdivision (c)(2) prescribes the methods for satisfying the notice requirements. Basically, the defense must make either a written or oral offer of proof establishing that its evidence satisfies one of the exceptions listed in subparagraph (b). If defense counsel cannot bring the evidence under one of the three exceptions, then the trial judge will rule the proffered evidence inadmissible. However, the court must keep in mind that that at the outset all the accused need do is show that his evidence falls within one of subparagraph (b)'s exceptions.

If the trial judge determines the accused's proof satisfies one of subdivision (b)'s exceptions, then an Article 39(a) session should be conducted. The hearing must be held out of the court-members presence, and it may be closed to the public. The purpose of this proceeding is to determine the testimony's admissibility, and its content. Both parties may call witnesses, including the victim.

Subdivision (c)(3) provides the bench with a standard for determining the ultimate admissibility and use of the evidence. Two separate considerations are involved here. First, the judge must be satisfied that the evidence of sexual conduct is "relevant." Relevance is defined in Rule 401. If it is, the Rule also requires that the evidence be more probative than prejudicial. The balance here is not towards admissibility as it is under Rule 403. Unless the judge decides it is more probative than prejudicial, it is excluded.

In striking the balance, the judge should consider how probative a jury could find the evidence, if the court-members believe it. Although the Federal Rule seems to indicate that notwithstanding Rule 104(b), the federal trial judge is to decide on the credibility of this kind of evidence, Military Rule 412 continues to employ the traditional relationship between judge and court-members and thus to avoid the very real constitutional problem presented by the Federal Rule.

If the judge decides to admit Rule 412 evidence, he is specifically required to determine how much of the proffered evidence will be admitted and how extensive an examination of the victim will be permitted. In making this determination, the trial judge should be guided by Rule 412's basic purpose — to limit victim harassment and embarrassment. Consistent with these responsibilities, the bench should carefully instruct counsel both as to how far, and to what degree, the victim and other witnesses may be examined.

One final procedural point should be mentioned here. The way subdivision (b)(1) is worded suggests that when constitutionally required evidence is involved, it cannot be excluded on the ground that it is not shown to be more probative than prejudicial. Presumably, however, before a ruling is made under (b)(1) that evidence cannot constitutionally be excluded, its prejudicial effect will be taken into account.

It also should be observed that the drafters' *Analysis* treats prior false complaints by a victim as outside the scope of this Rule. They will fall within Rules 403 and 404(b).

DRAFTERS' ANALYSIS

Rule 412 is taken from the Federal Rule. Although substantially similar in substantive scope to Federal Rule of Evidence 412, the application of the Rule has been somewhat broadened and the procedural aspects of the Federal Rule have been modified to adapt them to military practice.

Rule 412 is intended to shield victims of sexual assaults from the often embarrassing and degrading cross-examination and evidence presentations common to prosecutions of such offenses. In so doing, it recognizes that the present rule, which it replaces, often yields evidence of at best minimal probative value with great potential for distraction and incidentally discourages both the reporting and prosecution of many sexual assaults. In replacing the unusually extensive rule now found in *Manual* ¶ 153*b*(2)(b), which permits evidence of the victim's "unchaste" character regardless of whether he or she has testified, the Rule will significantly change present military practice and will restrict defense evidence. The Rule recognizes, however, in Rule 412(b)(1) the fundamental right of the defense under the Fifth Amendment to the Constitution of the United States to present relative defense evidence by admitting evidence that is "constitutionally required to be admitted." Further, it is the Committee's intent that the Rule not be interpreted as a rule of absolute privilege. Evidence that is constitutionally required to be admitted on behalf of the defense remains admissible notwithstanding the absence of express authorization in Rule 412(a). It is unclear whether reputation or opinion evidence in this area will rise to a level of constitutional magnitude, and great care should be taken with respect to such evidence.

Rule 412 applies to a "nonconsensual sexual offense" rather than only to "rape or assault with intent to commit rape" as prescribed by the Federal Rule. The definition of "nonconsensual sexual offense" is set forth in Rule 412(e) and "includes rape, forcible sodomy, assault with intent to commit rape or forcible sodomy, indecent assault, and attempts to commit such offenses." This modification to the Federal Rule resulted from a desire to apply the social policies behind the Federal Rule to the unique military environment. Military life requires that large numbers of young men and women live and work together in close quarters which are often highly isolated. The deterrence of sexual offenses in such circumstances is critical to military efficiency. There is thus no justification for limiting the scope of the Rule, intended to protect human dignity and to ultimately encourage the reporting and prosecution of sexual offenses, only to rape and/or assault with intent to commit rape.

Rule 412(a) generally prohibits reputation or opinion evidence of an alleged victim of a nonconsensual sexual offense.

Rule 412(b)(1) recognizes that evidence of a victim's past sexual behavior may be constitutionally required to be admitted. Although there are a number of circumstances in which this language may be applicable, *see, e.g.,* S. SALTZBURG & K. REDDEN, FEDERAL RULES OF EVIDENCE MANUAL 92-93 (2d ed. Supp. 1979), giving examples of potential constitutional problems offered by the American Civil Liberties Union during the House hearings on Rule 412, one may be of particular interest. If an individual has contracted for the sexual services of a prostitute and subsequent to the performance of the act the prostitute demands increased payment on pain of claiming rape, for example, the past history of that person will likely be constitutionally required to be admitted in a subsequent prosecution in which the defense claims consent to the extent that such history is relevant and otherwise admissible to corroborate the defense position. Absent such peculiar circumstances, however, the past sexual behavior of the alleged victim, not within the scope of Rule 412(b)(2), is unlikely to be admissible regardless of the past sexual history. The mere fact that an individual is a prostitute is not normally admissible under Rule 412.

Evidence of past false complaints of sexual offenses by an alleged victim of a sexual offense is not within the scope of this Rule and is not objectionable when otherwise admissible.

Rule 412(c) provides the procedural mechanism by which evidence of past sexual behavior of a victim may be offered. The Rule has been substantially modified from the Federal Rule in order to adapt it to military practice. The requirement that notice be given not later than fifteen days before trial has been deleted as being impracticable in view of the necessity for speedy disposition of military cases. For similar reasons, the requirement for a written motion has been omitted in favor of an offer of proof, which could, of course, be made in writing, at the discretion of the military judge. Reference to hearings in chambers has been deleted as inapplicable; a hearing under Article 39(a), which may be without spectators, has been substituted. The propriety of holding a hearing without spectators is dependent upon its constitutionality which is in turn dependent upon the facts of any specific case.

Although Rule 412 is not per se applicable to such pretrial procedures as Article 32 and Court of Inquiry hearings, it may be applicable via Rule 303 and Article 31(c). *See* the *Analysis* to Rule 303.

It should be noted as a matter related to Rule 412 that the present *Manual's* prohibition in ¶ 153a of convictions for sexual offenses that rest on the uncorroborated testimony of the alleged victim has been deleted. Similarly, an express hearsay exception for fresh complaint has been deleted as being unnecessary. Consequently, evidence of fresh complaint will be admissible under the Military Rule only to the extent that it is either nonhearsay, *see, e.g.,* Rule 801(d)(1)(B), or fits within an exception to the hearsay rule. *See, e.g.,* subdivisions (1), (2), (3), (4) and (24) of Rule 803.

SECTION V. PRIVILEGES

Rule 501. General Rule.

Rule 502. Lawyer-Client Privilege.
    (a) General rule of privilege.
    (b) Definitions.
    (c) Who may claim the privilege.
    (d) Exceptions.
        (1) Crime or fraud.
        (2) Claimants through same deceased client.
        (3) Breach of duty by lawyer or client.
        (4) Document attested by lawyer.
        (5) Joint clients.

Rule 503. Communications to Clergy.
    (a) General rule of privilege.
    (b) Definitions.
    (c) Who may claim the privilege.

Rule 504. Husband-Wife Privilege.
    (a) Spousal incapacity.
    (b) Confidential communication made during marriage.
        (1) General rule of privilege.
        (2) Definition.
        (3) Who may claim the privilege.
    (c) Exceptions.
        (1) Spousal incapacity only.
        (2) Spousal incapacity and confidential communications.

Rule 505. Classified Information.
    (a) General rule of privilege.
    (b) Definitions.
        (1) Classified information.
        (2) National security.
    (c) Who may claim the privilege.
    (d) Action prior to referral of charges.
    (e) Pretrial session.
    (f) Action after referral of charges.
    (g) Disclosure of classified information to the accused.
        (1) Protective order.
        (2) Limited disclosure.
        (3) Disclosure at trial of certain statements previously made by a witness.
            (A) Scope.
            (B) Closed session.
        (4) Record of trial.
    (h) Notice of the accused's intention to disclose classified information.
        (1) Notice by the accused.
        (2) Continuing duty to notify.
        (3) Content of notice.
        (4) Prohibition against disclosure.
        (5) Failure to comply.
    (i) In camera proceedings for case involving classified information.
        (1) Definition.
        (2) Motion for in camera proceeding.
        (3) Demonstration of national security nature of the information.
        (4) In camera proceeding.
            (A) Procedure.
            (B) Standard.
            (C) Ruling.
            (D) Alternatives to full disclosure.
            (E) Sanctions.
    (j) Introduction of classified information.

　　　　(1) Classification status.
　　　　(2) Precautions by the military judge.
　　　　(3) Contents of writing, recording, or photograph.
　　　　(4) Taking of testimony.
　　　　(5) Closed session.
　　　　(6) Record of trial.
　　(k) Security procedures to safeguard against compromise of classified information disclosed to courts-martial.

Rule 506. Goverment Information Other Than Classified Information.
　　(a) General rule of privilege.
　　(b) Scope.
　　(c) Who may claim the privilege.
　　(d) Action prior to referral of charges.
　　(e) Action after referral of charges.
　　(f) Pretrial session.
　　(g) Disclosure of government information to the accused.
　　(h) Prohibition against disclosure.
　　(i) In camera proceedings.
　　　　(1) Definition.
　　　　(2) Motion for in camera proceeding.
　　　　(3) Demonstration of public interest nature of the information.
　　　　(4) In camera proceeding.
　　　　　　(A) Procedure.
　　　　　　(B) Standard.
　　　　　　(C) Ruling.
　　　　　　(D) Sanction.
　　(j) Introduction of government information subject to a claim of privilege.
　　　　(1) Precautions by military judge.
　　　　(2) Contents of writing, recording, or photograph.
　　　　(3) Taking of testimony.
　　(k) Procedures to safeguard against compromise of government information disclosed to courts-martial.

Rule 507. Identity of Informant.
　　(a) Rule of privilege.
　　(b) Whom may claim the privilege.
　　(c) Exceptions.
　　　　(1) Voluntary disclosures; informant as witness.
　　　　(2) Testimony on the issue of guilt or innocence.
　　　　(3) Legality of obtaining evidence.
　　(d) Procedures.

Rule 508. Political Vote.

Rule 509. Deliberations of Courts and Juries.

Rule 510. Waiver of Privilege by Voluntary Disclosure.

Rule 511. Privileged Matter Disclosed Under Compulsion or Without Opportunity to Claim Privilege.

Rule 512. Comment Upon or Inference from Claim of Privilege; Instruction.
　　(a) Comment or inference not permitted.
　　(b) Claiming privilege without knowledge of members.
　　(c) Instruction.

Rule 501. General Rule

(a) A person may not claim a privilege with respect to any matter except as required by or provided for in:

　　(1) The Constitution of the United States as applied to members of the armed forces;

(2) An Act of Congress applicable to trials by courts-martial;

(3) These rules or this Manual; or

(4) The principles of common law generally recognized in the trial of criminal cases in the United States district courts pursuant to Rule 501 of the Federal Rules of Evidence insofar as the application of such principles in trials by courts-martial is practicable and not contrary to or inconsistent with the Uniform Code of Military Justice, these rules, or this Manual.

(b) A claim of privilege includes, but is not limited to, the assertion by any person of a privilege to:

(1) Refuse to be a witness;

(2) Refuse to disclose any matter;

(3) Refuse to produce any object or writing; or

(4) Prevent another from being a witness or disclosing any matter or producing any object or writing.

(c) The term "person" includes an appropriate representative of the federal government, a State, or political subdivision thereof, or any other entity claiming to be the holder of a privilege.

(d) Notwithstanding any other provision of these rules, information not otherwise privileged does not become privileged on the basis that it was acquired by a medical officer of civilian physician in a professional capacity.

EDITORIAL COMMENT

Like Section III, which adds criminal procedure rules to the basic model of the Federal Rules of Evidence, Section V adds substantial material not found in the Federal Rules of Evidence. Article V of the Federal Rules contains only one Rule — Rule 501 — as a result of a sometimes bitter struggle over specific rules of privilege. Rather than delay the adoption of the rest of the evidence rules while it debated privilege rules, Congress opted to follow the common law approach previously mandated by Rule 26 of the Federal Rules of Criminal Procedure.

Section V of the Military Rules does follow the Federal Rule to the extent that it recognizes federal common law, but also t provides for eight specific privileges. Additional privileges are located in Rules 301, 302, and 303.

The drafters chose to include specific privileges in order to provide concrete guidance to a world-wide criminal justice system which makes wide use of lay persons in disposing of criminal charges. The specific provisions draw heavily from both prior *Manual* provisions in ¶ 151*b* and the proposed Federal Rules on Privilege which were rejected by Congress. For a more complete discussion of the debate over the rejected federal privileges *see* S. Saltzburg & K. Redden, Federal Rules of Evidence Manual 200-201 (2d ed. 1977). The rejected Rules and the accompanying Advisory Committee's Notes can be found in that same reference at 748.

The privileges in Section V apply in virtually all proceedings conducted pursuant to provisions of the Uniform Code of Military Justice. This includes pretrial investigations, hearings on vacations of suspended sentences, search authorizations, and pretrial confinement determinations. *See* Rule 1101.

Section V covers not only oral testimony, but also situations in which a person claims a privilege not to testify at all or a privilege to decline to produce real evidence. It governs claims by witnesses, potential witnesses and non-witnesses who wish to prevent disclosure of material.

Rule 501 presents the general rule. Subdivision (a) notes the recognized sources of privileges: the Constitution, statutes, the Military Rules of Evidence, the *Manual,* and the federal common law. The federal common law privileges, as noted in (a)(4) may be available only to the extent that they do not conflict with the practicalities of court-martial practice and are not consistent with the U.C.M.J., the Military Rules of Evidence, or the *Manual.* A specific limitation on this broad provision is found in subdivision (d) which continues pre-Rules practice by specifically declining to recognize a doctor-patient privilege. *See Manual* ¶ 151*b* and *In re Grand Jury Subpoena,* 460 F. Supp. 150 (W.D. Mo. 1978) (court found no doctor-patient privilege in federal law). According to the drafters' *Analysis,* subdivision (d) does not affect the limited privilege stated in Rule 302 (Privilege Concerning Mental Examination of an Accused). That privilege is closely related to the privilege against self-incrimination. The strong antimedical privilege position of the Rule is reflected in the drafters' *Analysis,* which states that the military will not look to the law of another jurisdiction in analyzing medical privilege claims. However, it is unclear whether a narrow psychotherapist-patient privilege, rather than a broader doctor-patient privilege is barred by this subdivision. We would think that it would not be barred in light of the extraordinary need for confidentiality between psychotherapist and patient that is as important in military as in civilian life.

Subdivision (b) is patterned after the Supreme Court's proposed Rule 501. Under subdivision (c), patterned after Federal Rule 501, the broad definition of "person" permits representatives of entities to claim the privilege on behalf of the entity. For specific direction on who may claim the privileges, *see* Rules 502(c), 503(c), 504(b) (3), 505(c), 506(c), and 507(b).

DRAFTERS' ANALYSIS

Section V contains all of the privileges applicable to military criminal law except for those privileges which are found within Rules 301, Privilege Concerning Compulsory Self-Incrimination; Rule 302, Privilege Concerning Mental Examination of an Accused; and Rule 303, Degrading Questions. Privilege rules, unlike other Military Rules of Evidence, apply in "investigative hearings pursuant to Article 32; proceedings for vacation of suspension of sentence under Article 72; proceedings for search authorization; proceedings involving pretrial restraint; and in other proceedings authorized under the Uniform Code of Military Justice or this *Manual* and not listed in rule 1101(a)." Rule 1101(c); *see also* Rule 1101(b).

In contrast to the general acceptance of the proposed Federal Rules of Evidence by Congress, Congress did not accept the proposed privilege rules because a consensus as to the desirability of a number of specific privileges could not be achieved. *See generally* S. SALTZBURG & K. REDDEN, FEDERAL RULES OF EVIDENCE MANUAL 200-201 (2d ed. 1977). In an effort to expedite the Federal Rules generally, Congress adopted a general rule, Rule 501, which basically provides for the continuation of common law in the privilege area. The Committee deemed the approach taken by Congress in the Federal Rules impracticable within the armed forces. Unlike the Article III court system, which is conducted almost entirely by attorneys functioning in conjunction with permanent courts in fixed locations, the military criminal legal system is characterized by its dependence upon large numbers of laymen, temporary courts, and inherent geographical and personnel instability due to the worldwide deployment of military personnel. Consequently, military law requires far more stability than civilian law. This is particularly true because of the significant number of non-lawyers involved in the military criminal legal system. Commanders, convening authorities, non-lawyer investigating officers, summary court-martial officers, or law enforcement personnel need specific guidance as to what material is privileged and what is not.

Section V combines the flexible approach taken by Congress with respect to privileges with that provided in the present *Manual*. Rules 502-509 set forth specific rules of privilege to provide the certainty and stability necessary for military justice. Rule 501, on the other hand, adopts those privileges recognized in common law pursuant to Federal Rule of Evidence 501 with some limitations. Specific privileges are generally taken from those proposed Federal Rules of Evidence which although not adopted by Congress were non-controversial, or from the present Manual.

Rule 501 is the basic rule of privilege. In addition to recognizing privileges required by or provided for in the Constitution, an applicable Act of Congress, the Military Rules of Evidence, and the *Manual for Courts-Martial*, Rule 501(a) also recognizes privileges "generally recognized in the trial of criminal cases in the United States district courts pursuant to Rule 501 of the Federal Rules of Evidence insofar as the application of such principles in trials by court-martial is practicable and not contrary to or inconsistent with the Uniform Code of Military Justice, these rules, or this Manual." The latter language is taken from present *Manual* paragraph 137. As a result of Rule 501(a)(4), the common law of privileges as recognized in the Article III courts will be applicable to the armed forces except as otherwise provided by the limitation indicated above. Rule 501(d) prevents the application of a doctor-patient privilege. Such a privilege was considered to be totally incompatible with the clear interest of the armed forces in ensuring the health and fitness for duty of personnel. *See* present *Manual* paragraph 151c. The privilege expressed in Rule 302 and its conforming *Manual* change in paragraph 121, is not a doctor-patient privilege and is not affected by Rule 501(d).

It should be noted that the law of the forum determines the application of privilege. Consequently, even if a service member should consult with a doctor in a jurisdiction with a doctor-patient privilege for example, such a privilege is inapplicable should the doctor be called as a witness before a court-martial.

Subdivision (b) is a non-exhaustive list of actions which constitute an invocation of a privilege. The subdivision is derived from Federal Rule of Evidence 501 as originally proposed by the Supreme Court, and the four specific actions listed are also found in the Uniform Rules of Evidence. The list is intentionally non-exclusive as a privilege might be claimed in a fashion distinct from those listed.

Subdivision (c) is derived from Federal Rule of Evidence 501 and makes it clear that an appropriate representative of a political jurisdiction or other organizational entity may claim an applicable privilege. The definition is intentionally non-exhaustive.

Rule 502. Lawyer-Client Privilege

(a) General rule of privilege. A client has a privilege to refuse to disclose and to prevent any other person from disclosing confidential communications made for the purpose of facilitating the rendition of professional legal services to the client, (1) between the client or the client's representative and the lawyer or the lawyer's representative, (2) between the lawyer and the lawyer's representative, (3) by the client or the client's lawyer to a lawyer representing another in a matter of common interest, (4) between representatives of the client or between the client and a representative of the client, or (5) between lawyers representing the client.

(b) Definitions. As used in this rule:

(1) A "client" is a person, public officer, corporation, association, organization, or other entity, either public or private, who receives professional legal services from a lawyer, or who consults a lawyer with a view to obtaining professional legal services from the lawyer.

(2) A "lawyer" is a person authorized, or reasonably believed by the client to be authorized, to practice law; or a member of the armed forces detailed, assigned, or otherwise provided to represent a person in a court-martial case or in any military investigation or proceeding. The term "lawyer" does not include a member of the armed forces serving in a capacity other than as a judge advocate, legal officer, or law specialist as defined in Article 1, unless the member: (a) is detailed, assigned, or otherwise provided to represent a person in a court-martial case or in any military investigation or proceeding; (b) is authorized by the armed forces, or reasonably believed by the client to be authorized, to render professional legal services to members of the armed forces; or (c) is authorized to practice law and renders professional legal services during off-duty employment.

(3) A "representative" of a lawyer is a person employed by or assigned to assist a lawyer in providing professional legal services.

(4) A communication is "confidential" if not intended to be disclosed to third persons other than those to whom

disclosure is in furtherance of the rendition of professional legal services to the client or those reasonably necessary for the transmission of the communication.

*(c) **Who may claim the privilege.*** The privilege may be claimed by the client, the guardian or conservator of the client, the personal representative of a deceased client, or the successor, trustee, or similar representative of a corporation, association, or other organization, whether or not in existence. The lawyer or the lawyer's representative who received the communication may claim the privilege on behalf of the client. The authority of the lawyer to do so is presumed in the absence of evidence to the contrary.

*(d) **Exceptions.*** There is no privilege under this rule under the following circumstances:

*(1) **Crime or fraud.*** If the communication clearly contemplated the future commission of a fraud or crime or if services of the lawyer were sought or obtained to enable or aid anyone to commit or plan to commit what the client knew or reasonably should have known to be a crime or fraud;

*(2) **Claimants through same deceased client.*** As to a communication relevant to an issue between parties who claim through the same deceased client, regardless of whether the claims are by testate or intestate succession or by inter vivos transaction;

*(3) **Breach of duty by lawyer or client.*** As to a communication relevant to an issue of breach of duty by the lawyer to the client or by the client to the lawyer;

*(4) **Document attested by lawyer.*** As to a communication relevant to an issue concerning an attested document to which the lawyer is an attesting witness; or

*(5) **Joint clients.*** As to a communication relevant to a matter of common interest between two or more clients if the communication was made by any of them to a lawyer retained or consulted in common, when offered in an action between any of the clients.

EDITORIAL COMMENT

The traditional testimonial privilege protecting the lawyer-client relationship is now found in Rule 502, which generally follows the Supreme Court's proposed Federal Rule of Evidence 503. The proposed rule and the accompanying Advisory Committee Notes are included in S. SALTZBURG & K. REDDEN, FEDERAL RULES OF EVIDENCE MANUAL 752-756 (2d ed. 1977). Rule 502 also incorporates the tenor of *Manual* ¶ 151*b*(2) which had provided only generalized guidance on the nature and extent of the privilege.

Subdivision (a) is taken from proposed Federal Rule of Evidence 503(b) and presents a familiar statement of the general privilege rule. The privilege specifically rests with a client who may refuse to divulge, and who may block disclosure of, confidential communications made to a lawyer for the purpose of obtaining legal services. The Rule specifically notes that more than communications from the client to the lawyer are covered. For example, confidential communications from the lawyer's assistant to a representative of the client could be privileged. Discussions between lawyers working on the client's case and discussions between representatives of the client are also potentially within the general rule. Under (a)(3), communications in a joint conference between clients and their respective lawyers may also be privileged; each client has a privilege not to have his statements divulged.

The privilege extends to initial discussions between the parties even though the relationship does not continue. *Levin v. Ripple Twist Mills, Inc.*, 416 F. Supp. 876 (E.D. Pa. 1976). Communications not involving legal advice are not privileged. *See, e.g., Coastal States Gas Corp. v. Dep't of Energy*, 617 F.2d 854 (D.C. Cir. 1980); *United States v. Amerada Hess Corp.*, 619 F.2d 980 (3d Cir. 1980).

Definitions of the key terms used in the general rules are set out in subdivision (b). Under (b)(1) the term "client" includes more than natural persons. Corporations, organizations, and other legal entities are included. But the Rule provides no specific guidance on who speaks for the entity for purposes of the privilege. The federal courts have split on the issue. Prior to 1981, the more limited "control group" test seemed to be the most widely accepted. Under that standard a corporate or "entity" client is entitled to the privilege for communications made by an employee who is in a position to control or to take a substantial role in a decision involving the attorney's advice or is an authorized member of a group which has the authority. In effect, that employee personifies the organization. *See Mead Data Central Inc. v. Department of the Air Force*, 566 F.2d 242 (D.C. Cir. 1977); *City of Philadelphia v. Westinghouse Electric Corp.*, 210 F. Supp. 483 (E.D. Pa. 1962).

Broader tests of privilege were found in *United States v. United Shoe Machinery Corp.*, 89 F. Supp. 357 (D. Mass. 1950) (all communications by any employee are protected); *Harper and Row Publishers, Inc. v. Decker*, 423 F.2d 487 (7th Cir. 1970) (scope of employment test), aff'd, 400 U.S. 348 (1971); *Diversified Industries, Inc. v. Meredith*, 572 F.2d 596 (8th Cir. 1978) (en banc) (subject matter test). *See generally Attorney-Client Privilege in Federal Courts: Under What Circumstances Can Corporation Claim Privilege for Communications from Its Employees and Agents to Corporation's Attorney*, 9 A.L.R. FED. 685 (1971).

The Supreme Court in *Upjohn Co. v. United States*, 101 S. Ct. —— (1981), rejected the "control group" test and opted in favor of greater protection for employees' statements. Whether the Court will use the same broad approach in dealing with government agencies claiming privilege is not yet determined.

Occasionally, a question arises concerning whether a commander is entitled to invoke the lawyer-client privilege in conjunction with confidential discussions with a military lawyer. An analogous situation was addressed in *In re Grand Jury Proceedings*, 434 F. Supp. 648 (E.D. Mich. 1977), aff'd, 570 F.2d 562 (6th Cir. 1978), where the court distinguished between a corporate officer speaking for himself and speaking for the organization:

> If the communicating officer seeks legal advice himself and consults a lawyer about his problems, he may have a privilege. If he makes it clear when he is consulting the company lawyer that he personally is consulting the lawyer and the lawyer sees fit to accept and give communication knowing the possible conflicts that could arise, he may have a privilege. But in the absence of any indication to the company's lawyer that the lawyer is to act in any other capacity than as lawyer for the company in giving and receiving communications from control group personnel, the privilege is and should remain that of the company and not that of the communicating officer.

Subdivision (b)(2) addresses the definition of "lawyer." The definition includes not only attorneys authorized to practice law and those individuals reasonably believed by the client to be so authorized, *see, e.g., United States v. Ostrer*, 422 F. Supp. 93 (S.D.N.Y. 1976) (good faith belief), but also military personnel who are representing clients before military criminal or administrative proceedings. *See* Article 27, U.C.M.J. and *Manual* ¶ 151*b*(2). The Advisory Committee's Note on proposed Federal Rule of Evidence 503(a)(2), which serves in part as the basis for subdivision (b)(2), states that "authorized . . . to practice law" means that the lawyer must be licensed.

The second sentence of (b)(2) was apparently included to make clear that not all licensed attorneys serving in the armed forces necessarily act as lawyers while serving. The following personnel, including attorneys, who are not serving as judge advocates, legal officers, or law specialists, see Article 1, U.C.M.J., fit into one of the three listed categories in (b)(2) and fall within the zone of the privilege:

> (a) those representing individuals before military criminal or administrative proceedings;
> (b) those authorized to give professional legal services or reasonably believed by client to be authorized to do so; or
> (c) those licensed attorneys authorized to practice and actually practicing law while off-duty.

The definition of "representative" of a lawyer is addressed in subdivision (b)(3) and is a slight modification of proposed Federal Rule 503(a)(3). As under *Manual* ¶ 151*b*(2), individuals working for, or with, a lawyer may fit within the definition. The Rule, which includes individuals who are assigned or employed to assist a lawyer, probably should not be read so narrowly as to exclude volunteers who are actively assisting lawyers. Application of the privilege should not turn on detailing orders or remuneration but should depend upon whether a person is working for — *i.e.,* under the supervision or control — of a lawyer. The federal courts have applied the privilege to situations involving a client's communications with an accountant, *United States v. Kovel,* 296 F.2d 918 (2d Cir. 1961); law clerks, *Cold Metal Process Co. v. Aluminum Co. of America,* 7 F.R.D. 684 (D. Mass. 1947); stenographers, *Himmelfarb v. United States,* 175 F.2d 924 (9th Cir. 1949); engineers, *Lewis v. United Air Lines Transport Corp.,* 32 F. Supp. 21 (W.D. Pa. 1940). *Cf. Dabney v. Investment Corp. of America,* 82 F.R.D. 464 (E.D. Pa. 1979) (law student, not admitted to practice, was not agent of a duly licensed attorney).

Although no psychiatrist-patient privilege is recognized in the Rules, in some instances a psychiatrist may be considered a member of the defense team. *See, e.g., United States v. Alvarez,* 519 F.2d 1036 (3d Cir. 1975). *See generally* Saltzburg, *Privileges and Professionals; Lawyers and Psychiatrists,* 66 VA. L. REV. 597 (1980). *See also United States ex rel. Edney v. Smith,* 425 F. Supp. 1038 (E.D.N.Y. 1976), aff'd, 556 F.2d 556 (2d Cir.), cert. denied, 431 U.S. 958 (1977).

The privilege extends only to "confidential communications." Subdivision (b)(4) defines that term and requires an examination of the communicating party's intent. If the communication was intended to be confidential, interception by a third party (inadvertent or intentional) will not destroy the privilege. *Cf. Manual* ¶ 151*b*(2).

Although communications in the presence of third parties may destroy confidentiality — *see, e.g., United States v. Landof,* 591 F.2d 36 (9th Cir. 1978) (another lawyer, not acting as attorney or agent, was present) — disclosure to third parties who are outside the immediate circle of the lawyer, client, and their representatives, will not always result in a loss of the privilege. If communications are deemed to be "in furtherance of the rendition of professional legal services," the privilege may stand notwithstanding disclosure to third parties. The Advisory Committee Notes on the proposed Federal Rule 503(a)(4) noted that disclosure to spouses, parents, business associates, or joint clients might in some cases be necessary. *See Saltzburg & Redden, supra* at 754. However, public disclosure will constitute waiver of the privilege. *See* Rules 510, 511. Where the communication involves many individuals, the claimant may have the burden of showing that it remained within privileged channels. *See Coastal Corp. v. Duncan,* 86 F.R.D. 514 (D. Del. 1980).

The rule does not define "communication" but should encompass both oral and written communications as long as they are communications made for the purpose of getting advice. Documents that are prepared independently of the lawyer-client relationship cannot be given to a lawyer in order to conceal them. *See Fisher v. United States,* 425 U.S. 391 (1976).

The client, not the lawyer, holds the privilege, although under subdivision (c) the lawyer, his representatives, and specified representatives of the client may claim the privilege on behalf of the client. Subdivision (c) is identical to proposed Federal Rule 503(c) and slightly expands *Manual* ¶ 151*b*(2). Unless contrary evidence is presented, the lawyer's authority to claim the privilege on behalf of the client is presumed. The lawyer may not claim the privilege on his own behalf.

Subdivision (d) contains five "exceptions" to the privilege. Subdivisions (d)(2), claimants through same deceased client, and (d)(4), document attested by lawyer, are not likely to be encountered in military practice. The others, however, are more familiar. Under (d)(1), the client's communications concerning involvement in future crimes are not privileged. *United States v. Rosenstein,* 474 F.2d 705 (2d Cir. 1973); *United States v. Shewfelt,* 455 F.2d 836 (9th Cir. 1972). *See also In re Grand Jury Proceedings,* 604 F.2d 798 (3d Cir. 1979) (crime-fraud exception may also be applied to work-product privilege). The Advisory Committee's Note on the proposed Federal Rule states that in applying (d)(1) it would be appropriate to specifically focus, through questions, on what transpired between the lawyer and the client to avoid broad inquiries into lawyer-client communications.

The privilege may also be waived under (d)(3) where a question concerning alleged breaches of duty, by either the client or the lawyer, are raised. In military practice this exception will normally be raised where the accused client is raising post-conviction questions regarding his lawyer's competency, *see United States v. Allen,* 8 C.M.A. 504, 25 C.M.R. 8 (1957).

Under (d)(5), where a lawyer has initially undertaken to represent several co-accused, communications made by one or more of them are protected in a prosecution against any of them. Only when they sue each other does the privilege disappear. It should also be remembered that under subdivision (a)(3), *supra,* clients represented by different lawyers may share information with lawyers representing others with common interests. *See United States v. McPartlin,* 595 F.2d 1321 (7th Cir.), cert. denied, 444 U.S. 833 (1979).

If an accused claims good faith reliance on the advice of counsel as a defense this will be deemed to be a waiver of confidentiality, and the privilege will be lost. *See, e.g., United States v. Miller,* 600 F.2d 498 (5th Cir. 1979).

DRAFTERS' ANALYSIS

(a) General rule of privilege. Rule 502(a) continues the substance of the attorney-client privilege now found in ¶ 151*b*(2) of the present *Manual.* The Rule does however, provide additional detail. Subdivision (a) is taken verbatim from subdivision (a) of Federal Rule of Evidence 503 as proposed by the Supreme Court. The privilege is only applicable when there are "confidential communications made for the purpose of facilitating the rendition of professional legal services to the client." A mere discussion with an attorney does not invoke the privilege when the discussion is not made for the purpose of obtaining professional legal services.

(b) Definitions.

(1) Client. Rule 502(b) (1) defines a "client" as an individual or entity who receives professional legal services from a lawyer or consults a lawyer with a view to obtaining such services. The definition is taken from proposed Federal Rule 503(a) (1) as ¶ 151*b*(2) of the present *Manual* lacks any general definition of a client.

(2) Lawyer. Rule 502(b) (2) defines a "lawyer". The first portion of the paragraph is taken from proposed Federal Rule of Evidence 503(a) (2) and explicitly includes any person "reasonably believed by the client to be authorized" to practice law. The second clause is taken from present *Manual* paragraph 151*b*(2) and

recognizes that a "lawyer" includes "a member of the armed forces detailed, assigned, or otherwise provided to represent a person in a court-martial case or in any military investigation or proceeding" regardless of whether that person is in fact a lawyer. *See* Article 27. Thus an accused is fully protected by the privilege even if defense counsel is not an attorney.

The second sentence of the subdivision recognizes the fact, particularly true during times of mobilization, that attorneys may serve in the armed forces in a nonlegal capacity. In such a case, the individual involved is not treated as an attorney under the Rule unless the individual fits within one of the three specific categories recognized by the subdivision. Subdivision (b)(2)(b) recognizes that a servicemember who knows that an individual is a lawyer in civilian life may not know that the lawyer is not functioning as such in the armed forces and may seek professional legal assistance. In such a case the privilege will be applicable so long as the individual was "reasonably believed by the client to be authorized to render professional legal services to members of the armed forces."

(3) Representative of a lawyer. Rule 502(b)(3) is taken from proposed Federal Rule of Evidence 503(a)(3) but has been modified to recognize that personnel are "assigned" within the armed forces as well as employed. Depending upon the particular situation, a paraprofessional or secretary may be a "representative of a lawyer." *See* ¶ 151*b*(2) of the present *Manual.*

(4) Confidential communication. Rule 502(b)(4) defines a "confidential" communication in terms of the intention of the party making the communication. The Rule is similar to the substance of present *Manual* paragraph 151*b*(2) which omits certain communications from privileged status. The new Rule is somewhat broader than the present *Manual's* provision in that it protects information which is obtained by a third party through accident or design when the person claiming the privilege was not aware that a third party had access to the communication. Compare Rule ¶ 151*a* of the present *Manual.* The broader rule has been adopted for the reasons set forth in the Advisory Committee's notes on proposed Federal Rule 504(a) (4). The provision permitting disclosure to persons in furtherance of legal services or reasonably necessary for the transmission of the communication is similar to the provision in the current manual for communications through agents.

Although ¶ 151*c* of the present *Manual* precludes a claim of the privilege when there is transmission through wire or radio communications, the new Rules protect statements made via telephone, or, "if use of such means of communication is necessary and in furtherance of the communication", by other "electronic means of communication". Rule 511(b).

(c) Who may claim the privilege. Rule 502(c) is taken from proposed Federal Rule 503(b) and expresses who may claim the lawyer-client privilege. The Rule is similar to but slightly broader than ¶ 151*b*(2) of the present *Manual.* The last sentence of the subdivision states that "the authority of the lawyer to claim the privilege is presumed in the absence of evidence to the contrary."

The lawyer may claim the privilege on behalf of the client unless authority to do so has been withheld from the lawyer or evidence otherwise exists to show that the lawyer lacks the authority to claim the privilege.

(d) Exceptions. Rule 502(d) sets forth the circumstances in which the lawyer-client privilege will not apply notwithstanding the general application of the privilege.

Subdivision (d) (1) excludes statements contemplating the future commission of crime or fraud and combines the substance of present *Manual* paragraph 151*b*(2) with proposed Federal Rule of Evidence 503(d). Under the exception a lawyer may disclose information given by a client when it was part of a "communication [which] clearly contemplated the future commission of a crime or fraud", and a lawyer may also disclose information when it can be objectively said that the lawyer's services "were sought or obtained to commit or plan to commit what the client knew or reasonably should have known to be a crime or fraud." The latter portion of the exception is likely to be applicable only after the commission of the offense while the former is applicable when the communication is made.

Subdivisions (d) (2) through (d) (5) provide exceptions with respect to claims through the same deceased client, breach of duty by lawyer of client, documents attested by lawyers, and communications to an attorney in a matter of common interest among joint clients. There are no parallel provisions in the present *Manual* for these rules which are taken from proposed Federal Rule 503(d). The provisions are included in the event that the circumstances described therein arise in military practice.

Rule 503. Communications to Clergy

(a) General rule of privilege. A person has a privilege to refuse to disclose and to prevent another from disclosing a confidential communication by the person to a clergyman or to a clergyman's assistant, if such communication is made either as a formal act of religion or as a matter of conscience.

(b) Definitions. As used in this rule:

> (1) A "clergyman" is a minister, priest, rabbi, chaplain, or other similar functionary of a religious organization, or an individual reasonably believed to be so by the person consulting the clergyman.

> (2) A communication is "confidential" if made to a clergyman in the clergyman's capacity as a spiritual adviser or to a clergyman's assistant in the assistant's official capacity and is not intended to be disclosed to third persons other than those to whom disclosure is in furtherance of the purpose of the communication or to those reasonably necessary for the transmission of the communication.

(c) Who may claim the privilege. The privilege may be claimed by the person, by the guardian or conservator, or by a personal representative if the person is deceased. The clergyman or clergyman's assistant who received the communication may claim the privilege on behalf of the person. The authority of the clergyman or clergyman's assistant to do so is presumed in the absence of evidence to the contrary.

EDITORIAL COMMENT

The testimonial privilege protecting communications of a penitent to a clergyman which is now included in Rule 503 is drawn from proposed Federal Rule 506. *See* S. SALTZBURG & K. REDDEN, FEDERAL RULES OF EVIDENCE MANUAL 761-763 (2d ed. 1977). The Rule resembles prior *Manual* ¶ 151*b*(2).

The general rule, stated in subdivision (a), continues the pre-Rules practice of not extending the privilege to all confidential communications with clergy, but limiting it to those communications made either as a formal act of religion, such as religious confession, or as a matter of conscience. Proposed Federal Rule 506 would have extended the privilege to all confidential communications with a clergyman in his professional capacity. The Military Rule is likely to be as protective.

Subdivision (a) seems consistent with what little military and federal case law exists. *See, e.g., United States v. Kidd,* 20 C.M.R. 713 (A.B.R. 1955) (chaplain's stated opinion of accused revealed no confidences relating to matters of faith or conscience); *United States v. Wells,* 446 F.2d 2 (2d Cir. 1971) (letter given to priest was not privileged); *Mullen v. United States,* 263 F.2d 275 (D.C. Cir. 1958) (defendant's confession to Lutheran minister was privileged). The Rule differs from *Manual* ¶ 151*b*(2) in that the holder of the privilege may prevent disclosure by a third party eavesdropper. *See also* (b) (2).

The definitions of "clergyman" and "confidential" communication are addressed in subdivision (b). The definition of clergyman specifically notes those individuals who may qualify. It is not so broad as to include self-styled or self-determined ministers. In this regard the Advisory Committee Note on the proposed federal rule states that:

> A fair construction of the language requires that the person to whom the status is sought to be attached be regularly engaged in activities conforming at least in a general way with those of a Catholic priest, Jewish rabbi, or minister of an established Protestant denomination, though not necessarily on a full time basis. No further specification seems possible in view of the lack of licensing and certification procedures for clergymen.

See Saltzburg & Redden, supra, at 762. The communications also qualify if made to a person reasonably believed by the penitent to be a "clergyman" — *see* the comparable "reasonable belief" provision in Rule 502(b)(2), — or if made to a clergyman's assistant. *See generally* Note, *Catholic Sisters, Irregularly Ordained Women and the Clergy Penitent Privilege,* 9 U. CAL. DAVIS L. REV. 523 (1976).

The definition of confidential communications is found in subdivision (b)(2). It parallels a similar provision in Rule 502(b)(4). As we noted in our discussion of that provision, the definition turns on the penitent's intent and is broad enough to include oral and written statements if made to the clergyman in confidence for the purpose of seeking spiritual counseling. *Cf. United States v. Wells, supra.* (Letter given to priest was not privileged because it was not confidential.)

Under subdivision (c) the privilege may be claimed by the clergyman, not on his own behalf but rather on behalf of the individual. *See Manual* ¶ 151*b*(2). The Rule recognizes the prima facie authority on the part of a clergyman to so claim the privilege.

The Rule contains no specific exceptions. In particular, the penitent's stated intent to commit a crime does not negate the privilege. The Advisory Committee's Note on 506(b), the counterpart to the general rule in subdivision (a), states that "[t]he nature of what may reasonably be considered spiritual advice makes it unnecessary to include in the rule a specific exception for communications in furtherance of crime or fraud as in [the lawyer-client privilege]." *See* Rule 510 for waiver of privilege through voluntary disclosure.

DRAFTERS' ANALYSIS

(a) General rule of privilege. Rule 503(a) states the basic rule of privilege for communications to clergy and is taken from proposed Federal Rule of Evidence 506(b) and present *Manual* paragraph 151*b*(2). Like the present *Manual,* the Rule protects communications to a clergyman's assistant in specific recognition of the nature of the military chaplaincy, and deals only with communications "made either as a formal act of religion or as a matter of conscience."

(b) Definitions.

    (1) Clergyman. Rule 503(b)(1) is taken from proposed Federal Rule of Evidence 506(a)(1) but has been modified to include specific reference to a chaplain. The Rule does not define "a religious organization" and leaves resolution of that question to precedent and the circumstances of the case. "Clergyman" includes individuals of either sex.

    (2) Confidential. Rule 503(b)(2) is taken generally from proposed Federal Rule of Evidence 506(a)(2) but has been expanded to include communications to a clergyman's assistant and to explicitly protect disclosure of a privileged communication when "disclosure is in furtherance of the purpose of the communication or to those reasonably necessary for the transmission of the communication." The Rule is thus consistent with the definition of "confidential" used in the lawyer-client privilege, Rule 502(b)(4), and recognizes that military life often requires transmission of communications through third parties. The proposed Federal Rule's limitation of the privilege to communications made "privately" was deleted in favor of the language used in the actual Military Rule for the reasons indicated. The Rule is somewhat more protective than the present *Manual* because of its application to statements which although intended to be confidential are overheard by others. *See* Rules 502(b)(4) and 510(a) and the Analysis thereto.

(c) Who may claim the privilege. Rule 503(c) is derived from proposed Federal Rule of Evidence 506(c) and includes the substance of the present *Manual* paragraph 151 *b*(2) which provides that the privilege may be claimed by the "penitent." The Rule supplies additional guidance as to who may actually claim the privilege and is consistent with the other Military Rules of Evidence relating to privileges. *See* Rules 502(c); 504(b)(3); 505(c); 506(c).

Rule 504. Husband-Wife Privilege

(a) Spousal incapacity. A person has a privilege to refuse to testify against his or her spouse.

(b) Confidential communication made during marriage.

(1) General rule of privilege. A person has a privilege during and after the marital relationship to refuse to disclose, and to prevent another from disclosing, any confidential communication made to the spouse of the person while they were husband and wife and not separated as provided by law.

(2) Definition. A communication is "confidential" if made privately by any person to the spouse of the person and is not intended to be disclosed to third persons other than those reasonably necessary for transmission of the communication.

(3) Who may claim the privilege. The privilege may be claimed by the spouse who made the communication or by the other spouse on his or her behalf. The authority of the latter spouse to do so is presumed in the absence of evidence of a waiver. The privilege will not prevent disclosure of the communication at the request of the spouse to whom the communication was made if that spouse is an accused regardless of whether the spouse who made the communication objects to its disclosure.

(c) Exceptions.

(1) Spousal incapacity only. There is no privilege under subdivision (a) when, at the time the testimony of one of the parties to the marriage is to be introduced in evidence against the other party, the parties are divorced or the marriage has been annulled.

(2) Spousal incapacity and confidential communications. **There is no privilege under subdivisions (a) or (b):**

(A) In proceedings in which one spouse is charged with a crime against the person or property of the other spouse or a child of either, or with a crime against the person or property of a third person committed in the course of committing a crime against the other spouse;

(B) When the marital relationship was entered into with no intention of the parties to live together as spouses, but only for the purpose of using the purported marital relationship as a sham, and with respect to the privilege in subdivision (a), the relationship remains a sham at the time the testimony or statement of one of the parties is to be introduced against the other; or with respect to the privilege in subdivision (b), the relationship was a sham at the time of the communication; or

(C) In proceedings in which a spouse is charged, in accordance with Articles 133 and 134, with importing the other spouse as an alien for prostitution or other immoral purpose in violation of section 1328 of title 8, United States Code; with transporting the other spouse in interstate commerce for immoral purposes or other offense in violation of sections 2421-2424 of title 18, United States Code; or with violation of such other similar statutes under which such privilege may not be claimed in the trial of criminal cases in the United States district courts.

EDITORIAL COMMENT

The military and federal courts have generally recognized two distinct privileges related to marital relationships. One relates to the capacity of one spouse to testify against the other. The second relates to confidential communications made during the marriage. Rule 504 addresses both.

The capacity of a spouse to testify is laid out in subdivision (a). It adopts the approach of *Trammel v. United States,* 445 U.S. 40 (1980), and changes the pre-Rules practice which had permitted each spouse to prevent the other from testifying. *See Manual* ¶ 148e. *See, e.g., United States v. Lovell,* 8 M.J. 613 (A.F.C.M.R. 1979); *United States v. Gibbs,* 4 M.J. 922 (A.F.C.M.R. 1978); *United States v. Seiber,* 12 C.M.A. 520, 31 C.M.R. 106 (1961). Now, only the testifying spouse may decide whether or not to testify, and even that choice is denied under 504(c)(1) if at the time of the testimony the parties are divorced or the marriage has been annulled. The privilege is available, however, while the parties are married, even if the testimony in question involves events occurring prior to a *valid* (not a sham) marriage.

A spouse's privilege to prevent disclosure of confidential communications is provided in subdivision (b), which is comparable to the privileges in Rules 502 and 503. Note that this privilege is distinct from the capacity privilege, although both may arise in the same case. The general rule for marital communications is stated in subdivision (b)(1). An individual forever may block disclosure of confidential communications made to his spouse during their marriage. The privilege applies even after the marriage has ended. *Pereira v. United States,* 347 U.S. 1 (1954). But any communications made when the parties were legally separated are not covered by this provision. If the parties are still married, though separated at the time of trial, a testifying spouse might refuse to testify against the accused spouse under the incapacity privilege, unless it is barred under subdivision (c).

Communications under subdivision (b)(2) are considered confidential only if made in private. This is a variance on comparable provisions in Rules 502(b)(4) and 503(b)(2) which contain no "privacy" requirement; the presence of third parties in those instances will not in itself negate the confidentiality. Here the presence of third parties generally negates any presumption of privacy. *See, e.g., Pool v. United States,* 260 F.2d 57 (9th Cir. 1958). Disclosures to those third parties who are reasonably required to transmit the intended confidential communications are permitted, however. As in Rules 502 and 503, the communicating spouse may prevent disclosure of any confidential communications (made in private) which were overheard by third parties. *Cf. Manual* ¶ 151*b*(2).

Subdivision (b)(3) makes it clear that the privilege to prevent disclosure by anyone of confidential communications is held by the spouse who made them. The privilege may be claimed either by the communicating spouse or by the other in the former's behalf; the authority to do so is presumed. However, according to (b)(3), the privilege will not prevent an accused from disclosing or requiring his spouse to disclose communications, even if they were made by that spouse to the accused and the communicating spouse objects. This is generally consistent with *Manual* ¶ 151*b*(2). Many common law cases give the privilege to both spouses, but this Rule is more limited.

Subdivision (c) lists several situations where either or both the "spousal incapacity" privilege in subdivision (a) and the "confidential communications" privilege in subdivision (b) may not be invoked. Also, as noted earlier, a spouse has no grounds to refuse to testify against an accused spouse where the marriage has ended. *See* (c)(1).

Under (c)(2) both privileges fall where anti-marital acts are involved. The provisions of (c)(2)(A) and (c)(2)(C) are for the most part consistent with *Manual* ¶ 148*e,* except that under (c)(2)(A) a crime against the child of either spouse now will also negate both privileges under this Rule. This provision rests in part on *Wyatt v. United States,* 362 U.S. 525 (1960). *See also* proposed Federal Rule of Evidence 505(c)(1), included in S. Saltzburg & K. Redden, Federal Rules of Evidence Manual 759-61 (2d ed. 1977). And violation of federal statutes similar to those noted in (c)(2)(C) will also remove both privileges.

The exception stated in subdivision (c)(2)(B) generally follows *Manual* ¶ 148*e* and 151*b*(2) and limits application of both privileges where the marriage is a sham. For purposes of the capacity of a spouse to testify under (a), a sham marriage in effect at the time a witness is called to testify negates the privilege. *Lutwak v. United States,* 344 U.S. 604 (1953). The privilege for confidential communications under (b) does not exist if at the time of the communications the marriage was a sham even if it later ripened into a valid marriage. It is apparent the military judges will have to engage in some preliminary fact-finding as to the validity of the marriage when ruling on claim of both marital privileges. *See* our discussion of Rule 104.

DRAFTERS' ANALYSIS

(a) Spousal incapacity. Rule 504(a) is taken generally from *Trammel v. United States*, 445 U.S. 40 (1980) and significantly changes military law in this area. Under present law, *see* present *Manual* paragraph 148e, each spouse has a privilege to prevent the use of the other spouse as an adverse witness. Under the new rule, the *witness* spouse is the holder of the privilege and may choose to testify or not to testify as the witness spouse sees fit. *But see* Rule 504(c) (exceptions to the privilege). Implicit in the rule is the presumption that when a spouse chooses to testify against the other spouse the marriage no longer needs the protection of the privilege. Rule 504(a) must be distinguished from Rule 504(b), *Confidential communication made during marriage*, which deals with communications rather than the ability to testify generally at trial.

Although the witness spouse ordinarily has a privilege to refuse to testify against the accused spouse, under certain circumstances no privilege may exist, and the spouse may be compelled to testify. *See* Rule 504(c).

(b) Confidential communication made during marriage. Rule 504(b) deals with communications made during a marriage and is distinct from a spouse's privilege to refuse to testify pursuant to Rule 504(a). *See* present *Manual* paragraph 151b(2).

(1) General rule of privilege. Rule 504(b)(1) sets forth the general rule of privilege for confidential spousal communications and provides that a spouse may prevent disclosure of any confidential spousal communication made during marriage even though the parties are no longer married at the time that disclosure is desired. The accused may always require that the confidential spousal communication be disclosed. Rule 504(b)(3).

No privilege exists under subdivision (b) if the communication was made when the spouses were legally separated.

(2) Definition. Rule 504(b)(2) defines "confidential" in a fashion similar to the definition utilized in Rules 502(b)(4) and 503(b)(2). The word "privately" has been added to emphasize that the presence of third parties is not consistent with the spousal privilege, and the reference to third parties found in Rules 502 and 503 has been omitted for the same reason. Rule 504(b)(2) extends the definition of "confidential" to statements disclosed to third parties who are "reasonably necessary for transmission of the communication." This recognizes that circumstances may arise, especially in military life where spouses may be separated by great distances or by operational activities, in which transmission of a communication via third parties may be reasonably necessary.

(3) Who may claim the privilege. Rule 504(b)(3) is consistent with present *Manual* paragraph 151b(2) and gives the privilege to the spouse who made the communication. The accused may, however, disclose the communication even though the communication was made to the accused.

(c) Exceptions.

(1) Spousal incapacity only. Rule 504(c)(1) provides exceptions to the spousal incapacity rule of Rule 504(a). The rule is taken from present *Manual* paragraph 148e and declares that a spouse may not refuse to testify against the

other spouse when the marriage has been terminated by divorce or annulment. Annulment has been added to the present military rule as being consistent with its purpose. Separation of spouses via legal separation or otherwise does not affect the privilege of a spouse to refuse to testify against the other spouse. For other circumstances in which a spouse may be compelled to testify against the other spouse *see* Rule 504(c)(2).

Confidential communications are not affected by the termination of a marriage.

(2) Spousal incapacity and confidential communications. Rule 504(c)(2) prohibits application of the spousal privilege, whether in the form of spousal incapacity or in the form of a confidential communication, when the circumstances specified in paragraph (2) are applicable. Subparagraphs (A) and (C) deal with anti-marital acts, *e.g.,* acts which are against the spouse and thus the marriage. The Rule expressly provides that when such an act is involved a spouse may not refuse to testify. This provision is taken from proposed Federal Rule 505(c)(1) and reflects in part the Supreme Court's decision in *Wyatt v. United States,* 362 U.S. 525 (1960). *See also Trammel v. United States,* 445 U.S. 40 (1980). The Rule thus recognizes society's overriding interest in prosecution of anti-marital offenses and the probability that a spouse may exercise sufficient control, psychological or otherwise, to be able to prevent the other spouse from testifying voluntarily. The Rule is similar to present *Manual* paragraph 148*e* but has deleted the *Manual's* limitation of the exceptions to the privilege to matters occurring after marriage or otherwise unknown to the spouse as being inconsistent with the intent of the exceptions.

Rule 504(c)(2)(B) is derived from paragraphs 148*e* and 151*b*(2) of the present *Manual.* The provision prevents application of the privilege as to privileged communications if the marriage was a sham at the time of the communication, and prohibits application of the spousal incapacity privilege if the marriage was begun as a sham and is a sham at the time the testimony of the witness is to be offered. Consequently, the Rule recognizes for purposes of subdivision (a) that a marriage that began as a sham may have ripened into a valid marriage at a later time. The intent of the provision is to prevent individuals from marrying witnesses in order to effectively silence them.

Rule 505. Classified Information

(a) General rule of privilege. Classified information is privileged from disclosure if disclosure would be detrimental to the national security.

(b) Definitions. As used in this rule:

    (1) Classified information. "Classified information" means any information or material that has been determined by the United States Government pursuant to an executive order, statute, or regulation, to require protection against unauthorized disclosure for reasons of national security and any restricted data, as defined in section 2014(y) of title 42, United States Code.

    (2) National security. "National security" means the national defense and foreign relations of the United States.

(c) Who may claim the privilege. The privilege may be claimed by the head of the executive or military department or government agency concerned based on a finding that the information is properly classified and that disclosure would be detrimental to the national security. A person who may claim the privilege may authorize a witness or trial counsel to claim the privilege on his or her behalf. The authority of the witness or trial counsel to do so is presumed in the absence of evidence to the contrary.

(d) Action prior to referral of charges. Prior to referral of charges, the convening authority shall respond in writing to a request by the accused for classified information if the privilege in this rule is claimed for such information. The convening authority may:

    (1) Delete specified items of classified information from documents made available to the accused;

    (2) Substitute a portion or summary of the information for such classified documents;

    (3) Substitute a statement admitting relevant facts that the classified information would tend to prove;

    (4) Provide the document subject to conditions that will guard against the compromise of the information disclosed to the accused; or

(5) Withhold disclosure if actions under (1) through (4) cannot be taken without causing identifiable damage to the national security.

Any objection by the accused to withholding of information or to the conditions of disclosure shall be raised through a motion for appropriate relief at a pretrial session.

(e) Pretrial session. At any time after referral of charges and prior to arraignment, any party may move for a session under Article 39(a) to consider matters relating to classified information that may arise in connection with the trial. Following such motion or sua sponte, the military judge promptly shall hold a session under Article 39(a) to establish the timing of requests for discovery, the provision of notice under subdivision (h), and the initiation of the procedure under subdivision (i). In addition, the military judge may consider any other matters that relate to classified information or that may promote a fair and expeditious trial.

(f) Action after referral of charges. If a claim of privilege has been made under this rule with respect to classified information that apparently contains evidence that is relevant and material to an element of the offense or a legally cognizable defense and is otherwise admissible in evidence in the court-martial proceeding, the matter shall be reported to the convening authority. The convening authority may:

(1) institute action to obtain the classified information for use by the military judge in making a determination under subdivision (i);

(2) dismiss the charges;

(3) dismiss the charge or specifications or both to which the information relates; or

(4) take such other action as may be required in the interests of justice.

If, after a reasonable period of time, the information is not provided to the military judge in circumstances where proceeding with the case without such information would materially prejudice a substantial right of the accused, the military judge shall dismiss the charges or specifications or both to which the classified information relates.

(g) Disclosure of classified information to the accused.

(1) Protective order. If the government agrees to disclose classified information to the accused, the military judge, at the request of the government, shall enter an appropriate protective order to guard against the compromise of the information disclosed to the accused. The terms of any such protective order may include provisions:

(A) Prohibiting the disclosure of the information except as authorized by the military judge;

(B) Requiring storage of material in a manner appropriate for the level of classification assigned to the documents to be disclosed;

(C) Requiring controlled access to the material during normal business hours and at other times upon reasonable notice;

(D) Requiring appropriate security clearances for persons having a need to examine the information in connection with the preparation of the defense;

(E) Requiring the maintenance of logs regarding access by all persons authorized by the military judge to have access to the classified information in connection with the preparation of the defense;

(F) Regulating the making and handling of notes taken from material containing classified information; or

(G) Requesting the convening authority to authorize the assignment of government security personnel and the provision of government storage facilities.

(2) Limited disclosure. The military judge, upon motion of the government, shall authorize

(A) the deletion of specified items of classified information from documents to be made available to the defendant,

(B) the substitution of a portion or summary of the information for such classified documents, or

(C) the substitution of a statement admitting relevant facts that the classified information would tend to prove, unless the military judge determines that disclosure of the classified information itself is necessary to enable the accused to prepare for trial. The government's motion and any materials submitted in support thereof shall, upon request of the government, be considered by the military judge in camera and shall not be disclosed to the accused.

(3) Disclosure at trial of certain statements previously made by a witness.

(A) Scope. After a witness called by the government has testified on direct examination, the military judge, on motion of the accused, may order production of statements in the possession of the United States under section 3500(b) of title 18, United States Code. This provision does not preclude discovery or assertion of a privilege otherwise authorized under these rules or this Manual.

(B) Closed session. If the privilege in this rule is invoked during consideration of a motion under section 3500 of title 18, United States Code, the government may deliver such statement for the inspection only by the military judge in camera and may provide the military judge with an affidavit identifying the portions of the statement that are classified and the basis for the classification assigned. If the military judge finds that disclosure of any portion of the statement identified by the government as classified could reasonably be expected to cause damage to the national security in the degree required to warrant classification under the applicable executive order, statute, or regulation and that such portion of the statement is consistent with the witness' testimony, the military judge shall excise the portion from the statement. With such material excised, the military judge shall then direct delivery of such statement to the accused for use by the accused. If the military judge finds that such portion of the statement is inconsistent with the witness' testimony, the government may move for a proceeding under subdivision (i).

(4) Record of trial. If, under this subdivision, any information is withheld from the accused, the accused objects to such withholding, and the trial is continued to an adjudication of guilt of the accused, the entire unaltered text of the relevant documents as well as the government's motion and any materials submitted in support thereof shall be sealed and attached to the record of trial as an appellate exhibit. Such material shall be made available to reviewing authorities in closed proceedings for the purpose of reviewing the determination of the military judge.

(h) Notice of the accused's intention to disclose classified information.

(1) Notice by the accused. If the accused reasonably expects to disclose or to cause the disclosure of classified information in any manner in connection with a court-martial proceeding, the accused shall notify the trial counsel in writing of such intention and file a copy of such notice with the military judge. Such notice shall be given within the time specified by the military judge under subdivision (e) or, if no time has been specified, prior to arraignment of the accused.

(2) Continuing duty to notify. Whenever the accused learns of classified information not covered by a notice under (1) that the accused reasonably expects to disclose at any such proceeding, the accused shall notify the trial counsel and the military judge in writing as soon as possible thereafter.

(3) Content of notice. The notice required by this subdivision shall include a brief description of the classified information.

(4) Prohibition against disclosure. The accused may not disclose any information known or believed to be classified until notice has been given under this subdivision and until the government has been afforded a reasonable opportunity to seek a determination under subdivision (i).

(5) Failure to comply. If the accused fails to comply with the requirements of this subdivision, the military judge may preclude disclosure of any classified information not made the subject of notification and may prohibit the

examination by the accused of any witness with respect to any such information.

(i) In camera proceedings for cases involving classified information.

(1) Definition. For purposes of this subdivision, an "in camera proceeding" is a session under Article 39(a) from which the public is excluded.

(2) Motion for in camera proceeding. Within the time specified by the military judge for the filing of a motion under this rule, the government may move for an in camera proceeding concerning the use at any proceeding of any classified information. Thereafter, either prior to or during trial, the military judge for good cause shown or otherwise upon a claim of privilege under this rule may grant the government leave to move for an in camera proceeding concerning the use of additional classified information.

(3) Demonstration of national security nature of the information. In order to obtain an in camera proceeding under this rule, the government shall submit the classified information for examination only by the military judge and shall demonstrate by affidavit that disclosure of the information reasonably could be expected to cause damage to the national security in the degree required to warrant classification under the applicable executive order, statute, or regulation.

(4) In camera proceeding.

(A) Procedure. Upon finding that the government has met the standard set forth in subdivision (i)(3) with respect to some or all of the classified information at issue, the military judge shall conduct an in camera proceeding. Prior to the in camera proceeding, the government shall provide the accused with notice of the information that will be at issue. This notice shall identify the classified information that will be at issue whenever that information previously has been made available to the accused in connection with proceedings in the same case. The government may describe the information by generic category, in such form as the military judge may approve, rather than

identifying the classified information when the government has not previously made the information available to the accused in connection with pretrial proceedings. Following briefing and argument by the parties in the in camera proceeding the military judge shall determine whether the information may be disclosed at the court-martial proceeding. Where the government's motion under this subdivision is filed prior to the proceeding at which disclosure is sought, the military judge shall rule prior to the commencement of the relevant proceeding.

(B) Standard. Classified information is not subject to disclosure under this subdivision unless the information is relevant and material to an element of the offense or a legally cognizable defense and is otherwise admissible in evidence.

(C) Ruling. Unless the military judge makes a written determination that the information meets the standard set forth in (B), the information may not be disclosed or otherwise elicited at a court-martial proceeding. The record of the in camera proceeding shall be sealed and attached to the record of trial as an appellate exhibit. The accused may seek reconsideration of the determination prior to or during trial.

(D) Alternatives to full disclosure. If the military judge makes a determination under this subdivision that would permit disclosure of the information or if the government elects not to contest the relevance, materiality, and admissibility of any classified information, the government may proffer a statement admitting for purposes of the proceeding any relevant facts such information would tend to prove or may submit a portion or summary to be used in lieu of the information. The military judge shall order that such statement, portion, or summary be used by the accused in place of the classified information unless the military judge finds that use of the classified information itself is necessary to afford the accused a fair trial.

(E) Sanctions. If the military judge determines that alternatives to full disclosure may not be used and the government continues to object to disclosure of the information, the military judge shall issue any order that the interests of justice require. Such an order may include an order:

(i) striking or precluding all or part of the testimony of a witness;

(ii) declaring a mistrial;

(iii) finding against the government on any issue as to which the evidence is relevant and material to the defense;

(iv) dismissing the charges, with or without prejudice; or

(v) dismissing the charges or specifications or both to which the information relates.

Any such order shall permit the government to avoid the sanction for nondisclosure by permitting the accused to disclose the information at the pertinent court-martial proceeding.

(j) Introduction of classified information.

(1) Classification status. Writings, recordings, and photographs containing classified information may be admitted into evidence without change in their classification status.

(2) Precautions by the military judge. In order to prevent unnecessary disclosure of classified information, the military judge may order admission into evidence of only part of a writing, recording, or photograph or may order admission into evidence of the whole writing, recording, or photograph with excision of some or all of the classified information contained therein.

(3) Contents of writing, recording, or photograph. The military judge may permit proof of the contents of a writing, recording, or photograph that contains classified information without requiring introduction into evidence of the original or a duplicate.

(4) Taking of testimony. During the examination of a witness, the government may object to any question or line of inquiry that may require the witness to disclose

classified information not previously found to be relevant and material to the defense. Following such an objection, the military judge shall take such suitable action to determine whether the response is admissible as will safeguard against the compromise of any classified information. Such action may include requiring the government to provide the military judge with a proffer of the witness' response to the question or line of inquiry and requiring the accused to provide the military judge with a proffer of the nature of the information the accused seeks to elicit.

(5) Closed session. If counsel for all parties, the military judge, and the members have received appropriate security clearances, the military judge may exclude the public during that portion of the testimony of a witness that discloses classified information.

(6) Record of trial. The record of trial with respect to any classified matter will be prepared under paragraph 82 *d* of this Manual.

(k) Security procedures to safeguard against compromise of classified information disclosed to courts-martial. The Secretary of Defense may prescribe security procedures for protection against the compromise of classified information submitted to courts-martial and appellate authorities.

EDITORIAL COMMENT

Rule 505 creates a privilege for classified information that, together with Rule 506, is similar to an "executive privilege" that some civilian courts have recognized. In substance, the Rule generally follows a similar privilege recognized in *Manual* ¶ 151*b*. In form, it is closely patterned after H.R. 4743, 96th Cong., 1st Sess. (1979), which addressed in detail the handling of classified information in pretrial, trial, and appellate proceedings. Also evident in the Rule is the impact of the Supreme Court's decisions in *United States v. Reynolds,* 345 U.S. 1 (1953) and *United States v. Nixon,* 418 U.S. 683 (1974).

Rule 505 itself serves as a model for Rule 506, which provides a privilege for government information which is not of a classified nature. Although both Rules involve privileges that can be stated rather easily, they are extremely complex Rules because of the procedures that are established in an effort to protect unnecessary exposure of sensitive governmental information without prejudicing an accused's chance for a fair trial. As a practical matter, classified information or evidence is only rarely used. However, when the issue is raised all parties must be attuned to the technical requirements of this Rule — noting in particular special notice and written response and findings requirements not found in most of the other privilege rules.

Subdivisions (a), (b), and (c) of Rule 505 set out the basics of the privilege. The remaining subdivisions, (d) through (k), are primarily concerned with the procedures to be used in applying the privilege.

Classified information may be privileged from disclosure only when disclosure would be detrimental to national security, that is, the national defense or foreign relations of the United States. *See United States v. Reynolds,* 345 U.S. 1 (1953). Information may be "classified" by an executive order, statute or regulation. In addition, the privilege extends to "restricted data" as defined by 42 U.S.C. § 2014(y):

> (y) The term "Restricted Data" means all data concerning (1) design, manufacture, or utilization of atomic weapons; (2) the production of special nuclear material; or (3) the use of special nuclear material in the production of energy, but shall not include data declassified or removed from the Restricted Data category pursuant to section 2162 of this title.

According to subdivision (c), the privilege may be claimed either by the appropriate head of the executive or military department or government agency; a witness or prosecutor may claim it on behalf of that head if so authorized. The authority to do so is presumed; this is not the case in many civilian courts. *See, e.g., Coastal Corp. v. Duncan,* 86 F.R.D. 514 (D. Del. 1980) (requiring showing that head of agency wished to invoke privilege). Before claiming the privilege, the claimant must first determine that the information is properly classified and that disclosure would be detrimental to national security.

The Rule takes into account that the issue of disclosure of classified information may arise at any stage of the proceedings. If the privilege is claimed prior to referral of charges to trial, the defense counsel should first attempt to obtain discovery through the convening authority. Subdivision (d) notes that if such a request is made the convening authority must respond in writing. Although no mention is made of a written defense request for the information, that would seem to be the preferred method. The convening authority's options include limited disclosure, either through substitutions or deletions, control of over access to the documents, and withholding disclosure. If limited disclosure is made, the accused can ask for greater disclosure later.

If the defense is not satisfied with the convening authority's response then the issue may be raised through motion at a pretrial session as provided for in subdivision (e). At that Article 39(a) session, to be conducted after referral of charges, any party may raise the discovery issue, even if it has not been first raised with the convening authority. The military judge is apparently given some leeway here to determine the appropriate method of handling the issue, which includes deciding on the timing of discovery requests by the defense, providing for notice by the defense of an intent to disclose classified information, *see* (h), and for necessary in camera hearings, *see* (i). And if the parties are ready, he may proceed with an in camera proceeding to determine whether a privilege exists. *See* subdivision (i).

Although it is not clear from the Rule itself, the drafters apparently intended that subdivision (f) would address the options available to the government following a preliminary determination by the military judge that the confidential material is relevant and apparently could be admissible if it were disclosed. The convening authority may obtain the pertinent information to present to the judge for his determination of the privilege claim or he may take one of the other options noted in that subdivision, including dismissal of the charges. *See Manual* ¶ 33f and Article 43(e), U.C.M.J., which address the appropriateness of delay in prosecuting cases involving matters affecting national security. Note that subdivision (f) requires that a military judge must, under some circumstances of undue delay, dismiss charges or specifications that cannot fairly be tried without the information sought by the accused.

Subdivision (g) generally addresses those situations in which disclosure of classified information is voluntarily made to the defense. The government, under (g) (1), may request the military judge to issue a protective order which may include any of the suggested provisions noted in that subdivision — *e.g.*, storage, access, security clearance, and record keeping requirements. Under (g) (2), the government may also request authorization from the military judge to make only a limited disclosure — either through substitutions and/or deletions. The government's motion to do so may include a request that the motion and supporting matters be considered by the military judge alone and not be disclosed to the accused. Subdivision (g)(3) covers those situations where pursuant to the Jencks Act, 18 U.S.C. § 3500, the defense is entitled to see other documents or prior statements of a witness. Where the Jencks Act material is classified, the prosecution may provide the information for inspection by the military judge, in camera, along with an affidavit identifying the classified portions and the reasons for the classification. If the designated portions are classified and could "reasonably be expected" to damage national security and are consistent with the witness' testimony, they may be deleted. However, if the designated portions are inconsistent with the witness' testimony then the prosecution may request an in camera proceeding under subdivision (i). If information is kept from an accused who objects, a record of the entire document is to be made and kept under seal in the event of an appeal.

Subdivision (h) provides for defense notice of an intent to disclose classified information in a court-martial. The notice must be written and copies served on both the prosecution and military judge either within the time specified by the military judge or before arraignment. The Rules includes a continuing duty to give notice and prohibits disclosure prior to giving notice and providing the prosecution with a reasonable opportunity to request an in camera proceeding under subdivision (i). Failure to comply with these requirements may result in the court's barring the use of the information. *See* (h)(5). *Cf.* 506(h). The privilege itself extends, of course, to pretrial proceedings, but it is not entirely clear from the plain language of subdivision (h) whether the defense must give notice to the government prior to disclosing classified information at, for example, an Article 32 investigation. The better practice would be to read the requirement broadly and provide some notice to the government.

Should the prosecution wish to contest the disclosure of classified information, before or after a claim of privilege has formally been made, subdivision (i) provides for an "in camera proceeding," something generally new to military practice. An in camera proceeding according to the Rule is an Article 39(a) session closed to the public. The prosecution triggers the process with a timely motion and presentation of the classified information itself to the military judge alone for his consideration. In addition, the prosecution must present an affidavit demonstrating a reasonable expectation of damage to national security. See (i)(3). If the prosecution meets the requirements of (i) (3), an in camera proceeding is held after appropriate notice to the defense concerning the information at issue. See (i)(4)(A). The information may be described by generic category when it has not yet been disclosed to the defense and the government wishes to guard against revelation. After hearing the parties' positions, the military judge must make his rulings prior to the proceeding during which disclosure is sought.

Only classified information that is "relevant and material to an element of the offense or a legally cognizable defense and is otherwise admissible" is subject to disclosure. See (i)(4)(B). The word disclosure has a dual meaning. It means disclosure to the defense if that has not already occurred and also disclosure as evidence at trial. Failure of the judge to make a *written* determination that the information meets this standard will prevent disclosure. See (i)(4)(C). The record of the proceedings will be sealed and attached to the record as an appellate exhibit, however. Also, the accused may seek reconsideration of his disclosure request.

In lieu of disclosing classified information, the prosecution under (i)(4)(D) may either admit the relevant facts or provide a summary. Unless the classified information itself is necessary for a fair trial, the judge should order the accused to use the alternative forms offered by the prosecutor. See also (g) (1), (2). On the other hand, if the offered alternatives are not acceptable to the military judge and the prosecution still objects to disclosure, the judge may impose sanctions, some of which are noted in (i)(4)(E).

Subdivision (j) generally addresses the handling of classified information at trial and affords the military judge broad discretion in dealing with such evidence. As under the in camera proceedings noted in (i), here the military judge must do some balancing of competing interests: the government's claim of damage to national security and the accused's right to disclosure of all relevant facts necessary for a fair trial. Parts of documents may be excluded, for example, and the scope of questioning may be carefully controlled. An interesting option is for the judge to close the proceedings to the public when counsel, the judge and the court-members have security clearances. Also of particular note is subdivision (j) (3) which apparently provides an exception to the best evidence, or original document Rule. See Rules 1002, 1004. See also Rule 506(j) (2).

In addition to the procedural precautions noted in subdivision (j), the Secretary of Defense, under subdivision (k), may provide additional security procedures.

DRAFTERS' ANALYSIS

Rule 505 is based upon H.R. 4745, 96th Cong., 1st Sess. (1979), which was proposed by the Executive Branch as a response to what is known as the "graymail" problem in which the defendant in a criminal case seeks disclosure of sensitive national security information, the release of which may force the government to discontinue the prosecution. The Rule is also based upon the Supreme Court's discussion of executive privilege in *United States v. Reynolds,* 345 U.S. 1 (1953) and *United States v. Nixon,* 418 U.S. 683 (1974). The Rule attempts to balance the interests of an accused who desires classified information for his or her defense and the interests of the government in protecting that information.

(a) *General rule of privilege.* Rule 505(a) is derived from *United States v. Reynolds,* 345 U.S. 1 (1953) and present *Manual* paragraph 151. Classified information is only privileged when its "disclosure would be detrimental to the national security."

(b) *Definitions.*

(1) *Classified information.* Rule 505(b)(1) is derived from section 2 of H.R. 4745. The definition of "classified information" is a limited one and includes only that information protected "pursuant to an executive order, statute, or regulation," and that material which constitutes restricted data pursuant to 42 U.S.C. 2014(y) (1976).

(2) *National security.* Rule 505(b)(2) is derived from section 2 of H.R. 4745.

(c) *Who may claim the privilege.* Rule 505(c) is derived from present paragraph 151 of the *Manual* and is consistent with similar provisions in the other privilege rules. *See, e.g.,* Rule 501(c). The privilege may be claimed *only* "by the head of the executive or military department or government agency concerned" and then only upon "a finding that the information is properly classified and that disclosure would be detrimental to the national security." Although the authority of a witness or trial counsel to claim the privilege is presumed in the absence of evidence to the contrary, neither a witness nor a trial counsel may claim the privilege without prior direction to do so by the appropriate department or agency head. Consequently, expedited coordination with senior headquarters is advised in any situation in which Rule 505 appears to be applicable.

(d) *Action prior to referral of charges.* Rule 505(d) is taken from section 4(b)(1) of H.R. 4745. The provision has been modified to reflect the fact that pretrial discovery in the armed forces, prior to referral, is officially conducted through the convening authority. The convening authority should disclose the maximum amount of requested information as appears reasonable under the circumstances.

(e) *Pretrial session.* Rule 505(e) is derived from section 3 of H.R. 4745.

(f) *Action after referral of charges.* Rule 505(f) provides the basic procedure under which the government should respond to a determination by the military judge that classified information "apparently contains evidence that is relevant and material to an element of the offense or a legally cognizable defense and is otherwise admissible in evidence." *See generally* the *Analysis* to Rule 507(d).

It should be noted that the government may submit information to the military judge for in camera inspection pursuant to subdivision (i). If the defense requests classified information that it alleges is "relevant and material . . .," and the government refuses to disclose the information to the military judge for inspection, the military judge may presume that the information is in fact "relevant and material . . . ."

(g) *Disclosure of classified information to the accused.* Paragraphs (1) and (2) of Rule 505(g) are derived from section 4 of H.R. 4745. Paragraph (3) is taken from section 10 of H.R. 4745 but has been modified in view of the different application of the Jencks Act, 18 U.S.C. § 3500 (1976) in the armed forces. Paragraph (4) is taken from sections 4(b) (2) and 10 of H.R. 4745. The reference in H.R. 4745 to a recess has been deleted as being unnecessary in view of the military judge's inherent authority to call a recess.

(h) Notice of the accused's intention to disclose classified information. Rule 505(h) is derived from section 5 of H.R. 4745. The intent of the provision is to prevent disclosure of classified information by the defense until the government has had an opportunity to determine what position to take concerning the possible disclosure of that information. Pursuant to Rule 505(h) (5), failure to comply with subdivision (h) may result in a prohibition on the use of the information involved.

(i) In camera proceedings for cases involving classified information. Rule 505(i) is derived generally from section 5 of H.R. 4745. The "in camera" procedure utilized in subdivision (i) is generally new to military law. Neither the accused nor defense counsel may be excluded from the in camera proceeding. However, nothing within the Rule requires that the defense be provided with a copy of the classified material in question when the government submits such information to the military judge pursuant to Rule 505(i) (3) in an effort to obtain an in camera proceeding under this Rule. If such information has not been disclosed previously, the government may describe the information by generic category, rather than by identifying the information. Such description is subject to approval by the military judge, and if not sufficiently specific to enable the defense to proceed during the in camera session, the military judge may order the government to release the information for use during the proceeding or face the sanctions under subdivision (i)(4)(E).

(j) Introduction of classified information. Rule 505(j) is derived from section 8 of H.R. 4745 and *United States v. Grunden,* 2 M.J. 116 (C.M.A. 1977).

(k) Security procedures to safeguard against compromise of classified information disclosed to courts-martial. Rule 505(k) is derived from section 9 of H.R. 4745.

Rule 506. Government Information Other Than Classified Information

(a) General rule of privilege. Except where disclosure is required by an Act of Congress, government information is privileged from disclosure if disclosure would be detrimental to the public interest.

(b) Scope. "Government information" includes official communications and documents and other information within the custody or control of the federal government. This rule does not apply to classified information (rule 505) or to the identity of an informant (rule 507).

(c) Who may claim the privilege. The privilege may be claimed by the head of the executive or military department or government agency concerned. The privilege for investigations of the Inspectors General may be claimed by the authority ordering the investigation or any superior authority. A person who may claim the privilege may authorize a witness or the trial counsel to claim the privilege on his or her behalf. The authority of a witness or the trial counsel to do so is presumed in the absence of evidence to the contrary.

(d) Action prior to referral of charges. Prior to referral of charges, the government shall respond in writing to a request for government information if the privilege in this rule is claimed for such information. The government shall:

(1) delete specified items of government information claimed to be privileged from documents made available to the accused;

(2) substitute a portion or summary of the information for such documents;

(3) substitute a statement admitting relevant facts that the government information would tend to prove;

(4) provide the document subject to conditions similar to those set forth in subdivision (g) of this rule; or

(5) withhold disclosure if actions under (1) through (4) cannot be taken without causing identifiable damage to the public interest.

(e) Action after referral of charges. After referral of charges, if a claim of privilege has been made under this rule with

respect to government information that apparently contains evidence that is relevant and material to an element of the offense or a legally cognizable defense and is otherwise admissible in evidence in the court-martial proceeding, the matter shall be reported to the convening authority. The convening authority may:

> (1) institute action to obtain the information for use by the military judge in making a determination under subdivision (i);

> (2) dismiss the charges;

> (3) dismiss the charges or specifications or both to which the information relates; or

> (4) take other action as may be required in the interests of justice.

If, after a reasonable period of time, the information is not provided to the military judge, the military judge shall dismiss the charges or specifications or both to which the information relates.

(f) Pretrial session. At any time after referral of charges and prior to arraignment any party may move for a session under Article 39(a) to consider matters relating to government information that may arise in connection with the trial. Following such motion, or sua sponte, the military judge promptly shall hold a pretrial session under Article 39(a) to establish the timing of requests for discovery, the provision of notice under subdivision (h), and the initiation of the procedure under subdivision (i). In addition, the military judge may consider any other matters that relate to government information or that may promote a fair and expeditious trial.

(g) Disclosure of government information to the accused. If the government agrees to disclose government information to the accused subsequent to a claim of privilege under this rule, the military judge, at the request of the government, shall enter an appropriate protective order to guard against the compromise of the information disclosed to the accused. The terms of any such protective order may include provisions:

> (1) Prohibiting the disclosure of the information except as authorized by the military judge;

(2) Requiring storage of the material in a manner appropriate for the nature of the material to be disclosed;

(3) Requiring controlled access to the material during normal business hours and at other times upon reasonable notice;

(4) Requiring the maintenance of logs recording access by persons authorized by the military judge to have access to the government information in connection with the preparation of the defense;

(5) Regulating the making and handling of notes taken from material containing government information; or

(6) Requesting the convening authority to authorize the assignment of government security personnel and the provision of government storage facilities.

(h) Prohibition against disclosure. The accused may not disclose any information known or believed to be subject to a claim of privilege under this rule until the government has been afforded a reasonable opportunity to seek a determination under subdivision (i).

(i) In camera proceedings.

(1) Definition. For purposes of this subdivision, an "in camera proceeding" is a closed session under Article 39(a).

(2) Motion for in camera proceeding. Within the time specified by the military judge for the filing of a motion under this rule, the government may move for an in camera proceeding concerning the use at any proceeding of any government information that may be subject to a claim of privilege. Thereafter, either prior to or during trial, the military judge for good cause shown or otherwise upon a. claim of privilege may grant the government leave to move for an in camera proceeding concerning the use of additional government information.

(3) Demonstration of public interest nature of the information. In order to obtain an in camera proceeding under this rule, the government shall demonstrate through submission of affidavits and the information for examination only by the military judge that disclosure of the information reasonably could be expected to cause identifiable damage to the public interest.

(4) **In camera proceeding.**

(A) **Procedure.** Upon finding that the disclosure of some or all of the information submitted by the government under subsection (1) reasonably could be expected to cause identifiable damage to the public interest, the military judge shall conduct an in camera proceeding. Prior to the in camera proceeding, the government shall provide the accused with notice of the information that will be at issue. This notice shall identify the information that will be at issue whenever that information previously has been made available to the accused in connection with proceedings in the same case. The government may describe the information by generic category, in such form as the military judge may approve, rather than identifying the specific information of concern to the government when the government has not previously made the information available to the accused in connection with pretrial proceedings. Following breifing and argument by the parties in the in camera proceeding, the military judge shall determine whether the information may be disclosed at the court-martial proceeding. When the government's motion under this subdivision is filed prior to the proceeding at which disclosure is sought, the military judge shall rule prior to commencement of the relevant proceeding.

(B) **Standard.** Government information is subject to a disclosure under this subdivision if the party making the request demonstrates a specific need for information containing evidence that is relevant to the guilt or innocence of the accused and otherwise admissible in the court-martial proceeding.

(C) **Ruling.** Unless the military judge makes a written determination that the information is not subject to disclosure under the standard set forth in (B) the information may be disclosed at the court-martial proceeding. The record of the in camera proceeding shall be sealed and attached to the record of trial as an appellate exhibit. The accused may seek reconsideration of the determination prior to or during trial.

(D) Sanction. If the military judge makes a determination under this subdivision that permits disclosure of the information and the government continues to object to disclosure of the information, the military judge shall dismiss the charges or specifications or both to which the information relates.

(j) Introduction of government information subject to a claim of privilege.

(1) Precautions by military judge. In order to prevent unnecessary disclosure of government information after there has been a claim of privilege under this rule, the military judge may order admission into evidence of any part of a writing, recording, or photograph or may order admission into evidence of the whole writing, recording, or photograph, with excision of some or all of the government information contained therein.

(2) Contents of writing, recording, or photograph. The military judge may permit proof of the contents of a writing, recording, or photograph that contains government information that is the subject of a claim of privilege under this rule without requiring introduction into evidence of the original or a duplicate.

(3) Taking of testimony. During examination of a witness, the prosecution may object to any question or line of inquiry that may require the witness to disclose government information not previously found relevant and material to the defense if such information has been or is reasonably likely to be the subject of a claim of privilege under this rule. Following such an objection, the military judge shall take such suitable action to determine whether the response is admissible as will safeguard against the compromise of any government information. Such action may include requiring the government to provide the military judge with a proffer of the witness' response to the question or line of inquiry and requiring the accused to provide the military judge with a proffer of the nature of the information the accused seeks to elicit.

(k) Procedures to safeguard against compromise of government information disclosed to courts-martial. The Secretary of Defense may prescribe procedures for protection against

the compromise of government information submitted to courts-martial and appellate authorities after a claim of privilege.

EDITORIAL COMMENT

Government information which is not classified within the meaning of Rule 505, *supra,* may nonetheless be privileged under Rule 506. This Rule is generally modeled after Rule 505 but contains a number of significant, yet subtle, differences which may trap the unwary litigant.

As a general rule, government information, which includes, but is not limited to, official communications, documents and other information within the control of the federal government, is privileged if it would be detrimental to the public interest. *See generally Manual* ¶¶ 151*b*(1) and 151*b*(3). The exception lies in those Acts of Congress which may require disclosure. *See, e.g.,* 5 U.S.C. § 552 (Freedom of Information Act) and 18 U.S.C. § 3500 (Jencks Act). Thus the privilege here is narrower than that in Rule 505. Classified government information and the identity of an informant are covered in Rules 505 and 507, respectively.

In addressing the question of who may claim the privilege, subdivision (c) makes a distinction between government information and information derived from Inspector General investigations. The former may be claimed by the appropriate agency head; the latter may be claimed by the authority ordering the investigation or "any superior authority." The claimants in either case may authorize either a witness or trial counsel to claim the privilege on their behalf, and authorization is presumed as under Rule 505.

Like their counterparts in Rule 505, subdivisions (d) through (k) lay out some rather technical procedural requirements. Here, too, the defense should first go through pretrial discovery methods if the privilege is claimed prior to referral of charges. Unfortunately, subdivision (d) only indicates that the "government" must provide a written response to a request for information. The drafters' *Analysis* is silent on the subject of who actually must respond, but directs the reader to the drafters' *Analysis* for Rule 505(d), which notes that pretrial requests for evidence often are forwarded to the convening authority. Since the language of 506(d) is open-ended, in an appropriate case someone other than a convening authority — for example, one of the prosecutors—may act for the government. As a practical matter, the defense request for information should be directed through the prosecutor to the convening authority.

After preferral of charges, subdivision (e) explicitly requires that the convening authority be advised when the privilege has been claimed and the information requested appears to be otherwise admissible and relevant to an element of an offense or a valid defense. The Rule is silent as to who must determine that the requested information meets those requirements. Again, the drafters' *Analysis* to Rule 505(f), the counterpart to (e), assumes that this process will normally take place after a military judge, in a pretrial session, has made that determination. Note that under (e), if the information has been requested by the military judge for examination and the information is not turned over within a reasonable time, the military judge *must* dismiss the appropriate charges or specifications. The drafters do not provide any reasons for such a potentially harsh rule, which on its face greatly extends the powers of a military judge. An analogous situation has existed for some time in the area of witness production. Although in theory a military judge could dismiss charges for failure of the government to provide a defense witness, many military judges have opted for "abatement" of the proceedings until the government produced the witness or dismissed the charges. Apparently, the Rule intends to bar all unnecessary delays regarding non-classified information which can be screened in camera without the problems presented by classified material.

Subdivision (f) is similar to 505(e) and deals with using Article 39(a) sessions to establish some of the basic ground rules for discovery requests and privilege claims. Subdivision (g) is a streamlined version of 505(g); the government may request a protective order, although limited disclosure is apparently not an option under this Rule. *Cf.* Rule 505(g).

Subdivision (h) requires the defense to delay disclosing information which might be claimed under this privilege until the government has an opportunity to move for an in camera proceeding under (i). The provision has no teeth to it, however. *Compare* Rule 505(h). The drafters' *Analysis* provides no reasons for the absence of a sanction. That does not mean, however, that the disclosed information is admissible. The in camera proceedings noted in Rule 505 and used to determine admissibility of classified information are also available here for determining whether the unclassified government information is privileged and inadmissible. To obtain the in camera proceeding, the government bears the burden of first demonstrating that the disclosure reasonably could be expected to cause identifiable damage to the public interest. If the standard is satisfied, the accused is given notice of the proposed hearing. Information not previously disclosed to the accused may be referred to by generic category. The standard for disclosure under (i)(4)(B) is much lower than for disclosure of classified information under 505 (i)(4)(B). Under this Rule, the defense is entitled to the information if it is relevant to the issue of guilt or innocence and is otherwise admissible. There is no provision in subdivision (i) for alternatives to complete disclosure. *Compare* 505(i)(4)(D). Continued government objection to disclosure may trigger dismissal of appropriate charges. No lesser sanctions are specified.

Under subdivision (j) the military judge is given the authority to take precautions to prevent unnecessary disclosure. Specific provision is made in (j)(2) for consideration of other proof of contents of an original document containing privileged information. *See also* Rule 1002 and Rule 505(j)(3). Not surprisingly, there is no provision for closed hearings under this Rule, since no classified information is involved.

DRAFTERS' ANALYSIS

(a) General rule of privilege. Rule 506(a) states the general rule of privilege for nonclassified government information. The Rule recognizes that in certain extraordinary cases the government should be able to prohibit release of government information which is detrimental to the public interest. The Rule is modeled on Rule 505 but is more limited in its scope in view of the greater limitations applicable to nonclassified information. *Compare United States v. Nixon,* 418 U.S. 683 (1974) *with United States v. Reynolds,* 345 U.S. 1 (1953). Rule 506 addresses those similar matters found in present · *Manual* paragraphs 151*b*(1) and 151*b*(3). Under Rule 506(a) information is privileged only if its disclosure would be "detrimental to the public interest." It is important to note that pursuant to Rule 506(c) the privilege may be claimed only "by the head of the executive or military department or government agency concerned" unless investigations of the Inspectors General are concerned.

Under Rule 506(a) there is no privilege if disclosure of the information concerned is required by an Act of Congress such as the Freedom of Information Act, 5 U.S.C. § 552 (1976). Disclosure of information will thus be broader under the Rule than under the present *Manual. See United States v. Nixon,* 418 U.S. 683 (1974).

(b) Scope. Rule 506(b) defines "Government information" in a nonexclusive fashion, and expressly states that classified information and information relating to the identity of informants are solely within the scope of other Rules.

(c) Who may claim the privilege. Rule 506(c) distinguishes between government information in general and investigations of the Inspectors General. While the privilege for the latter may be claimed "by the authority ordering the investigation or any superior authority," the privilege for other government information may be claimed *only* "by the head of the executive or military department or government agency concerned." *See generally* the *Analysis* to Rule 505(c).

(d) Action prior to referral of charges. Rule 506(d) specifies action to be taken prior to referral of charges in the event of a claim of privilege under the Rule. *See generally* Rule 505(d) and its *Analysis.* Note that disclosure can be withheld *only* if action under paragraphs (1)-(4) of subdivision (d) cannot be made "without causing *identifiable* damage to the public interest." [Emphasis added].

(e) Action after referral of charges. See generally Rule 505(f) and its *Analysis.* Note that unlike Rule 505(f), however, Rule 506(e) does not require a finding that failure to disclose the information in question "would materially prejudice a substantial right of the accused." Dismissal is required when the relevant information is not disclosed in a "reasonable period of time."

(f) Pretrial session. Rule 506(f) is taken from Rule 505(e). It is the intent of the Committee that if classified information arises during a proceeding under Rule 506, the procedures of Rule 505 will be used.

(g) Disclosure of government information to the accused. Rule 506(g) is taken from Rule 505(g) but deletes references to classified information and clearances due to their inapplicability.

(h) Prohibition against disclosure. Rule 506(h) is derived from Rule 505(h) (4). The remainder of Rule 505(h) (4) and Rule 505(h) generally has been omitted as being unnecessary. No sanction for violation of the requirement has been included.

(i) In camera proceedings. Rule 506(i) is taken generally from Rule 505(i), but the standard involved reflects present *Manual* paragraph 151 and the Supreme Court's

decision in *United States v. Nixon,* 418 U.S. 683 (1974). In line with *Nixon,* the burden is on the party claiming the privilege to demonstrate why the information involved should not be disclosed. References to classified material have been deleted as being inapplicable.

(j) Introduction of government information subject to a claim of privilege. Rule 506(j) is derived from Rule 505(j) with appropriate modifications being made to reflect the nonclassified nature of the information involved.

(k) Procedures to safeguard against compromise of government information disclosed to courts-martial. Rule 506(k) is derived from Rule 505(k). Such procedures should reflect the fact that material privileged under Rule 506 is not classified.

Rule 507. Identity of Informant

(a) Rule of privilege. The United States or a state or subdivision thereof has a privilege to refuse to disclose the identity of an informant. An "informant" is a person who has furnished information relating to or assisting in an investigation of a possible violation of law to a person whose official duties include the discovery, investigation, or prosecution of crime. Unless otherwise privileged under these rules, the communications of an informant are not privileged except to the extent necessary to prevent the disclosure of the informant's identity.

(b) Who may claim the privilege. The privilege may be claimed by an appropriate representative of the United States, regardless of whether the information was furnished to an officer of the United States or of a state or subdivision thereof. The privilege may be claimed by an appropriate representative of a state or subdivision if the information was furnished to an officer thereof, except the privilege shall not be allowed if the prosecution objects.

(c) Exceptions.

(1) Voluntary disclosures; informant as witness. No privilege exists under this rule: (A) if the identity of the informant has been disclosed to those who would have cause to resent the communication by a holder of the privilege or by the informant's own action; or (B) if the informant appears as a witness for the prosecution.

(2) Testimony on the issue of guilt or innocence. If a claim of privilege has been made under this rule, the military judge shall, upon motion by the accused, determine whether disclosure of the identity of the informant is necessary to the accused's defense on the issue of guilt or innocence. Whether such a necessity exists will depend on the particular circumstances of each case, taking into consideration the offense charged, the possible defenses, the possible significance of the informant's testimony, and other relevant factors. If it appears from the evidence in the case or from other showing by a party that an informant may be able to give testimony necessary to the accused's defense on the issue of guilt or innocence, the military

255

judge may make any order required by the interests of justice.

(3) Legality of obtaining evidence. If a claim of privilege has been made under this rule with respect to a motion under rule 311, the military judge shall, upon motion of the accused, determine whether disclosure of the identity of the informant is required by the Constitution of the United States as applied to members of the armed forces. In making this determination, the military judge may make any order required by the interests of justice.

(d) Procedures. If a claim of privilege has been made under this rule, the military judge may make any order required by the interests of justice. If the military judge determines that disclosure of the identity of the informant is required under the standards set forth in this rule, and the prosecution elects not to disclose the identity of the informant, the matter shall be reported to the convening authority. The convening authority may institute action to secure disclosure of the identity of the informant, terminate the proceedings, or take such other action as may be appropriate under the circumstances. If, after a reasonable period of time disclosure is not made, the military judge, sua sponte or upon motion of either counsel and after a hearing if requested by either party, may dismiss the charges or specifications or both to which the information regarding the informant would relate if the military judge determines that further proceedings would materially prejudice a substantial right of the accused.

EDITORIAL COMMENT

Recognizing the strong policy of preserving the anonymity of informants, who fulfill an important law enforcement function, in order to protect them from retaliation, Rule 507 adopts the familiar informant privilege. *See Roviaro v. United States*, 353 U.S. 53 (1957). It generally follows the format of proposed Federal Rule 510 and continues the coverage of former *Manual* ¶ 151*b*(1). *See generally United States v. Ness*, 13 C.M.A. 18, 32 C.M.R. 18 (1962); *United States v. Hawkins*, 6 C.M.A. 135, 19 C.M.R. 261 (1955). For the proposed Federal Rule and the accompanying Advisory Committee Note *see* S. SALTZBURG & K. REDDEN, FEDERAL RULES OF EVIDENCE MANUAL 768-770 (2d ed. 1977).

The general rule of privilege is set out in subdivision (a) which states that federal, state and local authorities may block disclosure of the identity of an informant (although under (b) state and local claims cannot withstand the objection of the prosecution). An informant is defined in broad fashion and includes ordinary citizens who offer information, as well as paid undercover agents. The communications must have been made to a person whose official duties involve discovery, investigation and prosecution of crime. Thus, statements to public officials not involved in law enforcement would not qualify under the Rule. The privilege is limited to "identity" and does not block disclosure of any statements made by the informant unless they too might directly or indirectly identify the informant. *See Roviaro v. United States, supra,* and *Bowman Dairy Co. v. United States,* 341 U.S. 214, 221 (1951).

According to subdivision (b), both federal and state authorities are potential claimants of the privilege. Federal authorities may claim it regardless of whether the recipient of the information was a federal or state officer. But authorities of a state or its subdivisions may claim it only if the information was given to one of *its* officers, and as noted above, only if the prosecution does not object. The Rule specifically notes that an "appropriate representative" of either entity may claim the privilege but does not further define that term. The drafters' *Analysis* to this Rule and the Advisory Committee Note to the proposed federal rule indicate that the prosecutor will normally be the appropriate claimant. This certainly will not always be the case, however. Under the facts of a particular case, a military investigator might be the proper claimant. *See, e.g., Bocchicchio v. Curtis Publishing Co.,* 203 F. Supp. 403 (E.D. Pa. 1962) (civil action in which local policeman successfully claimed the privilege).

Subdivision (c) covers those situations where the privilege does not apply. First, under (c)(1) the privilege is not available where the informant's identity has already been disclosed to "those who would have cause to resent the communication." *Roviaro v. United States, supra.* This would generally not include disclosures to other law enforcement agencies. The disclosure may come from either a holder of the privilege or the informant himself — a twist on other privilege rules where only the holder may waive a privilege. The Rule implicitly recognizes that once such disclosure has been made it is no longer possible to conceal the identity of the person who cooperated with enforcement officials. And if the informant testifies for the prosecution, the defense should be permitted to inquire into the relationship between the government and the witness. *See, e.g., Harris v. United States,* 371 F.2d 365 (9th Cir. 1967). The idea here is that the fact that the person is appearing as a government witness, means that the accused has reason to resent the person, and that disclosure of the informant is likely to add little to the hostility that the accused already may feel toward the person. The privilege does not fall, however, where the defense calls the witness in an attempt to discover whether he is an informant, since the accused remains unsure whether he has reason to be hostile to the informant and the Rule does not want to encourage hostility.

Second, where the defense can show that the informant's identity is necessary to determine guilt or innocence, the privilege gives way under (c)(2) to the defendant's need for evidence. This exception is based in part on compulsory process considerations and the Sixth Amendment right of an accused to present a defense. *See, e.g., United States v. Silva,* 580 F.2d 144 (5th Cir. 1978). The Rule here follows *Manual* ¶ 151*b*(1) and provides no concrete guidance on when disclosure is required — only that specific facts and circumstances will play a large part in the determination. As a general rule, the defense burden will not be satisfied by mere speculation that an informant might be helpful. *United States v. Marshall,* 532 F.2d 1279 (9th Cir. 1976). Not specifically noted in (c)(2), but nonetheless important as a "relevant" factor, is the potential harm to an informant. In the balance, mere tipsters will normally not be identified, *cf.* subdivision (c)(3), while those informants who were active participants in, or eyewitnesses to, the crime generally will be. *See United States v. Skeens,* 449 F.2d 1066 (D.C. Cir. 1971).

Finally, (c)(3) addresses those situations where an informant's identity may be constitutionally required in an inquiry into the validity of a search or seizure under Rule 311. *See generally Franks v. Delaware,* 442 U.S. 928 (1978); *McCray v. Illinois,* 386 U.S. 300 (1967). The provision is generally patterned after proposed Federal Rule of Evidence 510(c)(3), but unlike that provision the Military Rule offers no specific guidance. The proposed Federal Rule would have permitted disclosure if the judge was "not satisfied that the information [used to support obtaining the evidence] was received from an informer reasonably believed to be reliable or credible." Although the plain language of the Military Rule does not so provide, the drafters suggest in their *Analysis* that the military judge should consider the "prevailing case law utilized in the trial of criminal cases in the Federal district courts." This law generally holds that the identity of the informant is not revealed when the informant's only relationship to the case is that officers relied upon him in making an arrest or obtaining a warrant. *See McCray v. Illinois, supra.* In an exceptional case in which the good faith of the officers who acted is in question, the identity may be revealed, perhaps only to the judge at first, but possibly also to the accused.

Some general guidance on handling claims of informant privilege is included in subdivision (d), which requires some decisions by the convening authority if the prosecution decides to withhold disclosure after a military judge has ruled that disclosure of an informant's identity is required. Failure to disclose may result in dismissal of charges.

Noticeably absent from both the Rule and the drafters' *Analysis* is any reference to the possibility of holding in camera proceedings to determine whether disclosure is required. Such private consideration by the judge is specifically noted in proposed Federal Rule, Rule 507(c), and seems to find some support in pre-Rules military case law. *See, e.g., United States v. Bennett,* 3 M.J. 903, 906, n.2 (A.C.M.R. 1977). Although not required, or even recommended by Rule 507, that practice is commendable. In addressing in camera hearings in this area the Advisory Committee Note on the proposed Federal Rule states that:

> The limited disclosure to the judge avoids any significant impairment of secrecy, while affording the accused a substantial measure of protection against arbitrary police action. The procedure is consistent with [*McCray v. Illinois,* 386 U.S. 300 (1967)] and the decisions there discussed.

That rationale seems equally applicable under the Military Rule.

DRAFTERS' ANALYSIS

(a) Rule of privilege. Rule 507(a) sets forth the basic rule of privilege for informants and contains the substance of present *Manual* paragraph 151*b*(1). The new Rule, however, provides greater detail as to the application of the privilege than does the present *Manual.*

The privilege is that of the United States or political subdivision thereof and applies only to information relevant to the identity of an informant. An "informant" is simply an individual who has supplied "information resulting in an investigation of a possible violation of law" to a proper person and thus includes good citizen reports to command or police as well as the traditional "confidential informants" who may be consistent sources of information.

(b) Who may claim the privilege. Rule 507(b) provides for claiming the privilege and distinguishes between representatives of the United States and representatives of a state or subdivision thereof. Although an appropriate representative of the United States may always claim the privilege when applicable, a representative of a state or subdivision may do so only if the information in question was supplied to an officer of the state or subdivision. The Rule is taken from proposed Federal Rule of Evidence 510(b), with appropriate modifications, and is similar in substance to paragraph 151*b* (1) of the present *Manual* which permits "appropriate governmental authorities" to claim the privilege.

The Rule does not specify who an "appropriate representative" is. Normally, the trial counsel is an appropriate representative of the United States. The Rule leaves the question open, however, for case by case resolution. Regulations could be promulgated which could specify who could be an appropriate representative.

(c) Exceptions. Rule 507(c) sets forth the circumstances in which the privilege is inapplicable.

(1) Voluntary disclosures; informant as witness. Rule 507(c)(1) makes it clear that the privilege is inapplicable if circumstances have nullified its justification for existence. Thus, there is no reason for the privilege, and the privilege is consequently inapplicable, if the individual who would have cause to resent the informant has been made aware of the informant's identity by a holder of the privilege or by the informant's own action or when the witness testifies for the prosecution thus allowing that person to ascertain the informant's identity. This is in accord with the intent of the privilege which is to protect informants from reprisals. The Rule is taken from paragraph 151*b*(1) of the present *Manual.*

(2) Testimony on the issue of guilt or innocence. Rule 507(c)(2) is taken from present *Manual* paragraph 151*b*(1) and recognizes that in certain circumstances the accused may have a due process right under the fifth amendment, as well as a similar right under the Uniform Code of Military Justice, to call the informant as a witness. The subdivision intentionally does not specify what circumstances would require calling the informant and leaves resolution of the issue to each individual case.

(3) Legality of obtaining evidence. Rule 507(c)(3) is new. The Rule recognizes that circumstances may exist in which the Constitution may require disclosure of the identity of an informant in the context of determining the legality of obtaining evidence under Rule 311; *see, e.g., Franks v. Delaware,* 442 U.S. 154, 167 (1978); *McCray v. Illinois,* 386 U.S. 300 (1967) (both cases indicate that disclosure may be required in certain unspecified circumstances but do not in fact require such disclosure). In view of the highly unsettled nature of the

issue, the Rule does not specify whether or when such disclosure is mandated and leaves the determination to the military judge in light of prevailing case law utilized in the trial of criminal cases in the Federal district courts.

(d) Procedures. Rule 507(d) sets forth the procedures to be followed in the event of a claim of privilege under Rule 507. If the prosecution elects not to disclose the identity of an informant when the judge has determined that disclosure is required, that matter shall be reported to the convening authority. Such a report is required so that the convening authority may determine what action, if any, should be taken. Such actions could include disclosure of the informant's identity, withdrawal of charges, or some appropriate appellate action.

Rule 508. Political Vote

A person has a privilege to refuse to disclose the tenor of the person's vote at a political election conducted by secret ballot unless the vote was cast illegally.

EDITORIAL COMMENT

Rule 508 is identical to proposed Federal Rule of Evidence 507 and like its counterpart recognizes that not only should secrecy in balloting be protected but also that secrecy after a vote is cast also should be maintained. Such secrecy is an integral part of a democracy and is considered especially important in a military system sensitive to remaining apolitical. *See* 18 U.S.C. § 596 (proscribes polling of armed forces regarding balloting).

The privilege may not be claimed if the vote was illegally cast. However, the voter would normally be able to claim the privilege against self-incrimination. *See generally* Article 31(a), U.C.M.J. and Rule 301.

DRAFTERS' ANALYSIS

Rule 508 is taken from proposed Federal Rule of Evidence 507 and expresses the substance of 18 U.S.C. § 596 (1976) which is applicable to the armed forces. The privilege is considered essential for the armed forces because of the unique nature of military life.

Rule 509. Deliberations of Courts and Juries

Except as provided in rule 606, the deliberations of courts and grand and petit juries are privileged to the extent that such matters are privileged in trial of criminal cases in the United States district courts, but the results of the deliberations are not privileged.

EDITORIAL COMMENT

Both military and civilian law endeavor to preserve the sanctity of the deliberative process of the fact-finder. Rule 509 follows *Manual* ¶ 151*b* in stating that the deliberations of courts and grand and petit juries are privileged. The Rule specifically notes that the results of deliberation are not privileged. No federal evidence rule covers this privilege; a similar privilege is recognized in decided cases, however. The drafters wrote the Rule so that it will track the approach of the federal courts over time. One exception to the privilege is found in Military Rule 606(b), which permits intrusion into the deliberative process when there are questions whether (1) extraneous prejudicial information was improperly brought to court-members' attention; or (2) any outside interference was improperly brought to bear upon any court-member; or (3) there was unlawful command influence. We further discuss these narrowly drawn exceptions under Rule 606. If the privilege does not apply, then either testimony or affidavits may be considered in assessing whether something so tainted judicial deliberations that the result should be set aside.

Although it is not clear in the Rule itself, if the privilege applies the members and third parties are precluded from disclosing the deliberations in courts martial. *See United States v. Harris,* 32 C.M.R. 878 (A.F.B.R. 1962); *United States v. Bourchier,* 5 C.M.A. 15, 17 C.M.R. 15 1954).

Unfortunately, the Rule provides no procedural guidance for determining who is to claim the privilege. Rule 606(b) also is silent on this point. Generally, the party relying on the result of the deliberations can be expected to object, although the court may raise the issue sua sponte.

To determine if the privilege is properly raised, the military judge may have to slightly intrude into the deliberations in order to determine whether an exception exists under 606(b). *See* J. WEINSTEIN & M. BERGER, WEINSTEIN'S EVIDENCE, § 104[04] (1978).

DRAFTERS' ANALYSIS

Rule 509 is taken from present *Manual* paragraph 151 but has been modified to ensure conformity with Rule 606(b) which deals specifically with disclosure of deliberations in certain cases.

Rule 510. Waiver of Privilege by Voluntary Disclosure

(a) A person upon whom these rules confer a privilege against disclosure of a confidential matter or communication waives the privilege if the person or the person's predecessor while holder of the privilege voluntarily discloses or consents to disclosure of any significant part of the matter or communication under such circumstances that it would be inappropriate to allow the claim of privilege. This rule does not apply if the disclosure is itself a privileged communication.

(b) Unless testifying voluntarily concerning a privileged matter or communication, an accused who testifies in his or her own behalf or a person who testifies under a grant or promise of immunity does not, merely by reason of testifying, waive a privilege to which he or she may be entitled pertaining to the confidential matter or communication.

EDITORIAL COMMENT

The privileges noted in these Rules are generally justified on the ground that it is important to maintain confidentiality or secrecy in some contexts in order to promote or to preserve the privacy of various relationships or the security of certain sensitive information. Once the holder of the privilege discloses the protected matter under circumstances indicating that the privacy of the relationship or the security of the information apparently is not critical, the privilege evaporates under Rule 510. Naturally, the holder of a privilege or his predecessor may voluntarily disclose, or consent to disclosure of, confidential matters or communications. Once this occurs, however, the privilege is removed and usually cannot be restored. (Note that involuntary disclosures are covered in Rule 512).

The waiver part of the Rule is drawn from proposed Federal Rule of Evidence 511 and is consistent with *Manual* ¶ 151a which also permitted waiver of privileges. Waiver occurs only when the confidential matter or communication — *i.e.,* whatever the privilege covers — is disclosed inappropriately. Thus, a client may disclose that he has retained a lawyer, which fact usually is considered outside the protection of the privilege, without losing the protection for privileged communications with counsel. *See United States v. Aronoff,* 466 F. Supp. 855 (S.D.N.Y. 1979). If a "significant part" of the actual privileged communications is disclosed, waiver results.

The Rule plainly contemplates that not all disclosures of privileged material will constitute a waiver. One type of disclosure that does not result in waiver involves disclosure of some privileged matter in the context of another privileged communication. For example, one spouse may report to the other what he or she said to a lawyer without losing the privilege. Or, one spouse may tell the lawyer what was said to the other spouse and keep the privilege. Even outside privileged relationships, as noted above, waiver will only be found where, under the circumstances, following disclosure of privileged material it would not be appropriate to permit the holder afterwards to claim the privilege. The Rule itself does not elaborate on when a disclosure is appropriate but the drafters' *Analysis* uses the example of disclosure of an informant's identity to another law enforcement agency to illustrate what possibly may be an appropriate disclosure. *See also United States v. Lipshy,* 492 F. Supp. 35 (N.D. Tex. 1979).

Although the standard for a voluntary waiver is an intentional relinquishment of a known right, *see Johnson v. Zerbst,* 304 U.S. 458 (1938), the Rule implictly recognizes that once confidentiality is destroyed, a holder's attempts to claim the privilege will not restore it. The waiver here will stand even if the disclosure was made without the holder realizing the impact of the disclosure. Since the holder has destroyed the privacy or security afforded by the privilege by disclosure repair cannot be made. It might be argued that the Rule is flexible enough to treat some unknowing disclosures as situations in which it would be appropriate to permit the holder subsequently to claim the privilege. For example, if the privileged material is disclosed by mistake following the exercise of due care, some civilian courts will allow the privilege to be retained, especially if privileged material is mistakenly included when massive amounts of documents are made available for discovery.

Subdivision (b) simply provides that by testiying an accused does not waive a privilege relating to confidential matters. *Compare* Rule 301(e) (accused waives privilege against self-incrimination by voluntarily testifying). The same holds true for witnesses testifying under a grant or promise of immunity.

DRAFTERS' ANALYSIS

Rule 510 is derived from proposed Federal Rule of Evidence 511 and is similar in substance to present *Manual* paragraph 151a which notes that privileges may be waived. Rule 510(a) simply provides that "disclosure of any significant part of the matter or communication under such circumstances that it would be inappropriate to claim the privilege" will defeat and waive the privilege. Disclosure of privileged matter may be, however, itself privileged; *see* Rules 502(b)(4); 503(b)(2); 504(b)(2). Information disclosed in the form of an otherwise privileged telephone call (*e.g.,* information overheard by an operator) is privileged, Rule 511(b), and information disclosed via transmission using other forms of communication may be privileged; Rule 511(b). Disclosure under certain circumstances may not be "inappropriate" and the information will retain its privileged character. Thus, disclosure of an informant's identity by one law enforcement agency to another may well be appropriate and not render Rule 507 inapplicable.

Rule 510(b) is taken from present paragraph 151*(b)* (1) of the *Manual* and makes it clear that testimony pursuant to a grant of immunity does not waive the privilege. Similarly, an accused who testifies in his or her own behalf does not waive the privilege unless the accused testifies voluntarily to the privileged matter of communication.

Rule 511. Privileged Matter Disclosed Under Compulsion or Without Opportunity to Claim Privilege

(a) Evidence of a statement or other disclosure of privileged matter is not admissible against the holder of the privilege if disclosure was compelled erroneously or was made without an opportunity for the holder of the privilege to claim the privilege.

(b) The telephonic transmission of information otherwise privileged under these rules does not affect its privileged character. Use of electronic means of communication other than the telephone for transmission of information otherwise privileged under these rules does not affect the privileged character of such information if use of such means of communication is necessary and in furtherance of the communication.

EDITORIAL COMMENT

As a general rule once privileged matter has been disclosed, confidentiality is also gone and may not later be recaptured. *See* our discussion of Rule 510. Rule 511, however, permits some relief for the holder of the privilege by creating an exclusionary rule of sorts.

The Rule is patterned after proposed Federal Rule of Evidence 512 and effects some changes in military practice. Under prior *Manual* ¶ 151*b*(1), evidence of privileged information could be used if it had been obtained by a third party whether that party came upon the information by design or inadvertence. As we have noted in our discussion of the specific privilege rules found in Section V, some of the privileges permit a matter to remain privileged, even though a third person may be told of the matter, since disclosure of the information may further the interests that the privilege is intended to promote. And we have noted that Rule 510 permits disclosure of privileged information as part of another privileged communication and limits the waiver doctrine to disclosures that are "inappropriate."

Rule 511 covers the situation in which there is no voluntary disclosure of privileged information; rather, the privileged material is improperly coerced from the holder or someone else or is obtained under circumstances in which the holder has no opportunity to claim the privilege.

Subdivision (a) requires exclusion of privileged matters "when offered against the privilege holder" in two instances.

First, exclusion is called for where the disclosure was "compelled erroneously." The Rule draws no fine lines as to who may do the compelling, but practice indicates, and the Rule apparently assumes, that it will most often arise in a judicial setting when a judge erroneously rejects a privilege claim. If erroneous disclosure is ordered by the judge over the objection of the holder and is discovered while the trial is still in progress, the evidence may be stricken unless it is such inflammatory material that only a mistrial will correct the error. If the error is not discovered until after trial, then the appellate court will assess the damage caused to the holder by the erroneous disclosure at trial. Second, exclusion is required under subdivision (a) where the disclosure was made without the holder being given an opportunity to claim the privilege. Examples here would include discovery by eavesdroppers or persons who fortuitously overhear or see something not intended for their ears and eyes.

Subdivision (b) makes a special exception for use of telephones and other electronic means of communication. Privileged communications relayed over the telephone do not lose their privileged status. The drafters' *Analysis* explains the breadth of this provision by noting that the privileged status remains even where the parties know that their telephone conversations are being monitored. It is not clear, however, how this section will work. If *A* knows that *B* is listening in on his conversation with a lawyer, then is *A* making confidential communications? If not, there is no privilege to begin with. And in this example, we think there is no privileged communication. A sensible rule is one that presumes that parties who use the phone believe that their conversations are not being overheard but that denies a privilege to one who chooses to say things knowing they will be overheard. Privileged communications through other electronic means — *e.g.*, radio or telegraph — remain privileged only if the means are necessary and in furtherance of the communication. It matters not that the communication itself is unnecessary as long as the actual "means" used are considered necessary for the communication.

This Rule operates on the principle that "the cat may be out of the bag" when privileged material is discovered by a third party, but that it is still important that the holder, who has relied on the privilege and not waived it, be able to protect against having the disclosure intrusion compounded by the use of the material in court. Yet, this Rule protects only the holder against the injury associated with the use of the evidence. Once there is no longer a secret, the Rule does not protect others against whom the privileged material might be used. Of course, the hearsay rules of Section VIII might bar the use of the evidence anyway.

DRAFTERS' ANALYSIS

Rule 511(a) is similar to proposed Federal Rule of Evidence 512. Placed in the context of the definition of "confidential" utilized in the privilege rules, *see, e.g.*, Rule 502(b) (4), the Rule is substantially different from present military law inasmuch as present law permits utilization of privileged information which has been gained by a third party through accident or design. *See* present *Manual* paragraph 151*b*(1). Such disclosures are generally safeguarded against via the definition of "confidential" used in the new Rules. Generally, the Rules are more protective of privileged information than is the present *Manual*.

Rule 511(b) is new and deals with electronic transmission of information. It recognizes that the nature of the armed forces today often requires such information transmission. Like present *Manual* paragraph 151*b*(1), the new Rule does not make a nonprivileged communication privileged; rather, it simply safeguards already privileged information under certain circumstances.

The first portion of subdivision (b) expressly provides that otherwise privileged information transmitted by telephone remains privileged. This is in recognition of the role played by the telephone in modern life and particularly in the armed forces where geographical separations are common. The Committee was of the opinion that legal business cannot be transacted in the 20th century without customary use of the telephone. Consequently, privileged communications transmitted by telephone are protected even though those telephone conversations are known to be monitored for whatever purpose.

Unlike telephonic communications, Rule 511(b) protects other forms of electronic communication only when such means "is necessary and in furtherance of the communication." It is irrelevant under the Rule as to whether the communication in question was in fact necessary. The only relevant question is whether, once the individual decided to communicate, the *means* of communication was necessary and in furtherance of the communication. Transmission of information by radio is a means of communication that must be tested under this standard.

Rule 512. Comment Upon or Inference from Claim of Privilege; Instruction

(a) Comment or inference not permitted.

(1) The claim of a privilege by the accused whether in the present proceeding or upon a prior occasion is not a proper subject of comment by the military judge or counsel for any party. No inference may be drawn therefrom.

(2) The claim of a privilege by a person other than the accused whether in the present proceeding or upon a prior occasion normally is not a proper subject of comment by the military judge or counsel for any party. An adverse inference may not be drawn therefrom except when determined by the military judge to be required by the interests of justice.

(b) Claiming privilege without knowledge of members. In a trial before a court-martial with members, proceedings shall be conducted, to the extent practicable, so as to facilitate the making of claims of privilege without the knowledge of the members. This subdivision does not apply to a special court-martial without a military judge.

(c) Instruction. Upon request, any party against whom the members might draw an adverse inference from a claim of privilege is entitled to an instruction that no inference may be drawn therefrom except as provided in subdivision (a)(2).

EDITORIAL COMMENT

Permitting comment on the invocation of a privilege whittles away at the privilege by placing a price on its assertion. *See Griffin v. California*, 380 U.S. 609, 614 (1965). Rule 512 is an attempt to reduce, if not eliminate, the costs of asserting a privilege. It is generally new to military practice, insofar as it affects privileges other than the privilege against self-incrimination, and is patterned after proposed Federal Rule of Evidence 513.

Subdivision (a)(1) bars comments from both the military judge and counsel on an accused's claim of privilege regardless of when the claim was made. In addition, no adverse inference may be drawn from the claim. *See also* Rule 301(f). We assume that the Rule bars comment and adverse inferences only where a claim of privilege by an accused is valid. If an accused refuses to answer questions, some relating to direct examination, comment would be proper and an adverse inference could be drawn. Similarly, if an accused refuses to reveal a communication that the court rules is not privileged, comment and an adverse inference might follow.

Slightly different treatment is afforded to persons other than accuseds under (a)(2). "Normally," no comment is permitted. An inference may be drawn only where the judge determines that the interests of justice require it. The Rule provides no further guidance on what might trigger a comment or negative inference. Although the drafters' *Analysis* uses an example where an inference might be drawn following a government claim of privilege, there is no reason to prohibit an inference to be drawn under (a)(2) against either side if the interests of justice so dictate. However, before an adverse inference can be drawn against an accused it is likely that the court will have to find that the accused is somehow responsible for the privilege assertion that troubles the court.

Subdivision (b) is intended to give meaning to (a) and requires the parties, where practicable, to conceal from the court-members the fact that a privilege has been claimed. This is consistent with military and civilian case law, *see, e.g., Namet v. United States,* 373 U.S. 179 (1963); *United States v. Bricker,* 35 C.M.R. 566 (A.B.R. 1965) and the applicable ABA Standards Relating to Administration of Criminal Justice. Standards 3-5.7 and 4-7.6 provide that a lawyer should not call a witness who he knows will claim a valid privilege not to testify, for the purpose of impressing upon the jury the fact of the claim of privilege. In some instances, doing so will constitute unprofessional conduct. To handle the problem of potential claims, the drafters' *Analysis* suggests that out-of-court hearings or sidebar conferences should be used to determine whether a privilege will be claimed and its likely impact, if any, on the trial. Sidebar conferences may often be insufficient to protect the privilege, however. The Advisory Committee Note on the proposed federal rule counterpart addresses that point:

> The value of a privilege may be greatly depreciated by means other than expressly commenting to a jury upon the fact that it was exercised. Thus, the calling of a witness in the presence of the jury and subsequently excusing him after a sidebar conference may effectively convey to the jury the fact that a privilege has been claimed, even though the actual claim has not been made in their hearing. Whether a privilege will be claimed is usually ascertainable in advance and the handling of the entire matter outside the presence of the jury is feasible. Destruction of the privilege by innuendo can and should be avoided. Tallo v. United States, 344 F.2d 467 (1st Cir. 1965); United States v. Tomaiolo, 249 F.2d 683 (2d Cir. 1957); San Fratello v. United States, 343 F.2d 711 (5th Cir. 1965); Courtney v. United States, 390 F.2d 521 (9th Cir. 1968); 6 Wigmore § 1808, pp. 275-276; 6 U.C.L.A. L. Rev. 455 (1959). This position is in accord with the general agreement of the authorities that an accused cannot be forced to make his election not to testify in the presence of the jury. 8 Wigmore § 2268, p. 407 (McNaughton Rev. 1961).

> Unanticipated situations are, of course, bound to arise, and much must be left to the discretion of the judge and the professional responsibility of counsel.

Much debate has centered on the effectiveness of an instruction by the judge not to draw any inferences from the claim of a privilege. Subdivision (c) does not settle the question but rather simply permits counsel to request such an instruction. There is apparently no sua sponte duty on the military judge to give the instruction in the absence of a request. If a request is made, however, the instruction must be given except where the judge determines that justice requires an inference under Rule 512(a)(2). *See also* Rule 301(g).

DRAFTERS' ANALYSIS

(a) Comment or inference not permitted. Rule 512(a) is derived from proposed Federal Rule 513. The Rule is new to military law but is generally in accord with the Analysis of Contents of the present *Manual;* United States Department of the Army. Pamphlet No. 27-2, Analysis of Contents, *Manual for Courts-Martial,* 1969, Revised Edition 27-33, 27-38 (1970).

Rule 512(a)(1) prohibits any inference or comment upon the exercise of a privilege by the accused and is taken generally from proposed Federal Rule of Evidence 513(a).

Rule 512(a)(2) creates a qualified prohibition with respect to any inference or comment upon the exercise of a privilege by a person not the accused. The Rule recognizes that in certain circumstances the interests of justice may require such an inference and comment. Such a situation could result, for example, when the government's exercise of a privilege has been sustained, and an inference adverse to the government is necessary to preserve the fairness of the proceeding.

(b) Claiming privilege without knowledge of members. Rule 512(b) is intended to implement subdivision (a). Where possible claims of privilege should be raised at an Article 39(a) session or, if practicable, at sidebar.

(c) Instruction. Rule 512(c) requires that relevant instructions be given "upon request." *Cf.* Rule 105. The military judge does not have a duty to instruct sua sponte.

SECTION VI. WITNESSES

Rule 601. General Rule of Competency

Every person is competent to be a witness except as otherwise provided in these rules.

EDITORIAL COMMENT

At common law, and under ¶ 149 of the *Manual,* witnesses could be prohibited from testifying if they suffered from certain categorical disabilities. At various times these were: mental infirmities, infamy, extreme youth, senility, bias or interest in the proceedings, spousal incapacity, co-accused or conspiratorial affiliations, religious beliefs, or official connections with the tribunal. Rule 601 alters these limitations by providing that every person is competent to be a witness with a few exceptions found in other Section VI Rules. These other Rules cover the oath or affirmation requirement (Rule 603), interpreters (Rule 604), the disqualification of military judges (Rule 605) and court-members (Rule 606). *See also* Section V on privileges.

The military version of Rule 601 follows the Federal Rule. It has been altered to eliminate any reference to state law in civil cases.

In declaring that all persons are competent to testify, the Rule raises a question concerning the trial judge's power at common law to voir dire witnesses to insure that their capabilities to observe, understand, recollect and communicate are adequate. We believe that the policy of the Rule is against exclusion of witnesses because of arbitrary classifications such as developed at common law. However, some voir dire questions may aid the judge in making rulings under Rules 403 and 611(a) concerning a witness' testimony.

We also believe that there is no reason to permit an intoxicated witness to testify while under the influence. It is not adequate to say that intoxication goes to the weight to be given to the testimony, because the intoxicated state may make cross-examination difficult, if not impossible. Moreover, there is something offensive about a court's acceptance of a drugged witness in a search for truth. A continuance and a medical examination will assure the appearance of fairness and an adequate opportunity for cross-examination. *See generally United States v. Meerbeke,* 548 F.2d 415 (2d Cir. 1976). The witness who is intoxicated at trial must be distinguished from the witness who is sober at trial, but was intoxicated at the time of the events observed. No continuance will aid the latter type of witness, and his testimony probably should be admitted unless its prejudicial effect substantially outweighs its probative value.

In any event, even before Rule 601 was adopted, the basic tendency in federal and military courts was to allow virtually all witnesses to testify. This tradition, coupled with Rule 601, means that counsel will have to shift their attention from challenging a witness' competency *before* he testifies, to litigating the weight his testimony should be given *after* he testifies. The Rule's objective is to provide court-members with the greatest amount of arguably reliable evidence possible, with the expectation that court-members can decide the appropriate weight to be given imperfect witnesses. They should not be denied the benefit of evidence that has some probative value unless there is a good reason to keep the evidence from them.

Recent federal litigation indicates the trend is to follow the Rule as written and to allow all witnesses to testify. In *United States v. McRary,* 616 F.2d 181 (5th Cir. 1980), for example, the accused was charged with kidnapping. In order to establish his mental responsibility, defense counsel attempted to call the accused's wife as a witness. Even though she had previously been found mentally incompetent to stand trial with respect to her participation in the charged criminal venture, the court said, in the process of reversing the conviction on other grounds, that mental incompetence rarely, if ever, could be a ground for disqualification. *See also, United States v. Mills,* 597 F.2d 693 (9th Cir. 1979), rejecting infamy as a reason not to permit a witness to testify.

DRAFTERS' ANALYSIS

Rule 601 is taken without change from the first portion of Federal Rule of Evidence 601. The remainder of the Federal Rule was deleted due to its sole application to civil cases.

In declaring that subject to any other Rule, all persons are competent to be witnesses, Rule 601 supersedes ¶ 148 of the present *Manual* which requires, among other factors, that an individual know the difference between truth and falsehood and understand the moral importance of telling the truth in order to testify. Under Rule 601 such matters will go only to the weight of the testimony and not to its competency. The Rule's reference to other rules includes Rules 603 (Oath or Affirmation), 605 (Competency of Military Judge as Witness), 606 (Competency of Court Member as Witness), and the rules of privilege.

The plain meaning of the Rule appears to deprive the trial judge of any discretion whatsoever to exclude testimony on grounds of competency unless the testimony is incompetent under those specific rules already cited *supra, see, e.g., United States v. Fowler,* 605 F.2d 181 (5th Cir. 1979), a conclusion bolstered by the Federal Rules of Evidence Advisory Committee's Note S. SALTZBURG & K. REDDEN, FEDERAL RULES OF EVIDENCE MANUAL 270 (2d ed. 1977). Whether this conclusion is accurate, especially in the light of Rule 403, is unclear. *Id.* at 269; *see also United States v. Callahan,* 442 F. Supp. 1213 (D. Minn. 1978).

Rule 602. Lack of Personal Knowledge

A witness may not testify to a matter unless evidence is introduced sufficient to support a finding that the witness has personal knowledge of the matter. Evidence to prove personal knowledge may, but need not, consist of the testimony of the witness. This rule is subject to the provisions of rule 703, relating to opinion testimony by expert witnesses.

EDITORIAL COMMENT

Taken from its federal counterpart, and having its genesis in ¶ 138*d* of the *Manual,* Rule 602 provides that a lay witness may not testify unless evidence is introduced establishing that the witness has personal knowledge of what he says. The Rule goes on to state that such a foundation may, but need not, be established through the witness himself. Thus, it is to be expected that traditional military practice should continue under this Rule, and counsel will be able to initiate testimony without qualifying the witness in any formal sense; only if it becomes apparent during the witness' testimony that a factual foundation is absent, should an inquiry be conducted. Under these circumstances the court-members must be excluded, and evidence must be presented to demonstrate how the witness gained the information he is relating. Of course, if opposing counsel has interviewed a witness prior to trial and has a good faith belief that the witness has no personal knowledge to support all or part of his testimony, he may seek a hearing before the witness takes the stand in order to avoid having the court-members hear testimony that does not satisfy the Rule.

Rule 602 provides a mechanism for insuring that only reliable evidence reaches the triers of fact. This goal complements Section VIII's hearsay provisions, and Section X's best evidence requirements, but it is different from both. A witness who says "I only know what Corporal Jones told me. He said ...." has personal knowledge of what he heard. What Jones said may be hearsay, however. But that is a different problem. And a witness who says "I only know what the paper said. It said ...." has personal knowledge, but there may be a best evidence problem. Practically, this Rule assures that hearsay and best evidence problems are not obscured by witnesses who purport to have first-hand knowledge that they really do not have and that witnesses testify to what they know, not what they surmise to be true. The trial judge decides under this Rule not whether the evidence offered actually is believable, but whether, as a matter of law, a reasonable court-member could believe it. In other words, there is a difference between improbable evidence, which the trial judge should admit, and completely unbelievable evidence which should be excluded.

The Rule does not address matters of weight or credibility which are reserved entirely for the finders of fact. To implement the Rule, the trial bench should not exclude evidence merely because a witness is uncertain or hesitant about his testimony. Uncertainty or hesitancy affects only the evidence's weight.

A limited exception to Rule 602 deals with an accused's admissions or confessions. Here, even though defense counsel can establish that the accused had no basis in fact for a statement, it will still be admitted under the usual approach to personal admissions, covered by Rule 801(d)(2)(A). Naturally, at trial the accused cannot make self-serving statements while testifying unless there is personal knowledge to support them.

The final sentence of Rule 602 concerns the provision's interaction with expert or opinion testimony under Rule 703. This sentence was inserted to underscore the drafter's intent that the requirement of personal knowledge would not limit an expert's testimony. Expert witnesses still will be permitted to offer their opinions, even though they may be based on information provided by others, and even though the information itself might not be independently admissible as evidence.

DRAFTERS' ANALYSIS

Rule 602 is taken without significant change from the Federal Rule and is similar in content to ¶ 138d of the present *Manual*. Although the *Manual* expressly allows an individual to testify to his or her own age or date of birth, the Rule is silent on the issue.

Notwithstanding that silence, however, it appears that it is within the meaning of the Rule to allow such testimony. Rule 804(b)(4) [Hearsay Exceptions; Declarant Unavailable — Statement of Personal or Family History] expressly permits a hearsay statement "concerning the declarant's own birth . . . or other similar fact of personal or family history, even though declarant had no means of acquiring personal knowledge of the matter stated." It seems evident that if such a hearsay statement is admissible, in-court testimony by the declarant should be no less admissible. It is probable that the expression "personal knowledge" in Rule 804(b)(4) is being used in the sense of "first hand knowledge" while the expression is being used in Rule 602 in a somewhat broader sense to include those matters which an individual could be considered to reliably know about his or her personal history.

Rule 603. Oath or Affirmation

Before testifying, every witness shall be required to declare that the witness will testify truthfully, by oath or affirmation administered in a form calculated to awaken the witness's conscience and impress the witness's mind with the duty to do so.

EDITORIAL COMMENT

Like its federal counterpart, Rule 603 requires that a witness swear or affirm that he will tell the truth before he is permitted to testify. The Rule establishes no specific colloquy to be used in carrying out this requirement. Any process that is sufficient to "awaken the witness's conscience . . ." is satisfactory. The object here is to impress upon prospective witnesses that they have a duty to tell the truth while testifying. To a large extent these requirements codify existing military practice. *See Manual* Chapter XXII generally, and ¶ 114 specifically, for applicable oaths.

The oath requirement is part of the Rules' effort to insure that only accurate information reaches fact-finders. Recent commentaries question the oath's continued validity. But no one has demonstrated that it is not an effective symbol for some witnesses of the importance the law places on honesty.

The new Rule is written to permit atheists, conscientious objectors, children and individuals with emotional difficulties to satisfy the basic criterion. The idea is to find a procedure that will establish the witness' willingness to tell the truth and the concomitant acceptance of responsibility for false statements. As a procedural matter, counsel who knows that a witness will not swear, but will affirm, should so indicate before the witness takes the stand to avoid embarrassment and even possible confusion among court-members who hear the witness refuse to swear to tell the truth.

A witness who refuses to promise to testify truthfully may be excluded. *See, e.g., United States v. Fowler,* 605 F.2d 181 (5th Cir. 1979). But, absent a valid privilege claim, no witness can refuse to provide testimony when summoned. The contempt power remains available to compel a recalcitrant witness to provide evidence, and it may have to be exercised on behalf of an accused in order to satisfy his compulsory process right.

If the court decides under Rule 104(a) that a witness is incapable of understanding the duty to tell the truth, the drafters' *Analysis* to Rule 601 suggests that the witness may be excluded. Thus, the old mental incompetency standard, abolished under Rule 601, may rear its head again here. We would suggest, however, that a witness be barred from testifying only as a last resort, after the judge has tried every form of oath or affirmation or substitute therefore that might awaken the witness's conscience.

Finally, we anticipate that the application of Rule 603 will still be limited during the sentencing portion of a court-martial. It is consistent with Rule 1101(c) and permissible under ¶ 75c (2) of the *Manual* for an accused to take the stand and make an unsworn statement. Although the government is prohibited from cross-examining the accused with respect to this statement, it may present evidence in rebuttal.

DRAFTERS' ANALYSIS

Rule 603 is taken from the Federal Rule without change. The oaths found within Chapter XXII of the Manual satisfy the requirements of Rule 603. Pursuant to Rule 1101(c), this Rule is inapplicable to the accused when he or she makes an unsworn statement under ¶ 75c (2) of the *Manual*.

Rule 604. Interpreters

An interpreter is subject to the provisions of these rules relating to qualification as an expert and the administration of an oath or affirmation that the interpreter will make a true translation.

EDITORIAL COMMENT

Because court-martials are conducted all over the world, large numbers of non-English speaking witnesses play a role in military justice. A reasonable requirement that their testimony be accurately communicated to those court-members and judges who may understand only English is found in Rule 604. The Rule is taken from its federal counterpart and does not substantially alter prior *Manual* practice. *See Manual* ¶ 141 generally, and ¶ 114e for specific interpreter oaths.

The new Rule establishes certain procedures for using an interpreter. First, the interpreter must be qualified in the same manner as any expert witness. This includes proof that the interpreter is competent to translate the foreign language into English, and that he is able to perform this function during the trial itself. To insure that the translation will be accurate, Rule 604 requires that the interpreter swear or affirm that he will "make a true translation." This last requirement means that the interpreter will not analyze the testimony during translation, but will provide an exact English version of it.

Rule 604 does not indicate when an interpreter is required. We believe that confrontation and compulsory process rights require an interpreter (1) when it is reasonably possible that without one, a witness may not understand questions or be understood by the tribunal and (2) when the defendant makes a timely request that an interpreter be appointed. Rule 1101(d) states that the Military Rules of Evidence (other than privilege rules) do not apply to Article 32 hearings and related processes. It must be noted that in these hearings defense counsel may be unable to adequately prepare a defense without an interpreter — *e.g.,* when some of the government's witnesses are foreign nationals, defense counsel unassisted by an interpreter will be unable to meaningfully discuss the case with these witnesses. Thorough preparation and cross-examination will then be undermined. Appointment of an interpreter in these hearings would be useful. If an interpreter is appointed, then there is no reason why a court would not be able to use this Rule as persuasive authority, even though it is not binding under Rule 1101.

The new Rule and the drafters' *Analysis* also fail to discuss how an accurate "transcript" can be assured when an interpreter is used. A court reporter will not be transcribing what he hears said to or by a non-English-speaking witness, but will record what is said to or by the interpreter. If an audio recording of the entire proceeding is not kept for appellate review, evidence of possible inaccuracies may be lost. Thus, we recommend tape recording whenever an interpreter is used.

DRAFTERS' ANALYSIS

Rule 604 is taken from the Federal Rule without change and is consistent with ¶ 141 of the present *Manual.* The oath found in *Manual* ¶ 114e satisfies the oath requirement of Rule 604.

Rule 605. Competency of Military Judge as Witness

(a) The military judge presiding at the court-martial may not testify in that court-martial as a witness. No objection need be made to preserve the point.

(b) This rule does not preclude the military judge from placing on the record matters concerning docketing of the case.

EDITORIAL COMMENT

Trial judges play a central role in determining how evidence will be presented, but Rule 605 prohibits them from being witnesses in cases they judge. Subdivision (a) of the Rule is taken from its federal counterpart, and resembles Article 26(d) of the Uniform Code of Military Justice. Subdivision (b) is not found in the Federal Rules, having been added to clarify existing military practice.

Rule 605(a) is a simple statement of judicial incapacity. It categorically prohibits the military judge from serving as a witness while presiding at a court-martial. The drafters felt this provision was so important that they created an exception to Rule 103's general requirement of a timely and specific objection and provided that counsel need not object to the judge's testimony in order to preserve a claim of error on appeal. The resulting "automatic exception" recognizes the reality that counsel generally will be reluctant to challenge a judge who is so bold as to believe that he can be an impartial judge of his own testimony, and that judges ought to be aware of the impropriety of assuming the role of evidence-giver and evidence-assessor in the same case.

It could be argued that Rule 605 is not needed, as general due process considerations should prohibit the trial judge from testifying, and thus aligning himself with one party or the other. *Cf. Connally v. Georgia*, 429 U.S. 245 (1977). But the Rule avoids any constitutional problem and any need for constitutional decision making.

Article 26(d) of the Code already provides the accused with protection in this area by stating that "no person is eligible to act as military judge in a case if he is . . . a witness for the prosecution. . . ." Rule 605 extends this protection to the government as well. Although one might argue that had Congress intended Article 26(d)'s provisions to protect the government, it would have included them in the Code itself, that argument seems weak. Congress apparently wanted to assure that the defendant would never be prejudiced but in no way indicated that the government should be prejudiced. Probably, Congress thought it more likely that a judge would be inclined to testify for the prosecution and absolutely prohibited that. This Rule goes further but is consistent with the goal of Congress.

Two exceptions to Rule 605(a) should be mentioned. First, there is no incapacity with respect to a trial judge testifying during subsequent proceedings which concern a trial he presided over. This could occur with respect to limited rehearings ordered pursuant to *United States v. Dubay*, 17 C.M.A. 147, 37 C.M.R. 411 (1967); or *United States v. Ray*, 20 C.M.A. 331, 43

C.M.R. 171 (1971). Second, a trial judge might avoid subdivision (a)'s prohibitions by taking judicial notice of facts. Judicial notice would not result in either counsel's examining the bench with respect to the accuracy or foundation of such facts. Notice of adjudicative facts would only be taken in accordance with Rule 201.

Rule 605(b) was created in response to military exigencies. Due to the lack of trial court clerks, and similar administrative assistants, military judges must often manage their own dockets. This situation could present problems of proof in litigating speedy trial motions. As a result, subdivision (b) specifically allows the bench to spread documentary and related matters on the record with respect to its docketing of the case. This is similar to Rule 103(b). Unfortunately, the Rule and the drafters' *Analysis* fail to define how this should be accomplished. The bench would be well-advised to provide the parties, as well as the reporter, with a statement, in writing if possible, of the matters involved and the facts to be recorded. This should minimize errors and assure that the parties have a chance to be heard on disputed points. It must also be recognized that speedy trial motions will be litigated during Article 39(a) sessions, which means that the Rules of Evidence will be relaxed, allowing testimony that may moot the judge's need to supplement the record. *See* our discussion of Rule 104(a).

DRAFTERS' ANALYSIS

Rule 605(a) restates the Federal Rule without significant change. Although Article 26(d) of the Uniform Code of Military Justice states in relevant part that "no person is eligible to act as a military judge if he is a witness for the prosecution. . . ." and is silent on whether a witness for the defense is eligible to sit, the Committee believes that the specific reference in the Code was not intended to create a right and was the result only of an attempt to highlight the more grievous case. In any event, Rule 605, unlike Article 26(d), does not deal with the question of eligibility to sit as a military judge, but deals solely with the military judge's competency as a witness. The rule does not affect voir dire.

Rule 605(b) is new and is not found within the Federal Rules of Evidence. It was added because of the unique nature of the military judiciary in which military judges often control their own dockets without clerical assistance. In view of the military's stringent speedy trial rules, see, e.g., *United States v. Burton*, 21 C.M.A. 112, 44 C.M.R. 166 (1971), it was necessary to preclude expressly any interpretation of Rule 605 that would prohibit the military judge from placing on the record details relating to docketing in order to avoid prejudice to a party. Rule 605(b) is consistent with present military law.

Rule 606. Competency of Court Member as Witness

(a) At the court-martial. A member of the court-martial may not testify as a witness before the other members in the trial of the case in which the member is sitting. If the member is called to testify, the opposing party, except in a special court-martial without a military judge, shall be afforded an opportunity to object out of the presence of the members.

(b) Inquiry into validity of findings or sentence. Upon an inquiry into the validity of the findings or sentence, a member may not testify as to any matter or statement occurring during the course of the deliberations of the members of the court-martial or to the effect of anything upon the member's or any other member's mind or emotions as influencing the member to assent to or dissent from the findings or sentence or concerning the member's mental process in connection therewith, except that a member may testify on the question whether extraneous prejudicial information was improperly brought to the attention of the members of the court-martial, whether any outside influence was improperly brought to bear upon any member, or whether there was unlawful command influence. Nor may the member's affidavit or evidence of any statement by the member concerning a matter about which the member would be precluded from testifying be received for these purposes.

EDITORIAL COMMENT

The court-members determine guilt and innocence. If an accused ultimately is convicted they also assess an appropriate sentence. The drafters recognized that these important responsibilities could be compromised if the members simultaneously served as witnesses. Subdivisions (a) and (b) of the Rule generally are taken from and consistent with the Federal Rule, and also are consistent with, but somewhat more expansive than, past military practice. *See generally Manual* ¶¶ 62f and 63.

Subdivision (a) of the new Rule states that a court-member should not testify as a witness when sitting as factfinder. The Rule is not one of strict incompetence, as its second sentence indicates that opposing counsel must object to such conduct in order to preserve any possible error for appeal. (Compare our discussion of Rule 605(a), indicating that no objection is necessary when the trial judge testifies as a witness.)

By prohibiting the triers of fact from testifying, the drafters recognized that it is not possible for court-members to sit as neutral arbiters and to evaluate, without bias, their own testimony. Other pragmatic considerations also support the Rule. Counsel will generally desire to talk with a witness just prior to direct examination. This could not be accomplished if the witness is also a court-member. More importantly, how aggressive could opposing counsel be in cross-examining or impeaching a witness if that same witness must later sit in judgment of counsel's case?

While 606(a) mandates that counsel not plan on using court-members during their case-in-chief, it does not address what should be done when it is determined *during* trial that a court-member may have relevant testimony to offer. This event is more likely to occur in military than in federal practice, because many military communities are small and closely knit. The problem envisioned here could easily arise as follows: During trial the government learns that an unanticipated witness must be called. In response, defense counsel discovers that a court-member is the sole source of valuable impeachment evidence concerning that witness. However, Rule 606(a) will not permit the court-member to testify over a timely government objection. This result raises problems of constitutional magnitude, as the accused's ability to present his defense is severely limited.

In this situation, it is doubtful that the trial judge could allow the court-member to testify for the very reasons that give rise to Rule 606(a). Hence, trial counsel will insist upon a mistrial as the only appropriate remedy. It is unlikely that the judge can save the case by excusing the testifying court-member, even if sufficient members are left to constitute a quorum. Government counsel still would feel that any attempt to impeach the court-member or to vigorously cross-examine him would prejudice his case in the remaining members' eyes.

Although no single solution will settle all 606(a) problems, a thorough *voir dire* of prospective court-members should help to minimize them. In this respect, counsel for both sides should insure that the triers of fact do not have personal knowledge of the facts and that they are not too closely associated with any potential witnesses. Care in voir dire may avoid trouble later.

Subdivision (b) addresses the role court-members play in post-trial challenges to the proceedings. Initially, it prohibits a member from testifying about his or any other member's: (1) actual deliberations, (2) impressions, (3) emotional feelings or (4) mental processes used to resolve an issue at bar. The Rule also states that if the court-members cannot testify, then their affidavits or similar documentary statements will not be admissible. *See United States v. Higdon,* 2 M.J. 445, 455 (A.C.M.R. 1975) where Federal Rule 606(b) was used to reject a court-member's affidavit alleging improper balloting techniques.

Alternatively, 606(b) allows court-members to testify if the possibility exists of: (1) extra-record prejudicial information being brought to their attention, (2) outside influence being exerted upon them, or (3) command control being used to guide the proceedings' outcome. This aspect of subdivision (b) is virtually identical with its federal counterpart, except that the drafters added a specific provision addressing command influence. *See* Article 37(a), Uniform Code of Military Justice, and ¶ 74d(1) of the *Manual* for prohibitions in this area. *See also United States v. Howard,* 23 C.M.A. 187, 48 C.M.R. 939 (1974), where the Court of Appeals reversed a conviction because it appeared that the convening authority attempted to influence the treatment of soldiers tried before general courts-martial. The addition of a specific Rule that will serve as a vehicle for publicizing these rare improprieties is consistent with executive and Congressional desires to demonstrate the independence of military tribunals.

By allowing court-members to testify under some circumstances, and not others, subdivision (b) represents the military drafters' adoption of a congressional compromise. The balance is struck between the necessity for accurately resolving criminal trials in accordance with rules of law on the one hand, and the desirability of promoting finality in litigation and of protecting members from harassment and second-guessing on the other hand. The result permits court-members to testify with respect to *objective* manifestations of impropriety — *e.g.*, that inadmissible evidence was placed in their deliberation room, *see United States v. Pinto*, 486 F. Supp. 578 (E.D. Pa. 1980) — but prohibits their testimony if the alleged transgression is *subjective* in nature — *e.g.*, allegations that the court members ignored the trial judge's instructions and convicted the accused because he failed to take the stand in his own defense, *see United States v. Edwards*, 486 F. Supp. 673 (S.D.N.Y. 1980). Recent federal litigation demonstrates that 606(b) will prevent counsel from examining court-members to determine whether they followed the bench's instructions, violated their juror oaths, or were emotionally influenced by some event at trial. *See United States v. Greer*, 620 F.2d 1382 (10th Cir. 1980). *See also* WEINSTEIN AND BERGER, WEINSTEIN'S EVIDENCE, 606-631 to 606-634 (1978), for other examples of subjective and objective criteria.

DRAFTERS' ANALYSIS

(a) At the court-martial. Rule 606(a) is taken from the Federal Rule without substantive change. The Rule alters present military law only to the extent that a member of the court could testify as a defense witness under prior precedent. Rule 606(a) deals only with the competency of court members as witnesses and does not affect other *Manual* provisions governing the eligibility of individuals to sit as members due to their potential status as witnesses. *See, e.g.,* ¶¶ 62*f* and 63. The Rule does not affect voir dire.

(b) Inquiry into validity of findings or sentence. Rule 606(b) is taken from the Federal Rule with only one significant change. The Rule, retitled to reflect the sentencing function of members, recognizes unlawful command influence as a legitimate subject of inquiry and permits testimony by a member on that subject. The addition is required by the need to keep proceedings free from any taint of unlawful command influence and further implements Article 37(a) of the Uniform Code of Military Justice. Use of superior rank or grade by one member of a court to sway other members would constitute unlawful command influence for purposes of this Rule under ¶ 74*d*(1). Rule 606 does not itself prevent otherwise lawful polling of members of the court, *see generally, United States v. Hendon*, 6 M.J. 171, 174 (C.M.A. 1979) and does not prohibit attempted lawful clarification of an ambiguous or inconsistent verdict. Rule 606(b) is in general accord with present military law.

Rule 607. Who May Impeach

The credibility of a witness may be attacked by any party, including the party calling the witness.

EDITORIAL COMMENT

At common law, and under previous *Manual* provisions, a party was prohibited from impeaching his own witness except in special circumstances — *e.g.,* the witness was hostile, he surprised counsel with damaging testimony, or he was essential to the calling party's case. Rule 607, which is identical with its federal counterpart, rejects the common law idea that a party calling a witness is required to vouch for the witness' testimony. Now counsel, on direct examination, may impeach a witness he has called.

Commentators have long called for this change. They perceived that the traditional practice artificially limited counsel's ability to accurately present a case. The common law practice assumed that proponents of witnesses had some real choice as to whom to call as witnesses. In most cases this is unrealistic. Parties must use those witnesses who have knowledge of the facts of a case. Those who participate in a crime will have knowledge. Those who witness it may have additional knowledge. People to whom confessions are made may have something to add. But these people all must be taken as they are. Counsel cannot substitute for them. Impeachment is less important with respect to witnesses who are carefully selected, screened and prepared before trial. It also is less likely to occur. Rarely does a party impeach his own expert or character witness. In fact, such witnesses are worth little if they are impeached.

The defense's need to impeach its own witnesses has been recognized by the Supreme Court as rising to the level of a constitutional right under limited circumstances. In *Chambers v. Mississippi,* 410 U.S. 284 (1973), the accused was charged with murder of a policeman. As part of its case, the defense called an individual named McDonald in order to establish that McDonald had previously confessed to the crime. During its direct examination the defense introduced one of McDonald's out-of-court statements, but McDonald recanted and sought to explain giving the statement. When the defense moved to cross-examine McDonald about three other statements, the trial judge denied the motion because of Mississippi's voucher rule. In reversing, the Supreme Court found that the state's use of its voucher rule had denied the accused his right to a fair trial, and his ability to present an adequate defense. *See also United States v. Johnson,* 3 M.J. 143 (C.M.A. 1977) adopting the holding for military practice.

Rule 607 is intended to permit impeachment, not to permit the introduction of inconsistent statements where there is no reason for impeachment other than to attempt to bring hearsay before court-members. If a witness's prior statement satisfies Rule 801(d)(1)(A)'s provisions, it will be admissible as substantive evidence. Any witness can be called and asked about statements that are non-hearsay and admissible under Rule 801(d)(1)(A). However, if a statement does not qualify under Rule 801 as non-hearsay, it is improper for a party to call the witness for the sole purpose of bringing out the prior statements. If the proponent of the witness does elicit some helpful material from the witness but also is damaged by portions of the witness' testimony, impeachment with inconsistent statements directed at the damaging testimony should be allowed. Also, if a party is surprised and hurt by a witness' testimony, impeachment is certainly proper. To be avoided, however, is the calling of a witness who counsel knows has nothing favorable to say in order to bring out inconsistent statements. Since the witness says nothing that helps the calling party, it is clear that this procedure is an attempt to avoid Rule 801 and to smuggle inconsistent statements into a trial in the hope that despite a limiting instruction under Rule 105, court-members will use the statements substantively.

We believe the proponent of a witness should be permitted to use evidence of "prior bad acts" to impeach his own witness under Rule 608(b). The same result should obtain under Rule 609 with respect to evidence of previous convictions. A party should not be forced to await impeachment by an opponent; he should be allowed to show that a witness has blemishes. Some courts call this taking the "sting" out of impeachment by an opponent. The legislative history of the Federal Rules displays no Congressional intent to limit their application of Rules 608 and 609 to only "cross-examination." *See* S. SALTZBURG & K. REDDEN, FEDERAL RULES OF EVIDENCE MANUAL, 398-399 (2d ed. 1977) for a more detailed discussion of this area. Here, the drafters' *Analysis* is much clearer than anything in the legislative history of the Federal Rules of Evidence and supports our suggestion.

The Rule does not set forth the types of impeachment that are permissible. Subsequent Rules cover many of the most familiar modes of impeachment, and Rule 402 would indicate that as long as the credibility of a witness is pertinent, relevant evidence detracting from it should be admitted unless another Rule stands in the way.

DRAFTERS' ANALYSIS

Rule 607 is taken without significant change from the Federal Rule. It supersedes *Manual* ¶ 153b (1) which restricts impeachment of one's own witness to those situations in which the witness is indispensable or the testimony of the witness proves to be unexpectedly adverse.

Rule 607 thus allows a party to impeach its own witness. Indeed, when relevant, it permits a party to call a witness for the sole purpose of impeachment. It should be noted, however, that an apparent inconsistency exists when Rule 607 is compared with Rules 608(b) and 609(a). Although Rule 607 allows impeachment on direct examination, Rules 608(b) and 609(a) would by their explicit language restrict the methods of impeachment to cross-examination. The use of the expression "cross-examination" in these rules appears to be accidental and to have been intended to be synonymous with impeachment while on direct examination. *See generally* S. SALTZBURG & K. REDDEN, FEDERAL RULES OF EVIDENCE MANUAL 298-299 (2d ed. 1977). It is the intent of the Committee that the Rules be so interpreted unless the Article III courts should interpret the Rules in a different fashion.

Rule 608. Evidence of Character, Conduct, and Bias of Witness

(a) Opinion and reputation evidence of character. The credibility of a witness may be attacked or supported by evidence in the form of opinion or reputation, but subject to these limitations: (1) the evidence may refer only to character for truthfulness or untruthfulness, and (2) evidence of truthful character is admissible only after the character of the witness for truthfulness has been attacked by opinion or reputation evidence or otherwise.

(b) Specific instances of conduct. Specific instances of conduct of a witness, for the purpose of attacking or supporting the credibility of the witness, other than conviction of crime as provided in rule 609, may not be proved by extrinsic evidence. They may, however, in the discretion of the military judge, if probative of truthfulness or untruthfulness, be inquired into on cross-examination of the witness (1) concerning character of the witness for truthfulness or untruthfulness, or (2) concerning the character for truthfulness or untruthfulness of another witness as to which character the witness being cross-examined has testified. The giving of testimony, whether by an accused or by another witness, does not operate as a waiver of the privilege against self-incrimination when examined with respect to matters which relate only to credibility.

(c) Evidence of bias. Bias, prejudice, or any motive to misrepresent may be shown to impeach the witness either by examination of the witness or by evidence otherwise adduced.

EDITORIAL COMMENT

Criminal proceedings are a search for the truth, and a search for truth depends on the honesty of the participants. The various witnesses who testify only advance the cause if they are truthful. Rule 607 recognizes the importance of witness credibility and Rule 608 covers several common forms of impeachment. The new Military Rule is more complete than its federal counterpart. It specifically provides that evidence of bias or prejudice may be used for impeachment. The new Rule is also broader than previous *Manual* renditions which placed limitations on character impeachment. *See Manual* ¶ 153*b*. *See United States v. Tomchek,* 4 M.J. 66 (C.M.A. 1977) for a discussion of Federal Rule 608 and court-martial practice.

Subdivision (a) prescribes how a witness' character for truthfulness may be attacked. It provides that reputation or opinion evidence may be used to demonstrate that the witness's character for truthfulness is bad. Only after some attack on credibility has been made may the witness's character be rehabilitated with opinion or reputation evidence. Thus, the Rule does not permit counsel to bolster an unattacked witness's testimony. The attack that triggers the opportunity for rehabilitation need not take form of negative character testimony. Anything that implies the untruthfulness of the witness — slashing cross-examination for example, *see United States v. Medical Therapy Sciences, Inc.*, 583 F.2d 36 (2d Cir. 1978), cert. denied, 439 U.S. 1130 (1979) — may satisfy the "or otherwise" language of the Rule. Rule 403 may be used to limit the amount of evidence accepted for impeachment and rehabilitation use.

It is rather surprising that the drafters of this Rule failed to provide the same complete treatment of reputation evidence that is provided in connection with Rule 405. Is the definition of "reputation" the same under both Rules? We think that the answer is "yes" despite Rule 608's silence. The two definitions of reputation traditionally are identical at common law, and it is doubtful that the drafters would have used the same word in Rule 608 as in Rule 405 without intending that the user of the Rules should look to Rule 405 for guidance as to what the word means. More troublesome is the question whether the affidavit evidence that is acceptable under Rule 405(c) also is acceptable under Rule 608. Arguably, Rule 405(c) evidence is more central to the merits and warrants special treatment. We do not think so, however. Although the intent of the drafters is not evident, we would hope that affidavits will be as readily admissible under Rule 608 as under Rule 405, since the reasons for accepting them are the same under both Rules, and the need to assess credibility often may be paramount in cases turning on the testimony of a small number of witnesses.

Rule 608(b)(2) provides that a character witness can be asked questions about specific acts of the person whose credibility has been rehabilitated or attacked as a way of impeaching the character witness. This is identical to the cross-examination that is permitted under Rule 405 and that is discussed there. Thus, we shall not repeat our treatment of this type of cross-examination here. We do note, however, that the cross-examination must relate to acts that might reasonably call into question reputation or opinion as to truthfulness, that the examiner is not permitted actually to offer extrinsic evidence to prove the acts and that there must be a good faith basis for any questions that are asked.

Rule 608(b) generally provides that a party may not offer evidence of specific instances of past conduct of a witness to attack or to support the witness' veracity. However, this general prohibition is subject to several exceptions. For instance, evidence of previous convictions may be admissible under Rule 609. More importantly for purposes of Rule 608, subdivision (b) allows a witness (including the accused — this Rule unlike previous *Manual* ¶ 153*b* does not distinguish the accused from other witnesses) to be asked about specific instances of conduct that might be probative of credibility. But, the Rule does not permit the questioner to introduce extrinsic evidence in support of his inquiry. The drafters were concerned that the introduction of extrinsic evidence would cause confusion and tend to distract the court-members. The general prohibition on extrinsic evidence does not necessarily mean that the questioner "must take the witness's answer," and abandon his inquiry once a "no" is given; counsel may pursue the investigation by pressing the witness for an admission as long as the questioning is reasonable under Rule 611(a). The Rule depends upon the trial judges to assure that the inquiry relates to truthfulness and not to general character. *See, e.g., United States v. Fortes,* 619 F.2d 108 (1st Cir. 1980), in which defense counsel attempted to cross-examine a government witness about his involvement in drug trafficking. The court of appeals held that the trial judge properly exercised his discretion to exclude the evidence as not sufficiently probative of truthfulness. In exercising discretion the trial judge might want to make a special effort to assure that the accused is not unfairly treated. Rules 403 and 611(a) may be useful here also.

Some question exists with respect to whether specific instances of conduct may be inquired into on direct as well as cross-examination. Recognizing that the text of the Rule would seem to restrict the use of the evidence to cross-examination, the military drafters have nevertheless suggested that the better approach here is to permit the direct examiner to impeach his witness. It may be that the Federal Rules, from which Rule 608 is taken, frequently use the words "cross-examine," when they mean "impeach." If so, this is a liability the Military Rules now share. *See* S. SALTZBURG & K. REDDEN, FEDERAL RULES OF EVIDENCE MANUAL 312-313 (2d ed. 1977), for a more detailed discussion of the issue. Although the military drafters' *Analysis* of how 608(b) evidence should be used is reasonable, it should be noted that no clear federal authority has yet evolved in the civilian courts.

The last sentence of subdivision (b) provides that all witnesses, including the accused, retain their privilege against self-incrimination as to questions asked about specific acts that relate only to credibility. The Rule accommodates Fifth Amendment interests and recognizes that they may predominate over impeachment needs. Its benefits can be seen in the following example. If the accused is charged with robbery, and takes the stand in his own defense, he does not waive his rights against self-incrimination with respect to any examination about unrelated forgery offenses that might shed light on credibility. The idea here is that a "waiver" rule would place too great a price upon the accused's right to testify in his own defense. It should be noted, however, that the Rule does not prohibit questions with respect to previous convictions governed by Rule 609 or interrogation about other misconduct if it is relevant to an issue other than credibility — *e.g.,* under Rule 404(b) it might be used to show plan, design, intent, knowledge and other issues. Thus, what may be inadmissible as character evidence under Rule 608(b) may be admissible as substantive evidence of guilt under Rule 404(b).

Subdivision (c) of the Military Rule allows a witness to be impeached by evidence of bias, prejudice, or motive to misrepresent. It adopts ¶ 153*d* of the previous *Manual.* No similar provision is found in the Federal Rule. However, most commentators agree that its omission is not significant and the federal courts have consistently admitted such evidence. *See United States v. Leja*, 568 F.2d 493 (6th Cir. 1977). Indeed, when the defense offers such evidence, it may deny confrontation rights to exclude it. *See, e.g., Davis v. Alaska*, 415 U.S. 308 (1974). To implement 608(c), the military drafters provide that evidence of bias or prejudice may be introduced through the examination of witnesses, "or by evidence otherwise adduced." Thus, extrinsic evidence plainly is allowed under (c), although not under (b).

DRAFTERS' ANALYSIS

(a) Opinion and reputation evidence of character. Rule 608(a) is taken verbatim from the Federal Rule. The Rule, which is consistent with the philosophy behind Rule 404(a), limits use of character evidence in the form of opinion or reputation evidence on the issue of credibility by restricting such evidence to matters relating to the character for truthfulness or untruthfulness of the witness. General good character is not admissible under the Rule. Rule 608(a) prohibits presenting evidence of good character until the character of the witness for truthfulness has been attacked. The Rule is similar to ¶ 153*b* of the present *Manual* except that the Rule, unlike ¶ 153*b*, applies to all witnesses and does not distinguish between the accused and other witnesses.

(b) Specific instances of conduct. Rule 608(b) is taken from the Federal Rule without significant change. The Rule is somewhat similar in effect to the military practice now found in ¶ 153*b*(2) of the *Manual* in that it allows use of specific instances of conduct of a witness to be brought out on cross-examination but prohibits use of extrinsic evidence. Unlike ¶ 153*b*(2), Rule 608(b) does not distinguish between an accused and other witnesses.

The fact that the accused is subject to impeachment by prior acts of misconduct is a significant factor to be considered by the military judge when he or she is determining whether to exercise the discretion granted by the Rule. Although the Rule expressly limits this form of impeachment to inquiry on cross-examination, it is likely that the intent of the Federal Rule was to permit inquiry on direct as well, *see* Rule 607, and the use of the term "cross-examination" was an accidental substitute for "impeachment." *See* S. SALTZBURG & K. REDDEN, FEDERAL RULES OF EVIDENCE MANUAL 312-313 (2d ed. 1977). It is the intent of the Committee to allow use of this form of evidence on direct-examination to the same extent, if any, it is so permitted in the Article III courts.

The Rule does not prohibit receipt of extrinsic evidence in the form of prior convictions, Rule 609, or to show bias, Rule 608(c). *See also* Rule 613 (Prior statements of witnesses). When the witness has testified as to the character of another witness, the witness may be cross-examined as to the character of that witness. The remainder of Rule 608(b) indicates that testimony relating only to credibility does not waive the privilege against self-incrimination. *See generally* Rule 301.

Although Rule 608(b) allows examination into specific acts, counsel should not, as a matter of ethics, attempt to elicit evidence of misconduct unless there is a reasonable basis for the question. *See generally* ABA PROJECT ON STANDARDS FOR CRIMINAL JUSTICE, STANDARDS RELATING TO THE PROSECUTION FUNCTION AND THE DEFENSE FUNCTION, Prosecution Function 5.7(d); Defense Functions 7.6(d) (Approved draft 1971).

(c) Evidence of bias. Rule 608 (c) is taken from present Manual ¶ 153*d* and is not found within the Federal Rule. Impeachment by bias was apparently accidentally omitted from the Federal Rule, *see, e.g.,* S. SALTZBURG & K. REDDEN, FEDERAL RULES OF

EVIDENCE MANUAL 313, 314 (2d ed. 1977), but is acceptable under the Federal Rules; *see, e.g., United States v. Leja,* 568 F.2d 493 (6th Cir. 1977); *United States v. Alvarez-Lopez,* 559 F.2d 1155 (9th Cir. 1977). Because of the critical nature of this form of impeachment and the fact that extrinsic evidence may be used to show it, the Committee believed that its omission would be impracticable.

It should be noted that the Federal Rules are not exhaustive and that a number of different types of techniques of impeachment are not explicitly codified.

The failure to so codify them does not mean that they are no longer permissible. *See, e.g., United States v. Alvarez-Lopez,* 559 F.2d 1155 (9th Cir. 1977); Rule 412. Thus, impeachment by contradiction, *see also* Rules 304(a)(2); 311(j), and impeachment via prior inconsistent statements, Rule 613, remain appropriate. To the extent that the Military Rules do not acknowledge a particular form of impeachment, it is the intent of the Committee to allow that method to the same extent it is permissible in the Article III courts. *See, e.g.,* Rules 402; 403.

Impeachment of an alleged victim of a sexual offense through evidence of the victim's past sexual history and character is dealt with in Rule 412, and evidence of fresh complaint is admissible to the extent permitted by Rules 801 and 803.

Rule 609. Impeachment by Evidence of Conviction of Crime

(a) General rule. For the purpose of attacking the credibility of a witness, evidence that the witness has been convicted of a crime shall be admitted if elicited from the witness or established by public record during cross-examination but only if the crime (1) was punishable by death, dishonorable discharge, or imprisonment in excess of one year under the law under which the witness was convicted, and the military judge determines that the probative value of admitting this evidence outweighs its prejudicial effect to the accused, or (2) involved dishonesty or false statement, regardless of the punishment. In determining whether a crime tried by court-martial was punishable by death, dishonorable discharge, or imprisonment in excess of one year, the maximum punishment prescribed by the President under Article 56 at the time of the conviction applies without regard to whether the case was tried by general, special, or summary court-martial.

(b) Time limit. Evidence of a conviction under this rule is not admissible if a period of more than ten years has elapsed since the date of the conviction or of the release of the witness from the confinement imposed for that conviction, whichever is the later date, unless the court determines, in the interests of justice, that the probative value of the conviction supported by specific facts and circumstances substantially outweighs its prejudicial effect. However, evidence of a conviction more than ten years old as calculated herein, is not admissible unless the proponent gives to the adverse party sufficient advance written notice of intent to use such evidence to provide the adverse party with a fair opportunity to contest the use of such evidence.

(c) Effect of pardon, annulment, or certificate of rehabilitation. Evidence of a conviction is not admissible under this rule if (1) the conviction has been the subject of a pardon, annulment, certificate of rehabilitation, or other equivalent procedure based on a finding of the rehabilitation of the person convicted, and that person has not been convicted of a subsequent crime which was punishable by death, dishonorable discharge, or imprisonment in excess of one year, or (2) the conviction has been the subject of a pardon, annulment, or other equivalent procedure based on a finding of innocence.

(d) Juvenile adjudications. Evidence of juvenile adjudications is generally not admissible under this rule. The military judge, however, may allow evidence of a juvenile adjudication of a witness other than the accused if conviction of the offense would be admissible to attack the credibility of an adult and the military judge is satisfied that admission in evidence is necessary for a fair determination of the issue of guilt or innocence.

(e) Pendency of appeal. The pendency of an appeal therefrom does not render evidence of a conviction inadmissible except that a conviction by summary court-martial or special court-martial without a military judge may not be used for purposes of impeachment until review has been completed pursuant to Article 65(c) or Article 66 if applicable. Evidence of the pendency of an appeal is admissible.

(f) Definition. For purposes of this rule, there is a "conviction" in a court-martial case when a sentence has been adjudged.

EDITORIAL COMMENT

At common law and under previous *Manual* provisions, any witness, including an accused, could have his credibility challenged with evidence regarding previous convictions. The rationale for admitting this evidence was that convictions are relevant to credibility as they demonstrate that the witness has violated the law, and witnesses who have violated the law are more likely to lie than witnesses who have not.

Although the rationale applied to a testifying accused as much as to other witnesses, it was obvious that a danger existed that court-members might convict an impeached accused because they perceived him as a bad person, and not pay sufficient attention to whether the charged offense was proved beyond a reasonable doubt. The possibility of prejudice is the same as when other criminal acts are offered under Rule 404(b).

When the Federal Rules were being debated, Congress indicated concern for the accused and looked for a rule which would fairly assist fact-finders in assessing a witness' credibility, but one that would protect the accused from unfair prejudice. What emerged is now Military Rule 609.

Prior military authority bears little resemblance to the new Rule, which has adopted all the nuances of the federal provision and has added some wrinkles of its own.

Subdivision (a) of the new Rule provides that certain, but not all convictions, can be used to attack a witness's credibility. Those convictions that qualify for use can be proved in two ways: (1) counsel may ask a witness if the witness has ever been convicted of a crime; or (2) counsel may introduce a public record demonstrating the conviction.

The Rule identifies two distinct categories of qualifying convictions. Subdivision (a)(1) makes convictions for offenses punishable by death, dishonorable discharge, or imprisonment in excess of one year under the law of the prosecuting jurisdiction eligible for admission. With respect to previous military convictions, the Rule specifically provides that the maximum punishment is to be determined by reference to ¶ 127 of the *Manual*. As a result the level of court-martial trying the accused is not relevant; only the maximum possible punishment for the charged offense will affect admissibility. It also changes former *Manual* ¶ 153b(2)(b)(3), which had permitted certain non-federal convictions to be used if they were considered to be of comparable gravity to a federal felony; now the law of the convicting jurisdiction and the punishment provided there are looked to exclusively.

The second portion of (a)(1) provides a further limitation upon the government's ability to introduce evidence of previous convictions. It provides that before a conviction is to be used against "the accused," the trial judge first must determine that the probative value of the conviction outweighs its prejudicial effect to the accused. Unlike Rule 403, this Rule indicates that the judge must determine that the evidence actually is more helpful than harmful to a defendant before it is received. There is no presumption of admissibility where the accused might be harmed.

The following criteria are among those which can be considered in evaluating the Rule's balancing requirements. (1) Did the prior offense display a conscious disregard for the requirements of the law? (2) Was the prior crime so similar to the charged offense that it may tend to be misused as evidence of the accused's general bad character? (3) Is there other better impeachment evidence? (4) Is it unfair to permit the accused to be unimpeached if other witnesses are impeached? (5) Will the case turn in large measure on the credibility of the accused? (6) How old is the prior conviction? And (7) what has the witness' conduct been following the conviction? These are not easy factors to apply and judges will differ on how much weight to give each.

Many federal appellate courts have pointed out the wisdom of trial judges who state their reasons for Rule 609(a)(1) rulings. *See, e.g., United States v. Seamster,* 568 F.2d 188, 191 n.3 (10th Cir. 1978). The rationale for stating reasons is the same as that supporting a statement of reasons for Rule 403 determinations.

One problem in interpreting the Rule is to decide whether the drafters intended the (a)(1) balance to govern only the individual accused's convictions or the convictions of any witness called by the accused. Neither the Federal Rules nor the Military Rules provide much guidance here. The language of the Rule suggests that it protects the accused from any prejudice that *any* impeachment of a witness might engender. Although the chance of prejudice is lessened when the accused is not actually the witness who is attacked, attacks on family members, codefendants and close friends could rub off on the accused. Thus, we believe the accused gets the benefit of the (a)(1) balancing.

The balancing test does seem to provide an advantage to the defense without equivalent protection for the government. Actually, it is not clear that the Congress or the military drafters focused on the question whether the government should be protected against unfair impeachment of its witnesses. We believe that the prosecution may prevent unfair impeachment under (a)(1) by asking to have evidence excluded under Rules 403 and 611. The government will not receive as much protection under these Rules, but it needs less, since it is less likely that it will be prejudiced as easily as an accused might be. There is an argument that the "shall be admitted" language of (a) bars any protection for the government, but we do not think that this was the intent of the drafters. The balancing test used in the federal circuit courts, from which (a)(1) was drawn, protected the government, and there is no clear indication that such protection was to end under the new Rule.

Subdivision (a)(2) states the second category of convictions that may be admitted. In (a)(2) the balancing test is abandoned. In its place is a standard providing that all convictions involving "dishonesty or false statements" are admissible. This classification is meant to be more restrictive than (a)(1), allowing admission only if the previous offense, felony or misdemeanor involved crimen falsi; *i.e.,* the intent to lie or to make a false or misleading statement. As a result, prior military convictions for fraud against the government (Article 132); uttering worthless checks (Article 123(a)), and related offenses will be admissible even though their maximum punishments are below subdivision (a)(1)'s requirements. The drafters felt this result was necessary because crimen falsi convictions most clearly demonstrate a witness's credibility. Without (a)(1)'s balancing all crimen falsi convictions may be admissible against either party, absent constitutional problems of military due process and fundamental fairness or timeliness problems under Rule 609(b). Most courts perceive such evidence as being automatically admissible. *See, e.g., United States v. Dixon,* 547 F.2d 1079 (9th Cir. 1976).

If a conviction qualifies under (a)(2) as well as under (a)(1), then the limitation of the latter should be ignored. A substantial gray area exists with respect to offenses which are not crimen falsi per se, but which may actually have involved dishonesty or a false statement. Counsel relying on a conviction not plainly within (a)(2) should be permitted to demonstrate the conviction's crimen falsi characteristics by proving that the offense was committed through false statements or dishonesty. *See United States v. Hayes,* 553 F.2d 824, 827 (2d Cir.), cert. denied, 434 U.S. 867 (1977), in which the court discussed how a conviction for importing cocaine could come within (a)(2)'s definition, if the government established it was based upon false written or oral statements made to customs officials. However, if the crime was founded on nothing more than secrecy or stealth, then it would have to qualify under Rule 609(a)(1). In either event, the proponent must affirmatively establish the offense's crimen falsi properties if he is to be successful. *Accord, United States v. Smith,* 551 F.2d 348 (D.C. Cir. 1976).

Subdivision (a)(2) covers all witnesses, including an accused, and gives no more protection to an accused than it gives to the government.

Federal courts have differed on the question of how much detail about a conviction should be allowed. Some allow the punishment to be revealed. Others do not. *See, e.g., United States v. Tumblin,* 551 F.2d 1001 (5th Cir. 1977). Generally, there is agreement that it is wrong— *i.e.,* too prejudicial —

to inquire into the details of the prior offense, except to show that it is an (a)(2) offense. *See, e.g., United States v. Tumblin, supra.*

Under Rule 609(b) evidence of a conviction generally will not be admissible if it is more than ten years old. This timeliness requirement is not found in the common law, nor in previous *Manual* provisions. *See United States v. Weaver,* 1 M.J. 111 (C.M.A. 1975). The drafters have provided that the time be measured from the date of conviction or the date the witness was released from confinement, whichever is later in time. Consequently, if the witness was convicted of robbery in 1974 and confined for two years thereafter, he could be impeached with the conviction until 1986.

Rule 609(b)'s legislative history indicates that the drafters created a strong presumption against the use of stale convictions, but permitted it to be rebutted by a showing that (1) the interests of justice require admission of an old conviction; (2) its probative value, supported by *specific facts and circumstances,* substantially outweighs its prejudicial effect; and (3) the proponent of such evidence has provided the adverse party with "sufficient advance written notice" of an intent to use the evidence.

In *United States v. Cavender,* 578 F.2d 528 (4th Cir. 1978), the court examined the Rule's balancing requirements and determined that Congress intended that the trial judge make special findings of fact as part of any Rule 609(b) resolution. *Accord, United States v. Mahler,* 579 F.2d 730 (2d Cir. 1978). This is a sound reading of the Rule.

Rule 609(b) does not define the prior notice that is required. In the absence of a binding judicial definition we suggest that the following criteria be used: (1) Opposing counsel should be given written notice, or an oral representation should be made on the record of the proponent's intentions to use such evidence; (2) where possible, the notice should be served at least 24 hours before the date of trial to permit in limine motions and rulings; (3) the notice should include a copy of any official, public, or other documentary evidence which will be used to establish the conviction; or (4) if such documentary evidence is not available, opposing counsel should be provided with a statement specifying where the witness was convicted, upon what charges, and based on what plea. The statement should also specify what appellate review has taken place. The proponent should be asked on the record why the interests of justice require the admission of the evidence. The opponent should be given a chance to be heard. And the trial judge should state his ruling and the reasons therefor on the record.

Such a detailed requirement will limit frivolous issues, while providing opposing counsel with sufficient information upon which to prepare a challenge. However, as mentioned in our discussion of Rule 412's notice requirements, failure to comply should not result in prohibiting counsel's use of his evidence. Instead the proceedings should be delayed until adequate notice and preparation can be accomplished.

Rule 609(c) contains two specific limitations upon counsel's ability to use evidence of previous convictions. Subdivision (c)(1) states that if an otherwise admissible conviction has been the subject of a pardon, annulment, certificate of rehabilitation, or similar process which is predicated upon a finding that the witness has rehabilitated himself, then evidence of that conviction will not be admissible. If a witness has demonstrated conduct inconsistent with his criminal past, the drafters concluded that past should not be used to impeach him. However, if after his rehabilitation the witness is convicted of a crime punishable by death, dishonorable discharge, or confinement for more than a year, then evidence of the previous conviction will be admissible. Of course the timeliness limitations of Rule 609(b) apply here.

Subdivision (c)(2) states that if a conviction has been the subject of a pardon, annulment or related proceeding based on a finding of not guilty, then evidence of the conviction is not admissible. This second aspect of the Rule is more absolute than the first. If the witness is subsequently convicted of another offense of any description, proof of the original conviction still will be excluded, since the accused is deemed innocent and the conviction cannot, therefore, properly support an impeachment attempt.

Future military litigation will certainly consider whether completion of the Army's course of instruction at the Retraining Brigade, or at the Air Force's 3320th Correction and Rehabilitation Squadron will qualify under the new Rule's definition of rehabilitation. *See generally* Schinasi and Green, *Impeachment by Prior Conviction Military Rule of Evidence 609,* THE ARMY LAWYER, January 1981 at 1. Both military facilities have been created to rehabilitate first offenders and to return them to duty. The philosophy of the Department of Defense in operating its correctional facilities is to rehabilitate those servicemembers coming within its jurisdiction. Based on these criteria, we believe 609(c) should be applicable. The drafters' *Analysis* is in accord with our view.

Rule 609(d) provides that evidence of juvenile adjudications generally is not admissible, and in no event may it be used against an accused. The Rule permits impeachment of witnesses other than the accused if the trial judge believes it is necessary to a fair resolution of the case, and the impeachment evidence would have been admissible had the witness previously been tried as an adult.

The drafters of subdivision (d) were sensitive to the public policy requirements that juveniles should not be stigmatized by their youthful misconduct. But the drafters also were concerned with problems of confrontation and compulsory process. The balance struck in 609(d) is consistent with the Supreme Court's Sixth Amendment decisions. *Cf. Davis v. Alaska,* 415 U.S. 308 (1974), for example, in which the court recognized that society's desire to protect juveniles could not be used to frustrate an accused's constitutional right to a fair trial (although *Davis* involved bias, not prior conviction type impeachment). *Cf. Burr v. Sullivan,* 618 F.2d 583 (9th Cir. 1980) (where the court found that the accused's state conviction had to be reversed because the trial judge improperly prevented defense counsel from using evidence of juvenile adjudications against government witnesses who were also co-conspirators); *United States v. Bates,* 617 F.2d 585 (10th Cir. 1980) (the accused's conviction for being an accessory to murder was reversed because defense counsel seeking impeachment evidence was denied a transcript of a previous juvenile proceeding involving a participant in the murder who was a key government witness).

Taken together, subdivisions (e) and (f) specify when the court-martial proceeding itself becomes a conviction for purposes of admissibility. Prior military authority permitted admission of convictions only after the appellate process was completed. The New Military Rule partially changes past practice, and partially adopts the current Federal Rule.

Rule 609(f) states that a conviction occurs when the court-martial adjudges a sentence. Subdivision (e) states that if the case was tried by a general court-martial, or a special court-martial empowered to adjudge a bad conduct discharge, then evidence of the conviction is admissible at any time after the sentence is adjudged. However, with respect to summary courts-martial and non-bad conduct discharge special courts-martial, the conviction is not admissible until it has been reviewed by a judge advocate or similarly legally-trained officer (see Article 65 (c)), and has undergone further appellate review where appropriate (*see* Article 66). Evidence that an appeal is pending will be admissible with respect to a general or punitive discharge special court-martial. Such evidence may weaken the force of the impeachment but does not affect the admissibility of the conviction itself.

These changes in military practice pose interesting practical problems. For instance, how will the accused's conviction be viewed if during a trial he was impeached with evidence of a prior conviction, which was subsequently reversed? What if a key defense witness was impeached with a conviction that is subsequently reversed? The first case, where the accused is the impeached witness, poses the greater chance of prejudice. But both situations raise the issue of whether a conviction should stand when a key witness is impeached on the basis of a conviction that is held to be invalid. A reviewing court would have to consider the following things: the importance of the impeached witness' credibility; the emphasis placed on the overturned conviction; the other impeachment evidence used against the witness; the likely impact of the evidence that the overturned conviction was on appeal; the nature of the conviction and its likely impeachment effect; and the possibility that the prior case will be retried and the conviction reinstated.

DRAFTERS' ANALYSIS

(a) General Rules. Rule 609(a) is taken generally from the Federal Rule but has been slightly modified to adapt it to military law. For example, an offense for which a dishonorable discharge may be adjudged may be used for impeachment. This continues the present rule as found in ¶ 153*b*(2)(b)(1) of the present *Manual*. In determining whether a military offense may be used for purposes of impeachment under Rule 609(a)(1), recourse must be made to the maximum punishment imposable if the offense had been tried by general court-martial. The Table of Maximum Punishments, ¶ 127*c*, and related sentencing provisions should be consulted.

Rule 609(a) differs slightly from the present military rule. Under Rule 609(a)(1), a civilian conviction's availability for impeachment is solely a function of its maximum punishment under "the law in which the witness was convicted." This is different from ¶ 153*b*(2)(b)(3) of the present *Manual* which allows use of a non-federal conviction analogous to a federal felony or characterized by the jurisdiction as a felony or "as an offense of comparable gravity." Under the new rule, comparisons and determinations of relative gravity will be unnecessary and improper.

Convictions that "involve moral turpitude or otherwise affect ... credibility are admissible for impeachment under ¶ 153*b*(2)(b) of the present *Manual*. The list of potential convictions expressed in ¶ 153*b*(2)(b) is illustrative only and non-exhaustive. Unlike the *Manual* rule, Rule 609(a) is exhaustive.

Although a conviction technically fits within Rule 609(a)(1), its admissibility remains subject to a finding by the military judge that its probative value outweighs its prejudicial effect to the accused.

Rule 609(a)(2) makes admissible convictions involving "dishonesty or false statement, regardless of punishment." This is similar in intent to ¶ 153*b*(2)(b)(4) of the present *Manual* which makes admissible "a conviction of any offense involving fraud, deceit, larceny, wrongful appropriation, or the making of false statement." The exact meaning of "dishonesty" within the meaning of Rule 609 is unclear and has already been the subject of substantial litigation. The Congressional intent appears, however, to have been extremely restrictive with "dishonesty" being used in the sense of untruthfulness. *See generally* S. SALTZBURG & K. REDDEN, FEDERAL RULES OF EVIDENCE MANUAL 336-345 (2d ed. 1977). Thus, a conviction for fraud, perjury, or embezzlement would come within the definition, but a conviction for simple larceny would not. Pending further case development in the Article III courts, caution would suggest close adherence to this highly limited definition.

It should be noted that admissibility of evidence within the scope of Rule 609(a)(2) is not explicitly subject to the discretion of the military judge. The application of Rule 403 is unclear.

While the language of Rule 609(a) refers only to cross-examination, it would appear that the Rule does refer to direct examination as well. *See* the *Analysis* to Rules 607 and 608(b).

As defined in Rule 609(f), a court-martial conviction occurs when a sentence has been adjudged.

(b) Time limit. Rule 609(b) is taken verbatim from the Federal Rule. As it has already been made applicable to the armed forces, *United States v. Weaver,* 1 M.J. 111 (C.M.A. 1975), it is consistent with the present military practice.

(c) Effect of pardon, annulment, or certificate of rehabilitation. Rule 609(c) is taken verbatim from the Federal Rule except that convictions punishable by dishonorable discharge have been added. Rule 609(c) has no equivalent in present military practice and represents a substantial change as it will prohibit use of convictions due to evidence of rehabilitation. In the absence of a certificate of rehabilitation, the extent to which the various Armed Forces post-conviction programs, such as the Air Force's 3320th Correction and Rehabilitation Squadron and the Army's Retraining Brigade, come within Rule 609(c) is unclear, although it is probable that successful completion of such a program is "an equivalent procedure based on the finding of the rehabilitation of the person convicted" within the meaning of the Rule.

(d) Juvenile adjudications. Rule 609(d) is taken from the Federal Rule without significant change. The general prohibition in the Rule is substantially different from ¶ 153*b*(2)(b) of the present *Manual* which allows use of juvenile adjudications other than those involving an accused. The discretionary authority vested in the military judge to admit such evidence comports with the accused's constitutional right to a fair trial, *Davis v. Alaska,* 415 U.S. 308 (1974).

(e) Pendency of appeal. The first portion of Rule 609(e) is taken from the Federal Rule and is substantially different from ¶ 153*b*(2)(b) of the present *Manual* which prohibits use of convictions for impeachment purposes while they are undergoing

appellate review. Under the Rule, the fact of review may be shown but does not affect admissibility. A different rule applies, however, for convictions by summary court-martial or by special court-martial without a military judge. The Committee believed that because a legally trained presiding officer is not required in these proceedings, a conviction should not be used for impeachment until legal review has been completed.

(f) Definition. This definition of conviction has been added because of the unique nature of the court-martial. Because of its recognition that a conviction cannot result until at least sentencing, *cf.* Lederer, *Reappraising the Legality of Post-trial Interviews,* THE ARMY LAWYER, July, 1977, at 12, the Rule may modify *United States v. Mathews,* 6 M.J. 357 (C.M.A. 1979).

Rule 610. Religious Beliefs or Opinions

Evidence of the beliefs or opinions of a witness on matters of religion is not admissible for the purpose of showing that by reason of their nature the credibility of the witness is impaired or enhanced.

EDITORIAL COMMENT

Rule 610 prohibits any party from impeaching or rehabilitating a witness's character with evidence of religious opinions or beliefs. No previous *Manual* provision addressed this topic. The Rule recognizes that to permit the questioning of a witness about religious views is to intrude upon a private area that receives First Amendment protection; that religious opinions or beliefs are not very probative; and that such evidence is emotional in nature, and may lead the court-members into distorting, ignoring or blindly accepting a witness' testimony because of antipathy or sympathy for his religious views.

The Rule bars only an inquiry into beliefs and opinions for the purpose of attacking or supporting credibility. It does not prohibit all mention of religion or religious matters. It may be permissible to inquire into the religious activities of a witness if the inquiry would produce relevant evidence. For example, a witness may have observed a criminal act from his seat in church. Rule 610 does not prevent counsel from establishing how and why his witness happened to be in a position to view the crime. Although this could be established, the philosophy of the Rule suggests that neither side should be permitted to argue either that the witness should be believed because of the church attendance or that the witness should be disbelieved because of membership in a particular church. Church affiliation also may be the subject of inquiry under some circumstances. For example, if a church official is charged with an offense, or is the victim of an offense, a witness's membership in the church might be used to show bias toward the accused or even toward the victim.

Nothing in the Rule covers the evidentiary use of political affiliations, which would raise many of the same concerns that gave rise to Rule 610. This shortcoming is important in today's military society where political, social and religious beliefs often become intertwined. There is good reason for a court to analogize to Rule 610 in making rulings regarding questions addressed to a witness about political or social beliefs and opinions. The bench should be careful to insure that its determinations do not violate the accused's ability to present his defense, but it also should be concerned with protecting the private thoughts and opinions of witnesses.

DRAFTERS' ANALYSIS

Rule 610 is taken without significant change from the Federal Rules and has no present equivalent in the *Manual for Courts-Martial.* The Rule makes religious beliefs or opinions inadmissible for the purpose of impeaching or bolstering credibility. To the extent that such opinions may be critical to the defense of a case, however, there may be a constitutional justification for overcoming the Rule's exclusion. *Cf. Davis v. Alaska,* 415 U.S. 308 (1974).

Rule 611. Mode and Order of Interrogation and Presentation

(a) Control by the military judge. The military judge shall exercise reasonable control over the mode and order of interrogating witnesses and presenting evidence so as to (1) make the interrogation and presentation effective for the ascertainment of the truth, (2) avoid needless consumption of time, and (3) protect witnesses from harassment or undue embarrassment.

(b) Scope of cross-examination. Cross-examination should be limited to the subject matter of the direct examination and matters affecting the credibility of the witness. The military judge may, in the exercise of discretion, permit inquiry into additional matters as if on direct examination.

(c) Leading questions. Leading questions should not be used on the direct examination of a witness except as may be necessary to develop the testimony of the witness. Ordinarily leading questions should be permitted on cross-examination. When a party calls a hostile witness or a witness identified with an adverse party, interrogation may be by leading questions.

EDITORIAL COMMENT

Since the Uniform Code of Military Justice was amended in 1968, military judges have been given broad discretion in controlling the court-martial process. *See* ¶ 149*a* and ¶ 137 of the former *Manual.* Rule 611(a) restates and codifies these powers and provides the judge with tremendous flexibility in running a trial.

Subdivision (a) states that the bench shall exercise reasonable control over the interrogation of witnesses and the presentation of evidence. The Rule requires that the bench involve itself in three important areas of litigation.

First, the military judge is to insure that evidence is presented so as to maximize its contribution to the search for truth. This restatement of common law principles allows the bench to control the use of real or demonstrative evidence, to determine whether counsel may ask for narrative testimony or must ask specific questions, and to control the order in which witnesses testify and even the internal ordering of a particular witness' testimony. *See .United States v. Jackson,* 549 F.2d 517 (8th Cir.), cert. denied, 438 U.S. 985 (1977). It may be used to control the extent of rebuttal evidence admitted. *See Smith v. Conley,* 584 F.2d 844 (8th Cir. 1978). The drafters have recognized that the trial judge's experience and common sense can assist in promoting a fair trial for both parties. *See United States v. Graves,* 1 M.J. 50 (C.M.A. 1975), where the Court of Military Appeals said that the trial judge is required to assure that the accused receives a fair trial.

Second, the judge shall endeavor to avoid the needless consumption of trial time. Control here is similar to that exercised under Rule 403, which allows the judge to exclude evidence to avoid "undue delay." Examinations into tangential or side issues can be limited under Rule 611 in order to focus attention on the real issues in a case. *See also* Rules 401 and 402 dealing with relevancy. Cumulative or redundant evidence can and should be controlled under Rule 611.

Third, the trial judge must protect witnesses from harassment or undue embarrassment. This requires the judge to draw a fine distinction between piercing, but effective examination, which is permissible, and interrogation aimed at belittling a witness and subjecting him to needless public ridicule, which is not. Impeachment and fair, even slashing examination is permitted, but attempts to confuse a witness, to bring out facts that do not amount to permissible impeachment, and to intimidate a witness are not.

The scope of permissible cross-examination is prescribed in Rule 611(b). It provides that cross-examination generally is permitted regarding the subject matter of direct examination and any matter affecting a witness' credibility or believability. *United States v. Wolfson,* 573 F.2d 216 (5th Cir. 1978), concludes that the scope of direct examination means the "subject matter" of the examination. The Rule also affords the judge discretion to allow additional cross-examination, but itself provides no guidelines for exercising this discretion.

Traditional military practice also limited a party's cross-examination to the subject matter of direct testimony plus examination directed at impeachment. The new Rule merely recodifies these standards and follows the Federal Rule. It is interesting to note that when the Federal Rule was drafted, the Advisory Committee was in favor of, and the Supreme Court actually adopted, a broader rule allowing more latitude in cross-examination. Ultimately, Congress rejected the "wide-open" approach, and the Military Rule also rejects it. As a result, if a party intends to exceed the bounds of direct examination, that inquiry usually should occur during the party's own case, and not as part of the opponent's. But the discretion afforded the judge permits more liberal cross-examination when it will assist in understanding evidence or is necessary to avoid burdening witnesses with several court appearances. If the cross-examiner exceeds the scope of direct examination, the new material must be elicited "as if on direct examination." This means no leading questions under subdivision (c) of the Rule, unless special circumstances would permit leading questions had the witness actually been called to testify by the cross-examiner.

Rule 611(b) does not address when and to what extent an accused may be cross-examined. The issue should be controlled largely by constitutional, not evidentiary, principles. The military drafters copied the Federal Rule which is silent on these questions. However, the military drafters did attempt to answer them in Rule 301, a provision with no federal counterpart. Although we will not repeat our discussion of Rule 301 here, it is important to note that Rule 301(e) states that when an accused voluntarily testifies, he waives his Fifth Amendment privilege only with respect to those matters contained in his direct examination. Government counsel may not expand the testimony into related or foundation areas. Rule 301(e) also provides that when the accused is tried for more than one offense, he may testify about only one of those charges, and thus not waive his protection against self incrimination with respect to the others. *See also* Rule 608(b).

Read together, Rules 611(b), 301 and 608(b) appear to take a restrictive approach toward cross-examination of an accused. This authority allows the accused to testify about only one of several specifications, limit cross-examination to only those matters covered on direct, to take the stand concerning any issue not dealing directly with guilt or innocence and to retain the privilege against self-incrimination. The Rules appear to be intended to encourage the accused to testify without impairing the government's ability to ask questions about the part of the case that the accused opens up. *See ¶ 72b* of the *Manual.*

Rule 611(c) covers leading questions. It largely restates the common law and previous *Manual* provisions which established that leading questions may be used on cross-examination, but generally cannot be used on direct examination. These are generalizations only. Sometimes leading questions are allowed on direct, but barred on cross-examination. The Rule itself recognizes this when it provides that the direct examiner may lead in order to develop a witness's testimony and to deal with hostile or adverse witnesses (discussed below). Leading questions on direct usually are allowed to identify a witness and his relationship to the military or offense in question. Witnesses also may be led through foundational matters to avoid wasting the court's time. Leading questions also may be allowed on direct examination when a party is examining a witness who requires special attention. Included in this category are children, timid or frightened adults, and witnesses who suffer memory lapses, or possess physical, emotional, or communicative disabilities. *See, e.g., United States v. Littlewind,* 551 F.2d 244 (8th Cir. 1977). *But see State v. Orona,* 92 N. Mex. 450, 589 P.2d 1041 (1979), for an example of abuses of leading questions condemned by the appellate court.

The second sentence of Rule 611(c) indicates that on cross-examination leading questions "ordinarily" will be permitted. They may not be allowed when one party questions a witness who is friendly to it and is considered adverse to the direct examiner.

The third sentence of 611(c) allows leading questions to be asked on direct examination when a party calls a hostile witness, or a witness identified with an adverse party. The drafters leave the term "hostile witness" undefined. Under previous *Manual* practice, counsel had to demonstrate a witness's hostility before he could ask leading questions. This meant something more than showing the witness was unfavorable. Counsel had to establish that the witness would not adequately respond to his questions and had been unwilling to cooperate during pretrial discussions. This situation is particularly likely to occur in the military where defense counsel will often have to call witnesses aligned with the command in order to establish its defense. Such witnesses may be unwilling to assist defense counsel. As a result normal direct examination will prove troublesome, and may in fact produce harmful testimony due to counsel's inability to effectively limit the witness' responses. Even if a witness cannot be shown to be "actually" hostile, it may be that most officers and senior enlisted men will be "identified" with the government. The "identified with" language of the Rule should make it less necessary in many cases to make a finding about actual hostility.

If the government calls a witness who actually is hostile to the accused or is identified with the government, it would seem, as noted above, that there is good reason to allow leading questions by a cross-examiner who is permitted to go beyond the scope of the direct examination. After all, if the witness were recalled by the cross-examiner, subdivision (c) would permit leading questions, and the reason for permitting broad cross-examination may be to avoid any recall for the convenience of the witness or the court-martial. This reason does not suggest that cross-examination beyond the scope of direct should be more restricted than direct examination upon recall would have been.

DRAFTERS' ANALYSIS

(a) *Control by the military judge.* Rule 611(a) is taken from the Federal Rule without change. It is a basic source of the military judge's power to control proceedings and replaces *Manual* ¶ 149a and that part of ¶ 137 dealing with cumulative evidence. It is within the military judge's discretion to control methods of interrogation of witnesses. The Rule does not change present law. Although a witness may be required to limit an answer to the question asked, it will normally be improper to require that a "yes" or "no" answer be given unless it is clear that such an answer will be a complete response to the question. A witness will ordinarily be entitled to explain his or her testimony at some time before completing that testimony. The *Manual* requirement that questions be asked through the military judge is now found in Rule 614.

Although the military judge has the discretion to alter the sequence of proof to the extent that the burden of proof is not affected, the usual sequence for examination of witnesses is: prosecution witnesses, defense witnesses, prosecution rebuttal witnesses, defense rebuttal witnesses, and witnesses for the court. The usual order of examination of a witness is: direct examination, cross-examination, redirect examination, recross-examination, and examination by the court, ¶ 54a.

(b) *Scope of cross-examination.* Rule 611(b) is taken from the Federal Rule without change and replaces ¶ 149b(1) of the present *Manual* which is similar in scope. Under the Rule the military judge may allow a party to adopt a witness and proceed as if on direct examination. *See* Rule 301(b)(2) (judicial advice as to the privilege against self-incrimination for an apparently uninformed witness); Rule 301(f)(2) (effect of claiming the privilege against self-incrimination on cross-examination); Rule 303 (Degrading Questions); and Rule 608(b) (Evidence of Character, Conduct, and Bias of Witness).

(c) *Leading questions.* Rule 611(c) is taken from the Federal Rule without significant change and is similar to ¶ 149c of the present *Manual*. The reference in the third sentence of the Federal Rule to an "adverse party" has been deleted as being applicable to civil cases only.

A leading question is one which suggests the answer it is desired that the witness give. Generally, a question that is susceptible to being answered by "yes" or "no" is a leading question.

The use of leading questions is discretionary with the military judge. Use of leading questions may be appropriate with respect to the following witnesses among others, children, persons with mental or physical disabilities, the extremely elderly, hostile witnesses, and witnesses identified with the adverse party.

It is also appropriate with the military judge's consent to utilize leading questions to direct a witness's attention to a relevant area of inquiry.

Rule 612. Writing Used to Refresh Memory

If a witness uses a writing to refresh his or her memory for the purpose of testifying, either

(1) while testifying, or

(2) before testifying, if the military judge determines it is necessary in the interests of justice,

an adverse party is entitled to have the writing produced at the hearing, to inspect it, to cross-examine the witness thereon, and to introduce in evidence those portions which relate to the testimony of the witness. If it is claimed that the writing contains privileged information or matters not related to the subject matter of the testimony, the military judge shall examine the writing in camera, excise any privileged information or any portions not so related, and order delivery of the remainder to the party entitled thereto. Any portion withheld over objections shall be attached to the record of trial as an appellate exhibit. If a writing is not produced or delivered pursuant to order under this rule, the military judge shall make any order justice requires, except that when the prosecution elects not to comply, the order shall be one striking the testimony or, if in discretion of the military judge it is determined that the interests of justice so require, declaring a mistrial. This rule does not preclude disclosure of information required to be disclosed under other provisions of these rules or this Manual.

EDITORIAL COMMENT

Rule 612 provides that a writing may be used to refresh a witness's memory while the witness is on the stand, or before the witness testifies. If the writing is used at trial, it must be made available to the opposing party, who can employ it in an effort to show that the witness is not really remembering but is being coached, which may effectively impeach the witness. Focusing on those portions of the document that relate to the witness's testimony may effectively impeach the witness. If memory was refreshed before trial, disclosure of the material used to refresh it may, but need not, be required by the trial judge in the interests of justice.

Although the Rule is limited to refreshing memory, there is a decided trend in civilian courts to treat any use of documents to "prepare" a witness as falling under the Rule. *See, e.g., Berkey Photo, Inc. v. Eastman Kodak Co.,* 74 F.R.D. 613 (S.D.N.Y. 1977), rev'd on other grounds, 603 F.2d 263 (2d Cir. 1979), cert. denied, 100 S. Ct. 1061 (1980).

A party's ability to obtain evidence is not absolute even under Rule 612(1). Statements used to refresh recollection may be protected from disclosure if they contain privileged information or matters not related to the content of the witness' testimony. If privilege or relevance claims are made, the trial judge shall order the document produced and examine it in camera. The bench must excise any privileged information or other matter not reasonably related to the witness's testimony. Once this redaction has occurred, the military judge should then order the remainder of the document turned over to opposing counsel. The Rule provides that if any material has been withheld by the bench, it must be appended to the record of trial so that appellate review will be facilitated. Although the Rule and its drafters' *Analysis* are silent on this matter, it is interesting to note that military authority requires a copy of the record of trial to be served on defense counsel and the accused. If the record contains privileged information, the original motivation for keeping it from the accused may be frustrated. We recommend that when the record is served the withheld material should be separately forwarded to the appellate agencies for review and consideration. *Compare* Rules 505 and 506.

If a privilege is waived by disclosure to a witness, then the waiver would allow the previously privileged material to be disclosed.

If the trial court's order to disclose evidence is not respected, then the bench may order corrective action. Any order that justice requires may be entered against the accused, but if the government withholds evidence, the court must strike the direct testimony, or in the judge's discretion, declare a mistrial when justice requires one. It should be noted that nothing in Rule 612 is intended to preempt the military's already broad discovery rules. *See* ¶ 44*h* of the *Manual,* which requires the prosecution to permit defense counsel to examine any document accompanying the charges "including the report of investigation and papers sent with the charges on a rehearing."

In large part the military version of Rule 612 mirrors its federal counterpart. However, the federal language dealing with the Jencks Act, 18 U.S.C. § 3500, was viewed as being more restrictive than the new provision, and as a result was omitted.

Rule 612 does alter some past military practices while leaving others unchanged. Paragraph 146*a* of the previous *Manual* permitted a witness's recollection to be refreshed with any form of documentary evidence as long as opposing counsel was given the opportunity to examine it and to introduce it if he felt it was inconsistent with the proponent's case or it would assist him in some other fashion. Experience under the federal version of Rule 612 indicates that virtually any document may be used to refresh a witness's recollection. This includes statements previously made by the witness or by someone other than the witness; originals, duplicates and copies of documents; even statements that may seem inconsistent or contrary to the witness's testimony. Past practice also demonstrates that counsel need do very little to take advantage of Rule 612. It is generally sufficient if the witness states that his present recollection of the events is now depleted, but if he were permitted to refer to a known document, his memory might be refreshed. *See United States v. Jiminez,* 613 F.2d 1373 (5th Cir. 1980). No further demonstration is necessary.

The second aspect of Rule 612 is new to military practice. It allows opposing counsel to determine whether a witness has used any document or writing in preparation for trial. If this has occurred, counsel may request that the document be produced during cross-examination. The court has discretion to allow this. Certainly, careful counsel will ask witnesses for the other side whether they have consulted documents in preparation for trial.

Neither the drafters' *Analysis* nor the Rule itself suggests any time restraints on the implementation of 612(2). It is uncertain whether a witness' reference to a document six weeks before trial would be as likely to result in an order to turn over the document as when memory is refreshed on the morning of trial. Would a gap of six months between refreshing and trial make a difference? No definitive answer is possible.

It does appear, however, that the witness must have used the document for the specific purpose of preparing for trial. Although the time lag between use and testimony need not be outcome-determinative in every case, it may be that fears concerning the "planting" of ideas with a witness increase the more a witness is focusing on the testimony to be given at trial. This is more likely to be the case when memory is refreshed immediately before or during the recess of a trial.

Difficulties in applying the Rule will arise when an otherwise proper request for a document conflicts with the attorney-client privilege or with the work product doctrine. For example, in preparing his client for trial, an attorney may have collected and organized certain information to facilitate a witness' testimony. This might include the accused's personal statement. Under Rule 1101 which makes privileges applicable throughout the proceedings, and under Rule 502, we believe an accused may refer to his own statement to refresh memory without waiving any privilege. We believe that there is less reason to be protective of work product and that if a witness uses work product to prepare testimony, it should be subject to disclosure under the Rule. *See United States v. Nobles,* 422 U.S. 225 (1975).

DRAFTERS' ANALYSIS

Rule 612 is taken generally from the Federal Rule but a number of modifications have been made to adapt the Rule to military practice. Language in the Federal Rule relating to the Jencks Act, 18 U.S.C. § 3500, which would have shielded material from disclosure to the defense under Rule 612 was discarded. Such shielding was considered to be inappropriate in view of the general military practice and policy which utilizes and encourages broad discovery on behalf of the defense.

The decision of the president of a special court-martial without a military judge under this Rule is an interlocutory ruling not subject to objection by the members, ¶ 57a.

Rule 612 codifies the doctrine of past recollection refreshed and replaces that portion of ¶ 146a of the present *Manual* which now deals with the issue. Although the present *Manual* rule is similar, in that it authorizes inspection by the opposing party of a memorandum used to refresh recollection and permits it to be offered into evidence by that party to show the improbability of it refreshing recollection, the Rule is somewhat more extensive as it also deals with writings used before testifying.

Rule 612 does not affect in any way information required to be disclosed under any other rule or portion of the *Manual. See, e.g.,* Rule 304(c)(1).

Rule 613. Prior Statements of Witnesses

(a) Examining witness concerning prior statement. In examining a witness concerning a prior statement made by the witness, whether written or not, the statement need not be shown nor its contents disclosed to the witness at that time, but on request the same shall be shown or disclosed to opposing counsel.

(b) Extrinsic evidence of prior inconsistent statement of witness. Extrinsic evidence of a prior inconsistent statement by a witness is not admissible unless the witness is afforded an opportunity to explain or deny the same and the opposite party is afforded an opportunity to interrogate the witness thereon, or the interests of justice otherwise require. This provision does not apply to admissions of a party-opponent as defined in rule 801(d)(2).

EDITORIAL COMMENT

The military drafters have adopted Rule 613 from its federal counterpart without change. The Rule addresses the use of prior statements. Its practical effect is limited to the use of prior inconsistent statements, although the word "inconsistent" is not used in the Rule's title.

Apparently, subdivision (a) addresses the use of any prior statement of a witness, whether offered as substantive or impeachment evidence and whether the statement is inconsistent or consistent with the witness's testimony. The drafters' *Analysis* questions this, but we think that the drafters' *Analysis* misses the connection between Rules 613 and 801(d)(1). Rule 801(d)(1) lays down the rule that governs the *substantive* use of inconsistent statements, consistent statements and prior identifications. Subdivision (a) of Rule 613 can be used in conjunction with that Rule. Presumably, it will be. Subdivision (b) of Rule 613 would seem to govern the use of a prior statement used as substantive evidence under Rule 801(d)(1), but Rule 801(d)(1) itself requires that the witness be subject to cross-examination on the prior statement and therefore Rule 613(b) adds nothing of importance to it. Rule 613(b) becomes important, however, when prior inconsistent statements not covered by Rule 801(d)(1)(A) are offered as impeachment evidence.

This Rule changes military practice. Prior military practice in this area was governed by *Manual* ¶ 153b(2)(c) which followed the common law. It specified that if a witness was to be impeached with a prior inconsistent statement, first a foundation had to be established. To accomplish this, counsel had to direct the witness's attention to the time and place of the statement, and the person or persons to whom it was made and then ask the witness if he made the statement. This provision applied whether the prior statement was oral or written. Like the common law, the military's prior rule operated to protect the witness from unfair surprise by informing him of his past statement. Some supporters of the Rule believed that when the witness was faced with his alleged prior statement, he was more likely to be truthful about it.

But many critics believed that the Rule had the opposite effect and that the process of establishing a foundation prior to using inconsistent statements allowed the dishonest witness to reshape his testimony, anticipate questions, and thus frustrate counsel by preventing his cross-examination from being an effective truth-developing mechanism.

Although the literature indicates that federal judges often failed to honor the common law foundational requirements, their military counterparts scrupulously enforced them. The new Rule abandons them, and provides that when counsel is examining a witness based on an inconsistent oral or written pretrial statement, that statement need not be shown to the witness, nor must its contents be disclosed to the witness during cross-examination. However, if opposing counsel requests the statement, it must be shown or disclosed to him. While the Rule is unclear as to how disclosure should be made, it appears that counsel need do no more than provide the opposing party with the statement in the same form it was received. Thus, if counsel obtained a document displaying the previous inconsistent statement, the document should be shown. If the information was transmitted in oral form, counsel need only disclose the statement, and its accompanying transmittal details. In either event, disclosure is not required until the witness is actually examined about his prior statement. It is important to note that no information need be given to opposing counsel unless a specific request is made for it.

Even more important is the fact that the prior inconsistent statement need not be offered or mentioned during cross-examination, but may be withheld until other witnesses are called. This may be particularly useful if counsel is attempting to demonstrate collusion among witnesses. Thus the statement may be offered to impeach a witness after the witness has left the stand. The Rule provides that the witness must be afforded an opportunity to explain or deny an inconsistent statement, but does not require that the opportunity be afforded before the statement is offered. A subsequent opportunity is acceptable. *See, e.g., United States v. King,* 560 F.2d 122 (2d Cir. 1977), cert. denied, 434 U.S. 925 (1978).

On its face, Rule 613(b) allows the impeacher an almost absolute right to delay the witness's opportunity to talk about his prior inconsistent statement and to explain it. The statement may be in evidence for some time before the witness is recalled. This may unfairly detract from the witness's ability to put the statement in perspective. Also, any delay associated with keeping the witness on call for the moment when the opportunity to explain is afforded will needlessly keep the witness at the courthouse or nearby. This is particularly troubling in the military, where witnesses for both sides may have substantial command responsibilities. Of course, the trial court retains its discretion to control the presentation of evidence and witnesses under Rule 611(a), and thus may order that any use of prior inconsistent statements proceed as at common law unless the court is shown a bona fide reason for departing from the familiar foundation requirement.

Subdivision (b) does make it clear that extrinsic evidence may not be admitted unless the witness is offered the opportunity to "explain or deny" the statement. As noted above, this may come after the statement is revealed through a third party. The party relying on the witness is entitled to an opportunity to explain the circumstances under which the statement was made and the reasons why the statements may have differed from trial testimony. For example, when the previous statement was made, the witness may have been acting in response to threats, fear, or unlawful command control. Similarly, the statement may appear to be inconsistent only because it has been taken out of context. Counsel also may be able to explain inconsistencies by showing that the witness merely misunderstood questions, or misspoke when the prior statement was made.

The last sentence of Rule 613(b) provides that the opportunity to explain or deny any inconsistency may be abrogated when the "interests of justice otherwise require." Neither the Rule itself, nor the drafters' *Analysis* illustrates when this exception is likely to be invoked. In the military, it might be important when a party discovers that an inconsistent statement exists after a witness is excused and the witness is then outside the trial court's jurisdiction or has been discharged from the service and cannot be located.

Nowhere in the Rule is it indicated which party must afford the impeached witness the opportunity to explain or to deny an inconsistent statement. Is it the responsibility of the party attacking the witness to give the witness a chance to explain? Or is this left to the party who is relying on the witness? In our view, the attacking party should bear the burden, since he knows the attack is coming and that the witness might not be available to explain or deny the statement if it is held in reserve rather than used while the witness first testifies. If the attacker does not indicate that the witness may have to be recalled, then the chances increase that the witness will become unavailable at the time the impeachment takes place. Moreover, at common law the attacker had to lay a foundation. We view Rule 613 as authorizing a delayed "foundation" or opportunity for the impeached witness to be heard and not as shifting the burden of providing the foundation.

Finally, it should be noted that Rule 613 does not govern if Rule 801(d)(2) admissions are introduced. They may be offered and accepted as *substantive* evidence without a foundation having been laid first.

DRAFTERS' ANALYSIS

(a) Examining witness concerning prior statement. Rule 613(a) is taken from the Federal Rule without change. It alters military practice inasmuch as it eliminates the foundation requirements found in *Manual* ¶ 153b(2)(c) of the present *Manual.* While it will no longer be a condition precedent to admissibility to acquaint a witness with the prior statement and to give the witness an opportunity to either change his or her testimony or to reaffirm it, such a procedure may be appropriate as a matter of trial tactics.

It appears that the drafters of Federal Rule 613 may have inadvertently omitted the word "inconsistent" from both its caption and the text of Rule 613(a). The effect of that omission, if any, is unclear.

(b) Extrinsic evidence of prior inconsistent statement of witness. Rule 613(b) is taken from the Federal Rule without change. It requires that the witness be given an opportunity to explain or deny a prior inconsistent statement when the party proffers extrinsic evidence of the statement. Although this foundation is not required under Rule 613(a), it is required under Rule 613(b) if a party wishes to utilize more than the witness' own testimony as brought out on cross-examination. The Rule does not specify any particular timing for the opportunity for the witness to explain or deny the statement nor does it specify any particular method. The Rule is inapplicable to introduction of prior inconsistent statements on the merits under Rule 801.

Rule 614. Calling and Interrogation of Witnesses by the Court-Martial

(a) Calling by the court-martial. The military judge may, sua sponte or at the request of the members or the suggestion of a party, call witnesses, and all parties are entitled to cross-examine witnesses thus called. When the members wish to call or recall a witness, the military judge shall determine whether it is appropriate to do so under these rules or this Manual.

(b) Interrogation by the court-martial. The military judge or members may interrogate witnesses, whether called by the military judge, the members, or a party. Members shall submit their questions to the military judge in writing so that a ruling may be made on the propriety of the questions or the course of questioning and so that questions may be asked on behalf of the court by the military judge in a form acceptable to the military judge. When a witness who has not testified previously is called by the military judge or the members, the military judge may conduct the direct examination or may assign the responsibility to counsel for any party.

(c) Objections. Objections to the calling of witnesses by the military judge or the members or to the interrogation by the military judge or the members may be made at the time or at the next available opportunity when the members are not present.

EDITORIAL COMMENT

This Military Rule of Evidence is consistent with past court-martial practice, *see Manual* ¶¶ 54a (which has been amended) and 149, and the common law. Although it is generally consistent with its federal rules counterpart, substantial additions were necessary to accommodate military procedures.

Subdivision (a) recognizes that even though counsel will generally present all witnesses possessing relevant and important testimony, the trial bench and the court-members may sua sponte call or recall witnesses. The bench may also be asked to call witnesses by either party. Any witness called by the judge or court-members may be examined by both sides as if on cross-examination; thus, leading questions may be used. When the members desire to call or recall a witness, their request must be approved by the bench. Either party may object. The ultimate resolution of any objection naturally resides with the trial judge. *See* Rule 611(a). In determining how to exercise its discretion, the court should balance the need to clarify or supplement the evidence presented by the parties against the possibility of interfering with the parties' control of their cases. Additionally, the bench, which may have substantial influence on members or witnesses, does not want to be viewed as being so involved with a party or witness that it favors or disfavors that party or witness, lest its impartiality be questioned.

Unlike its federal counterpart, Rule 614(b) allows court-members, as well as the military judge and counsel, to interrogate witnesses. The Rule applies whether the witness was called by the members, the judge or the parties. In this respect, the military drafters have continued traditional court-martial practice, but have formalized the procedure so that it is necessary for members' questions to be submitted in writing to the bench before they can be asked. *Compare Manual* ¶ 149*b*(3) which made this requirement discretionary. Note also that the drafters have corrected this practice at ¶ A8-22 of the *Manual.* Requiring questions first to be submitted to the bench allows the trial judge and counsel to cure defective questions and to reject improper ones. The traditional practice of attaching all questions to the trial record as appellate exhibits should be continued.

The last sentence of 611(b) provides that if the court-members desire a witness's presence, and the trial judge determines the request is proper, the judge may assign the responsibility of initiating examination to either party, or the bench may examine the witness itself. Past practice indicates that this examination usually will be conducted by the party standing to benefit most from such evidence. In any event, as noted above, both parties — even the party who conducts the first examination — may proceed as if on cross-examination and may use leading questions. We believe the drafters' use of the phrase "direct examination" in 614(b) means initial examination as opposed to a restrictive form of questioning. Any other reading would be inconsistent with subdivision (a).

Military judicial authority has closely examined the trial judge's role in obtaining testimony, particularly from the accused. In *United States v. Shackleford,* 2 M.J. 17 (C.M.A. 1976) the court reversed appellant's conviction, finding that he had been denied a fair trial due to the bench's examination, which included information obtained from an "improvidenced" guilty plea. Before the trial judge examines a witness or permits the members to examine a witness, he should determine whether that witness's testimony needs clarification or completion. If the bench believes it does, questioning should be conducted with the greatest restraint. The military judge and the members must continue to appear and must in fact be neutral; they must not prematurely lean toward any position, they must not impose on the presumption of innocence; and the judge must not attempt to invade the province of the court-members.

Rule 607 will probably reduce the already infrequent incidents of judges or court-members having to call witnesses. Now that a party may impeach his own witness, a barrier to obtaining testimony has been removed, and the need for the court to call a witness to avoid restrictive impeachment is gone.

Read together, subdivisions (a) and (b) allow the judge and members to obtain testimony which may be essential to a party's case. The classic situation concerns the prosecution's failure to present evidence on an element of the offense. Under these circumstances, if the accused were charged with larceny of personal property valued at more than $100, and the prosecution presented no evidence concerning the property's value, the court-members or the bench could require that a witness be called or further examined in order to determine if that element can be proved. Although previous military authority was unclear on this point, such practices have been permitted because they are essential to a fair and just resolution of the case. However, any appearance of impropriety here may be limited if instead of eliciting the testimony itself the bench merely suggests to counsel that inquiry into the area is necessary. In fact the more essential the testimony the greater the need is for the court and the members to appear neutral. *See United States v. Karnes*, 531 F.2d 214 (4th Cir. 1976).

Subdivision (c) provides that if counsel has an objection to any examination conducted by the members or the judge, or to the judge's decision to call or recall a witness, that objection need not be made in the members' presence, but may be raised "at the next available opportunity when the members are not present." While this appeared to be in conflict with Rule 103's requirement for timely objections, the drafters recognized that a timely objection here may either alienate the court-members, or demonstrate a conflict with the judge.

There is no reason why a military judge who sees a party making an obvious error should refrain from calling the error to the party's attention, and if a party forgets to offer promised evidence, the judge may remind the party of the gap in the proof. Court-members and the court should not have to sit idly by, confused, when a proper question might provide necessary understanding. But the court and the members must understand that the parties are entitled to present their cases in what they believe is the most effective way and to present them to a neutral factfinder. Thus, too much premature questioning by the court and the members may impair a party's opportunity to present evidence and the appearance of impartiality. For suggested guidelines for judges, *see* Saltzburg, *The Unnecessarily Expanding Role of the American Trial Judge*, 64 Va. L. Rev. 1 (1978). Questioning by jurors (members) is discussed in the article at pages 63-65.

DRAFTERS' ANALYSIS

(a) Calling by the court-martial. The first sentence of Rule 614(a) is taken from the Federal Rule but has been modified to recognize the power of the court members to call and examine witnesses. The second sentence of the subdivision is new and reflects the members' power to call or recall witnesses. Although recognizing that power, the Rule makes it clear that the calling of such witnesses is contingent upon compliance with these Rules and this *Manual*. Consequently, the testimony of such witnesses must be relevant and not barred by any Rule or *Manual* provision.

(b) Interrogation by the court-martial. The first sentence of Rule 614(b) is taken from the Federal Rule but modified to reflect the power under these Rules and *Manual* of the court-members to interrogate witnesses. The second sentence of the subdivision is new and modifies ¶ 54a and ¶ 149a of the present *Manual* by requiring that questions of members be submitted to the military judge in writing. This change in current practice was made in order to improve efficiency and to prevent prejudice to either

party. Although the Rule states that its intent is to ensure that the questions will "be in a form acceptable to the military judge," it is not the intent of the Committee to grant carte blanche to the military judge in this matter. It is the Committee's intent that the military judge alter the questions only to the extent necessary to ensure compliance with these Rules and *Manual*. When trial is by special court-martial without a military judge, the president will utilize the same procedure.

(c) Objections. Rule 614(c) is taken from the Federal Rule but modified to reflect the powers of the members to call and interrogate witnesses. This provision generally restates present law but recognizes counsel's right to request an Article 39(a) session to enter an objection.

Rule 615. Exclusion of Witnesses

At the request of the prosecution or defense the military judge shall order witnesses excluded so that they cannot hear the testimony of other witnesses, and the military judge may make the order sua sponte. This rule does not authorize exclusion of (1) the accused, or (2) a member of an armed service or an employee of the United States designated as representative of the United States by the trial counsel, or (3) a person whose presence is shown by a party to be essential to the presentation of the party's case.

EDITORIAL COMMENT

At common law and under ¶ 53f of the *Manual,* prospective witnesses were not permitted to be in the court-room while other witnesses were testifying. A perceived need for this sequestration was based upon the belief that if witnesses were allowed to hear each other's testimony, the possibility of collusion or the unconscious melding of stories was too great.

Like the Federal Rule on which it is based, Military Rule 615 provides that either party, or the trial judge sua sponte, may require all propective witnesses to be excluded during testimony. The Rule does not apply to arguments, instructions or ministerial aspects of a proceeding. Although the court may have inherent power to exclude witnesses from all aspects of a trial— *see, e.g., United States v. Juarez,* 573 F.2d 267 (5th Cir.), cert. denied, 439 U.S. 915 (1978) — no party has a right to sequester witnesses except during testimony.

Rule 615 has been interpreted as elevating sequestration to a right, but a right that is not absolute. The Rule recognizes three exceptions to the sequestration right. The Military and Federal Rules differ in their treatment of these exceptions, because the Military Rule is confined to criminal cases.

Rule 615(1) states that sequestration does not apply to the accused even if he is to be a witness. Defense counsel need do nothing in order to avoid the Rule, as the accused's right to be in the court-room is controlled by the Sixth Amendment, not the Rules of Evidence. *See Geders v. United States,* 425 U.S. 80 (1976). If an accused voluntarily absents himself from the court-room after being arraigned, ¶ 13c of the *Manual* provides that the accused may be tried in absentia.

Subdivision (2) indicates that if the prosecutor designates a member of the military or an employee of the United States as a representative of the government, that individual, even though he may testify, need not be sequestered. This aspect of Rule 615 is like its federal counterpart and the common law, which permitted a government agent familiar with the case to sit at counsel table and assist the prosecutor. Although in past court-martial practice, this right has not often been utilized, federal district courts have recognized that an agent's presence, particularly during long and complex trials, or trials which concern specialized subject matters, allows the government to be better prepared to meet the uncertainties of litigation. *See, e.g., In re United States,* 584 F.2d 666 (5th Cir. 1978), where the court held that a government agent could be the prosecution's representative under Rule 615(2). The court opined, however, that the trial judge, via Rule 611(a), can require the government to present such a designated agent-witness at the beginning of its case, thus limiting the possibility of collusion or undue influence upon his testimony by other witnesses. The judge can require this but need not. If the government can establish that presenting the witness's testimony out of sequence would substantially harm its case, then the judge may permit the witness to testify after remaining in the courtroom. In either event, the government should be able to use the witness during rebuttal should it be necessary. Of course, rebuttal also can be controlled under Rule 611. We anticipate Rule 615(2) will be interpreted by military courts as it has been by civilian courts.

Subdivision (3) contains the final exception to sequestration. It provides that a witness need not be excluded if a party can demonstrate that the witness is essential to its presentation. This determination is made by the trial judge after balancing the party's need for the witness and the type of assistance the witness will provide against the public policy considerations giving rise to the sequestration rule. This exception will most commonly be exercised in the military in connection with expert witnesses, particularly psychiatrists. *See* Rule 703. *See also Government of the Virgin Islands v. Edinborough,* 625 F.2d 472 (3d Cir. 1980) (suggesting that the mother of minor rape victim may be essential to the prosecutor's case and may be present while her daughter testifies). While the responsibility to establish a witness's "essentiality" is upon counsel, the bench probably may make such a finding sua sponte.

In order for sequestration to be effective, the trial judge should instruct each witness not to discuss his testimony with anyone other than counsel for either side and should instruct counsel not to discuss what other witnesses have said with witnesses yet to testify. It may be difficult for counsel to prepare witnesses without suggesting what the prior testimony has been, but that is just what counsel must try to do. If the witness fails to heed this advice, sequestration will be useless. However, no effective remedy for treating violations of a sequestration order has been developed. Military judges probably do not have the power to cite such witnesses for contempt. *See* Article 48 of the Uniform Code of Military Justice and ¶ 118 of the *Manual.* Other remedies are available though. The bench should permit counsel to bring out and comment on the sequestration violation. Certainly, it relates to witness credibility. The court could add its own comment on the violation. The bench also could prohibit a witness from testifying or strike his testimony. This remedy has not been widely used since it deprives a party and the fact-finder of testimony that might be critical to a fair decision. *See, e.g., United States v. Oropeza,* 564 F.2d 316 (9th Cir. 1977), cert. denied, 434 U.S. 1080 (1978). Since courts have been reluctant to embrace this remedy, it is not surprising that even harsher remedies — like dismissing a case or striking a defense — have not been popular.

DRAFTERS' ANALYSIS

Rule 615 is taken from the Federal Rule with only minor changes of terminology. The first portion of the Rule is in conformity with present practice; *e.g.,* ¶ 53f. The second portion, consisting of subdivisions (2) and (3), represents a substantial departure from current practice and will authorize the prosecution to designate another individual to sit with the trial counsel. Rule 615 thus modifies ¶ 53f. Under the Rule, the military judge lacks any discretion to exclude potential witnesses who come within the scope of Rule 615(2) and (3) unless the accused's constitutional right to a fair trial would be violated. Developing Article III practice recognizes the defense right, upon request, to have a prosecution witness, not excluded because of Rule 615, testify before other prosecution witnesses.

Rule 615 does not prohibit exclusion of either accused or counsel due to misbehavior when such exclusion is not prohibited by the Constitution of the United States, the Uniform Code of Military Justice, this *Manual* or these Rules.

SECTION VII. OPINIONS AND EXPERT TESTIMONY

Rule 701. Opinion Testimony by Lay Witnesses

If the witness is not testifying as an expert, the testimony of the witness in the form of opinions or inferences is limited to those opinions or inferences which are (a) rationally based on the perception of the witness and (b) helpful to a clear understanding of the testimony of the witness or the determination of a fact in issue.

EDITORIAL COMMENT

Rule 701, identical to Federal Rule 701, governs the testimony of ordinary or "lay" witnesses. Experts are covered by Rules 702, 703 and 705.

Opinions, as opposed to facts, are traditionally not preferred by the law. Evidence rules have developed to encourage witnesses to state what they have perceived so that the trier of fact can draw inferences and conclusions from reports of perceptions. When witnesses summarize or offer shortcuts in the form of conclusions or opinions, it is feared that they invade the province of the fact-finder by depriving the fact-finder of the opportunity to draw its own inferences and conclusions rather than accepting those of witnesses.

Most modern evidentiary rules have recognized that it is almost impossible to draw any sharp line between fact and opinion. Former *Manual* ¶ 138e restricted opinion testimony to opinions that were commonly drawn and could not be conveyed to a court by "a mere recitation of the observed facts." Rule 701 is much more permissive. It allows lay witnesses to testify in the form of opinions or inferences as long as they are helpful to a clear understanding of the testimony of the witness or they are helpful to a determination of a fact in issue. It is not altogether clear what the distinction is between understanding the testimony of a witness and determining a fact in issue, since it appears that any improvement in the understanding of testimony would also improve the determination of a fact in dispute. It probably is not important that the distinction be drawn in most cases. What is important is that helpful opinion be admitted. The Rule does require, however, that the opinion or inference be "rationally based on the perception of the witness." It should be emphasized that there are two requirements here. The first is that the witness have perceived that which the witness testifies about. This may mean that the witness has seen something; it may mean that the witness has heard something; or in some cases it may mean that the witness has felt or touched something. All of these would qualify as perceptions of the witness. The second requirement is that the perceptions be rationally based. A witness may only testify as to perceptions that most people would say are rationally based on experiences of the witness. For example, it is doubtful that ESP would be accepted as a rational perception, at least not at the present time.

It is likely that Rule 701 will shift the debate about opinion evidence to where it belongs. Rather than arguing about whether it is *necessary* to have opinion evidence, lawyers will argue about whether it is *helpful.* If such evidence is helpful, courts will welcome the help.

In using Rule 701, courts will have to be aware of the dangers of certain types of opinion evidence. For example, when witnesses are called to identify photographs depicting someone involved in a criminal act, it is better to use identification witnesses who are not police or parole officers to avoid suggesting to the factfinder a prior criminal record, which might not be admissible under other rules like Rules 404 and 609. *See United States v. Butcher,* 557 F.2d 666 (9th Cir. 1977).

Rule 701 must be read in conjunction with Rule 704, which permits opinions on the ultimate issue in the case. Yet, in using both Rules, courts must remember that only helpful opinions should be accepted. Opinions that attempt to tell court-members how to decide a case often are not helpful. For example, no witness should offer an opinion that a defendant is guilty. In some cases the line between permissible and impermissible opinion is indeed fine. *See, e.g., United States v. Smith,* 550 F.2d 277 (5th Cir. 1977) (witness permitted to testify that defendant knew and understood the requirements of a statute). *Compare id.* with *United States v. Phillips,* 600 F.2d 535 (5th Cir. 1979) (court suggests that a social security agent probably should not have been permitted to testify that a defendant understood the meaning of the word "disability").

DRAFTERS' ANALYSIS

Rule 701 is taken from the Federal Rule without change and supersedes that portion of ¶ 138e which deals with opinion evidence by law witnesses. Unlike the present *Manual* Rule which prohibits lay opinion testimony except when the opinion was of a "kind which is commonly drawn and which cannot, or ordinarily cannot, be conveyed to the court by a mere recitation of the observed facts," the Rule permits opinions or inferences whenever rationally based on the perception of the witness and helpful to either a clear understanding of the testimony or the determination of a fact in issue. Consequently, the Rule is broader in scope than the *Manual* provision it replaces. The specific examples listed in the *Manual,* "the speed of an automobile, whether a voice heard was that of a man, woman or child, and whether or not a person was drunk" are all within the potential scope of Rule 701.

Rule 702. Testimony by Experts

If scientific, technical, or other specialized knowledge will assist the trier of fact to understand the evidence or to determine a fact in issue, a witness qualified as an expert by knowledge, skill, experience, training, or education, may testify thereto in the form of an opinion or otherwise.

EDITORIAL COMMENT

Rule 702 sets forth a standard for the use of expert witnesses. If an expert can "assist the trier of fact" the expert may be permitted to testify. The assistance may help the trier of fact understand other evidence in the case or understand the way in which the evidence relates to legal questions in the case. Like Rule 701, which covers ordinary lay witnesses, Rule 702 is a permissive rule that encourages the use of witnesses who can help court members or judges decide cases before them. There is no requirement under the Rule that an expert be absolutely necessary or that the subject matter of expert testimony be totally beyond the ken of court members. The test is whether the expert can be helpful.

This Rule should result in greater admissiblity of expert testimony than was the case under prior Manual ¶ 138e. The adoption of this Rule has also resulted in the deletion of former ¶ 142e of the *Manual.* This paragraph had made inadmissible polygraph test results and the results of procedures involving drugs or hypnosis. With the deletion of this paragraph, Rule 702 leaves the court with leeway to admit any expert testimony that it finds to be helpful. But the drafters' *Analysis* makes it clear that it was not intended that the elimination of ¶ 142e should be taken as an indication that the testimony that was formerly inadmissible should now be admitted. Rather, courts are to evaluate expert evidence in light of the current scientific evidence that is available when the expert is called to testify and in light of the problems that often are associated with certain forms of evidence. *See generally,* Oeveren, *Admissibility of Polygraph Results Under Military and Federal Rules of Evidence,* 12 THE ADVOCATE 257 (1980); Williams, *Admissibility of Polygraph Results Under the Military Rules of Evidence,* THE ARMY LAWYER, June 1980, at 1.

Nothing in Rule 702 requires that expert testimony be based on scientific principles that are generally accepted in the scientific community. With respect to polygraph tests, such a requirement had been established in the famous case, *Frye v. United States,* 293 F. 1013 (D.C. Cir. 1923). It should be noted, however, that Rule 703, which states the permissible bases for expert opinions, requires that an expert rely upon data "reasonably relied upon by experts in the particular field." This would suggest that some acceptance of scientific evidence in the general fields in which the expert works is necessary if an expert is to satisfy that Rule. The drafters' *Analyses* of Rules 702 and 703 indicate that the exact standard of scientific certainty is not yet well established in civilian courts under the Federal Rules of Evidence. It is probable, therefore, that it will take some time in the military courts for a workable standard to be developed. The reason why a certain level of acceptance in the scientific community has been required by many courts is that trials produce a final result between the parties. If testimony is based on principles that prove to be invalid, punishment may be imposed upon persons without proper justification. In the scientific community generally, scientists can correct their mistakes and admit past errors and are encouraged to do so. In the litigation context, it is difficult to reopen old cases. It may be that a standard of "reasonable scientific acceptance" is a workable one that will provide adequate protection against premature use of new scientific techniques, without unduly restricting courts from utilizing reliable technological advances.

A person may qualify as an expert as a result of special knowledge, skill, experience, training or education. In other words, anything that makes someone more knowledgeable, skillful or experienced than the average person might qualify one as an expert. The general rule is that trial judges have great discretion in controlling expert testimony. *See e.g., United States v. Lopez,* 543 F.2d 1156 (5th Cir. 1976). Judges should remember, however, that Rule 401 establishes a low threshold of relevance, and Rule 402 creates a presumption that relevant evidence should be admissible. Thus, judges should not arbitrarily exclude evidence that might be helpful. *See, e.g., United States v. Garvin,* 565 F.2d 519 (8th Cir. 1977). The expert who is called to testify need not be "an outstanding practitioner," but need only be a person who can help the jury. *See, e.g., United States v. Barker,* 553 F.2d 1013 (6th Cir. 1977). It is important that the expert not be permitted to testify on extraneous matters, especially where those matters might be highly prejudicial. *See, e.g., United States v. Green,* 548 F.2d 1261 (6th Cir. 1977).

DRAFTERS' ANALYSIS

Rule 702 is taken from the Federal Rule verbatim, and replaces that portion of *Manual* ¶ 138e dealing with expert testimony. Although the Rule is similar to the present manual rule, it may be broader and *may* supersede *Frye v. United States,* 293 F. 1013 (D.C. Cir. 1923), an issue now being extensively litigated in the Article III courts. The Rule's sole explicit test is whether the evidence in question "will assist the trier of fact to understand the evidence or to determine a fact in issue." Whether any particular piece of evidence comes within this test is normally a matter within the military judge's discretion.

Under Rule 103(a) any objection to an expert on the basis that the individual is not in fact adequately qualified under the Rule will be waived by a failure to so object.

¶ 142e of the present *Manual,* "Polygraph tests and drug-induced or hypnosis-induced interviews," has been deleted as a result of the adoption of Rule 702. ¶ 142e states: "The conclusions based upon or graphically represented by a polygraph test and the conclusions based upon, and the statements of the person interviewed made during a drug-induced or hypnosis-induced interview are inadmissible in evidence." The deletion of the explicit prohibition on such evidence is not intended to make such evidence per se, admissible and is not an express authorization for such procedures. Clearly, such evidence must be approached with great care. Considerations surrounding the nature of such evidence, any possible prejudicial effect on a fact finder, and the degree of acceptance of such evidence in the Article III courts are factors to consider in determining whether it can in fact "assist the trier of fact." As of late 1979, the Committee was unaware of any significant decision by a United States Court of Appeals sustaining the admissibility of polygraph evidence in a criminal case, *see, e.g., United States v. Masri,* 547 F.2d 932 (5th Cir. 1977); *United States v. Cardarella,* 570 F.2d 264 (8th Cir. 1978), although the Seventh Circuit, *see, e.g., United States v. Bursten,* 560 F.2d 779 (7th Cir. 1977) (holding that polygraph admissibility is within the sound discretion of the trial judge), and perhaps the Ninth Circuit, *United States v. Benveniste,* 564 F.2d 335, 339 n. 3 (9th Cir. 1977), at least recognize the possible admissibility of such evidence. There is reason to believe that evidence obtained via hypnosis may be treated somewhat more liberally than is polygraph evidence. *See, e.g., Kline v. Ford Motor Co.,* 523 F.2d 1067 (9th Cir. 1975).

Rule 703. Bases of Opinion Testimony by Experts

The facts or data in the particular case upon which an expert bases an opinion or inference may be those perceived by or made known to the expert, at or before the hearing. If of a type reasonably relied upon by experts in the particular field in forming opinions or inferences upon the subject, the facts or data need not be admissible in evidence.

EDITORIAL COMMENT

Identical to Federal Rule 703, Military Rule 703 expands the bases upon which expert opinion may rest. The traditional common law approach was to restrict expert testimony to opinions or inferences based upon facts presented in evidence. Since the expert usually had no personal knowledge of the facts, a hypothetical question, often lengthy and complicated, was put to the expert and the expert was asked to offer views assuming the facts stated in the question were correct. Proof supporting the assumed facts was required from other witnesses. The new Rule adopts a much more flexible approach to expert testimony.

Under Rule 703, an expert may base an opinion upon facts or data that he has perceived or that he has been told about, either while watching the trial or hearing or before, as long as the facts or data upon which the expert relies are "reasonably relied upon by experts in the particular field." This is so even though the facts or data would not otherwise be admissible in evidence.

There are two principal problems that arise under Rule 703. The first is how to determine what experts in the particular field reasonably rely upon. To make the determination, the judge may consider: the testimony of the expert who is called; literature that is offered in support of, or in opposition to, the testimony; and the testimony of other experts. When making the decision to admit or to exclude expert testimony, the judge is making a preliminary decision on an evidence question that is covered by Rule 104(a). This means that in a hearing on the evidence question the judge is not bound by the Rules of Evidence other than the privilege rules; this signifies that the judge can consider hearsay testimony, which often may take the form of books, especially learned treatises.

The hardest question the judge may face in deciding on which facts or data are reasonably relied upon is how much scientific acceptance is required before certain tests may be deemed to be valid. This problem is discussed in the Editorial Comment to Rule 702. For a good discussion on the general subject of when information relied upon outside of courts should be deemed to be reliable enough for use in court, see McElhaney, *Expert Witnesses and the Federal Rules of Evidence*, 28 MERCER L. REV. 463 (1977).

The other problem that arises under the Rule is whether the expert who has relied upon facts or data not themselves admissible in evidence may report the facts or data in explaining an opinion or inference. If the expert is denied an opportunity to relate the facts or data that explain an opinion, it is difficult for the judge or court-members to evaluate the legitimacy of the opinion. Thus, it would seem imperative that some explanation for the expert opinion be permitted. It is also clear, however, that unless care is taken in utilizing Rule 703, parties can "smuggle" much hearsay evidence into a case, when such evidence is not properly admitted for its truth. We suggest that Rule 403 is an appropriate tool for handling the problem. Some explanation for the expert opinion should be provided, but the judge should make sure that no party takes unfair advantage of Rule 703. Of course, when the expert relies upon information that is not admissible for its truth, a limiting instruction can be given under Rule 105, and it will be given upon request.

Rule 705 governs the order in which an expert is entitled to present testimony.

DRAFTERS' ANALYSIS

Rule 703 is taken from the Federal Rule without change. The Rule is similar in scope to ¶ 138e of the present *Manual,* but is potentially broader as it allows reliance upon "facts or data" whereas the present *Manual's* limitation is phrased in terms of the personal observation, personal examination or study, or examination or study "of reports of others of a kind customarily considered in the practice of the expert's specialty." Hypothetical questions of the expert are not required by the Rule.

A limiting instruction may be appropriate if the expert while expressing the basis for an opinion states facts or data that are not themselves admissible. *See* Rule 105.

Whether Rule 703 has modified or superseded the *Frye* test for scientific evidence, *Frye v. United States,* 293 F. 1013 (D.C. Cir. 1923) is unclear and is now being litigated within the Article III courts.

Rule 704. Opinion on Ultimate Issue

Testimony in the form of an opinion or inference otherwise admissible is not objectionable because it embraces an ultimate issue to be decided by the trier of fact.

EDITORIAL COMMENT

Taken from Federal Rule 704 without change, Military Rule 704 states that testimony in the form of an opinion or inference is not objectionable on the ground that it embraces an ultimate issue that the trier of facts must decide. In common law courts, an objection that an opinion on an ultimate issue invaded the province of the fact-finder usually would be sustained. This produced substantial and confusing litigation on the subject of what was an ultimate issue and what kinds of testimony amounted to usurpation of the fact-finder's function. Prior to the adoption of Rule 704, the approach in the military courts to the problem was uncertain. Rule 704 clarifies matters.

It should be noted that the Rule does not distinguish between lay and expert witnesses. Any opinion that is otherwise admissible can be admitted despite the fact that it relates to an ultimate issue in the case. But it is important to keep in mind that the testimony must otherwise qualify for admission. This means that lay witness testimony must satisfy the requirements of Rule 701, and that expert testimony must satisfy the requirements of Rules 702 and 703. This means that unhelpful testimony — *e.g.*, testimony not based on the rational perceptions of a lay witness or expert testimony based on facts or data not reasonably relied upon by similar experts — would not be admissible.

The drafters' *Analysis* plainly states that the Rule "does not permit the witness to testify as to his or her opinion as to the guilt or innocence of the accused or to state legal opinions." It is for the judge to state the law for court-members. *See United States v. Popejoy*, 578 F.2d 1346 (10th Cir.), cert. denied, 439 U.S. 896 (1978). And no witness helps the court-members by offering a judgment on ultimate guilt and innocence. This adds nothing to the information about the case that the court-members have to assist them in their decision. In some instances, the line between impermissible and permissible opinion is difficult to draw. *See, e.g., United States v. Hearst*, 563 F.2d 1331 (9th Cir. 1977), cert. denied, 435 U.S. 1000 (1978) (upholding the introduction of expert opinion on human motivation to rob a bank). For a discussion of various ultimate issue problems, *see* Traster, *The Ultimate Issue Rule in State and Federal Courts*, 27 Defense L.J. 307 (1978).

Whenever a question is put to a witness, the interrogator should assure that the question does not assume that the witness understands legal terms that might be unfamiliar to people untrained in the law. An expert witness, for example, should not be asked whether in his opinion an accused is legally sane. A medical expert might not understand the legal definition of sanity. The questioner should make clear what the standard is and then ask the expert for an opinion.

DRAFTERS' ANALYSIS

Rule 704 is taken from the Federal Rule verbatim. The *Manual* for Courts-Martial is silent on the issue and current military law is unsettled. The Rule does not permit the witness to testify as to his or her opinion as to the guilt or innocence of the accused or to state legal opinions. Rather it simply allows testimony involving an issue which must be decided by the trier of fact. Although the two may be closely related, they are distinct as a matter of law.

Rule 705. Disclosure of Facts or Data Underlying Expert Opinion

The expert may testify in terms of opinion or inference and give the expert's reasons therefor without prior disclosure of the underlying facts or data, unless the military judge requires otherwise. The expert may in any event be required to disclose the underlying facts or data on cross-examination.

EDITORIAL COMMENT

Rule 705 is taken verbatim from Federal Rule 705. It governs the form in which an expert's testimony may be offered.

Under the Rule an expert may give opinions or state inferences on direct examination without disclosing the underlying facts or data. On cross-examination, the Rule states that the expert "may in any event be required to disclose the underlying facts." This is a confusing Rule.

It seems that the drafters intended to assure that the cross-examiner always would be able to probe the bases for an expert opinion. Yet, the second sentence of the Rule seems to suggest that the trial judge *may* permit the cross-examiner to inquire into the underlying facts, but that there is some discretion to deny an opportunity to do so. We can think of few, if any, circumstances in which cross-examination about the bases of expert opinion should be denied. Of course, under Rule 403 this examination may be restricted in length and scope in order to avoid confusion and waste of time. But some cross-examination would seem to be required. Indeed, some courts have suggested that the government has an obligation "not to obstruct a criminal defendant's cross-examination of expert testimony." *United States v. Mangan,* 575 F.2d 32 (2d Cir.), cert. denied, 439 U.S. 931 (1978).

The first sentence of the Rule gives the trial judge authority to require an expert to disclose the facts or data upon which an opinion or inference is based before stating the opinion or inference. In our view, if it is likely that a challenge will be made to the propriety of admitting a particular opinion, it would make sense for the trial judge to assure that the facts or data upon which the opinion is based are first presented in order to prevent any opinion that might not be permissible from actually coming before court members, who might have a difficult time striking it from their minds later.

Counsel should be aware that it usually is to the advantage of the direct examiner to bring out the facts or data upon which an opinion is based, because the opinion is worth no more than the facts that support it. It is dangerous for a direct-examiner to refrain from asking questions about the facts or data, because the cross-examiner also may choose not to ask them and the answers may never find their way into evidence.

DRAFTERS' ANALYSIS

Rule 705 is taken from the Federal Rule without change and is similar in result to the requirement in ¶ 138e of the present *Manual* that the "expert may be required, on direct or cross-examination, to specify the data upon which his opinion was based and to relate the details of his observation, examination, or study." Unlike the present *Manual,* Rule 705 requires disclosure on direct examination only when the military judge so requires.

Rule 706. Court Appointed Experts

(a) Appointment and compensation. The trial counsel, the defense counsel, and the court-martial have equal opportunity to obtain expert witnesses under Article 46. The employment and compensation of expert witnesses is governed by paragraphs 115 and 116 of this Manual.

(b) Disclosure of employment. In the exercise of discretion, the military judge may authorize disclosure to the members of the fact that the military judge called an expert witness.

(c) Accused's experts of own selection. Nothing in this rule limits the accused in calling expert witnesses of the accused's own selection and at the accused's own expense.

EDITORIAL COMMENT

Military Rule 706 is very different from its federal counterpart. Under Article 46 of the Uniform Code of Military Justice, trial counsel, defense counsel and the court have equal opportunities to obtain expert witnesses. *Manual* ¶¶ 115 and 116 cover compensation. Because of the Code and *Manual* provisions, parts of the Federal Rule are unnecessary in the Military Rules of Evidence.

An expert witness, like any other witness (*see* Rule 614), may be called to testify by the military judge. Subdivision (b) authorizes the military judge to inform court-members of the fact that an expert witness has been called by the judge. This presents a problem much like that presented when the judge calls any other witness: There is a danger that the court-members will associate the witness with the judge and will tend to give the witness special consideration or deference. If the judge does inform the court-members that he has called an expert, the judge should be very careful to instruct the members that they are to judge the witness' credibility as they would judge that of any other witness and that there is no special significance in the fact that the court has called the witness. For a discussion of the problems that may arise when the judge becomes identified with witnesses, *see* Saltzburg, *The Unnecessarily Expanding Role of the American Trial Judge,* 64 VA. L. REV. 1 (1978).

Subdivision (c) is included to make it clear that nothing in this Rule limits the accused in calling expert witnesses that the accused has retained and selected. The accused is entitled to obtain help of an expert witness under Article 46. But the accused may also obtain expert witnesses on his own. The only limitation upon the calling of witnesses will be found in the relevance provisions, Rule 402 and Rule 403.

DRAFTERS' ANALYSIS

(a) Appointment and compensation. Rule 706(a) is the result of a complete redraft of subdivision (a) of the Federal Rule that was required to be consistent with Article 46 of the Uniform Code of Military Justice which is implemented in ¶¶ 115 and 116 of the *Manual.* Rule 706(a) states the basic rule that prosecution, defense, military judge, and the court members all have equal opportunity under Article 46 to obtain expert witnesses. The second sentence of the subdivision replaces subdivision (b) of the Federal Rule which is inapplicable to the armed forces in the light of ¶ 116.

(b) Disclosure of employment. Rule 706(b) is taken from FED. R. EVID. 706(c) without change. The *Manual* is silent on the issue, but the subdivision should not change military practice.

(c) Accused's expert of own selection. Rule 706(c) is similar in intent to subdivision (d) of the Federal Rule and adapts that Rule to military practice. The subdivision makes it clear that the defense may call its own expert witnesses at its own expense without the necessity of recourse to ¶ 116.

SECTION VIII. HEARSAY

Rule 801. Definitions.
    (a) Statement.
    (b) Declarant.
    (c) Hearsay.
    (d) Statements which are not hearsay.
        (1) Prior statement by witness.
        (2) Admission by party-opponent.

Rule 802. Hearsay Rule.

Rule 803. Hearsay Exceptions; Availability of Declarant Immaterial.
    (1) Present sense impression.
    (2) Excited utterance.
    (3) Then existing mental, emotional, or physical condition.
    (4) Statements for purposes of medical diagnosis or treatment.
    (5) Recorded recollection.
    (6) Records of regularly conducted activity.
    (7) Absence of entry in records kept in accordance with the provisions of paragraph (6).
    (8) Public records and reports.
    (9) Records of vital statistics.
    (10) Absence of public record or entry.
    (11) Records of religious organizations.
    (12) Marriage, baptismal, and similar certificates.
    (13) Family records.
    (14) Records of documents affecting an interest in property.
    (15) Statements in documents affecting an interest in property.
    (16) Statements in ancient documents.
    (17) Market reports, commercial publications.
    (18) Learned treatises.
    (19) Reputation concerning personal or family history.
    (20) Reputation concerning boundaries or general history.
    (21) Reputation as to character.
    (22) Judgment of previous conviction.
    (23) Judgment as to personal, family or general history, or boundaries.
    (24) Other exceptions.

Rule 804. Hearsay Exceptions; Declarant Unavailable.
    (a) Definition of unavailability.
    (b) Hearsay exceptions.
        (1) Former testimony.
        (2) Statement under belief of impending death.
        (3) Statement against interest.
        (4) Statement of personal or family history.
        (5) Other exceptions.

Rule 805. Hearsay Within Hearsay.

Rule 806. Attacking and Supporting Credibility of Declarant.

Rule 801. Definitions

The following definitions apply under this section:

(a) Statement. A "statement" is (1) an oral or written assertion or (2) nonverbal conduct of a person, if it is intended by the person as an assertion.

(b) Declarant. A "declarant" is a person who makes a statement.

335

(c) Hearsay. "Hearsay" is a statement, other than one made by the declarant while testifying at the trial or hearing, offered in evidence to prove the truth of the matter asserted.

(d) Statements which are not hearsay. A statement is not hearsay if:

(1) Prior statement by witness. The declarant testifies at the trial or hearing and is subject to cross-examination concerning the statement, and the statement is (A) inconsistent with the declarant's testimony, and was given under oath subject to the penalty of perjury at a trial, hearing, or other proceeding, or in a deposition, or (B) consistent with the declarant's testimony and is offered to rebut an express or implied charge against the declarant of recent fabrication or improper influence or motive, or (C) one of identification of a person made after perceiving the person; or

(2) Admission by party-opponent. The statement is offered against a party and is (A) the party's own statement in either the party's individual or representative capacity, or (B) a statement of which the party has manifested the party's adoption or belief in its truth, or (C) a statement by a person authorized by the party to make a statement concerning the subject, or (D) a statement by the party's agent or servant concerning a matter within the scope of the agency or employment of the agent or servant, made during the existence of the relationship, or (E) a statement by a co-conspirator of a party during the course and in furtherance of the conspiracy.

EDITORIAL COMMENT

This is one of the most complicated of all the Military Rules of Evidence. It offers a definition of hearsay that covers all of the provisions in Section VIII, and then creates exemptions from the definitions that used to be known as exceptions to the hearsay rule. As a result, the structure of the Rule, identical to its federal counterpart, leaves users not only confused but also tongue-tied in attempting to invoke the Rule at trial.

Subdivision (a) defines hearsay. A typical hearsay problem arises when someone makes an oral statement or writes something out of court and the statement or the writing is offered as evidence in court. The less common and more difficult hearsay problem arises when someone does something outside of court which does not involve the use of words, but which is offered as if the conduct of the person were the equivalent of a communication or an assertion. Subdivision (a) defines a "statement" as an oral or written assertion or other non-verbal conduct that is intended by the person who is acting to be an assertion. The definition of "statement" is important because the word is used in subdivision (c) in the actual definition of hearsay.

By excluding conduct not intended to be an assertion from the definition of "statement," the Rule is similar to ¶ 139a of the former *Manual*. Although a person's out-of-court actions that are not intended to be assertions may be ambiguous, the current trend is to exclude them from definitions of hearsay on the ground that problems of sincerity are considerably reduced when the person is not intending to make an assertion at the time action is taken. This trend is evident in the new Rule.

Subdivision (b) defines the word "declarant" as a person who makes a statement. This is a standard definition and is important because it too is used in defining hearsay under subdivision (c).

It is in subdivision (c) that hearsay is defined as a statement that is offered to prove the truth of the matter asserted unless the statement was made by the declarant while testifying at the trial or hearing in which it is offered as evidence. In other words, there are two parts to the definition. First, statements made at a trial or hearing by a witness that are subject to examination and cross-examination are not hearsay; only statements made outside of a trial or hearing can be hearsay. Even these out-of-court statements will not be hearsay unless they are offered in evidence at the trial or hearing to prove the truth of what it is that the declarant asserted. Much of the difficulty in hearsay analysis arises when counsel and the court analyze whether a statement is being offered for its truth.

Sometimes a statement is offered not for its truth, but simply because it was made. Two good examples are found in the drafters' *Analysis*. The first is in example 1. If a witness hears a person say, "I am going to kill you" to another person (who becomes the accused), and the accused offers testimony of the witness as to what he heard in support of a self-defense claim, the statement that the witness relates is not hearsay. The important thing is not that the statement was true, but that it was made. The fact that it was made may have entitled the accused to respond to the statement with self-protective action. The other helpful example of the drafters is 3. If a person is being tried for disobeying an order, someone who overheard the order being given may testify to what he heard. The order itself is relevant because the words were uttered. An order is neither true nor false. Either it was issued or it was not. The words that were uttered are important simply because they were said. This is not hearsay.

One way to analyze the question whether a statement is being offered for its truth is to ask whether the proponent of the statement is asking the trier of fact to treat the statement as if it were made by a witness on the stand and to place faith in it as a true representation of some fact. If the answer is no, the statement is not hearsay. If the answer is yes, the statement probably qualifies as hearsay under the definition of subdivision (c).

A harder class of cases arises when a statement is offered not for its truth and not simply because it was made, but to show the belief of the declarant. If, for example, one soldier said to another, "There goes General Jones," and later the declarant wanted to offer the testimony of the other soldier to whom he made the statement to show that he thought a particular person was General Jones, the statement would not be hearsay. It would not be offered to show that the person indeed was General Jones, but to show the belief of the declarant. Unless the statement actually is offered for the truth of the contents, it will not be hearsay.

Although the definition of hearsay under subdivision (c) is slightly different from that found in former *Manual* ¶ 139a, the difference is not very important, and practice under subdivision (c) should resemble former practice.

It is subdivision (d) that makes some lawyers tongue-tied in using the Rule. This subdivision states that some statements are not hearsay and goes on to list eight different categories of statements that are treated as non-hearsay. What makes this confusing is that most, if not all, of these statements are assertions made out of court that are offered for their truth. Thus, they meet the definition of hearsay that is set forth in subdivision (c). What subdivision (d) actually does is to say that despite the fact that the statements that fall within it qualify under subdivision (c) as hearsay, they receive special treatment and are not subject to the same definition as other statements. The result is that they are not excluded on hearsay grounds when offered as evidence. Statements that qualify under (d) need not also qualify under the exceptions to the hearsay rule that are found in Rules 803 and 804.

Subdivision (d) is divided into two parts. The first part takes up statements by witnesses who are present at a trial or hearing and are subject to cross-examination concerning prior out-of-court statements. It is important to note that the fact that a witness is present to testify and to be examined does not by itself mean that any former statements by the witness can be admitted without violating the hearsay rule. At common law, statements by anyone, including witnesses present at trial, were hearsay if they were offered for their truth outside of court at a time when cross-examination was not possible, unless they qualified under the usual hearsay exceptions. Subdivision (d) (1) departs from the common law and provides that three categories of former statements may be used as long as the person who made the statement is present at trial and is subject to cross-examination.

The first class of prior statements that may be admitted is comprised of some prior inconsistent statements. These statements must have been given under oath and subject to the penalty of perjury "at a trial, hearing, or other proceeding, or in a deposition." There is no requirement that there has been an opportunity for prior cross-examination. The oath is an absolute requirement, and the only other requirement is that there has been some kind of formal proceeding. Apparently, the formal proceeding guarantees an accurate record and suggests to the person who makes the statement the importance of telling the truth and thus adds to the oath requirement a guarantee of trustworthiness. As the drafters' *Analysis* properly notes, some courts have read this provision broadly and have allowed in statements that may not have been made under the most reliable circumstances. *See, e.g., United States v. Castro-Ayon,* 537 F.2d 1055 (9th Cir.), cert. denied, 429 U.S. 983 (1976) (admitting tape-recorded statements given under oath at a border patrol station). The drafters suggest that the provision clearly should apply to Article 32 hearings, and this seems to be an eminently reasonable position.

The importance of this provision should be clear. It marks a change from prior law. *See* former *Manual* ¶ 139a; *United States v. Burge,* 1 M.J. 408 (C.M.A. 1976) (Cook, J., concurring). When a statement qualifies under this provision, it can be used as substantive evidence, not just for impeachment purposes. Thus, no limiting instruction on the use of the evidence would be given. If a witness is present at trial and has made statements that qualify under this provision, the witness can be called for the sole purpose of bringing out such statements, since this is the elicitation of substantive evidence and is permissible, therefore this is to be distinguished from the situation in which prior inconsistent statements that do not qualify under this provision have been made and a party tries to call a witness for the sole purpose of bringing out those inconsistent statements. This problem is discussed under Rule 607.

Subdivision (d)(1)(B) covers prior consistent statements. Unlike prior inconsistent statements, consistent statements need not have been made under oath, nor need they have been made in a prior proceeding. Any statement made previously to anyone might qualify. However, the language covers only those statements that are offered to rebut an express or implied charge against the declarant of recent fabrication, improper influence or bad motive. This limitation reflects the common law view that someone who repeats the same story over and over is not necessarily likely to be more truthful than someone who says the same thing just once. A lie often repeated does not become the truth. What the Rule does is to permit a party to show that a witness has been consistent in a story once it is suggested that the witness may have invented testimony. Most courts have read into the provision the traditional requirement that the prior statement had been made prior to the time at which a motive to falsify testimony would have arisen. This is more a relevance than a hearsay restriction. For a prior consistent statement to add much to a case, and to help to dispel a charge that the witness is lying, the statement should have been made prior to the time when the witness would have had a reason to lie. Thus, the cases cited in the drafters' *Analysis* do indicate that the common law limitation still is followed.

Rule 801(d)(1)(B) indicates that prior consistent statements can only be used as substantive evidence if they satisfy the requirement that the evidence be offered in response to an attack on the witness of the kind specified in the Rule. It is arguable that nothing in the Rule bars the offer of other prior consistent statements to bolster the credibility of the witness, not to prove the truth of their contents. However, most federal courts, interpreting the federal counterpart to the Military Rule, have determined that the common law rule — that prior consistent statements are generally inadmissible — is what the drafters of Rule 801 intended should remain in effect. *See, e.g., United States v. Quinto,* 582 F.2d 224 (2d Cir. 1978); *United States v. Check,* 582 F.2d 668 (2d Cir. 1978). Even though Senior Judge Henry Friendly has argued to the contrary, *see United States v. Rubin,* 609 F.2d 51, 66 (2d Cir. 1979), we think that the majority of the federal courts have adopted the correct approach. The problem is not really a hearsay problem. The trouble with prior consistent statements is that they are so easily manufactured. As noted above, at common law the judgment was that false statements repeated over time do not become any more true simply because they were made more than once. Thus, their probative value was viewed as low. The common law courts recognized an exception for cases in which a witness was attacked as a liar, and the fact that a prior statement was made tended to cast out on the attack. We think that Rule 801(d)(1)(B) does intend to follow the common law approach and that it recognizes that it is not important whether prior consistent statements are deemed to be substantive evidence or simply corroborative evidence, since the witness is repeating the same thing from the witness stand as the witness said in the prior statement.

The third category of prior statements by a witness that qualify for admission is prior identifications. Any identification of a person made "after perceiving the person" identified may be admitted. It is difficult to imagine an identification made *before* perceiving the person; thus, the language that we have quoted from the Rule is probably unnecessary. But it does little harm. It is important to keep in mind, however, that prior identification means at any time prior to the trial or hearing. There is no time restraint on when the identification must have been made. Of course, the identification must comply with the requirements of law. *See* Rule 321. An identification need not have been made under oath. It can be used whether or not there is any suggestion that the witness is lying. There is no requirement that the witness have any loss of memory as a prerequisite to the use of the statement. Rule 801(d)(1)(C) reflects a modern trend that adopts the view that earlier identifications are more likely to be trustworthy than later identifications, and that due process requirements assure that the identifications will be reliable enough to be used as evidence.

For all of these categories to be applicable, the witness must be subject to cross-examination. It seems evident that a witness who refuses to respond to questions on cross-examination would not satisfy the Rule and any (d)(1) statements of such a witness would have to be stricken. Closer questions arise when a witness claims a slight loss of memory or the witness is evasive. The question for the trial judge is whether the cross-examiner has a fair chance to test the witness and to ask the witness about the prior statements. The fact that a witness may deny having made a prior statement does not prevent it from being admitted through another witness. And the fact that the witness has denied having made the prior statement may not mean that proof of the statement through the testimony of someone else will amount to a confrontation violation. *See Nelson v. O'Neil,* 402 U.S. 622 (1971).

The other part of subdivision (d) covers five kinds of statements that used to comprise a familiar exception to the hearsay rule. The exception was the admissions exception. Although the five admissions found in subdivision (d)(2) are now deemed to be non-hearsay, the effect of the new Rule is to admit these statements as evidence just as they were admitted when they were hearsay exceptions. Nevertheless, this is not to say that the placement of admissions in Rule 801 may not be significant. Under Rules 803 and 804, there are residual exceptions to the hearsay rule that permit courts to admit evidence that technically does not qualify under a traditional exception, but that seems to be reliable enough to be admitted. It is not clear that under these residual exceptions an analogy can be drawn to admissions, because admissions are not treated as hearsay exceptions. This may be important when the residual exceptions are implemented.

Subdivision (d)(2)(A) covers the most familiar of all admissions, the personal admission. It provides that a party's own statements may be used against the party. Such statements are admissible under former *Manual* ¶ 140a. Naturally, any statement that is made would be excluded if it violated a constitutional or procedural rule. *See* Rules 304 and 305.

The provision in (d)(2)(B) covers adoptive admissions. The clearest case of an adoptive admission is when a declarant says something like the following: "I agree with you. That is correct." When a person remains silent, it may be more difficult to decide whether silence is intended to be acquiescence in a statement. If so, it may be admitted, just as it could have been admitted under former *Manual* ¶ 140a (4). It should be noted that Rule 304(h)(3) limits the use of silence when a person is under official investigation or is in confinement, arrest or custody.

The third type of admission found in (d)(2)(C) covers statements by authorized spokespersons. The rationale here is self-evident. If one person asks someone else to speak for him, the requesting party is treated as if he had made the statements personally. Although the former *Manual* did not have a specific provision for such statements, the drafters of the new Rule indicate that these statements would have qualified under an agency theory under former law.

A second kind of agent's admission is covered by subdivision (d)(2)(D), which treats as nonhearsay statements by a party's agent or servant concerning a matter within the scope of the agency or employment while the agency or employment relationship continues. This provision allows in evidence more statements than were admitted at common law. It may turn out that the Rule has special significance for the accused. It would seem to make any person who is working for the government and who makes statements about his work for the government a government agent and thus make his statements concerning his employment admissible. Some civilian courts have suggested that statements by government employees do not fall within this provision. *See, e.g., United States v. Kampiles,* 609 F.2d 1233 (7th Cir. 1979). But it is difficult to see why government agents should be treated differently from the agents of other entities. There may be some reason why informants should not be treated as traditional government agents. But in the armed services, it would be difficult to argue that the agents that the government trusts with national security cannot be deemed agents for purposes of a hearsay exemption.

The final admission also rests on an agency theory. It is the traditional admission for coconspirators' statements. The Rule provides that statements by one conspirator made during the course of and in furtherance of the conspiracy may be admitted against other conspirators. It is for the judge to decide whether the statement was made during the course of the conspiracy, and this may require a determination as to when the conspiracy actually ended. *See, e.g., United States v. Floyd,* 555 F.2d 45 (2d Cir.), cert. denied, 434 U.S. 851 (1977). The judge also must decide whether the statement was in furtherance of the conspiracy. Many courts do not treat this requirement very seriously. *See, e.g., United States v. Harris,* 546 F.2d 234 (8th Cir. 1976). A few courts do enforce the requirement with more vigor, however. *See, e.g., United States v. Castillo,* 615 F.2d 878 (9th Cir. 1980); *United States v. Lang,* 589 F.2d 92 (2d Cir. 1978).

Civilian courts have had the most difficulty in deciding how much independent evidence of conspiracy must be shown to exist before conspirators' statements may be admitted. It might seem odd that there is no requirement on the face of the Rule that a conspiracy be proved by independent evidence, but in order to determine that statements are made in furtherance of and during a conspiracy, the Rule assumes that the trial judge must have found that a conspiracy existed. The confusion of civilian courts is attributable to a number of different approaches to the independent evidence problem that existed well before the Federal Rules of Evidence were adopted. There was agreement that the trial judge had to decide that there was sufficient independent evidence in the case, but disagreement on how the finding was to be made.

Most civilian courts now take the view, and it seems to be the proper view, that Rule 104(a) governs and that the trial judge must make a preliminary finding that a conspiracy exists before admitting conspirators' statements. The traditional view with respect to preliminary questions of fact is that the judge will make the ruling by using a preponderance of the evidence standard and that the party, usually the government, claiming that conspiracy exists bears the burden of convincing the judge by a preponderance of the evidence of the conspiracy before the hearsay exemption will be deemed to apply. The question that divides the courts is whether the hearsay statements that are the subject of the challenge can be considered when the judge makes the finding of conspiracy. Some courts take the view that the statements can be, because Rule 1101 indicates that the Rules of Evidence do not apply in preliminary fact-finding. *See, e.g., United States v. Petrozziello,* 548 F.2d 20 (1st Cir. 1977). Other courts take the view that to allow the conspirators' statements themselves to be used to prove conspiracy would be "bootstrapping," which means that the statements that are subject to challenge would themselves be used as a basis for finding the conspiracy that is necessary to qualify the statements for admission. Thus, these courts would exclude the statements themselves from consideration on the issue of whether a conspiracy exists. *See; e.g., United States v. James,* 590 F.2d 575 (5th Cir.) (en banc), cert. denied, 442 U.S. 917 (1979).

Our view is that bootstrapping ought not to be permitted. Even in those courts that permit the statements to be considered, there usually is language in the opinions that the statements themselves are not to be given much weight. The difficulty is that it is difficult to tell how much weight the trial judge is giving to the conspirators' statements that are subject to challenge.

Since the reason for admitting conspirators' statements is that if a conspiracy exists, it is fair to hold one person responsible for statements that are made in furtherance of the conspiracy, at least while the conspiracy continues, it is essential for the trial judge to make a fair finding that a conspiracy does exist. We do not believe that it is unduly burdensome for the government to meet the preponderance of the evidence standard by using the independent evidence alone.

Of course, the statements themselves must be considered when the issue of whether they are in furtherance of the conspiracy arises, since the contents of the statement will be important in making this determination.

A number of courts have struggled with the question of what kind of hearing should be held when ruling on the admissibility of conspirators' statements. With respect to many hearsay questions, and many other questions of evidence law that the judge decides, it is possible to have a hearing outside the presence of the jury in which the judge listens to all relevant evidence in order to make the preliminary determination on the question of admissibility. When conspirators' statements are offered, this procedure often is unrealistic. It may be that the independent evidence that the government relies on amounts to most of the government's case. To make the government put on that evidence in a preliminary hearing is to try the case twice. Thus, a trial judge in federal court often will allow the government to introduce conspirators' statements with the promise that sufficient independent evidence will be offered to convince the judge to make a ruling, using the preponderance of the evidence standard, that a conspiracy has been proven on the basis of independent evidence. If the government fails to keep its promise, any conspirators' statements that had been conditionally admitted will be stricken, or a mistrial will be declared when that is necessary to protect the accused. *See* ¶ 74 *a* (2) of the *Manual* which has been amended to deal with the trial judge's instructional responsibilities in this area. Some courts have suggested that the government should try to offer its independent evidence first, before offering conspirators' statements. This is a suggestion that may work in a simple conspiracy case, but that will cause problems that may disrupt any orderly mode of proof in a complex case. There probably is no escape from the proposition that unless courts are willing to take the time to have hearings that are not much different from full scale trials, they may have to rely on representations by government counsel as to the sufficiency of the independent evidence. One technique that some judges have used is to ask the government to state orally or in writing the independent evidence that it intends to rely upon. This gives the judge a chance to make an initial judgment as to whether the independent evidence is so weak that the government should be compelled to put it on first before offering conspirators' statements. Also, the trial judge who has an initial statement from the government describing the independent evidence could decide to have a preliminary hearing in some cases, especially when the independent evidence is weak, the conspirators' statements are critical to the government's case, and it might appear unfair to the bench to make the accused stand trial before a decision is made on the admissibility of the conspirators' statements.

There is a dispute among the civilian courts over the timing for a ruling on the admissibility of conspirators' statements which have been conditionally admitted — *i.e.,* on the condition that the judge ultimately find by a preponderance of the evidence that a conspiracy exists, that the person who made the statement was a member of the conspiracy, that the person against whom it is offered also is a member of the conspiracy, that the conspiracy was ongoing at the time the statement was made and that the statement was in furtherance of the conspiracy. It seems that in all the federal circuits, trial judges must rule at the conclusion of the government's case on the admissibility of conspirators' statements. If the government has satisfied the preponderance standard at this time, this is not the end of the matter. It is important to recall that the defendant will not yet have presented evidence. In any ordinary hearing on an evidence question, both sides have a chance to be heard, and this should be true also under the conspirators' hearsay rule. Thus, the trial judge should reconsider the preponderance of the evidence ruling at the close of all the evidence. In some circuits, it is at this time that the judge makes a formal ruling to admit evidence. In other circuits the judge simply reconsiders a prior formal ruling. The difference is not important.

It should be noted that just as the trial judge must decide that a conspiracy exists before admitting statements under (d)(2)(E), the judge must make a similar determination under subdivision (d)(2)(C) and (D). Under these subdivisions the judge must decide that someone is indeed authorized or actually an agent before admitting statements.

The fact that a statement qualifies for admission under Rule 801 does not necessarily mean that a confrontation challenge cannot be made. But, after *Dutton v. Evans,* 400 U.S. 74 (1970), it is not likely that a challenge will succeed.

One familiar class of admissions, statements by predecessors in interest, is not included within Rule 801(d). As noted above, it is doubtful that the residual exceptions found in Rules 803 and 804 can be expanded to cover admissions, since admissions are not treated as exceptions by the Military Rules of Evidence; they are just non-hearsay. Thus, statements by predecessors in interest will be excluded when offered for their truth unless they qualify under some exception to the hearsay rule — e.g., they are declarations against interest. This should serve as a reminder that when statements are offered that fall within the basic hearsay definition of Rule 801(c), counsel must consult Rule 801(d) as well as both Rules 803 and 804 before being able to decide whether the statement is likely to be admitted.

Finally, counsel always should keep in mind that statements that are not offered for their truth need not satisfy either Rule 801(d) or Rules 803 or 804. This is important in thinking about statements like conspirators' statements, which may be offered as acts of the conspiracy, not for their truth. If this is the case, there is no need to struggle with the tricky problems of Rule 801(d)(2)(E).

DRAFTERS' ANALYSIS

(a) Statement. Rule 801 (a) is taken from the Federal Rule without change and is similar to ¶ 139*a* of the present *Manual.*

(b) Declarant. Rule 801 (b) is taken from the Federal Rule verbatim and is the same definition used in present military practice.

(c) Hearsay. Rule 801 (c) is taken from the Federal Rule verbatim. It is similar to the present *Manual* definition, found in ¶ 139*a*, which states: "A statement which is offered in evidence to prove the truth of the matters stated therein, but which was not made by the author when a witness before the court at a hearing in which it is so offered, is hearsay." Although the two definitions are basically identical, they actually differ sharply as a result of the Rule's exceptions which are discussed *infra.*

(d) Statements which are not hearsay. Rule 801 (d) is taken from the Federal Rule without change and removes certain categories of evidence from the definition of hearsay. In all cases, those categories represent hearsay within the meaning of the present *Manual* definition.

 (1) Prior statement by witness. Rule 801 (d) (1) is taken from the Federal Rule without change and removes certain prior statements by the witness from the definition of hearsay. Under the present *Manual* rule, an out-of-court statement not within an exception to the hearsay rule and unadopted by the testifying witness, is inadmissible hearsay notwithstanding the fact that the declarant is now on the stand and able to be cross-examined, ¶ 139*a; United States v. Burge,* 1 M.J. 408 (C.M.A. 1976) (Cook, J., concurring). The justification for the present *Manual* rule is presumably the traditional view that out of court statements cannot be adequately tested by cross-examination because of the time differential between the making of the statement and the giving of the in-court testimony. The Federal Rules of Evidence Advisory Committee rejected this view in part believing both that later cross-examination is sufficient to ensure reliability and that earlier statements are usually preferable to later ones because of the possibility of memory loss. *See generally,* 4 J. WEINSTEIN & M. BERGER, WEINSTEIN'S EVIDENCE ¶ 801 (d) (1) [01] (1978). Rule 801 (d) (1) thus not only makes an important shift in the military theory of hearsay, but also makes an important change in law by making admissible a number of types of statements that are either inadmissible or likely to be inadmissible under present military law.

 Rule 801 (d) (1) (A) makes admissible on the merits a statement inconsistent with the in-court testimony of the witness when the prior statement "was given under oath subject to the penalty of perjury at a trial, hearing, or other proceeding, or in a deposition." The Rule does not require that the witness has been subject to cross-examination at the earlier proceeding, but requires that the witness must have been under oath and subject to penalty of perjury. Although the definition of "trial, hearing, or other proceeding" is uncertain, it is apparent that the Rule was intended to include grand jury testimony and may be extremely broad in scope. *See, e.g., United States v. Castro-Ayon,* 537 F.2d 1055 (9th Cir.), cert. denied, 429 U.S. 983 (1976) (tape recorded statements given under oath at a Boarder Patrol station found to be within the Rule). It should clearly apply to Article 32 hearings. The Rule does require as a prerequisite a statement "given under oath subject to the penalty of perjury." The mere fact that a statement was given under oath may not be sufficient. No foundation other than that indicated as a condition precedent in the Rule is apparently necessary to admit the statement under the Rule. *But see* WEINSTEIN'S EVIDENCE 801-874 (1978).

Rule 801 (d) (1) (B) makes admissible on the merits a statement consistent with the in-court testimony of the witness and "offered to rebut an express or implied charge against the declarant of recent fabrication or improper influence or motive." Unlike Rule 801 (d) (1) (A), the earlier consistent statement need not have been made under oath or at any type of proceeding. On its face, the Rule does not require that the consistent statement offered has been made prior to the time the improper influence or motive arose or prior to the alleged recent fabrication. Notwithstanding this, at least two circuits have read such a requirement into the rule, *United States v. Quinto*, 582 F.2d 224 (2d Cir. 1978); *United States v. Scholle*, 553 F.2d 1109 (8th Cir. 1977). *See also United States v. Dominguez*, 604 F.2d 304 (4th Cir. 1979).

The propriety of this limitation is clearly open to question. *See generally United States v. Rubin*, 609 F.2d 51 (2d Cir. 1979). The limitation does not, however, prevent admission of consistent statements made after the inconsistent statement but before the improper influence or motive arose. *United States v. Scholle, supra*. Rule 801 (d) (1) (B) provides a possible means to admit evidence of fresh complaint in prosecutions of sexual offenses. Although limited to circumstances in which there is a charge, for example, of recent fabrication, the Rule, when applicable, would permit not only the fact of fresh complaint, as is presently possible, but also the entire portion of the consistent statement.

Under Rule 801 (d) (1) (C) a statement of identification is not hearsay. The content of the statement as well as the fact of identification is admissible. This Rule must be read in conjunction with Rule 321 which governs the admissibility of statements of pretrial identification.

(2) Admission by party opponent. Rule 801 (d) (2) eliminates a number of categories of statements from the scope of the hearsay rule. Unlike those statements within the purview of Rule 802 (d) (1), these statements would have come within the exceptions to the hearsay rule as recognized in the *Manual*. Consequently, their "reclassification" is a matter of academic interest only. No practical difference results. The reclassification results from a belief that the adversary system impels admissibility and that reliability is not a significant factor.

Rule 801 (d) (2) (A) makes admissible against a party a statement made in either the party's individual or representative capacity. This is treated as an admission or confession under ¶ 140a of the present *Manual*, and is an exception to the present hearsay rule.

Rule 801 (d) (2) (B) makes admissible "a statement of which the party has manifested the party's adoption or belief in its truth." This is an adoptive admission and is an exception to the present hearsay rule. *Cf.* ¶ 140a(4) of the present *Manual*. While silence may be treated as an admission on the facts of a given case, *see, e.g.*, Rule 304 (h) (3) and the analysis thereto, under Rule 801 (a) (2) that silence must have been intended by the declarant to have been an assertion. Otherwise, the statement will not be hearsay within the meaning of Rule 801 (a) (2) and will presumably be admissible, if at all, as circumstantial evidence.

Rule 801 (d) (2) (C) makes admissible "a statement by a person authorized by the party to make a statement concerning the subject." While this is not expressly dealt with by the *Manual*, it would be admissible under present law as an admission; *cf.* ¶ 140b, utilizing agency theory.

Rule 801 (d) (2) (D) makes admissible "a statement by the party's agent or servant concerning a matter within the scope of the agency or employment of the agent or servant, made during the existence of the relationship." These statements would appear to be admissible under present law. Statements made by interpreters, as by an individual serving as a translator for a servicemember in a foreign nation who is, for example, attempting to consummate a drug transaction with a non-English speaking person, should be admissible under Rule 801 (d) (2) (D) or Rule 801 (d) (2) (C).

Rule 801 (d) (2) (E) makes admissible "a statement by a co-conspirator of a party during the course and in furtherance of the conspiracy." This is similar to the military hearsay exception found in ¶ 140*b* of the present *Manual.* Whether a conspiracy existed for purposes of this Rule is solely a matter for the military judge. Although this is the prevailing Article III rule, it is also the consequence of the Military Rules' modification to Federal Rule of Evidence 104(b). Rule 801 (d) (2) (E) does not address many critical procedural matters associated with the use of co-conspirator evidence. *See generally* Comment, *Restructuring the Independent Evidence Requirement of the Coconspirator Hearsay Exception,* 127 U. Pa. L. Rev. 1439 (1979). For example, the burden of proof placed on the proponent is unclear although a preponderance appears to be the developing Article III trend. Similarly, there is substantial confusion surrounding the question of whether statements of an alleged co-conspirator may themselves be considered by the military judge when determining whether the declarant was in fact a co-conspirator. This process, known as bootstrapping, is not permitted under present military law. *See, e.g., United States v. Duffy,* 49 C.M.R. 208, 210 (A.F.C.M.R. 1974); *United States v. LaBossiere,* 13 C.M.A. 337, 339, 32 C.M.R. 337, 339 (1962). A number of circuits have suggested that Rule 104(a) allows the use of such statements, but at least two circuits have held that other factors prohibit bootstrapping. *United States v. James,* 590 F.2d 575 (5th Cir.) (en banc), cert. denied, 442 U.S. 917 (1979); *United States v. Cambindo Valencia,* 609 F.2d 603 (2d Cir. 1979). Until such time as the Article III practice is settled, discretion would dictate that present military law be followed and that bootstrapping not be allowed. Other procedural factors may also prove troublesome although not to the same extent as bootstrapping. For example, it appears to be appropriate for the military judge to determine the co-conspirator question in a preliminary Article 39(a) session. Although receipt of evidence "subject to later connection" or proof is legally possible, the probability of serious error, likely requiring a mistrial, is apparent.

Rule 801(d)(2)(E) does not appear to change what may be termed the "substantive law" relating to statements made by co-conspirators. Thus, whether a statement was made by a co-conspirator in furtherance of a conspiracy is a question for the military judge, and a statement made by an individual after he or she has withdrawn from a conspiracy is not made "in furtherance of the conspiracy."

Official statements made by an officer — as by the commanding officer of a battalion, squadron, or ship, or by a staff officer, in an indorsement or other communication — are not excepted from the operation of the hearsay rule merely by reason of the official character of the communication or the rank or position of the officer making it.

The following examples of admissiblity under this Rule may be helpful:

(1) A is being tried for assaulting B. The defense presents the testimony of C that just before the assault C heard B say to A that B was about to kill A with B's knife. The testimony of C is not hearsay, for it is offered to show that A acted in self-defense because B made the statement and not to prove the truth of B's statement.

(2) A is being tried for the rape of B. If B testifies at trial, the testimony of B that she had previously identified A as her attacker at an identification lineup would be admissible under Rule 801 ((d) (1) (C) to prove that it was A who raped B.

(3) Private A is being tried for disobedience of a certain order given him orally by Lieutenant B. C is able to testify that he heard Lieutenant B give the order to A. This testimony, including testimony of C as to the terms of the order, would not be hearsay.

(4) The accused is being tried for the larceny of clothes from a locker. A is able to testify that B told A that B saw the accused leave the quarters in which the locker was located with a bundle resembling clothes about the same time the clothes were stolen. This testimony from A would not be admissible to prove the facts stated by B.

(5) The accused is being tried for wrongfully selling government clothing. A policeman is able to testify that while on duty he saw the accused go into a shop with a bundle under his arm; that he entered the shop and the accused ran away; that he was unable to catch the accused; and that thereafter the policeman asked the proprietor of the shop what the accused was doing there; and that the proprietor replied that the accused sold him some uniforms for which he paid the accused $30. Testimony by the policeman as to the reply of the proprietor would be hearsay if it was offered to prove the facts stated by the proprietor. The fact that the policeman was acting in the line of his duty at the time the proprietor made the statement would not render the evidence admissible to prove the truth of the statement.

(6) A defense witness in an assault case testifies on direct examination that the accused did not strike the alleged victim. On cross-examination by the prosecution, the witness admits that at a preliminary investigation he stated that the accused had struck the alleged victim. The testimony of the witness as to this statement will be admissible if he was under oath at that time and subject to a prosecution for perjury.

Rule 802. Hearsay Rule

Hearsay is not admissible except as provided by these rules or by any Act of Congress applicable in trials by court-martial.

EDITORIAL COMMENT

The military's adoption of Rule 802, borrowed from Federal Rule 802, redefines much of military hearsay practice. It states that hearsay is not admissible unless these Military Rules or an act of Congress made specifically applicable to court-martial practice provide otherwise. The federal version of this Rule is similar, but also recognizes the Supreme Court's power to promulgate hearsay provisions.

Under ¶ 139a of the previous *Manual,* hearsay evidence not covered by an exception was *incompetent,* not merely inadmissible. The distinction was important. For example, if an accused were charged with larceny and the only evidence establishing lawful ownership in someone other than the accused were proved through inadmissible hearsay evidence, an appellate court would have reversed, even though the defense made no objection to this evidence. *See, e.g., United States v. Zone,* 7 M.J. 21 (C.M.A. 1979).

Rule 802, in conjunction with Rule 103(a) and (d) may now alter the treatment such evidence will receive on appeal. Since Rule 802 makes hearsay evidence only inadmissible, counsel's failure to object waives the delict, unless plain error is found.

The drafters of Rule 802 intended it to eliminate judicial power to create new hearsay exceptions. The Rule states that only Congress may create such Rules. Congress, acting through the President and Article 36(a) of the Uniform Code of Military Justice, has provided all the available exceptions. *See also* Rule 801(d) which provides exemptions from the ban on hearsay evidence. This means only that new categories of exceptions may not be created judicially. It should be noted, however, that Rules 803(24) and 804(b)(5) allow for hearsay evidence to be admitted on a case-by-case basis, even though it would not be admissible under any specific exception. In order to meet both Rules' requirements, counsel must satisfy criteria aimed at assuring the evidence's truthful character and the trial court's need for the evidence, as well as providing opposing counsel with advance notice of its intended use. Congress intended that both Rules not be used so as to provide an escape from Rule 802. If the evidence is admissible under the residual exceptions it must be because of the particular circumstances at bar. Federal decisions appear in accord, emphasizing as they do a narrow construction of the residual exceptions. *See, e.g., United States v. White,* 611 F.2d 531 (5th Cir. 1980).

DRAFTERS' ANALYSIS

Rule 802 is taken generally from the Federal Rule but has been modified to recognize the application of any applicable Act of Congress.

Although the basic rule of inadmissibility for hearsay is identical with that found in ¶ 139a of the present *Manual,* there is a substantial change in military practice as a result of Rule 103(a). Under the present *Manual*, hearsay is incompetent evidence and does not require an objection to be inadmissible. Under the new Rules, however, admission of hearsay will not be error unless there is an objection to the hearsay. *See* Rule 103(a).

Rule 803. Hearsay Exceptions; Availability of Declarant Immaterial

The following are not excluded by the hearsay rule, even though the declarant is available as a witness:

(1) Present sense impression. A statement describing or explaining an event or condition made while the declarant was perceiving the event or condition or immediately thereafter.

(2) Excited utterance. A statement relating to a startling event or condition made while the declarant was under the stress of excitement caused by the event or condition.

(3) Then existing mental, emotional, or physical condition. A statement of the declarant's then existing state of mind, emotion, sensation, or physical condition (such as intent, plan, motive, design, mental feeling, pain, and bodily health), but not including a statement of memory or belief to prove the fact remembered or believed unless it relates to the execution, revocation, identification, or terms of declarant's will.

(4) Statements for purposes of medical diagnosis or treatment. Statements made for purposes of medical diagnosis or treatment and describing medical history, or past or present symptoms, pain, or sensations, or the inception or general character of the cause or external source thereof insofar as reasonably pertinent to diagnosis or treatment.

(5) Recorded recollection. A memorandum or record concerning a matter about which a witness once had knowledge but now has insufficient recollection to enable the witness to testify fully and accurately, shown to have been made or adopted by the witness when the matter was fresh in the witness's memory and to reflect that knowledge correctly. If admitted, the memorandum or record may be read into evidence, but may not itself be received as an exhibit unless offered by an adverse party.

(6) Records of regularly conducted activity. A memorandum, report, record, or data compilation, in any form, of acts, events, conditions, opinions, or diagnoses, made at or near the time by, or from information transmitted by, a person with knowledge, if kept in the course of a regularly conducted business activity, and if it was the regular practice of that business activity to make the memorandum, report, record, or data compilation, all as shown by the testimony of the custodian or other qualified

witness, unless the source of information or the method or circumstances of preparation indicate lack of trustworthiness. The term "business" as used in this paragraph includes the armed forces, a business, institution, association, profession, occupation, and calling of every kind, whether or not conducted for profit. Among those memoranda, reports, records, or data compilations normally admissible pursuant to this paragraph are enlistment papers, physical examination papers, outline-figure and fingerprint cards, forensic laboratory reports, chain of custody documents, morning reports and other personnel accountability documents, service records, officer and enlisted qualification records, logs, unit personnel diaries, individual equipment records, daily strength records of prisoners, and rosters of prisoners.

(7) Absence of entry in records kept in accordance with the provisions of paragraph (6). Evidence that a matter is not included in the memoranda, reports, records, or data compilations, in any form, kept in accordance with the provisions of paragraph (6), to prove the nonoccurrence or nonexistence of the matter, if the matter was of a kind of which a memorandum, report, record, or data compilation was regularly made and preserved, unless the sources of information or other circumstances indicate lack of trustworthiness.

(8) Public records and reports. Records, reports, statements, or data compilations, in any form, of public office or agencies, setting forth (A) the activities of the office or agency, or (B) matters observed pursuant to duty imposed by law as to which matters there was a duty to report, excluding, however, matters observed by police officers and other personnel acting in a law enforcement capacity, or (C) against the government, factual findings resulting from an investigation made pursuant to authority granted by law, unless the sources of information or other circumstances indicate lack of trustworthiness. Notwithstanding (B), the following are admissible under this paragraph as a record of a fact or event if made by a person within the scope of the person's official duties and those duties included a duty to know or to ascertain through appropriate and trustworthy channels of information the truth of the fact or event and to record such fact or event: enlistment papers, physical examination papers, outline-figure and fingerprint cards, forensic

laboratory reports, chain of custody documents, morning reports and other personnel accountability documents, service records, officer and enlisted qualification records, records of court-martial convictions, logs, unit personnel diaries, individual equipment records, guard reports, daily strength records of prisoners, and rosters of prisoners.

(9) ***Records of vital statistics.*** Records or data compilations, in any form, of births, fetal deaths, deaths, or marriages, if the report thereof was made to a public office pursuant to requirements of law.

(10) ***Absence of public record or entry.*** To prove the absence of a record, report, statement, or data compilation in any form, or the nonoccurrence or nonexistence of a matter of which a record, report, statement, or data compilation, in any form, was regularly made and preserved by a public office or agency, evidence in the form of a certification in accordance with rule 902, or testimony, that diligent search failed to disclose the record, report, statement, or data compilation, or entry.

(11) ***Records of religious organizations.*** Statements of births, marriages, divorces, deaths, legitimacy, ancestry, relationship by blood or marriage, or other similar facts of personal or family history contained in a regularly kept record of a religious organization.

(12) ***Marriage, baptismal, and similar certificates.*** Statements of fact contained in a certificate that the maker performed a marriage or other ceremony or administered a sacrament, made by a clergyman, public official, or other person authorized by the rules or practices of a religious organization or by law to perform the act certified, and purporting to have been issued at the time of the act or within a reasonable time thereafter.

(13) ***Family records.*** Statements of fact concerning personal or family history contained in family Bibles, genealogies, charts, engravings on rings, inscriptions on family portraits, engravings on urns, crypts, or tombstones, or the like.

(14) ***Records of documents affecting an interest in property.*** The record of a document purporting to establish or affect an interest in property, as proof of the content of the original recorded document and its execution and delivery by each person by whom it purports to have been executed, if the record is a record of a public office and an applicable statute authorizes the recording of documents of that kind in that office.

(15) Statements in documents affecting an interest in property. A statement contained in a document purporting to establish or affect an interest in property if the matter stated was relevant to the purpose of the document, unless dealings with the property since the document was made have been inconsistent with the truth of the statement or the purport of the document.

(16) Statements in ancient documents. Statements in a document in existence twenty years or more the authenticity of which is established.

(17) Market reports, commercial publications. Market quotations, tabulations, directories, lists (including government price lists), or other published compilations, generally used and relied upon by the public or by persons in particular occupations.

(18) Learned treatises. To the extent called to the attention of an expert witness upon cross-examination or relied upon by the expert in direct examination, statements contained in published treatises, periodicals, or pamphlets on a subject of history, medicine or other science or art, established as a reliable authority by the testimony or admission of the witness or by other expert testimony or by judicial notice. If admitted, the statements may be read into evidence but may not be received as exhibits.

(19) Reputation concerning personal or family history. Reputation among members of the person's family by blood, adoption, or marriage, or among the person's associates, or in the community, concerning the person's birth, adoption, marriage, divorce, death, legitimacy, relationship by blood, adoption, or marriage, ancestry, or other similar fact of the person's personal or family history.

(20) Reputation concerning boundaries or general history. Reputation in a community, arising before the controversy, as to boundaries of or customs affecting lands in the community, and reputation as to events of general history important to the community or State or nation in which located.

(21) Reputation as to character. Reputation of a person's character among the person's associates or in the community.

(22) Judgment of previous conviction. Evidence of a final judgment, entered after a trial or upon a plea of guilty (but not upon a plea of nolo contendere), adjudging a person guilty of a crime punishable by death, dishonorable discharge, or imprisonment in excess of one year, to prove any fact essential to

sustain the judgment, but not including, when offered by the Government for purposes other than impeachment, judgments against persons other than the accused. The pendency of an appeal may be shown but does not affect admissibility. In determining whether a crime tried by court-martial was punishable by death, dishonorable discharge, or imprisonment in excess of one year, the maximum punishment prescribed by the President under Article 56 at the time of the conviction applies without regard to whether the case was tried by general, special, or summary court-martial.

(23) Judgment as to personal, family or general history, or boundaries. Judgments as proof of matters of personal, family, or general history, or boundaries essential to the judgment, if the same would be provable by evidence of reputation.

(24) Other exceptions. A statement not specifically covered by any of the foregoing exceptions but having equivalent circumstantial guarantees of trustworthiness, if the court determines that (A) the statement is offered as evidence of a material fact; (B) the statement is more probative on the point for which it is offered than any other evidence which the proponent can procure through reasonable efforts; and (C) the general purposes of these rules and the interests of justice will best be served by admission of the statement into evidence. However, a statement may not be admitted under this exception unless the proponent of it makes known to the adverse party sufficiently in advance of the trial or hearing to provide the adverse party with a fair opportunity to prepare to meet it, the intention to offer the statement and the particulars of it, including the name and address of the declarant.

EDITORIAL COMMENT

When read together, Rules 801(d), 803 and 804 present an organized codification of hearsay authority. Rule 801(d) excludes from the basic definition of hearsay (801(c)) much of what the military and common law traditionally labeled hearsay; 804 provides hearsay exceptions applicable when the declarant is unavailable; and 803 lists hearsay exceptions applicable whether or not the declarant is available. However, 801(d), 803 and 804 only provide that evidence falling within these exceptions is not excluded. Nothing in the Rules requires such evidence to be admitted. In order to reach the finder of facts, the evidence still will have to satisfy authentication, best evidence and relevancy criteria. Even then the trial judge may exclude it under Rule 403 as being substantially more prejudicial than probative. Defense counsel can also object that such evidence violates the Sixth Amendment's confrontation clause.

Rule 803 lists 24 exceptions to the general hearsay prohibition found in Rule 802. Twenty-three cover specific categories of exceptions. There is one residual exception at the end. Because the 803 exceptions are so expansive, it can be helpful to consider them by categories. The numbered paragraphs of the Rule will be referred to either as exception (1), etc., or paragraph (1), etc., in the rest of this comment.

The first category, paragraphs (1) through (4), concerns the admissibility of evidence dealing with the declarant's state of mind, emotional or physical condition.

Exception (1) is taken from the Federal Rules without change. It is similar to the *Manual's* past treatment of spontaneous exclamations. Under paragraph (1), the present sense impression of a declarant is admissible if it describes or explains an event or condition and was made while in the act of perceiving an event or condition or immediately thereafter.

At common law, this evidence was often referred to as "res gestae" (a term also used by various courts to describe exceptions (2), (3), and (4)). Commentators have thoroughly discredited the term as being virtually meaningless and it is not used in this Rule. Wigmore, for example, described res gestae as being so ambiguous and potentially harmful that it "ought therefore wholly to be repudiated as a vicious element in our legal phraseology." 6 WIGMORE, EVIDENCE § 1767, at 182 (3d ed. 1940).

The common law treatment of present sense impression evidence generally required that an exciting event trigger the statement. Although this necessity is now confined to another exception — excited utterances under paragraph (2) — the Rule still seeks to avoid calculated or planned statements when possible, because these are not as likely to be as sincere as spontaneous statements. Thus, the Rule applies only to statements made at the time of the event or immediately thereafter. The term "immediately thereafter" is not defined in the Rule or its drafters' *Analysis.* To avoid undue extension of this exception, we believe that a statement must be made as soon as the opportunity to speak arises. *See Wolfson v. Mutual Life Insurance Co. of New York,* 455 F. Supp. 82 (M.D. Pa.), aff'd, 588 F.2d 825 (3d Cir. 1978) (one hour is too long a time gap). *But see United States v. Blakey,* 607 F.2d 779 (7th Cir. 1979) (23 minutes is acceptable). The burden is on the person who claims the benefit of this or another exception to show entitlement to it. *See United States v. Cain,* 587 F.2d 678 (5th Cir.), cert. denied, 440 U.S. 975 (1979).

Exception (2), identical to the Federal Rule, permits a declarant's excited utterance to be admitted. The Rule, like its federal counterpart, recognizes that statements made during a startling event or while under the stress of excitement, possess inherent reliability. The excitement and associated spontaneity remove an opportunity for calculation. However, the commentators have noted that such circumstances may also cause error in perception and interpretation leading to inaccurate statements.

In distinguishing between paragraphs (1) and (2) of the Rule, it should be noted that while (1) allows statements explaining or describing the event to be admitted, statements falling under (2) must only "relate" to the startling event itself. *See, e.g., United States v. Napier,* 518 F.2d 316 (9th Cir.), cert. denied, 423 U.S. 895 (1975). The drafters properly note that the Rule does not on its face require independent proof of the startling event, but the trial judge under Rule 104(a) must find that the exception is satisfied before admitting evidence. Usually this will involve independent evidence, since somehow the judge must find excitement.

Paragraph (3) exempts a statement of the declarant's then existing state of mind, emotional or physical condition from the hearsay ban. This Rule concerns such issues as intent, motive, design or plan as well as statements concerning physical or mental ailments. The Rule generally does not permit evidence of present memory or belief to prove the existence of a past condition or fact. The Rule thus follows the Supreme Court's traditional distinction between statements of present status (including forward-looking statements — *see Mutual Life Insurance Co. v. Hillmon,* 145 U.S. 285 (1892) — which do not present memory problems) and backwards-looking statements which do. *See Shepard v. United States,* 290 U.S. 96 (1933). An exception to the memory prohibition is created for memory relating to the execution, revocation, identification or tenor of the declarant's will. The legislative history of this "exception to the exception" indicates the drafters of the Federal Rule felt that such evidence was especially necessary in will contests and that a person could be trusted to recall accurately his actions in connection with disposition of his property.

The following examples help demonstrate the military's codification of the Rule. Assume the declarant said, "I'm going to miss tomorrow's morning formation," and he subsequently failed to appear. This statement may be introduced against the declarant to show his intention to be away. However, if the declarant stated, "I missed yesterday's formation," that statement is inadmissible under exception (3) to show that he was not present. A memory problem arises with the second statement.

The federal drafters may have intended Rule 803(3) to permit statements to be used only to show the declarant's state of mind. If so, then a declaration that the declarant and another individual intended to miss formation would not be admissible to show what the other individual did. The military drafters' *Analysis* appears to have adopted this view of the Rule, although it is not clear that the drafters of the Federal Rule were so restrictive. Most, but not all, courts have permitted these declarations to be used to show what both persons did. *See, e.g., United States v. Pheaster,* 544 F.2d 353 (9th Cir. 1976), cert. denied, sub nom. *Inciso v. United States,* 429 U.S. 1099 (1977).

The same logic applies to statements of existing physical conditions. The declarant's protestation, "my arm hurts" falls within the exception, while his statement, "my arm hurt yesterday" is excluded when both are offered for their truth.

Exception (4) allows statements made for the purpose of medical diagnosis or treatment to be admitted when they describe the declarant's medical history, past or present symptoms, or sensations. While 803(4) is identical with the federal rule, it is broader than its military precursor in that it admits evidence which describes the inception, general character or external cause of the injury, as long as this evidence is reasonably pertinent to diagnosis or treatment.

Rule 803(4) does not appear to be limited to statements made to doctors for treatment purposes. It includes doctors who diagnose as well as those who treat. For some reason the drafters' *Analysis* appears to miss this point. Any doubt that the Rule is meant to cover diagnosing physicians is removed if one looks to the Advisory Committee's Note accompanying Federal Rule 803(4) from which the Military Rule is taken.

Under the Rule, statements need not be made directly to a physician; they need only be made for the purpose of diagnosis or treatment. Thus, statements to nurses or hospital staff or ambulance personnel would qualify under the Rule. And the statements need not have come from the patient. Statements of family members and friends may qualify.

Although there is overlap between (3) and (4), Rule 803(4) does extend paragraph (3) in two important aspects. First, it allows evidence of the individual's medical history (*i.e.,* backwards-looking statements) to be admitted as an exception to the hearsay rule. Second, statements relating to the cause of an injury, pain or sensation may be admitted if reasonably necessary to the doctor's treatment or diagnosis. This means that statements concerning *who* caused the injury are unlikely to be admissible, but statements describing *how* and *when* the injury occurred will be admissible. The Rule depends on the expertise of doctors to ferret out false statements.

Before leaving this first category of exceptions, it is important to note that the drafters have not included a provision admitting evidence of "fresh complaint" here. Paragraph 142c of the prior *Manual* allowed such evidence to be admitted in sexual offense prosecutions. Its use was limited to proving that the victim complained and identified the offender. The evidence was admissible only for "corroborating the testimony of the victim." Even though no specific mention has been made of fresh complaint in the new Rules, the drafters indicate that paragraphs (1) through (4) may be used to prove many of the same things that fell within the former fresh complaint Rule.

Exceptions (5) through (18) concern the admissibility of writings or documents. These exceptions are particularly important in court-martial practice due to the world-wide nature of military jurisdiction, the unavailability of witnesses resulting from lack of subpoena power outside the United States, discharged and unlocatable witnesses within the United States, and the impracticability of transporting obtainable witnesses thousands of miles between their present duty station and the situs of trial. Many of these Rules are copied directly from the Federal Rules. Two exceptions, (6) and (8), are substantially different and deserve special attention.

Paragraph (5) is identical to the Federal Rule and similar to ¶ 146a and ¶ 149 c(1)(b) of the previous *Manual*. It provides that when a witness has no present recollection concerning matters he once knew, a memorandum or record displaying his past knowledge can be used to prove that knowledge. The document or memorandum must have been adopted by the witness when the information was fresh in the witness' mind. It must also accurately reflect what the knowledge once was. If the trial judge admits the memorandum or record, it may be read into evidence. This procedure is different than prior *Manual* practice which allowed the proponent to admit the document. The federal drafters felt that permitting the triers of fact to obtain the document and take it to the deliberation room with them unfairly emphasized the evidence. Although the proponent cannot present the document to the fact-finders the opponent may do so, if he wishes, in order to establish some inconsistency or inaccuracy.

The guarantee of reliability is found in the timing requirements of the Rule and the opportunity to examine the declarant about the circumstances in which the statement was made. Note that oral statements that were not recorded when made, do not qualify under the Rule.

In order to use 803(5) counsel must first establish that the witness' memory is impaired. Once this is accomplished, counsel should attempt to refresh the witness' recollection with the document. *See* Rule 612. If memory cannot be refreshed, then the document's contents will be admissible. This sequence of events is recommended because it places a premium upon the witness' ability to testify, and not on the recordation of that testimony. If recollection can be refreshed with the document, then the witness may testify and be fully cross-examined.

The next important criterion here is that the record must have been made when the information was fresh in the witness' mind. It is of no consequence that the witness himself did not make the recording; what is important is that the witness, at some time prior to the court-martial, adopted the information contained in the document. Also, it should be satisfactory if the witness made an oral statement and someone else accurately recorded it. At least, we think this is the intent of the drafters. However, Congress changed the wording of the Rule so that on its face it appears to require that the witness has made or adopted the statement. At common law it was enough if the witness made the statement and someone else wrote it down as long as both were present to testify. We believe that the common law approach still is valid in view of Congress' desire to expand, not contract, the Federal Rule despite unfortunate drafting.

Exception (6) permits records of regularly conducted activities to be admitted as an exception to the hearsay rule. The guarantee of reliability is in the regularity of the record-keeping and the reliance of the business on the records. The military provision is taken generally from the Federal Rule, but the definition of "business" is expanded and a final sentence has been added by the military drafters to address Court of Military Appeals decisions in the area. A business entry can be defined as:

(a) Any memorandum, report or data compilation;

(b) Concerning acts, events, opinions or diagnosis;

(c) When made at or near the time of the event;

(d) From information transmitted by a person with a duty to the business and with knowledge of the information;

(e) If the information was recorded in the regular course of business;

(f) And it was the regular practice of the business to record such information.

The drafters intended that the word "memorandum" should be broadly construed so that virtually any document will satisfy its mandate. Similarly, the military drafters have defined the word "business" in its broadest sense to specifically include the armed forces. This exception also allows opinions to be admitted as business entries. Prior military practice required live testimony for such evidence.

Paragraph (6) plainly requires an adequate foundation for every business record. Past military practice allowed evidence custodians and unit personnel clerks to lay the foundation. We foresee no change in this practice with the adoption of the new exception.

Opposing counsel will generally attack the offer of a business document on the ground that its lack of trustworthiness requires exclusion. This could mean that the document's author was not being provided with accurate or reliable information. It could also mean that because the document was prepared with a view toward prosecution, the author, as well as those feeding him information, had a motive to lie. *Manual* ¶ 144*d* prohibited statements from qualifying as business records if made principally with a view toward prosecution. It is unlikely that much will change now that the specific prohibition is removed, since documents made with an eye to use at trial are not likely to be viewed as ordinary business records.

The last sentence of paragraph (6) will cause military practitioners the most concern. It specifically makes admissible government and police documents which are often used to prepare the prosecution's case. Some of these previously have been held inadmissible. The two most important examples under this Rule concern forensic laboratory reports and chain of custody documents. Both of these are integral aspects of drug prosecutions.

In the past, the Court of Military Appeals refused to treat all the evidence falling within 803(6) as presenting the same problem of trustworthiness. In *United States v. Evans,* 21 C.M.A. 579, 45 C.M.R. 353 (1972), and *United States v. Miller,* 23 C.M.A. 247, 49 C.M.R. 380 (1974), the court established that laboratory reports were admissible under the business entry exception to the hearsay rule. Thus, the chemist who analyzed the contraband in question did not have to be produced during the government's case-in-chief, even over defense objections. However, defense counsel could obtain the witness for his case if he wanted to test the chemist's competency or the techniques used in evaluating the evidence. In *United States v. Vietor,* 10 M.J. 69 (C.M.A. 1980) the court stated that in order for defense counsel to actually obtain the chemist's presence at trial, the defense must demonstrate that competency or examination techniques are really in question. Thus, there is no absolute right to the chemist's presence. *See United States v. Strangstalien,* 7 M.J. 225 (C.M.A. 1979) and *United States v. Herrington,* 8 M.J. 194 (C.M.A. 1980), where the court reaffirmed its view that laboratory reports are made by neutral and detached chemists who are not part of the prosecution team, and thus the chemists could be trusted to portray accurately their analyses in the reports. The court chose to find that laboratory reports were, as a result, not made principally for the purposes of prosecution.

The court went in the opposite direction with respect to chain of custody documents. These government forms are used to trace the handling of evidence. They do not warrant that the individuals controlling the substance have failed to alter or tamper with it; they merely determine who handled the evidence. When the government attempted to use chain of custody documents to demonstrate that fungible contraband seized from the accused was the same contraband analyzed by the forensic chemist, the Court of Military Appeals reversed convictions, finding that these documents were prepared by law enforcement personnel who, by definition, were concerned with obtaining convictions. The documents were thus viewed as prosecutorial in nature and inadmissible. *See United States v. Nault,* 4 M.J. 318 (C.M.A. 1978); *United States v. Porter,* 7 M.J. 32 (C.M.A. 1979); and *United States v. Nuetze,* 7 M.J. 30 (C.M.A. 1979). In *United States v. McKinney,* 9 M.J. 86 (C.M.A. 1980) the court affirmed the authority listed above, but in a footnote implied that the Military Rules of Evidence might change things. The court was indeed prescient.

It is interesting to note that the Court of Military Appeals recently has withdrawn from its original position requiring strict tracing of contraband, as explained in *Nault, supra. See United States v. Fowler,* 9 M.J. 149 (C.M.A. 1980); and *United States v. Courts,* 9 M.J. 285 (C.M.A. 1980), which cited *United States v. Lane,* 591 F.2d 961, 962 (D.C. Cir. 1979), among other federal authorities. *See also* our discussion of Rule 901.

Plainly, confrontation challenges will be raised when the last sentence of the Rule is used. *See United States v. Oates,* 560 F.2d 45 (2d Cir. 1977) for a particularly enlightening discussion of the confrontation issue. *Compare* Imwinkelried, *The Constitutionality of Introducing Laboratory Report Against Criminal Defendants,* 30 HASTINGS L.J. 621 (1979) *with* Weinstein, *Three Years of the Federal Rules of Evidence,* N.Y.L.J. 7 February 1978 at 1, col. 2.

We have said that the business duty requirement that is imposed in most jurisdictions still remains part of the Military Rule. The Rule itself does not make this clear, but this is because of a Congressional change in the wording of Federal Rule 803(6) that has found its way into the Military Rule. Congress never expressed any desire to eliminate the business duty requirement, and we believe it is an essential guarantee of the reliability of business records. Most federal courts have recognized this. *See, e.g., United States v. Davis,* 571 F.2d 1354 (5th Cir. 1978); *United States v. Plum,* 558 F.2d 568 (10th Cir. 1977).

Exception (7) is taken verbatim from the Federal Rules and is similar to prior *Manual* authority. It provides that if a specific matter is not noted in a record of regularly conducted activity as described in (6) above, that fact may be shown to prove the nonoccurrence or nonexistence of the matter. The information in question must be the type which would normally have been made in the regular course of activity, and the records consulted must qualify under paragraph (6).

Many commentators believe paragraph (7) is not required because the existence or nonexistence of a record is not hearsay evidence. Legislative history indicates Congress merely wanted to assure that the evidence would be admissible and that it provided an exception just in case one is needed. *See, e.g.,*

United States v. Rich, 580 F.2d 929 (9th Cir.), cert. denied, 439 U.S. 935 (1978).

Exception (8) is one of the most complex and controversial provisions in the Rules. It is a combination of previous *Manual* practice, the Federal Rule, and the military drafters' additions to the Federal Rule. This provision is broader than its federal counterpart, admitting a wide scope of otherwise inadmissible government documents. Like the last sentence of exception (6), the last sentence of this Rule is not consistent with prior federal and military judicial authority and raises Sixth Amendment confrontation issues. Our comments on exception (6) should be consulted when using the final sentence of this Rule.

Public records, reports, statements or data compilations, no matter what their form, may be admissible if they are made by or in a public office or agency and if they satisfy subsection (A), (B) or (C) of the Rule. Records and reports of an agency's activities satisfy (A). The drafters' *Analysis* suggests a useful limitation on the concept of an "activity." Matters observed by someone who had a duty to observe such matters and report them are admissible if contained in public records and reports under subsection (B), except that matters observed by police officers and persons acting in a law enforcement capacity are excluded. (Compare this provision with the last sentence of paragraph (8), discussed *infra*). Unlike (C), (B) does not distinguish between evidence offered by the government and evidence offered by the accused. This has caused problems for civilian courts, since some evidence arguably could fall under either (B) or (C). To avoid a conflict, federal courts have interpreted the exclusion of law enforcement observations only when offered by the government. *See, e.g., United States v. Smith,* 521 F.2d 957 (D.C. Cir. 1975). Subsection (C) of the Rule allows factual findings made pursuant to government authorized investigations to be admitted against the government unless the information is untrustworthy. (It is uncertain whether the "untrustworthy clause" modifies only (C) or all subsections. We believe it probably modifies them all. *Compare* Rule 803(6)). It should be noted that subsection (C) is limited to factual findings, but any finding can involve an evaluation of data or evidence. For a good discussion of evaluative reports, *see Melville v. American Home Assurance Co.,* 443 F. Supp. 1064 (E.D. Pa. 1977), rev'd on other grounds, 584 F.2d 1306 (3d Cir. 1978).

The last sentence of paragraph (8) provides that, notwithstanding (B) and (C), a great many government and police related documents are admissible if they record a fact or event, were made by a person who was acting within his official duties, those duties including the obligation to know or ascertain the information's accuracy and trustworthiness, and that the individual thereafter had the duty to record such factors or events. Once these criteria are established, forensic laboratory reports, chain of custody documents, all officer and enlisted records, finger-print cards and related documents become admissible public records. These records are discussed in connection with exception (6).

The drafters' *Analysis* opines that evidence excluded under Rule 803(8)(B) should probably be excluded also under Rule 803(6), or the former Rule would be meaningless. In our view, this is incorrect. An activity must be regularly conducted under exception (6); it need not be under exception (8). If it is regularly conducted it may be reliable enough to be admitted. If not, then the case for exclusion is strengthened. Many observations not part of regularly conducted activities can be excluded under 803(8)(B) even if some observations occurring during regularly conducted activities are admissible. *See United States v. King,* 613 F.2d 670 (7th Cir. 1980).

Exception (9) concerns the admissibility of records or data compilations made in any form which concern birth, death, marriage and related vital public statistics. The report must have been made to a public office charged by law with collecting such information in order to be admissible as an exception to the hearsay rule.

Exception (10) performs the same function as Rule 803(7). It provides that if a diligent search of public records is made, a document certified in accordance with Rule 902 may be admitted to show the absence of a record or the nonoccurrence or nonexistence of a matter which otherwise would have been recorded. *See, e.g., United States v. Johnson,* 577 F.2d 1304 (5th Cir. 1978); *United States v. Lee,* 589 F.2d 980 (9th Cir. 1979).

Exception (11) is in many ways a combination of Rules 803(6) and 803(10). However, it is broader than both Rules. It allows admission of religious records which establish birth, death, marriage and similar events, even though the transmitting agent does not have a duty to transmit, and even though he has no formal relationship with the religious organization involved. As long as the information in question is kept in the organization's regular course of activity, it will be admissible.

Exception (12) allows marriage, baptism and similar events to be proved by documentary evidence if such documents were executed by the clergyman, public official or other person authorized to conduct the ceremony in question, at the time the ceremony was held, or within a reasonable time thereafter. The Rule provides that practices of the religious organization or a public law be consulted in order to determine whether the maker of the document was authorized to so act.

Exception (13) is well recognized but little used in the federal law. It permits facts concerning family or personal history to be proved through genealogies, family portraits, family Bibles or other related materials.

Exception (14) covers documents that purport to establish or affect an interest in property. The Rule requires that the document used to prove this issue be one that is authorized to be recorded and that it actually be recorded in a public office. The document may be used to prove the contents of the original recorded document and its execution by each person by whom it purports to have been executed.

Exception (15) establishes that statements contained in documents that purport to establish or affect property interests may be used if the matter stated was relevant to the purpose for which the document was created, and if no inconsistent dealings have subsequently occurred.

Exceptions (11), (12), (14) and (15) rest on the assumption that public officials or persons entrusted to perform various ceremonial activities are unlikely to be dishonest. Exception (13) assumes that people generally have no reason to lie in family records.

Exception (16) recognizes that ancient documents may be admitted as an exception to the hearsay rule if the document has been in existence twenty years or more. Of course the common problem in dealing with ancient documents generally does not concern hearsay issues; it concerns authentication problems. *But see* Rule 901(8) (easing authentication requirement). Age is some guarantee that a document is not created to obtain an advantage in litigation.

Exception (17) has been taken from the Federal Rule and ¶ 144f of the *Manual.* It allows market quotations, directories, government pricing lists and any other published compilations to be admitted for the purpose of establishing value or price, for example. The Rule encompasses virtually any published compilation relied upon by the public or persons in a particular occupation. It does not refer, as did the *Manual,* to an absence of entries in reports or publications. *Compare* exceptions (7) and (10).

Exception (18) allows learned treatises to be admitted as an exception to the hearsay rule. Whereas Rule 703 permits an expert to rely on inadmissible data, the instant Rule provides for the use of the contents of learned treatises as substantive evidence. This goes beyond prior *Manual* ¶ 138e. Learned treatises, defined in the Rule as published documents, periodicals or pamphlets concerning medical, scientific, historic or artistic information, may be used in connection with direct or cross-examination of an expert. The exception may not be used except in conjunction with expert testimony. To be used, treatises must be reliable. Reliability can be established through the witness' testimony, through subsequent expert testimony, or by judicial notice. If reliable, the treatise can be used on direct examination if relied upon by the expert, and on cross-examination if called to the attention of the expert. The cross-examiner may use the treatise whether or not the expert agrees that it is reliable and whether or not the expert ever has seen the treatise before. A treatise may be read to the finders of fact, but may not be given to them as an exhibit, unless it is not feasible to read the treatise. *See United States v. Mangan,* 575 F.2d 32 (2d Cir.), cert. denied, 439 U.S. 931 (1978). Both this exception and exception (17) rely on practices to guarantee trustworthiness; courts will use what is relied upon outside of court to govern important decisions.

Paragraphs (19), (20) and (21) cover reputation evidence. Paragraphs (19) and (20) have no counterpart in previous military authority. Paragraph (21) can be traced to ¶ 138f of the *Manual.* Reputation is trusted as to certain matters about which the community is likely to know and when there may be no good substitute evidence.

Exception (19) expands paragraphs (11), (12) and (13) with respect to establishing marriage, divorce, death, legitimacy and related family and personal history matters. Rule 803(19) allows such information to be proved by family reputation testimony, or by reputation testimony from personal associates, community members or related organizations. We believe military organizations and installations will qualify as communities. *See* Rule 405.

Exception (20) is an extension of paragraphs (14) and (15). It permits reputation evidence to be used for the purpose of determining boundaries or community land usage. Such evidence must have existed prior to the court-martial's formation. Paragraph (20) includes reputation evidence dealing with private boundaries and private customs as well.

Exception (21) concerns the type of reputation evidence admitted in Rules 405 and 608. It allows reputation evidence of a person's character among his associates or community members to be admitted as an exception to the hearsay rule. By definition, reputation evidence amounts to what the witness has heard other people say about an individual. These community statements are used and relied upon for their truthfulness.

Rules 803(22) and (23) allow evidence of previous judgments concerning convictions, family history or borders to be admitted as exceptions to the hearsay rule.

Exception (22) admits evidence of a final judgment entered after trial or after a plea of not guilty (not nolo contendere) to be admitted to prove any fact essential to sustaining the judgment. To be admissible, the conviction must be for a crime punishable by death, imprisonment for more than one year, or dishonorable discharge. The reliability comes from the "against interest" aspect of a guilty plea and the proof beyond a reasonable doubt advanced in litigated cases. A party may establish that an appeal from the conviction is pending, but such appeal will not prohibit the fact of conviction from being used. As in Rule 609, the felony characteristics of military offenses are to be measured by Article 56 of the Uniform Code of Military Justice, through ¶ 127 of the *Manual,* and are based on the date of conviction. The exception allows convictions anywhere to be used as evidence. The drafters' *Analysis* suggests that foreign convictions were not contemplated by the authors of the Federal Rules from which the Military Rule is taken. But civilian courts have recognized the legitimate use of foreign convictions. *See, e.g., Lloyd v. American Export Lines,* 580 F.2d 1179 (3d Cir.), cert. denied, 439 U.S. 969 (1978); *cf. United States v. Veltre,* 591 F.2d 347 (5th Cir. 1979) (Rule 609). It is very important to keep in mind that prior convictions are admissible, not conclusive, under the Rule. Still, they may be challenged on confrontation grounds where a judge or court-members convicted but cannot be questioned about the rationale under Rule 606(b).

Exception (23) is linked with paragraphs (19) and (20) described above. This Rule includes evidence of judgments concerning personal, family or property boundaries within the exception. The Rule's legislative history indicates that judgments are sufficiently reliable to justify their admission as substantive evidence.

The legislative history of Federal Rule 803(24) indicates that Congress had substantial doubts about its wisdom. At one point, the House deleted the provision from the Rules. However, the Senate was able to resurrect the Rule after including important restrictions on its use. Many commentators and courts agree that this Rule's history and construction indicate that it should be narrowly construed. *See, e.g., United States v. White,* 611 F.2d 531 (5th Cir. 1980). Because the military drafters did not alter the federal format, it appears that they also intended a restrictive interpretation of the Rule, although the drafters' *Analysis* suggests that if civilian courts become more liberal in using the Rule, military courts may follow suit.

Exception (24) often is known as the "catch-all" or residual exception. It allows hearsay evidence to be admitted even though it does not fall within any specific exception. In order to qualify for admission, the evidence must have circumstantial guarantees of truthworthiness equivalent to those supporting the 23 specific exceptions. Moreover, the trial judge must determine that (A) the statement is offered to prove a material (which we think must mean important) fact; (B) is more probative of the fact than any other evidence reasonably available; and (C) admission of the evidence will not frustrate the interests of justice or the purposes of these Rules.

In order to meet this burden, the proponent will have to address and satisfy each element of the Rule. This is an affirmative obligation; it cannot be satisfied by a general plea for admission. Because paragraph (24) contains so many variables, we believe that without special findings, an appellate court cannot determine whether the trial bench properly evaluated the issues before it. Evidence which may be admissible under this provision is by definition unusual. It does not fit within this Rule's other 23 exceptions; nor does it fit the various exemptions in 801 or the exceptions in 804. As a result, a decision admitting or rejecting the evidence should be accompanied by a reasoned explanation, particularly because the trial bench must simultaneously consider not only the various requirements of the Rule, but also the "interests of justice" and the "general purposes of these rules."

The notice requirement is important. Although the Rule does not specify how far in advance notice must be given, the Rule states that the notice must provide the opponent with a fair opportunity to meet the evidence. Thus, timing may depend on how much preparation an opponent would need to fairly respond to the hearsay. The notice also must describe what the evidence is and how it will be offered, which includes information concerning the name and address of the declarant. Federal courts have split in determining how strictly the time requirement will be enforced. *Compare United States v. Evans*, 572 F.2d 455 (5th Cir. 1978) (taking a flexible approach) with *United States v. Oates, supra* (taking a restrictive approach).

DRAFTERS' ANALYSIS

Rule 803 is taken generally from the Federal Rule with modifications as needed for adaptation to military practice. Overall, the Rule is similar to practice under *Manual* ¶¶ 142 and 144 of the present *Manual*. The Rule is, however, substantially more detailed and broader in scope than the present *Manual*.

(1) Present sense impression. Rule 803(1) is taken from the Federal Rule verbatim. The exception it establishes is not now recognized in the Manual for Courts-Martial. It is somewhat similar to a spontaneous exclamation, but does not require a startling event. A fresh complaint by a victim of a sexual offense may come within this exception depending upon the circumstances.

(2) Excited utterance. Rule 803(2) is taken from the Federal Rule verbatim. Although similar to ¶ 142b, of the present *Manual* with respect to spontaneous exclamations, the Rule would appear to be more lenient as it does not seem to require independent evidence that the startling event occurred. An examination of the Federal

Rules of Evidence Advisory Committee Note indicates some uncertainty, however. S. SALTZBURG & K. REDDEN, FEDERAL RULES OF EVIDENCE MANUAL 540 (2d ed. 1977). A fresh complaint of a sexual offense may come within this exception depending on the circumstances.

(3) Then existing mental, emotional, or physical condition. Rule 803(3) is taken from the Federal Rule verbatim. The Rule is similar to that found in present *Manual* ¶ 142*d* but may be slightly more limited in that it may not permit statements by an individual to be offered to disclose the intent of another person. Fresh complaint by a victim of a sexual offense may come within this exception.

(4) Statements for purposes of medical diagnosis or treatment. Rule 803(4) is taken from the Federal Rule verbatim. It is substantially broader than the state of mind or body exception found in ¶ 142*d* of the present *Manual.* It allows, among other matters, statements as to the cause of the medical problem presented for diagnosis or treatment. Potentially, the Rule is extremely broad and will permit statements made even to non-medical personnel (*e.g.,* members of one's family) and on behalf of others so long as the statements are made for the purpose of diagnosis or treatment. The basis for the exception is the presumption that an individual seeking relief from a medical problem has incentive to make accurate statements. *See generally,* 4 J. WEINSTEIN & M. BERGER, WEINSTEIN'S EVIDENCE ¶ 804(4)[01] (1978). The admissibility under this exception of those portions of a statement not relevant to diagnosis or treatment is uncertain. Although statements made to a physician, for example, merely to enable the physician to testify, do not appear to come within the Rule, statements solicited in good faith by others in order to ensure the health of the declarant would appear to come within the Rule. Rule 803(4) may be used in an appropriate case to present evidence of fresh complaint in a sexual case.

(5) Recorded recollection. Rule 803(5) is taken from the Federal Rule without change, and is similar to the present exception for past recollection recorded found in ¶¶ 146*a* and 149*c*(1)(b) of the present *Manual* except that under the Rule the memorandum may be read but not presented to the fact finder unless offered by the adverse party.

(6) Record of regularly conducted activity. Rule 803(6) is taken generally from the Federal Rule. Two modifications have been made, however, to adapt the rule to military practice. The definition of "business" has been expanded to explicitly include the armed forces to ensure the continued application of this hearsay exception, and a descriptive list of documents, taken generally from present *Manual* ¶ 144*d,* has been included. Although the activities of the armed forces do not constitute a profit making business, they do constitute a business within the meaning of the hearsay exception, *see* ¶ 144*c,* of the present *Manual,* as well as a "regularly conducted activity".

The specific types of records included within the Rule are those which are normally records of reguarly conducted activity within the armed forces. They are included because of their importance and because their omission from the Rule would be impracticable. The fact that a record is of a type described within the subdivision does not eliminate the need for its proponent to show that the *particular* record comes within the Rule when the record is challenged; the Rule does establish that the *types* of records listed are normally business records.

Chain of custody receipts or documents have been included to emphasize their administrative nature. Such documents perform the critical function of accounting for property obtained by the United States Government. Although they may be used as prosecution evidence, their primary purpose is simply one of property accountability. In view of the primary administrative purpose of these matters, it was necessary to provide expressly for their admissibility as an exception to the hearsay rule in order to clearly reject the interpretation of ¶ 144*d* of the present *Manual* with respect to chain of custody forms as set forth in *United States v. Porter*, 7 M.J. 32 (C.M.A. 1979) and *United States v. Nault*, 4 M.J. 318 (C.M.A. 1978) insofar as they concerned chain of custody forms.

Laboratory reports have been included in recognition of the function of forensic laboratories as impartial examining centers. The report is simply a record of "regularly conducted" activity of the laboratory. *See, e.g., United States v. Strangstalien*, 7 M.J. 225 (C.M.A. 1979); *United States v. Evans*, 21 C.M.A. 579, 45 C.M.R. 353 (1972).

Paragraph 144*d* prevented a record "made principally with a view to prosecution, or other disciplinary or legal action . . ." from being admitted as a business record. This limitation has been deleted, *but see* Rule 803(8)(B) and its *Analysis*. It should be noted that a record of "regularly conducted activity" is unlikely to have a prosecutorial intent in any event.

The fact that a record may fit within another exception, *e.g.*, Rule 803(8), does not generally prevent it from being admissible under this subdivision although it would appear that the exclusion found in Rule 803(8)(B) for "matters observed by police officers and other personnel acting in a law enforcement capacity" prevents any such record from being admissible as a record of regularly conducted activity. Otherwise the limitation in subdivision (8) would serve no useful purpose. *See also Analysis* to Rule 803(8)(B).

Rule 803(6) is generally similar to the present *Manual* rule but is potentially broader because of its use of the expression "regularly conducted" activity in addition to "business". It also permits records of opinion which are prohibited by ¶ 144*d* of the present *Manual*. Offsetting these factors is the fact that the Rule requires that the memorandum was "made at or near the time by, or from information transmitted by a person with knowledge . . .", but ¶ 144*c* of the present *Manual* rule expressly does not require such knowledge as a condition of admissibility.

(7) Absence of entry in records kept in accordance with the provisions of paragraph (6). Rule 803(7) is taken verbatim from the Federal Rule. The Rule is similar to ¶¶ 143*a*(2)(h) and 143*b*(3) of the present *Manual*.

(8) Public records and reports. Rule 803(8) has been taken generally from the Federal Rule but has been slightly modified to adapt it to the military environment. Rule 803(8)(B) has been redrafted to apply to "police officers and other personnel acting in a law enforcement capacity" rather than the Federal Rule's "police officers and other law enforcement personnel". The change was necessitated by the fact that all military personnel may act in a disciplinary capacity. Any officer, for example, regardless of assignment, may potentially act as a military policeman. The capacity within which a member of the armed forces acts may be critical.

The Federal Rule was also modified to include a list of records that, when made pursuant to a duty required by law, will be admissible notwithstanding the fact that they may have been made as "matters observed by police officers and other personnel acting in a law enforcement capacity." Their inclusion is a direct result of the fact, discussed above, that military personnel may all function within a law enforcement capacity. The committee determined it would be impracticable and contrary to the intent of the Rule to allow the admissibility of records which are truly administrative in nature and unrelated to the problems inherent in records prepared only for purposes of prosecution to depend upon whether the maker was at that given instant acting in a law enforcement capacity. The language involved is taken generally from ¶ 144*b* of the present *Manual*. Admissibility depends upon whether the record is "a record of a fact or event if made by a person within the scope of his official duties and those duties included a duty to know or ascertain through appropriate and trustworthy channels of information the truth of the fact or event. . . ." Whether any given record was obtained in such a trustworthy fashion is a question for the military judge. The explicit limitation on admissibility of records made "principally with a view to prosecution" now found in ¶ 144*d* has been deleted.

The fact that a document may be admissible under another exception to the hearsay rule, *e.g.,* Rule 803(6), does not make it inadmissible under this subdivision.

Military Rule of Evidence 803(8) raises numerous significant questions. Rule 803(8)(A) extends to "records, reports, statements, or data complications" of "public offices or agencies, setting forth (A) the activities of the office or agency." The term "public office or agency" within this subdivision is defined to include any government office or agency including those of the armed forces. Within the civilian context, the definition of "public offices or agencies" is fairly clear and the line of demarcation between governmental and private action can be clearly drawn in most cases. The same may not be true within the armed forces. It is unlikely that every action taken by a servicemember is an "activity" of the department of which he or she is a member. Presumably, Rule 803(8) should be restricted to activities of formally sanctioned instrumentalities roughly similar to civilian entities. For example, the activities of a squadron headquarters or a staff section would come within the definition of "office or agency". Pursuant to this rationale, there is no need to have a military regulation or directive to make a statement of a "public office or agency" under Rule 803(8)(A). However, such regulations or directives might well be highly useful in establishing that a given administrative mechanism was indeed an "office or agency" within the meaning of the Rule.

Rule 803(8)(B) encompasses "matters observed pursuant to duty imposed by law as to which matters there was a duty to report . . . ." This portion of Rule 803(8) is broader than subdivision (8)(A) as it extends to far more than just the normal procedures of an office or agency. Perhaps because of this extent, it requires that there be a specific duty to observe and report. This duty could take the form of a statement, general order, regulation or any competent order.

The exclusion in the Federal Rule for "matters observed by police officers" was intended to prevent use of the exception for evaluative reports as the House Committee believed them to be unreliable. Because of the explicit language of the exclusion, normal statutory construction leads to the conclusion that reports which would be within Federal or Military Rule 803(8) but for the exclusion in (8)(B) are not otherwise admissible under Rule 803(6). Otherwise the inclusion of the limitation would serve virtually no purpose whatsoever. There is no contradiction between the exclusion in Rule 803(8)(B) and the specific documents made admissible in Rule 803(8) (and Rule 803(6)) because those documents are not matters "observed by police officers and other personnel acting in a law enforcement capacity." To the extent that they might be so considered, the specific language included by the committee is expressly intended to reject the subdivision (8)(B) limitation. Note, however, that all forms of evidence not within the specific item listing of the Rule but within the (8)(B) exclusion will be inadmissible insofar as Rule 803(8) is concerned, whether the evidence is military or civilian in origin.

A question not answered by Rule 803(8) is the extent to which a regulation or directive may circumscribe Rule 803(8). Thus, if a regulation establishes a given format or procedure for a report which is not followed, is an otherwise admissible piece of evidence inadmissible for lack of conformity with the regulation or directive? The committee did not address this issue in the context of adopting the Rule. However, it would be at least logical to argue that a record not made in substantial conformity with an implementing directive is not sufficiently reliable to be admissible. *See, e.g.,* Rule

403. Certainly, military case law predating the Military Rules may resolve this matter to the extent to which it is not based purely on now obsolete *Manual* provisions. As the modification to subdivision (8) dealing with specific records retains the present *Manual* language, it is particularly likely that present case law will survive in this area.

Rule 803(8)(C) makes admissible, but only against the government, "factual findings resulting from an investigation made pursuant to authority granted by law, unless the sources of information or other circumstances indicate lack of trustworthiness." This provision will make factual findings made, for example, by an Article 32 Investigating Officer or by a Court of Inquiry admissible on behalf of an accused. Because the provision applies only to "factual findings," great care must be taken to distinguish such factual determinations from opinions, recommendations and incidental inferences.

(9) Records of vital statistics. Rule 803(9) is taken verbatim from the Federal Rule and has no express equivalent in the present *Manual.*

(10) Absence of public record or entry. Rule 803(10) is taken verbatim from the Federal Rule and is similar to present *Manual* ¶ 143a(2)(g).

(11-13) Records of religious organizations; Marriage, baptismal, and similar certificates; Family records. Rule 802(11)-(13) are all taken verbatim from the Federal Rule and have no express equivalents in the present *Manual.*

(14-16) Records of documents affecting an interest in property; Statements in documents affecting an interest in property; Statements in ancient documents. Rules 803(14)-(16) are taken verbatim from the Federal Rule and have no express equivalent in the present *Manual.* Although intended primarily for civil cases, they all have potential importance to courts-martial.

(17) Market reports, commercial publications. Rule 803(17) is taken generally from the Federal Rule. Government price lists have been added because of the degree of reliance placed upon them in military life. Although included within the general Rule, the committee believed it inappropriate and impracticable not to clarify the matter by specific reference. The Rule is similar in scope and effect to *Manual* ¶ 144f except that it lacks the *Manual's* specific reference to an absence of entries. The effect, if any, of the difference is unclear.

(18) Learned treatises. Rule 803(18) is taken from the Federal Rule without change. Unlike ¶ 138e of the present *Manual,* which allowed use of such statements only for impeachment, this Rule allows substantive use on the merits of statements within treatises if relied upon in direct testimony or called to the expert's attention on cross-examination. Such statements may not, however, be given to the fact finder as exhibits.

(19-20) Reputation concerning personal or family history; Reputation concerning boundaries or general history. Rules 803(19)-(20) are taken without change from the Federal Rule and have no express equivalents in the present *Manual.*

(21) Reputation as to character. Rule 803(21) is taken from the Federal Rule without change. It is similar to ¶ 138f of the present *Manual* in that it creates an exception to the hearsay rule for reputation evidence. "Reputation" and "community" are defined in Rule 405(d) and "community" includes a "military organization regardless of size". Affidavits and other written statements are admissible to show character under Rule 405(c), and, when offered pursuant to that Rule, are an exception to the hearsay rule.

(22) Judgment of previous conviction. Rule 803(22) is taken from the Federal Rule but has been modified to recognize convictions of a crime punishable by a dishonorable discharge, a unique punishment not present in civilian life. *See also* Rule 609 and its *Analysis.*

There is no equivalent to this Rule in military law. Although the Federal Rule is clearly applicable to criminal cases, its original intent was to allow use of a prior criminal conviction in a subsequent civil action. To the extent that it is used for criminal cases, significant constitutional issues are raised, especially if the prior conviction is a foreign one, a question almost certainly not anticipated by the Federal Rules Advisory Committee.

(23) Judgment as to personal, family or general history, or boundaries. Rule 803(23) is taken verbatim from the Federal Rule, and has no express equivalent in the present *Manual.* Although intended primarily for civil cases, it clearly has potential use in courts-martial for such matters as proof of jurisdiction.

(24) Other exceptions. Rule 803(24) is taken from the Federal Rule without change. It has no express equivalent in the present *Manual* as it establishes a general exception to the hearsay rule. The Rule implements the general policy behind the Rules of permitting admission of probative and reliable evidence. Not only must the evidence in question satisfy the three conditions listed in the Rule (materiality, more probative on the point than any other evidence which can be reasonably obtained, and admission would be in the interest of justice) but the procedural requirements of notice must be complied with. The extent to which this exception may be employed is unclear. The Article III courts have divided as to whether the exception may be used only in extraordinary cases or whether it may have more general application. It is the intent of the committee that the Rule be employed in the same manner as it is generally applied in the Article III courts. Because the general exception found in Rule 803(24) is basically one intended to apply to highly reliable and necessary evidence, recourse to the theory behind the hearsay Rule itself may be helpful. In any given case, both trial and defense counsel may wish to examine the hearsay evidence in question to determine how well it relates to the four traditional considerations usually invoked to exclude hearsay testimony: How truthful was the original declarant? To what extent were his or her powers of observation adequate? Was the declaration truthful? Was the original declarant able to adequately communicate the statement? Measuring evidence against this framework should assist in determining the reliability of the evidence. Rule 803(24) itself requires the necessity which is the other usual justification for hearsay exceptions.

Rule 804. Hearsay Exceptions; Declarant Unavailable

(a) Definitions of unavailability. "Unavailability as a witness" includes situations in which the declarant—

(1) is exempted by ruling of the military judge on the ground of privilege from testifying concerning the subject matter of the declarant's statement; or

(2) persists in refusing to testify concerning the subject matter of the declarant's statement despite an order of the military judge to do so; or

(3) testifies to a lack of memory of the subject matter of the declarant's statement; or

(4) is unable to be present or to testify at the hearing because of death or then existing physical or mental illness or infirmity; or

(5) is absent from the hearing and the proponent of the declarant's statement has been unable to procure the declarant's attendance (or in the case of a hearsay exception under subdivision (b)(2), (3), or (4), the declarant's attendance or testimony) by process or other reasonable means; or

(6) is unavailable within the meaning of Article 49(d)(2).

A declarant is not unavailable as a witness if the declarant's exemption, refusal, claim of lack of memory, inability, or absence is due to the procurement or wrongdoing of the proponent of the declarant's statement for the purpose of preventing the witness from attending or testifying.

(b) Hearsay exceptions. The following are not excluded by the hearsay rule if the declarant is unavailable as a witness:

> *(1) Former testimony.* Testimony given as a witness at another hearing of the same or different proceeding, or in a deposition taken in compliance with law in the course of the same or another proceeding, if the party against whom the testimony is now offered had an opportunity and similar motive to develop the testimony by direct, cross, or redirect examination. A record of testimony given before courts-martial, courts of inquiry, military commissions, other military tribunals, and before proceedings pursuant to or equivalent to those required by Article 32 is admissible under this subdivision if such record is a verbatim record. This paragraph is subject to the limitations set forth in Articles 49 and 50.

(2) Statement under belief of impending death. In a prosecution for homicide or for any offense resulting in the death of the alleged victim, a statement made by a declarant while believing that the declarant's death was imminent, concerning the cause or circumstances of what the declarant believed to be the declarant's impending death.

(3) Statement against interest. A statement which was at the time of its making so far contrary to the declarant's pecuniary or proprietary interest, or so far tended to subject the declarant to civil or criminal liability, or to render invalid a claim by the declarant against another, that a reasonable person in the position of the declarant would not have made the statement unless the person believed it to be true. A statement tending to expose the declarant to criminal liability and offered to exculpate the accused is not admissible unless corroborating circumstances clearly indicate the trustworthiness of the statement.

(4) Statement of personal or family history. (A) A statement concerning the declarant's own birth, adoption, marriage, divorce, legitimacy, relationship by blood, adoption, or marriage, ancestry, or other similar fact of personal or family history, even though declarant had no means of acquiring personal knowledge of the matter stated; or (B) a statement concerning the foregoing matters, and death also, of another person, if the declarant was related to the other by blood, adoption, or marriage or was so intimately associated with the other's family as to be likely to have accurate information concerning the matter declared.

(5) Other exceptions. A statement not specifically covered by any of the foregoing exceptions but having equivalent circumstantial guarantees of trustworthiness, if the military judge determines that (A) the statement is offered as evidence of a material fact; (B) the statement is more probative on the point for which it is offered than any other evidence which the proponent can procure through reasonable efforts; and (C) the general purposes of these rules and the interest of justice will best be served by admission of the statement into evidence. However, a

statement may not be admitted under this exception unless the proponent of it makes known to the adverse party sufficiently in advance of the trial or hearing to provide the adverse party with a fair opportunity to prepare to meet it, the intention to offer the statement and the particulars of it, including the name and address of the declarant.

EDITORIAL COMMENT

Rule 804 provides the second major set of exceptions to the ban on hearsay evidence that is found in Rule 802. Whereas Rule 803 provides exceptions that do not depend on a showing that the hearsay declarant is unavailable at trial, Rule 804 conditions the use of the exceptions found therein on the unavailability showing. It certainly is arguable that a number of the exceptions found in Rule 804 are every bit as reliable as those found in Rule 803. Former testimony, for example, could be viewed as one of the most reliable of all the hearsay exceptions. The fact remains, however, that the requirement that the declarant be unavailable suggests that courts are especially hesitant in using the Rule 804 exceptions.

At common law, each hearsay exception that was conditioned on unavailability had its own requirement for the type of unavailability that would satisfy the exception. Instead of distinguishing among hearsay exceptions, Rule 804(a) provides a definition of unavailability that governs the use of all the exceptions contained in the Rule.

The first situation in which a hearsay declarant is unavailable is the case in which the declarant claims a privilege at trial and the claim is sustained by the military judge. For example, a declarant may have made a declaration against interest that can be used at trial, but if called to testify, the declarant would assert the privilege against self-incrimination. Assuming that the declarant faces some potential criminal liability, a trial judge would have to sustain the claim, and the declaration against interest could be offered under subdivision (b). The declarant would be unavailable under subdivision (a)(1).

The second situation in which a declarant is unavailable is when the declarant refuses to testify concerning the subject matter of a prior statement even though the trial judge has ordered him to give testimony. A witness who will not talk is no better than a witness who is not present. It is important that the trial judge attempt to get the witness to answer questions that are asked, rather than to assume that the initial reluctance of the witness to speak must immediately be respected. If the trial judge is unable to hold the witness in contempt, as may be the case, then there may be little the trial judge can do to force the witness to comply with the order of the court.

A third example of unavailability is that of a forgetful witness who claims lack of memory concerning the subject matter of a prior statement. This category can prove to be troublesome. If a witness testifies to a lack of memory with respect to the subject matter of the statement, there is no problem if the trial judge believes that the witness truly has a loss of memory, but if the trial judge decides that the witness is faking a memory loss in order to avoid providing testimony, there is a good argument that the trial judge should attempt to convince the witness that it is important to provide the testimony that is needed in the case. If this argument is accepted, the trial judge would make the same kind of effort that was discussed in the previous paragraph. If, however, the witness persists in refusing to testify, even if the witness is feigning a memory loss, the witness is unavailable for all practical purposes and the hearsay exception may be relied upon.

The fourth example is perhaps the most familiar of all. A witness who is dead or who is unable to be present because of a physical or mental illness or infirmity is unavailable within the meaning of the Rule. This is a familiar example at common law.

A fifth situation in which a declarant is unavailable is one in which the declarant is absent from the trial and the person offering a prior statement of the declarant has been unable to procure the attendance of the declarant, and with respect to dying declarations, declarations against interest and statements of personal history, the person offering the statement has been unable to get any testimony from the declarant in the form of a deposition or any other statement that an opponent would have a chance to cross-examine. The preference is for cross-examination, if possible, except when the declarant has no need for it, as under Rule 801(d)(2)(A) and (B).

Finally, subdivision (a) states that a witness is unavailable if the witness is deemed to be unable to be present at trial under Article 49(d)(2) of the Uniform Code of Military Justice. The drafters' *Analysis* indicates that the meaning of "military necessity" associated with the Article "must be determined by reference to the cases construing Article 49." *See, e.g., United States v. Obligacion,* 37 C.M.R. 861 (A.F.B.R. 1967) requiring an actual showing of unavailability based upon government counsel's investigation and attempt to obtain witness; *United States v. Chavez-Rey,* 49 C.M.R. 517 (A.F.C.M.R. 1974) witness unavailable based on "consideration[s] of time, expense, and personal safety of the two witnesses." *See also United States v. Ledbetter,* 2 M.J. 37 (C.M.A. 1976).

When subdivision (a) is compared to its federal counterpart, it is apparent that the two Rules are quite similar, except for the addition of the sixth definition of unavailability, which is unique to the military. The subdivision is similar to former ¶¶ 145a and 145b of the *Manual.* However, 804(a)(3) is somewhat broader than the prior *Manual* provisions, and Rule 804 does not distinguish between capital and non-capital cases as did the prior *Manual.*

It should be noted that the Supreme Court has indicated that the government must make a good faith effort to produce witnesses at trial in order to satisfy the confrontation clause of the Sixth Amendment under some circumstances, especially with respect to the former testimony exception considered below. The seminal case was *Barber v. Page,* 390 U.S. 719 (1968). After deciding *Barber,* the Court backed off from a stringent good faith requirement somewhat in *Mancusi v. Stubbs,* 408 U.S. 204 (1972). Most recently, in *Ohio v. Roberts,* 100 S. Ct. 2531 (1980), the Court again indicated that the government's efforts may not have to be as strenuous as was thought after

Barber. But it is clear that the government is going to have to do something more than offer evidence that would allow the judge to speculate that witnesses might be unavailable. *See, e.g., Government of the Canal Zone v. P. (Pinto),* 590 F.2d 1344 (5th Cir. 1979). Also, the government is going to have to make efforts to assure that witnesses do not become absent because of its fault. *See, e.g., United States v. Mann,* 590 F.2d 361 (1st Cir. 1978).

Only after a declarant is found to be unavailable may the five exceptions found in subdivision (b) be considered. These exceptions include four specific provisions and one residual exception that resembles the exception found in Rule 803(24).

The first exception in (b)(1) governs testimony that someone gave as a witness at another hearing, whether of the same or a different case, or during the taking of a deposition, as long as the person *against whom* the former testimony is now offered had an opportunity and similar motive to develop the testimony of the missing witness. *See* amended ¶ 117*b*(11) of the *Manual* concerning depositions used at trial. The opportunity need not have been on cross-examination. It can have come on direct examination or on redirect examination. And it does not matter whether in the case in which the former testimony is offered, the posture of the party against whom it is offered has changed. For example, the fact that someone was a plaintiff in a previous case and is now a defendant does not affect the former testimony rule. What a court must do is examine the prior case in order to see what motive the person had to examine the witness. If the motive is similar to the motive in the case in which the former testimony is offered and if the opportunity for examination were present at the former time, whether the opportunity was taken advantage of or not, then the former testimony rule is satisfied. It is important to know that the Rule does not require that the issues in the two cases be identical or that the parties be identical. The Rule focuses on the fair opportunity for a prior examination of a witness at a time when a party had an incentive to fully examine the witness. It may be easier for a court to find similar motive when the issues are identical or similar, but in some cases the issues may be different and yet a motive to examine the witness fully may be found.

It should be clear that the former testimony exception to the hearsay rule is one that has a very strong foundation. After all, the person against whom the testimony is offered has had a chance to examine the witness. The witness has been under oath, there has been a record made of the proceedings. In fact, unlike the Federal Rule, Military Rule 804(b)(1) explicitly states that a record of testimony before various military tribunals is admissible "if such record is a verbatim record." This is to emphasize the importance of accuracy in the use of former testimony. As long as former testimony is accurate, the fact that it has been given under oath when a party has had a chance to examine a witness means that the only thing that is missing is that the fact finder will not be able to observe the demeanor of the witness. Few exceptions have such a strong basis. This may raise the question of why former testimony is included under Rule 804, rather than under Rule 803. The answer is that live testimony generally is preferred to a record of testimony, precisely because demeanor and an opportunity for first-hand observation of the witness are important. Only when the witness is unavailable is former testimony to be used.

It appears that the most controversial aspect of former testimony will arise in connection with Article 32 proceedings. Much of the drafters' *Analysis* concerns this issue. Whereas the Federal Rules of Criminal Procedure now make clear that a preliminary hearing is not a discovery device, Article 32 hearings serve the function of a preliminary hearing as well as the function of a discovery device. Thus, a defense counsel who wants to engage in discovery runs the risk that questions prematurely put to witnesses will be viewed as creating former testimony should the witness become unavailable at trial. The drafters state that former testimony arising from an Article 32 proceeding is admissible only if the motive for the Article 32 examination is the same as at trial. This, of course, is what (b)(1) states. The drafters suggest that defense counsel sometimes should assert that they plan not to examine witnesses fully, but only for purposes of discovery, because this would alert the judge in subsequent trials to the fact that defense counsel did not wish to create former testimony. The problem with this suggestion is that it will probably produce automatic statements by diligent defense counsel as to their intent to limit the examination of a witness. We do not think that any disclaimer by defense counsel ought to be binding on the court. Rather, careful defense counsel should indicate why it is that an examination is being limited — *e.g.,* investigation is not complete, certain witnesses have not been found, etc. If this is stated on the record during the Article 32 proceeding, the case for treating the Article 32 examination as falling outside the hearsay exception is strengthened. No matter what, we think that the judge at trial is going to have to examine the record of the Article 32 proceeding if the government claims that it is entitled to use the former testimony exception. The judge will look to see the completeness of the examination, whether defense counsel sought to attack the witness, and whether there were gaps in the questioning that were consistent with the protestations by defense counsel as to the examination's being a limited one.

If defense counsel's examination of witnesses at the Article 32 proceeding is outside the realm of former testimony, this does not mean that the government's examination of witnesses also falls outside the exception. It very well may be that the government is prepared to go forward with full examination when defense counsel is not, and that its investigating officer will do a complete job. If so, there may be a different treatment of the government and the defendant. *Cf. United States v. Klauber,* 611 F.2d 512 (4th Cir. 1979) (indicating that the court might follow *United States v. Driscoll,* 445 F. Supp. 864 (D.N.J. 1978) and treat grand jury testimony as admissible against the government).

Generally, the actual record of a proceeding will be offered to satisfy the former testimony rule. But it appears that only the verbatim record of military proceedings is required by the exception. As at common law, witnesses who have heard testimony in other proceedings outside the military sphere apparently are still free to testify under the exception.

The second exception for unavailable declarants is the traditional dying declaration; it is found in (b) (2). Although the Rule is similar to the Federal Rule, it eliminates any reference to civil cases. The exception covers statements made by a declarant who believes that death is imminent as long as the statement concerns the cause or circumstances of the perceived impending death. Dying declarations are admissible in prosecutions for homicide or for any offense that results in the death of the alleged victim. Thus, if a lesser included offense is charged, but death has resulted from the offense, the statement may be admissible. It is very important to keep in mind that there is no requirement that the declarant has died as a result of the offense. As long as the declarant is unavailable, the hearsay exception may be used. Of course, there must be a showing that the declarant believed death was imminent when the statement was made. Often, death will follow. But the fact that the declarant misperceived the situation and did not die does not mean that the declaration fails to qualify under the exception. It qualifies as long as the declarant later becomes unavailable. The exception expands somewhat ¶ 142 *a* of the present *Manual,* but is based on the familiar rationale that people do not lie as they contemplate death and the possibility of "meeting their Maker."

The third exception is the familiar exception for statements against interest. These statements are to be distinguished from admissions, which are covered by Rule 801(d)(2). A declaration against interest is a statement that was against the interest of the declarant when made; an admission is a statement that is offered against a party by an opponent, even though the admission may have been self-serving to the declarant when made. A declaration against interest may be made by anyone; an admission is a statement by a party or someone associated with the party. Interestingly, the prior *Manual* had no provision for declarations against interest, although they were recognized in military case law. *See, e.g., United States v. Johnson,* 3 M.J. 143 (C.M.A. 1977).

The Military Rule follows the Federal Rule. It expands the class of statements that qualify as declarations against interest beyond those recognized at common law. The Rule recognizes that statements may be against pecuniary or proprietary interests, which was the situation at common law, or against penal interests. The penal interest part of the Rule is the expansion that many commentators have advocated for some time. The Rule indicates that statements qualify as being against interest if they would have subjected someone to civil or criminal liability at the time that they were made. The test under the Rule is whether "a reasonable person in the position of the declarant would not have made the statement unless the person believed it to be true." The rationale of the rule is that people are reluctant to say things against their self-interest unless those things happen to be the truth. Thus, it is important to determine whether a person would have thought the statement was against interest when made, because, if not, there is no guarantee of trustworthiness.

The last sentence of the exception states that a declaration against interest that tends to expose a declarant to criminal liability and is offered to exculpate an accused is not admissible unless corroborating circumstances clearly indicate the trustworthiness of the statement. The reason for this limitation is that the drafters of the exception believed that when several people were involved in criminal activity, once one is convicted that person has no reason to refrain from taking the blame for the offense in an effort to help his confederates. And the drafters feared that someone imprisoned for a long period of time has little to lose by confessing to a crime that may have been committed by someone else. Thus, the Rule requires corroboration and civilian courts seem to take the requirement quite seriously. *See, e.g., United States v. Mackin*, 561 F.2d 958 (D.C. Cir.), cert. denied, sub nom. *Gibson v. United States*, 434 U.S. 959 (1977). One court has held that when the government offers declarations against interest by a declarant other than a defendant, corroborating circumstances also are required. *See United States v. Alvarez*, 584 F.2d 694 (5th Cir. 1978). *Alvarez* may seem to be justifiable on the theory that the government should be no better off than the defendant, but arguably it is an unnecessary decision. Most courts have indicated grave problems when a statement by a declarant is a declaration against his own interest but it also includes references to third parties. It is common practice to redact the statements to avoid references to the third parties. *See, e.g., United States v. White*, 553 F.2d 310 (2d Cir. 1977), cert. denied, 431 U.S. 972 (1978).

It is somewhat surprising to us that the drafters' *Analysis* seems to take lightly the arguments against admitting statements by one person implicating another; the drafters apparently accept the theory that any declaration against interest is reliable. But, the point about the reliability of declarations against interest is that reasonable people do not make statements against their *own* interest, yet, reasonable people do make statements implicating others more readily than they make statements concerning their own liability. We believe that there are serious confrontation problems with using statements of unavailable witnesses that include references to third persons. Typically, common law courts have avoided the problem through redaction. We see no reason why redaction should not be utilized in the future as well.

Although statements that tend to exculpate the accused need corroboration, it is clear that, if corroborated, statements need not *necessarily* subject a declarant to liability. The Rule requires only that the statement tend to subject the declarant to civil or criminal liability. *See, e.g., United States v. Thomas*, 571 F.2d 285 (5th Cir. 1978); *United States v. Satterfield*, 572 F.2d 687 (9th Cir.), cert. denied, 439 U.S. 840 (1978).

The fourth hearsay exception covers statements of personal or family history. It is divided into two parts. A person's statements concerning his own birth, adoption, marriage and family relations are admissible even though the person had no means of acquiring personal knowledge of the matter stated. The second part of the exception covers statements by someone about another's family history. A person can make a statement about another if the speaker is related by blood, adoption or marriage, or even if the speaker was so intimately associated with the family of the other person as to be likely to have accurate information concerning the matter declared. This is a very broad rule. It allows statements to be admitted even though they were made after a dispute arose and even though the declarant may not have personal knowledge about the matter stated. It remains to be seen whether this Rule will often be used in the military. It had no counterpart in the prior *Manual*.

It seems that the reliability of many of the statements covered by this exception is suspect. At common law, the statements seeking to qualify under the exception had to have been made before a dispute arose — i.e., at a time when a person would have had no reason to lie about the matters covered by the exception. But this requirement is eliminated. Apparently, the drafters believed that a person generally does not tell lies about these matters. It also may be that such lies are likely to be noticed by people who are familiar with the person, his family and his background. Courts may find that statements made by a friend of the family or relative are more reliable than one made by a person about himself, since his own statements might be self-serving. Of course, statements that are very suspect because of the circumstances in which they were made could conceivably be excluded under Rule 403.

The final exception (b)(5) is the exception that parallels the one found in Rule 803(24). It is known as the "catch-all" or the residual hearsay exception. Like its counterpart under Rule 803, it provides that a statement that is not specifically covered by any of the four previous exceptions can be admitted if the statement has equivalent circumstantial guarantees of trustworthiness, it is offered as evidence of a material (which presumably means important) fact, it is more probative than other evidence that can be secured, and the general purposes of the Rules and the interests of justice are better served by admitting the statement than by excluding it. A notice requirement also is imposed upon a person seeking to utilize the exception.

Because there are residual exceptions in both Rules 803 and 804, it is apparent that analogies can be drawn to any of the exceptions found in either of the Rules. One of the reasons that we have indicated some of the rationales behind certain Rules is that these become important when the residual exceptions are utilized. There seems to be close judicial scrutiny of statements admitted against an accused under the residual exception. *See, e.g., United States v. Bailey,* 581 F.2d 341 (3d Cir. 1978); *United States v. Gonzalez,* 559 F.2d 1271 (5th Cir. 1977). The broadest use of the residual exception is found in *United States v. West,* 574 F.2d 1131 (4th Cir. 1978); *United States v. Garner,* 574 F.2d 1141 (4th Cir.), cert. denied, 439 U.S. 936 (1978).

DRAFTERS' ANALYSIS

(a) Definition of unavailability. Subdivisions (a)(1)-(a)(5) of Rule 804 are taken from the Federal Rule without change and are generally similar to the relevant portions of ¶¶ 145*a* and 145*b* of the present *Manual,* except that Rule 804(a)(3) provides that a witness who "testifies as to a lack of memory of the subject matter of the declarant's statement" is unavailable. The Rule also does not distinguish between capital and non-capital cases.

Rule 804(a)(6) is new and has been added in recognition of certain problems, such as combat operations, that are unique to the armed forces. Thus, Rule 804(a)(6) will make unavailable a witness who is unable to appear and testify in person for reason of military necessity within the meaning of Article 49(d)(2). The meaning of "military necessity" must be determined by reference to the cases construing Article 49. The expression is not intended to be a general escape clause, but must be restricted to the limited circumstances that would permit use of a deposition.

(b) Hearsay exceptions.

(1) Former testimony. The first portion of Rule 804(b)(1) is taken from the Federal Rule with omission of the language relating to civil cases. The second portion is new and has been included to clarify the extent to which those military tribunals in which a verbatim record normally is not kept come within the Rule.

The first portion of Rule 804 (b) (1) makes admissible former testimony when "the party against whom the testimony is now offered had an opportunity and similar motive to develop the testimony by direct, cross, or redirect examination." Unlike ¶ 145*b* of the present *Manual,* the Rule does not explicitly require that the accused, when the evidence is offered against him or her, have been "afforded at the former trial an opportunity to be adequately represented by counsel." Such a requirement should be read into the Rule's condition that the party have had "opportunity and similar motive." In contrast to the present *Manual,* the Rule does not distinguish between capital and non-capital cases.

The second portion of Rule 804(b)(1) has been included to ensure that testimony from military tribunals, many of which ordinarily do not have verbatim records, will not be admissible unless such testimony is presented in the form of a verbatim record. The committee believed substantive use of former testimony to be too important to be presented in the form of an incomplete statement.

Investigations under Article 32 of the Uniform Code of Military Justice present a special problem. Rule 804(b)(1) requires that "the party against whom the testimony is now offered had an opportunity and similar motive to develop the testimony" at the first hearing. The "similar motive" requirement was intended primarily to ensure sufficient identity of issues between the two proceedings and thus to ensure an adequate interest in examination of the witness. *See, e.g.,* 4 J. WEINSTEIN & M. BERGER, WEINSTEIN'S EVIDENCE ¶ 804 (b) (1) [(04)] (1978). Because Article 32 hearings represent a unique hybrid of preliminary hearings and grand juries with features dissimilar to both, it was particularly difficult for the committee to determine exactly how subdivision (b) (1) of the Federal Rule would apply to Article 32 hearings. The specific difficulty stems from the fact that Article 32 hearings were intended by Congress to function as discovery devices for the defense as well as to recommend an appropriate disposition of charges to the convening authority. *Hutson v. United States,* 19 C.M.A. 437, 42 C.M.R. 39 (1970); *United States v. Samuels,* 10 C.M.A. 206, 212, 27 C.M.R. 280, 286 (1959). *See generally, Hearing on H.R. 2498 Before a Subcomm. of the House Comm. on Armed Services,* 81st Cong., 1st Sess., 997 (1949). It is thus permissible, for example, for a defense counsel to limit cross-examination of an adverse witness at an Article 32 hearing using the opportunity for discovery, alone, for example, rather than impeachment. In such a case, the defense would not have the requisite "similar motive" found within Rule 804(b)(1).

Notwithstanding the inherent difficulty of determining the defense counsel's motive at an Article 32 hearing, the Rule is explicitly intended to prohibit use of testimony given at an Article 32 hearing unless the requisite "similar motive" was present during that hearing. It is clear that some Article 32 testimony is admissible under the Rule notwithstanding the congressionally sanctioned discovery purpose of the Article 32 hearing. Consequently, one is left with the question of the extent to which the Rule actually does apply to Article 32 testimony. The only apparent practical solution to what is otherwise an irresolvable dilemma is to read the Rule as permitting only Article 32 testimony preserved via a verbatim record that is not objected to as having been obtained without the requisite "similar motive." While defense counsel's assertion of his

381

or her intent in not examining one or more witnesses or in not fully examining a specific witness is not binding upon the military judge, clearly the burden of establishing admissibility under the Rule is on the prosecution and the burden so placed may be impossible to meet should the defense counsel adequately raise the issue. As a matter of good trial practice, a defense counsel who is limiting cross-examination at the Article 32 hearing because of discovery should announce that intent sometime during the Article 32 hearing so that the announcement may provide early notice to all concerned and hopefully avoid the necessity for counsel to testify at the later trial.

The Federal Rule was modified by the committee to require that testimony offered under Rule 804(b) (1) which was originally "given before courts-martial, courts of inquiry, military commissions, other military tribunals, and before proceedings pursuant to or equivalent to those required by Article 32" and which is otherwise admissible under the Rule be offered in the form of a verbatim record. The modification was intended to ensure accuracy in view of the fact that only summarized or minimal records are required of some types of military proceedings.

An Article 32 hearing is a "military tribunal." The Rule distinguishes between Article 32 hearings and other military tribunals in order to recognize that there are other proceedings which are considered the equivalent of Article 32 hearings for purposes of former testimony under Rule 804 (b) (1).

(2) Statement under belief of impending death. Rule 804 (b) (2) is taken from the Federal Rule except that the language, "for any offense resulting in the death of the alleged victim," has been added and reference to civil proceedings has been omitted. The new language has been added because there is no justification for limiting the exception only to those cases in which a homicide charge has actually been preferred. Due to the violent nature of military operations, it may be appropriate to charge a lesser included offense rather than homicide. The same justifications for the exception are applicable to lesser included offenses which are also, of course, of lesser severity. The additional language, taken from ¶ 142a, thus retains the present *Manual* rule, modification of which was viewed as being impracticable.

Rule 804 (b) (2) is similar to the dying declaration exception found in ¶ 142a of the present *Manual*, except that the Military Rule does not require that the declarant be dead. So long as the declarant is unavailable and the offense is one for homicide or other offense resulting in the death of the alleged victim, the hearsay exception may be applicable. This could, for example, result from a situation in which the accused, intending to shoot A, shoots both A and B; A utters the hearsay statement, under a belief of impending death, B dies, and although A recovers, A is unavailable to testify at trial. In a trial of the accused for killing B, A's statement will be admissible.

There is no requirement that death immediately follow the declaration, but the declaration is not admissible under this exception if the declarant had a hope of recovery. The declaration may be made by spoken words or intelligible signs or may be in writing. It may be spontaneous or in response to solicitation, including leading questions. The utmost care should be exercised in weighing statements offered under this exception since they are often made under circumstances of mental and physical debility and are not subject to the usual tests of veracity. The military judge may exclude those declarations which are viewed as being unreliable. *See, e.g.,* Rule 403.

A dying declaration and its maker may be contradicted and impeached in the same manner as other testimony and witnesses. Under the present law, the fact that the deceased did not believe in a deity or in future rewards or punishments may be offered to affect the weight of a declaration offered under this Rule but does not defeat admissibility. Whether such evidence is now admissible in the light of Rule 610 is unclear.

(3) Statement against interest. Rule 804(b) is taken from the Federal Rule without change, and has no express equivalent in the *Manual*. It has, however, been made applicable by case law, *United States v. Johnson,* 3 M.J. 143 (C.M.A. 1977). It makes admissible statements against a declarant's interests, whether pecuniary, proprietary, or penal when a reasonable person in the position of the declarant would not have made the statement unless such a person would have believed it to be true.

The Rule expressly recognizes the penal interest exception and permits a statement tending to expose the declarant to criminal liability. The penal interest exception is qualified, however, when the declaration is offered to exculpate the accused by requiring the "corroborating circumstances clearly indicate the trustworthiness of the statement." This requirement is applicable, for example, when a third party confesses to the offense the accused is being tried for and the accused offers the third party's statement in evidence to exculpate the accused. The basic penal interest exception is established as a matter of constitutional law by the Supreme Court's decision in *Chambers v. Mississippi,* 410 U.S. 284 (1973), which may be broader than the Rule as the case may not require either corroborating evidence or an unavailable declarant.

In its present form, the Rule fails to address a particularly vexing problem — that of the declaration against penal interest which implicates the accused as well as the declarant. On the face of the Rule, such a statement should be admissible, subject to the effects, if any, of *Bruton v. United States,* 391 U.S. 123 (1968) and Rule 306. Notwithstanding this, there is considerable doubt as to the applicability of the Rule to such a situation. *See generally,* 4 J. WEINSTEIN & M. BERGER, WEINSTEIN'S EVIDENCE 804-93, 804-16 (1978). Although the legislative history reflects an early desire on the part of the Federal Rules of Evidence Advisory Committee to prohibit such testimony, a provision doing so was not included in the material reviewed by Congress. Although the House included such a provision, it did so apparently in large part based upon a view that *Bruton, supra,* prohibited such statements — arguably an erroneous view of *Bruton, supra, see, e.g., Bruton v. United States,* 391 U.S. 123, 128, n. 3 (1968); *Dutton v. Evans,* 400 U.S. 74 (1970). The Conference Committee deleted the House provision, following the Senate's desires, because it believed it inappropriate to "codify constitutional evidentiary principles" WEINSTEIN'S EVIDENCE at 804-16 (1978) citing CONG. REC. H 11931-32 (daily ed. Dec. 14, 1974). Thus, applicability of the hearsay exception to individuals implicating the accused may well rest only on the extent to which *Bruton, supra,* governs such statement. The committee intends that the Rule extend to such statements to the same extent that subdivision 804(b)(4) is held by the Article III courts to apply to such statements.

(4) Statement of personal or family history. Rule 804 (b) (4) of the Federal Rule is taken verbatim from the Federal Rule, and has no express equivalent in the present *Manual.* The primary feature of Rule 803 (b) (4) (A) is its application, even though the "declarant had no means of acquiring personal knowledge of the matter stated."

(5) Other exceptions. Rule 804 (b) (5) is taken without change from the Federal Rule and is identical to Rule 803(24). As Rule 803 applies to hearsay statements regardless of the declarant's availability or lack thereof, this subdivision is actually superfluous. As to its effect, *see* the *Analysis* to Rule 803(24).

Rule 805. Hearsay Within Hearsay

Hearsay included within hearsay is not excluded under the hearsay rule if each part of the combined statements conforms with an exception to the hearsay rule provided in these rules.

EDITORIAL COMMENT

This one sentence Rule states that double or multiple hearsay is not excluded under Rule 802, if an exception to the hearsay rule satisfies each hearsay problem associated with the statement.

The first step in utilizing Rule 805 is to decide whether more than one level of hearsay (as defined in Rule 801(c)) is involved in a particular case. Consider, for example, a case in which an accused is charged with assault and claims self-defense. An investigating officer called to the scene of the dispute talked to a witness who said that he saw someone hand the accused a piece of paper with the words on it "Jones (the alleged victim of the assault) has a gun and is going to kill you." The witness is unavailable at trial and the officer wishes to relate the witness' statement. This is not a double hearsay problem. The only hearsay issue involves the witness' statement to the officer about what he saw. The witness' statement would be offered for its truth and would be hearsay under the definition of Rule 801(c). What was written on the note would not be offered for its truth. True or false, the fact that it was relayed to the accused helps to explain the accused's action. Thus, this is a situation involving one ordinary hearsay problem.

Consider another example. Following an automobile accident an investigator goes to the scene and talks to the accused. The accused admits fault and is subsequently charged with vehicular or negligent homicide. The officer recorded the statement of the accused in a report of the investigation, but the officer is not present to testify at trial. The officer's report might qualify as a business record or an official record (although it probably would not qualify as a public record if the officer were acting in a law enforcement capacity). Assuming that the report itself qualified, it could be used to show what it was the officer heard. As for what the accused said, it would be an admission and admissible as non-hearsay under Rule 801(d)(2)(A). Because of the way Rule 801 defines hearsay and exempts admissions from the definition, this again technically is a problem of one level of hearsay.

An example of a case in which Rule 805 would be important is a situation in which an officer conducts an investigation and comes upon a person who makes a statement in an excited state. The officer records the statement as part of his report. Assuming that the report qualifies as an admissible document under either Rule 803(6) or 803(8), the excited utterance also could qualify under Rule 803(2). The report would be offered to prove what the officer heard — *i.e.*, the truth of what the officer stated in his report that he heard. And the excited utterance would be used to prove the truth of its contents also. It requires a second hearsay exception.

There is no doubt that it is easy to mistake a double hearsay for an ordinary hearsay situation. An example is *United States v. Ruffin,* 575 F.2d 346 (2d Cir. 1978). The Court of Appeals was reviewing the testimony of an expert who testified about a public record that he had examined. The court found that the public record came within Rule 803(14) but said that the trial judge had erred in permitting the expert to relate what he had observed because there was no hearsay exception to cover this. In saying this, the court erred, since a person present to testify about what he saw is not relating hearsay information at all. He is giving first-hand testimony about personal observations and can be cross-examined about them.

Although Rule 805 admits hearsay within hearsay as long as there are exceptions that satisfy each hearsay problem, it probably is the case that the more levels of hearsay pyramided together the more likely it is that the court will exclude evidence under Rule 403. It also is likely that confrontation arguments will be taken more seriously when one piece of evidence presents more than one hearsay problem.

DRAFTERS' ANALYSIS

Rule 805 is taken verbatim from the Federal Rule. Although the *Manual* does not explicitly address the issue, the Military Rule is identical with the new Rule.

Rule 806. Attacking and Supporting Credibility of Declarant

When a hearsay statement, or a statement defined in rule 801(d)(2)(C), (D), or (E), has been admitted in evidence, the credibility of the declarant may be attacked, and if attacked may be supported, by any evidence which would be admissible for those purposes if declarant had testified as a witness. Evidence of a statement or conduct by the declarant at any time, inconsistent with the declarant's hearsay statement, is not subject to any requirement that the declarant may have been afforded an opportunity to deny or explain. If the party against whom a hearsay statement has been admitted calls the declarant as a witness, the party is entitled to examine the declarant on the statement as if under cross-examination.

EDITORIAL COMMENT

Rule 806 indicates that a statement that is hearsay or that is introduced as a vicarious admission against a party gives rise to a right on the part of the party against whom the evidence is offered to impeach the credibility of the hearsay declarant. The Rule states that the credibility of the declarant may be attacked by any evidence which would be admissible to attack the declarant if he had testified as a witness. Thus, the declarant may be shown to be biased. An attack through character evidence may be made. An effort may be made to show that the declarant was incapable of observing events or hearing statements. Once a declarant is attacked, the declarant may be supported. This is consistent with the rule that rehabilitation of an individual, declarants as well as witnesses, is not to be attempted until an attack takes place. *Accord,* Rule 608(a).

One of the traditional forms of impeachment, showing that the witness or declarant has made a prior inconsistent statement, is explicitly permitted by the second sentence of Rule 806. This sentence indicates that when a hearsay declarant, unlike the usual witness, is impeached with an inconsistent statement, there is no requirement that the declarant be afforded an opportunity to deny or explain the statement. Thus, the prior inconsistent statement is automatically admissible to impeach a hearsay declarant or a person whose vicarious admissions have been offered against a party.

The third sentence of the Rule covers a situation in which a party is not satisfied simply with impeaching the declarant; he wants to call the declarant to testify as a witness. If he does so, the party is entitled to examine the declarant on the statement as if under cross-examination. Thus, the party who calls the witness may ask leading questions about the statement that has been offered against him. If the party goes beyond asking questions about the statement, then it would seem that the party must proceed as if on direct examination, unless the court orders otherwise under Rule 611.

One thing that is not clear in Rule 806 is whether a prior inconsistent statement of a person who has made a vicarious admission may be offered without a foundation. It is interesting that the vicarious admissions are specifically mentioned in the first sentence of the Rule, but are not mentioned in the second. We view this as inadvertent and would suggest that the party who wishes to impeach the declarant who has made a vicarious admission can do so through an inconsistent statement. We would also take the same view with respect to the third sentence. Thus, we believe that a party can call a person who made a vicarious statement to ask about the statement and proceed as if on cross-examination. Thus far there has been little litigation under this Rule in the federal courts. The Military Rule is identical to Federal Rule 806, and it may be that there will be little litigation in the military courts as well.

Examples of the few cases in which the Rule has been cited are *United States v. Check,* 582 F.2d 668 (2d Cir. 1978); *United States v. Lawson,* 608 F.2d 1129 (6th Cir. 1979).

It is likely that specific act impeachment of a declarant under Rule 608(b) probably cannot be accomplished unless the declarant is called to testify, since the Rule bars extrinsic evidence.

DRAFTERS' ANALYSIS

Rule 806 is taken from the Federal Rule without change. It restates the present military rule that a hearsay declarant or statement may always be contradicted or impeached. The Rule eliminates any requirement that the declarant be given "an opportunity to deny or explain" an inconsistent statement or inconsistent conduct when such statement or conduct is offered to attack the hearsay statement. As a result, Rule 806 supersedes Rule 613(b) which would require such an opportunity for a statement inconsistent within court testimony.

SECTION IX. AUTHENTICATION AND IDENTIFICATION

Rule 901. Requirement of Authentication or Identification.
    (a) General provision.
    (b) Illustrations.
        (1) Testimony of witness with knowledge.
        (2) Nonexpert opinion on handwriting.
        (3) Comparison by trier or expert witness.
        (4) Distinctive characteristics and the like.
        (5) Voice identification.
        (6) Telephone conversations.
        (7) Public records or reports.
        (8) Ancient documents or data compilation.
        (9) Process or system.
        (10) Methods provided by statute or rule.
Rule 902. Self-Authentication.
    (1) Domestic public documents under seal.
    (2) Domestic public documents not under seal.
    (3) Foreign public documents.
    (4) Certified copies of public records.
    (4a) Documents or records of the United States accompanied by attesting certificates.
    (5) Official publications.
    (6) Newspapers and periodicals.
    (7) Trade inscriptions and the like.
    (8) Acknowledged documents.
    (9) Commercial paper and related documents.
    (10) Presumptions under Acts of Congress and regulations.

Rule 903. Subscribing Witness' Testimony Unnecessary.

Rule 901. Requirement of Authentication or Identification

(a) General provision. The requirement of authentication or identification as a condition precedent to admissibility is satisfied by evidence sufficient to support a finding that the matter in question is what its proponent claims.

(b) Illustrations. By way of illustration only, and not by way of limitation, the following are examples of authentication or identification conforming with the requirements of this rule:

(1) Testimony of witness with knowledge. Testimony that a matter is what it is claimed to be.

(2) Nonexpert opinion on handwriting. Nonexpert opinion as to the genuineness of handwriting, based upon familiarity not acquired for purposes of the litigation.

(3) Comparison by trier or expert witness. Comparison by the trier of fact or by expert witnesses with specimens which have been authenticated.

(4) Distinctive characteristics and the like. Appearance, contents, substance, internal patterns, or other distinctive characteristics, taken in conjunction with circumstances.

(5) Voice identification. Identification of a voice, whether heard firsthand or through mechanical or electronic transmission or recording, by opinion based upon hearing the voice at any time under circumstances connecting it with the alleged speaker.

(6) Telephone conversations. Telephone conversations, by evidence that a call was made to the number assigned at the time by the telephone company to a particular person or business, if (A) in the case of a person, circumstances, including self-identification, show the person answering to be the one called, or (B) in the case of a business, the call was made to a place of business and the conversation related to business reasonably transacted over the telephone.

(7) Public records or reports. Evidence that a writing authorized by law to be recorded or filed and in fact recorded or filed in a public office, or a purported public record, report, statement, or data compilation, in any form, is from the public office where items of this nature are kept.

(8) Ancient documents or data compilation. Evidence that a document or data compilation, in any form, (A) is in such condition as to create no suspicion concerning its authenticity, (B) was in place where it, if authentic, would likely be, and (C) has been in existence 20 years or more at the time it is offered.

(9) Process or system. Evidence describing a process or system used to produce a result and showing that the process or system produces an accurate result.

(10) Methods provided by statute or rule. Any method of authentication or identification provided by Act of Congress, by rules prescribed by the Supreme Court pursuant to statutory authority, or by applicable regulations prescribed pursuant to statutory authority.

EDITORIAL COMMENT

In introducing evidence a proponent must show that the evidence is what he says it is and that it satisfies minimum evidentiary standards. With ordinary witnesses, the foundation is relevance, personal knowledge and competence. (Rules 401, 601 and 602). With experts, the foundation is relevance, expertise and a reasonable basis for testimony. (Rules 401, 702 and 703). Other evidence may require more of a foundation. The process of laying this foundation is generally labeled "authentication" — a generic term employed to describe identification of physical or voice evidence, or verification of charts, diagrams and documents. Rule 901 prescribes a general requirement for authentication or identification and also provides illustrations of proper ways to satisfy the requirement. With only a minor change in paragraph (b)(10), the Rule is identical to its federal counterpart. The Rule makes it easier for the proponent to authenticate evidence than under prior law.

Subdivision (a) addresses the general requirement for authentication or identification: Before admitting a piece of evidence, the military judge must be satisfied that the court-members could find that the evidence is what it purports to be. This subdivision, identical in approach to Rule 104(b), treats authentication as a matter of conditional relevancy. The proferred evidence must, of course, be admissible under other Rules, such as Section IV (relevancy); Section VIII (hearsay); and Section X (best evidence). Authentication is therefore only one of several hurdles a proponent must leap. For a discussion of the interplay between the concepts of authentication, best evidence, and hearsay, *see* Greenberg, *Introduction of Documentary Evidence in Civil Cases under the New Federal Rules of Evidence,* 9 CLEARING HOUSE REV. 1 (1975).

The new Rule apparently only requires a prima facie showing of authenticity through either direct or circumstantial evidence. The opponent may offer rebuttal or contradictory proof, but the judge decides only whether court-members reasonably could find the evidence to be what its proponent claims it is. Whether or not to believe it is a decision for the court-members. Still reserved for the military judge are the evidentiary questions of relevancy, hearsay, and best evidence (except for Rule 1008).

What impact will Rule 901(a) have on military practice? On its face, subdivision (a) portends abandonment of many step-by-step authentication techniques recognized in pre-Rules practice. Arguably, such abandonment could be viewed as consistent with the Rules' overall approach, which generally is to prefer admission of evidence. But neither the legislative history of the Federal Rules nor federal case-law precisely defines the relationship of Rule 901(a) to common law authentication rules.

The drafters' *Analysis* to this Rule recognizes a "substantial question" as to its impact on pre-Rules authentication requirements. Despite the apparent minimal requirement of subdivision (a), the drafters' *Analysis* suggests that the Rule requires more to authenticate evidence than one might think. For example, a chain of custody is still required. This is generally consistent with the federal cases which have continued to apply traditional techniques in a flexible fashion. In *United States v. Fuentes,* 563 F.2d 527 (2d Cir. 1977), for instance, the court rejected any rigid formula for authenticating tape-recordings, but noted that the government must produce clear and convincing evidence of authenticity and accuracy as a foundation for admission. The court stated that common law techniques of authentication could serve as a valuable formulation of factors to be considered by the trial judge in determining admissibility. We think that in criminal cases there is a continuing need for careful screening by the military judge where evidence is not unique and stable and might change in form or quality between the time it is gathered and the time it is offered at trial. The drafters' *Analysis* is consistent with our approach and is in harmony with existing case law requiring minimal guarantees of reliability as a condition to admission of evidence in criminal trials. *See* S. SALTZBURG & K. REDDEN, FEDERAL RULES OF EVIDENCE MANUAL 641-644 (2d ed. 1977).

Counsel and judges should therefore employ existing military and federal law as a template for treatment of chains of custody. That is, if fungible evidence is being offered, the government must be prepared to show continuous custody which preserves the evidence in substantially the same condition it was in when obtained. *See, e.g., United States v. Clark,* 425 F.2d 827, 833 (3d Cir. 1970) (drugs); *United States v. Fowler,* 9 M.J. 149 (C.M.A. 1980) (drugs); and *United States v. Nault,* 4 M.J. 318, 319 (C.M.A. 1978) (drugs). *See also, United States v. Zink,* 612 F.2d 511 (10th Cir. 1980) (chain of custody for sack of money). Minor breaks in the chain do not necessarily render the evidence inadmissible but rather present issues of weight. *United States v. Henderson,* 588 F.2d 157 (5th Cir.), cert. denied 440 U.S. 945 (1979), *United States v. Courts,* 9 M.J. 285 (C.M.A. 1980). But the absence of care that produces a major break in the chain of custody may require that the evidence be rejected. Apparently, this is contemplated in the drafters' *Analysis. See also* our discussion of the admissibility of the chain of custody documents at Rule 803(6) and (8).

Subdivision (b) provides ten non-exhaustive illustrations of authentication or identification. On the whole, these examples broaden the proponent's horizons for authenticating evidence in military practice. The point here is that the Rule recognizes that there are many ways, often overlapping, to authenticate evidence. None of the illustrations are inconsistent with pre-Rules practice; although several were not specifically included in the former *Manual* provisions — *e.g.,* (b)(6), (b)(8). *See also Manual* ¶ 54 for guidance on handling real evidence, charts, diagrams, etc., at trial.

Illustration (1). A time-honored method of authenticating or identifying evidence is to elicit testimony from a witness who is familiar with the proferred evidence — *e.g.,* the witness saw the accused sign the false pay voucher or recognizes the victim's bloody shirt. *United States v. Johnson,* — F.2d — (9th Cir. 1980) (ax was sufficiently identified by witness who was "pretty sure" that it was the one used in the assault). The traditional chain of custody and other recognized methods of identifying physical evidence would also be examples of this illustration in operation. *See generally* Imwinkelried, *The Identification of Original, Real Evidence,* 61 MIL. L. REV. 145 (1973).

Illustration (2). Any lay witness familiar with the handwriting in question may identify it as long as the familiarity was not acquired solely for purposes of the court-martial. *See United States v. Pitts,* 569 F.2d 343 (5th Cir.), cert. denied, 436 U.S. 959 (1978) (lay opinion rejected where familiarity acquired for purposes of the trial). This example of authentication, distinguishable from expert testimony governed by Rule 702 and ¶ (b)(3) follows, *infra, Manual* ¶ 143 b. *See, e.g., United States v. Ocamb,* 12 C.M.A. 492, 31 C.M.R. 78 (1961) (witness competent to identify signature if he has previously seen him sign his name).

Illustration (3). This illustration addresses authentication of a wide variety of evidence such as blood, ballistics, fingerprints, and handwriting. Proffered evidence may be authenticated by allowing court-members or an expert witness to compare it with an authenticated specimen. The specimen may be used if the court-members could find it to be genuine. Where the comparison involves specialized or scientific principles, the proponent should normally employ expert testimony. *See generally* our discussion at Rule 702. This provision apparently expands *Manual* ¶ 144e, which had limited comparison of fingerprints to persons skilled in that craft.

Illustration (4). Evidence may in some instances be authenticated by simply showing the characteristics of the item itself. For example, in *United States v. Stearns,* 550 F.2d 1167 (9th Cir. 1977) the contents of a photograph, in conjunction with other circumstantial or indirect evidence, could serve as authentication in the absence of testimony to establish what the pictures represented. The better practice of course is to establish authenticity through the testimony of a witness who is familiar with the exhibit. *See* (b)(1). Another common example here would be the application of the reply letter doctrine formerly referenced in *Manual* ¶ 143b(1).

Illustration (5). A voice may be identified by a witness who has either directly or indirectly heard the voice; the witness need not testify as an expert unless the identification process entails analysis of voiceprints. *See, e.g., United States v. Wright,* 17 C.M.A. 183, 37 C.M.R. 447 (1967) (expert interpreted voiceprint). For a general discussion of use of voice spectrographs *see* Gorecki, *Evidentiary Use of Voice Spectrograph in Criminal Proceedings,* 77 MIL. L. REV. 167 (1977).

Illustration (6). If counsel cannot establish the identity of a voice through a witness's familiarity under paragraph (b)(5), other circumstantial proof may suffice. This illustration is grounded upon the common everyday assumptions and assurances of reliability associated with telephonic communications. For example, if the proponent can show that the witness determined the phone number of Sergeant X, dialed that number and talked to a person identifying himself as Sergeant X, the ensuing conversation will probably have been authenticated. *See, e.g., United States v. Sawyer,* 607 F.2d 1190 (7th Cir. 1979) (telephone conversation authenticated by showing defendant's telephone number and that conversation centered on IRS matters personal to the defendant). *See generally* Shumkler, *Voice Identification in Criminal Cases Under Article IX of the Federal Rules of Evidence,* 49 TEMP. L.Q. 867 (1976). Likewise, a telephone conversation with a business may be authenticated if the witness dialed the number assigned to the business and the conversation involved business reasonably transacted over the telephone. Radio transmissions could be authenticated in similar fashion.

Illustration (7). Public records, including computer data may be authenticated, as under pre-Rules practice, by showing custody either through live testimony or the commonly used authenticating or attesting certificates. *See Manual* ¶ 143*b*. Accompanying hearsay and secondary evidence (best evidence) principles are covered in Sections VIII and X, respectively. *See also* Rule 902 for records which may be self-authenticating.

Illustration (8). The "ancient documents" method of authentication was not officially recognized in the *Manual* and will probably not find much use in contemporary military practice. Note that the Rule reduces the common law requirement of 30 years to 20 and shifts the emphasis from the document's appearance of authenticity to custody or location of the document.

Illustration (9). Where the proffered evidence is the result of a process or system, the proponent may authenticate the evidence by establishing that the process or system produces accurate results. Authentication of x-rays, computer print-outs and tape recordings would be examples of evidence included in this illustration. The reliability of the system may be judicially noticed. *See* Rule 201.

Illustration (10). This provision was included in the Federal Rule to specifically recognize the continued viability of a variety of authentication methods prescribed in the Bankruptcy Act and the Civil and Criminal Rules of Procedure. The Military Rule has been modified to permit future promulgation of methods of authentication or identification.

DRAFTERS' ANALYSIS

(a) General provision. Rule 901(a) is taken verbatim from the Federal Rule, and is similar to ¶ 143*b* of the present *Manual,* which states in pertinent part that: "A writing may be authenticated by any competent proof that it is genuine — is in fact what it purports or is claimed to be." Unlike the *Manual* provision, however, Rule 901(a) is not limited to writings and consequently is broader in scope. The Rule supports the requirement for logical relevance. *See* Rule 401.

There is substantial question as to the proper interpretation of the Federal Rule equivalent of Rule 901(a). The Rule requires only "evidence sufficient to support a finding that the matter in question is what its proponent claims." It is possible that this phrasing supersedes any formulaic approach to authentication and that rigid rules such as those that have been devised to authenticate taped recordings, for example, are no longer valid. On the other hand, it appears fully appropriate for a trial judge to require such evidence as is needed "to support a finding that the matter in question is what its proponent claims," which evidence may echo in some cases the common law formulations. There appears to be no reason to believe that the Rule will change the present law as it affects chains of custody for real evidence — especially if fungible. Present case law would appear to be consistent with the new Rule because the chain of custody requirement has not been applied in a rigid fashion. A chain of custody will still be required when it is necessary to show that the evidence is what it is claimed to be and, when appropriate, that its condition is unchanged. Rule 901(a) may make authentication somewhat easier, but is unlikely to make a substantial change in most areas of military practice.

As is generally the case, failure to object to evidence on the grounds of lack of authentication will waive the objection, *see* Rule 103(a).

(b) Illustrations. Rule 901(b) is taken verbatim from the Federal Rule with the exception of a modification to Rule 901(b)(10). Rule 901 (b)(10) has been modified by the addition of "or by applicable regulations prescribed pursuant to statutory authority." The new language was added because it was viewed as impracticable in military practice to require statutory or Supreme Court action to add authentication methods. The world wide disposition of the armed forces with their frequent redeployments may require rapid adjustments in authentication procedures to preclude substantial interference with personnel practices needed to ensure operational efficiency. The new language does not require new statutory authority. Rather, the present authority that exists for the various Service and Departmental Secretaries to issue those regulations necessary for the day to day operations of their departments is sufficient.

Rule 901(b) is a non-exhaustive list of illustrative examples of authentication techniques. None of the examples are inconsistent with present military law and many are found within the present *Manual, see, e.g.,* ¶ 143*b.* Self-authentication is governed by Rule 902.

Rule 902. Self-Authentication

Extrinsic evidence of authenticity as a condition precedent to admissibility is not required with respect to the following:

(1) Domestic public documents under seal. A document bearing a seal purporting to be that of the United States, or any State, district, Commonwealth, territory, or insular possession thereof, or the Panama Canal Zone, or the Trust Territory of the Pacific Islands, or of a political subdivision, department, officer, or agency thereof, and a signature purporting to be an attestation or execution.

(2) Domestic public documents not under seal. A document purporting to bear the signature in the official capacity of an officer or employee of any entity included in paragraph (1) hereof, having no seal, if a public officer having a seal and having official duties in the district or political subdivision of the officer or employee certifies under seal that the signer has the official capacity and that the signature is genuine.

(3) Foreign public documents. A document purporting to be executed or attested in an official capacity by a person authorized by the laws of a foreign country to make the execution or attestation, and accompanied by a final certification as to the genuineness of the signature and official position (A) of the executing or attesting person, or (B) of any foreign official whose certificate of genuineness of signature and official position relates to the execution or attestation or is in a chain of certificates of genuineness of signature and official position relating to the execution or attestation. A final certification may be made by a secretary of embassy or legation, consul general, consul, vice consul, or consular agent of the United States, or a diplomatic or consular official of the foreign country assigned or accredited to the United States. If reasonable opportunity has been given to all parties to investigate the authenticity and accuracy of official documents, the court may, for good cause shown, order that they to be treated as presumptively authentic without final certification or permit them to be evidenced by an attested summary with or without final certification.

(4) Certified copies of public records. A copy of an official record or report or entry therein, or of a document authorized by

law to be recorded or filed and actually recorded or filed in a public office, including data compilations in any form, certified as correct by the custodian or other person authorized to make the certification, by certificate complying with paragraphs (1), (2), or (3) of this rule or complying with any Act of Congress, rule prescribed by the Supreme Court pursuant to statutory authority, or an applicable regulation prescribed pursuant to statutory authority.

(4a) Documents or records of the United States accompanied by attesting certificates. Documents or records kept under the authority of the United States by any department, bureau, agency, office, or court thereof when attached to or accompanied by an attesting certificate of the custodian of the document or record without further authentication.

(5) Official publications. Books, pamphlets, or other publications purporting to be issued by public authority.

(6) Newspapers and periodicals. Printed materials purporting to be newspapers or periodicals.

(7) Trade inscriptions and the like. Inscriptions, signs, tags or labels purporting to have been affixed in the course of business and indicating ownership, control, or origin.

(8) Acknowledged documents. Documents accompanied by a certificate of acknowledgment executed in the manner provided by law by a notary public or other officer authorized by law to take acknowledgments.

(9) Commercial paper and related documents. Commercial paper, signatures thereon, and documents relating thereto to the extent provided by general commercial law.

(10) Presumptions under Acts of Congress and regulations. Any signature, document, or other matter declared by Act of Congress or by applicable regulation prescribed pursuant to statutory authority to be presumptively or prima facie genuine or authentic.

EDITORIAL COMMENT

The traditional burden of authenticating certain familiar evidence has been considerably eased by Rule 902, which relieves the proponent from offering extrinsic evidence to establish that the evidence is what it purports to be. The Rule, which deals only with the question of authenticity of evidence, takes the view that some evidence is so likely to be genuine that its proponent should not be compelled to lay a formal foundation. Instead, the evidence authenticates itself. (Rule 901(b)(4) may reach similar results in some cases.)

Underlying the Rule is the philosophy that extrinsic evidence should only be required when reasonable people might question the genuineness of evidence. Technical and time-consuming foundation requirements are reserved for cases in which they serve a valid purpose. It should be emphasized that nothing in the Rule prevents an opponent of evidence from contesting its authenticity. The Rule assumes that evidence falling into one of the specified classes is so likely to be what it purports to be that no extrinsic evidence is required of the proponent. But nothing inhibits the opponent from offering evidence to prove to the court that an exhibit that has been admitted is not authentic.

The Rule is almost identical to its federal counterpart; paragraph (4a) is added, however, and minor changes are made in paragraph (10). On the whole the Rule makes no substantial change in pre-Rules practices.

Each category of evidence covered by the Rule is addressed below.

(1) If a public document bears one of the designated official seals and is accompanied by a signature it is self-authenticating. The signature may be on the document itself or a copy thereof (execution) or on an accompanying attestation certificate. This paragraph is identical to the Federal Rule. The drafters' *Analysis* states that judicial notice of seals and signatures is not required. *Manual* ¶ 147a. *See also Manual* ¶ 143b(2)(c) and (d) which provided for authentication of United States and State records.

(2) A public document not bearing a seal may be self-authenticating if it bears an appropriate signature and if a public officer having a seal certifies under seal that (1) the document's signer has the official capacity and (2) the signature on the document is genuine. The paragraph, identical to the Federal Rule, seems to cover only those situations where the officer or employee signing the document has no seal. What of the situation where the individual has a seal but has not used it? Neither the legislative history of the Federal Rule or the drafters' *Analysis* address this point. We see no reason to distinguish between that situation and one where the signing official does not have a seal. In both cases, it is the certification of the official, under seal, which provides self-authentication.

(3) A foreign document may be self-authenticating under this paragraph if it is executed or attested to by an individual authorized to do so by the foreign country's laws and is accompanied by a "final certification." The final certification relates to the genuineness of (1) the signature and (2) the official position of the individual executing or attesting the document. The Rule also provides for chains of certificates of genuineness. That is, the signature and official position of the original signer may in some instances be accompanied by a chain of certificates until an authorized final certification is made. For

example, *A* executes a foreign document; *B* (not authorized under the Rule to provide a final certification) attests to *A*'s signature and official position, and *C*, a counsel general, provides a final certification to *B*'s signature and official position. *See, e.g., United States v. Rodriguez Serrate,* 534 F.2d 7 (1st Cir. 1976) (copy of foreign birth certificate was authenticated using a chain of certifications). *See generally,* Annot., 41 A.L.R. FED. (1979), Proof of Foreign Official Record Under Rule 44(a)(2) of Federal Rules of Civil Procedure.

This paragraph, identical to the Federal Rule, is patterned after Federal Rules of Civil Procedure 44(a)(2) and generally follows pre-Rules practice with two exceptions. First, this paragraph restricts the authority to issue final certification to civilian authorities. *Manual* ¶ 143*b*(2)(e) had permitted United States military personnel to do so. Second, the Rule does not permit self-authentication if the authentication process is based solely on the foreign country's laws. *Manual* ¶ 143*b*(2)(e).

In any event, the paragraph permits relaxation of the requirement of final certification if all parties have had a reasonable opportunity to examine the documents and good cause is shown. *See, e.g., In re Sterling Navigation Co.,* 444 F. Supp. 1043 (S.D.N.Y. 1977) (trial judge relied on Rule 902(3)).

This paragraph covers foreign public documents. Copies of foreign public records may be self-authenticating, however, under paragraph (4). On November 28, 1979, the Senate gave its consent to the ratification by the United States of an international Convention making it easier for parties than it is under Rule 902 to authenticate foreign public documents. Under the Convention, each country designates public officials by title who may stamp what is called an "apostille," a form of certification, on the document itself or affix it to an accompanying paper. The apostille states that the document was signed by an individual acting in his official capacity and that the official's stamp or seal is genuine.

(4) Copies of official records, reports, and data compilations properly on file may be self-authenticating if they are accompanied by a certificate from a custodian or other authorized person and conform with paragraphs (1), (2), or (3). They are also self-authenticating if the certificates conform to Acts of Congress, rules prescribed by the Supreme Court, or to applicable regulations. This paragraph differs from the Federal Rule in that provision is made here for regulatory prescription of the certification process. The certificate is itself a public document. It permits any official public record or report and any document filed in accordance with applicable law to be self-authenticating. This can be an expansive category.

Occasionally, counsel will want to show that a report or record does not exist. Either this paragraph or paragraphs (1), (2), and (3) in conjunction with Rule 803(10), permit counsel to do so by using a certified affidavit of the official who conducted the search. *See, e.g., United States v. City of McAlester,* 410 F. Supp. 848 (E.D. Okla. 1976) (search revealed no reference in records to litigation involving city) and *Robbins v. United States,* 476 F.2d 26 (10th Cir. 1973) (absence of firearm registration). If some public record accompanies the certificate, this paragraph probably governs. Otherwise, paragraphs (1), (2), and (3) probably are controlling.

The contents of the authenticating certificate are not prescribed and any format which certifies correctness should suffice. *But see United States v. Stone,* 604 F.2d 922 (5th Cir. 1979) (authenticating affidavit by the custodian contained inadmissible hearsay.)

(4a) Spawned by military necessity and derived from *Manual* ¶ 143*b*(2)(c), this new paragraph provides for self-authentication of both United States documents and records which are kept in accordance with applicable laws or regulations and are accompanied by an attesting certificate. The paragraph applies to both originals and copies and requires that the "custodian" execute the attesting certificate. The drafters' *Analysis* causes some confusion by defining an attesting certificate as "a certificate or statement, signed by the custodian of the record *or the deputy or assistant of the custodian...*" [emphasis added]. The drafters' definition is taken from *Manual* ¶ 143*b*(2)(a) and apparently does not make allowance for the plain language of the Rule which limits self-authentication to evidence attested to by the custodian. This provision will allow for continuation of the common pre-Rules practice of authenticating evidence such as laboratory reports, personnel records and accountability reports with certificates.

Particular attention should be paid to the self-authentication of chain of custody forms and laboratory reports. This paragraph does not really change the common pre-Rules practice of authenticating lab reports, but it may ease the proponent's burden of showing a chain of custody. In the past the chain was normally proved by live testimony. Chain of custody forms were held to be inadmissible hearsay. *See United States v. Porter,* 7 M.J. 32 (C.M.A. 1979). Applied broadly, this paragraph, operating in conjunction with Rule 901(a), Rule 803(6), and (8), could revolutionize prosecution of drug cases. *See* our more detailed discussion of Rule 803(6) and (8), indicating that chain of custody forms and lab reports may now be admissible without live witness foundations.

Evidence offered under this paragraph must still qualify under best evidence and hearsay principles, and the proponent may, in limited circumstances, be required to show that the proffered document or record is kept under authority of the United States or a subordinate entity. Should the authority be questioned, the proponent will normally be able to satisfy this paragraph by presenting the applicable statute or regulation. Alternatively the military judge could take judicial notice of the authority. *See* Rule 201A.

There is a rebuttable presumption that the custodian's signature, which must be legible, *see, e.g., United States v. Lawson,* 42 C.M.R. 847 (A.C.M.R. 1970), is genuine.

(5) Official publications or copies thereof may be self-authenticating if they are purportedly issued by public authority. This provision clearly applies to United States publications. But what of a regulation published by order of the commanding general of an installation? A regulation published by the ship's captain? No specific guidance on this point can be found in the Rule, the legislative history or the drafters' *Analysis.* The Rule assumes that few people will fraudulently hold out a publication as a government publication, and we believe this holds true for regulations as well. Moreover, the Rule's preference for admissibility would seem to support self-authentication of local official

publications or their equivalent. The problem can most often be avoided by employing judicial notice under Rule 201 or 201A.

(6) Periodicals and newspapers may now be self-authenticating. Again, these documents in themselves exhibit sufficient reliability to escape the requirement for extrinsic evidence. Does this paragraph, which is identical to the Federal Rule, apply if counsel merely offers a newspaper clipping or excerpt from a periodical? Probably not. But they could be authenticated under Rule 901. What if a microfilm copy of a newspaper is offered? This would be permissible under Rule 1003.

(7) This paragraph, which is identical to its federal counterpart, treats tags, labels, inscriptions, and the like as self-authenticating if they are supposed to have been affixed in a course of business. Generally, this provision will find little use in military criminal trials. It might be helpful, however, in establishing government ownership in a case involving, for example, larceny of government property which clearly bears a *U.S.* stamp. *Cf. United States v. Gibson,* 13 C.M.R. 825 (A.F.B.R. 1953) (lay witnesses identification at time of larceny of stolen blankets bearing markings of *U.S. Army* and *U.S. Navy* held insufficient to establish ownership).

(8) Documents accompanied by a certificate of acknowledgement by either a notary or other properly authorized officer are self-authenticating. Under the federal counterpart, the acknowledgment will normally be executed by a notary. However, Article 136, U.C.M.J. confers upon a large category of military personnel the "general powers of a notary public. ..." Under this Rule, documents properly acknowledged by those personnel would probably be self-authenticating. The certificate need not be affixed with a seal. *See generally* Annot., *Sufficiency of Certificate of Acknowledgment,* 25 A.L.R.2d 1124, 1129 (1952).

(9) Certain commercial paper may be self-authenticating under the provisions of "general commercial law," *i.e.,* the Uniform Commercial Code. For example, under 3-307 of the Code, signatures on negotiable instruments are presumed genuine. *See, e.g., United States v. Carriger,* 592 F.2d 312 (6th Cir. 1979) (mere production of promissory note is prima facie evidence of validity); *United States v. Little,* 567 F.2d 346, 349 n.1 (8th Cir. 1977), cert. denied, 435 U.S. 969 (1978) (corporate checks admissible under Rule 902(a)). *See also* Uniform Commercial Code §§ 1-202 (third-party documents), 3-510 (evidence of dishonor and notice of dishonor); 8-105(2) (signature on negotiable instrument). This paragraph apparently eases the pre-Rules practice requiring a three-step foundation for returned checks. *See, e.g., United States v. Baugh,* 33 C.M.R. 913 (A.F.B.R. 1963). Other banking or commercial records could be self-authenticating under paragraph (4).

(10) This final paragraph is a modification of the Federal Rule. Language was added to permit designation of additional matters worthy of self-authentication.

DRAFTERS' ANALYSIS

Rule 902 has been taken from the Federal Rule without significant change except that a new subdivision, 4a, has been added and subdivisions (4) and (10) have been modified. The Rule prescribes forms of self-authentication.

(1) Domestic public documents under seal. Rule 902(1) is taken verbatim from the Federal Rule, and is similar to aspects of ¶¶ 143*b*(2)(c) and (d) of the present *Manual.* The Rule does not distinguish between original documents and copies. A seal is self-authenticating and, in the absence of evidence to the contrary, is presumed genuine. Judicial notice is not required.

(2) Domestic public documents not under seal. Rule 902(2) is taken from the Federal Rule without change. It is similar in scope to aspects of ¶¶ 143*b*(2)(c) and (d) of the present *Manual* in that it authorizes use of a certification under seal to authenticate a public document not itself under seal. This provision is not the only means of authenticating a domestic public record under this Rule. *Compare* Rule 902(4); 902(4a).

(3) Foreign public documents. Rule 902(3) is taken without change from the Federal Rule. Although the Rule is similar to ¶¶ 143*b*(2)(e) and (f) of the present Manual, the Rule is potentially narrower than the present military one as the Rule does not permit "final certification" to be made by military personnel as does the *Manual* rule nor does it permit authentication made solely pursuant to the laws of the foreign nation. On the other hand, the Rule expressly permits the military judge to order foreign documents to "be treated as presumptively authentic without final certification or permit them to be evidenced by an attested summary with or without final certification."

(4) Certified copies of public records. Rule 902(4) is taken verbatim from the Federal Rule except that it has been modified by adding "or applicable regulation prescribed pursuant to statutory authority." The additional language is required by military necessity and includes the now existing statutory powers of the President and various Secretaries to promulgate regulations. *See, generally,* Analysis to Rule 901(b).

Rule 902(4) expands upon prior forms of self-authentication to acknowledge the propriety of certified public records or reports and related materials domestic or foreign, the certification of which complies with subdivisions (1), (2), or (3) of the Rule.

(4a) Documents or records of the United States accompanied by attesting certificates. This provision is new and is taken from the third subparagraph of ¶ 143 *b*(2)(c) of the present *Manual.* It has been inserted due to the necessity to facilitate records of the United States in general and military records in particular. Military personnel do not have seals and it would not be practicable to either issue them or require submission of documents to those officials with them. In many cases, such a requirement would be impossible to comply with due to geographical isolation or the unwarranted time such a requirement could demand.

An "attesting certificate" is a certificate or statement, signed by the custodian of the record or the deputy or assistant of the custodian, which in any form indicates that the writing to which the certificate or statement refers is a true copy of the record or an accurate "translation" of a machine, electronic, or coded record, and that the signer of the certificate or statement is acting in an official capacity as the person having custody of the record or as the deputy or assistant thereof.

Paragraph 143(2)(a) of the present *Manual.* An attesting certificate does not require further authentication and, absent proof to the contrary, the signature of the custodian or deputy or assistant thereof on the certificate is presumed to be genuine.

(5-9) Official publications; Newspapers and periodicals; Trade inscriptions and the like; Acknowledged documents; Commercial paper and related documents. Rules 902(5)-(9) are taken verbatim from the Federal Rule and have no equivalents in the *Manual* or in Military law.

(10) Presumptions under Acts of Congress and regulations. Rule 902(10) was taken from the Federal Rule but was modified by adding "and Regulations" in the caption and "or by applicable regulation prescribed pursuant to statutory authority." *See, generally* the *Analysis* to Rule 901(10) for the reasons for the additional language. The statutory authority referred to includes the presently existing authority for the President and various Secretaries to prescribe regulations.

Rule 903. Subscribing Witness' Testimony Unnecessary

The testimony of a subscribing witness is not necessary to authenticate a writing unless required by the laws of the jurisdiction whose laws govern the validity of the writing.

EDITORIAL COMMENT

Normally, writings may be authenticated under either Rule 901 or 902. However, if a statute (almost always a state statute) requires the testimony of a subscribing or attesting witness to authenticate a document, then under Rule 903 that state requirement controls.

The common law recognized a preference for the live testimony of the individual who had signed the proffered document as either a subscribing or attesting witness. Only after producing the witness, or sufficiently explaining his absence, could the proponent resort to other methods of authentication. The subscribing witnesses' testimony was not binding, however, and could be explained or contradicted by other evidence. Most states have abolished the requirement of authentication through subscribing witnesses' testimony; those remaining statutes would normally require it in authenticating wills or marriage contracts. *See generally,* J. WEINSTEIN and M. BERGER, WEINSTEIN'S EVIDENCE ¶ 903[02] (1978).

Even assuming a state statute exists, this Rule, which is identical to the Federal Rule, comes into play only when the document is being offered to show execution. Rule 903 could have an impact on the government and defense in military cases. For example, a marriage contract might be offered in defense to a charge of violation of Article 132, U.C.M.J. (*e.g.,* false claim for dependent travel). Or, a properly executed marriage contract may be relied upon by the prosecution where the accused is charged with bigamy. In either instance, the state statutes controlling the execution and authentication of the offered marriage contract should be consulted. If they do not require a subscribing witness's testimony, counsel may authenticate the evidence under Rule 901 or 902.

Congress could, of course, require subscribing witnesses to be called to authenticate federal writings, but it has shown no inclination to embrace the common law requirement that most states have repudiated.

DRAFTERS' ANALYSIS

Rule 903 is taken verbatim from the Federal Rule and has no express equivalent in the present *Manual.*

SECTION X. CONTENTS OF WRITINGS, RECORDINGS, AND PHOTOGRAPHS

Rule 1001. Definitions.

For purposes of this section the following definitions are applicable:

(1) Writings and recordings. "Writings" and "recordings" consist of letters, words, or numbers, or their equivalent, set down by handwriting, typewriting, printing, photostating, photographing, magnetic impulse, mechanical or electronic recording, or other form of data compilation.

(2) Photographs. "Photographs" include still photographs, X-ray films, video tapes, and motion pictures.

(3) Original. An "original" of a writing or recording is the writing or recording itself or any counterpart intended to have the same effect by a person executing or issuing it. An "original" of a photograph includes the negative or any print therefrom. If data are stored in a computer or similar device, any printout or other output readable by sight, shown to reflect the data accurately, is an "original".

(4) Duplicate. A "duplicate" is a counterpart produced by the same impression as the original, or from the same matrix, or by means of photography, including enlargements and miniatures, or by mechanical or electronic rerecording, or by chemical reproduction, or by other equivalent techniques which accurately reproduce the original.

EDITORIAL COMMENT

The Best Evidence Rule requires that where the proponent is seeking to prove the contents of a writing, he must present the "original" unless an exception exists. Rules 1001, 1002, 1003 and 1004 now comprise the military's basic Best Evidence Rule. It formerly was included in *Manual* ¶ 143a. Rules 1005-1008 cover special aspects of best evidence problems.

Rule 1001 sets forth those underlying definitions which serve as the framework for the three succeeding Rules. This Rule is identical to its federal counterpart and makes no substantial change in military practice.

Paragraph (1) defines "writings" and "recordings" in broad fashion as "letters, words, or numbers, or their equivalent" produced through a variety of methods. It is comparable to *Manual* ¶ 143d which had defined a writing to be "every method of recording data upon any medium."

Paragraph (2) states that photographs include not only commonly used still photographs, but also X rays, video tapes and motion pictures. This section has no counterpart in former *Manual* provisions, but is consistent with pre-Rules practice.

Section (3) defines an "original" writing, recording and photograph. The writing or recording itself is an original, as is any counterpart intended to be treated as an original. *Manual* ¶ 143a(1) treated complete carbon copies as duplicate originals. Identical photostatic copies were also considered as duplicate originals if they were intended to serve as originals. Under Paragraph (3), carbon copies will now be considered as originals only if they were intended to serve as such. Otherwise they are "duplicates" within the definition of Paragraph (4).

An original photograph under Section (3) includes both the negative and any prints made from the negative. Computer printouts are also treated as originals.

Paragraph (4) defines the term "duplicate" as a counterpart produced by the same impression as the original or by other accurate means of reproduction. The means or process used to create the duplicate is not crucial as long as it represents a technique insuring accuracy. A duplicate may be created simultaneously with the original or at a later time. Not within this definition are those copies subsequently produced manually, i.e., handwritten or typed.

Paragraph (4), as applied, may work a change in former military practice and relax the Best Evidence Rule. Photostatic copies of original documents were normally considered under pre-Rules practice to be secondary evidence if they were not intended to serve as originals. *Manual* ¶ 143a(1). Now, although they remain duplicates and are not treated as originals, they are generally admissible under Rule 1003. But this section also may be more demanding in part, than pre-Rules practice, which treated complete carbon copies as duplicate originals, whether or not they were intended to serve as originals. *Manual* ¶ 143a(1). Now, absent that intent, they will be treated as duplicates and not originals. In defining pre-Rules practice, the drafters' *Analysis* makes nothing of the distinction between the two categories of duplicate originals. The drafters' *Analysis* may therefore be misleading insofar as it suggests that all documents formerly labelled as "duplicate originals" are now governed by

Paragraph (4). In our view, duplicate originals that are intended to be originals, whether carbon copies or otherwise, were treated as originals before and are still originals under Paragraph (3). Only when there is no intent that a duplicate be treated as an original is Paragraph (4) used, and this is where the Rule, as applied to carbons, differs from pre-Rules practice.

DRAFTERS' ANALYSIS

(1) Writings and recordings. Rule 1001(1) is taken verbatim from the Federal Rule and is similar in scope to *Manual* ¶ 143*d* of the present *Manual.* Although the present *Manual* is somewhat more detailed, the *Manual* was clearly intended to be expansive. The Rule adequately accomplishes the identical purpose through a more general reference.

(2) Photographs. Rule 1001(2) is taken verbatim from the Federal Rule and has no express equivalent in the present *Manual.* It does, however, reflect current military law.

(3) Original. Rule 1001(3) is taken verbatim from the Federal Rule and is similar to ¶ 143*a*(1) of the present *Manual.* The present *Manual,* however, treats "duplicate originals," *i.e.,* carbon and photographic copies made for use as an original, as an "original" while Rule 1001(4) treats such a document as a "duplicate."

(4) Duplicate. Rule 1001(4) is taken from the Federal Rule verbatim and includes those documents ¶ 143*a*(1) of the present *Manual* defines as "duplicate originals." In view of Rule 1003's rule of admissibility for "duplicates," no appreciable negative result stems from the reclassification.

Rule 1002. Requirement of an Original.

To prove the content of a writing, recording, or photograph, the original writing, recording, or photograph is required, except as otherwise provided in these rules, this Manual, or by Act of Congress.

EDITORIAL COMMENT

The traditional Best Evidence Rule (more accurately, the Original Document Rule), now captured in Rule 1002 requires a party wanting to prove the contents of a writing, recording or photograph to produce the *original* unless otherwise exempted. This Rule is substantially similar to the Federal Rule, although a minor textual change recognizes that the *Manual* itself might provide an exception to the requirement of an original.

The Rule generally follows pre-Rules practice, *see Manual* ¶ 143a, but will change military practice insofar as most of the pre-Rules *Manual* exceptions to the requirement of an original are not specifically recognized in Section X. *See, e.g., Manual* ¶ 143a(f) (fingerprints comparison). However, as the drafters' *Analysis* notes, this will be offset by other Rules which will normally allow admission of the same evidence. For example, Rules 1003 to 1007, provide exceptions to Rule 1002, and a substantial number of federal statutes relieve the proponent from presenting the original. For a listing of examples, *see generally* 5 J. WEINSTEIN AND M. BERGER, WEINSTEIN'S EVIDENCE ¶ 1002[04] (1978).

Defining what constitutes the original should normally not present a problem. *See* our discussion of Rule 1001(3). One of the most commonly encountered problems, however, is to determine whether the proponent of evidence is attempting to prove the contents of the writing, recording or photograph. There seems to be a universal urge to object on "best evidence" grounds whenever testimony draws attention to a document. That an event or statement has been reduced to writing or recorded on videotape does not in itself trigger the Rule and prevent a witness from testifying as to the event or statement. *United States v. Jewson,* 1 C.M.A. 652, 5 C.M.R. 80 (1952). The Rule does not apply, for instance, when a writing is used to support a witness' opinion or when it is used in court to refresh recollection. And in *United States v. Rose,* 590 F.2d 232 (7th Cir. 1978), cert. denied, 442 U.S. 929 (1979) a witness' testimony concerning a tape-recorded conversation did not violate the Best Evidence Rule, because the testimony concerned the contents of the conversation not the contents of the tape recording. Usually, a picture or film is offered as a representation of what a witness saw, or a tape recording is offered to illustrate what a witness heard. In these instances, the picture, film or tape is not offered to prove its contents, but to illustrate or to complete testimony, and the Best Evidence Rule is inapplicable. If, however, the film or picture is allegedly obscene, the contents are being proved when it is offered, and Rule 1002 is applicable.

By the same token, the mere fact that a laboratory report has been prepared on a marihuana sample does not require its production under this Rule to establish the sample's identity; the identity may be independently established through testimony of the chemist. The identity of the drug is in issue, not the contents of the lab report — unless of course the proponent offers the report into evidence. The point here is that the proponent may often avoid potential Best Evidence Rule problems by simply relying upon testimony which relates, not the contents of a writing, but rather the event itself.

Some of the confusion among counsel in application of the Best Evidence Rule centers on misapplication of what might be loosely termed a "best" or most persuasive evidence notion. In a drug case, the laboratory report is normally the most persuasive evidence of the drug's identity, and in proving a confession, the most persuasive evidence of what the accused said usually lies in his signed written statement. But the fact that more persuasive evidence exists in the form of a writing, recording or photograph does not trigger Rule 1002 when oral testimony is offered. The Rule only operates when someone is trying to prove the contents of an item. Note, however, that the existence of better evidence may result in exclusion of evidence to save time under Military Rules 403 or 611, or to vindicate the reliability concerns of particular provisions like Military Rules 803(6), 803(24), and 804(b)(5).

Rule 1002 is only one of several interrelated hurdles to admissibility. Offered writings, recordings and photographs are subject to the limitations of Section VIII (hearsay) and Section IX (authentication). For discussions of applicability of this Rule *see generally* Berger, *Article X, Contents of Writings, Recordings, and Photographs,* 33 FED. B.J. 87 (1974); Note, *Contents of Writings, Recordings and Photographs,* 27 ARK. L. REV. 357 (1973).

DRAFTERS' ANALYSIS

Rule 1002 is taken verbatim from the Federal Rule except that "this Manual" has been added in recognition of the efficacy of other *Manual* provisions. The Rule is similar in scope to the best evidence rule found in ¶ 143a(19) of the present *Manual* except that specific reference is made in the rule to recordings and photographs. Unlike the present *Manual,* the Rule does not contain the misleading reference to "best evidence" and is plainly applicable only to writings, recordings or photographs.

It should be noted that the various exceptions to Rule 1002 are similar to but not identical with those found in the present *Manual. Compare* Rules 1005-1007 *with* ¶ 143 a(2)(f) of the present *Manual.* For example, ¶¶ 143a(2)(e) and 144c of the present *Manual* exempt banking records and business records from the rule as categories while the Rule does not. The actual difference in practice, however, is not likely to be substantial as Rule 1003 allows admission of duplicates unless, for example, "a genuine question is raised as to the authenticity of the original." This is similar in result to the *Manual's* treatment of business records in ¶ 144c of the present *Manual.* Omission of other *Manual* exceptions, *e.g.,* certificates of fingerprint comparison and identity, *see* Rules 703; 803; evidence of absence of official or business entries, and copies of telegrams and radiograms, do not appear substantial when viewed against the entirety of the Military Rules which are likely to allow admissibility in a number of ways.

The Rule's reference to "Act of Congress" will now incorporate those statutes that specifically direct that the best evidence rule be inapplicable in one form or another.

See, e.g., 1 U.S.C. § 209 (copies of District of Columbia Code of Laws). As a rule, such statutes permit a form of authentication as an adequate substitute for the original document.

Rule 1003. Admissibility of Duplicates

A duplicate is admissible to the same extent as an original unless (1) a genuine question is raised as to the authenticity of the original or (2) in the circumstances it would be unfair to admit the duplicate in lieu of the original.

EDITORIAL COMMENT

A "duplicate," as defined in Rule 1001(4), is as readily admissible as an original unless there is a genuine question about the original's authenticity or fairness dictates that under the circumstances the duplicate should not be admitted. In short, duplicates are admissible unless the opponent can show good reason for requiring production of the original. *See, e.g., United States v. Morgan,* 555 F.2d 238 (9th Cir. 1977) (applying Rule 1003, court held xerox copy to be presumptively admissible). The rationale for this liberal rule, which presumes reliability, rests in large part on technology capable of producing virtually identical duplicates, thereby insuring a high degree of accuracy and precision.

Identical to its federal counterpart, this Rule changes pre-Rules practice, which permitted only duplicate originals to be treated as originals. *See Manual* ¶ 143*a*(1). Identical carbon copies were considered duplicate originals regardless of any intent to treat them as originals. However, photocopies were duplicate originals only if they were intended to be treated, or were in fact treated, as originals. Thus, under pre-Rules practice if counsel subsequently made a xerox copy of the document solely for purposes of trial, it was not considered a duplicate original, but was treated as secondary evidence.

Now, the term "duplicate original" is gone, carbon copies receive no special status, and photocopies are made solely for purposes of trial will normally be admissible under this Rule. But duplicates intended to have the same effect as originals are still treated as originals. *See* our discussion of Rules 1001(3) and 1002.

Probably the most important issue at trial with respect to 1003 will center on when a duplicate will not be treated as an original. The Rule states that a duplicate should not receive favored treatment if a "genuine" question of the authenticity of the original is raised. This clearly places a burden on the opponent to present information, or at least a particularized claim, which indicates specifically what is wrong with the duplicate. The authenticity question may be raised on the face of the offered duplicate where, for example, a number of handwritten annotations have been made, or where portions of the document are blurred. Extrinsic evidence, such as another conflicting duplicate that is supposedly also an accurate copy of the original may raise a serious question of authenticity. *See United States v. Enstam,* 622 F.2d 857 (5th Cir. 1980) (genuine question not raised where prosecution could not explain original's disappearance and duplicate did not show original's colorations). The Rule also will not admit a duplicate where it would be unfair to do so. Fairness might dictate exclusion where, for instance, the duplicate represents only an extract of the original and the missing portions would be useful for cross-examination.

Rule 1003 is intended to do away with purely technical objections, but not to claims that a duplicate is incomplete, altered or otherwise misleading or incorrect. Judges faced with an objection to admissibility must decide whether there is a good reason to require the original to be produced or to have its absence explained. The nature of the objection, the quality of the duplicate, its role in the trial, and lastly, the equities of the specific trial setting should be considered. *See, e.g., Amoco Production Co. v. United States,* 619 F.2d 1383 (10th Cir. 1980) (duplicate file copy excluded because critical part was not completely reproduced). If a duplicate is not admissible under this Rule, it may be admissible under Rule 1004, as long as the absence of an original is properly explained.

DRAFTERS' ANALYSIS

Rule 1003 is taken verbatim from the Federal Rule. It is both similar to and distinct from the present *Manual.* To the extent that the Rule deals with those copies which were intended at the time of their creation to be used as originals, it is similar to the present *Manual's* treatment "duplicate "dupliatcate originals". ¶ 143a(1), except that under the present *Manual* there is no distinction to be made between originals and "duplicate originals". Accordingly, in this case the Rule would be narrower than the present *Manual.* To the extent that the Rule deals with copies not intended at their time of creation to serve as originals, however, *e.g.,* when copies are made of preexisting documents for the purpose of litigation, the Rule is broader than the present *Manual* because the present *Manual* would prohibit such evidence unless an adequate justification for the non-production of the original existed.

Rule 1004. Admissibility of Other Evidence of Contents

The original is not required, and other evidence of the contents of a writing, recording, or photograph is admissible if:

(1) Originals lost or destroyed. All originals are lost or have been destroyed, unless the proponent lost or destroyed them in bad faith; or

(2) Original not obtainable. No original can be obtained by any available judicial process or procedure; or

(3) Original in possession of opponent. At a time when an original was under the control of the party against whom offered, the party was put on notice, by the pleadings or otherwise, that the contents would be a subject of proof at the hearing, and the party does not produce the original at the hearing; or

(4) Collateral matters. The writing, recording, or photograph is not closely related to a controlling issue.

EDITORIAL COMMENT

A proponent may offer secondary evidence in lieu of an original writing, recording or photograph if he does so through a recognized exception to the Best Evidence Rule. Rule 1004, identical to the Federal Rule, notes four commonly recognized exceptions. Others are presented in Rules 1005 (Public Records), 1006 (Summaries), and 1007 (Testimony or Written Admission of Party). Once an exception is shown, and Rule 1002 is overcome, the proponent is free to rely upon any form of secondary evidence. In theory, once the door is opened there are no technical degrees of secondary evidence. As a practical matter, however, counsel will normally want to present the most persuasive evidence available. *See United States v. Gerhart,* 538 F.2d 807 (8th Cir. 1976) (secondary evidence subject to opponent's attack on question of weight). Rule 1004 provides no major changes in military practice, although minor changes are apparent as we note in the following discussions on the four exceptions.

Section (1) is consistent with *Manual* ¶ 143a(2) and excuses production of an original which has been lost or destroyed, other than in bad faith. *See, e.g., United States v. Rhodes,* 3 C.M.A. 73, 11 C.M.R. 73 (1953) (copies could be used after destruction of letters by co-conspirator); *Schiavone-Chase Corp. v. United States,* 553 F.2d 658 (Ct. Cl. 1977) (copies could be used when standard government procedure resulted in destruction of documents). Traditionally, the proponent bears the burden of showing that the original has been destroyed or that a reasonable search has failed to locate the original. In determining the sufficiency of the proponent's search one commentator has suggested consideration of four factors: (a) suspicion of fraud, (b) importance of the instrument, (c) age of the instrument, and (d) lapse of time since the instrument was last seen. 5 J. WEINSTEIN AND M. BERGER, WEINSTEIN'S EVIDENCE, ¶ 1004(1)[04] (1978). A lost or destroyed original must still be authenticated under Section IX. This normally requires the proponent to establish that the original existed, was executed, and was later lost or destroyed. The particular order of proof here is not crucial. However, the military judge may prescribe the order under Rule 611(a). Questions of whether the original ever existed are for the court-members, *see* Rule 1008, but whether an original has been lost or destroyed is a question for the military judge. *See also* Rule 104.

Section (2) permits a proponent to offer secondary evidence if the original cannot be secured through available judicial process or procedure. This provision arguably narrows similar pre-Rules practice which had permitted secondary evidence where production of the original was not feasible. *Manual* ¶ 143a(2). If production is possible, yet costly in time or money, it is unclear whether the proponent may employ this exception to escape the requirement of producing the original. One commentator has suggested that the absolute terms of this provision should implicitly include the phrase "to the extent practicable and reasonable" and permit judges to fully exercise their discretion. 5 J. WEINSTEIN AND M. BERGER, WEINSTEIN'S EVIDENCE, ¶ 1004(2)[01] (1978). The drafters' *Analysis* is silent on this point. But the Advisory Committee's Note that accompanied the identical Federal Rule indicates that the drafters of that rule contemplated making a party utilize a subpoena *duces tecum* accompanying a deposition in another jurisdiction, which suggests that some expense is contemplated. Thus, it seems that the plain wording of Rule 1004(2) controls.

Under Section (3), a proponent may use secondary evidence if the original is in the hands of the opponent who fails to produce it at trial after receiving notice to do so. This section is similar to *Manual* ¶ 143a(2) except that now notice must first be given to the opponent. No special format is required for the notice as long as it is reasonable. If the accused has need of the original, because it is better evidence for some reason, the prosecution cannot validly refuse an order to turn it over to the defense. Because of potential self-incrimination problems, the prosecution should not demand in open court production of an original in possession of the accused. *McKnight v. United States,* 115 F. 972 (6th Cir. 1902) (reversible error to require prosecutor in open court to demand defendant to produce); *United States v. DeBell,* 11 C.M.A. 45, 28 C.M.R. 269 (1959) (dissenting opinion noted that prosecutor's tactic of demanding production in open court was a deliberate invasion of privilege against self-incrimination).

Section (4) generally follows pre-Rules case law and excuses production of the original if it is relevant only to collateral matters. *See, e.g., United States v. Jewson,* 1 C.M.A. 652, 5 C.M.R. 80 (1952) (secondary evidence admissible to impeach accused). This provision is grounded on expediency and inserts a needed degree of flexibility into a potentially technical Best Evidence Rule. When faced with matters which are potentially collateral, military judges should measure the importance of the offered evidence and its role in the trial. In many cases close examination of the evidence will reveal that the Best Evidence Rule should not even come into play because the contents of the original are not in question although a witness had made a passing reference to it. *See* our discussion at Rule 1002.

DRAFTERS' ANALYSIS

Rule 1004 is taken from the Federal Rule without change, and is similar in scope to the present *Manual*. Once evidence comes within the scope of Rule 1004, secondary evidence is admissible without regard to whether "better" forms of that evidence can be obtained. Thus, no priority is established once Rule 1002 is escaped. Although the present *Manual* states in ¶ 143a(2) that "the contents may be proved by an authenticated copy or by the testimony of a witness who has seen and can remember the substance of the writing" when the original need not be produced, that phrasing appears illustrative only and not exclusive. Accordingly, the Rule, the *Manual,* and common law are in agreement in not requiring categories of secondary evidence.

(1) Originals lost or destroyed. Rule 1004(1) is similar to the present *Manual* except that the Rule explicitly exempts originals destroyed in "bad faith." Such an exemption is implicit in the present *Manual.*

(2) Original not obtained. Rule 1004(2) is similar to the justification for nonproduction in ¶ 143a(2) of the present *Manual,* "an admissible writing . . . cannot feasibly be produced."

(3) Original in possession of opponent. Rule 1004(3) is similar to the present *Manual* provision in ¶ 143a(2) that when a document is in the possession of the accused, the original need not be produced except that the present *Manual* explicitly does not require notice to the accused, and the Rule may require such notice. Under the Rule, the accused must be "put on notice, by the pleadings or otherwise, that the contents would be a subject of proof at the hearing." Thus, under certain circumstances, a formal notice to the accused may be required. Under no circumstances should such a request or notice be made in the presence of the court-members. The only purpose of such notice is to justify use of secondary evidence and does not serve to compel the surrender of evidence from the accused. It should be noted that Rule 1004(3) acts in favor of the accused as well as the prosecution and allows notice to the prosecution to justify defense use of secondary evidence.

(4) Collateral matters. Rule 1004 is not found within the *Manual* but restates present military law. The intent behind the Rule is to avoid unnecessary delays and expense. It is important to note that important matters which may appear collateral may not be so in fact due to their weight. *See, e.g., United States v. Parker,* 13 C.M.A. 579, 33 C.M.R. 111 (1963). (Validity of divorce decree of critical prosecution witness not collateral when witness would be prevented from testifying due to spousal privilege if the divorce were not valid). The Rule incorporates this via its use of the expression "related to a controlling issue."

Rule 1005. Public Records

The contents of an official record, or of a document authorized to be recorded or filed and actually recorded or filed, including data compilations in any form, if otherwise admissible, may be proved by copy, certified as correct or attested to in accordance with rule 902 or testified to be correct by a witness who has compared it with the original. If a copy which complies with the foregoing cannot be obtained by the exercise of reasonable diligence, then other evidence of the contents may be given.

EDITORIAL COMMENT

Rule 1005 presents an exception to the requirement of Rule 1002 that an original writing or recording must be used to prove the contents thereof. This Rule provides that copies of official records or documents authorized and actually to be recorded or filed may be presented instead of the original. It is a rule of preference. Although duplicates generally benefit from a presumption of reliability, see Rule 1003, Rule 1005 indicates two preferred methods of dealing with duplicates of public documents. This Rule therefore appears to preempt Rule 1003 insofar as the contents of public documents are in question. The legislative history of the almost identical Federal Rule indicates that the special treatment for public documents represented a judgment that it should never be necessary to disrupt public offices by having original documents produced, but that there should be some guarantee that substitute evidence is reliable. In lieu of even requiring production of an original, the drafters favored two forms of secondary evidence. If these cannot be submitted, other evidence may be offered.

To satisfy the Rule, a proponent may either have the copy certified as correct under Rule 902(4), (4a) or compared with the original by a witness who can testify that the offered copy is a correct reproduction. Only if reasonable diligence does not produce a certified, attested or a compared copy, may the proponent rely upon other forms of secondary evidence. It should be obvious that as long as the original public record is available, it should be possible to use the forms of proof preferred by this Rule.

The Rule is substantially similar to the Federal Rule; the words "or attested to" were added in recognition of Rule 902(4a). The changes to military practice should be slight. *Manual* ¶ 143a(2)(c) exempted "official records" from the Best Evidence Rule and ¶ 143a(2)(e) exempted banking entries. Rule 1005 is clearly broad enough to cover both provisions. Apparently not covered, however, is a related *Manual* provision which formerly permitted the head of an executive or military department or agency to certify that release of certain records would be contrary to public interest. *See Manual* ¶ 143a(2)(d). This may be covered by the privilege rules, however. *See* Rules 505(a), (c); 506(a), (c).

DRAFTERS' ANALYSIS

Rule 1005 is taken verbatim from the Federal Rule except that "or attested to" has been added to conform the Rule to the new Rule 902(4a). The Rule is generally similar to *Manual* ¶ 143*a*(2)(c) of the present *Manual* although some differences do exist, however. The Rule is somewhat broader in that it applies to more than just "official records." Further, although the present *Manual* permits "a properly authenticated" copy in lieu of the official record, the Rule allows secondary evidence of contents when a certified or attested copy "cannot be obtained by the exercise of reasonable diligence." The Rule does, however, have a preference for a certified or attested copy.

Rule 1006. Summaries

The contents of voluminous writings, recordings, or photographs which cannot conveniently be examined in court may be presented in the form of a chart, summary, or calculation. The originals, or duplicates, shall be made available for examination or copying, or both, by other parties at reasonable time and place. The military judge may order that they be produced in court.

EDITORIAL COMMENT

Numerous or bulky originals often represent an inconvenient form of evidence. Rule 1006 represents a time-honored exception to the Best Evidence Rule and permits admission of evidence in the form of summaries, charts, or calculations when the originals cannot be conveniently examined in court. *See, e.g., Nichols v. Upjohn Co.,* 610 F.2d 293 (5th Cir. 1980) (94,000 page document summarized by testimony); *United States v. Seelig,* 622 F.2d 207 (6th Cir. 1980) (chart summarized 161 underlying exhibits involving 1,409 transactions; *United States v. Denton,* 556 F.2d 811 (6th Cir.), cert. denied, 434 U.S. 892 (1977) (composite tape recording). As a pre-condition to admissibility of this secondary evidence, the proponent must provide a reasonable opportunity for the opponent to examine or copy the originals which serve as the foundation for the summary. What constitutes a reasonable opportunity will depend on the circumstances of the case, although the military judge should be satisfied that the opponent has had ample time to prepare for cross-examination or to gather rebuttal evidence. Presentation of bulky or numerous originals for the first time at trial will normally call for a continuance. In any event, the judge may require production of the originals in court to examine them for himself.

The Rule expands pre-Rules practice which required that the summarization had to be prepared by a person trained or qualified to do so. *Manual* ¶ 143a (2)(b). This individual was then to be called as the foundation witness. *United States v. Calhoun,* 7 M.J. 905 (A.F.C.M.R. 1979), pet. denied, 8 M.J. 176 (C.M.A. 1979) (witness not qualified). Rule 1006 contains no such limitations, although in highly technical matters the proponent will normally wish to rely upon the testimony of a qualified witness. Furthermore, the Rule does not limit the type of secondary evidence to summaries as the *Manual* did. *See* ¶ 143a (2)(b); charts and calculations will do.

Before authenticating the secondary evidence the proponent must establish that the underlying originals are otherwise admissible; a summary, chart or calculation based on inadmissible evidence will itself be inadmissible. *See, e.g., United States v. Johnson,* 594 F.2d 1253 (9th Cir.), cert. denied, — U.S. — (1979) (underlying materials not shown to be within exception to hearsay rule). If an expert is testifying, a summary used to explain his opinion may be based on inadmissible data reasonably relied upon by the expert. Of course, the judge may exclude under Rule 403 any summary that is likely to be misused by court-members.

DRAFTERS' ANALYSIS

Rule 1006 is taken from the Federal Rule without change, and is similar to the exception to the best evidence rule now found in ¶ 143a(2)(b) of the present *Manual*. Some difference between the Rule and the present *Manual* exists, however, because the Rule permits use of "a chart, summary, or calculation" while the *Manual* permits only "a summarization." Additionally, the Rule does not include the present *Manual* requirement that the summarization be made by a "qualified person or group of qualified persons," nor does the Rule require, as the *Manual* appears to, that the preparer of the chart, summary or calculation testify in order to authenticate the document. The nature of the authentication required is not clear although some form of authentication is required under Rule 901 (a).

It is possible for a summary that is admissible under Rule 1006 to include information that would not itself be admissible if that information is reasonably relied upon by an expert preparing the summary. *See generally* Rule 703 and S. Saltzburg & K. Redden, Federal Rules of Evidence Manual 694 (2d ed. 1977).

Rule 1007. Testimony or Written Admission of Party

Contents of writings, recordings, or photographs may be proved by the testimony or deposition of the party against whom offered or by the party's written admission, without accounting for the nonproduction of the original.

EDITORIAL COMMENT

In lieu of presenting or accounting for an original, a proponent may offer an opponent's admission of the contents of the original. To insure the reliability of this brand of secondary evidence, the admissions must be either in the form of testimony or depositions given under oath or written admissions. This rule of convenience is identical to Federal Rule 1007, but finds no equivalent in either the *Manual* or military case law.

Although the Rule will probably not find much use, its relationship to other Rules should be recognized. For example, Rule 1007 does not bar a proponent from using an opponent's oral unsworn admissions to prove the contents of an original; the original will have to first be accounted for, however. *See, e.g.,* Rule 1004 (originals lost or destroyed, etc.). Application of this Rule should not be confused with a situation where primary evidence is offered to establish an event which may have been memorialized in a writing, recording or photograph. In that case the Best Evidence Rule and its exceptions are inapplicable. See our discussion at Rule 1002.

The Hearsay Rule is also potentially involved here. Rule 801(d)(2), treats admissions of an opponent as nonhearsay. It would also seem to permit admissions by authorized speakers, employees, or co-conspirators to be used under Rule 1007 against an opponent to establish the contents. *See* S. SALTZBURG & K. REDDEN, FEDERAL RULES OF EVIDENCE MANUAL, 697 (1977). However, Rule 1007 acts as a limitation on Rule 801(d)(2) insofar as only written or sworn admissions could be used to prove the contents of an original.

An example of the potential interplay of these principles might be demonstrated in a case where the accused has confessed both orally and in writing to sending a written threat. His confessions describe in detail the contents of the threat which has since been lost. How may the prosecution establish the contents of the written threat? The prosecution may account for the lost original under Rule 1004(1) and proceed to offer either the oral or written confessions of the accused as secondary evidence. The prosecution may employ Rule 1007 and offer the accused's written confession without accounting for the lost original. The oral statements could be used to prove that a threat, otherwise proved, was mailed, because that can be used for a purpose other than to prove the contents of a writing.

DRAFTERS' ANALYSIS

Rule 1007 is taken from the Federal Rule without change and has no express equivalent in the present *Manual*. The Rule establishes an exception to Rule 1002 by allowing the contents of a writing, recording or photograph to be proven "by the testimony or deposition of the party against whom offered or by the party's written admission."

Rule 1008. Functions of Military Judge and Members

When the admissibility of other evidence of contents of writings, recordings, or photographs under these rules depends upon the fulfillment of a condition of fact, the question whether the condition has been fulfilled is ordinarily for the military judge to determine in accordance with the provisions of rule 104. However, when an issue is raised (a) whether the asserted writing ever existed, or (b) whether another writing, recording, or photograph produced at trial is the original, or (c) whether other evidence of contents correctly reflects the contents, the issue is for the trier of fact to determine as in the case other issues of fact.

EDITORIAL COMMENT

Rule 1008 is one of several Military Rules addressing the respective functions of the military judge and the court-members. *See* our discussions of Rules 104(b), 401, 402, 602, and 901 (a). The Rule is identical to the Federal Rule and differentiates between questions which go to the competency (*i.e.,* the technical rules of evidence) of the evidence and those which go to conditional relevance (*i.e.,* whether to believe admitted evidence). As a general rule, competency questions are decided only by the military judge. Included within this realm are application of rules of exclusion, privileges, relevance, and hearsay.

The first sentence of Rule 1008 addresses a basic competency question that arises under Section X: The judge must determine whether the requirements of the exceptions to the Best Evidence Rule have been met before permitting use of secondary evidence. For example, under Rule 1003 the judge must first determine whether:

(1) the offered evidence constitutes a "duplicate"; and

(2) a genuine question has been raised about the original's authenticity; or

(3) it would be unfair to admit the duplicate.

Under Rule 1004 the military judge must decide whether:

(1) the original is lost or destroyed;

(2) the proponent destroyed or lost the original in bad faith;

(3) the original is obtainable through judicial process;

(4) notice was given to the opponent who has control of the original;

(5) the offered evidence goes to a collateral matter.

And under Rule 1005 the judge must decide whether the proponent exercised reasonable diligence in attempting to obtain a properly certified or compared copy.

The second sentence of Rule 1008 places in the hands of the court-members the responsibility to decide, when the issue is raised, (a) whether the asserted writing ever existed, (b) whether another writing, recording, or photograph produced at trial is the original, and (c) whether the secondary evidence accurately reflects the original's contents. This provision requires the judge not to engage in fact-finding, but to decide only whether there is enough evidence on the issue to persuade a reasonable court member. *See also* our discussion of Rules 104(b) and 901(a). These three questions arguably involve technical rules of evidence and could have been given to the judge, but they are sent to the court-members because they go to the heart of a dispute and the Rule's drafters apparently and wisely decided that no legal knowledge is needed to decide these questions.

DRAFTERS' ANALYSIS

Rule 1008 is taken from the Federal Rule without change, and has no formal equivalent in current military practice. The Rule specifies three situations in which the members must determine issues which have been conditionally determined by the military judge. The members have been given this responsibility in this narrow range of issues because the issues that are involved go to the very heart of a case and may prove totally dispositive. Perhaps the best example stems from civil practice. Should the trial judge in a contract action determine that an exhibit is in fact the original of a contested contract, that admissibility decision could determine the ultimate result of trial if the jury were not given the opportunity to be the final arbiter of the issue. A similar situation could result in a criminal case for example in which the substance of a contested written confession is determinative (this would be rare because in most cases the fact that a written confession was made is unimportant, and the only relevant matter is the content of the oral statement that was later transcribed) or in a case in which the accused is charged with communication of a written threat. A decision by the military judge that a given version is authentic could easily determine the trial. Rule 1008 would give the members the final decision as to accuracy. Although Rule 1008 will rarely be relevant to the usual court-martial, it will adequately protect the accused from having the case against him or her depend upon a single best evidence determination by the military judge.

SECTION XI. MISCELLANEOUS RULES

Rule 1101. Applicability of Rules

(a) Rules applicable. Except as otherwise provided in this Manual, these rules apply generally to all courts-martial, including summary courts-martial; to proceedings pursuant to Article 39(a); to limited factfinding proceedings ordered on review; to proceedings in revision; and to contempt proceedings except those in which the judge may act summarily.

(b) Rules of privilege. The rules with respect to privileges in Sections III and V apply at all stages of all actions, cases, and proceedings.

(c) Rules relaxed. The application of these rules may be relaxed in sentencing proceedings as provided under paragraph 75c and otherwise as provided in this Manual.

(d) Rules inapplicable. These rules (other than with respect to privileges) do not apply in investigative hearings pursuant to Article 32; proceedings for vacation of suspension of sentence pursuant to Article 72; proceedings for search authorizations; proceedings involving pretrial restraint; and in other proceedings authorized under the Uniform Code of Military Justice or this Manual and not listed in rule 1101(a).

EDITORIAL COMMENT

Military Rule 1101 is modeled after its federal counterpart, but because of procedural and jurisdictional differences between the two systems, alterations in the Military Rule were required. Subdivision (a) states that unless the *Manual* provides otherwise, these Rules are applicable to all courts-martial, including summary courts, Article 39(a) sessions, limited factfinding proceedings ordered by reviewing agencies, proceedings in revision, and non-summary contempt proceedings.

We have extensively discussed these matters in Rule 104, and therefore will not repeat our discussion here. It is important to note, however, that the Rules of Evidence generally will be applicable during those portions of the court-martial aimed at resolving the ultimate issues at bar. Most of the Rules will not apply when litigating pretrial evidentiary or constitutional matters, but subdivision (b) requires that the privileges of Section V "apply at all stages of all actions, cases and proceedings."

Unlike federal criminal trials, courts-martial extend litigation through sentencing. Subdivision (c) continues traditional military practice by allowing the evidentiary rules to be relaxed here. *See ¶ 75c* of the *Manual.* This provision also recognizes that other *Manual* paragraphs may impact on the Rule, and have allowed for their application.

Rule 1101(d) provides that except with respect to privileges, the Military Rules of Evidence also do not apply to Article 32 investigations; proceedings to vacate suspensions of sentences under Article 72; proceedings involving search authorizations; and proceedings regarding restraints or confinements.

Although Rules 104, 1101(a), (c) and (d) specify that evidentiary limitations are not applicable to a wide range of proceedings, this does not mean all evidentiary constraints are gone. Federal experience indicates that judges and magistrates will still heavily borrow from the Rules to facilitate hearings and to insure that their determinations are founded on evidence of a type usually relied upon by tribunals. Trial courts will still find indispensable the requirement that witnesses who do not understand English and their interpreters both take an oath. It seems that many of the exceptions for various proceedings in Rule 1101 serve principally to avoid cumbersome hearsay and authentication problems.

DRAFTERS' ANALYSIS

The Federal Rule has been revised extensively to adapt it to the military criminal legal system. Subdivision (a) of the Federal Rule specifies the types of courts to which the Federal Rules are applicable, and Subdivision (b) of the Federal Rule specifies the types of proceedings to be governed by the Federal Rules. These sections are inapplicable to the military criminal legal system and consequently were deleted. Similarly, most of Federal Rule of Evidence 1101(d) is inapplicable to military law due to the vastly different jurisdiction involved.

(a) Rules applicable. Rule 1101(a) specifies that the Military Rules are applicable to all courts-martial, including summary courts-martial, to Article 39(a) proceedings, limited factfinding proceedings ordered on review, revision proceedings and contempt proceedings. This limited application is a direct result of the limited jurisdiction available to courts-martial.

(b) Rules of privilege. Rule 1101(b) is taken from subdivision (c) of the Federal Rule and is similar to present military law. Unlike the Federal Rules, the Military Rules contain detailed privileges rather than a general reference to common law. *Compare* Federal Rule of Evidence 501 with Military Rule of Evidence 501-512.

(c) Rules relaxed. Rule 1101(c) conforms the rules of evidence to military sentencing procedures as set forth in *Manual ¶ 75c.* Courts-martial are bifurcated proceedings with sentencing being an adversarial proceeding. Partial application of the rules of evidence is thus appropriate. The Rule also recognizes the possibility that other *Manual* provisions may now or later affect the application of the rules of evidence.

(d) Rules inapplicable. Rule 1101(d) is taken in concept from subdivision (d) of the Federal Rule. As the content of the Federal Rule is, however, generally inapplicable to military law, the equivalents of the Article III proceedings listed in the Federal Rule have been listed here. They include Article 32 investigative hearings, the partial analog to grand jury proceedings, proceedings for search authorizations, and proceedings for pretrial release.

Rule 1102. Amendments

Amendments to the Federal Rules of Evidence shall apply to the Military Rules of Evidence 180 days after the effective date of such amendments unless action to the contrary is taken by the President.

EDITORIAL COMMENT

One criticism of prior *Manual* practice was that it could not easily assimilate improvements developed in federal, state or military courts. In order to change a *Manual* provision, the President had to authorize the alteration and then promulgate it by Executive Order. The realities of this process inhibited amendments. What resulted was a series of ad hoc judicial actions which sought to keep military practice in line with federal developments. *See, e.g.,* Article 36; and *United States v. Weaver,* 1 M.J. 111 (C.M.A. 1975), where the Court of Military Appeals adopted Federal Rule 609(b).

Rule 1102 should remove these liabilities. It provides that 180 days after the Federal Rules are amended, the Military Rules will adopt the amendment. The Rule also states that such changes to military practice will automatically occur unless the President takes action to the contrary. This period will begin to run from the effective date of the federal amendment's implementation, not from the date the amendment is proposed by the Supreme Court.

DRAFTERS' ANALYSIS

Rule 1102 has been substantially revised from the original Federal Rule which sets forth a procedure by which the Supreme Court promulgates amendments to the Federal Rules subject to Congressional objection. Although it is the Committee's intent that the Federal Rules of Evidence apply to the armed forces to the extent practicable, *see* Article 36(a), the Federal Rules are often in need of modification to adapt them to the military criminal legal system. Further, some rules may be impracticable. As Congress may make changes during the initial period following Supreme Court publication, some period of time after an amendment's effective date was considered essential for the armed forces to review the final form of amendments and to propose any necessary modifications to the President. Six months was considered the minimally appropriate time period.

Amendments to the Federal Rules are not applicable to the Armed Forces until 180 days after the effective date of such amendment, unless the President directs earlier application. In the absence of any Presidential action, however, an amendment to the Federal Rules of Evidence will be automatically applicable on the 180th day after its effective date. The President may, however, affirmatively direct that any such amendment not apply, in whole or part, to the armed forces and that direction shall be binding upon courts-martial.

Rule 1103. Title

These rules may be known and cited as the Military Rules of Evidence.

EDITORIAL COMMENT.

The drafters' *Analysis* indicates that they adopted the title "Military Rules of Evidence" to highlight the commonality of these Rules and the Federal Rules of Evidence.

DRAFTERS' ANALYSIS

In choosing the title, Military Rules of Evidence, the Committee intends that it be clear that military evidentiary law should echo the civilian federal law to the extent practicable, but should also ensure that the unique and critical reasons behind the separate military criminal legal system be adequately served.

TABLE OF CASES

C

D

E

F

G

H

Johnstone, United States v.
Jones v. United States, 362 U.S. 257 (1960) — Rule 311.
Jones, United States v.
Jordan, United States v.
Juarez, United States v.
Justice, United States v.

K

Kampiles, United States v.
Karnes, United States v.
Kastigar v. United States, 406 U.S. 441 (1972) — Rule 301.
Katz v. United States, 389 U.S. 347 (1967) — Rule 317.
Kellam, United States v.
Keller, United States v.
Kelly, United States v.
Kentucky, Rawlings v.
Kercheval v. United States, 274 U.S. 220 (1927) — Rule 410.
Kick, United States v.
Kidd, United States v.
Kim, United States v.
Kincheloe, United States v.
King, United States v.
Kirby v. Illinois, 406 U.S. 682 (1972) — Rule 321.
Kirby, United States v.
Kitchens v. Smith, 401 U.S. 847 (1971) — Rule 406.
Klauber, United States v.
Klein, Hodges v.
Klein, Spevak v.
Kline v. Ford Motor Co., 523 F.2d 1067 (9th Cir. 1975) — Rule 702.
Kotteakos v. United States, 328 U.S. 750 (1946) — Rule 103.
Kovel, United States v.
Krejce, United States v.

L

LaBossiere, United States v.
Lakeside v. Oregon, 435 U.S. 333 (1978) — Rule 301.
Land, United States v.
Landof, United States v.
Lane, United States v.
Lange, United States v.
Lawson, United States v.
Ledbetter, United States v.
Lee, United States v.
Lego v. Twomey, 404 U.S. 477 (1972) — Rule 311.
Leja, United States v.
Lenz, United States v.
Levesque, United States v.
Levi, Wolfish v.
Levy, Parker v.

M

McPartlin, United States v.
McRary, United States v.
Mead Data Central Inc. v. Department of the Air Force, 566 F.2d 242 (D.C. Cir. 1977) — Rule 502.
Medical Therapy, United States v.
Meerbeke, United States v.
Melville v. American Home Assurance Co., 443 F. Supp. 1064 (E.D. Pa. 1977), rev'd on other grounds, 584 F.2d 1306 (3d Cir. 1978) — Rule 803.
Mendenhall, United States v.
Meredith, Diversified Industries, Inc. v.
Mespoulede, United States v.
Michelson v. United States, 335 U.S. 469 (1948), Rule 405.
Michigan v. Mosley, 423 U.S. 96 (1975) — Rules 304, 305.
Middendorf v. Henry, 425 U.S. 25 (1976) — Rules 101, 102.
Middleton, United States v.
Milburn, United States v.
Milhollan, United States v.
Miller, United States v.
Mills, United States v.
Miranda v. Arizona, 384 U.S. 436 (1966) — Rule 305.
Mississippi, Chambers v.
Mitchell, Zweibon v.
Mohel, United States v.
Montgomery, United States v.
Moore v. United States, 429 U.S. 20 (1976) — Rule 102.
Moore, United States v.
Morales, United States v.
Morgan, United States v.
Morris, United States v.
Mosley, Michigan v.
Mullen v. United States, 263 F.2d 275 (D.C. Cir. 1958) — Rule 502.
Muncy, United States v.
Municipal Court, Camera v.
Mutual Life Ins. Co. v. Hillmon, 145 U.S. 285 (1892) — Rule 803.
Mutual Life Ins. Co. of New York, Wolfson v.

N

Namet v. United States, 373 U.S. 179 (1963) — Rule 512.
Napier, United States v.
Nault, United States v.
Neil v. Biggers, 409 U.S. 188 (1972) — Rule 321.
Nelson v. O'Neil, 402 U.S. 622 (1971) — Rules 306, 801.
Ness, United States v.
New Hampshire, Coolidge v.
New Jersey v. Portash, 440 U.S. 450 (1979) — Rule 302.
New York, Dunaway v.
New York, Harris v.
New York, Lo-Ji Sales, Inc. v.

Pitts, United States v.
Plum, United States v.
Pool v. United States, 260 F.2d 57 (9th Cir. 1958) — Rule 504.
Popejoy, United States v.
Portash, New Jersey v.
Porter, United States v.
Powell, United States v.
Pringle, United States v.
Pyburn, United States v.

Q

Quintana, United States v.
Quinto, United States v.

R

Ragghianti, United States v.
Rakas v. Illinois, 439 U.S. 128 (1978) — Rule 311.
Randolph, Parker v.
Rawlings v. Kentucky, 444 U.S. 989 (1980) — Rule 311.
Ray, United States v.
Reagan, United States v.
Reynolds, United States v.
Rhode Island v. Innis, 440 U.S. 934 (1980) — Rule 305.
Rhodes, United States v.
Ricardo, United States v.
Rice, United States v.
Rich, United States v.
Rivas, United States v.
Rivera, United States v.
Robbins v. United States, 476 F.2d 26 (10th Cir. 1973) — Rule 902.
Roberts, Ohio v.
Roberts, United States v.
Robertson, United States v.
Rocha, United States v.
Rochin v. California, 342 U.S. 165 (1952) — Rule 312.
Rodriguez Serrate, United States v.
Rosado, United States v.
Rosato, United States v.
Rose, United States v.
Rosenstein, United States v.
Ross, United States v.
Roviaro v. United States, 353 U.S. 53 (1957) — Rule 507.
Rubin, United States v.
Ruffin, United States v.
Ruiz, United States v.
Rumsfeld, Berlin Democratic Club v.

S

Saint John, United States v.

T

U

United States v. O'Brien, 601 F.2d 1067 (9th Cir. 1979) — Rule 103.
United States v. Obligacion, 37 C.M.R. 861 (A.B.M.R. 1967) — Rule 804.
United States v. Ocamb, 12 C.M.A. 492, 31 C.M.R. 78 (1961) — Rule 901.
United States v. Oropeza, 564 F.2d 316 (9th Cir. 1977), cert. denied, 434 U.S.
    1080 (1978) — Rule 615.
United States v. Ostrer, 422 F. Supp. 93 (S.D.N.Y. 1976) — Rule 502.
United States v. Paige, 7 M.J. 480 (C.M.A. 1979) — Rule 314.
United States v. Parker, 13 C.M.A. 579, 33 C.M.R. 111 (1963) — Rule 1004.
United States v. Passini, 10 M.J. 108 (C.M.A. 1980) — Rule 103.
United States v. Penn, 18 C.M.A. 194, 39 C.M.R. 194 (1969) — Rule 305.
United States, Pereira v.
United States v. Pheaster, 544 F.2d 353 (9th Cir. 1976), cert. denied, sub nom.
    Inciso v. United States, 429 U.S. 1099 (1977) — Rule 803.
United States v. Phillips, 600 F.2d 535 (5th Cir. 1979) — Rule 615.
United States v. Pinto, 486 F. Supp. 578 (E.D. Pa. 1980) — Rule 606.
United States v. Pitts, 569 F.2d 343 (5th Cir.), cert. denied, 436 U.S. 959 (1978)
    — Rule 901.
United States v. Plum, 558 F.2d 568 (10th Cir. 1977) — Rule 803.
United States, Pool v.
United States v. Popejoy, 578 F.2d 1346 (10th Cir.), cert. denied, 439 U.S. 896
    (1978) — Rule 704.
United States v. Porter, 7 M.J. 32 (C.M.A. 1979) — Rules 803, 902.
United States v. Powell, 8 M.J. 260 (C.M.A. 1980) — Rule 315.
United States v. Pringle, 3 M.J. 308 (C.M.A. 1977) — Rules 105, 306.
United States v. Pyburn, 47 C.M.R. 896 (A.F.C.M.R. 1973) — Rule 312.
United States v. Quintana, 5 M.J. 484 (C.M.A. 1978) — Rule 305.
United States v. Quinto, 582 F.2d 224 (2d Cir. 1978) — Rule 801.
United States v. Ragghianti, 560 F.2d 1376 (9th Cir. 1977) — Rule 105.
United States v. Ray, 20 C.M.A. 331, 43 C.M.R. 171 (1971) — Rule 605.
United States v. Reagan, 7 M.J. 490 (C.M.A. 1980) — Rule 103.
United States v. Reynolds, 345 U.S. 1 (1953) — Rules 505, 506.
United States v. Rhodes, 3 C.M.A. 73, 11 C.M.R. 73 (1953) — Rule 1004.
United States v. Ricardo, 619 F.2d 1124 (5th Cir. 1980) — Rule 403.
United States v. Rice, 550 F.2d 1364 (5th Cir. 1977) — Rule 103.
United States v. Rich, 580 F.2d 929 (9th Cir.), cert. denied, 439 U.S. 935 (1978)
    — Rule 803.
United States v. Rivas, 3 M.J. 282 (C.M.A. 1977) — Rule 301.
United States v. Rivera, 23 C.M.A. 430, 50 C.M.R. 389 (1975) — Rule 302.
United States v. Rivera, 1 M.J. 107 (C.M.A. 1975) — Rule 301.
United States v. Rivera, 4 M.J. 215 (C.M.A. 1978) — Rule 314.
United States, Robbins v.
United States v. Roberts, 2 M.J. 31 (C.M.A. 1976) — Rule 313.
United States v. Robertson, 582 F.2d 1356 (5th Cir. 1978) — Rule 410.
United States v. Rocha, 553 F.2d 615 (9th Cir. 1977) — Rule 404.
United States v. Rodriguez Serrate, 534 F.2d 7 (1st Cir. 1976) — Rule 902.
United States v. Rosado, 2 M.J. 763 (A.C.M.R. 1976) — Rule 311.
United States v. Rosato, 3 C.M.A. 143, 11 C.M.R. 143 (1953) — Rule 312.
United States v. Rose, 590 F.2d 232 (7th Cir. 1978), cert. denied, 442 U.S. 929
    (1979) — Rule 1002.

United States v. Strangstalien, 7 M.J. 225 (C.M.A. 1979) — Rule 803.

United States v. Sturdivant, 9 M.J. 923 (A.C.M.R. 1980) — Rule 317.

United States v. Surry, 6 M.J. 800 (A.C.M.R. 1978) — Rule 201.

United States, Tallo v.

United States v. Temperly, 22 C.M.A. 383, 47 C.M.R. 235 (1973) — Rule 305.

United States v. Tempia, 16 C.M.A. 629, 37 C.M.R. 249 (1967) — Rules 304, 305, 410.

United States v. Terrell, 4 M.J. 720 (A.C.M.R. 1978), aff'd on other grounds, 6 M.J. 13 (C.M.A. 1978) — Rule 301.

United States v. Texidor Perez, 7 M.J. 356 (C.M.A. 1979) — Rule 316.

United States v. Thomas, 1 M.J. 397 (C.M.A. 1976) — Rule 313.

United States v. Thomas, 571 F.2d 285 (5th Cir. 1978) — Rule 804.

United States v. Tibbetts, 1 M.J. 1024 (N.C.M.R. 1976) — Rule 305.

United States v. Tomaiolo, 249 F.2d 683 (2d Cir. 1957) — Rule 512.

United States v. Tomchek, 4 M.J. 66 (C.M.A. 1977) — Rule 608.

United States, Trammel v.

United States v. Tua, 4 M.J. 761 (A.C.M.R. 1977) — Rule 403.

United States v. Tumblin, 551 F.2d 1001 (5th Cir. 1977) — Rule 609.

United States v. Turck, 49 C.M.R. 49 (A.F.C.M.R. 1974) — Rule 311.

United States v. Turner, 5 M.J. 148 (C.M.A. 1978) — Rule 305.

United States v. United Shoe Machinery Corp., 89 F. Supp. 357 (D. Mass. 1950) — Rule 502.

United States v. United States District Court, 407 U.S. 297 (1972) — Rule 317.

United States v. Unrue, 22 C.M.A. 466, 47 C.M.R. 556 — Rule 313.

United States v. Upjohn, 600 F.2d 1223 (6th Cir. 1979), cert. granted, 100 S. Ct. 925 (1980) — Rule 502.

United States v. Vaile-Valdez, 554 F.2d 911 (9th Cir. 1977) — Rule 103.

United States v. Vanderpool, 10 C.M.R. 664 (A.F.B.R. 1953) — Rule 103.

United States v. Veltre, 591 F.2d 347 (5th Cir. 1979) — Rule 803.

United States v. Vietor, 10 M.J. 69 (C.M.A. 1980) — Rule 803.

United States v. Villines, 9 M.J. 807 (N.C.M.R. 1980) — Rule 301.

United States v. Vitale, 596 F.2d 688 (5th Cir. 1979) — Rules 103, 105.

United States v. Wade, 388 U.S. 218 (1967) — Rules 301, 321.

United States, Walder v.

United States v. Waller, 3 M.J. 32 (C.M.A. 1977) — Rule 311.

United States v. Ward, 1 M.J. 176 (C.M.A. 1975) — Rule 103.

United States v. Washington, 592 F.2d 680 (2d Cir. 1979) — Rule 105.

United States v. Watson, 423 U.S. 411 (1976) — Rule 314.

United States v. Weaver, 1 M.J. 111 (C.M.A. 1975) — Rules 406, 609, 1102.

United States v. Webster, 1 M.J. 216 (C.M.A. 1975) — Rule 301.

United States v. Weckner, 3 M.J. 546 (A.C.M.R. 1977) — Rule 316.

United States v. Wells, 446 F.2d 2 (2d Cir. 1971) — Rule 503.

United States v. Weshenfelder, 20 C.M.A. 416, 43 C.M.R. 256 (1971) — Rule 314.

United States v. West, 574 F.2d 1131 (4th Cir. 1978) — Rule 804.

United States v. Westmore, 17 C.M.A. 406, 38 C.M.R. 204 (1968) — Rule 304.

United States v. Whipple, 4 M.J. 773 (C.G.C.M.R. 1978) — Rule 312.

United States v. White, 17 C.M.A. 211, 38 C.M.R. 9 (1967) — Rule 305.

V

W

INDEX

A

ACCIDENT REPORTS.
Expert, Rule 702.
Policy, Rule 803(6), (8).

ACCUSED IN CRIMINAL CASE.
Character Evidence.
Admissibility, Rule 404(a)(1).
Compulsory Self-Incrimination.
See Self-Incrimination.
Cross-Examination.
Preliminary matters.
Cross-examination of accused testifying on preliminary matters, Rule 104(d).
Failure to Testify, Rule 301.
Preliminary Matters.
Testimony on preliminary matter does not subject accused to cross-examination as to other issues, Rules 104(d), 304, 311, 321.

ACKNOWLEDGMENTS.
Authentication and Identification.
Acknowledged documents.
Self-authentication, Rule 902(8).

ADJUDICATIVE FACTS.
Judicial Notice.
See Judicial Notice of Adjudicative Facts.

ADMISSIBILITY.
Bodily Evidence, Rule 312.
Character Evidence.
Not admissible to prove conduct, Rule 404.
Exceptions, Rule 404.
Witnesses, Rule 608.
Compromise.
Compromise and offers to compromise, Rule 408.
Conduct.
Witnesses, Rule 608.
Confessions.
Generally, Rule 304.
Hearings on admissibility of confessions.
Conducted out of hearing of court-members, Rule 104(c).
Conviction of Crime.
Purposes of impeachment, Rule 609.

455

BLUEPRINTS.
  Copies, Rule 1001(3).

BODY EVIDENCE.
  Blood Samples, Rules 301, 312.
  Handwriting Samples, Rule 301.
  Searches for, Rule 312.
  Self-incrimination, Rules 301, 312.
  Surgical Intrusions, Rule 312(c).
  Visual Examination of Body, Rule 312(b).

BURDEN OF PROOF.
  Admissibility of Admissions, Confessions, Rule 304(e).
  Eyewitness Identification, Rule 321(d).
  Unlawful Search and Seizure, Rule 311(e).

BUSINESS CUSTOM.
  Admissibility, Rule 406.
  Authentication, Rule 901(b)(6).

BUSINESS RECORDS.
  Hearsay Exception, Rule 803(6).

C

CHAIN OF CUSTODY.
  See also Authentication and Identification.
  Requirements of, Rule 901.

CHARACTER EVIDENCE.
  Accused in Criminal Case.
    Admissibility, Rule 404(a)(1).
  Admissibility.
    Not admissible to prove conduct, Rule 404.
      Exceptions, Rule 404.
    Witnesses, Rule 608(a).
  Conduct.
    Character evidence not admissible to prove conduct, Rule 404.
    Specific instances of conduct.
      When allowed to prove character, Rule 405(b).
  Hearsay.
    Reputation as to character.
      Exception to hearsay rule, Rule 803(21).
  Impeachment, Rules 405, 608.
  Methods of Proving Character, Rule 405.
  Opinion.
    Method of proving character, Rule 405(a).
  Reputation.
    Method of proving character, Rule 405(a).
  Victim in Criminal Case.
    Admissibility, Rule 404(a)(2).
    Nonconsensual sexual offenses, Rule 412.
  Witnesses, Rule 608(a).

CROSS-EXAMINATION.
Accused in Criminal Case.
Preliminary matters.
Cross-examination of accused testifying on preliminary matters,
Rules 104(d), 304(f), 311(f), 321(e).
Leading Questions, Rule 611(c).
Scope, Rule 611(b).

D

DATA COMPILATIONS.
Authentication, Rule 901(b)(8).
Business Records, Rule 803(6).

DEAD MAN'S ACTS.
Disqualification, Rule 601.

DEFINITIONS.
Admission, Rule 304(c)(2).
Classified Information, Rule 505(b).
Clergyman, Rule 503(b).
Client, Rule 502(b).
Community, Rule 405(d).
Confession, Rule 304(c)(1).
Convictions, Rule 609(f).
Duplicate of Writing or Recording, Rule 1001(4).
Hearsay, Rule 801.
Unavailability, Rule 804(a).
In Camera Proceedings, Rules 505(i), 506(i).
Involuntary, Rule 304(c)(2).
Lawyer, Rule 502(b).
Military Community, Rule 405(d).
Nonconsenual Sexual Offense, Rule 412(e).
Original Writing or Recording, Rule 1001(3).
Past-Sexual Behavior, Rule 412(d).
Photographs, Rule 1001(2).
Recordings, Rule 1001(1).
Relevant Evidence, Rule 401.
Reputation Evidence, Rule 405(d).
Unlawful Eyewitness Identification, Rule 321(b).
Writings, Rule 1001(1).

DISCLOSURE OF EVIDENCE.
See also Notice Requirements; Privileges.
Classified Information.
Disclosure by military judge, Rule 505(g)(2).
Disclosure to accused, Rule 505(g).
Report to convening authority of, Rule 505(f).
Communications, Privileged.
See Privileges.
Deliberations of Courts, Rule 509.

H

HABIT.
    Admissibility, Rule 406.
    Relevance, Rule 406.

HANDWRITING.
    Authentication and Identification.
        Comparison by trier or expert witness, Rule 901(b)(3).
        Nonexpert opinion, Rule 901(b)(2).
    Harmless Error, Rule 103.

HEARSAY.
    Admission by Party-Opponent.
        Not hearsay, Rule 801(d).
    Ancient Documents.
        Exception to hearsay rule, Rule 803(16).
    Character Evidence.
        Reputation as to character.
            Exception to hearsay rule, Rule 803(21).
    Conspirators' Statements.
        Not hearsay, Rule 801(d).
    Conviction of Crime.
        Judgment of previous conviction.
            Exception to hearsay rule, Rule 803(22).
    Credibility of Declarant.
        Attacking and supporting, Rule 806.
    Declarant.
        Availability of declarant.
            Exceptions to hearsay rule, Rule 803.
        Credibility of declarant.
            Attacking and supporting, Rule 806.
        Defined, Rule 801(b).
        Exceptions to hearsay rule.
            Availability of declarant immaterial, Rule 803.
            Unavailability of declarant, Rule 804.
        Unavailability.
            Exceptions to hearsay rule, Rule 804.
    Declaration Against Interest, Rule 804(b)(3).
    Definitions, Rule 801.
        Unavailability, Rule 804(a).
    Dying Declarations.
        Exception to hearsay rule, Rule 804(b)(2).
    Exceptions.
        Ancient documents, Rule 803(16).
        Boundaries.
            Judgment as to boundaries, Rule 803(23).
            Reputation concerning boundaries, Rule 803(20)
        Business records, Rules 803(6), 803(7).

JUDICIAL NOTICE OF ADJUDICATIVE FACTS—Cont'd
Time.
Instructions to court-members, Rule 201(g).
When notice may be taken, Rule 201(f).

JUDICIAL NOTICE OF LAW.
Domestic Law, Rule 201A(a).
Foreign Law, Rule 201A(b).

JUVENILE ADJUDICATIONS.
Impeachment, Rule 609(d).

L

LAWYER-CLIENT PRIVILEGE.
Scope, Rule 502.

LAY WITNESSES.
Opinion, Rule 701.

LEADING QUESTIONS.
See also Questions.
Cross-examination, Use in, Rule 611(c).
Exceptions, Rule 611(c).
General Rule, Rule 611(c).

LEARNED TREATISES.
Hearsay Exception, Rule 803(18).

LEGISLATIVE FACTS.
Judicial Notice, Rule 201.

LETTERS.
Authentication, Rules 901, 902.

LIABILITY INSURANCE.
Admissibility, Rule 411.
Relevance, Rule 411.
Witnesses.
Bias or prejudice.
Admissible to show bias or prejudice of witness, Rule 411.

LIMITING INSTRUCTION.
Required, Rule 105.

LINEUPS.
See Eyewitness Identification.

LOST DOCUMENTS.
Admissible, Rule 1004(1).

M

MARITAL PRIVILEGES.
Scope, Rule 504.

N

X